KT-547-968

Special Events

The Wiley Event Management Series

Series Editor: Dr. Joe Goldblatt, CSEP

Special Events: A New Generation and the Next Frontier, Sixth Edition
by Dr. Joe Goldblatt, CSEP

The Complete Guide to Careers in Special Events: Step Toward Success!
by Gene Columbus

The Dictionary of Event Management
by Dr. Joe Goldblatt, CSEP and Carol F. McKibben, CSEP

The International Dictionary of Event Management, Second Edition
by Dr. Joe Goldblatt, CSEP, and Kathleen S. Nelson, CSEP

Corporate Event Project Management
by William O'Toole and Phyllis Mikolaitis

Event Marketing: How to Successfully Promote Events, Festivals, Conventions, and Expositions
by Leonard H. Hoyle, CAE, CMP

Event Risk Management and Safety
by Peter E. Tarlow, Ph.D.

Event Sponsorship
by Bruce E. Skinner and Vladimir Rukavina

Professional Event Coordination
by Julia Rutherford Silvers, CSEP

The Complete Guide to Event Entertainment and Production
by Mark Sonder, MM, CSEP

The Guide to Successful Destination Management
by Pat Schaumann, CMP, CSEP

The Sports Event Management and Marketing Playbook
by Frank Supovitz

Art of the Event: Complete Guide to Designing and Decorating Special Events
by James C. Monroe, CMP, CSEP

Global Meetings and Exhibitions
by Carol Krugman, CMP, CMM, and Rudy R. Wright, CMP

Special Events

A New Generation and the Next Frontier

Sixth Edition

Dr. Joe Goldblatt, CSEP

John Wiley & Sons, Inc.

Photos were taken by the author unless otherwise noted.

This book is printed on acid-free paper. ♾

Published by John Wiley & Sons, Inc., Hoboken, New Jersey.
Published simultaneously in Canada.

Library of Congress Cataloging-in-Publication Data:
Goldblatt, Joe
Special events: a new generation and the next frontier / Joe Goldblatt.—6th ed.
p. cm.—(The Wiley event management series ; 13)
Includes bibliographical references and index.
ISBN 978-0-470-44987-5 (hardback)
1. Special events—Management. I. Title.
GT3405.G65 2010
394.2—dc22

Printed in the United States of America

10 9 8 7 6 5 4 3

DEDICATION

The **Sixth Edition** *of* **Special Events** *is dedicated to three extraordinary women whose lives and careers have served as a profound inspiration to many others: Jean McFaddin, Nina de Courson, and Dr. Kathy Nelson, CMP, CSEP.*

Jean McFaddin is the legendary producer of the Macy's Thanksgiving Day Parade, one of the most widely viewed annual events in the entire world. Jean directed, and, according to The History Channel™, "transformed" the parade during her long tenure. She has also used her immense talents to inspire and transform the lives and careers of thousands of others as an engaging speaker. She is a popular mentor to college students throughout the world, and continues to challenge and motivate the next generation to forge new frontiers, as she has done through her highly successful career. In the vast constellation of talent within the global special events industry, she will always be my bright north star.

Over half a century ago, our favorite aunt, Nina de Courson, traveled all the way from the state of Iowa in the United States to Europe. She did this at a time when women from small towns, such as hers, rarely traveled at all. Upon arriving in Europe, she used her acclaimed singing talent to perform with leading opera companies on the continent. Later in her career, her tenacity and talent led her to successfully transition to the world of business, where she triumphed once again. Aunt Nina has never stopped learning new things. She generously shares her knowledge and wisdom with others. Her generosity, creativity, and courage inspire me, my wife, Nancy, and many others every day.

Dr. Kathy Nelson, CMP, CSEP was a pioneering educator and researcher in the field of special events. Among her many achievements, she led the Certified Special Events Professional (CSEP) committee for the International Special Events Society during a critical time in its development. She was a charter member of the Event Management Body of Knowledge (EMBOK) project and greatly contributed to the formal codification of this emerging field of study and practice. I had the great pleasure of working with Kathy to co-author the **International Dictionary of Special Events** *(Wiley, 2001). Her devotion to her family, husband Dan, daughter Chloe, and her extended family, friends, and colleagues was boundless. Despite her untimely death in July of 2010, her legacy will stretch beyond her years on earth to inform, illuminate, and inspire many future generations of event professionals to come.*

Therefore, it is with great admiration and profound respect that I dedicate this book to three remarkably resilient, and, indeed, modern renaissance women, Jean McFaddin, Nina de Courson, and Dr. Kathy Nelson, CMP, CSEP.

Professor Joe Goldblatt, CSEP
Edinburgh, Scotland

> As is the generation of leaves, so is that of humanity. The wind scatters the leaves on the ground, but the live timber burgeons with leaves again in the season of spring returning. So one generation will grow while another dies.
>
> Homer (900–800 B.C.), *The Iliad*

Note to the reader: The Greek poet Homer reportedly wrote (with others) the epic poem, *The Iliad*. This poem eloquently recounts the end of the Trojan War (1194–1184 B.C.). As ***Special Events, Sixth Edition*** is being published at what is hopefully the end of a period of severe economic turmoil, it is my firm belief that the next generation of special event professionals will explore new frontiers, and, as Homer imagined, continually grow from strength to strength.

CONTENTS

APPENDICES

FOREWORD

For more than thirty years there have been many innovations in the special events industry. One of the most important innovations being the availability of process training on researching, designing, planning, coordinating, and evaluating events, rituals and ceremonies. At the forefront of this effort is Dr. Joe Goldblatt, CSEP, working to ensure the next generation benefits from his experience, hard work, on-the-job training, successes, and failures in this industry. He is one of the early pioneers who examined the process and results in his own business, The Wonder Company, which successfully produced events from the smallest party to presidential inaugurations. Now, you will benefit from his experience in this latest edition of ***Special Events***.

Dr. Goldblatt is really in the relationship business and his contacts include the names and numbers of industry leaders, educators, students, vendors, suppliers, and many good friends from around the world that share his interest and passion for the industry. He is loved and respected by his students and honored by members of the industry. Because of his exceptional relationship skills and his commitment to investing in the next generation, other industry professionals have willingly assisted Dr. Goldblatt by providing him with information on trends, and contributing to his many books and articles, including this ***Sixth Edition*** of ***Special Events***.

Dr. Goldblatt's first edition of *Special Events: The Art and Science of Celebration* was published twenty years ago and each new edition has been updated to include the most current and relevant information in the special events industry. This newest edition is very much a continuation of the art of bringing people together for celebrations. You will find it to be the ideal book to use to understand the scope of the many elements involved in special events. It is an "owner's manual" for event planning. It explains the language of the industry in great detail that is easy to understand and exciting to read. For example, "Eventology" explains the science of planning in addition to the creative development necessary for events. Every event professional should own a copy of ***Special Events***.

My first meeting with Dr. Goldblatt took place many years ago when he was the Founding President of the International Special Events Society (ISES) and I was the Manager of Convention/Resort Entertainment for Walt Disney World. I was immediately taken with Dr. Goldblatt's vision of establishing higher standards and creativity in the events industry. There was a great need but there were few training programs or books that addressed the complexity of planning events, festivals, parties, industrials, and other celebrations. Dr. Goldblatt shared his mission of establishing a certification, which ultimately resulted in his being part of the first group to receive the Certified Special Events Professional (CSEP) after taking part in the development of the curriculum. Dr. Goldblatt is a gifted educator with the ability to see the big picture and break it down into its component parts.

One only has to spend a few minutes with Joe to feel like he has known you for a very long time. Dr. Joe, as his students often call him, is a man always in motion even when standing or sitting still. His knowledge goes well beyond event planning. He has read many books, seen lots of movies, attended numerous theatre productions, met a great many people, remembers most names, can recall facts about people, places, and things better than anyone I have ever met. He has an extremely positive outlook on life and brings great energy to everything he does.

Most importantly, I am honored to say that Joe Goldblatt is my best friend. For those of you reading this, it may surprise you that so many individuals regard Joe as their best friend. And they are correct; Joe is your best friend, too. He is a kind and caring man with a great deal of knowledge which will become evident to you as you read this book. So when facing a challenge with an event you are planning, trust in your best friend by opening ***Special Events*** and getting back to the basics. You can't go wrong.

In this, the sixth edition of the world's first text book in the field of special events, Dr. Goldblatt provides the most up-to-date information concerning technology, corporate social responsibility and event environmental sustainability. This book will become your essential reference tool for producing high quality special events, whether you are a student or an experienced event professional.

Joe and I love our families, theatre, stories, helping others, and can spend hours talking about each topic. I must bow to the remarkable storytelling ability of my best friend. Joe shares personal stories about his experiences that are filled with humor and emotion that are guaranteed to entertain as well as inform those of us lucky enough to be on his mailing list. You will see what I mean when you begin reading the words of wisdom from this world traveler who is out to change the world one person, and one celebration, at a time.

GENE COLUMBUS
Executive Director
Orlando Repertory Theater
Orlando, Florida
Formerly, A Cast Member and Manager of Entertainment
Staffing for Walt Disney World for 38 Years

PREFACE

Auld Lang Syne
Should auld acquaintance be forgot,
And never brought to mind?
Should auld acquaintance be forgot,
And auld lang syne?

Robert Burns (1759–1796)

The poet laureate of my adopted homeland of Scotland was born in Alloway, only a few miles from where I am writing these lines. I have come to Ayrshire in Scotland to the lovely and warm home of my friend Allison Russell to research why, 250 years after his birth, millions of people throughout the world continue to celebrate the immortal memory of Robert Burns with traditional Burns suppers.

Mr. Burns is the author of over 6000 poems, including *Auld Lang Syne*. This is perhaps his best-known poem, because it has been transformed into one of the world's best-loved songs, ritually sung on New Year's Eve by hundreds of millions of people throughout the world. According to journalists, the only song that is sung more often than *Auld Lang Syne* is *Happy Birthday*. One song celebrates friendship and memories and the other celebrates new beginnings. In both songs we have the circle of life itself, as seen through musical celebration.

Above all else in life, Burns appreciated a robust party with friends and family. These celebrations, regardless of size, created the unique experience anthropologists and sociologists later recognized as *communitas*. Similarly, my friend Allison has turned her home into a celebration destination where her friends and family often dance in her living room and kitchen.

The term *communitas* was defined by another Scotsman, the sociologist Victor Turner from Glasgow. Turner described it as "an intimate moment of sharing" that achieved the effect of creating "time out of time" (Turner 1977). Through *ceildhs* (Scottish dance parties) and other social events, Robert Burns and his friends and family would come together, tell stories, and enjoy food and beverage while remembering auld lang syne (old times since).

For Burns, the practice of celebration provided the ultimate *raison d'etre* (reason for living) despite often-recurring catastrophic conditions.

At the same time I am investigating Burns, the world appears to be once again facing another crisis as the banking industry and financial markets experience severe distress requiring massive government intervention. With the sometimes overwhelming and seemingly endless myriad problems plaguing the twenty-first century, now more than ever, we seek refuge in and strength through our celebrations to transcend what appears to be desperate times.

Throughout history, people have recognized the power of celebration to inspire hope and provide fortitude for daily living. When I interviewed the five earth scientists who lived for nearly one year in the Biosphere, a closed-environment research laboratory in the Arizona desert, I asked them how they managed to survive in this isolated scientific environment for so long.

They replied, "We survived because of science. We *lived* because of celebrations. Every month we celebrated birthdays, anniversaries, births of new creatures and our personal and professional triumphs. These celebrations sustained our spirits" (Biosphere 1998).

Once when lecturing in Trinidad and Tobago, a student said to me, half apologizing, "When major disasters happen in other parts of the world we feel threatened as well. So we immediately return to our celebrations to remind us of why we are alive and to give us strength to go on."

Following the tragic aftermath of Hurricane Katrina, I visited New Orleans during the first Mardi Gras celebrations to be held since the natural disaster. The mayor and other leaders were doubtful that the city could host a major special event, and some argued that the celebrations should be canceled.

However, the citizens of New Orleans prevailed. On the first night of the first Mardi Gras parade since Hurricane Katrina, I stood in the French Quarter surrounded by mostly the citizens of New Orleans. We huddled together against the unusually cool winds. The mood was somber, as would be expected among so many who had lost their homes, their jobs, and even loved ones.

Within a few minutes the spirits changed as we heard the slow and then rapid drum beats of one of the jazz bands as it began to turn a corner and enter the street where we silently stood waiting. Suddenly, this silence turned into cheers and loud clapping, as the city welcomed back its parade and its raison d'etre.

As people began once more to dance in the streets of the French Quarter, I recognized, as did Barbara Ehrenrich, author of *Dancing in the Streets, A Collective History of Joy*, our infinite capacity for human joy and celebration (Ehrenrich 2007). When the leaders of New Orleans questioned whether their celebrations could or should continue, the people demonstrated that cold night that, without their celebrations, they could not continue.

From the first dawn of human history, human beings have come together, first to gain sustenance from food and drink, later to tell stories around the prehistoric campfire, and, today, in the postmodern Internet social media chat room. In every instance we are celebrating and commemorating what makes us infinitely human.

In his poem *Auld Lang Syne*, Burns asks rhetorically, "Should auld (old) acquaintance be forgot and never brought to mind?" He is asking a universal question about the precious connection between human beings and memory, human beings and relationships, and, ultimately, human beings and their sacred bond to one another.

I will continue to argue in this book that we must never forget the traditions of celebration that bind society together. It is through special events and celebrations that we continue to remember our shared history, our friends, and family. The complex celebrations that you will produce will create new milestones and enduring memories that will make our lives worth living and, for those who follow us, worth remembering—*auld lang syne*.

That is one of the major purposes of this ***Sixth Edition*** of ***Special Events: A New Generation and the Next Frontier.*** Since its inception, this book has chronicled and championed the development, changes, and challenges faced by the global celebrations industry.

I am more convinced than ever before that you, and the events you design and produce, will, similar to Burns poetry, help us and others find the kinship, courage, and commitment to transcend all the troubles of the past and overcome the challenges of the future.

The planned events of our lives often give us purpose and bring us together to achieve common positive goals. I describe this process as cultural progression through *eventology*.

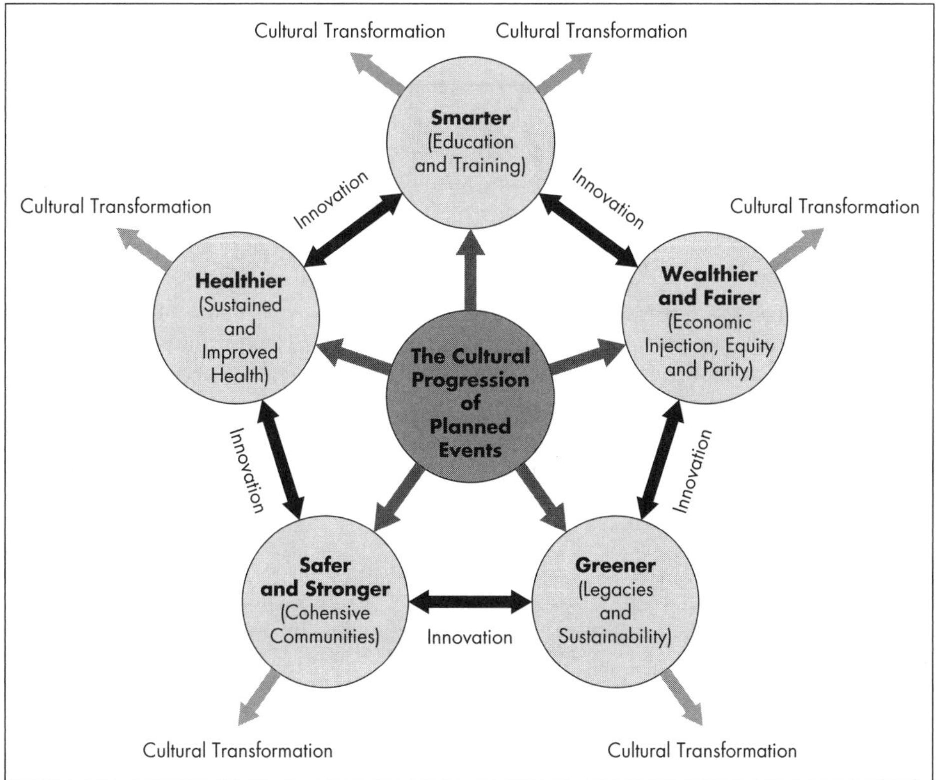

Figure P.1 Goldblatt Model of Cultural Progression Through Planned Events

Figure P.1 demonstrates how planned events and their creativity may produce positive social benefits through innovation.

Eventology is the study of planned events to promote positive societal benefits (Goldblatt 2008). The term *event* is derived from the Latin word *e-venire*, which means outcome. Therefore, *eventology* is the scientific process through celebration to promote positive outcomes for all of society.

One of the most important outcomes is the opportunity to unite the global human society through events. Whether you produce events for associations, corporations, exhibitions, incentives, schools, sports, or even zoos, from A to Z, there are increasingly more opportunities than ever before to bring people together for mutual benefit. Burns understood this well as he chronicled his friends' and family's celebration through his poetry.

Many years ago, I was invited to read from one of my books at a library book-signing program. A female poet was also invited to read during the same program. While we were awaiting the program to begin, we eyed each other curiously, and finally I asked the poet: "Why would an event producer and a poet be invited to share the same platform?"

The poet thought about it and replied, "An event is a poem. Like poetry, a beautiful event is eternal."

As we celebrate the twentieth anniversary of the first publication of this book, I am more committed than ever before to never let our old acquaintance be forgot. We must eternally celebrate our memories through events while also making new ones that continually advance human society to help our culture progress into a future that is truly boundless.

Sadly, Robert Burns only lived to age 37. He lived fully and often joyously every day, due in large part to the many celebrations he hosted or attended. As a member of the global celebrations family, and in commemoration of Burns's 250th birthday, I am rededicating my career to making certain that all the days of our lives may one day be described by those who follow us as special events.

Through the pages of this ***Special Events, Sixth Edition***, I invite you to join me and meet the individuals and organizations that share our common devotion to and passion for human celebration. And now, as I walk through the purple heather of Scotland, I invite you to stroll alongside and, perhaps, even rekindle the spirit of Robert Burns as together we rediscover and better understand why events are indeed like poems. Through this rededication and rediscovery we will, unless old acquaintance be forgot, learn that every event we may produce can result in an outcome of eternal beauty that will be cherished and remembered.

The Sixth Edition

The contents of the ***Sixth Edition*** of ***Special Events*** are drawn from the many great continents of the earth. In my travels around the globe, I have searched for the reasons we celebrate and how special events bring meaning to our lives and those of our guests.

Since the publication of the previous edition, I have traveled throughout six continents: Africa, Asia, Australia, Europe, and North and South America in search of the rituals, ceremonies, customs, and traditions from whence our contemporary celebrations have developed.

In Malaysia, I discovered how ancient rituals are being preserved and given new meaning by the current generation. In Australia, while conducting research at the Strehlow Institute in Alice Springs, I learned about men's and women's secret rituals that are thousands of years old. Throughout Africa, Brazil, Canada, the Caribbean, France, Germany, Kazakhstan, Qatar, Russia, Switzerland, Thailand, and now Scotland, I have observed and learned why and how people celebrate their triumphs, their joys, and even their sorrows (Turner 1977). These lessons will serve as further instruction for you, the next generation of tribal leaders and poets who will create and produce new rituals, ceremonies, and celebrations. You will compose the event poetry that, through its beauty, endures forever.

Through my travels I have discovered that there is no universally accepted definition of the person who plans and produces events. Some refer to this person as event manager, others as event planner and still others as event director. In previous definitions I have used the term event leader. However, in this edition, the terms *event planner* and *event leader* are used interchangeably. Perhaps one day a universally accepted definition will emerge. For the purposes of this book, the event planner and/or event leader represent the individual responsible for the research, design, coordination, planning, and coordination of planned events.

Each new edition of this book also represents a unique gathering of new associates as well as a reunion (old times since) of those who have joined us once again. Indeed, each new edition represents our collective history as well as the opening of a new window to explore the future of this fascinating field of study.

Nearly everywhere in the world, human beings take part in rituals and ceremonies to recall their collective history and express their individual aspirations.

Wilson and Goldfarb (1994) further define ceremony and ritual:

> *A ceremony is a formal religious or social occasion, usually led by a designated authority figure, such as a priest or chief; examples would include a graduation or inauguration and a marriage ceremony. A ritual is the acting out of an established, prescribed procedure; rituals can range from a family event, such as Thanksgiving or Christmas dinner, to elaborate religious events, such as the Roman Catholic mass and the Jewish Yom Kippur service during the High Holy Days.*

In the postmodern world, the designated authority figure is often the event planner or leader. This is the trained professional who researches, designs, plans, coordinates, and evaluates the ritual or ceremony. Now, thanks in large part to readers like you who are committed to continuing professional education, the planned events profession is firmly established and generally recognized throughout the world.

As I travel throughout the world, I have noted that, for the first time, federal governments are taking a sincere interest in our profession and are seeking methods to study, evaluate, and determine how best to benefit from the assets event leaders bring to their nations. For example, the federal government of Canada conducted a landmark study to identify international standards for event professionals. If adopted by governments throughout the world, these standards will enable the event management profession to join other recognized fields of study such as engineering and medicine as a professional field of study with globally recognized standards, qualifications, and credentials.

Whether it is the 2016 Summer Olympic Games in Rio de Janeiro, Brazil, or the 2008 European Capital of Culture programs in Liverpool, England, and Stavanger, Norway, national and local governments throughout the world actively compete through million-dollar annual investments to attract special events to their destination cities. Government leaders realize that events such as meetings, conventions, exhibitions, incentives, festivals, fairs, weddings, and others not only represent big business, but they also produce new jobs and establish or promote the overall image of a destination, which is a central part of the global tourism industry. In fact, when well planned and coordinated, events contribute significantly to the quality of place, something that citizens and businesses desire and political leaders must provide.

Events not only help establish a quality of place, they often transform communities. In Providence, Rhode Island, the *Waterfire*™ event (www.waterfire.org) has helped transform a decaying urban center into a thriving entertainment district. *Waterfire* is an event conceived by the artist Barnaby Evans using the basic elements of water, fire, and music to create a dramatic and inspiring tourism experience. One hundred bonfires are placed in metal cauldrons in the middle of a river in the center of Providence. Using highly fragrant wood, New Age and classical music, and hundreds of volunteers as bonfire builders and lamplighters, this event has literally helped rekindle the tourism economy of Providence.

This is but one example of the hundreds of thousands of small and large events being produced throughout the world where ceremonies and rituals draw on ancient symbols to create new outcomes. This edition of ***Special Events*** reminds us how modern events such as *Waterfire* use rituals and ceremonies to explore how planned events promote both continuity and stability within human societies. In this edition, you will discover, as Victor Turner stated, the *fons et origo* (fountainhead and origin) of social structure. Perhaps through this discovery you will find the resources, ideas, and inspiration to raise this ancient tradition and modern profession to a higher level of excellence and meaning.

New to This Edition

The ***Sixth Edition*** of ***Special Events*** differs from all others by providing the following new enhancements to the text.

- **New interviews** with experienced event practitioners, distinguished event studies university faculty, event students currently studying in university, as well as successful graduates of event studies programs. Through these profiles in each chapter you will meet the experienced pioneers and their protégées. You will learn what makes the great ones great and their events truly spectacular.

- New chapters include:
  - **Chapter 6: Green Events.** Thanks to Sam Goldblatt, in this first-ever chapter on environmental sustainability for meetings and events, you will discover the latest trends, techniques, and tips for recycling, reducing the carbon footprint, and reusing elements of your event to create sustainable outcomes.
  - **Chapter 13: Doing the Right Thing, Corporate Social Responsibility (CSR).** This chapter explores the emerging focus on CSR in organizations such as Meeting Professionals International and includes case examples of programs that focus on linking event outcomes to improving society.
  - **Chapter 16: The New Best Practices in Planned Events**. This chapter takes you behind the scenes of two of the most amazing, remarkable, and successful international and national planned events of the recent past, the opening ceremonies of the Beijing, China 2008 Summer Olympic Games and the year long Homecoming Scotland 2009 celebrations featuring hundreds of creative and innovative events.
  - **Chapter 17: New Frontiers in Twenty-First-Century Planned Events.** This chapter includes new theoretical case studies for a number of different event fields, such as attractions, catering, conventions, government, festivals, sports, and more.
- **Event measurement, evaluation,** and **assessment topics** are integrated throughout a number of the chapters in ***Special Events***. As governments and other funders increasingly ask for valid and reliable data about the impact of your event, this coverage provides you with the strategies and tools to collect, analyze, and disseminate information that will help you attract greater support in the future for your events.
- Over 200 new **web resources** in the text and appendices will help you save money, save time, and improve the overall quality of your events.
- A **comprehensive listing of schools of** event management is provided for further study.
- An **expanded case studies** section based on the Harvard Business Review model as well as five new best practice events serve as sterling models for your future event.
- Dozens of **new photographs** illustrating the vast depth and breadth of global planned events. All photos were taken by the author unless otherwise credited.
- Finally, throughout ***Special Events, Sixth Edition***, you will learn how **technology** may be harnessed to help you improve your events' financial, quality, environmental, and other strategic outcomes.

Supplement Offerings

A comprehensive ***Instructor's Manual*** (ISBN 978-0-470-64189-7) accompanies this book. It can be obtained by contacting your Wiley sales representative. If you do not know who your representative is, please visit **www.wiley.com**, click on Resources for Instructors, and click on Who's My Rep? An electronic version of the ***Instructor's Manual*** is available to qualified instructors, and ***PowerPoint slides*** are available to students and instructors on the companion website, at **www.wiley.com/college/goldblatt.**

The ***Test Bank*** has been specifically formatted for Respondus, an easy-to-use software program for creating and managing exams that can be printed to paper or published directly to Blackboard, WebCT, Desire2Learn, eCollege, ANGEL, and other eLearning systems. Instructors who adopt ***Special Events*** can download the test bank for free. Additional Wiley resources also can be uploaded into your LMS course at no charge.

Many of the appendices that appeared in previous editions of ***Special Events*** have been removed from the print book and are available on the students and instructor's website for the book at **www.wiley.com/college/goldblatt.** Please visit the resources for more information on the following topics:

Appendix 4: Organizations and Resources
Appendix 5: Internet Sites
Appendix 6: Periodicals
Appendix 7: APEX Resources
Appendix 8: Directories
Appendix 9: Audio and Visual Resources
Appendix 10: Software
Appendix 11: Sample Client Agreement
Appendix 12: Sample Vendor Agreement
Appendix 13: Sample Insurance Certificate
Appendix 14: Sample Catering Menus
Appendix 15: Sample Incident Report
Appendix 16: Sample Purchase Order
Appendix 17: Sample Event Evaluations
Appendix 18: Sample Event Attendee Survey
Appendix 19: International Events Management Standards DACUM Chart

Next Generation Event Leaders

Throughout this book, you will see numerous examples of how the profession of Event Leadership has evolved both naturally and strategically to focus more and more on the leadership skills that are needed for long-term career success. Furthermore, you will discover how the next generation of event leaders is rapidly conquering the new frontiers of the profession through technology, environmental sustainability, and a greater focus on events whose purposes are now beyond generating economic impacts.

A recent comprehensive study led by Philip Mondor of the Canadian Tourism Human Resource Council identified the increasingly complex and integrated tasks associated with twenty-first century event leadership. The International Event Management Standards

(IEMS) study was the outgrowth of a group of industry leaders who first identified a preliminary Event Management Body of Knowledge (EMBOK).

Although one could argue that creativity is a continuous thread throughout all of the duties associated with the event manager, the IEMS study determined that the priority of responsibilities, and the knowledge associated with those priorities, have indeed expanded, as outlined in the online appendices for this book.

The emerging research within the special events profession continues to validate and confirm the findings of the event professionals. There appears to be a newfound body of knowledge linking the modern process of event management with the more established field of project management. Project management requires a clear identification of the goals and objectives of the event and a thorough review and evaluation of each milestone that is established. Event planners are increasingly being held accountable for understanding and embracing similar competencies. With this book, you will be able to develop and expand your competency as an event professional and therefore increase your marketability and career options.

New Data Create the Knowledge You Need to Lead

Education

According to the Association of Event Management Educators (AEME) in Great Britain, applications for event management programs in higher education in the United Kingdom increased by 450 percent between 1997 and 2007 (AEME 2008). The majority of event education programs are located in North America (the United States and Canada); however, the second largest percentage of programs is located in what could be easily described on a per capita basis as the world capital for event education, Australia. The third-largest percentage of centers for event education is throughout Europe. Figure P.2 depicts where the programs are located throughout the world. A sampling of schools of event management, along with their contact details, is listed in the appendices.

Employment

According to the *Event Solutions* 2007 Annual Forecast survey of the events industry, "lack of qualified employees" ranks as the fourth most significant issue facing today's events companies. Furthermore, industry growth is slow but steady, with 46 percent of all event suppliers anticipating no decrease in staffing in the near future. Education, training, and certification are desired traits in tomorrow's events work force.

Internet Innovation

In my studies with ISES members, the number of Internet users increased from 56 to nearly 100 percent from 2000 to 2005, and continues to grow. As Internet use becomes increasingly common, web sites have become essential attributes for events companies,

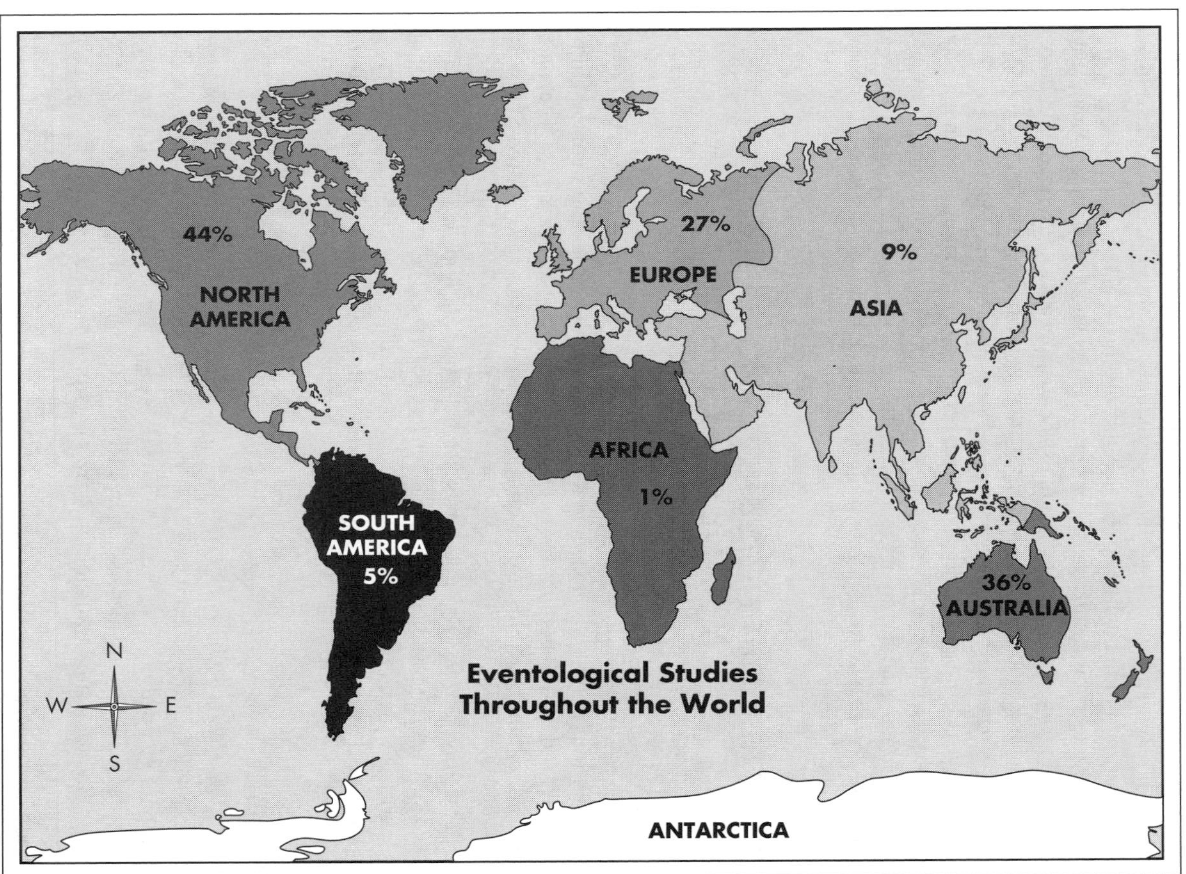

Figure P.2 Map of Event Management Programs

which are utilizing new Internet tools. *Events Solutions* reports an increased use of online registration, e-newsletters, interactive calendars, and webcasting.

Certification

Events professionals are increasingly seeking certification from recognized bodies within the industry. According to the *Event Solutions* 2007 survey, 34 percent of all event professionals hold a certification, the most popular being Certified Meeting Professional (CMP) and Certified Special Events Professional (CSEP).

Gross Revenues

In 2004, *Event Solutions* reported that in all categories, event professionals' gross revenues were under $250,000 per year. This corresponds with the surveys I have conducted with ISES members, showing that most event organizations are small businesses. However, as a result of the global financial crisis of 2008 and 2009, many organizations report reduced earnings, especially in the corporate sector.

Event Budgets

With small revenues, events companies continue to produce large-scale productions. Small event budgets under $5,000 have decreased since 2001, while most events in 2007 were budgeted between $50,000 and $99,999, an increase from 2004, according to *Event Solutions*. And while budgets rose, 40 percent of event planners did not predict a change in their fees in 2007 and 37 percent of event suppliers only predicted a price increase of 1 to 5 percent.

Compensation

There is a wide range of healthy salaries across the events industry, from assistant trade show/conference manager (average 2007 salary: $37,500) to meeting planner (average 2007 salary: $62,213) to food and beverage director (average 2007 salary: $93,000). The event production segment, with its knowledge of special technology, offers the highest average salary, at almost $70,000. Always strong, trade shows, conferences and conventions ranks second highest in terms of compensation. The catering industry, with many low-level jobs, has the lowest average salary (under $60,000) but also the highest overall job—the average director of catering made $87,000 in 2007.

Corporate and Association Event Planner Salaries

Event Solutions discovered that there was a 15 percent decrease in corporate event planner salaries from 2003 to 2004. Perhaps this trend is due, as *Event Solutions* postulates, to the hiring of many new entry-level employees at typically lower salaries. Or could this signal the maturation of this industry in terms of employment? This could be an early indicator that event professionals, especially in the corporate sector, must work harder to justify fair and equitable compensation for the complex and high-level tasks they perform.

However, the salaries are still healthy in this sector, with a senior event producer earning on average over $55,000 per year. By comparison, the association planners reported an average salary for a senior event producer or meeting manager of $47,000. Their salaries also decreased from those reported in 2003. Generally, salaries may be seen as flat or slightly increased when all categories and factors are considered. Therefore, event professionals must continue to demonstrate the added value for their services to help promote well-deserved increases in the future (www.event-solutions.com).

Festival Executives and Special Event Director/Operations Compensation and Benefits

In 2006, the International Festivals and Events Association (IFEA) again conducted a compensation and benefits survey to identify trends in this important budget area. The largest single percentage of the 779 respondents managed events with budgets between $250,000 and $500,000.

According to the 2003 survey, most festival organizations have small staffs of fewer than six persons; however, they average per-festival involvement of 533 volunteers. These organizations are highly dependent on volunteer labor, including interns.

In the survey, 206 individuals responded to the question regarding compensation for Executive Director or Chief Executive Officer (CEO) and stated that the average salary was $65,000. Of these respondents, 50 percent received bonuses ranging from $100 to a maximum of $86,500. Moreover, 62 percent of the respondents reported receiving raises in 2005.

By contrast, those individuals reporting their title as Special Events Director/Operations earned, on average, $55,000 (www.ifea.com).

Exhibition Industry Growth

According to the Center for Exhibition Industry Research (CEIR), the U.S. exhibition industry maintains steady growth. There was the construction of 23 new buildings and the expansion of 63 buildings in the exhibitions sector in 2007. Total exhibition space in the United States and Canada increased from 80 million in 2004 to 84.5 million square feet in 2007 (www.ceir.org).

Convention Industry Impact

The Convention Industry Council (CIC) reported in their 2007 Certified Meeting Professional Report that the meetings industry is the twenty-ninth largest contributor to the U.S. gross national product. In 2007, total direct spending amounted to over $122 billion (www.conventionindustry.org). The CIC and its industry partners are conducting in 2010 a major economic impact study of the convention industry to provide further evidence of the strength and importance of this profession.

Global Event Growth

The International Congress and Convention Association (ICCA) is the leading global association for members of the meetings, incentives, conventions, and exhibitions (MICE) industry. ICCA members reported producing over 6,500 association events in 2007, or 800 more than were produced in 2006, and this number has maintained steady growth since the new millennium. The United States continues its lead as the country hosting the most international association events, followed closely by Germany, Spain, and the United Kingdom. The busiest city for these events, however, remains Vienna, Austria, followed by Berlin, Singapore, and Paris. Beijing made the top ten, and after hosting the 2008 Olympic Games, we may expect to see a rise in the number of international events in China, a country with great potential in this industry (www.iccaworld.com).

The New Generation and the New Frontier

All industries experience different economic periods over time. Generally, economic downturns in the tourism industry are not long lasting due to the continued need of human beings to experience periods of leisure. Exogenous shocks, such as the global financial crisis or terrorism attacks or the rising cost of energy (automobile and airplane fuel especially), could slow the growth of the events industry in the future.

However, the global events industry also has the benefit of providing goods and services that are always in demand as individuals mark and therefore celebrate the many milestones (births, deaths, and everything in between) in their lives. The worldwide phenomenon of aging populations is rapidly influencing the modern events industry; more events are celebrated as people are living longer.

Furthermore, the demand for professional event planners may grow due to the increasing work requirements of most adults that leave little time to plan even the simplest of celebrations. Finally, the harder one works often correlates with the level of stress in one's daily life.

Therefore, the forces of aging, increased work leading to greater stress, and reduced time for planning events may help fuel the sustained growth of the global events industry. This industry will need event leaders like you to plan and produce these events. And to succeed, you will need to continue to learn, grow, and demonstrate through credentials such as professional certification and successful events the added value of your efforts.

Many readers of this book represent the next generation of event planners who, individually and together, will push the frontiers of the profession to new and unprecedented horizons.

Conclusions

The events industry is indeed going through a period of unprecedented change. These changes are the result of both internal and external forces and trends. The advancement in event research and education, the adoption by governments of international standards for events management, the rapid expansion of technological platforms for communication, and the increased focus on the development of environmentally sustainable events are harbingers of great promise for an industry that is still in its early stages of evolution.

However, the deeply troubling global economic crisis of 2008–2009, coupled with the continuing threats posed by global terrorism, remind all who seek to build a future for this industry that we must be ever vigilant as we combat forces that appear to be beyond our immediate control.

Despite the global financial troubles that have led to nationalization of many banks throughout the world, there still appears to be interest and curiosity by the financial community in how they may benefit from investing in the global celebrations industry. While I was preparing the ***Fifth Edition*** of this book, the government of Kazakhstan was preparing to conduct a feasibility study to invest hundreds of millions of dollars in the construction of its first major Congress center.

As I prepared this ***Sixth Edition***, I received a communication from a major international banking firm inquiring if there is any research documenting the economic value of the suppliers to the global events industry. When I asked why he wished to conduct research in the celebrations industry, he replied, "This is one of the industries of the future, and we are preparing to invest in it." His inquiry, interestingly, was not unusual or even unique. As banks tumble and the stock market crashes, celebrations continue. Unemployment may rise and mortgages may be difficult to obtain, but weddings, bar and bat mitzvahs, anniversaries, meetings, and other valuable products and services in the twenty-first century celebrations industry continue to not merely survive, but thrive, in times where other industries suffer or vanish entirely. Just as they have for thousands of years, they will continue to flourish throughout the future.

BBC Television interviewed me at the height of the global banking crisis in 2009 and asked if I thought the Edinburgh international festivals would suffer as a result of these severe economic challenges. I replied that while many other industries have indeed fallen into decline, I predicted that our festivals and events would rise to unprecedented heights as human beings needed, wanted, and desired, perhaps now more than ever, the spiritual fulfillment they provide at a great value. As evidence of strength of the event industry, the Edinburgh Festival Fringe sold more tickets (over 1.8 million) in 2009 and set new records for both attendance and performer participation.

This book is your tool for ensuring these celebrations continue throughout the world of tomorrow. As a new generation of leaders of planned events prepares to explore the next frontier, we may march forward with confidence due to the indelible ability of celebrations, much like poems, to infuse our lives with hope and provide memories that, as Burns noted 250 years ago, shall never be forgotten.

Professor Joe Goldblatt, CSEP
Executive Director
International Centre for the Study of Planned Events
School of Business, Enterprise, and Management
Queen Margaret University
Edinburgh, Scotland

ACKNOWLEDGMENTS

Special Events has been in continuous publication for over 20 years. Now, as it enters its ***Sixth Edition***, it is important to acknowledge the many hands that have helped it reached this special milestone. I wish to acknowledge the following individuals and organizations whose intellectual and creative contributions have helped forge these new frontiers for many future generations to come.

Sixth Edition Pioneers and Protégés

Richard Aaron
Cynthia Bernabe
Clara Bignami
Orit Blatt
Raymond Bremer
Liane Boucher
Alicia Brett
Robyn Brown
Dianne Devitt
Joan Eisenstodt
Dr. Rebecca Finkel
Robin Holt
Anthony Lack
Trevor Laffin
Sharon McElhinney
Andrea Michaels
Anders Muller
Dr. Kathy Nelson (deceased)
Kari Felicia Nestande
Arlene Rush
Ira Rosen
Steven Wood Schmader
Astrid Schrier
Liam Sinclair
Rai Shacklock
Dr. Karen Silva-Sabatoni
Stuart Turner
Liz Glover-Wilson
Cheng So Yin

Additional Contributors:

Alis Aimone (deceased)
Betsy Barber, PhD
Eva Barkoff
Angelo Bonita
Paul Bush
Jeffrey Campbell
Shelia Ann Trapp Campbell
Canadian Tourism Human Resource Council
Professor Anthony Cohen, CBE, FRSE
Sara Cohen
Gene Columbus
Alice Conway, CSEP
Christine Cox
John J. Daly, CSEP
Nina de Courson
Julie Day
Ysabel de la Rosa
Professor Mike Donnelly, PhD
Edinburgh International Conference Centre
Robert Estrin
Susan Faulk

Linda Faulkner
Max Goldblatt (deceased)
Max Darwin Goldblatt
Rosa Goldblatt (deceased)
Sam DeBlanc Goldblatt
Dr. Joseph Arthur Greenberg
Sir Thomas and Lady Emma Ingilby
Klaus Inkamp (deceased)
Jeffrey Hamberger, J.D.
Dr. Donald E. Hawkins
Linda F. Higgison (deceased)
International Special Events Society
Bertha Jacob (deceased)
Johnson & Wales University
Carola Jacob
Sam Jacob (deceased)
Alex Khripunov
Louise E. Knowles
Leah and Stephen Lahasky
Faith Liddell
Michael Loshin, J.D.
Tim Lundy, CSEP
Kath Mainland
Jean McFaddin
Dr. Cathy Matheson
Meeting Professionals International
Jeffrey Montague
Bill Morton
Jack Morton (deceased)
National Association of Catering Executives
Gabrielle Pointer
Leah Pointer (deceased)
Leith's
Queen Margaret University School of Business, Enterprise, and Management
Jason Quinn
Ridgewells Caterers
Professor Russell Rimmer, PhD
Allison Russell
Lynne Russell
Ira Rosen, CFEE
Dr. Ira Shapiro
Julia Schiptsova
Steven Wood Schmader, CFEE
Wright K. Smith (deceased)
Temple University
JoAnna Turtletaub
The George Washington University
The International Special Events Society (ISES)
The Professional Convention Management Association (PCMA)
Harith Wickrema
Sarah Whigham
Dr. Brunetta Wolfman
David Wolper

The John Wiley & Sons, Inc. editorial team for this book, so capably led by Mary Cassells, has provided a seamless and professional transition between each edition. I very much appreciate their professionalism, talent, and friendship. These outstanding Wiley team members include Richard DeLorenzo, Julie Kerr, and Jenni Lee.

And most especially, I am grateful to my senior editor, Sam Goldblatt, for this, the ***Sixth Edition*** of ***Special Events***. His constant devotion to this project, as perhaps best exemplified in his groundbreaking chapter on Greener Events, is most appreciated by both author and very proud father (one and the same).

Finally, were it not for my partner of 33 years, I would not have had the time, encouragement, inspiration, or support needed to complete this work. Therefore, my most sincere appreciation goes to Nancy Lynner, whose amazing talent, boundless love, and devotion provide the very best foundation for my life and work.

Professor Joe Goldblatt, CSEP
September 2010

PART ONE

Theory of Event Leadership

IMEX is the largest business event tourism program in Frankfurt, Germany and one of the largest in Europe. IMEX welcomes thousands of hosted buyers and destinations who come to expand the global meetings and events industry through this important industry event.

CHAPTER 1

Welcome to Planned Events

In this chapter you will learn how to:

- Understand and appreciate the importance of economic, social, cultural, political, and environmental sustainability for planned events
- Recognize and understand the economic, social, political, cultural, and environmental changes that are affecting the global events industry
- Identify and benefit from the demographic changes affecting the global event industry
- Utilize the psychographic changes affecting event length, purpose, and outcomes to improve performance
- Recognize and analyze the multitudinous challenges facing the events industry including financial, security, labor, ecological, and other critical areas
- Identify new and emerging career opportunities in this growing field
- Understand why education has become the most important factor in the growth of planned events
- Identify industry certification programs
- Advance your career throughout the twenty-first century
- Develop new ways to sustain your career

The professional event host knows that the word "Welcome!" is an essential part of the guest experience at any event. Therefore, I warmly welcome you to the sixth edition of *Special Events*. However, in the global spirit of this book, allow me to add:

- Beruchim Habaim (Hebrew)
- Benvenuto (Italian)
- Bien venue (French)
- Bienvenidos (Spanish)
- Dobre doshli (Bulgarian)
- Dobro pozhalovat! (Russian)
- Fáilte (Scots Gaelic)
- Fair faa ye (Ulster Scots)
- Fun ying (Cantonese Chinese)
- G'day (Australian English)
- Hos geldin (Turkish)
- Huan ying (Mandarin Chinese)
- Kali meta (Greek)
- Khosh aamadid (Farsi: Iran, Afghanistan and Tajikistan)
- Kwaribu (Swahili)
- Laipni ludzam (Latvian)
- Sabah al kher (Arabic)
- Swaagatam (India)
- Tusanyuse Kulamba (Bugandan)
- Urakasa neza (Kinyarwandan)
- Urseo oh se yo (Korean)
- Velkomst (Danish)
- Willkommen (German)
- Yokoso (Japanese)

The Internet has changed and is rapidly changing the world. For example, to learn how to say "welcome" in hundreds of different languages, visit www.elite.net/~runner/jennifers/welcome.htm.

The local or regional nature of planned events was replaced with lightning speed by global connections throughout the world. I discovered this while seated at my home computer receiving e-mail messages from distant lands. "Thanks for your excellent book—it changed my perspective about the profession," wrote one industry member from the Far East. These types of messages were quickly followed by requests for information and, ultimately, offers to fly me to lands that I had only read about. The Internet has had as much influence as Gutenberg's printing press—perhaps more. The World Wide Web has woven the Event Leadership profession together into a new global community. As a result of this new "Web," each of us now has far greater opportunities for career and business development than we previously imagined or aspired to.

Event Aspect	From:	To:
Event organization	Amateur	Professional
Event guests	Younger, monocultural	Older, multicultural
Event technology	Incidental	Integral and ubiquitous
Event markets	Local	Global
Event education	Nonessential	Essential, qualifications (certifications and degrees valued by employers)
Event evaluation	Narrow	Comprehensive

Figure 1.1 A Generation of Change

In the past two decades since the first edition of *Special Events*, the field of planned events has seen numerous changes. Figure 1.1 summarizes these paradigm shifts.

These six aspects of the profession reflect how the Event Leadership field has experienced sweeping changes in the past decade. The letters above the massive doors to the National Archives in Washington, DC, read "Where Past is Prologue." And so it is with our profession. To go forward, we must first reflect on the historical roots of our field of study.

A New Generation and the Next Frontier

Although the field of special events, celebrations, rituals, and rites may date back to the early beginning of humankind, you, as a member of the current and future generation of professional practitioners, may have a greater impact on this field than that of all those who have come before you. That is why the sixth edition of this 20-year-old volume is titled "A New Generation and The Next Frontier." The purpose of this book is not to prepare you for your first job. It is to prepare you for your last one.

Throughout your career you will face many daunting challenges, including the recent global financial turmoil, ecological issues and continuing security threats. In addition, I am certain you will face challenges we have not even imagined as of this time.

Therefore, in order to prepare for the future, it is important to understand the past. The history of special events is rich with personalities, innovation, and creativity. During your time, you will add to this lore with your own contributions. However, now I invite you to take a walk up the Main Street of special event history and meet some of the interesting persons whose seminal contributions developed the field that you will soon help advance into the next frontier.

Once Upon a Time and Not Too Long Ago

The term *special events* may have first been used at what is often described as the "happiest place on earth." In 1955, when Walt Disney opened Disneyland in Anaheim, California, he turned to one of his imagineers, Robert Jani, and asked him to help solve a big problem. Each day at 5:00 P.M., thousands of people, in fact almost 90 percent of the guests, would leave the park. The problem with this mass exodus was that Walt's happiest place on earth remained open until 10:00 P.M. This meant that he had to support a payroll of thousands of workers, utilities, and other expenses for five hours each day with no income.

To correct this problem, Robert Jani, then director of public relations for Disneyland and later the owner of one of the most successful special event production companies in the world, Robert F. Jani Productions, proposed the creation of a nightly parade that he dubbed the "Main Street Electric Parade." Dozens of floats with thousands of miniature lights would nightly glide down Main Street, delighting thousands of guests who remained to enjoy the spectacle. This technique is used today in all Disney parks, with perhaps the best example at Epcot, where a major spectacular is staged every night. According to the producers, this spectacle results in millions of dollars of increased spending annually.

One of the members of the media turned to Robert Jani during the early days of the Main Street Electric Parade and asked, "What do you call that program?" Jani replied, "A special event." "A special event—what's that?" the reporter asked. Jani thoughtfully answered with what may be the simplest and best definition: A special event is that which is different from a normal day of living. According to Jani, nowhere on earth does a parade appear on the main street every night of the year. Only at Disneyland, where special events are researched, designed, planned, managed, coordinated, and evaluated, does this seemingly spontaneous program take place every night. Jani, who would later produce National Football League Super Bowl half-time spectaculars as well as the legendary Radio City Music Hall Christmas Show (among many other unique events), was a man whose motto was "Dream big dreams and aim high."

Anthropological and Sociological Origins

Emile Durkheim (1858–1978) was a French scientist whose theories and discoveries helped form the basis of the fields of sociology and anthropology. Durkheim was mainly concerned with how societies maintain their integrity and intactness in the modern era. He believed that the relationship between people and the supernatural being was similar to that of the relationship between people and the community. Durkheim classified religion into four categories:

1. Disciplinary: forcing or administrating discipline
2. Cohesive: bringing people together, a strong bond
3. Vitalizing: making things more lively or vigorous, vitality, boosting spirits
4. Euphoric: conveying happiness, a good feeling, confidence, well being

It may be argued that planned events, celebrations, rituals, and rites accomplish many of these same outcomes. There is a certain discipline within events, they bring people together, they often boost spirits, and they can lead to euphoria. However, they differ in one significant way from Durkheim's theories. Planned events are designed to produce outcomes.

Ten years after Durkheim's death, in the first edition of this book, I defined a special event as a *unique moment in time celebrated with ceremony and ritual to satisfy specific needs.* My definition emerged from that of anthropologist Victor Turner, who wrote: "Every human society celebrates with ceremony and ritual its joys, sorrows, and triumphs." According to Turner and other researchers whom I had studied in my exploration of anthropology, ceremony and ritual were important factors in the design, planning, management, and coordination of special events.

The term *event* is derived from the Latin word "e-venire," which means "outcome." Therefore, every event is, in fact, an outcome produced by a team that is led by the Event Leader. After interviewing thousands of experts in Event Leadership for the past five editions of *Special Events*, I have discovered that, while special events may represent many professions, one person is always at the helm of this large vessel. That person is the Event Leader.

Growth Opportunities

Only six decades ago, when an orchestra was needed to provide music for a wedding or social event, one consulted an orchestra leader. Very often, the orchestra leader would provide references for additional talent to enhance the event. Mike Lanin, of Howard Lanin Productions of New York City, tells the story of a meeting his father, Howard Lanin, the renowned society maestro, had with a client in Philadelphia during the late 1920s. Having already asked Lanin to provide music for her daughter's coming-out party being held at the Bellevue-Stratford Hotel (now the Park Hyatt at the Bellevue), the client asked that he provide décor as well. When Lanin asked how much the client would like to spend, the client replied, "Just make it lovely, Howard—just make it lovely." Lanin immediately realized that making this huge ballroom "lovely" might require an investment of five figures. With inflation, the cost of such an undertaking today would well exceed six figures. But Lanin was fortunate to have earned his client's total trust. Without further discussion, the orchestra leader and decorator went to work. Few clients of any era would offer such an unlimited budget. But more and more often, special events professionals such as the Lanins are being asked to provide more diversified services. And although orchestra leaders may have been comfortable recommending decorations and other services and products for social events three decades ago, they and others with specific areas of expertise found that, when it came to events designed for advertising and public relations opportunities, they required specialized assistance.

Public Relations

Public relations is a proud ancestor of the celebrations industry. Less than 50 years ago, the modern profession of public relations and advertising became an accepted tool in American commerce. When a corporation wished to introduce a new product, increase sales, or motivate its employees, its corporate leaders turned to public relations and advertising professionals to design a plan. Today, the celebrations industry includes tens of thousands of hardworking professionals, who, for the first time in the industry's history, are truly working together to offer their clients the excellent services and products they deserve. As an example of the growth of Event Leadership in the public relations field, consider this comment from the first person in the United States to receive a master's degree in public relations, Carol Hills, now a professor at Boston University: "My students are extremely interested in events. They recognize that public relations and events are inseparable. Event leadership is certainly a growth area in public relations practice."

Marketing and Retail Sales

According to the International Council of Shopping Centers (ICSC) in New York, marketing directors who produce events for local and regional shopping centers can earn healthy incomes. Marketing professionals have recognized the need for specialized training and the benefits of certification within their industry. Events help attract and influence consumers to purchase specific products and services from small retail stores up to major regional shopping centers. In this age of entrepreneurship, the creation of new business is far greater than the growth of established firms. With each new business created, there is a new opportunity to celebrate through a grand opening or other special event. There are millions of new businesses created annually throughout the world that may require an Event Leader to produce an opening celebration.

Global Business

According to the World Economic Forum, there are 12 pillars of competitiveness within the global economy:

1. Institutions
2. Infrastructure
3. Macroeconomic stability
4. Health and primary education
5. Higher education and training
6. Goods market efficiency
7. Labor market efficiency
8. Financial market sophistication
9. Technological readiness
10. Market size
11. Business sophistication
12. Innovation

These pillars are closely interrelated in any economy. In order for your events business to effectively compete in the global marketplace, it is important for you to identify the countries in the world that are leading in these competitive areas. The World Economic Forum 2008–2009 Global Competitiveness Report of 134 economies throughout the world listed, in order of competitiveness, the United States, Switzerland, Denmark, Sweden, and Singapore as the most competitive economies. However, the United Kingdom dropped from ninth to twelfth position in this report (World Economic Forum 2008–2009 Global Competitiveness Report).

From this report and others, despite the continuing economic challenges being experienced throughout the world, Event Leaders may begin to see new opportunities for event growth and development. The Nordic countries and Asia (most notably Singapore) demonstrate great competitiveness and may provide new and stronger opportunities for event development in the future. For example, in 2010, Singapore will host the first Youth Olympic Games, a pioneering development by the International Olympic Committee designed for youths 14 to18 years of age.

Leisure and Recreation

According to recent studies conducted by the International Amusement Parks and Attractions Association (IAAPA), the changing lifestyle trends bear watching. Fifty percent of the new so-called baby boomer or limbo generations now have more discretionary income. Due to longevity and what is defined as *vacation starvation,* they are spending this income on leisure products.

Many of these individuals are described as "wanderlust singletons" because most are indeed single adults. They are socially aware and environmentally sensitive, support fair trade, and desire nature-based tourism experiences.

They have a strong need to escape a working environment that is increasingly stressful, and therefore they seek experiences in the great outdoors, where there is a greater opportunity for controlled risk through activities such as whitewater rafting with an experienced guide.

One final psychographic change identified by IAAPA was the development of *tribing* and mass customization. Seth Godin in his book *Tribes* states that people form tribes with or without leaders and that the key is for leaders and organizations to work for the tribe and make it something better (Godin 2008).

Affinity or special interest groups—where individuals can bond with people of similar interests and experience levels—and the need to customize experiences are both growing in importance. The ability to satisfy both needs, tribal as well as individual activities, will determine in the future which Event Leaders will succeed and which may fail.

Demographers believe that India and China will soon emerge as the major exporters of tourists due to the population density and the rising average income. However, in developed countries such as the United States, a new group nicknamed "SKIN" is developing. SKIN means "spending kids' inheritance now." As adults find new ways to extend the longevity and quality of their lives, leisure, sought through special events, will become even more popular.

An Event Leader historically was a person responsible for researching, designing, planning, coordinating, and evaluating events, and you will learn about each of these phases in the pages to come. However, the logical question one may ask is: What is the Event Leadership profession?

The Event Leadership Profession

According to experts in the field of professional certification, all professions are represented by three unique characteristics: (1) the profession must have a unique body of knowledge; (2) the profession typically has voluntary standards that often result in certification; and (3) the profession has an accepted code of conduct or ethics. Event leadership meets each of these qualifications. Although it can be argued that, like tourism, Event Leadership actually comprises many industries, increasingly, as data are gathered and scientific tests conducted, it becomes more apparent that Event Leadership represents a unique body of knowledge.

Event leadership is a profession that, through planned events, requires public assembly for the purpose of celebration, education, marketing, and reunion. Let us explore this further. The term *public assembly* means events managed by professionals who typically bring people together for a purpose. Although one person can certainly hold an event by him- or herself, arguably it will not have the complexities of an event with 10 or 10,000 people. Therefore, the size and type of group will determine the level of skills required by a professional Event Leader.

The next key word is *purpose*. In daily lives, events take place spontaneously and, as a result, are sometimes not orderly, effective, or on schedule. However, professional Event Leaders begin with a specific purpose in mind and direct all activities toward achieving this purpose. Event leaders are purposeful about their work.

The third and final key component consists of the four activities that represent these purposes: celebration, education, marketing, and reunion.

Celebration

Celebration is characterized by festivities ranging from fairs and festivals to social life-cycle events. Although the term *celebration* can also be applied to education, marketing, and reunion events, it serves to encompass all aspects of human life where events are held for the purpose of celebration.

When one hears the word *celebration,* typically one has an image of fireworks or other festivities. In fact, the word is derived from the Latin word *celebro,* meaning "to honor." Another commonly accepted definition is "to perform," as in a ritual. Therefore, celebrations usually refer to official or festive functions such as parades, civic events, festivals, religious observances, political events, bar and bat mitzvahs, weddings, anniversaries, and other events tied to a person's or organization's life-cycle or of historical importance.

Education

From the first event in preschool or kindergarten to meetings and conferences where many adults receive continuing education throughout their entire adult lives, educational events mark, deliver, test, and support growth for all human beings. This growth may be social, such as the high school prom, or it may be professional, such as a certification program. Regardless of the purpose, a school public assembly may be primarily or secondarily educationally related.

The term educate is also derived from Latin and means "to lead out." Through education events, Event Leaders lead out new ideas, emotions, and actions that improve society. Examples of education events include convocations, commencements, alumni events, training at a corporation, meetings and conferences with specific educational content, and an activity known as edutainment. *Edutainment* results from the use of entertainment devices (e.g., singers and dancers) to present educational concepts. Through entertainment, guests may learn, comprehend, apply (through audience participation), analyze, and even evaluate specific subject matter. Entertainment may be used to lead out new ideas to improve productivity.

Marketing

Event marketing, according to *Advertising Age,* is now an intrinsic part of any marketing plan. Along with advertising, public relations, and promotions, events serve to create awareness and persuade prospects to purchase goods and services. These events may be private, such as the launch of a new automobile to dealers or the public. Retailers have historically used events to drive sales, and now other types of businesses are realizing that face-to-face events are an effective way to satisfy sales goals. The appearance of soap opera stars at a shopping center is an example of many types of promotions used to attract customers to promote sales.

Reunion

When human beings reunite for the purposes of remembrance, rekindling friendships, or simply rebonding as a group, they are conducting a reunion activity. Reunion activities are present in all the Event Leadership subfields because once the initial event is successful, there may be a desire to reunite. The reunion activity is so symbolic in the American system that President Bill Clinton used this theme for his inaugural activities.

Event Leadership Subfields

The desire and need to celebrate are unique characteristics that make us human. The humorist Will Rogers is reported to have said: "Man is the only animal that blushes . . . or needs to!" Human beings are the only animals that celebrate, and this not only separates us from the lower forms but also perhaps raises us to a transcendent or even spiritual level. The growth of Event Leadership subfields certainly reflects this extraordinary capability for celebration to transform individual humans and entire industries.

As noted earlier, anthropology historically has recognized a four-field approach to Event Leadership. However, the profession encompasses many specialized fields: advertising, attractions, broadcasting, civic, corporate, exposition, fairs, festivals, government, hospitality, meetings, museums, retail, and tourism. Event leaders may specialize in any of these fields; however, rarely is an Event Leader an expert in more than a few of these areas. For example, a director of Event Leadership for a zoological society may plan events for the zoo, and some of those events may involve retail promotions. Therefore, knowledge of education and marketing, as well as administration and risk management, is important.

These subfields are not scientifically categorized—there are many cross-linkages. However, this list provides an overview into the possibilities for Event Leaders as they seek to chart their future course of study:

- Civic events
- Expositions/exhibitions
- Fairs and festivals
- Hallmark events
- Hospitality
- Meetings and conferences

- Retail events
- Social life-cycle events
- Sports events
- Tourism

Once trained in the fundamentals, event planners may wish to specialize or concentrate their studies in one or two event subfields. By concentrating in more than one area, they are further protected from a downturn in a specific market segment. For example, if association meeting planners suddenly were no longer in demand, due to outsourcing, cross-training in government or corporate event planning may allow them to make a smooth transition to this new field. Use the descriptions of subfields that follow as a guide to focus your market or future employment options. The appendixes list contact details for many of the industry organizations.

Civic Events

Beginning with the U.S. bicentennial celebration in 1976 and continuing with individual centennials, sesquicentennials, and bicentennials of hundreds of towns and cities, Americans in the twentieth century created more events than at any other time in the history of the republic. In both Europe and Asia, celebration is rooted in long-standing religious, cultural, and ritual traditions. Civic events may include public demonstrations through planned events such as marches to protest certain laws or policies or to advocate for a cause.

The United States has not only blended the traditions of other cultures but has created its own unique events, such as the annual Doo-Dah Parade in Pasadena, California. Anyone and everyone can participate in this event, and they do. There is a riding-lawn-mower brigade, a precision briefcase squad, and other equally unusual entries. As the United States matures, its celebrations will continue to develop into authentic made-in-the-U.S.A. events.

In Edinburgh, Scotland, the Beltane Festival (later resulting in the tradition known as May Day) is held in early May of each year on Calton Hill and involves hundreds of celebrants recreating ancient Celtic rites and rituals as well as through contemporary celebration creating new ones. It is known as a complement to Samhain (All Hallow's Eve), when the other world visits us, and Beltane, where we can visit the otherworld. The citizens of Edinburgh and tourists visiting the city observe and participate during this ritualistic celebration that involves reenactment of ancient ceremonies. This reenactment of ancient rituals in a contemporary context often creates discomfort and therefore the organizers feel the need to notify the guests of what they may experience. The ticket that is issued for admission clearly states, "CAUTION: After 8 P.M. there may be partial nudity and inappropriate behavior."

Civic events may not always result in civilized activities as expected in the traditional sense, as exemplified by the Beltane Festival. However, the term *civil* suggests that the behavior of the group will conform to the social norm. In the case of the Beltane Festival, the social norm that dates back to Celtic period is imposed on a contemporary setting with many different reactions from the participants, guests, and media who participate and observe.

Expositions/Exhibitions

Closely related to fairs and festivals is the exposition. Although divided into two categories—public and private—the exposition has historically been a place where retailers meet wholesalers or suppliers to introduce their goods and services to buyers. Some marketing analysts have suggested that it is the most cost-effective way to achieve sales, as people who enter the exposition booth are more qualified to buy than is a typical sales suspect. Furthermore, the exposition booth allows, as do all events, a multisensory experience that influences customers to make a positive buying decision. A major shift in this field has been to turn the trade show or exposition into a live multisensory event with educational and entertainment programs being offered in the various booths. Like many others, this field presents growth opportunity. The third richest man in America, Sheldon Adelson, earned his fortune running a computer trade show during the tech boom. Although some smaller trade shows have consolidated with larger ones, just as many or perhaps more shows are being created each year. This spells opportunity for savvy event marketers who wish to benefit from this lucrative field.

Fairs and Festivals

Just as in ancient times, when people assembled in the marketplace to conduct business, commercial as well as religious influences have factored into the development of today's festivals, fairs, and public events. Whether a religious festival in India or a music festival in the United States, each is a public community event symbolized by a kaleidoscope of experiences that finds meaning through the lives of the participants. This kaleidoscope comprises performances, arts and crafts demonstrations, and other media that bring meaning to the lives of participants and spectators.

These festivals and fairs have shown tremendous growth as small and large towns seek tourism dollars through such short-term events. Some communities use these events to boost tourism during the slow or off-season, and others focus primarily on weekends to appeal to leisure travelers. Regardless of the reason, fairs (often not-for-profit but with commercial opportunities) and festivals (primarily not-for-profit events) provide unlimited opportunities for organizations to celebrate their culture while providing deep meaning for those who participate and attend.

Hallmark Events

The growth of the Olympic Games is but one example of how hallmark events have grown in both size and volume during the past decade. A hallmark event, also known as a mega event, is best defined as a one-time or recurring event of major proportions, such as the Summer or Winter Olympic Games, the National Football League Super Bowl, or other event projects of similar size, scale, scope, and budget. According to Colin Michael Hall (*GeoJournal* 1989), a hallmark event may also be defined as "major fairs, expositions, cultural and sporting events of international status which are held on either a regular or a one-off basis. A primary function of the hallmark event is to provide the host community with an opportunity to secure high prominence in the tourism market place. However, international or regional prominence may be gained with significant social and environmental costs." From the Olympic Games to the global millennium celebrations, the 1980s and 1990s were a period of sustained growth for such mega-events. Although television certainly helped propel this growth, the positive impact of tourism dollars has largely driven the development of these events.

Birthright Israel, an initiative of the Israeli government to bring young Diaspora Jews from around the world to Israel, produces a similar event, appropriately titled the Mega Event. Held in a large Jerusalem hotel, the Mega Event features singers, dancers, pyrotechnics, lasers, and celebrity appearances, all crafted as a celebration of Israel. When my son attended in 2008, President Shimon Peres himself took the stage to welcome the Diaspora Jews to the Promised Land. This use of grandiose spectacle to forge national identity and promote tourism shows how the concept of mega events can be reinterpreted.

Ironically, the World's Fair movement appears to have ebbed in the current era of globalization. This is perhaps due to the fact that the inventions showcased in previous World's Fairs (space travel, computers, teleconferencing) have become commonplace and because supposedly futuristic innovations actually appeared before some fairs opened. This provides an opportunity to reinvent, revive, and perhaps sustain this hallmark event.

Hospitality

In the hospitality industry, hotels throughout the world are expanding their business interests from merely renting rooms and selling food and beverages to actually planning events. Nashville's Opryland Hotel may have been the first to create a department for special events as a profit center for the corporation. It was followed by Hyatt Hotels Regency Productions, and now other major hotel chains, such as Marriott, are exploring ways to move from fulfilling to actually planning and profiting from events. According to Maricar Donato, president of WashingTours, cultural sensitivity in hospitality will grow rapidly as events increasingly become multicultural experiences due to the diverse composition of event guests.

Meetings and Conferences

According to the Convention Industry Council, an organization that represents 34 associations whose members plan or supply meetings, conferences, and expositions, these combined industries contribute over $122.31 billion annually to the U.S. economy (Convention Industry Council Economic Industry Report 2004). As a result of this impact, the U.S. convention industry is the twenty-ninth largest contributor to gross domestic product. Since widespread use of the jet airplane in the 1950s, meetings and conferences have multiplied by the thousands as attendees jet in and out for three- and four-day events. These events are primarily educational seminars that provide networking opportunities for association members and corporate employees. Despite the recent challenges of terrorism and environmental concerns over rising fuel prices, the globalization of the economy has produced significant growth in international meetings. As a result, Event Leaders are now traveling constantly, both domestically and internationally.

However, there is much controversy regarding economic impact studies related to tourism and conventions in particular. In 2004, Boston, Massachusetts, hosted the U.S. Democratic Convention. As this was the first convention to be held since the terrorist attacks in New York City in 2001, the costs for security and safety were enormous. However, the mayor of Boston predicted a net economic benefit for the city of $154 million. A subsequent study by the Beacon Hill Institute at Suffolk University identified the actual net economic benefits to Boston as only $14 million. Although this was still a positive benefit, it was nowhere near the estimate predicted by the mayor (Beacon Hill Institute, Suffolk University, 2004).

Retail Events

From the earliest days of ancient markets, sellers have used promotions and events to attract buyers and drive sales. The paradigm has shifted in this subindustry from the early 1960s and 1970s, when retailers depended on single-day events to attract thousands of consumers to their stores. Soap opera stars, sports celebrities, and even live cartoon characters during a Saturday appearance could increase traffic and, in some cases, sales as well. Today, retailers are much more savvy and rely on marketing research to design long-range promotional events that use an integrated approach, combining a live event with advertising, publicity, and promotions. They are discovering that cause marketing, such as aligning a product with a worthy charity or important social issue (e.g., education), is a better way to build a loyal customer base and improve sales. This shift from short-term quick events to long-term integrated event marketing is a major change in the retail events subindustry.

Social Life-Cycle Events

Bar and bat mitzvahs, weddings, golden wedding anniversaries, and other events that mark the passage of time with a milestone celebration are growing. As the age of Americans rises due to improvements in health care, there will be many more opportunities to celebrate. Only a few years ago, a fiftieth wedding anniversary was a rare event. Today, most retail greeting-card stores sell golden-anniversary greeting cards as but just one symbol of the growth of these events.

In the wedding industry, it is not uncommon to host an event that lasts three or more days, including the actual ceremony. This is due to the great distances that families must travel to get together for these celebrations. It may also be due to the fast-paced world in which we live, which often prevents families and friends from coming together for these milestones. Whatever the reason, social life-cycle events are growing in both length of days and size of budgets.

Funeral directors report that business is booming. Coupled with the increase in number of older U.S. citizens is the fact that many people are not affiliated with churches or synagogues. Therefore, at the time of death, a neutral location is required for the final event. Most funeral chapels in the United States were constructed in the 1950s and now must be expanded to accommodate the shift in population. New funeral homes are being constructed and older ones are being expanded.

In the first edition of this book, I predicted that in the not-too-distant future, funerals might be held in hotels to provide guests with overnight accommodations and a location for social events. Now I predict that in some large metropolitan areas, due to aging demographics, funeral home construction will be coupled with zoning decisions regarding hotel and motel accommodations to provide a total package for out-of-town guests. With the collapse of the traditional family of the 1950s and Americans' proclivity for relocation, it is not unreasonable to assume that weddings, funerals, and reunions are central to our lives for reconnecting with family and friends. Perhaps one growth opportunity for future Event Leaders will be to design a total life-cycle event environment providing services, including accommodations, for these important events in a resort or leisure setting.

Social life-cycle events have always been important. While conducting focus group research at a local nursing home, a 97-year-old woman told me: "When you get to be my age, you forget almost everything. What you do remember are the important things: your daughter's wedding, your fiftieth wedding anniversary, and other milestones that make life so meaningful." Increasingly, due to limited time availability, people are turning to Event Leaders to organize these important milestone events.

Sports Events

One example of the growth in popularity in professional sports is the rapid development of sports hall of fame and museum complexes throughout the United States. The 1994 World Cup soccer craze generated excitement, visibility, and, in some cases, significant revenue for numerous destinations throughout the United States. Before, during, or following the big game, events are used to attract, capture, and motivate spectators, regardless of the game's outcome, to keep supporting their favorite team. In fact, the line has been blurred between sport and entertainment, due largely to the proliferation of events such as pregame giveaways, postgame fireworks and musical shows, and even promotions such as trivia contests during the game. In 2010, Singapore will host the International Youth Olympic Games and Johannesburg, South Africa, will host the World Cup. While in 2012, London, England, will host the Summer International Olympic Games, and then Scotland will host both the Commonwealth Games and the Ryder Cup in 2014. The estimated total combined economic impact from these three events in the United Kingdom between 2012 and 2014 would be over 2.5 billion pounds, as well as the creation of thousands of jobs to support these events (Blake, Nottingham University 2005; Scottish Parliament 2008; Anderson Economic Group 2006).

Tourism

Since the U.S. bicentennial in 1976, when literally thousands of communities throughout the United States created celebrations, event tourism has become an important phenomenon. According to a study I conducted in 1994, those communities that do not have the facilities to attract the largest conventions are turning increasingly to event tourism as a means of putting heads in beds during the off-season and weekends. Whether it is in the form of arts and crafts shows, historical reenactments, music festivals, or other events that last anywhere from 1 to 10 days, Americans are celebrating more than ever before and profiting from event tourism.

From taxpayers to political leaders to business leaders, more and more stakeholders are becoming invested in event tourism. According to studies by the Travel Industry Association of America, an increasing number of adults visit a special event (fair, festival, other) while on vacation. In fact, the 2003 edition of Historic/Cultural Traveler reports that 48 percent of all travelers visited a fair or exhibition and 31 percent of all travelers attended an organized sporting event during their trip (Travel Industry Association 2003). In this period immediately after the terrorist attacks of September 11, 2001, when transportation for leisure tourists rapidly changed from flying to driving, many local events such as agricultural fairs and festivals benefited from nearby visitors who took advantage of the opportunity to experience a local festival, often for the first time.

One of the best examples of this growth is the 2009 Homecoming Scotland programme of event. Scotland significantly increased their tourism arrivals through the orchestration of a year long program of successful tourism events celebrating Scottish culture and heritage. This program is featured as a international best practice at the conclusion of this book.

Some see local event tourism as a growth area. The term *staycation,* or *portmanteau* (stay-at-home vacation), was first coined by the Canadian comedian and television star Brent Butt, when he sent his friends exotic post cards whilst actually vacationing in a field across the street from his place of work.

Stakeholders

Stakeholders are people or organizations who have invested in an event. For example, the stakeholders of a festival may include the board of directors, the political officials, the municipal staff, the participants (craftspeople), the utility companies, and others. Event planners must scan the event environment to identify internal as well as external stakeholders. An internal stakeholder may be a member of the board, the professional staff of the organization, a guest, or other closely related person. External stakeholders may include media, municipal officials, city agencies, or others. A stakeholder does not have to invest money in an event to be considered for this role. Emotional, political, or personal interest in a cause is evidence of investment in an event.

The Event Leadership Professional Model

The analysis herein, from defining the profession, to identifying the principal activities conducted within this profession, to listing some of the subfields where event planners work, is not intended to be comprehensive. Rather, it is a framework within which you can begin to see a pattern emerge. This pattern is reflected in Figure 1.2, a model that depicts the linkages among the definition, activities, subfields, and stakeholders. It will be useful to you as you begin or continue your studies in planned events, as it provides a theoretical framework supporting the organization of this profession. The term *eventology* was first introduced in North America in 2003 by Linda Higgison (1947–2007). Higgison was a prolific writer, speaker, and successful business entrepreneur. The concept was first explored 20 years earlier by the Institute for Eventology in Japan. This scientific field of study incorporates previous studies in sociology, anthropology, psychology, business, communications, technology, theology, and other more-established scientific fields. Eventology is a synthesis of studies conducted in previous fields that advances these fields of study to systematically explore the outcomes resulting from human events.

THE PROFESSION

PLANNED EVENTS

The function that requires human assembly for the purpose of celebration, education, marketing, and reunion

⇓

THE PROFESSIONAL TITLE(s)

EVENT PRODUCER, DIRECTOR, MANAGER

The person responsible for researching, designing, planning, coordinating, and evaluating an event

⇓

SUBFIELD SPECIALIZATION

Examples of subfields: civic events, conventions, expositions, fairs and festivals, hallmark events, hospitality, incentive travel, meetings and conferences, retail events, reunions, social life-cycle events, sport events, and tourism

⇓

STAKEHOLDERS

Individuals or organizations financially, politically, emotionally, or personally invested in an event

Figure 1.2 Goldblatt Model for the Event Leadership Profession

Change, Creativity, and Innovation: The Three Constants in Event Leadership

A six-year study titled *The Profile of Event Management* (International Special Events Society 1999) identified many significant changes in the Event Leadership profession. Many of these shifts were identified in Figure 1.1; now let's explore these changes further and see how they may affect your career.

Demographic Change

Within the next few years, nearly 70 million Americans will turn 50 years of age. As a result of the graying of America, not only will millions of Americans celebrate a major milestone (middle age) but Event Leaders will be forced to rethink the types of events they design. For example, as Americans age, it is likely that they will experience more health problems, such as loss of hearing and vision and restriction of movement. Therefore, we must respond to these changes with improved resources, such as large-type printed programs, infrared assisted-listening devices, and event ramps and handrails to accommodate persons with physical challenges. The good news is that, as people age, so do their institutions, creating a multiplier effect for the number of celebrations that will be held. The other news is that Event Leaders must anticipate the requirements the aging population will have and be prepared to adapt their event design to satisfy these emerging physical and psychological needs.

Furthermore, the cultural composition of society is changing rapidly as well. It is projected that the minority will become the majority in the United States by 2050. The U.S. Census Bureau stated in 2008 that by 2050, 54 percent of U.S. citizens will be nonwhite and the number of U.S. residents who are over 65 years of age will more than double.

Aging and multicultural change will be major factors in the design and planning of events throughout the remainder of the twenty-first century. Those who are attuned to the needs, wants, and desires of older persons attending their events and are sensitive to the myriad of multicultural nuances that will inform their event decisions will be most successful and develop sustainable careers.

Psychographic Change

Tourism researchers have identified the adventurist or allocentric tourist as the fastest-growing market in leisure travel. This projection is further evidenced by the rapid growth in ecotourism programs throughout the world. In both developed and developing countries, Event Leaders must rethink the approach to events to preserve the high-touch experience for guests. This need for high levels of stimulation may be a direct response to the decade-long fascination with the Internet, which is essentially a solitary endeavor. The Internet may have directly or indirectly created an even greater demand for high-touch, in-person, face-to-face events. By understanding the psychographic needs of event guests and providing high-touch experiences, Event Leaders may, in fact, have greater opportunities for maximizing the outcomes that guests desire.

Career Opportunities

Figure 1.3 lists 15 established and emerging careers in planned events. No one can determine accurately how many more careers may be added to this list in the near-, mid-, or

Event Management Position	Background and Experience Typically Required
Attraction Event Director	Organization, marketing, logistical, human relations, financial, negotiation
Catering Director	Food and beverage coordination, organization, financial, supervisory, sales, negotiation
Civic or Council Event Manager	Organization, legal and regulatory research ability, human relations, financial, marketing, logistical, negotiation
Convention Service Leader	Organization, supervisory, financial, logistical, human relations, negotiation
Cruise Event Director	Interest in cruising and leisure / recreation, ability to develop and lead leisure activities such as seminars, games, dances and other recreational activities to create events on cruise vessels
Education Event Manager	Understanding of principles of adult learning and curriculum development, marketing, finance, organization, volunteer coordination
Family Reunion Manager	Human relations, marketing, financial, organization, supervisory, negotiation
Festival Event Director	Organization, financial, marketing, volunteer coordination, supervisory, entertainment, cultural arts, negotiation
Fitness Event Director	Strong background in physical fitness and sports, interest in and knowledge of general nutrition, ability to use events to promote physical fitness through walking, running, and other fitness activities
Fundraising Event Director	Research, fundraising, proposal writing, marketing, human relations, volunteer coordination, financial

Figure 1.3 Planned Event Positions and Background and Experience Typically Required

Event Management Position	Background and Experience Typically Required
Health Event Manager	Strong background in healthy and physical fitness as well as nutrition, ability to organize events that produce healthy outcomes such as health fairs and exhibitions
Political Event Director	Affiliation with a cause or political party, volunteer coordination, financial, marketing, human relations, fundraising
Leisure Event Manager	Strong background in leisure and recreation, ability to develop events for leisure purposes
Meeting Director	Organization, education, marketing, volunteer coordination, financial
Public Relations Event Director	Writing, organization, research, financial, marketing, human relations, public relations, logistical, negotiation
Public Recreation Event Director	Strong understanding of principles of youth and adult recreation, strong human relations skills, good physical condition, ability to coach and mentor others
Retail Event Director	Marketing, advertising, organization, financial, human relations, logistical, negotiation
School Reunion Event Manager	Research, organization, financial, marketing, negotiation, volunteer coordination
Senior or Mature Commercial Recreation Event Director	Strong understanding of principles of aging, skilled in commercial recreation methods, respect for and dedication to working with older adults, ability to anticipate, market, engage and satisfy needs of this population
Social Life-cycle Event Director	Human relations, counseling, organization, financial, negotiation
Sport Event Director	General knowledge of sport, organization, financial, marketing, negotiation, volunteer coordination, supervisory
Tourism Event Manager	Organization, political savvy, financial, marketing, research
University/College Event Director	Organization, financial, supervisory, marketing, logistical, human relations, negotiation

Figure 1.3 *(Continued)*

long-term future. However, using the demographic and psychographic cues identified in this chapter, the event planner may begin to imagine what is most likely to develop in terms of future careers.

The aging population in North America will certainly require a strong health care system to provide a comfortable lifestyle. This growth in the field of health care will inevitably create new positions for event professionals in tourism, recreation, leisure, and education related directly to serving older people with programs tailored to their physical abilities and personal interests. When my students ask me what will be the hottest jobs of the future I always respond, "Anything that helps old people feel better." When they look at me quizzically, I remind them that there will be a lot of old people in the future due to the aging population throughout the world, and they need to be prepared to distract, entertain, improve, and engage them through events.

Technology will also offer many interesting vocational pursuits for Event Leaders of the next frontier. The rapid technological development we have experienced in the past decades will probably continue and even accelerate. Professional Event Leaders must meet the technological challenges of the twenty-first century through a commitment to continuing education. As these new technology platforms emerge, Event Leaders must improve their skills continually to meet these fierce challenges or risk being left behind as technology advances.

Will we see the emergence of an eventologist, one who combines high touch and high tech to provide a virtual and live event enabling guests to achieve high levels of customization, speed, and service through appropriate technology and greater emphasis on satisfying each person's unique needs? Although we cannot predict with total accuracy what will occur one year from today, much less five years from this moment, we must be prepared by accepting responsibility for harnessing new technologies that best serve event guests.

Gender Opportunities

Although studies of gender in Event Leadership consistently indicate that females outnumber males, the same studies reflect inequalities in this dichotomy. In a compensation study by the American Society of Association Executives (ASAE), the ASAE found that 80 percent of meeting planners for associations are females who earn a median salary of $71,000 (U.S. dollars). Their male counterparts earned a median salary of $90,000 (U.S. dollars) (ASAE 2006 compensation study).

Males will continue to enter the profession due to the rich array of career opportunities that await them and the lucrative salaries that are being offered. However, to achieve long-term success, the profession must provide upward mobility for all workers. Upward mobility is tied only partially to compensation. Greater upward mobility specifically requires that, as an Event Leadership employer, you must provide advancement, lifestyle, and training opportunities for event workers, to enable them to achieve professional growth within specific event organizations. Without these internal opportunities, Event Leaders will continue to seek new employment and take with them the institutional memory and experience they have gained while working for your firm.

Educational Opportunities

When the second edition of *Special Events* was written in 1996, I identified 30 to 40 colleges and universities that offered courses, degrees, and certificates in event-related studies. In a study commissioned in 1999 by the Council for Hospitality, Restaurant, and Institutional Education, I identified over 140 institutions of higher education that offer educational opportunities related to meetings, conferences, and special events. Now there were hundreds of institutions that offer courses in the fields related to eventology, and more emerge annually around the world, such as The Queen Margaret University International Centre for Planned Events. A listing of these schools may be seen at www.wiley.com/goldblatt.

Finally, the technological advancement we have experienced is directly responsible for the contraction and consolidation of global markets. To ensure future success and career advancement, an Event Leader must embrace the global market as an opportunity rather than a challenge. Through research, focus, and sensitivity to cultural differences, the professional Event Leader will be able to reap infinite benefits from the new global economy. In this book, we provide a strategic plan for learning how to identify and conquer these markets to ensure further long-term personal and professional growth. Perhaps the fastest growth has been in the development and delivery of distance learning programs. At The George Washington University, hundreds of registrations are received annually for their highly successful distance learning certificate program.

Certification

Historically, modern professions have used voluntary professional certification as a means to continually improve their practice and to slow or discourage regulatory bodies (e.g., local and state governments) from creating licensing requirements. When a profession can demonstrate the ability to regulate itself effectively, government may be less likely to interfere. The profession first addressed the issue of certification in 1985 with the delivery of the first Certified Meeting Professional (CMP) examination. Next, in 1988, the International Special Events Society (ISES) announced formation of the Certified Special Events Professional (CSEP) task force to develop a certification that would encompass a broader range of event competencies in addition to meetings and conventions. ISES studied a wide variety of certification programs, including the CMP, to identify models for the rapidly emerging event profession. Ultimately, the Canadian government model (Certified Event Coordinator and Certified Event Manager) emerged as the best template at that time from which to construct the CSEP program. In 2007 ISES revised and improved this program. Current information regarding the CSEP program is available from www.ises.com.

Developing your Career

Now that event planning has emerged as a professional career, it is essential that you manage your growth carefully to sustain your development for many years to come. There are numerous challenges in developing any professional career, whether in medicine, law, or Event Leadership. Identifying these challenges and developing a strategic plan to address them is the most effective way to build long-term success. The four primary challenges that professionals encounter are time, finances, technology, and human resources. They are the four pillars upon which you will construct a successful career (see Figure 1.4). This chapter will help you transform these challenges into opportunities for professional growth and better understand the emerging resources available in this new profession.

Mastering Yourself

The first person to be managed is you. Your ability to organize, prioritize, supervise, and delegate to others is secondary to being able to manage your time and professional resources efficiently and effectively. Once you are sufficiently well managed, you will find that managing others is much easier. Managing yourself essentially involves setting personal and professional goals and then devising a strategic plan to achieve them. Doing this involves making choices. For example, you may want to spend more time with your family, and that will determine in what field you elect to specialize. Certain fields will rob you of time with your family and friends, especially as you are building your career; others will allow you to work a semi-regular schedule. Association or corporate meeting planning

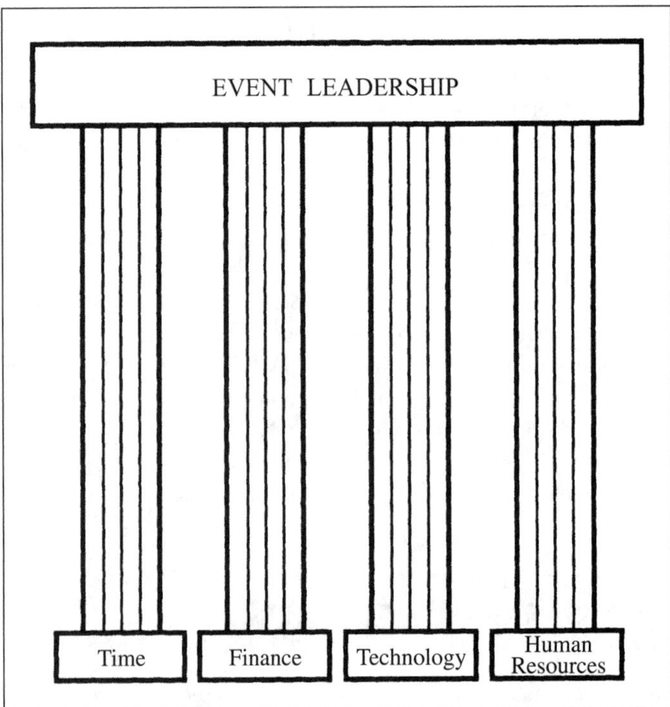

Figure 1.4 Four-Pillar Approach: Foundation for Success

may require that you work 9:00 A.M. to 5:00 P.M. for 40 weeks of the year and 7:00 A.M. to 10:00 P.M. or later during convention preparation and production. Hospitality Event Leadership positions, by contrast, may require long hours every day for weeks on end. After all, the primary resource of the Event Leader is time. It is the one commodity that, once invested, is gone forever. Setting personal and professional goals has a direct correlation with the type of work you will perform. It is hoped that the fruits of your labors will represent an excellent return on your investment.

Mastering Time Management

One key element in effective time management is the ability to use your time effectively by distinguishing between what is urgent and what is important. Urgency is often the result of poor research and planning. Importance, however, results from knowledge of priorities of time, resources, and the overarching goals of the event. I recognized this principle when I sold my business, when for the first time in my adult life I was able to distinguish between my personal and my professional time. Too often, the event planner—one who usually loves what he or she is doing for a living (thereby distinguishing this person from most of the working population of the world)—combines personal and professional time to his or her detriment. In my own experience, I carefully analyzed the capacity for personal and professional time each week and learned that only 168 hours are available. Of these hours, 56 are invested in sleeping and 21 in eating, leaving 91 hours for work and personal commitments. For nearly 15 years I had used between 70 and 80 of these valuable hours for work-related activities, leaving only 10 or so per week for my family and myself. After I had completed this analysis, I set about matching my time to my new goals.

One of the reasons I sold my business was to spend more time with my family and improve myself both mentally and physically. I realized that, by working smarter instead of longer, I could accomplish in 50 hours the tasks that it had formerly taken me 25 percent more time to do. This new plan would allow me to spend additional time with my family and work toward achieving other personal goals that I had set.

Effective time management must begin with setting personal and professional priorities, especially as this profession is one with a high degree of burnout. Finding a healthy balance among the worlds of work, family, leisure, recreation, and spiritual pursuits is essential to your long-term success as an Event Leader. This book will not only help you find this balance but also show you how to integrate time management principles into every aspect of your Event Leadership professional career. This integration of time management principles will ultimately allow you more hours for recreation, leisure, and self-improvement, while providing increased earnings with fewer working hours. The 10 suggestions for event time management will help you develop an effective system suitable for your personal and professional style:

1. *Budget your time and relate this budget directly to your financial and personal priorities.* For example, if you value your family life, budget a prescribed period of time to be with your family each week.
2. *Determine, by an analysis of your overhead, what your time is worth hourly.* Remind yourself of the value of your time by placing a small sign with this amount on or

near your telephone. Condense extraneous phone calls and other activities that are not profit producing.

3. *Make a list of tasks to complete the next day before you leave the office or go to bed.* Include in this list all telephone calls to be made, and carry it with you for ready reference. In the age of cellular communications, you can return calls from anywhere. As each task is completed, cross it off triumphantly. Move uncompleted tasks to the next day's list.
4. *Determine whether meetings are essential and the best way to communicate information.* Many meetings can be conducted via telephone conference call rather than in person. Other meetings can be canceled and the information communicated through memoranda, newsletters, or even video or audio recordings.
5. *When receiving telephone calls, determine if you are the most appropriate person to respond to the caller.* If you are not the most appropriate person, direct the caller to the best source. For example, when people contact you for information about the Event Leadership industry, refer them immediately to the ISES or IFEA Web sites (www.ises.com and www.ifea.com, respectively). Tell them that if they have additional questions, you will be pleased to answer them after they contact ISES or IFEA.
6. *Upon opening e-mail, mail or reading faxes, handle each item only once.* Respond to casual correspondence by writing a note on the document and returning it with your business card. Not only is this efficient, but it is also good for the environment. Respond to business documents upon receipt by setting aside a prescribed time of day to handle this important task. Place a message on your outgoing voice and email letting your clients and others know how soon you will respond to their query.
7. *When traveling for more than three business days, have your mail sent to you through an overnight service.* Doing this allows you to respond in a timely manner and not miss important opportunities.
8. *Prepare a written agenda for every meeting, no matter how brief.* Distribute the agenda in advance and see that each item includes a time for discussion. When appropriate, ask meeting participants to prepare a written summary of their contributions and deliver them to you prior to the start of the meeting. This summary will assist you in better preparing for the contributions of the meeting participants.
9. *Establish a comprehensive calendar that includes the contact name, address, and telephone number of people with whom you are meeting.* Use computer software contact-information programs and a personal digital assistant consolidate and take this information on the road with you.
10. *Delegate nonessential tasks to capable assistants.* The only true way to multiply your creativity is to clone yourself. A well-trained, well-rewarded administrative assistant will enhance your productivity and even allow you occasionally to take some well-deserved time off.

Mastering Finance

Becoming a wise and disciplined money manager is another pillar upon which you can construct a long-term career. During your Event Leadership career, you will be required to read and interpret spreadsheets filled with financial data. When interviewing students for admission to university programs, I have found that over 90 percent are not comfortable with their financial or accounting skills and do not have a personal budget. However, you cannot entrust this to others. Instead, you must be able to understand their interpretations of these data and then make judgments based on your final analysis.

Sharon Siegel, executive vice president of Deco Productions in Miami, Florida, has owned her company for several years and understands the importance of prudent financial management. "Watching your overhead is extremely important," she says, "especially if you are constructing and storing props." Siegel, former owner of Celebrations, merged her company with an entertainment firm and provides full-service destination management services, including design and fabrication of decorations. To help control overhead, her firm is located in the building that houses her husband's large party rental operation. Not only does this protect the bottom line, but it improves gross income through referral business generated through the party rental operation.

Sound financial practices allow savvy Event Leaders to better control future events by collecting and analyzing the right information with which to make wise decisions. In this book, we look at many ways in which you may become more comfortable with accounting. As a result of your new confidence, you will greatly improve your profitability to ensure a long, prosperous future in this profession. These five techniques will assist you with establishing your own framework for long-term profitability:

1. Set realistic short-, mid-, and long-term financial goals.
2. Seek professional counsel.
3. Identify and use efficient financial technology.
4. Review your financial health frequently and systematically.
5. Control overhead and build wealth.

Mastering Technology

New advances ranging from personal digital assistants (PDAs) as well as Radio Frequency Identification (RFID) to the broadband capability of the Internet itself (social media such as Facebook, Twitter, Bebo, and others) are rapidly transforming the way in which we conduct business. As an example, most résumés that I review describe computer skills and software literacy. Although this is a basic requirement for most administrative jobs, it is surprising that some Event Leaders are still somewhat intimidated by the computer age.

Overcoming this intimidation through the selection of proper tools to solve daily challenges is an essential priority for modern Event Leaders. These basic tools may include software programs for word processing, financial management, and database management.

Word-processing skills allow you to produce well-written proposals, agreements, production schedules, and other important documents for daily business easily and efficiently. Many successful Event Leaders incorporate desktop publishing software with word-processing tools to produce well-illustrated proposals and other promotional materials.

Financial spreadsheet software allows you to process quickly, efficiently, and accurately hundreds of monthly journal entries and determines instantly profit or loss information from individual events. These same software systems also allow you to produce detailed financial reports to satisfy tax authorities as well as to provide you with a well-documented history of income and expense. Most important, the use of electronic financial management tools will enable you to determine instantly your cash flow to further ensure that at the end of the month, you have enough income to cover bills and produce retained earnings for your organization.

Learning to use these systems is relatively simple, and most Event Leaders report that they are impressed with the ease and efficiency of this technology compared to the days of pencil or pen entries in financial journals. There are numerous brand names available for purchase, and I encourage you to determine at the outset your financial management needs and then select software that will meet those needs cost-effectively now and for the immediate future.

A database system will allow you to compile huge amounts of information, ranging from vendor to prospective client to guest lists, and organize this information for easy retrieval. Event professionals coordinate hundreds of resources per year, and the ability to store, organize, and retrieve this information quickly, cost-efficiently, and securely is extremely important for business operations and improved earnings.

There are numerous software systems available; many can be customized to fit the individual needs of your organization. However, Event Leaders may fail to recognize the time required to enter the data initially and the discipline required to continue to add to the original database in a systematic manner.

Whether for human, financial, or organizational purposes, information technology is the critical link between an average organization soon in decline or a great Event Leadership firm with expansive growth potential. Use the next five steps to acquire and maintain the right technology to match your needs:

1. Identify the technology needs within your organization.
2. Review and select appropriate technology.
3. Establish a schedule for implementation.
4. Provide adequate training for all personnel.
5. Review needs systematically and adapt to new technology.

Mastering Human Resource Skills

Empowering people is one of the most important human resource skills the Event Leader must master. Thousands of decisions must be made to produce successful events, and the Event Leader cannot make all of them. Instead, he or she must hire the right people and empower them to make a range of important decisions.

Although the empowerment of event staff and volunteers is important, the primary reason why most event planning organizations fail is not creativity but financial administration. Perhaps this is why in many companies the chief financial officer (CFO) is one of the best compensated at the executive level.

As you become more educated in finance, human resource management, and other business skills, they are actually demonstrating entrepreneurial skills to their current

Navigating the Internet for Event Leadership Success

Billions of people are currently using the Internet to satisfy their information, marketing, and other personal and professional needs. Will the Internet reduce or eliminate the need for human beings getting together in person? On the contrary, futurists such as Alvin Toffler and William Hallal predict that this unprecedented information technology will increase the desire for public assembly, as hundreds of millions of people assemble virtually and find common interests that require public assembly to fully satiate their needs.

The Internet is a complex network of millions of computers that sends and receives information globally. Initially conceived by the Department of Defense Advanced Research Projects Agency, the Internet was installed as a highly stable network with no single point of origin. Initially, only the government, university scientists, and technical specialists used the Internet to share information, due to its inherently technical interface. With the invention of the browser, a software program that allows the users to view parts of the Internet graphically (known as the World Wide Web), the Internet is now the fastest-growing communications device in the world. Not since the invention of the printing press has communications been so rapidly transformed.

To use the Internet, you will need to identify a local access server, such as one of the major online subscription services or one of hundreds of local access firms. Once you are admitted to cyber- (meaning "to steer") space, you may easily navigate between thousands of sites (or home pages) using search engines that allow you to search for information that has been indexed.

In the Event Leadership profession, there are hundreds of home pages on the Internet system (see Appendices 1 and 2 for some examples). Viewing sites with a browser on the World Wide Web using the point-and-click method is easy and fun. Many of the pages contain hyperlinks, which are a way to access more information. After you click your mouse on a highlighted key word (hypertext) on a home page, a related home page appears.

One of the easiest and fastest ways to conduct research is through the Internet. For example, the Event Leader who desires to identify sources for entertainment may either review a variety of home pages related to this subject or visit a chat room—a live link across the Internet—to query other people who are interested in the same subject.

If you can wait a day or two to retrieve the information you require, the bulletin board may be a feasible option. However, if you need the information now, you will want to go directly to the chat room or home page.

Regardless of what service you use, the Internet system is the Event Leader's most dynamic tool in transforming tomorrow's events through unlimited education and research. Get connected, log on, navigate, and surf the Event Leadership superhighway to find greater success.

employers. Many employers reward, these continuously improving professionals,) as they master and exhibit the skills needed to manage a complex competitive environment by working smarter rather than harder.

One of the benefits of mastering skills in Event Leadership is the ability to learn how to run your own business effectively to improve your performance as an employee. In addition, you may be improving your opportunity to one day own and operate your own successful Event Leadership consulting practice. As the chief event officer (CEO), you must empower others to lead as well.

There Is No Substitute for Performance

When meeting with his team and listening to their assurances of improving profits, Harold Gineen, the former chairman of International Telephone and Telegraph (ITT), would invoke the most sacred of all Event Leadership business principles: "There is no substitute for performance." Four pillars of long-term success in Event Leadership—time, financial, technology, and human resource management—must be applied to achieve consistent success. Setting benchmarks to measure your achievements will help you use these pillars to build a rock-solid foundation for your Event Leadership career. According to Sharon Siegel of Deco Productions of Florida and many of her colleagues, all Event Leaders are ultimately measured only by their last performances. Steadily applying these best practices will help ensure many stellar event performances to come.

Challenges and Opportunities

Three important challenges await you in developing a long, prosperous professional career in Event Leadership. Each of these challenges is related to the other. The environment in which business is developed, the rapid changes in available resources, and the requirement for continuous education form a dynamic triangle that will either support your climb or entrap you while limiting your success. You will find that your ability to master each of these challenges dramatically affects your success ratio throughout your career.

Business Development

Every organization faces increased competition as the world economy becomes smaller and you find that you no longer compete in a local market. Performing a competitive analysis in your market area is an important step in determining your present and future competitors and how you will differentiate yourself to promote profitability. One way to do this is to thoughtfully consider your organization's unique qualities. After you have identified these qualities, compare them to the perception your current and future customers have of other organizations. Are you really all that different from your competitors? If you have not identified your unique differentiating qualities, you may need to adjust the services or products you provide to achieve this important step. The five steps that follow are a guide to best practices in competitive advantage analysis:

1. Audit your organization's unique competitive advantage: quality, product offering, price, location, trained and experienced employees, reputation, safety, and so on.
2. Survey your current and prospective customers to determine their perception of your unique attributes compared to competing organizations.

3. Anonymously call and visit your competitors, and take notes on how they compare to your unique competitive advantage.
4. Share this information with your staff, and adjust your mission and vision to promote greater business development.
5. Review your position systematically every business quarter to determine how you are doing and adjust your plan when necessary.

Whether you are the owner, manager, or employee, maintaining a competitive advantage in Event Leadership is the secret to success in long-term business development. To maintain your most competitive position, combine this technique with constantly reviewing the trade and general business literature as well as information about emerging trends.

Relationship marketing is increasingly important since the development of affinity programs by retailers in the 1950s. Modern organizations are just now learning what buyers and sellers in markets knew thousands of years ago: All sales are based on relationships. Implied in that relationship is the reality that the buyer and seller like, respect, and trust one another. The higher the price, the more important this process becomes. Event leaders must use events to further this important process.

According to *Advertising Age* and other major chroniclers of global marketing relationships, relationship marketing is the fastest-growing segment in the entire marketing profession. Event professionals must invest the same time that larger organizations do to understand how to use events to build solid relationships that promote loyalty, word-of-mouth endorsement, and other important attributes of a strong customer and client relationship.

Resource Development

As more and more organizations create their own home pages on the World Wide Web, consumers will be increasingly exposed to infinite resources for Event Leadership. Your challenge is to select those resources that fit your market demand and cultivate them to ensure the highest consistent quality. One of the reasons that brand names have grown in importance is due to consumers' desire for dependability and reliability. Positioning yourself and your organization as a high-quality, dependable, and reliable service through your careful selection of product offerings will further ensure your long-term success. Whether you are selecting vendors or determining the quality of paper on which to print your new brochure, every decision will reflect your taste and, more important, that of your customers. Determine early on, through research, whom you are serving and then select those resources to match their needs, wants, desires, and expectations. This may be accomplished in five ways:

1. Identify through research the market(s) you are serving.
2. Establish a database to collect information about the needs, wants, desires, and expectations of your customers.
3. Regularly review new products (some Event Leaders set aside a specific day each month to see new vendors), and determine if they meet the standards set by your customers.

4. Match the needs, wants, desires, and expectations to every business development decision. For example, do your customers prefer to do business with you in the evening? If so, stay open late one night per week.
5. Regularly audit your internal procedures to make certain that you are developing new business by positioning your products and services as quality, dependable, and reliable resources for your customers.

Lifelong Learning: A User's Guide

If the twentieth century represented the age of innocence in Event Leadership, the twenty-first century may be described as "the renaissance." You are part of an era of unprecedented learning and expansion of knowledge in the field of Event Leadership. This book will serve as your primer to direct you to additional resources to ensure that you stay ahead of rather than behind the learning curve in this rapidly changing and expanding profession. One way to do this is to establish learning benchmarks for yourself throughout your career. Attending one or two annual industry conferences, participating in local chapter activities, or setting aside time each day to read relevant literature (see Appendices 1 and 4) about the profession will certainly help you stay current. Perhaps the best proven way to learn anything is to teach someone else what you have learned. Collecting information that can later be shared with your professional colleagues is an excellent way to develop the habit of lifelong learning. Consider these five techniques for lifelong learning:

1. Budget time and finances to support continuing education on an annual basis.
2. Require or encourage your employees to engage in continuous Event Leadership education by subsidizing their training. Ask them to contribute by purchasing books that are related to the course work.
3. Establish a study group to prepare for the certification examination.
4. Set aside a specific time each week for professional reading. Collect relevant information and then highlight, clip, circulate, or file this information at this time.
5. Participate in webinars and attend industry conferences and expositions to expose yourself to new ideas on an annual basis. Remember that, upon returning to your organization, you will be required to teach what you have learned to others. Therefore, become a scholar of your profession.

When you audit the business environment, select resources that demonstrate your quality, dependability, and reliability, and engage in a program of lifelong learning, you will be far ahead of your current and future competitors. This book will help you understand the profession of Event Leadership as both an art and a science, requiring not only your creativity but also your exacting reasoning ability. However, any book is only a catalyst for future exploration of a field of study. As a result of using this book to promote your future growth, you will have established the rigor required to become a scholar of Event Leadership and an authority in your organization. To maintain your position, you will need not only to return to this book as a central reference but to begin a comprehensive file of additional educational resources. This book provides several appendix resources from which you may assemble this base of knowledge. Upon completing this book, use Appendix 1 to expand your comprehension of the profession by contacting the organizations listed to request educational materials to improve and sustain your practice. Doctors, lawyers, and accountants, as well as numerous other established professionals, require continuous education to meet licensing or certification standards. Our profession must aspire to this same level of competence. Your use of this book and commitment to future educational opportunities will enhance your competence.

Getting Focused

Although ISES has identified nearly two dozen professions within the events industry, you must soon decide how you will focus your studies. After reading the preface and this chapter, you should be able to comprehend the macro profession of Event Leadership through brief descriptions of the many subfields. Now is the time to begin to focus your studies on one or two specific subfields, such as tourism, meetings, conventions, festivals, reunions, and social life-cycle Event Leadership. Use the list of Event Leadership positions described in Figure 1.3 as a tool to get focused, and select the one or two areas where you wish to concentrate your studies.

Did you note the similarities in background and experience in each position? The key to your success in this business (or any other, for that matter) is a thorough grounding in organization, creativity, innovation, negotiation, finance, and marketing. Human relations experience is also essential, as is the related volunteer coordination skill. Increasing in importance is your ability to design, conduct, and analyze research. Throughout the book each skill is discussed in detail. However, you must now begin to focus on how you will apply these skills to your particular career pursuits.

Event leadership is a profession that provides skills for use in a variety of related disciplines. The field is grounded in the science of management, but you will also learn skills in psychology, sociology, and even anthropology as you develop your career. As you move from one subfield to another, these foundational skills will serve you well. They are the portable elements of this curriculum that you may take with you and apply to a variety of different types of events.

How to Use this Book

Self-Education: The Reading Log

Each chapter of this book represents the sum of many years of professional reading by this author. Therefore, as you approach a new chapter, look for related writings in industry trade and professional journals as well as general media, such as *The New York Times*

(USA) or *The Guardian* (UK). As you identify these readings, save them for your study time. When you complete your two 20-minute study periods, give yourself a bonus by reading the related material and then noting in your reading log the title, author, date, and a short description. Developing this habit during your study period will begin a lifelong process that will reward you richly throughout your career. Make certain that you develop a filing system for these readings for future reference, and use the reading log as a classification system for easy reference.

Benchmark Checklists

Self-improvement is the goal of every successful person. It is a continuous process. Ensuring continuous self-improvement and business improvement requires utilizing an old tradition in a new context. The term *benchmarking* was first used by Xerox Corporation to describe the way its corporate leaders reinvented its organization to compete more effectively. This process was so successful that Xerox won the most coveted award in corporate America, the Malcolm Baldrige National Quality Award. The principles of benchmarking are simple; however, the application requires commitment and discipline.

Benchmarking is a management process in which you study similar organizations to determine what systems they are using that can become quality benchmarks for your own organization. Once you have identified these benchmarks, your organization's goal is to meet or exceed these standards within a specified period of time.

The checklists throughout this book are your benchmarks. They are the result of 25 years of study of successful individuals and organizations in the profession of Event Leadership. Your goals should be to develop the rigor to meet or exceed these standards during your career.

Critical Connections for Career Advancement

In addition to the numerous tables, charts, and models in this book, each chapter includes four critical connections to help you rapidly advance. The very nature of special events is to connect people through a shared activity; therefore, each chapter includes specific instructions for global, technological, resource, and learning connections. Make certain that you carefully review these sections at the end of each chapter to expand, reinforce, and strengthen your connections in the twenty-first-century global Event Leadership profession.

New Profiles: Pioneers and Protégés

This edition provides a series of new profiles of distinguished event pioneers and protégés throughout the world. The concept of the protégé dates back to the ancient Greeks, when the goddess Athena became the mentor of Telemachus to help him through his time of difficulty. This edition of *Special Events* for the first time introduces both a pioneer and a protégé in each chapter to help you understand through experience and aspiration the infinite opportunities that await you in this rapidly expanding field.

The pioneers who were selected for this edition will inspire you with their devotion to the field of special events leadership. The protégés will, through they ambition and optimism, help raise your sights to conquer new opportunities throughout your career.

Appendices

The numerous appendices are designed to provide you with extensive resources in one location to use throughout your professional life. Review these listings and determine what gaps you currently have in your operations, marketing, or other areas, and use these resources to add to your knowledge. As Event Leadership is an emerging discipline and rapidly expanding profession, you may notice gaps in the appendices that you can fill. Send me your resources at jgoldblatt@qmu.ac.uk, and you will be acknowledged in the next edition.

Role and Scope

This book's role is to expand the knowledge base in the emerging discipline of planned events. The scope of its task is to provide concrete techniques to immediately improve your practice. Your career needs will determine how you use this book to improve your business. However, if you are sincerely interested in expanding the knowledge base in planned events, your practice will improve in equal proportion to your level of commitment. This is so important that it bears repeating. If you are interested in expanding the body of knowledge in planned events, your skills will improve in equal proportion to your level of commitment.

Therefore, as in most professions, the harder you work, the more you will learn. And as is also true in all professions, the more you learn, the more you will earn. I encourage you to become a scholar of this fascinating profession and, as suggested earlier, read this book as if someday, somewhere, you will be requested to teach others. I challenge you to achieve mastery through these pages so that those you will influence will leave this profession even better prepared for those who will follow.

I, like you, am a student of this profession. There are new learning opportunities every day. Over two decades ago, I stood outside a hospital nursery window gazing lovingly on our newborn son, Sam. Only a few hours earlier, I had telephoned my cousin Carola in New Orleans to announce his birth and, choking back tears, to tell her and the family that he would be named for my beloved uncle Sam, her father, who had recently died. Celebrating this new life together, we laughed out loud about the "curse" that might come with my son's name. Would he be as funny, charming, irascible, and generous as my uncle Sam? His potential was limitless. Today, Sam has earned his master's degree in festival management, produces the Edinburgh 48 Hour Film Festival, is the editor of this book and has contributed the chapter entitled Greener Events. His own book, the first in the world on greener meetings and events, will be published by Wiley 2011.

Confucius declared several thousand years ago that "we are cursed to live in interesting times indeed." Like Sam, regardless of what road you take in the infinitely fascinating Event Leadership profession, you can be assured of finding many opportunities in these very interesting and challenging times. In the closing lines of his best-seller *Megatrends* (1982), John Naisbitt exalted the world he had spent years analyzing: "My God, what a fantastic time in which to be alive." The future that you and your colleagues will create will carry the curse of Confucius, the joy of Naisbitt, and the final assurance of the French poet Paul Valéry, who wrote: "The trouble with the future is it no longer is what it used to be." Your future is secure in knowing that there are millions of new births annually in the world and, therefore, just as many future events (and many more) for you to lead.

Career-Advancement Connections

Corporate Social Responsibility Connection

Identify a recurring event such as a meeting, a festival, or a exhibition and examine the composition of the membership of the profession in terms of gender and cultural heritage versus actual participation in the event. Design a corporate social responsibility approach to increasing participation in the event across all sectors that are underrepresented.

The Pioneer: Stuart Turner, International Events Director, Sport, EventScotland

Stuart Turner first developed an interest in planned events during the 1986 Commonwealth Games in Edinburgh, Scotland. According to Stuart, "That was the moment when I found my passion. I discovered that, while competition is important, it is just as important to bring people together through events." Fifteen years later, Turner was active in both the 2000 Summer Olympic Games in Sydney, Australia, where he worked in the Team Great Britain holding area and then in Salt Lake City, Utah (United States), for the 2002 Winter Olympic Games. "I was so passionate about being part of the games that I funded my own trip to Salt Lake to participate in this event."

He described his personal mentor, Pete Bilsborough of the University of Stirling athletic program, as someone who provided him with great wisdom during his days as a member of the Scottish canoe slalom team. "Pete allowed us to use the resources of the University for our practices, and throughout my entire career he has always been there to provide me with sage advice. We had the opportunity to work together when I worked for Sport Scotland on the area institute

Global Connection

Connect globally with Event Leaders throughout the world through an Internet Listserv, such as "World of Events," which is managed by Leeds Metropolitan University in Great Britain, or the "World Festival Network" on Facebook. "World of Events" provides a global forum for discussion of Event Leadership topics by researchers, academics, students, and practitioners throughout the world (www.worldofevents.net). Search for the Facebook (www.facebook.com) group "World Festival Network" and discover this Edinburgh Fringe-based community of international arts festivals around the world.

Technology Connection

Develop an interactive Web-based data management system to enable you to collect and access your Event Leadership data from throughout the world. The best system for achieving this is to create a password-protected Internet-based database that can be accessed by an authorized Event Leader from any remote point

network. He has been a genuine thread throughout my entire career."

During his 20-plus-year career in events, has seen the field change dramatically. "Perhaps one of the greatest challenges has been in the area of technology. Today with mobile phones, you can order your ticket to a event and then flash the ticket bar code from your telephone screen to gain admission to the venue. Further, education has truly advanced since I was in college. In those days, the major subjects were recreation and physical education, but now you can gain specialized study in events management. Finally, the environment has become a major force that is driving the greening of events. Young children are now studying ecology in school, and by the time they are old enough to attend an event they are much more sensitive to the importance of environmental sustainability. All events today must not only think about environmental impacts but also act as responsible stewards of the natural environment from the very beginning of their development and that is not something we would have considered as important only 20 years ago."

Turner's own sage advice to the next generation of event professionals is, "If you want to find out what is possible, you need to push things right to the limit, you will then find out what is possible." Throughout his long and distinguished career, Stuart Turner has witnessed from a front-row seat the rapid evolution of the events industry throughout the world. He has recognized from the example of his own mentor, as well as through mentoring young professionals himself, that successful careers in events management belong to those who have the passion, commitment, and courage to explore new frontiers for personal development and professional growth.

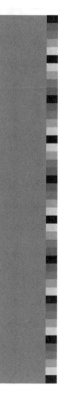

on earth. It is critical to protect your valuable data. The protection can be enforced by setting different levels of access: to review data only, to add data, or to delete and modify data.

Resource Connection

Use the appendices of the book to connect with associations for future study. Hundreds of colleges and universities throughout the world offer courses, curricula, degrees, certificates, and other resources. Visit www.qmu.ac.uk/be and click on research to access the International Centre for the Study of Planned

The Protégé: Clara Bignami, Graduate, Queen Margaret University Events Management Programme, Events Assistant, EventScotland

Clara Bignami's first memorable special events experience took place at The Wicker Man Festival, an alternative Scottish music fest near her hometown. "It's a lot less commercialized than the bigger festivals," she explains. "It's bang on in the countryside so there are nice surroundings. There are cows, and I don't think they mind the music." The many challenges of festival management, whether it be dealing with talent, vendors, or livestock, intrigued her.

When looking through the Queen Margaret University prospectus, the Event Management course jumped out at her as she remembered her festival experiences. She soon discovered the many disciplines of event management, such as risk management. "Anticipating risk is very important because, if

Events, where you will find a comprehensive listing of colleges that offer courses and curriculum in events management.

 Learning Connection

Construct a 1-, 3-, 5-, and 10-year plan or blueprint to identify your career goals and path. Assess your current skill and experience level and list the educational, practical, and theoretical resources that you will need to achieve your goals and objectives. Read *The Complete Guide to Careers in Special Events: Step Toward Success!* by Gene Columbus (2009) and *Dollars and Events. How to Succeed in the Special Events Business* by Dr. Joe Goldblatt and Frank Supovitz (1999).

something goes wrong, you lose customer satisfaction and can receive negative media attention. This is very dangerous for an event that may never happen again." Bignami describes how she uses this knowledge in her work for EventScotland: "We receive event applications for funding and we need to research them with all possible risks in mind, mainly because we are spending public funds and we want to support something that is successful either economically or in the media."

At EventScotland, Bignami sees the way in which events are used to drive tourism and offers her insider perspective. "So many events do not differentiate themselves from the same events in other cities, and competition is increasing." Noting that many event markets are reaching saturation, she predicts that "destinations or events will need to create a unique selling point, marketing themselves in a way to capture the imagination of the public."

Bignami also sees growth in environmental issues. "Local authorities are under increasing pressure to take the environment as a major issue." At the 2008 World Acrobatic Championship in Glasgow, EventScotland supported travel passes and free journeys to encourage public transportation and reduce carbon emissions. "The response was very happy," recalls Bignami, saying "we will certainly carry on for the 2014 Commonwealth Games in Glasgow."

Any successful event professional working in Scotland will need a firm grasp of the issues surrounding both destination event tourism and environmental concerns. In this regard, Clara Bignami is well poised for a bright future.

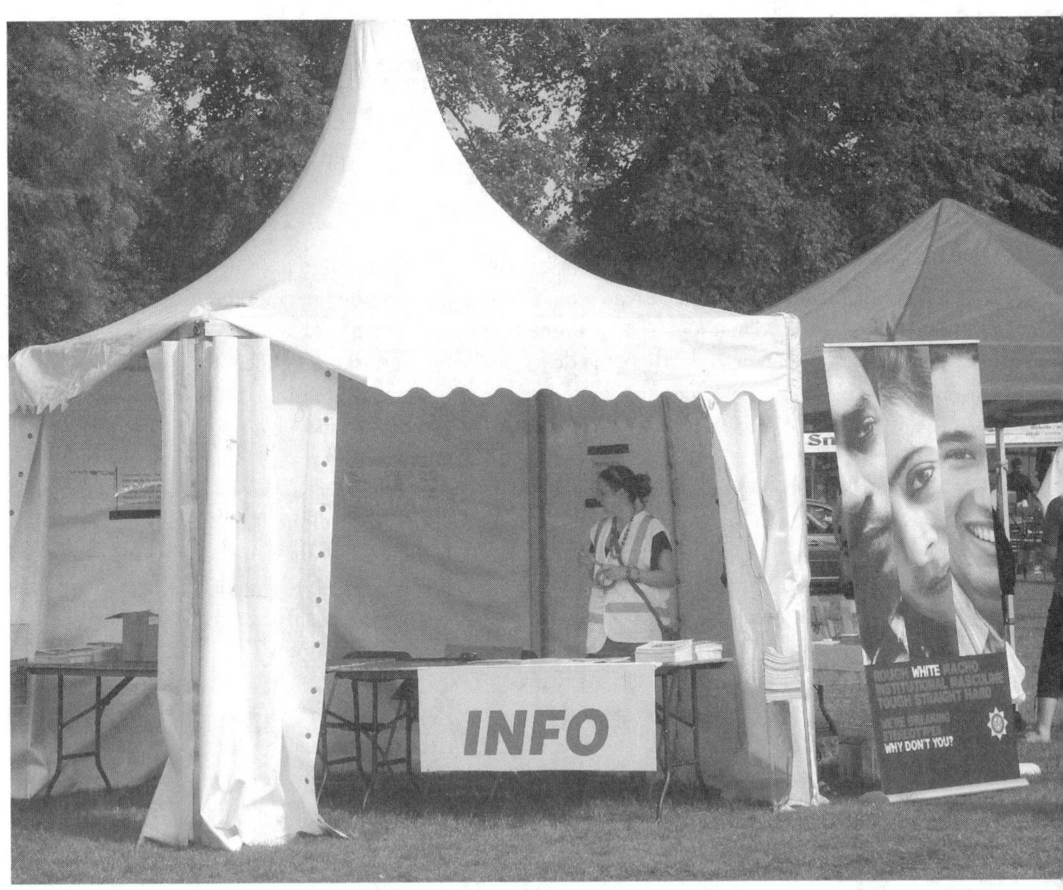

The Edinburgh Mela is a large multicultural festival held in Scotland each year. It is a model of global best practice in planned events.

CHAPTER 2

Models of Global Planned Events

In this chapter you will learn how to:

- Recognize and use the five phases of the modern event leadership process
- Identify the strengths, weaknesses, opportunities, and threats of your event
- Create an accurate blueprint for your event
- Conduct a comprehensive needs assessment
- Complete a gap analysis for your event
- Communicate effectively with event stakeholders
- Critically integrate Corporate Social Responsibility (CSR)

All successful events have five critical stages in common to ensure their consistent effectiveness. These five phases, or steps, of successful Event Leadership, are research, design, planning, coordination, and evaluation (see Figure 2.1). Underpinning each of these stages is the opportunity to demonstrate Corporate Social Responsibility (CSR) to promote greater sustainability for your event and the global events industry. In this chapter, we explore each phase to enable you to produce successful and sustainable events every time.

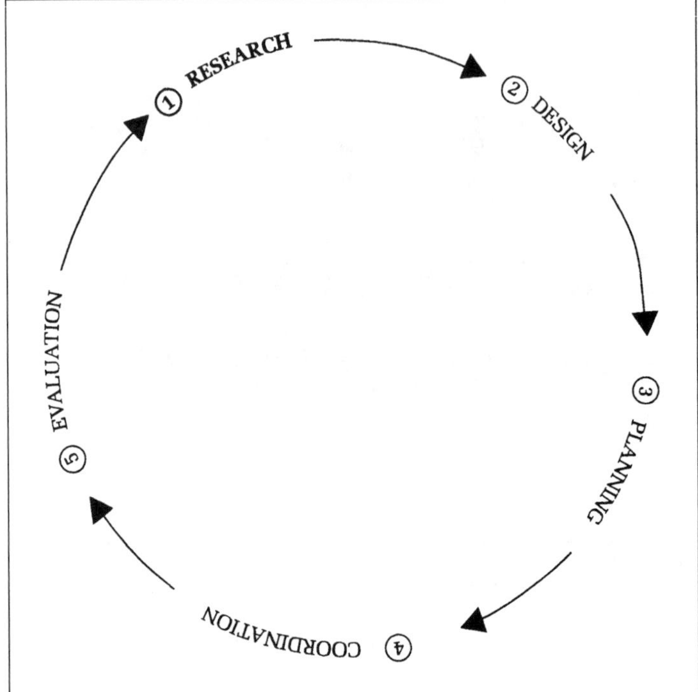

Figure 2.1 Event Leadership Process

Research

Excellent event research reduces risk. The better research you conduct prior to the event, the more likely you are to produce an event that matches the planned outcomes of the organizers or stakeholders. For many years, public relations professionals and other marketing experts have realized the value of using research to pinpoint the needs, wants, desires, and expectations of prospective customers. Government leaders regularly conduct feasibility studies prior to authorizing capital investments. These feasibility studies include exhaustive research. An event is a product that is placed before members of the public with the reasonable expectation that they will attend. Therefore, it is imperative that you conduct careful and accurate consumer research to reduce the risk of nonattendance.

I have interviewed hundreds of leading Event Leadership professionals, and they have stated their belief that more time must be devoted to research and evaluation of events. According to these experts, if more time were devoted to these phases of the

Event Leadership production process, less time and expense would ultimately be needed to complete the following steps.

Market Research Techniques

Before bringing a new product or service to market, the inventor or manufacturer will conduct market research to determine the needs, wants, desires, and expectations of the target market. Whether your event is a new or a preexisting product, market research is required to determine how to obtain the very best position in a sometimes crowded marketplace. Typically, qualitative and, in most cases, focus group research is used for this purpose.

Market research will help you determine the target or primary market, as well as the secondary and tertiary markets, for your event. Market research will also enable you to study the service levels expected by guests, as well as the perceptions by internal stakeholders of the services currently being delivered. By studying the market in depth, you can spot emerging trends, develop new service delivery systems, and solve minor problems before they become major catastrophes.

One example of this is the meeting planner who discovered through research that attendees could not register for the upcoming convention during normal business hours due to workplace regulations. Therefore, she rapidly moved her registration channel to the Internet to allow 24/7 access for her members. This new service was a major success, and registrations for the conference increased tenfold.

Quantitative versus Qualitative Research

The three types of pre-event research are quantitative, qualitative, or a combination or hybrid of both. Matching the research type to the event is important and is determined by the goals of the research, the time allowed for conducting the research, and the funds available.

Quantitative Pre-Event Research

Event Leaders primarily use quantitative research to determine demographic information such as gender, age, income, and other pertinent facts about the future market for an event. This research is relatively inexpensive to conduct and easy to tabulate and analyze with computers. Figure 2.2 provides a model of a typical quantitative pre-event research survey.

Whether you use a written survey, an in-person interview, or a telephone interview method of construction, the research survey is of prime importance. To achieve the greatest possible response, offer a reward, such as "enclose your business card and we will share the research findings with you," or offer an immediate incentive, such as enclosing a small monetary payment or other incentive.

Questions may be developed in two different styles. As noted in Figure 2.2, Question 4 uses a Likert scale to allow a respondent to select the response that states his or her opinion precisely. Question 5 uses a semantic differential scale to allow a respondent to select a continuum between two opposing adjectives. The number that the respondent chooses indicates the likelihood of attending or not attending an event.

This survey will enable the organizers of XYZ event to determine the feasibility of producing the following event. Your participation is important in this effort. Answer all questions by checking the appropriate box. Return this survey by January 1, 2011.

1. Gender? ☐ Male ☐ Female

2. Age? ☐ Under 25 ☐ 26–34 ☐ 35–44 ☐ 45–60 ☐ 61 and over

3. Income? ☐ Under $24,999 ☐ $25,000–44,999 ☐ Over $45,000

4. If the event were held during the summer I would: (*Likert scale*)

☐ Not attend ☐ Maybe attend ☐ No opinion ☐ Probably attend ☐ Positively attend

5. If the event were held during the fall I would: (*semantic differential scale*)

Not Attend ☐ 1 ☐ 2 ☐ 3 ☐ 4 ☐ 5 Positively attend

6. If you checked number 1 above, please describe your reasons for nonattendance in the space below: (*open-ended question*)

____

____

____

Return this survey by January 1, 2011 to:
Dr. Joe Goldblatt, CSEP
Queen Margaret University
Queen Margaret University Drive
Edinburgh, Scotland EH21 6UU
UK

To receive a free copy of the survey results, please include your business card or e-mail.

Figure 2.2 Quantitative Pre-Event Survey Model

Qualitative Pre-Event Research

Market research consultants rely on qualitative research to probe for hidden meanings in quantitative studies. Qualitative research tells the research organization what is beneath the numbers in quantitative research and, therefore, is an important step in the research process. This type of research may take the form of a focus group, participant observation, or a case study. Selecting the proper methodology depends on your goals, the time available, and the funding.

The focus group typically comprises 8 to 12 people of similar background and experience who assemble for the purpose of discussion. A trained facilitator leads the group through specific questions that will provide clues to the goals or outcomes desired from the research. A focus group may be one hour in length, although, in most cases, it lasts between 90 minutes and two hours. In some instances, a room with a one-way mirror is used to allow the other stakeholders to observe participants for subtle changes in body language, facial reactions, and other gestures that may reveal information in addition to their verbal opinion. The focus group is audio taped, and the tapes are later transcribed and analyzed to identify areas of agreement or discord.

The participant observation style of qualitative research involves placing the researcher in a host community to participate in and observe the culture of those being studied. For example, if you desire to determine whether a certain destination is appropriate for relocation of an event, you may wish to visit, participate, and observe for an extended period of time before making a decision. Interviews with key informants are essential to this research.

The third type of qualitative research is the case study. In this style, a preexisting event is singled out as a specific case to be studied in depth. The event may be studied from a historical context, or the stakeholders may be interviewed to determine how personality, skill, and other factors drive the success of the event. The case study enables the event researcher to draw conclusions based on the research gleaned from a comparable event.

Innovators

A leading innovator in measurement, assessment, and evaluation of meetings and events is the firm MeetingMetrics (www.meetingmetrics.com). The founder, Ira Kerns, worked for many years as a producer of meetings and events and recognized the critical need to more carefully and authentically evaluate these programs.

Therefore Kerns and his colleagues developed the MeetingMetrics system that incorporates a dashboard of tools including the discovery, pre-meeting, pulse, and post-meeting evaluation. During the discovery phase the event planner may convene a virtual focus panel to help develop questions for a pre- and post-meeting / event survey. Discovery uses open-ended questions, similar to the focus panel methodology, to help the planner identify issues and concerns that may be addressed later in the quantitatively designed pre- and post-meeting evaluation questions.

One of the major benefits of MeetingMetrics is that, loaded into the software, it has thousands of questions that may be selected for use in any of the survey phases, which simplifies the work of the meeting and event planner immensely. However, any question may be changed or entirely new questions may be submitted as well.

The entire system is Internet driven, so the survey respondents receive an introductory email from the event organizer alerting them that they are being asked to participate in a survey. The names, contact details and profiles of the respondents are captured in Excel™ and then uploaded into the MeetingMetrics framework. MeetingMetrics automatically sends out the survey to the respondents within a schedule set by the event organizer.

Finally, MeetingMetrics will then automatically produce detailed reports including charts and graphs to demonstrate the difference between the event attendees expectations and final perception of the event. Although the most popular phases are the discovery, pre- and post-meeting surveys, the pulse survey may be used to take the pulse of the event if the planning period is lengthy to make certain the program elements are still tracking closely with the needs of the attendees.

MeetingMetrics is one very profound example of how technology is enabling meeting and event planners to better align their final products with the expectations of their attendees. Measurement, assessment and evaluation is not only the wave of the future for meeting and event planners but is also the best way to justify future investment in your program and yourself (increased pay, bonuses and other performance based rewards).

Cost

Qualitative research is generally more expensive than quantitative research due to the time that is involved in probing for answers more complex and diverse than numerical data. The cost of training interviewers, the interviewers' time, the time for analyzing the data, and other costs contribute to this investment. Although the cost is greater, many Event Leaders require both qualitative and quantitative studies to validate their assumptions or research their markets.

Combined Research

In most cases, event planners use a combination of quantitative and qualitative research to make decisions about future events. Event Leaders obtain large volumes of information in a cost-efficient manner using the quantitative method and then probe for hidden meanings and subtle feelings using the qualitative approach.

Effective quantitative research includes elements of qualitative research to increase the validity of the questions. Event planners should use a small focus group or team of experts to review the questions before conducting a survey. These experts can confirm that a question is understandable and valid for the research being conducted. Figure 2.3 provides a simple way for Event Leaders to determine what research methodology is most effective for their purpose.

The goals and required outcomes of the research, combined with the time frame and funding available, will ultimately determine the best method for your pre-event research. Regardless of the type of research you conduct, it is important that you take care to produce valid and reliable information.

Goal	Method
Collect gender, age, and income data	Written survey
Collect attitudes and opinions	Focus group
Examine culture of community	Participant/observer
Identify comparable characteristics	Case study
Collect demographic and psychographic data	Combined methods

Figure 2.3 Selecting the Appropriate Pre-Event Research Method

Validity and Reliability: Producing Credible Pre-Event Research

All research must be defended. After you have decided, "What is it we need to know to be more successful?" and conducted discovery and pre-event surveys, your stakeholders will ask you bluntly, "How do you now know that you know?" If your research has high validity and reliability, you can provide greater assurance that your work is truthful. Validity primarily confirms that your research measures what it purports to measure. For example, if you are trying to determine if senior citizens will attend an event, you must include senior citizens in your sample of respondents to ensure validity. Furthermore, the questions you pose to these seniors must be understandable to them to ensure that their responses are truthful and accurate.

Reliability helps prove that your research will remain truthful and accurate over time. For example, if you were to conduct the same study with another group of senior citizens, would the answers be significantly different? If the answer is yes, your data may not be reliable. Designing a collection instrument that has high validity and reliability is a challenging and time-consuming task. You may wish to contact a university or college marketing, psychology, or sociology department for assistance by an experienced researcher in developing your instrument. Often, a senior-level undergraduate student or a graduate student may be assigned to help you develop the instrument and collect and analyze the data for college credit. The participation of the university or college will add credibility to your findings. Use software applications such as Microsoft Excel for analyzing data. For more complex analysis, use statistical applications such as SAS, Minitab, and SPSS.

Interpreting and Communicating Research Findings

Designing and collecting pre-event research is only the beginning of this important phase. Once you have analyzed the data carefully and identified the implications of your research, as well as provided some recommendations based on your study, you must present the information to your stakeholders. The way that you do this will determine the level of influence you wield with stakeholders.

If the stakeholders are academics or others who have a research background, using tables or a written narrative may suffice. However, if, as is most often the case, stakeholders are unsophisticated with regard to research, you may instead wish to use graphs, charts, and other visual tools to illustrate your findings. To paraphrase Confucius, "One picture is certainly worth a thousand numerals." Use these five steps to present your pre-event research findings effectively:

1. Determine your audience and customize your presentation to their personal communication learning style.
2. Describe the purpose and importance of the research.
3. Explain how the research was collected and describe any limitations.
4. Reveal your findings and emphasize the key points.
5. Invite questions.

Distributing a well-produced written narrative with copies of the information you are presenting (e.g., graphs from slides) will be helpful to the stakeholders, as they will need more time for independent study before posing intelligent questions. In the written narrative, include a section describing the steps you have taken to produce research that demonstrates high validity and reliability; also list any independent organizations (e.g., a university or college) that reviewed your study prior to completion.

Communicating your research findings is an essential phase in the research process. Prepare, rehearse, and then reveal your data thoughtfully and confidently. Summarize your presentation by demonstrating how the findings support the goals and objectives of your research plan.

The Five Ws: How to Produce Consistently Effective Events

Too often, students ask what event they should produce for a class project instead of why they should produce the event in the first place. After the economically rocky early 1990s, organizations began to analyze carefully why a meeting or event should occur. The five W's help answer that question.

The first step is to ask, "Why must we hold this event?" Not one but a series of compelling reasons must confirm the importance and viability of holding the event.

The second step is to ask, "Who will the stakeholders be for this event?" Stakeholders are both internal and external parties. Internal stakeholders may be the board of directors, committee members, staff, elected leaders, guests, or others. External stakeholders may be the media, politicians, bureaucrats, or others who will be investing in the event. Conducting solid research will help you determine the level of commitment of each of these parties and help you define for whom this event is being produced.

The third step is to ask, "When will the event be held?" You must ask yourself if the research-through-evaluation timeframe is appropriate for the size of the event. If this time period is not appropriate, you may need to rethink your plans and either shift the dates or streamline your operations. *When* may also determine *where* the event may be held.

The fourth step involved is to ask, "Where will the event will be held?" As you will discover in this chapter, once you have selected a site, your work becomes either easier or more challenging. Therefore, this decision must be made as early as possible, as it affects many other decisions.

The fifth and final W is to determine, from the information gleaned thus far, "What is the event product that you are developing and presenting?" Matching the event product to the needs, wants, desires, and expectations of your guests while satisfying the internal requirements of your organization is no simple task. You must analyze the what carefully and critically to make certain that the why, who, when, and where are synergized in this answer.

Once these five questions have been answered thoroughly, it is necessary to determine how the organization will allocate scarce resources to produce maximum benefit for the stakeholders. SWOT (strengths, weaknesses, opportunities, threats) analysis provides a comprehensive tool for ensuring that you review each step systematically.

SWOT Analysis: Finding the Strengths, Weaknesses, Opportunities, and Threats

Identifying and analyzing the strengths, weaknesses, opportunities and threats (SWOT) of your event assists you in identifying the internal and external variables that may prevent the event from achieving maximum success. The SWOT analysis is not the first step in research but it must be completed prior to designing the event to make certain you have comprehensively evaluated all of the internal and exogenous variables that could impact your outcomes.

Strengths and Weaknesses

The strengths and weaknesses of an event are primarily considerations that can be spotted before the event actually takes place. Typical strengths and weaknesses of many events are shown in Figure 2.4. The strengths and weaknesses may be uncovered through a focus group or through individual interviews with the major stakeholders. If the weaknesses outnumber the strengths and there is no reasonable way to eliminate the weaknesses and increase the strengths within the event planning period, you may wish to postpone or cancel the event.

Opportunities and Threats

Opportunities and threats are two key factors that generally present themselves either during an event or after it has occurred. However, during the research process, these factors should be considered seriously, as they may spell potential disaster for the event. Opportunities are activities that may be of benefit to an event without significant investment by your organization. One example is that of selecting a year in which to hold an event that coincides with your community's or industry's hundredth anniversary. Your event may benefit from additional funding, publicity, and other important resources

Strengths	Weaknesses
Strong funding	Weak funding
Good potential for sponsors	No potential for sponsors
Well-trained staff	Poorly trained staff
Many volunteers	Few volunteers
Good media relations	Poor media relations
Excellent site	Weak site

Figure 2.4 Event Strengths and Weaknesses

simply by aligning yourself with this hallmark event. Other possible beneficial outcomes, sometimes indirect, such as the potential of contributing to the political image of the event's host, are considered opportunities.

Threats are activities that prevent you from maximizing the potential of an event. The most obvious threat is weather; however, political threats may be just as devastating. Local political leaders must buy in to your civic event to ensure cooperation with all agencies. Political infighting may quickly destroy your planning. A modern threat is that of terrorism. The threat of violence erupting at an event may keep people from attending. A celebrity canceling or not attending can also create a significant threat to the success of an event. Typical opportunities and threats for an event are listed in Figure 2.5.

You will note that, although strengths and weaknesses are often related, opportunities and threats need not be. Once again, in making a decision to proceed with event planning, your goal is to identify more opportunities than threats. All threats should be considered carefully, and experts should be consulted to determine ways in which threats may be contained, reduced, or eliminated.

SWOT analysis (see Figure 2.6) is a major strategic planning tool during the research phase. By using SWOT analysis, an event planner can not only scan the internal and external event environment but also can proceed to the next step, which involves analyses of the weaknesses and threats, and provides solutions to improve the event planning process.

The research phase of the event administration process is perhaps most critical. During this period you will determine through empirical research whether you have both the internal and external resources essential to make a decision to produce an effective event. Your ability to select the appropriate research methodology, design the instrument, and collect, analyze, interpret, and present the data will ultimately determine whether an event has sufficient strength for future success. The first phase of the event planning process—research—is the foundation on which the four remaining phases will rest. Although each phase is equal in importance, the future success of an event depends on how well you conduct the research phase.

Opportunities	Threats
Civic anniversary	Hurricanes and tornadoes
Chamber of Commerce promotion	Political infighting
Celebrity appearance	Violence from terrorism
Align with environmental cause	Alcoholic consumption
Tie-in with media	Site in bad neighborhood
Winning elections	Celebrity canceling or not attending
Developing more loyal employees	Food poisoning

Figure 2.5 Event Opportunities and Threats

Known S = strengths		
1. Strong funding 2. Well-trained staff 3. Event well respected by media	Internal Internal External	
Known W = weaknesses		
1. Weak funding 2. Few human resources 3. Poor public-relations history	Internal Internal External	
Potential O = opportunities		
1. Simultaneous celebration of a congruent event 2. Timing of event congruent with future budget allocation	External Internal	
Potential T = threats		
1. Weather 2. New board of directors leading this event	External Internal	

Figure 2.6 SWOT Analysis

Design: Blueprint for Success

Having researched your event thoroughly and determined that it is feasible, time may now be allotted to use the right side of the brain—the creative capacity—to create a general blueprint for your ideas. There are numerous ways to begin this process, but it is important to remember that the very best event designers are constantly visiting the library, attending movies and plays, visiting art galleries, and reviewing periodicals to maintain their inspiration. This continuous research for new ideas will further strengthen the activities you propose for an event.

Brainstorming and Mind Mapping

Too often in volunteer-driven organizations, the very best ideas are never allowed to surface. This occurs because well-meaning volunteers (and some not so well-meaning volunteers) tell their colleagues, "This will never work," or, "This is impossible at this time." Although their opinions are certainly valid, the process of shooting down ideas before they are allowed to be fully developed is an unfortunate occurrence in many organizations. Event Leaders must encourage and support creativity because, ultimately, the product you will offer is a creative art. Creativity is an essential ingredient in every event management process.

When beginning the design phase of this Event Leadership process, conduct a meeting where creative people are encouraged to brainstorm the various elements of the event. The Event Leader is the facilitator of this meeting, and, in addition to various creative stakeholders, you may choose to invite other creative people from the worlds of theater, dance, music, art, literature, and other fields. At the outset of the meeting, use a flip chart to lay out the ground rules for the discussion. In large bold letters write, "Rule 1: There are no bad ideas. Rule 2: Go back and reread Rule 1."

You may wish to begin the session with an activity that will stimulate creativity. One activity I've used is to place an object in the center of the table and invite participants to describe what it might become. For example, a shoebox might become a tomb, a rocket, or a small dwelling. As each person offers his or her ideas, the others should be encouraged to be supportive.

Once you have completed these warm-up activities, members should be given simple suggestions regarding the why of the event. From these suggestions, they should be encouraged to provide creative ideas for who, when, where, what, and how. If one member (or more than one member) tends to dominate the discussion, ask him or her to summarize and then say "Thank you" as you quickly move on to others to solicit their ideas. Use the flip chart to list all the initial ideas, and do not try to establish categories or provide any other organizational structure.

Mind mapping allows an Event Leader to begin to pull together the random ideas and establish linkages that will later lead to logical decision making. Using the flip chart, ask each member of the group to revisit his or her earlier ideas and begin to link them to the five Ws, and ultimately help you see how the event should be developed. Write *Why? Who? When? Where? What?* and *How?* in the center of a circle on a separate page of the chart. From this circle, draw spokes that terminate in another circle. Leave the circles at the end of each spoke empty. The ideas of your team members will fill these circles, and they will begin to establish linkages between the goal (Why? Who? When? Where? What? and How?) and the creative method. Figure 2.7 is an example of a successful event mind-mapping activity.

Mind mapping is an effective way to synthesize the various ideas suggested by group members and begin to construct an event philosophy. The event philosophy will determine the financial, cultural, social, and other important aspects of the event. For example, if the sponsoring organization is a not-for-profit group, the financial philosophy will not support charging high fees to produce a disproportionate amount of funds, or the tax status may be challenged. Mind mapping allows you to sift through the ideas carefully and show how they support the goals of the event. As you do this, an event philosophy begins to emerge. Those ideas that do not have a strong linkage or support the philosophy should be placed on a separate sheet of flip chart paper for future use. Remember Rule 1?

Dr. Cathy Matheson of the Queen Margaret University International Centre for the Study of Planned Events uses mind mapping to coalesce and analyze ideas that she identifies while participating in professional meetings. She creates a core theoretical

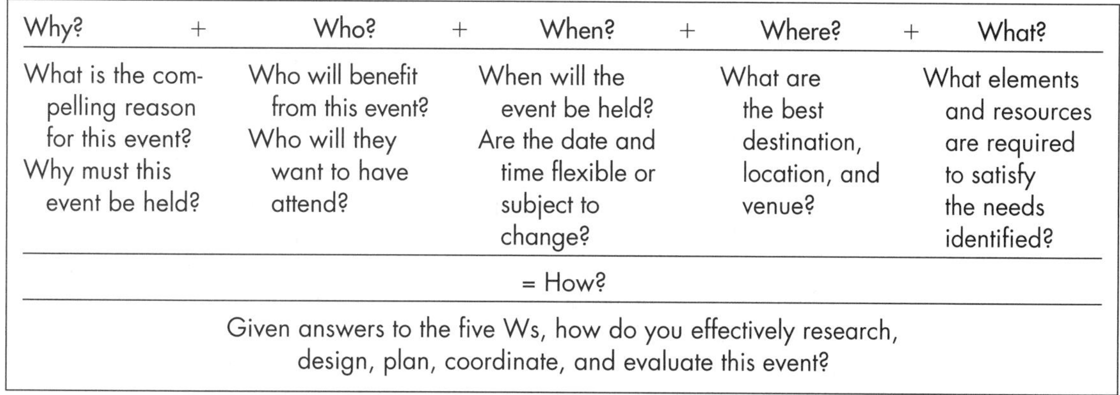

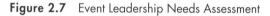

Why? +	Who? +	When? +	Where? +	What?
What is the compelling reason for this event? Why must this event be held?	Who will benefit from this event? Who will they want to have attend?	When will the event be held? Are the date and time flexible or subject to change?	What are the best destination, location, and venue?	What elements and resources are required to satisfy the needs identified?

= How?

Given answers to the five Ws, how do you effectively research, design, plan, coordinate, and evaluate this event?

Figure 2.7 Event Leadership Needs Assessment

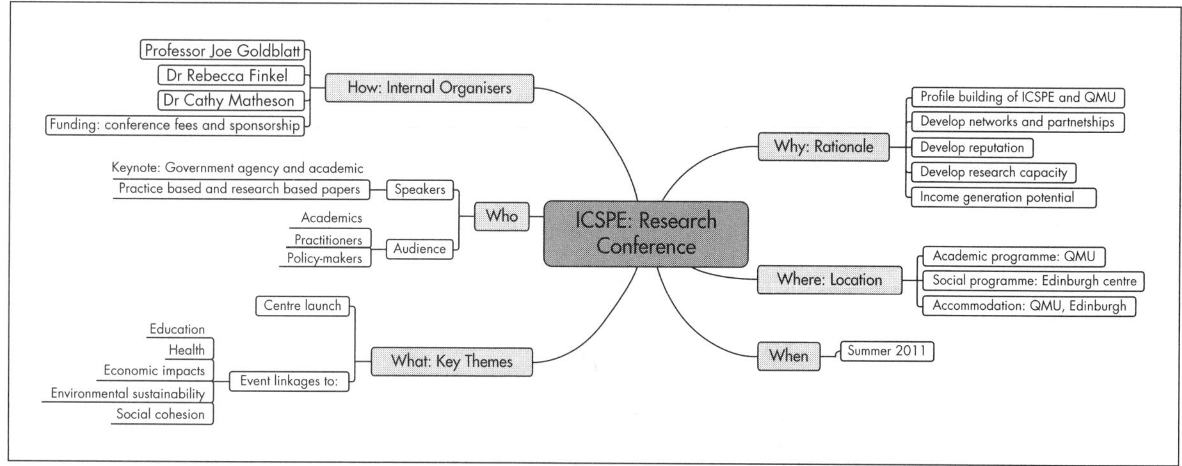

Figure 2.8 Example of Mind Map by Dr. Cathy Matheson at QMU

or topical element in the center of her mind map and then links all of the key elements to this core. Finally, she assesses each of the key elements to identify commonalities and linkages. Figure 2.8 is an example of how the mind map process may be used in the event design context.

The Creative Process in Event Leadership

Special events require people with the ability to move easily between the left and right quadrants of the cerebellum. The right side of the brain is responsible for creative, spontaneous thinking, while the left side of the brain handles the more logical aspects of our lives. To function effectively, Event Leaders must be both right- and left-brained. Therefore, if you have determined that one side of your brain is less strong than the other, you must take steps to correct this to achieve maximum success in Event Leadership.

Most of this book is concerned with logical, reasoning activities. Therefore, assuming that one of the aspects of Event Leadership that you find attractive is the creative opportunities afforded in this profession, I will provide some insight into ways to develop your creativity to the highest possible level. Remember that developing creativity is a continuous process. The reason that some corporations put their advertising accounts out for review to other agencies periodically is to be sure that the current agency is working at its highest possible creative level. As an Event Leader, you too must strive for constant review of your creative powers to make certain that you are in high gear. Following are some tips for continuously developing your creativity:

- Surf the Internet for new event models, theories, designs, scenarios, products and services.
- Visit one art gallery each month.
- Attend a live performance of opera, theater, or dance each month.
- Read great works of literature, on a continuing basis.
- Join a book discussion group to explore ideas about the literature you are reading.
- Enroll in a music, dance, literature, visual arts, or acting class or discussion group.
- Apply what you are discovering in each of these fields, where appropriate, to planned events.

Perhaps the best way to stretch your creativity continually is to surround yourself with highly creative people (see Figure 2.9). Whether you are in a position to hire creativity or must seek creative types through groups outside the office, you must find the innovators in order to practice innovation.

Malcolm Gladwell, the author of the bestselling books *The Tipping Point, Blink,* and *The Outliers,* sees the world through a prism of patterns and intuition. He describes his work as that of writing "intellectual adventure stories." For example, Gladwell states that through the process of rapid cognition—such as just looking around a person's bedroom—you may learn a great deal about the individual.

Gladwell argues in his latest book, *The Outliers,* that if individuals devote 10,000 or more hours to mastering their craft they will rapidly develop greater self-confidence and be perceived by others as authorities. Therefore, extensive professional experience (practice) as well as the acquisition of educational credentials through formal study are both essential if you are going to design a sustainable career in planned events.

The modern events industry demands rapid cognition in order for you to remain competitive. Therefore, surround yourself with visionaries and gurus such as Malcolm Gladwell, and your intellectual and creative bedroom décor will tell the world a lot about your curiosity and continuous pursuit of knowledge and wisdom.

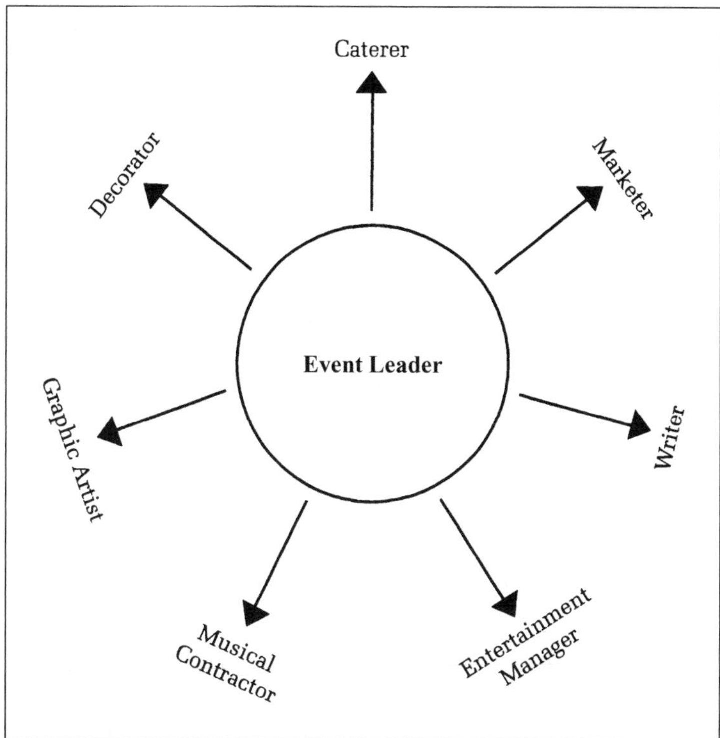

Figure 2.9 Creative Influences

Making the Perfect Match through Needs Assessment and Analysis

Once you have completed the brainstorming and mind-mapping activities satisfactorily, it is time to make certain that your creative ideas perfectly match the goals and objectives of your event. This is accomplished through needs assessment and analysis.

Needs assessment and analysis enables you to create an event that closely satisfies the needs of your stakeholders. You actually began this process by asking "Why?" and "Who?" Now it is time to take it one giant step forward and survey the stakeholders to determine if your creative solutions will satisfy their needs. To accomplish this part of the design phase, develop your ideas into a series of questions, query the key constituents for the event, and determine if the various elements you have created, from advertising to décor, from catering to entertainment, and everything in between, meet their expectations. Once you are confident that you have assessed the needs of the stakeholders adequately and confirmed that you have, through analysis, determined how to meet these needs, you are well prepared to confirm the final feasibility of your event design.

Is It Feasible?

Feasibility simply means that you have looked at the event design objectively to determine if what you propose is practical given the resources available. This is the final checkpoint before actual planning begins and, therefore, must be given adequate time for review. Municipalities often engage professional engineers or other consultants to conduct lengthy feasibility studies before approving new construction or other capital expenditures. Although you may not need a battery of consultants, it is important for you to review all previous steps thoroughly when determining the feasibility of an event plan.

The three basic resources that will be required are financial, human, and political. Each of these resources may have varying degrees of importance, depending on the nature of the event. For example, a for-profit or large hallmark event will require significant financial investment to succeed. A not-for-profit event will rely on an army of volunteers, and, therefore, the human element is more important. A civic event will require greater political resources to accomplish. Therefore, when assessing and analyzing feasibility, first determine in what proportions resources will be required for the event. You may wish to weigh each resource to help prepare your analysis.

Financial Considerations

You will want to know if sufficient financial resources are available to sustain development and implementation of the event. Furthermore, you must consider what will happen if the event loses money. How will creditors be paid? You will also want to know what resources you can count on for an immediate infusion of cash, should the event require this to continue development. Finally, you must carefully analyze the cash-flow projections for the event to determine how much time is to be allowed between payables and receivables.

The Human Dimension

In assessing the feasibility of an event, you must not only know where your human resources will come from but how they will be rewarded (financially or through intangibles, such as awards and recognition). Most important, you must know how they will work together as an efficient event team.

Politics as Usual

The increasingly important role of government leaders in event oversight must be viewed with a practiced eye. Politicians see events as both good (opportunities for publicity, constituent communications, and economic impact) and bad (drain on municipal services and potential for disaster). When designing civic events, it is particularly important that you understand and enlist the support of politicians and their bureaucratic ministers to ensure smooth cooperation for your event. Furthermore, for all events, it is essential that you carefully research the permit process to determine if the event you have designed is feasible according to the code within the jurisdiction where the event will be held.

The Approval Process

The research and design phases add to the event history once an event is approved. The approval process may be as simple as an acceptance by the client or as complex as requiring dozens of signatures from various city agencies that will interact with the event. Regardless of the simplicity or complexity of this step, you should view it as an important milestone that, once crossed, assures you that the plan has been reviewed and deemed reasonable and feasible, and has a high likelihood of success. All roads lead to official approval, whether in the form of a contract or as individual permits from each agency. Without official approval, an event remains a dream. The process for turning dreams into workable plans requires careful research, thoughtful design, and critical analysis. This could be called the *planning to plan* phase, because it involves so many complex steps related to the next phase. However, once the approval is granted, you are on your way to the next important phase: the actual planning period.

Project Management Systems for Event Leaders

According to William O'Toole and Phyllis Mikolaitis, CSEP, the authors of *Corporate Event Project Management* (2002), there are several reasons why project management offers you unique resources for improving your practice. Using a project management system will help you establish a systematic approach to all events. Like the five phases of Event Leadership, the project management system provides you with a superstructure to enable you to systematically approach every event using the same framework.

Many events—especially those in the social market—are driven by emotional decisions rather than systematic or logical approaches. The project management system will depersonalize the event as it provides you with an objective process for reviewing the event development.

Communication is critical throughout the Event Leadership process, and the project management system will help you facilitate clear communications with stakeholders from many different fields. Through meetings and documents, project management provides a transparent system to promote better communications.

Many corporate and government organizations already utilize project management systems; therefore, using this system will help you conform to those that are already in place in your clients' organizations.

Accountability is increasingly one of the more important outcomes of any event project. The project management system helps ensure accountability through the continuous outputs that are required to update the progress of the event.

O'Toole and Mikolaitis believe that, through the adoption of project management systems, you will be able to increase the visibility for the profession of Event Leadership. If your work is often invisible until the actual start of the event, the project management system will provide a continuous flow of information charting the progress of the event as it develops and will provide your client and others with an overview of the complexity of your job.

Training is critical for your staff and volunteers. By providing them with a project management system to follow, you simplify and expedite this training. The project management system will put your staff and volunteers to work more quickly and will motivate them to consistently perform better over the life span of the event.

In addition to facilitating training, project management competency helps develop transferable skills that will help you attract the best people. As a result of working within your project management system, your staff and volunteers will learn a system that can be transferred and applied to a seemingly infinite number of jobs and careers.

Finally, as an event project manager, you will establish a diverse body of knowledge that may be transmitted to other organizations. In addition, you will be able to accumulate and refine the knowledge you receive from specific events and related projects from around the world. Whether it is a moon landing mission by NASA or the development and deployment of the new Transportation Security Administration, you can benefit from the successful project management experiences of other organizations.

In traditional project management, a technique called the Project Breakdown Structure (PBS) is often used to establish the organizational structure. Similar to the traditional organizational chart, the PBS provides a thorough overview of all of the event requirements.

After the event has been thoroughly defined, the work that will be required must be carefully analyzed. During this decomposition period, the work that will be conducted for the event is broken down into smaller units of work called tasks. This process is described in project management as the Work Breakdown Structure (WBS). Tasks or activities are generally singular, independent entities that may be individually managed. They also have specific start and finish times. Finally, they require clearly assigned resources (labor, finance, time). When several tasks are bundled together, they form a work package. A milestone is the accomplishment or completion of an important task.

Scheduling is perhaps one of the most valuable advantages of using a project management system for your event. Tasks are usually divided into two types of scheduling systems. Parallel scheduling refers to tasks that may be performed at the same time. Serial scheduling refers to tasks that must be performed in a sequence, such as when the lighting company must first hang the lights before the rental company places the tables and chairs for a banquet. Timelines for your events may benefit from a pictorial tool, such as the Gantt chart or bar chart, which demonstrates the major tasks that need to be accomplished. Creating and documenting the critical tasks and critical path are major responsibilities for the event project manager. The ability of the event project manager to list, prioritize, and sequence the tasks will ultimately determine the overall success of the event from an operational and financial standpoint.

Influence diagrams and sensitivity analyses are used to mitigate future challenges. The influence diagram is a chart that demonstrates through boxes and arrows what tasks are interdependent on others. Most importantly, it clearly demonstrates that events are part of larger systems and that one change in the system can affect hundreds of other components in the event. The sensitivity analysis is the identification of the degree of influence any part of the event has on the entire event as a whole. This analysis also aids in the risk-management controls for the event because it demonstrates how a small change in one area can affect other areas of the entire event. As a result of this careful documentation, a series of outputs is created, including charts and reports. Later you can use these outputs to form a handbook or manual to educate or train others, as well as provide important documentation and historical detail of the event.

Event Leaders will greatly benefit from project management training. The use of this system, as outlined by O'Toole and Mikolaitis, provides Event Leaders with a system that bridges the most accepted practices of their clients. For this reason and many more, it is important that Event Leaders become familiar with how to apply project management techniques to their Event Leadership system.

Planning Consistently Effective Events

The planning period is typically the longest period of time in the Event Leadership process. Historically, this has been due to disorganization. Disorganization is best characterized by frequent changes resulting from substitutions, additions, or even deletions due to poor research and design. Ideally, the better the research and design, the simpler and briefer the planning period will be. Since events are planned by human beings for other human beings, this theory is fraught with exceptions. However, your goal should be to develop a smooth planning process based on careful research and design procedures. The planning phase involves using the time/space/tempo laws (see Figure 2.10) to determine how best to use your immediate resources. These three basic laws will affect every decision you make; how well you make use of them will govern the final outcome of an event.

Timing

The law of timing refers to how much time you have in which to act or react. The first question that many Event Leaders ask the client is: When would you like to schedule the event? The answer to that question tells you how much time you have to prepare. Often that timetable may seem incredibly short.

The length of time available for planning and for actual production will dramatically affect the cost and sometimes the success of the event. Equally important, as you discovered earlier, is how you use your time. According to the Greek philosopher Theophrastus, "Time is the most valuable thing a human can spend."

When budgeting time for a proposed event, some independent Event Leaders estimate the amount of time necessary for pre-event client meetings, site inspections, meetings with vendors, ongoing communications and contract preparations, actual event time from time of arrival through departure, and post-event billable time. You may wish to allocate your billable time to follow the five phases of the event process: research, design, planning, coordination, and evaluation.

Because you can only estimate the time involved in these tasks, you must add a contingency time factor to each phase. Mona Meretsky, president of Comcor Event and Meeting Production Inc. of Ft. Lauderdale, Florida (www.comcoreevents.com), believes that using a 10 percent contingency factor will help you cover extra time required but not originally projected.

Like Meretsky, Audrey Gordon, sole proprietor of Audrey Gordon Parties of Chicago, admits that her actual time often exceeds her projected time. "A Bar Mitzvah

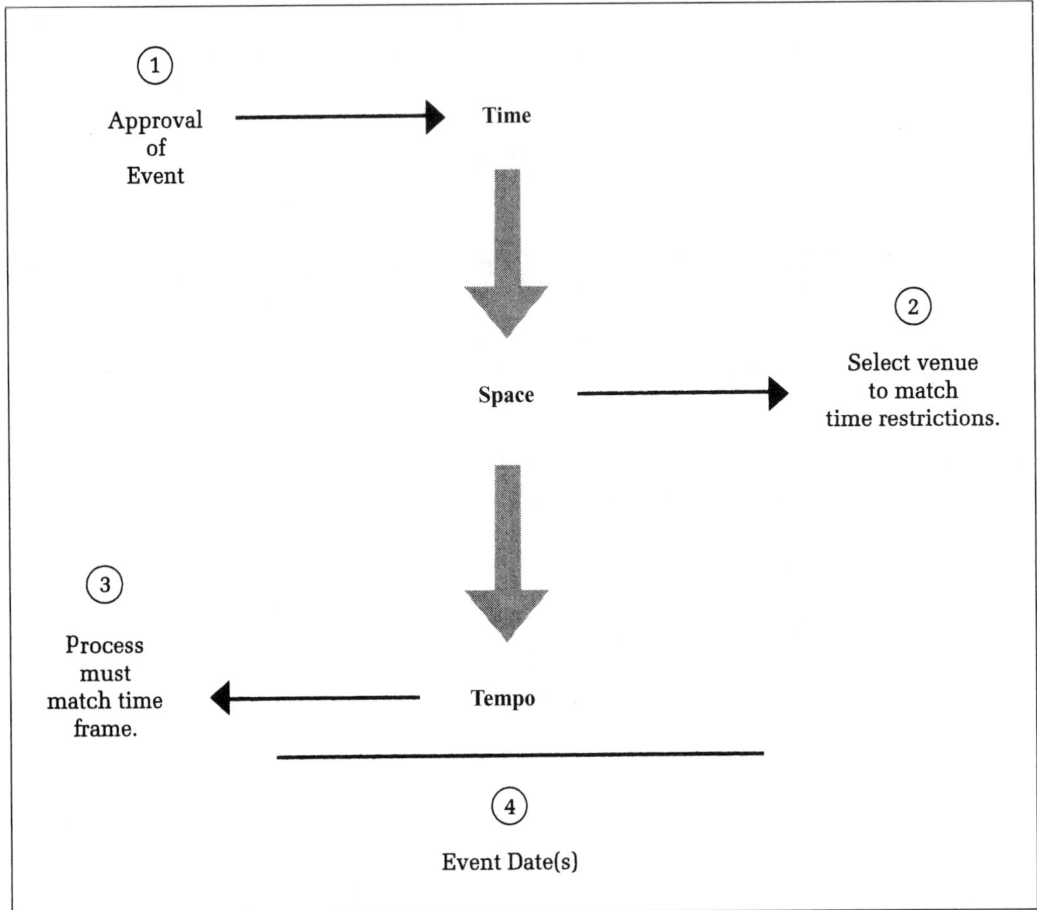

Figure 2.10 Time/Space/Tempo Laws

could, if necessary, be planned in one eight-hour day. The worst-case scenario is days of planning, as people usually change their minds often."

By paying careful attention to the research and design phase, you will be able to budget your time more precisely. This is particularly true for the event itself. This part of planning involves when to arrive for a particular event, when to cue the appropriate musician or performer, when to take breaks, and, of course, when to stop. Planning the time of an event is as important as managing your planning time.

Meretsky says, "I request that my personnel be set up for our events one hour in advance. In Florida, guests often arrive early, and we must be ready when they are."

Gordon, owner of a one-person firm, must rely on legions of vendors to produce her social life-cycle events. Her planning must be careful and precise, even to the point of listing what song is to be played at a specific time. The net result of her exhaustive preparation is that guests are able to relax and enjoy the event, as every element happens logically, sequentially, and on time.

The moment the client approves the date of an event, the Event Leader must begin assessing how the planning period will affect other business operations. Therefore, the law of timing sometimes requires that, when an unreasonable time frame is allotted to produce an event professionally, the Event Leader must decline to accept the opportunity. Ultimately, timing is the factor that will govern every decision when you ask yourself: "Given this amount of time, can I produce an event that displays the quality and professionalism I am known for without losing equal or possibly larger opportunities?" Your answer will determine whether the light turns green, fades to yellow, or becomes red.

Space

The law of space refers to both the physical space where an event will be held and the time between critical decisions pertaining to the event. The relationship of timing to space is one that is constant throughout the entire event process.

For the 1988 Super Bowl halftime show in Jack Murphy Stadium, Radio City Music Hall Productions designed an elaborate show featuring 88 grand pianos. Suddenly, without warning, the day before the actual production, the producer was instructed that his setup time for the production was reduced to only a few minutes. Further complicating matters, the groundskeepers at the stadium raised serious concerns that the movement of the pianos onto the field would affect the turf on the field. In this example and numerous others, the actual physical space governs the time required for various elements of the event.

When selecting a venue for an event, the location and physical resources present will significantly affect the additional time that must be invested. If you select a historic mansion with elaborate permanent décor, less time will be required to decorate the site. By comparison, if you select a four-walled venue, such as a hotel or convention center (where you are literally renting the four walls), significant time and expense must be invested to create a proper atmosphere for the event.

When considering the space for an event, some Event Leaders prepare an elaborate checklist to review each element carefully. The checklist should reflect the goals and objectives of the event and not merely replicate a form you have copied for convenience. One of the primary considerations when selecting space is the age and type of guest who will be attending. Older guests may not be able to tolerate extreme temperatures, and this may preclude you from selecting an outdoor venue. For events with young children, you may or may not wish to select a site in a busy urban setting. Go back to the research and needs assessment phase, and review why this event is important and who the stakeholders are. Then select a venue specifically to match their needs, wants, and expectations.

The terms *ingress* and *egress* are important concepts when reviewing a potential venue. Ingress defines the entrances or access to the venue, and egress refers to the exits or evacuation routes. When considering ingress and egress, you must consider not only people, including those with disabilities, but also vehicles, props, possibly animals, and indeed any element that must enter or exit the site. You must also keep in mind the time available for ingress or egress, as this will determine the number of portals (doors) that may need to be available for this purpose.

Parking, public transportation, and other forms of transportation, including taxis, limousines, and tour buses, must also be considered when analyzing a site. These considerations should include the number of parking spaces, including those for the disabled, the availability and security/safety of public transportation, and the time required to dispatch a taxi.

Tempo

The final law of event planning is concerned with the rate or tempo at which events take place during both production planning and the event itself. From the moment the client approves an agreement or authorizes you to proceed with planning to the final meeting, you must be aware of the projected rate at which events will happen. Improved technology, such as faxes and online services, has dramatically accelerated the process and the demands of clients to "do it now." However, "now" is often not as efficient as later. When an Event Leader is pressured to deliver a product before it is fully developed, the results may be less than exemplary. Therefore, as you manage the rate at which tasks will be completed and events will occur, it is important to consider if each action is being performed at the best time. "Maybe" is not an acceptable response. To determine if this is the best moment for this task to be handled, ask yourself if you have sufficient information and resources to implement it. If not, try to delay the action until you are better prepared.

Establishing the proper tempo is not an exact science. Rather, like a conductor of an orchestra, you must allow your personal taste, energy, and experience to guide you as you speed up or slow down the tempo as required. By analyzing the event site and estimating the time required for a project, the Event Leader is better able to set the tempo or schedule for the setup, production, and removal of the equipment. Without this advance analysis, the Event Leader becomes an orchestra conductor without benefit of a score, a musician without benefit of a maestro.

Understanding the needs of guests also helps establish and adjust the tempo during an event. If guests are concerned primarily with networking, a leisurely time frame should be followed to allow for plenty of interaction. For example, while the transition from cocktails to dinner may be brisk when the program is more important than networking, the transition may be slowed when the emphasis is on the connections the audience members make among themselves.

Jerry Edwards, CPCE, past president of the National Association of Catering Executives (NACE), and owner of Chef's Expressions, Inc., in Timonium, Maryland, is convinced that the best event planners are those who are focused on quality outcomes for their guests. "I was very fortunate to own a business in the era of high demand, and I was able to continually upgrade my staff. Now, thanks to The Food Channel and other food-related programming, customers are more sophisticated and demanding," says Edwards.

When Edwards began his catering business, there was little information regarding high-end catering or ethnic menus. Today, due to changing tastes, everyone is concerned with the food components and the final presentation. In terms of changing tastes, Edwards reports that the use of full-liquor bars is up by 21 percent in his events. "Perhaps the nostalgia exhibited by the baby boomers has brought back the name brand or call liquor consumption. They will actually pay for liquor but may not pay as much for food. Nine out of ten will ask for liquor by brand name. The drink reflects personal taste, sophistication, and success," says Edwards. The three-term president of NACE said that he learned the catering business through the NACE meetings he attended. His involvement in NACE helped take his business from $500,000 to over $2 million per year in revenues.

Edwards envisions that, through organizations such as NACE, Event Leaders in the near future will earn credentials from either certifications or college degrees and that specific career paths will be identified for young people to help them break the glass ceiling that continues to exist in the hospitality industry. Finally, he believes that human nature plays a significant role in developing Event Leaders, and that schools and associations must work closer together to promote leadership development. "We need to begin developing the next level of Event Leaders in the catering industry, and we can do this best by working together to help ensure the future for our profession," suggests the man who bought a small lunch counter for $2,000 and then developed a multimillion-dollar off-premise catering enterprise while serving as a leader for one of the industry's major associations.

These three basic laws—timing, space, and tempo—are as old as human creation itself, and govern the planning of all events. To become an expert Event Leader, you must master your ability to manage time in the most minute segments. You must develop the vision to perceive the strengths, weaknesses, opportunities, and threats of every space. Finally, you must be able to analyze the needs of your guests to set tempos that will ensure a memorable event.

Gap Analysis

Too often, event planners proceed by rote memory to produce an event in a style with which they are most familiar. In doing this, they often overlook critical gaps in the logical progression of event elements. Identifying these gaps and providing recommendations for closure is the primary purpose of *gap analysis*.

This planning tool involves taking a long, hard look at event elements and identifying significant gaps in the planning that could weaken the overall progression of the plan. An example is an event planner who has scheduled an outdoor event in September in Miami Beach, Florida. September is the prime month of the hurricane season. The event planner has created a wide gap in his or her plan that must be closed to strengthen the overall event. Therefore, finding a secure indoor location in case of a weather emergency would be a good beginning toward closing this gap.

Use a critical friend—a person whose expertise about the particular event is known to you—to review your plan and search for gaps in your logical thinking. Once you have identified the gaps, look for opportunities to close them. By implementing the findings from SWOT and gap analysis, you are able to begin executing your plan. This execution phase is known as coordination.

Coordination: Executing the Plan

As the light turns green, the tempo accelerates, and now you are faced with coordinating the minute-by-minute activities of the event itself. I was once asked, "What does it take to be a competent Event Leader?" "The ability to make good decisions," I swiftly answered. I realize now that it requires much more than good decision making. However, it is also true that during the course of coordinating an event you will be required to make not dozens but hundreds of decisions. Your ability to use your professional training and experience to make the correct decision will affect the outcome of the entire event. While it is true that Event Leaders should maintain a positive attitude and see problems as challenges in search of the right solution, it is also important that you apply critical analysis to every challenge that comes your way. These six steps are a simple but effective way to make these decisions:

1. Collect all the information. Most problems have many sides to review.
2. Consider the pros and cons of your decision in terms of who will be affected.
3. Consider the financial implications of your decision.
4. Consider the moral and ethical implications of your decision.
5. Do no harm. Your decision must not harm others or yourself if at all possible.
6. Make the decision and continue looking forward.

Evaluation: The Link to the Next Event

The planned event process, as shown in Figure 2.11, is a dynamic spiral that is literally without end. The first phase—research—is connected with the last—evaluation. In this last phase, you will ask, "What is it we wish to evaluate, and how will we best accomplish this?" You can evaluate events by each part of the Event Leadership process or through a general comprehensive review of all phases. It is up to you and your stakeholders to decide what information you require to improve your planning and then implement effective strategies to accomplish this phase.

Perhaps the most common form of event evaluation is the written survey. Usually, the survey is conducted immediately following the event, to identify the satisfaction level of the participants and spectators. As with any evaluation method, there are pros and cons to immediate feedback. One bias is the immediate nature of the feedback, which prohibits respondents from digesting the total event experience before providing feedback.

Another form of evaluation is the use of monitors. A monitor is a trained person who will observe an element of the event and provide both written and verbal feedback to the event planner. The event monitor usually has a checklist or survey to complete and will then offer additional comments as required. The benefit of this type of evaluation is that it permits a trained, experienced event staff member or volunteer to observe the event objectively while it is taking place and provide instructive comments.

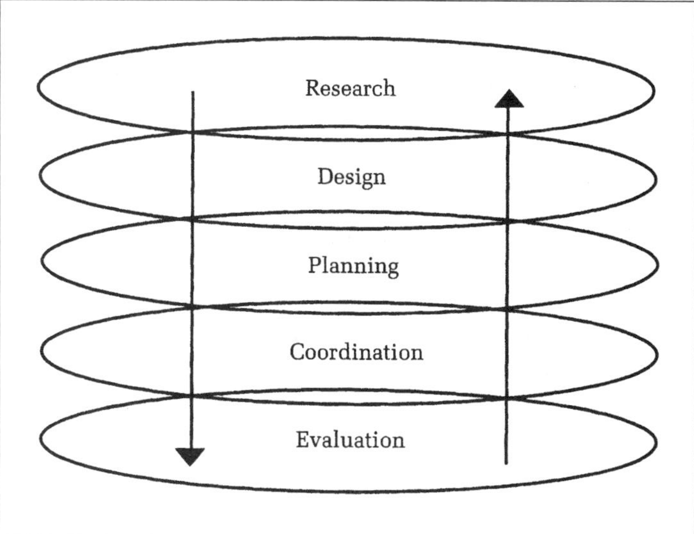

Figure 2.11 Planned Event Process

The third form of event evaluation is the telephone or mail survey conducted after the event. In this evaluation, the event planner surveys the spectators and participants after the event through either a mail or a telephone survey. By waiting a few days after the event to collect these data, the Event Leader is able to glean from the respondents how their attitudes have changed and developed after some time has passed since participating in the event.

A new form of evaluation that is growing in popularity is the pre- and post-event survey. This evaluation allows an event planner to determine the respondents' knowledge, opinions, and other important information both before and after their attendance at an event. This is especially helpful when trying to match expectations to reality. For example, an event guest may state upon entering an event that he or she expects, based on the advertising and public relations, to enjoy nonstop entertainment. However, upon completing the exit interview, the guest registers disappointment because of the gaps in the programming. This type of evaluation helps event organizers close gaps between over-promising and under-delivering certain aspects of an event. Registration mail-in rebates and other incentives may be offered for filling out both surveys.

Regardless of the form of evaluation you use, it is critical that you not wait until the end of the event to find out how you are doing. If you were to attend any banquet where I am responsible for the event, you might be surprised to see me wandering from table to table and asking guests how they are enjoying dinner. In doing this, I am able to uncover gaps in execution of the plan. One guest might say: "I ordered vegetarian and was served meat." I am able to correct this error immediately. If I had waited until the person had filled out an evaluation form, it would have been too late. Take the temperature of your guests hourly to make certain that you are on target in meeting your goals and objectives.

By doing this, you are able to reset your course immediately and ensure that, together, you will arrive at the same destination: a successful event.

Professor Helmut Schwagermann lectures at the University of Applied Science of Osnabrueck in Germany. A longtime veteran of the global meeting industry, Schwagermann has developed an original theory to control the outcome of events.

He recommends that the control of events take place in three phases.

1. Control the event concept in a pre-event test.
2. Control the event during the process itself using what he describes as the "in-between test."
3. Control the results of the event through a post-test. During this post-test, ask questions such as: Did the event satisfy the economic results and strategic communication goals?

Schwagermann cautions that so-called hard economic facts such as profits are not always justified. Long-term effects, such as changes in opinions and behavior as well as the effect on remembering and emotional excitement, can be measured with instruments of comprehensive event marketing research.

Whether in Germany or Australia, comprehensive measurement and evaluation is being given a high priority by event planners, clients, and government. Leo Jago, deputy chief executive officer and director of research of the Australian federal government's Sustainable Tourism Cooperative Research Center, has similarly conceived and tested a new Triple Bottom Line theory for event evaluation. According to Jago, events cannot be measured or evaluated in strictly economic terms. Rather, he recommends a triple evaluation process that includes comprehensive analysis of the economic, sociocultural, and ecological outcomes of the event.

The event evaluations standards being established in Australia may be the direct results of the successful Summer Olympic Games of 2000 that were held in Sydney. In preparation for the games, the Sydney Organizing Committee for the Olympic Games developed, in cooperation with the International Olympic Committee (IOC) and Monash University, an information-sharing and knowledge transfer program. The IOC requires every official organizing committee to provide a final comprehensive report. However, the Sydney Olympic Games were the first time this process was coordinated in a systematic process that was originally called "Athena" in honor of the Greek goddess of knowledge and wisdom. As a result of the Sydney initiatives, the IOC has formalized the knowledge transfer process as part of their Olympic Games operations plan.

The future of event evaluation and knowledge transfer will most certainly include more comprehensive processes as recommended and demonstrated by Schwagermann, Jago, and the IOC. Regardless of how you establish the metrics for final evaluation of your event, you must insure that you have provided the appropriate resources to evaluate the outcome of your efforts thoroughly and systematically. Evaluation is the fifth phase in the event management process; however, it propels the first phase of research by collecting and analyzing the history that is needed to continually improve your event process in the future.

This process is the conceptual framework for every effective event. The process is dynamic and selective, in that the Event Leader must determine where to begin and how to proceed to best accomplish the objectives. One event may be past the research stage, and the event planner may be retained merely to coordinate the elements. Still another may be midway through the planning phase. The effective event planner will immediately recognize that the event process cannot be complete or totally effective unless each phase is considered carefully. It does not matter where you begin the process. What is essential is that every phase be considered, visited, and understood.

Communications: The Tie That Binds

Event planning is a profession whose success or failure ratio often depends on people's ability to communicate effectively with one another. It does not matter whether this communication is oral, written, electronic, or all three. What is important is that event planners become practiced communicators in order to maintain clear communications with all stakeholders. Regardless of the communication channel that you are using, you want to make sure that you make your point clearly and establish the right priorities in your message.

Often both visual and auditory noise provides a barrier to open communication. Visual noise includes those visual distractions that take place when you are trying to communicate with others. Auditory noise may be music, traffic, or other distractions that interfere with others' ability to hear and concentrate on what you are saying. Remove all noise before trying to communicate with others. Find a quiet place to meet, remove visual distractions, and verify and confirm that those you are communicating with comprehend what you are sharing.

Written communications are essential not only for record keeping but also for purposes of mass distribution. It is impossible to transmit verbally to 1,000 people an event update without distortion. (Remember the children's game "telephone"?) Use memorandums, briefing statements, bulletins, and other documents to communicate effectively to one or many others. Memoranda should include an "Action Required" statement to inform the reader how best to respond and in what time frame.

Bulletins must be sporadic, or you run the risk of becoming the person who cried "wolf" once too often and now is ignored by everyone. Newsletters are a particularly effective tool for communications; however, use caution, as they are extremely labor intensive to continually write, edit, produce, and distribute on a regular basis.

Perhaps one of the best ways to communicate is through a meeting. When scheduling a meeting, make certain that you prepare an agenda in advance that lists the items for discussion. Distribute this document prior to the meeting to those who will attend and ask them to comment. This will help them prepare for the meeting. Use the agenda to guide the meeting, and, as the leader, serve as a facilitator for discussion. Using a flip chart will help you capture ideas while sticking to the agenda. One extremely effective device is to assign participants work prior to the meeting so that they come to the meeting prepared and ready to make specific contributions. Make sure that your meeting does not take much longer than initially planned; otherwise, you will give the impression of being a disorganized person who does not value your own time and the time that others invest in the meeting.

Digital technology has made audio and video communication more accessible than ever. Record meetings or dictate your thoughts onto a CD, DVD, MP3 recorder or even a cassette tape recorder or camcorder. The average person commutes to the office 20 or more minutes twice daily and can use this time to listen to prerecorded information such as meeting minutes or industry news. My son downloads free PodCasts about specific interests from iTunes and listens to them while commuting. As more computers come equipped with video editing software, making your own basic business videos is easier than ever. Thanks to the growth of Internet sites such as YouTube, short homemade videos are a huge part of today's culture. By creating your own digital audio or video based around your events business, you can generate excitement and capture the attention of staff and stakeholders in a contemporary and fun way.

While not the most reliable source of information, the blogosphere (the world of personal online journals) and accompanying online forums are certainly the easiest and fastest way to find information on or communicate about specific interests such as events. Google searches will invariably reveal that someone else in the world shares your interest, no matter how obscure, and is communicating about it online. Even when communicating on accredited Web sites such as those run by *Special Events* magazine, BizBash, or MPI, use the information as a stepping stone towards more reliable research sources. Remember to stay professional and formal even in anonymous online forums.

Videoconferencing has never been easier thanks to Web tools such as Skype, a free videoconferencing service that allows an Event Manager in Philadelphia to talk face-to-face with a client in Tokyo. For a successful videoconference, prepare the technology and have a backup, choose hours sensitive to the participant's time zone, and treat it like an in-person meeting. Don't make your caller get up at 3 A.M. to call you at 12 noon your time. Don't dress down or multitask while speaking—they can see you! Most importantly, videoconferencing is not always reliable and may result in an interrupted or distorted meeting. Sometimes, a simple phone call will do.

Event Management Body of Knowledge Project

In 2004, the first Event Management Body of Knowledge (EMBOK) Embizo was held at the Edeni Private Game Reserve near Kruger National Park in South Africa. The term *embizo* comes from the Sulu language and means "a gathering." The purpose of this historic meeting was to identify and develop a global model for producing professional live events. Many years earlier, the Project Management Institute (PMI) used a similar process to standardize the project management process. Therefore, the EMBOK participants used the PMI model as a way to standardize the body of knowledge in the global event industry.

The convener for this meeting was Janet Landey, CSEP, the managing director of the South African Institute for Event Management. The event educators included Glenn Bowdin of Leeds Metropolitan University; this author; Matthew Gonzalez of Events Education; Dr. Kathy Nelson of the University of Nevada at Las Vegas; William O'Toole of the University of Sydney, Australia; Julia Rutherford Silvers, CSEP of Speaking of Events; and Dr. Jane Spowart of the University of Johannesburg.

Following several days of intensive meetings and friendly but lively debate, a preliminary model was developed. A second Embizo was held in the summer of 2005,

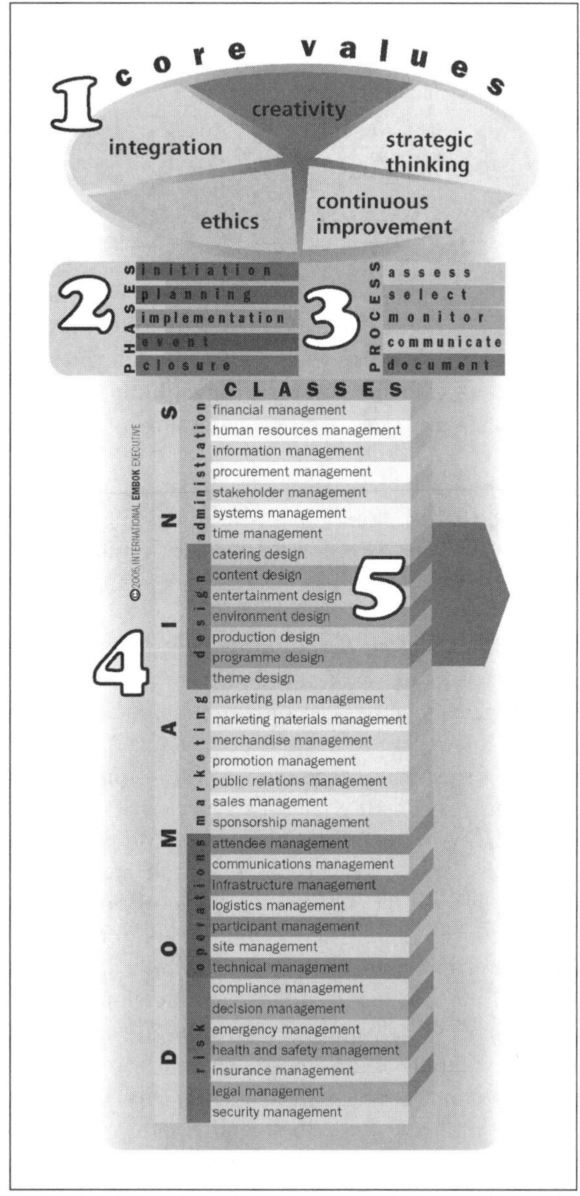

Figure 2.12 Model of Event Management Body of Knowledge (EMBOK) Project. Courtesy of Janet Landey, CSEP.

also in South Africa, and further work was completed regarding the development of the model and in establishing communications channels to share this valuable information with others. Figure 2.12 demonstrates one example of this model. EMBOK is still very much a work in progress, but it has tremendous potential in creating a set of unifying standards around which Event Leaders may work together to continuously improve the profession. For more information about EMBOK, visit the Web site at www.embok.org.

Synergy: Linking Administration, Coordination, Marketing, and Risk Management

At one time, the Walt Disney Company was the only organization of its size and type with an executive board position titled Vice President for Corporate Synergy. Due to the diversity in the Disney product line (theme parks, retail stores, movies, recordings, sport, television), the leaders of this successful organization believe that one person must be responsible for ensuring that there is synergy among all aspects of the business operation.

Up to one year in advance, before Disney rolls out a new movie, the retail stores are developing new products, the theme parks are planning new live shows, and the other aspects of the corporation are preparing for joint promotion and distribution of the new product. This kind of synergy allocates Disney's immense resources in the most efficient manner.

Your event also must manage resources efficiently. These resources include your ability to administrate, coordinate, market, and manage the risk for the event. You must link these four competencies together carefully throughout the event process in order to produce the very best and most profitable event product.

The administration process of an event serves as the foundation for the resources you will select and manage during the coordination process. Poor administration will later undermine your ability to coordinate the event. Strong coordination will result in better marketing results. Unless your operations people are aware that today's tickets are discounted, for example, all the advertising in the world will be wasted. The link between coordination and marketing, and for that matter administration, is vital. Finally, legal, ethical, and risk-management issues form a strong river current that runs through every decision you make in Event Leadership. If your marketing team leader overpromotes or inaccurately promotes an event, he or she will place those who must coordinate event operations at a great disadvantage. In subsequent chapters, we introduce each of these competencies in detail, but at this stage it is important for you to recognize the connection between them. Together, and with the potential adoption of EMBOK, they weave a strong tapestry that will help shield you from future problems and provide you with a rich understanding of how all team members must work together productively.

Corporate Social Responsibility (CSR) and Planned Events

The term *Corporate Social Responsibility* has been widely adopted in the past decade by both corporations as well as local, regional, and federal governments. The term *company* is derived from the Latin root words *cum* (together) and *pani* (the baking of bread). Therefore, when a company plans, organizes and delivers a special event, it is implicit that they do this in concert with others. David Packard, one of the founders of the computer giant Hewlett Packard, understood that the mission of a business was greater than financial gain. He stated, "When a group of people get together and establish something called a company they are able to accomplish something collectively that they could not accomplish separately—they make a contribution to society" (Packard 1939).

One of the primary reasons I was attracted to the higher purpose of planning events was the opportunity to draw people together for a positive societal outcome. Today, this is known as CSR. However, Mr. Packard and myself and other individuals throughout time have described this as the golden rule (do unto others as you would have them do unto you), or as one sage wrote, "If I am not for myself who will be for me? If I am not for others, what am I? And if not now, when?" (Rabbi Hillel 30 B.C.–9 A.D.).

CSR statements and outcomes now regularly appear in corporate reports as well as in tenders that are offered by corporations and governments. These aspirational and sometimes fundamentally important core values communicate to others what the organization stands for, how they are helping others, and when they are practicing CSR.

One example of CSR In the meetings and events industry is a project titled Hospitality Helping Hands. This highly successful program has resulted in hundreds of volunteers helping restore and rebuild cities where the PCMA has held its annual conventions for the past several years. In 2009, a group of Scottish students from Queen Margaret University in Edinburgh, Scotland, joined dozens of professional meeting and event planners in restoring and cleaning the historic cemeteries in New Orleans, Louisiana, which had suffered the ravages of Hurricane Katrina.

There are innumerable ways in which events may be used to demonstrate CSR. However, it is important to make certain it is carefully aligned with not only the core values of the event organizer but also the event sponsor's mission and values. Furthermore, it is equally important to remember that each event has the potential to incrementally improve the world. Therefore, look for the nuggets of gold within every event opportunity as you seek ways to promote fun and foster a better society at the same time.

Figure 2.13 provides some examples of how you may incorporate CSR into your future events.

In a broader global context, your organization may also wish to consider buying as much of your products and services from local providers, purchasing only fair-trade products, and ensuring that your products are made in an ethical manner—including only purchasing from firms that provide safe and secure working conditions for their workers. In a later chapter, we will explore the potential for greener events; however, every

1. Devote one morning or afternoon of the event to helping clean or restore a children's playground.
2. Use excess funds designated for a cocktail party or banquet to purchase equipment for a children's school or playground.
3. Reuse paper and other products left over from your meeting or event within local schools or community centers.
4. Invite individuals who could not ordinarily afford to attend your event to be your guests.
5. Develop a volunteer team to identify future opportunities for CSR and empower them to conduct research and make future recommendations.

Figure 2.13 Corporate Social Responsibility Opportunities within Planned Events

event should be considered an opportunity to reduce the carbon footprint and slow global warming through the planning and delivery of environmentally sustainable programs.

Indeed, the model of global Event Leadership is changing rapidly. As Gladwell suggests, stakeholders in planned events use rapid cognition to make conscious and unconscious decisions about who they want to work with and who they want to give their money to for planning events. The positive movement toward CSR can be seen as a critical step

The Pioneer: Professor Anthony Lack, Training and Events Manager, HTMI, Soerenberg, Switzerland

"Mr. Lack," as his students refer to him with great respect, has always been interested in planned events. "When we immigrated from South Africa to Europe we held a birthday party for our triplets and over 200 people attended. This required highly detailed planning to insure a successful outcome!" Anthony and his

students at the HTMI campus in the Swiss Alps annually produce a highly successful International Night. According to Anthony, this event enables the students to work closely together to produce a outcome that is enjoyed by all. Through the process of planning this complex event, which involves many different cultures, his students learn about organization,

in the right direction that will serve as the fundamental underpinning for future event decisions. If events are designed to serve others, one could then ask, "How may each and every event repair, improve, and advance human society through research, design, planning, coordination, and evaluation?"

Career-Advancement Connections

Corporate Social Responsibility Connection

Select a corporation and read its mission statement. Now, design an event for the corporation that includes elements of CSR as an implied and explicit outcome that matches, supports, or even advances its mission.

Global Connection

In celebration of the sixth edition of this textbook, we have created an online forum for people around the world to post case studies in Event Management. Go to http://eventstudies.wordpress.com and post a case study on an event you have experienced.

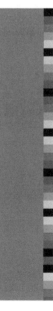

creativity, attention to detail, and the ability to get along with one another.

He was first inspired to enter the field of event planning whilst a student himself at the Hotel Institute of Management with Professor James Gallagher. Gallagher was a charismatic and dynamic professor that rapidly engaged Anthony's interest in convention and event planning. However, according to Anthony, "My first mentor was my mother. She organized beautiful parties and I helped her with the planning and service." These early mentors provided the foundation for his teaching practice today. He states, "For example, event planning is becoming highly competitive, and so my students must practice exceptional customer service, they must have strong advanced skills in technology, and they must recognize the value of corporate social responsibility through each event they produce."

Looking to the future, he believes that his students may even be planning events that take place not only on airplanes such as the Airbus A380 but also in outer space as well. "They must be prepared for the challenges as well as the opportunities of the future." The best single piece this pioneer offers to the next generation of event planners is to "Always stay several steps ahead in your industry. Constantly look around you for ideas such as trends and then be prepared to seize the future through your intuition, foresight, and ambition."

Technology Connection

Visit www.meetingmetrics.com or www.corbinball.com to learn how technology is being used to improve and advance the measurement, assessment, and evaluation of meetings and events.

Resource Connection

Contact meetings and event industry associations to stay abreast of quickly developing industry trends. The International Special Events Society (www.ises.com), Professional Convention Management Association (www.pcma.org), and Meeting Professionals International (www.mpiweb.org), among others, are committed to continuous education in the Event Leadership community. For

The Protégé: Cheng So Yin (Amy)

Amy So Yin is a recent graduate of HTMI, and Mr. Lack is her mentor. She has a global view of the events industry and relates it to tourism. She says that "Events, like tourism, are a way that world cultures are exposed to each other. We share our cultures and develop more respect through events and this leads to greater integration of organizations and people."

Amy became interested in events while participating in HTMI's annual international event. According to Amy, "Although I was not on the main organizing committee, I saw how people would get excited, energized and their lives were changed by working together so closely to produce this successful event. That is when I knew that this is what I wanted to do as my future career." She describes Mr. Lack as "Not only experienced but also passionate

a comprehensive listing of meetings and events professional organizations visit www.conventionindustry.org.

 Learning Connection

In this chapter, you have explored the five stages of each event and how corporate social responsibility may underpin each phase. To enhance your understanding of the chapter, complete this activity:

You are organizing a major rock music festival that will feature musicians from around the world. It is a three-day event and will include 500 performers and 50,000 guests. Describe how you will use each of the five steps to plan this event, and how you will imbed CSR in your planning process.

about this industry. His passion is infectious and makes us all want to work harder and accomplish more not only through our studies and events but also in our future careers."

In describing the major changes in planned events, she notes that, "through social media such as Facebook, the Internet is rapidly becoming the primary marketing tool for events. Therefore, we must continually improve our skills in this area. One way I do this is by surfing the Internet to identify new event Web sites and become aware of new products and services that may benefit my future clients." Her vision of the future is highly positive and includes greater use of video and Internet teleconferencing as a key component of events and meetings. Amy states, "Many hotels and conference centers have these capabilities, but I believe within a few years most, if not all, will use this technology to further advance communications beyond the site where the event is occurring. This will enable millions to participate in future events simultaneously, along with those who are at the site where the event is taking place."

She agrees with her mentor Mr. Lack that to be successful, we must always be several steps ahead of the industry in which we are working. Amy Cheng exemplifies this forward-thinking approach through her daily online review of newspapers, books, and other documents in her continuing quest to identify trends and forces that may impact the future of planned events.

PART TWO

Event Administration

A VIP dinner is meticulously planned by students at HTMI in Switzerland.

CHAPTER 3

Developing and Implementing the Event Plan

In this chapter you will learn how to:

- Conduct comprehensive research for your event
- Identify key sources of information for planning
- Design a program creatively
- Develop an appropriate theme
- Establish and manage an effective strategic plan
- Use emerging technologies to improve and accelerate your planning process
- Develop and manage the timeline for an event

Comprehensive administration is the foundation for all successful events. The administration of an event provides you and the stakeholders with data with which to design the dream that will produce the deliverables you desire.

During the administration process, the Event Leader must make certain that data identified during research are used to drive the design and ultimately to produce the measurable outcomes required by event stakeholders:

Research (data) + Design = Planned sucessful outcomes

Research without the important phase of design will result in a dry, one-dimensional, and perhaps boring event. To produce a multidimensional and multisensory event experience that transforms guests, you must research as well as design the event outcome. The research and design phases ultimately produce the tools with which you can construct a blueprint of the event plan. The final event plan is, in fact, a direct reflection of the research and design phases.

Stretching the Limits of the Event

Whereas research is either inductive or deductive in form and often proceeds in a linear fashion, the design phase is weblike and often kaleidoscopic. Just as the Internet provides you with literally millions of resources for event design, your own mental process must mirror this technology. During the design process, the professional Event Leader considers every possibility and challenges every assumption determined during the research phase. This pushing of the research envelope is essential if you are to produce innovative, highly creative, unique special events that will exceed guest expectations.

Joseph Pine and James H. Gilmore state in *The Experience Economy* (2000), "You are what you charge for." If you are to steadily increase the value of your work as an event researcher, designer, planner, coordinator, and evaluator, you must strive continually to collect the best information and resources to produce a solid plan that satisfies the needs, wants, desires, and, ultimately, expectations of event guests.

Designing the Event Environment

The playwright's work is restrained by what the theater's limited confines can accommodate. Event planners face a similar challenge each time they are called on to create an environment. Whether the site is a palatial mansion or a suburban park, the challenges remain the same. How can the site be adapted to meet the needs of guests? Ballrooms with their four bare walls, department stores filled with products, and even main streets upon which parades are staged offer the same problems and opportunities as those confronting playwrights and set designers.

When creating an environment, the special events professional must return to the basic needs of the guests. To be successful, the final design must satisfy these needs. Lighting, space, movement, decor, acoustics, and even such seemingly mundane concerns as restrooms all affect the comfort of the guests and so play vital roles in creating a successful environment.

Five-Card Draw: Playing the Five Senses

When attempting to satisfy the needs of guests, remember that the five senses are very powerful tools. Like five winning cards in the Event Leader's hand, combining the five senses—tactile, smell, taste, visual, and auditory—to satiate the needs of guests is the primary consideration when designing the event environment. The olfactory system creates instant emotional and creative reactions within your guests. How many times have you walked into a room, noticed a familiar smell, and suddenly experienced déjà vu? Event Leadership pioneer Jack Morton (1910–2004) stated that smell is the most powerful sense because of the memories it produces. In fact, smell may generally be the strongest sense in terms of generating emotional response; however, this will vary among individual guests. Therefore, as the Event Leader you must actively seek to employ in your environmental design elements that will affect all the senses.

When designing an *American Idol*–themed banquet, you may erect a backdrop that evokes memories of the popular television show, play the theme music, and even have Simon Cowell look-alikes at the door to greet your guests. However, the settings and actors are still lacking one critical sensory element. When you add a light scent of lemon or orange to the fog machine, the event suddenly becomes a total sensory experience set in Southern California.

Just as some guests are sensitive to certain stimuli, such as smell or hearing, other guests have a primary sense that they rely on. Due to the influence of television, many baby boomers may rely primarily on their visual sense. When designing the environment, this fact is important to recognize when you are trying to communicate your message quickly. Use the senses as instruments to tune the imagination of guests. Be careful to avoid playing sharp or flat notes by overdoing it. Find the perfect sensory melody and guests will become involved in your event creatively and emotionally.

Five procedures will enable you to survey guests to determine their level of sensitivity as well as their primary sensual stimuli in order to create an effective event sensory environment:

1. Use a focus group to determine the primary sensory stimuli of your guests.
2. Identify any oversensitivity or even allergies guests may have that could be irritated by certain sensory elements.
3. Use the draft diagram of the event environment to identify and isolate the location of certain sensory experiences.
4. Share this design tool with typical guests and solicit their attitudes and opinions.
5. Audit the venue to determine the preexisting sensory environment and what modifications you will be required to implement.

Soundscaping

To communicate with the guests at an event, you must design a sound system and effects that are unique and powerful enough to capture their attention. Do not confuse powerful with loud, however. Poignant background music at a small social event has as much power as a booming rock beat at a retail promotion. As with other components of event production, successful use of sound requires gauging and meeting the needs of the audience.

Sound by itself is a most powerful sensation. When asked which of her senses she would like to have returned to her, the late Helen Keller, blind and deaf since birth, explained that the ability to hear is more important than the ability to see. The eyes can deceive, but the way in which others speak and the thoughts they share reveal much about personality and intentions. (*Helen Keller in Scotland, A Personal Record Written By Herself*, London: Methuen,1933) Sound unlocks our imagination and allows us to visualize images buried in our subconscious. When planning the sound design for your event, many questions need to be considered. What is to be the dominant sensory element for the event? Sound may be the dominant sensory element for your event; for example, if live music or extensive speeches are the major component of your event, your investment in high-quality sound production may be paramount.

How will sound help support, reinforce, or expand the guests' perceptions of the event? Consider the theme of your event and devise ways in which sound can be used to convey that theme to the guests. For example, if you are planning a Polynesian theme event, the use of recorded island-type music at the entrance will help communicate that theme.

Are the architectural conditions in the venue optimal for sound reproduction? This question is most important considering the number of new sites being created every day. The majority of these sites were not designed for optimum sound reproduction, and the event planner or sound designer must, therefore, consider how to improve the sound conditions in the venue. In the five special events markets, sound design, like lighting, is growing tremendously. In the social market, not only are live bands used more than ever, but with the addition of new electronic instruments, the repertoire of a small live band can be increased many fold. Moreover, the rise of the disc jockey format and the more frequent use of videotape require that the sound quality must be better than ever before. As the sophistication of the audio components available to the average consumer has increased, the sound systems for retail events have had to improve in quality as well to match the sound many guests can experience in their living rooms. Whether it is a fashion show or a visit with Santa, excellent sound is required to give the event credibility and value in the eyes (or ears) of the guest. Millions of dollars' worth of merchandise may be on display, but if the sound system is poor, the guest perceives less value and is less inclined to buy.

Meetings and convention events also place more importance on sound reproduction for their programs. Gone are the days when a meeting planner was content to use the hotel house speakers for live music. Today, many musical groups carry their own speakers, mixing boards, and operators, or high-quality concert sound equipment must be provided by the event planner.

Visual Cues

Both the baby boomers and generation Y were raised in front of television sets and therefore require strong visual elements to assist them with experiencing your event. This includes using proper signs to orient the guest and provide clear direction. Additional visual elements that must be considered are the proper and repetitive use of key design elements such as the logo. A logo is the graphic symbol of the organization sponsoring the event. Not only must this symbol be represented accurately, but it also must always appear in the same manner to benefit from repetitive viewing and establish consistency to promote retention.

Touch

Whether you are considering the cloth that will dress the banquet table, the napkins, or the printed program, touch will immediately convey the quality of the event environment. To establish this sense, use several different textures and, while wearing a blindfold, touch the various elements to determine what feelings are promoted. When handling the cloth, do you feel as if you are attending a royal gala or a country picnic? When holding the program, are you a guest of the king or the court jester? This blindfold test can help you narrow your choices and effectively select the right fabric, paper, or other product to properly communicate the precise sense of touch you desire. Today, there are hundreds of different types of linens available to provide a strong sense of touch for your event. One of the largest linen providers is BBJ Linens, which has offices in over 20 different cities in the United States and ships worldwide. Its extensive inventory may be viewed at www.bbjlinens.com.

Another pioneering firm in the sense of touch for special events is Sculptware of Arizona. The founder, Mitch Keldorf, created in 1987 the concept of using stretch fabrics to cover chairs and tables for dazzling new looks. The Sculptware products may be seen at www.sculptwareonline.com.

Smell

Earlier we discussed the use of a smell such as lemons or oranges to stimulate the sense of memory through smell. Remember that throughout the event environment, a series of smells may be present that will either create the correct environment or confuse and irritate the guest. When conducting the site inspection, note if the public areas are overdeodorized. This smell is often a clue that chemicals are being used to mask a foul smell. Instead, you may wish to look for venues whose aromas are natural and the result of history, people, and, of course, natural products such as plants and flowers.

Some people are extremely sensitive to strong odors. Therefore, when using the sense of smell, do not overdo it. Instead, establish neutral areas where the smell of a scented candle, flowers, or food odors is not present, to provide the nose with a respite from this stimulation. However, establishing individual areas that have a strong aroma of pizza baking or chocolate melting is also important to both attract and convey the proper atmosphere. You may, for example, wish to incorporate the smell of barbecue into your western-themed event or pine trees into your Christmas wonderland. Again, when establishing these areas of smell, try to isolate them so that the guests can return to a neutral zone and not feel overwhelmed by this sense.

Taste

The sense of taste will be discussed later; however, the Event Leader must realize that the catering team members play a critical role in establishing a strong sensory feeling for the event. Consult in advance with the catering team and establish the goals and objectives of the food presentation. Then determine how best to proceed in combining the other four senses with the sense of taste to create a total olfactory experience for the guests. Keep in mind the age, culture, and lifestyle of the guests. Older guests may not be as sensitive to taste, whereas other guests may require spicier food combinations to engage their sense of taste. The taste sense historically has been linked with a strong sensual experience. Play the taste card for all it is worth, and you will transform guests from spectators to fully engaged participants who will long remember the succulent event you have designed.

Blending, Mixing, and Matching the Senses for Full Effect

Make certain that you carefully select those event-design sensory elements that will support the goals and objectives of the event. Do not confuse or irritate guests by layering too many different senses in an effort to be creative. Rather, design the sensory experience as you would select paint for a canvas. Determine in advance what you hope to achieve or communicate, and then use the five senses as powerful tools to help you accomplish your goals.

Bells and Whistles: Amenities that Make the Difference

Once you have established the atmosphere for your event environment and satisfied the basic needs of all guests, you have the opportunity to embellish or enhance their experience by adding a few well-chosen amenities. An amenity is best defined as a feature that increases attractiveness or value. In today's added value–driven business environment, amenities are more important than ever before. These amenities may include advertising specialty items given as gifts at the beginning or the end of the event, interactive elements such as karaoke, and even child care.

A popular way to stretch the budget is to transform the guests into décor elements. This is accomplished by distributing glow-in-the-dark novelty items, such as necklaces, pins, or even swizzle sticks. As guests enter the darkened event environment, their glowing presence suddenly creates exciting visual stimuli. Firms such as Oriental Trading (www.orientaltrading.com) specialize in providing these items.

Karaoke, Japanese for "empty orchestra," was invented in Japan in the 1980s as a way for party guests to sing along with their favorite pop songs. Patrons sing into a microphone over backing tracks, as the lyrics are shown on a TV screen. The growth in popularity was explosive for many years, and it remains a classic event activity. In the twenty-first century, however, karaoke technology has rapidly diversified. Events can now sing, dance, rap, or play musical instruments along with their favorite songs. Dance Dance Revolution (DDR) shows event patrons the dance moves so they can dance with their pop idols, and Rock Band gives patrons the ability to play electric guitar or drums along with rock stars. The popularity of Nintendo's Wii has shown that consumers demand more physical activity with their video games, and karaoke software remains a beloved party technology.

Whether dealing with glow-in-the-dark jewelry or karaoke software, you must evaluate consistently the needs, wants, and desires of guests to determine if the communications media you are using are effective and efficient. Using feedback from specific populations will help you achieve this purpose rapidly.

Identifying the Needs of Your Guests

Once you have gathered all the quantitative data from the site inspection, it is time to analyze your findings and determine what implications emerge for your event environment design. Important considerations include the legal, regulatory, and risk management issues that are uncovered during the site inspection.

Provision for Guests Having Disabilities

If the venue is not in full compliance with the United States Americans with Disabilities Act or comparable regulations in your country, you may need to make certain modifications in your design. Always check in advance with local authorities to determine if the regulations governing your event site require modification of your design. Regardless of the regulatory environment, it is critically important that your design provide a total sensorial experience that all guests may enjoy.

For example, if you are hosting a group of children or adults with visual challenges, you may wish to increase the tactile elements in your event or invite them backstage for a touch and feel of the costumers prior to the start of the event. If your guests have a auditory challenge, you may wish to augment their auditory experience with more tactile (Braille) or visual stimuli, such as signs or the use of sign language interpreters. For stage spectaculars, hiring an audio describer can give hearing-impaired patrons a rolling commentary of what is happening visually onstage.

Implications of Size, Weight, and Volume

Let us assume that your design requires massive scenery and that the ingress to your venue is a door of standard width and height. How do you squeeze the elephant through the keyhole? The answer is, of course, "Very carefully." Seriously, make certain that your design elements can be broken down into small units. Using component parts for the construction process will enable you to design individual elements that will fit easily through most doorways.

Weight is an important consideration, as many venues were not built with this factor in mind. Before bringing in elements that have extraordinary weight, check with the facility engineer to review the construction standards used in the venue and then determine if the stress factor is sufficient to accommodate your design. Shifting weight also can cause serious problems for certain venues. Therefore, if you are using a stage platform and simply placing a heavy prop, you may not experience any problems. However, if on this same platform you are showcasing 50 dancers performing high-energy routines, the platforms may not be sufficiently reinforced to handle this shifting weight. In addition to reviewing with the engineer or other expert the stress weight that the area can accommodate, conduct independent tests yourself by actually walking across the stage or examining the undergirders to ensure that what goes up will not come down.

The final consideration is volume. The fire marshal determines the number of persons who can be safely accommodated in the venue. You, however, greatly influence this number by the seating configuration, the amount of décor, and other technical elements that you include in the final event environment. Less equals more. Typically, the fewer design elements you incorporate, the more people you can accommodate. Therefore, when creating your total event design, first determine the number of people you must accommodate, then subtract the number of square feet required for the guests. The remainder will determine the volume of elements that contribute to the event environment.

Julia Rutherford Silvers, CSEP, in *Professional Event Coordination* (2003), notes:

> *A unique venue should be carefully examined to determine its capabilities and challenges. You should be looking at accessibility for the vendors providing the goods and services for the event, as well as accessibility for the guests, workable space for preparations and event activities, power and parking capabilities, safety and sanitation issues, and, of course, protection for the property rights of the venue as well as its neighbors—for example, in regard to noise, light, and other forms of disturbance or pollution.*

One example of protecting the property rights of neighbors is evident at the famous Hollywood Bowl amphitheater, which is located in a residential neighborhood in Hollywood, California. Prior to the start of the performance and immediately afterward, the audience is reminded through an audio announcement to please exit the venue quietly and not honk auto horns, play loud car radio music, or make other noise that will inconvenience the neighbors.

Similarly, when Unique Events of Edinburgh, Scotland, created a new event during its 2008 Edinburgh Christmas program, it decided to stage it in an area that had not been used before for live events. The Grass Market is a historic section in the old city of Edinburgh that combines both residential and commercial structures. In order to host this event there, the organizers sought permission from the home dwellers in advance.

Designing a successful outcome for your event requires always thinking about the safety and security of your guests. The governor of Rhode Island asked me to chair a task force to analyze how businesses in that state would be impacted by the tragic occurrence of The Station nightclub fire in 2003 in Providence, in which 100 persons died and many others were severely injured. This accident was caused by the use of pyrotechnics by the band that was performing in the nightclub. Furthermore, the insulation used by the nightclub was not fire retardant. When the pyrotechnic display was performed the low ceiling cause an instant inferno and many of the dead and injured were trampled to death as they tried to leave from the same door they entered the club. As a result of The Station nightclub fire, the National Fire Protection Association has revised its standards and now requires an announcement be made prior to the start of each performance notifying the audience members of the location of the nearest fire exits and how to exit the venue in an orderly manner.

Example: Calculating and Sizing the Event Environment

1. Identify the total number of persons and multiply the square feet (or meters) required for each person. For example:

   50 couples
   × 10 square feet per couple
   = 500 square feet

2. Subtract the total number of square feet required for the couples from the total space available. For example:

   1,000 square feet available for dance floor
   – 500 square feet required by couples
   = 500 square feet available for props, tables, chair, and other equipment

Do not do this in reverse. Some event leaders create a lavish design first, only to find later that the number of guests will not allow them to install this design.

Securing the Environment

The local or state fire marshal is responsible for determining occupancy and the police and local security officials will determine how to secure an environment to reduce the possibility of theft or personal injury. When considering the theme and other important design elements, remember that people will be walking under, over, and within this environment, and their safety must be paramount in your planning. Providing adequate lighting for traversing the event environment, securing cables and other technical components with tape or ramps, and posting notices of "Use Caution" or "Watch Your Step" are important considerations when designing beautiful, as well as safe, event environments.

Theft, sadly, is a major concern in designing an event environment. Do not make it easy to remove items from the event environment. Secure perimeter doors with guards or provide bag-check stations at the entrance to discourage unscrupulous persons from removing valuable event elements. This is especially important when designing expositions where millions of dollars of merchandise may be on display for long periods of time. Furthermore, do not allow event participants to store merchandise or personal goods, such as purses, in public areas. Instead, provide a secure area for these elements, to ensure a watchful eye.

In today's post–September 11 world, securing the environment also involves additional considerations. For example, Event Leaders must ask questions concerning biochemical risks, terrorism threats, communicable disease threats (pandemics and epidemics), and effective crowd-control procedures.

As a direct result of The Station nightclub fire mentioned earlier, several new laws have been adopted and the Rhode Island state legislature has outlawed the grandfathering of buildings. Adopting the National Fire Protection Association (NFPA) 101, the Life Safety Code, and the NFPA 1, the Uniform Fire Code™, as their guides, Rhode Island has virtually banned indoor pyrotechnics except in major theater auditoriums and arenas. In addition, the state is requiring venues to provide one trained crowd manager for all events with 300 or more persons and one additional trained crowd manager per each additional 300 persons. Within a few years, the majority of nightclubs, restaurants, and other event facilities will have fire-suppression equipment (sprinklers) as a direct result of the tragic loss of 100 lives in The Station nightclub fire. It is the responsibility of every Event Leader to anticipate potential risks and proactively create an environment that is as risk-free as possible.

Transportation and Parking Factors

Event safety and security expert Dr. Peter Tarlow, in his book *Event Risk Management and Safety* (Wiley, 2002), states that the area that unites security and safety is the parking lot. Tarlow reminds us that parking lots can be dangerous for six reasons.

1. *People tend to drive in parking lots as if there are no rules or laws.* Having parking attendants or traffic directors can help alleviate this problem.
2. *Pedestrians often assume that parking lots are safe and that drivers will follow the rules and see them.* The use of parking attendants will help separate unaware pedestrians from clueless drivers.
3. *Event attendees often lose their cars and may inadvertently set off the alarm of another car that looks like theirs.* This type of behavior could cause a panic, so it is best if signs are posted reminding drivers to note the location of their vehicle.
4. *Catastrophic weather conditions can create dangers for people who have parked in outdoor locations.* Providing enclosed shuttle buses or trams can help alleviate these problems.
5. *Poor lighting has been proven to promote criminal activity in parking lots.* When possible, make certain the parking areas have sufficient lighting and/or adequate patrols.
6. *Children can run off while parents are loading or unloading cars and can easily be injured.* Having a drop-off area for children where they can be safely secured before parents park their cars is an excellent way to mitigate this problem.

As you develop and implement the event plan, remember that often transportation and parking is the first and last impression. Therefore, it makes good sense to follow Dr. Tarlow's wise counsel. For example, a clean parking area and a spotless restroom create and sustain a lasting impression of professionalism and quality.

The venue may or may not provide easy vehicle ingress. Therefore, well in advance, you must locate the proper door for load-in of your equipment, the times the dock is available for your deliveries, and other critical factors that will govern your ability to transport equipment and park your vehicles. Another consideration for transportation relates to approved routes for trucks and other vehicles. In some jurisdictions, such as Washington, DC, truck and large vehicular traffic is strictly regulated. Once again, confer well in advance with transportation and venue officials to determine the most efficient route.

Whether you are parking your vehicles in a marshaling facility or on the street, security must be considered as well as easy access. Some venues may not be located in the safest of neighborhoods, and, therefore, securing your vehicles and providing safe and fast access to them are important. Well-lit, fenced-in areas are best for parking; however, the proximity of the vehicles to the loading area of the venue is the prime concern.

You may think that transportation and parking have little to do with creating a proper event environment, but these two considerations should be given significant attention. Many events have started late or suffered in quality due to late or lost vehicles and inefficient load-in operations. Remember, you may design the most incredible event environment, but until it is shipped, loaded in, and installed properly, it is only your idea. Proper transportation and installation will turn your idea into a dynamic event environment.

Effectively Manage the Event Environment

Understanding the basic needs of the guest is of paramount importance, especially when you are working with a smaller budget than you would like. In circumstances where the budget is severely restricted, there are ways, using your imagination, to stretch limited funds. Use your budget to enhance the beginning and the end, as these are what the guest will most remember. Following are some considerations for managing the design of an event environment.

Entrances and Reception Areas

The Event Leader must immediately establish the theme of the event with a comprehensive environmental design. The use of proper signs, bearing the group's name or logo, and appropriate décor will reassure guests that they are in the right place. Consider the arrival process from the guests' point of view. They received the invitation some time ago and probably did not bring it with them to the event. Therefore, they are relying on memory to guide them to the right building and the right room. Once they have located parking, they ask the attendant to direct them to XYZ event. The attendant is rushed, having to park several hundred cars for perhaps as many as six different functions, and cannot recall the exact location of the affair. Should the guests stumble upon your site and not recognize it because the logo is absent or the entrance does not communicate the theme of the party, they will become confused and lost. Providing your own personnel in costume or professional wardrobe will help guests locate your event, as will proper signage. Upon arrival, guests should have an "Aha!" experience, knowing that they have arrived at the right place at the right time. You can offer guests this experience and create a positive impression by proper design of the reception area at which they are greeted. When guests must wait in long lines, they often begin to resent the event or its hosts. You must plan for these delays and offer solutions.

Figures 3.1 to 3.4 demonstrate how to place greeters, or "damage control" hosts, to handle problems in the reception area. In Figure 3.1, the guests have begun to form a second row at the reception table. When this occurs, greeters should immediately invite the second-row guests to step forward to the additional tables set behind the primary tables. Having extra tables available will be perceived by guests as an added courtesy and will help ease heavy arrival times. Note that the guests at the primary tables enter between them so as not to conflict with the guests at the additional tables.

Figure 3.2 shows a solution to the problem of guests arriving without an invitation and without their names appearing on the list of invitees. To avoid embarrassment and delay, the guest is invited to step forward to the courtesy table, conveniently isolated from the general crowd flow. There the problem can be resolved quietly and courteously, or the guest may be ushered out a back door without disrupting the event.

The scenario depicted in Figure 3.3 is one that every experienced event planner has known. During heavy arrival time, such as the second half-hour of a one-hour cocktail party

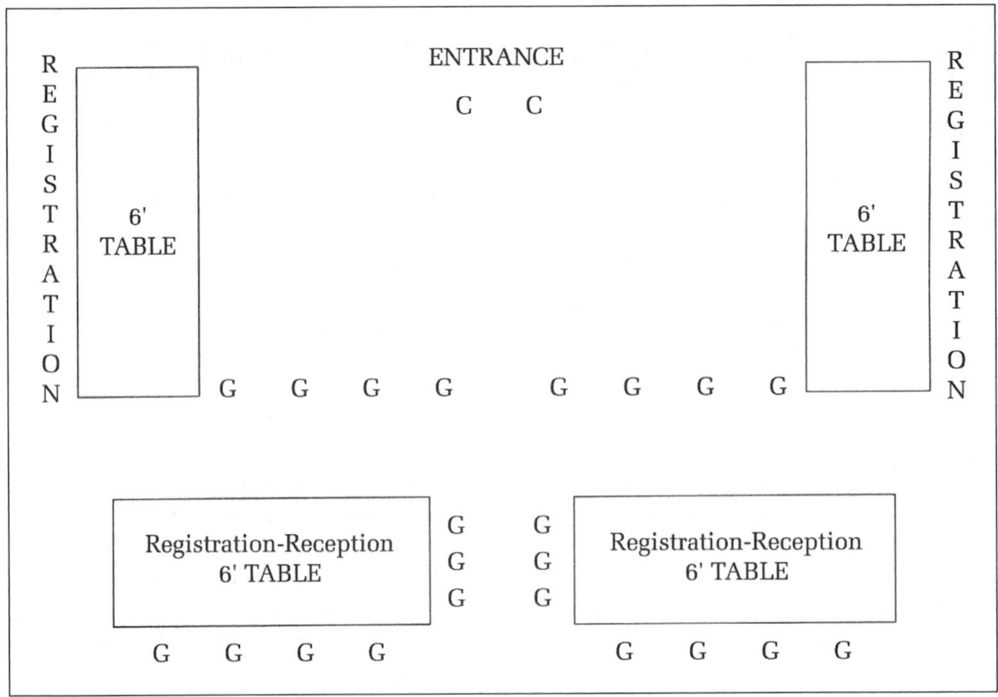

Figure 3.1 Registration-Reception Setup with Secondary Tables Supporting a Primary Table (G, guest; C, control)

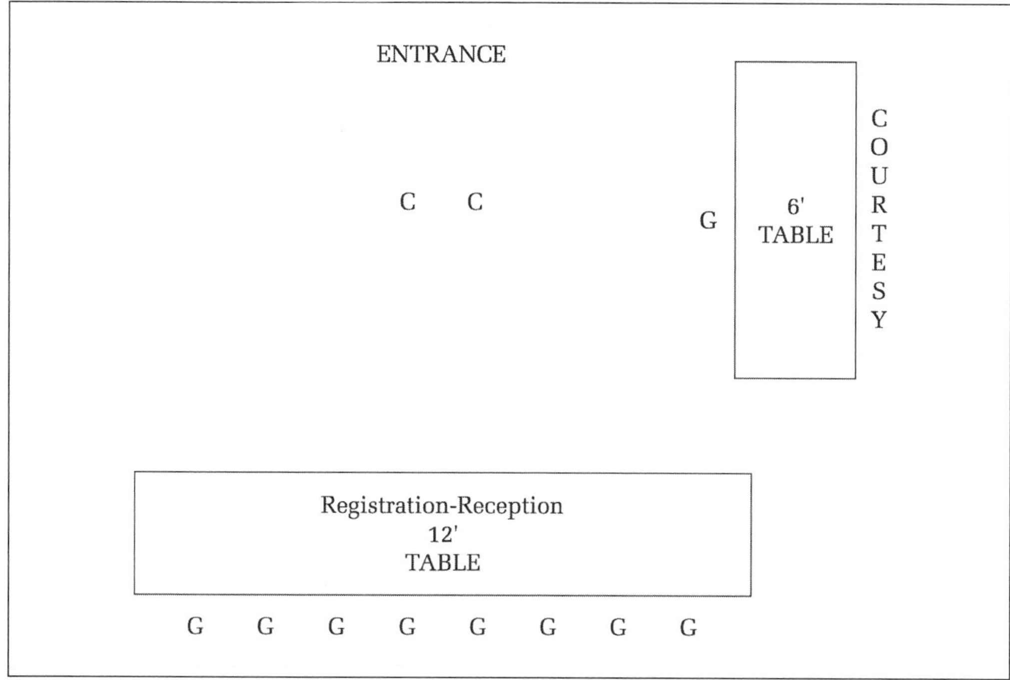

Figure 3.2 Registration-Reception Setup with a Secondary Courtesy Table (G, guest; C, control)

preceding the main event, long lines of guests are forming while those staffing the reception tables are trying to greet arrivals quickly and efficiently and keep the line moving. Professional greeters can make the guests' wait less annoying. Their job is simply to greet the guests in line, quietly thank them for coming, and answer any questions they may have while waiting. Often professional performers, such as strolling mimes, clowns, jugglers, or magicians, may be used in this area to entertain, thereby distracting guests while they wait in line.

When you expect long lines over a brief period, the best arrangement is a variation of Figure 3.1. By using two additional courtesy tables, positioned at an angle, as shown in Figure 3.4, you can alleviate crowding. The reception setup integrating the professional greeter into the flow of guest traffic further ensures the ease and comfort of guests.

In Figure 3.4, you can keep guests moving forward and handle disputes at the same time. The hosts and hostesses at these courtesy tables should be trained to resolve disputes quickly and know when to refer a guest to a supervisor for further assistance. Most disputes can be remedied simply, requiring no more than preparation of a name badge, a payment, or other minor business. If handled at the primary table, such tasks become cumbersome. Experienced planners know that the floor plan for the reception area should facilitate guests' arrivals and is critical to the success of the event. The way in which a guest is first received at an event determines all future perceptions that he or she will have

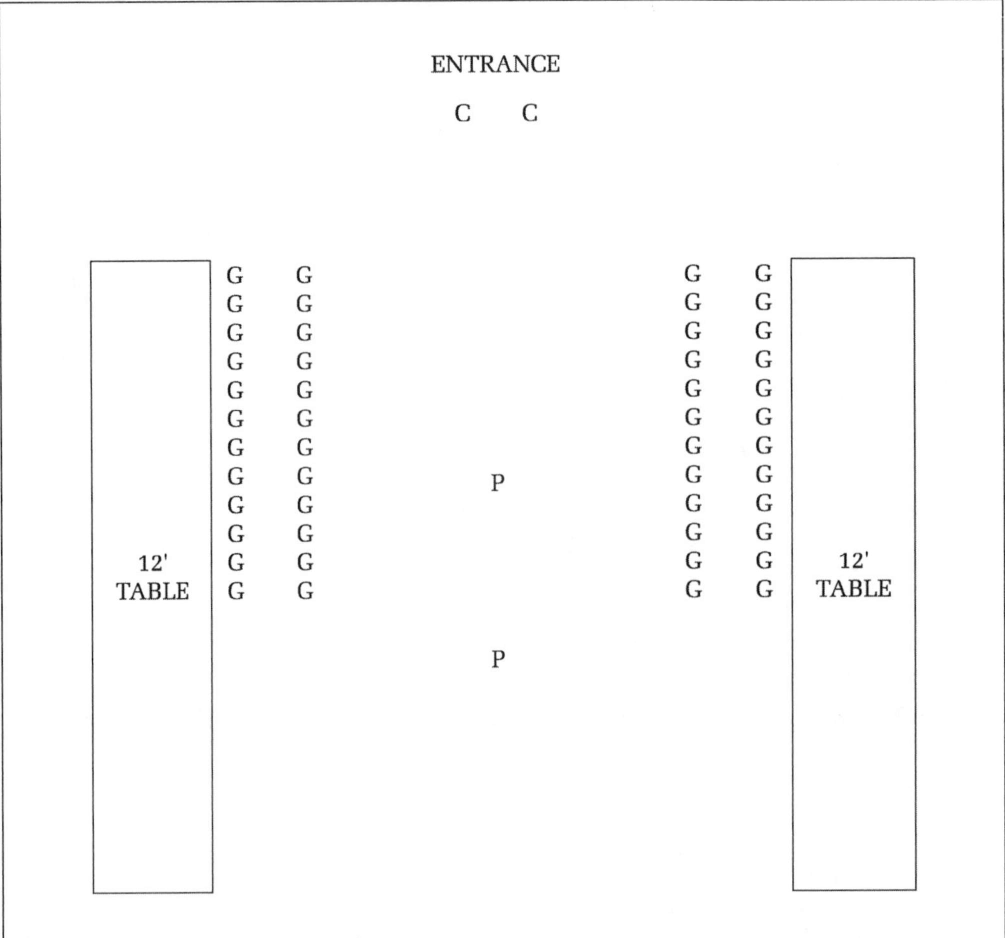

Figure 3.3 Reception Setup Integrating the Professional Greeter into the Flow of Guest Traffic (G, guest; C, control, P, professional greeter)

about the event program you have designed. Take time to plan this area carefully to ensure an efficient and gracious reception.

Function Areas

The reception area may create the first impression, but the main function area will determine the effectiveness of the overall design. This is the area in which guests will spend the most time, and this is the area where your principal message must be communicated to guests in a memorable manner. Traditional space designs are currently being rethought by meeting planners as well as psychologists to develop a more productive environment.

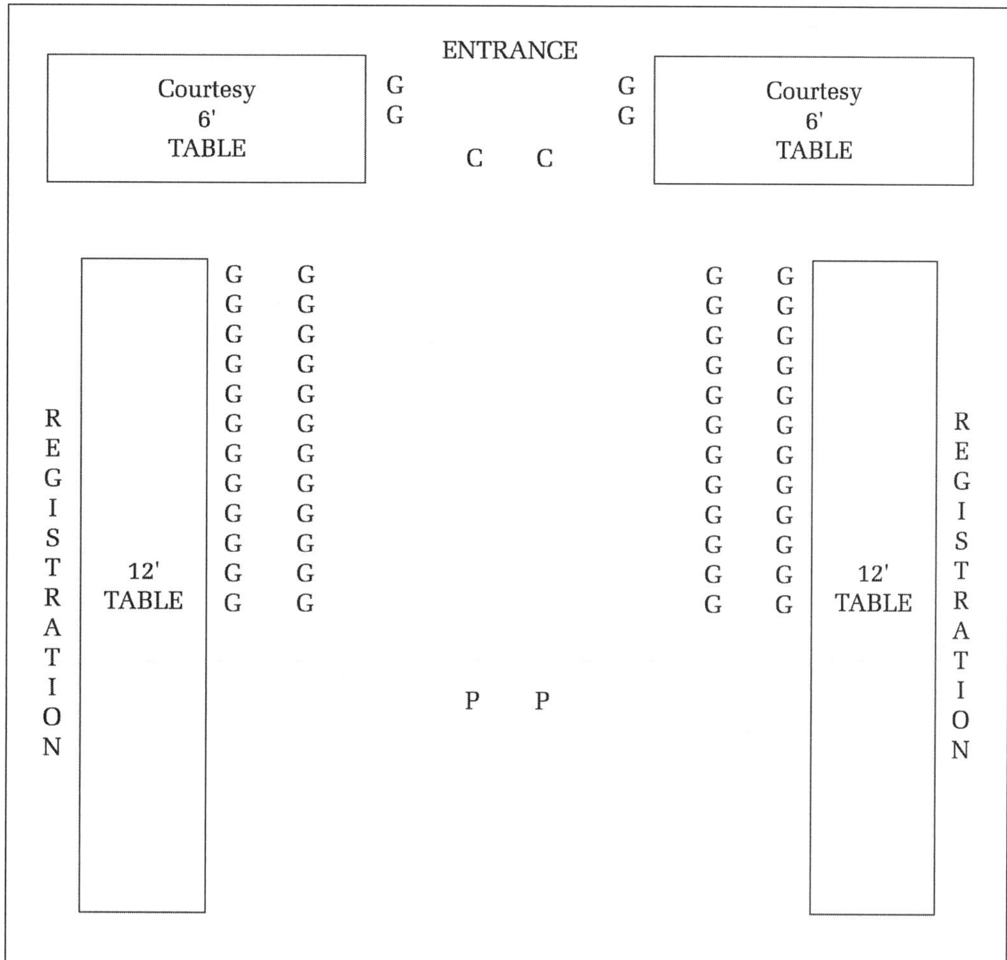

Figure 3.4 Reception Setup Using Two Additional Courtesy Tables Positioned at an Angle (G, guest; C, control; P, professional greeter)

Dr. Paul Radde is a psychologist who has pioneered the development of physical-space planning for conferences that provides a better environment in which to learn. Radde has, often to the chagrin of various hotel setup crews, determined that speakers prefer and often deliver a better talk when there is no center aisle. In the traditional theater- or classroom-style setup shown in Figure 3.5, all of the speaker's energy escapes through the center aisle. When this lane is filled with live bodies, the speaker's interaction is increased, as is the human connection among audience members themselves.

Figure 3.6 demonstrates the optimum setup, complete with wide aisles on each side to allow for proper egress. With this setting, each row should be at least 6 inches farther apart than in Figure 3.5, to allow for more efficient egress. Some fire marshals prohibit

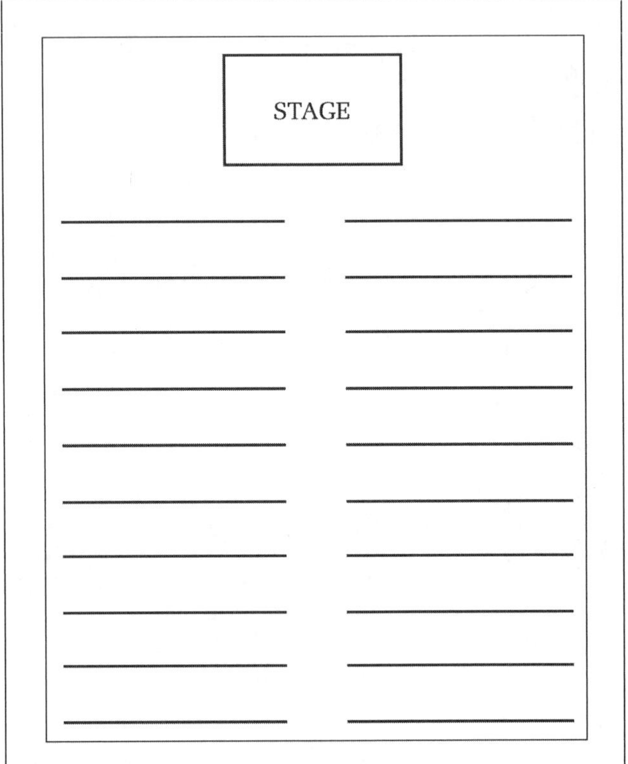

Figure 3.5 Traditional Theater- or Classroom-Style Setup

the arrangement in Figure 3.6 because some audience members will be seated too far from an aisle. An excellent alternative is shown in Figure 3.7, in which the front two rows are solid, with side aisles beginning behind the second row.

Perhaps the best adaptation is shown in Figure 3.8. In this arrangement, all rows except the first five are sealed, and the center aisle is easily reached by latecomers in the rear of the auditorium. Planning an effective seating arrangement is only the beginning. Masking tape or rope on stanchions can be used to seal the back rows, as shown in Figure 3.8, encouraging guests to fill in the front rows first.

Once the rows are filled with guests, the tape is removed. After 30 years of watching audiences head for the back rows, I experimented a few years ago with this method to determine if I could control seating habits without inconveniencing the audience unduly. Much to my delight, several audience members have thanked me for this subtle suggestion to move up front. Without this direction, audience members become confused and revert to old habits.

Interestingly, once a guest claims a seat, he or she will return to it throughout the event. However, unless I have predetermined that they will sit up front by making the back rows

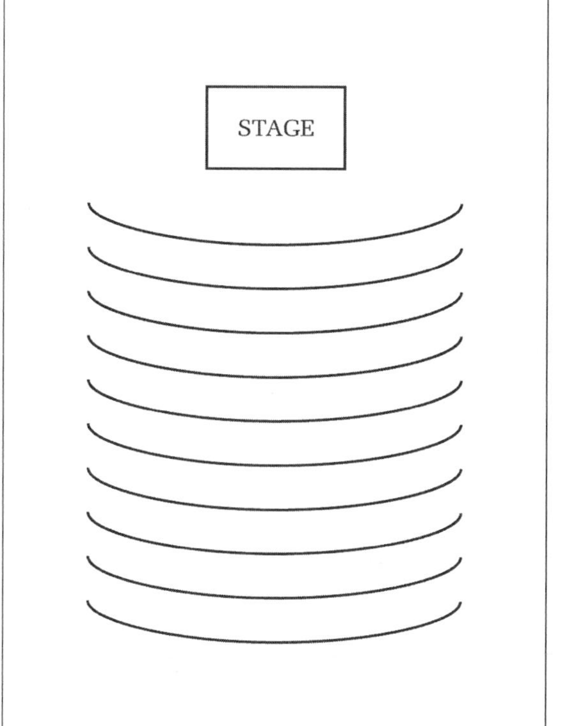

Figure 3.6 Optimum Theater- or Classroom-Style Setup

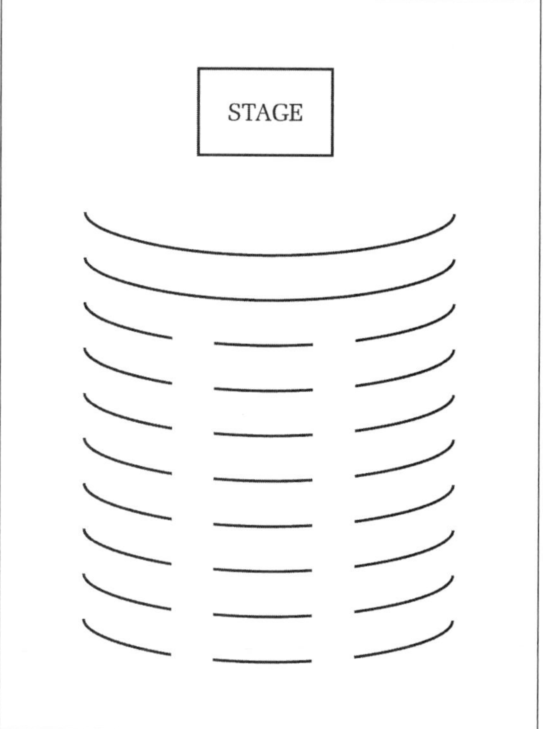

Figure 3.7 Modified Theater- or Classroom-Style Setup

unavailable, all of the coaxing and bribing (I once placed dollar bills under front-row seats) will not move audience members from the back-row comfort zone.

Innovative Sites

The purpose of creatively designing your environment is to provide a dynamic atmosphere within which your guest may experience the event. One innovative decorator staged a banquet in a tractor-trailer. The guests were escorted up the steps and dined inside an actual tractor-trailer decorated by the decorator's team of artists. The goal of this creative design was to surprise and intrigue guests, who were picked up in limousines and brought to this isolated and inelegant site. Inside the tractor-trailer, they found luxurious décor, complete with chandeliers, tapestries, and fine linens. The decorator stated that the total tab for the 40 guests, including catering, service, and décor, was roughly $16,000.

Not every client will allocate over $400 per person for an event. Nonetheless, the Event Leader is increasingly faced with the challenge of finding innovative, creative environments

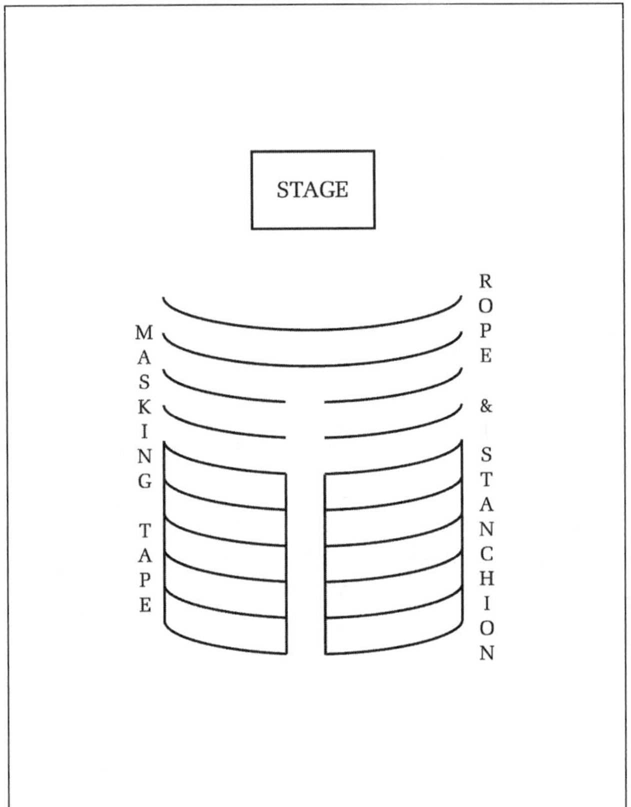

Figure 3.8 Modified Theater- or Classroom-Style Setup with Roped-off Rear Section

in which to stage events. Curators of museums and public buildings in record numbers throughout the United States have begun setting fees and offering their buildings to groups that wish to host a reception or meeting in a novel atmosphere.

With these new opportunities for use of public space come increased challenges for decorators, who must now cope with the increased demand for atmospheric props in place of flats, banners, murals, and other more traditional scenic devices. Figure 3.9 includes a sampling of ideas for unusual sites in which to hold special events. Use this list to brainstorm with your event stakeholders to determine the best venue for your next event. The possibilities for exciting, innovative, and offbeat event sites are infinite. It is important, however, that your selection be logical and practical in terms of location, parking, setup, budget, and use of space.

One important source for identifying a suitable venue for your event is BizBash. BizBash is a publication that promotes the special events industry in key cities including New York, Los Angeles, Toronto, Miami, and others. You may find BizBash at www.bizbash.com

Transit

Aircraft carrier	Moving railroad train	Stationary caboose
Blimp	Orient Express	Subway platform
Cruise ship	Paddle-wheel steamboat	Tractor-trailer
Double-decker bus	Roller coaster	Trolley
Segway® appetizer/starter stations	Space shuttle	Yacht
Golf cart mounted cocktail bars	Stage Coach buffet tables	Hot-air balloon
Monorail		

Design by Mother Nature

Apple orchard	Christmas-tree farm	National forest
Arboretum	Dude ranch	Pasture
Botanical center	Formal garden	Rose garden
Caverns	Greenhouse	Summer camp
Central Park	Meadow	Underneath a waterfall
Planetarium		

Music, Music, Music

American Idol stage set	*Dancing with the Stars* stage set	Rave nightclub
Grand Ole Opry stage	Symphony hall	Estate of deceased music star
Opera house	Television décor of The Grammy Awards™	Gazebo or bandshell in a park
Recording studio		Eurovision stage set
X Factor stage set	*Strictly Come Dancing* stage set	

On Stage

Circus center ring	Famous actor's dressing room	Theater green room
Circus museum	Professional theater—lobby backstage, on stage	Theatrical museum
Comedy nightclub		
	Community theater	

At the Movies

Any movie theater	Former movie or television location (such as the bridge in Madison County or Southfork Ranch in *Dallas* television show)	Former movie set (such as Universal Studios' back lot or Granada Studios tour)
Drive-in movie	Estate of a deceased film star	Historic movie theater
Radio City Music Hall		

Figure 3.9 Event Sites *(Continued)*

	Food, Glorious Food	
Orchard	Cornfield	Kitchen of a bakery
Bottling plant	Distillery	Vineyard
Cannery Farmer's Market		
	Infamous	
Alcatraz	Microbrewery	Saloon in a ghost town
Former speakeasy	Nightclub	Homes of famous outlaws (now often museums)
Former Bank or Investment Company building		
	Stately	
Castle	Convent	Monastery
Cathedral	Mansion stately home/Palace	
	The Child in You	
Amusement park	Clown alley at a circus	Laser-tag center
Arcade	Fairgrounds	Puppet theater
Children's museum	Family entertainment center	Virtual-reality center
Children's theater Putt-Putt (miniature golf) Water Park		
	Wild Places	
Animal shelter	Pet kennel	Wild-animal park
Aviary	Stable	Zoo
Local animal farm or ranch		
	In Scholarly Pursuits	
University/college dining hall	University/college private dining facility (president's dining room)	University/college theater, meeting room, chapel
University/college library		
	In Glass Cases	
Aquarium	Medical museum	Science museum
Art museum	Natural-history museum	Sculpture museum
Aviation museum	Planetarium	Textile museum
Historical society museum	Potter's studio	
	Behind the Scenes	
Aircraft hangar	Empty swimming pool	Movie sound stage
Baseball dugout	Football locker room	Presidential library
Current embassy	Former embassy	Television studio

Figure 3.9 *(Continued)*

Diplomatic reception rooms Radio station at the U.S. Department of State		
	The Winner Is You	
Basketball court	Hockey rink	Racetrack
Fifty-yard line of a football field	Home plate on a baseball diamond	Roller rink
	Miniature golf course	Former Olympic Games venue
Swimming pool		
	Ghoulish and Ghastly	
Abandoned hospital morgue	Cemetery	Mausoleum
Abandoned hospital operating room	Funeral home	Tombstone manufacturer

Figure 3.9 *(Continued)*

Wherever you turn, you will find new products and new services available to help you transform an environment for a creative special event. Many unusual products can be found at gift shows (trade shows featuring new and unusual gift items), antique stores and shows, flea markets, used and classic clothing stores, hotel closeout sales, and other businesses selling off stock. The ISES worldwide resource directory lists additional groups and organizations that can help create an environment for your next special event.

Amenities and Furnishings

The possibilities for linens, silverware, glassware, centerpieces, and even costumes for servers are greater in the profession today than ever before. Sites, sources, and suppliers for these items can be found in journals such as *Event Solutions* (www.event-solutions.com) and *Special Events* (www.specialevents.com) magazines, and various industry newsletters. See Appendices 4, 5, and 6 for dozens of additional resources.

Edible Centerpieces and Displays

The centuries-old European custom of including elaborately designed food displays as part of the décor is finally becoming popular—indeed, in some regions, de rigueur—in the United States. This important area of setting design can range from fancy carved crudités for the hors d'oeuvres to elaborate centerpieces carved from thick dark chocolate. Today's special events professionals are as concerned with the aesthetic appeal of food selections as they are with taste. In fact, food presentation has become an art form in the United States, one in which annual competitions are held in areas ranging from ice sculpture and sugar works to chocolate and pastry design. When incorporating food into an overall design, remember that, ultimately, most food is intended to be eaten. The display must be accessible to guests and still look appealing after they are served. If possible, a server should offer the first guests who visit the display a serving of the decorated or carved item. This will help encourage other guests to help themselves. You may wish to prepare two versions of an item: one for show on an elevated, lighted platform and one for serving, placed within reach of guests. This will allow every guest to appreciate the work of your culinary artists throughout the event.

Decorating the Environment

The decorating profession has undergone a rapid transformation since the 1920s, when Howard Lanin's client told him: "Just make it lovely." Today, making it lovely involves a specialized professional in touch with the latest styles and products with which to create specific environments that will satisfy guests' individual needs. Today's designers are creating more profound, if only temporary, works of art to frame special events. Sixty years ago, special events were most often held in private rooms, private clubs, churches, public sites, or hotels. Modern decorators are faced with the challenge of turning almost any conceivable space into a suitable environment for a special event. From football fields to tractor-trailers, today's decorators must display more imagination, creativity, and skill than ever before to keep pace with changing styles and trends. The designer/decorator's craft is one of transformation. Turning a polo field into a castle, a ballroom into the Land of Oz, or a black tent into an extraterrestrial fantasy, decorators transport guests from the ordinary to the extraordinary by creating a world of fantasy.

Regional customs and geographic location may determine, to some extent, what types of products are used for some events. Very often, for example, a client in Florida will request a mariachi theme, and a client from the Southwest will desire a Polynesian holiday. But expanded delivery services, which allow suppliers to send almost anything overnight, have enabled designers and decorators to obtain almost any product for a special event, regardless of location.

One challenge that decorators face is designing an environment that will satisfy both primary and secondary audiences. Creating designs and products that will translate to television, film, and still photography is becoming increasingly important. Consequently, when formulating design ideas, consider both the primary and secondary audiences: Who will view this event, and in what format? Perhaps the design will be detailed in such a way that it will show well in close-up photography. Many stock décor items available in today's events marketplace did not exist 60 years ago. Synthetic fibers and plastics have become increasingly sophisticated, enabling the fabrication of countless imaginative pieces. Even as these lines are written, products continue to be developed, providing greater selection at lower cost. Trying to describe all the products and techniques available to the event practitioner is impossible. The discussions that follow will introduce you to some of the more popular products and the imaginative ways that some innovative special events planners use them. Their continual exploration of new ways to satisfy clients' needs is the ultimate key to creative design.

Interactive Décor

Today's guests want to be more than just spectators at a special event—after all, movies and television provide plenty of opportunities to watch fantastic special effects and see gorgeous set designs and wonderful performances. To provide more than just a passive viewing experience, the event designer must create an environment that allows the guests to participate—to be actors in the decorator's dream world.

In Atlanta, Georgia, I experimented with this idea of interactive décor with an audience of prestigious and somewhat jaded professional catering executives. The challenge was to show these hospitality professionals something new, working, as always, within a specific budget. The theme of the banquet was "Starship NACE" (National Association of Catering Executives). As the guests entered the foyer, they passed between two 25-inch color television monitors that featured a close-up view of an extraterrestrial's face. As each guest passed, the alien greeted him or her by name and offered a warm welcome to the event. I stood in the shadows, out of sight, and watched the guests' reactions—they suddenly stopped and laughed, clearly baffled by how an image on a screen could recognize and greet them. In actuality, an actor was hidden in a side room. As each guest stepped into the reception area, a technician using a two-way radio revealed the name to the actor, who in turn announced the name on television. Fog machines were set a few feet beyond the television monitors; just as the guests were recovering from one experience, they would receive a small blast of dry chemical fog to surprise them again. Throughout the cocktail reception, a prerecorded endless-loop cassette tape featuring space sounds and a professional narrator making preboarding announcements was played. When the time came to open the ballroom doors for dinner, four astronauts dressed in white jumpsuits, with NACE embroidered on their breast pockets, and blue and white space helmets, also featuring the NACE emblem, appeared in front of each door. As the doors were slowly opened, more fog seeped from the ballroom into the cocktail area. The guests entered the ballroom via a tunnel constructed of black pipe and drape and hundreds of miniature white lights. They tiptoed over a moonscape atmosphere, created by thousands of Styrofoam peanuts covered by ground cloth. Walking through that tunnel, the guests were entering another world. Once inside the ballroom, a robot welcomed the guests from the dance floor and instructed them to "be seated quickly, as the starship will be departing soon." "Also Sprach Zarathustra," the music used in the movie *2001: A Space Odyssey*, played in the background, and the sound effects of sonic blasts were added, projected through four speakers to create a true sense of surround sound. One-dimensional scenic pieces of planets were hung from the walls, and miniature strobe lights created the effect of starlight.

Later chapters explore how the use of video and live action helped to provide constant interaction for the guests attending this event. At this point, it is sufficient to understand the importance of creating a design that will meet the needs of the guests. Today, any site can be transformed through décor, using a variety of products and techniques. Regardless of the site and the decoration details, however, the designer's objective remains the same: satisfying the guests. To accomplish this goal, the designer must involve the guests in the event as much as possible through their senses, their activities, and their emotions. Site design can facilitate such involvement, as the "Starship NACE" event demonstrates.

In another example of interactive décor, my firm was involved in designing a theme event titled "A Dickens of a Christmas," in which the streets of Victorian London were re-created to bring the feeling of Charles Dickens's England to a hotel exhibit room. Since one of Dickens's best-known tales is *A Christmas Carol,* we decided to employ a winter setting and scattered artificial snow throughout the hall. I was delighted to see the usually staid guests kicking the snow throughout the room as they traveled down each lane, participating actively in the setting. We also included a group of street urchins (actually, professional boys and girls with extensive Broadway credits), who were instructed to attempt to steal food from the lavish buffets throughout the room. Each time they snatched a scone, the waiters would grab them and say, "All right, if you want to eat, you must sing for your supper!" The children then proceeded to sing a 10-minute medley of holiday carols. The guests reacted first with surprise when the waiter reprimanded the children and then, within seconds, became emotionally involved as the adorable and talented children sang for their supper. A life-sized puppet of Ebenezer Scrooge was also used. As guests wandered by his house (a display piece), he popped his head out and shouted, "You're standing on my kumquats! Get out of my garden now! Bah, humbug!" The guests, of course, loved this Christmas nemesis. Those who were recognized by the puppeteer were called by name, much to their delight and the delight of their friends. Mr. Scrooge created gales of laughter, once again emotionally stimulating the guests.

The potential for effective design is truly greater than ever. To succeed, the guest must be involved sensuously, physically, and emotionally. The Bible tells us that "There is nothing new under the sun" (Ecclesiastes 1:9). The late Cavett Robert, chairman emeritus of the National Speakers Association, has said, "Much that is described as 'new' is actually old wine in new bottles." These maxims apply to the décor industry because, with every advancement of new technology, the basic principles of satisfying the guest's sensual, physical, and emotional needs remain unchanged.

Inside the World of Event Design

When the Barack Obama Presidential Inaugural Committee required an experienced and award winning official decorator for their balls and parade, they turned to Hargrove, Inc., which has been providing this service for over 50 years.

Hargrove, Inc., of Lanham, Maryland, was founded in the late 1930s by Earl Hargrove Sr., who specialized in what was then called window trimming, decorating store windows of retail establishments in the Washington, DC, area to promote sales. With the advent of television, Hargrove's clients began to funnel their advertising dollars into the new medium, and his business soared. When Hargrove's son, Earl Jr., returned home from a stint in the Marine Corps in the late 1940s, he joined his father's company. Earl Jr. wanted to pursue the new and lucrative field of convention and trade-show display and exposition decorating, but his father wanted to remain solely in the specialty decorating market. Although they separated for a time, Earl Jr. pursuing the convention market and Earl Sr. struggling in the specialty decorating market, they eventually rejoined forces.

Their longevity in the Washington, DC, events arena is best symbolized by their association with the national Christmas tree located beside the White House. In 1949, Earl Hargrove Jr. placed the star high atop the tree; in that same year, he and his father renewed their business partnership, and a new brilliance in special events décor began.

Today, that partnership includes many more members of the Hargrove family, a talented team of employees, and a large warehouse-studio filled with thousands of props, scenic items, and parade floats. When Earl Hargrove Jr. began in partnership with his father, he discovered the lucrative market for Washington social events. He recalls receiving an order in the early 1950s to decorate a country club for which the total bill was $350. Times certainly have changed, both in terms of budget and available products with which to decorate. Today a third-generation Hargrove, Carla Hargrove McGill, helps lead the organization that provides décor for major casinos, corporations, and associations, as well as private individuals who seek decorations for their bar and bat mitzvahs, weddings, and other celebrations. McGill believes that her mission in the social-event field is to bring the client's theme to life through décor. Doing so today, however, is trickier than in past years, in part because of more stringent fire regulations. According to McGill, "Many states have particularly tough fire laws governing interior décor, and others are following. Every product we use must be flame-proofed, which in the balloon industry, for example, is very difficult to accomplish, largely due to high manufacturers' costs." When Earl Jr. began with his father, the available materials were paper, cloth, and wood. Today the Hargroves enjoy many more options, including foam, fiberglass, a wide selection of flame-proofed fabrics, and a full range of plastics, to mention only a few. Forty years ago, guests were content merely to view the decoration. Today Hargrove, Inc., is challenged to give guests a feeling of participation and interaction with the décor.

Hargrove, Inc. designs sets for themed events using devices such as time tunnels, which the guests walk through to enter the main event, or three-dimensional props that the guests may touch. The Hargroves agree that a successful decorator must offer a full range of services and products to be successful. Hargrove, Inc., will rent out a single prop or create an entirely new themed event. This diversity has proven successful for over 40 years. The Hargroves, along with other professional decorators, suggest that, although there are millions of new decorating ideas for special events, not all of them are practical. Therefore, it is always important to consider these points when choosing decorations:

- What will the venue (site, building) allow in terms of interior/exterior décor?
- What are the policies regarding installation? What are the policies or laws of the local municipality regarding decorating materials?
- What is the purpose of the décor?
- Are you conveying a specific theme?
- Is there a specific message?
- What period or style are you attempting to represent?
- What are the demographics and psychographics of your attendees?
- Are they spectators or participants?
- What are the budgetary guidelines for the décor?
- How long will it be in use?
- Which existing scenic pieces can be modified to fit your theme or convey your message?

Parades and Float Design

Starting with the original Cherry Blossom parade in Washington, DC, the Hargrove artists have been recognized as leaders in the U.S. float design and construction industry. Many nationally known parades, including the annual Miss America parade in Atlantic City and the 1987 We the People parade in Philadelphia, celebrating the bicentennial of the U.S. Constitution, have featured Hargrove floats. Designing, building, transporting, and operating floats can be a costly enterprise. But the rewards for the sponsor, in terms of publicity, can be priceless, provided that the right steps are taken. These questions should be addressed before contracting to design a float:

- What does the parade committee or organization allow in terms of size, materials, and thematic design?
- Under what meteorological conditions and in what climate will the float be used? (Some float builders specialize in designs suitable for particular climates.)
- Will the float appear on television?
- What investment will the sponsor make?
- What constraints are imposed by the parade itself regarding construction, size, weight, materials, and themes? (For example, spatial constraints may limit a float's dimensions.)
- What message does the sponsor wish to convey?
- Where will the floats be stored prior to the parade?
- What is the physical environment of the parade route?

When asked why he continues to pursue this extremely labor-intensive sector of the decorating profession, Earl explained with a story: "Years ago, I was in Atlantic City with the Miss America Parade, and a man in the convention pipe-and-drape industry saw me watching my floats go down the boardwalk. He said, 'Earl, why don't you get out of the float business and just concentrate on the convention draping part? That's where the profits are.' Well, I didn't answer him, but I knew at that moment how different our company is from all the others. This guy was the unhappiest guy in the world. He didn't really love what he did. On the other hand, we do what we love to do, and I hope it shows in our work."

Parade floats are a perfect example of the need to consider the ultimate viewership of your design. Corporations sponsor floats in an effort to develop positive publicity and influence consumers to buy their products and services. Since only a few parades are televised nationally, most floats need only ensure that the sponsor's theme is conveyed to the live audience viewing the event. Many floats include people—pageant queens, actors, actresses, costumed characters, and celebrities—in their design. When planning the float design, it is essential to consider their place in the display. The wardrobe color of the person riding on the float, for example, will affect the total look of the float and, therefore, is an important design concern. Additionally, the lighting at the time of the parade will determine, to some extent, which colors and materials will best convey your message.

As I noted earlier, it is essential to review the parade organization's requirements for parade floats before making any design choices. In most cases, it will be appropriate to feature the float sponsor's name prominently in the design. The manner in which you incorporate the sponsor's name or logo into the float design will affect the integrity of the display itself. Be careful to make the sponsor's name and/or logo a cohesive part of the design whenever possible instead of merely tacking a loose sign on the side as if it were an afterthought. Your ability to incorporate the sponsor's message into your final design in a seamless manner will determine the effectiveness of the float in the eyes of both the viewer and the sponsor. Whether it's themed décor for social events or major parade floats for the Philadelphia Thanksgiving Day parade, the Hargrove family, starting with the founder, Earl Sr. and continuing today with Earl Jr. and his children, bring innovations to the art and science of décor. They are serious businesspeople concerned with profit and growth, but they are guided ultimately by the feeling that they bring a special magic to special events. The Hargrove family still ensures the placement of the star high atop the national Christmas tree; perhaps this is a symbol of the bright, shining influence their art has shone upon the special events universe.

Say It with Flowers

Flowers are usually more costly than stock rental decorations (props) because of their perishable nature. According to some designers, the markup for floral is often four times the cost. If the cost of the floral centerpiece is $20, the designer will sell it to the client for $80 or more to recover his or her labor, materials, and overhead costs, plus retain a margin of profit.

John Daly, CSEP, president of John Daly, Inc., of Santa Barbara, California, began his successful design firm with floral products. He suggests that, when designing vertical centerpieces, these guidelines should be observed: "The centerpiece height should not exceed 14 inches unless it is loose and airy, therefore see-through, over the 14-inch mark. This, of course, does not apply to the epergne arrangement. An epergne is a flower holder, such as a candelabra or mirrored stand, that raises the flowers from the table. When using the epergne, the base of the floral arrangement should begin at least 24 inches above table height."

Daly believes that event design has truly matured into both a fine art and a science because of the new materials available and the speed at which they can be obtained. Today, a wider range of floral products is available because of the advances in transportation and shipping. With the advent of overnight delivery systems, Daly can have virtually any product he wishes for any event in any location. As designer for events in Seoul, Korea, the Virgin Islands and throughout the world, this advantage has increased his ability to use fresh and exciting ideas in many far-off event sites.

Balloon Art

Balloon décor can range from a simple balloon arch to more elaborate designs, such as three-dimensional shapes or swags of balloons, intertwined with miniature lights, hung from the ceiling. Balloons can create special effects, such as drops, releases, and explosions. Balloon drops involve dropping balloons over the audience from nets or bags suspended from the ceiling. Releases, including setting helium-filled balloons free outdoors from nets, bags, or boxes, are commercially available. Explosions might include popping clear balloons filled with confetti or popping balloons mounted on a wall display to reveal a message underneath.

From centerpieces to massive walls of balloons, such as the U.S. flag displays that Treb Heining (Balloonart by Treb) created for the city of Philadelphia, balloon art has become an established part of the special events industry. Organizations such as the National Association of Balloon Artists (NABA) and Pioneers Balloon Company's Balloon Network are working to educate both balloon professionals and their clients to the uses of this art form, as well as to ensure greater responsibility in employing it.

Balloon art has become an integral part of event décor largely because of the innovations in the 1980s and 1990s by Treb Heining of California. From creating an enormous birthday cake for a tenth-anniversary celebration at a shopping mall to supervising the balloon effects for the opening and closing ceremonies of the Los Angeles Olympic Games to orchestrating the mammoth balloon drops for the U.S. national political conventions and coordinating the New Year's confetti blizzards In New York's Time Square, Heining has been at the forefront of his profession for many years. He began by selling balloons at Disneyland in Anaheim, California, and later used the same products for decoration at both social and corporate events.

In recent years, there has been much discussion regarding the effect of balloon releases on the environment. Marine biologists have determined that wind currents cause balloons to drift out over bodies of water, where they lose velocity and eventually fall into the waters below. They are concerned that sea animals may ingest these products and become ill or die. Although there is currently no conclusive evidence that balloon releases have harmed marine animals, what goes up must eventually come down, and both the balloon professional and his client must act responsibly. Electric power companies in some jurisdictions throughout the United States have reported incidences where foil balloons have become entangled in power lines following a release, causing power failures due to the conductivity of the metallic balloon. All balloon professionals disapprove of foil balloon releases, as well as releases where hard objects are included in or on the balloon itself. Although it is impossible to regulate a balloon's final destination after a release, it is possible to design and stage releases that will not adversely affect the environment. A tethered release—where the balloons are released on long tethers and not allowed to float freely—may be one alternative. In some jurisdictions, the Federal Aviation Administration requests notice of balloon releases in order to advise pilots in the area.

Tents: Beyond Shelter Is Décor

One example of a new adaptation of a classic environment is in the tenting industry. Developments in materials and workmanship in this industry have multiplied the design possibilities of tents. Half a century ago, the standard tent available for a special event was a drab olive U.S. Army tarpaulin. Flooring was rarely considered, and lighting was most elementary. Today, however, thanks to significant pioneers such as Bob Graves, former owner of the Van Tent company, Harry Oppenheimer, the founder of HDO Productions (www.hdotents.com), and major innovators such as Edwin Knight, CERP of EventQuip (www.eventquip.com), the tenting industry has truly come of age. Oppenheimer describes his service as "essentially solving a space problem. For that special occasion, such as a fiftieth anniversary, you don't have to build a family room to accommodate your guests. You can rent a tent with all of the same comforts of a family room."

Oppenheimer stated that the successful tenting professional prepares for the unforeseen, imagining the structure in snow, wind, rain, and perhaps hail. Most professionals in the tenting industry will not only carefully inspect the ground surface but will also bore beneath the surface to check for underground cables and pipes that might be disturbed by the tent installation. When Oppenheimer receives an inquiry for tenting from a prospective client, he first dispatches an account executive from his firm to meet with the client in person and view the site. Once the site has been inspected, the account executive is better prepared to make specific recommendations to the client. HDO Productions uses a computer network to track the client's order. The computer will first tell HDO if equipment and labor are available to install the tent on the date requested. The computer then lists the number of employees needed for the installation and prints the load sheet for the event.

Today's tent fabrics are synthetic rather than muslin. Synthetics provide a stronger structure that is easier to maintain and aesthetically more pleasing. Oppenheimer particularly likes such innovations as the parawing tent structure, which can be used indoors as well as outdoors in venues that need aesthetic enhancement to mask unfinished portions or obnoxious views. A parawing tent or marquee is a triangular or rectangular piece of fabric that is used to create a shelter for an event. It is stretched at each corner (tension point) to create a bold and often times dramatic covering for a stage, a booth or other event area. The addition of lighting to these sail-like images will make the event even more aesthetically pleasing. Heating, air conditioning, and flooring are also now available for tented environments. Each of these important elements can help ensure the success of your tented event. A competent tenting contractor will survey your installation area and determine if flooring is advisable, or perhaps essential, because of uneven topography. Listen carefully to his or her recommendations.

I had the misfortune of watching 3,000 women remove their fancy dress shoes as they sank ankle deep in mud under a tent. The client refused to invest in flooring, although the additional cost was quite minimal. A pouring rain arrived just before the guests stepped under the canopy and flooded the public areas of the tent. It is a wonder the client did not have to replace 3,000 pairs of ruined shoes. From wooden floors to Astroturf, your tent contractor can recommend the most cost-efficient ground surface for your event. In some instances, the location for the tent may require grading or other excavation to prepare the land for effective installation. Many tent contractors provide a preliminary evaluation and recommendation at no charge in order to prepare a proper bid for an event.

Heating or air conditioning can increase the comfort of your guests, thus helping increase attendance at your tented event. Once again, your tent contractor will assist you in determining whether to add these elements and what the cost will be. If you elect to air-condition or heat your tent, make certain that the engineer in charge of the temperature controls remains on-site during the entire event. The temperature will rise as the tent fills with guests, so the heating or air conditioning must be adjusted throughout the event to ensure comfort. When you use a tent, you not only take responsibility for ensuring the comfort and safety of the guests, but in some jurisdictions you are actually erecting a temporary structure that requires a special permit. Check with local authorities.

A tent provides a special aesthetic appeal; like balloons bobbing in the air, white tent tops crowned with colorful flags seemingly touching the clouds signal an event to your arriving guests. Few forms of décor make as immediate and dramatic an impression as a tent does. With a competent tent contractor, the problems you might anticipate are easily manageable, and the possibilities for an innovative event, year-round, are limitless.

Décor Costs

When hiring a design professional for an event, expect to cover not only the cost of labor, delivery, and the actual product, but also the designer's consultation fee. In some cases, this consultation fee may be included in the final bid for the job. If you are soliciting many different proposals, it is best to outline your budget range for the project to the prospective designers up front. This openness may dictate the selection of products for your event. Labor is a major component of design charges because the designer-decorator's craft is so time-consuming.

The complexity of the design will affect costs, as will the amount of time available for installation. The longer the time allowed for installation, the fewer persons required. I have seen décor budgets double when less than one hour was allotted for installation of a major set. Allow enough time for the designers to do their work from the very beginning, alleviating the need for extra last-minute labor to complete the job. While many variables are involved in pricing décor, a typical margin of profit above the direct cost of materials and labor is 40 percent. This does not include the general overhead associated with running a business, including insurance, rent, promotion, vehicles, and the like. Therefore, today's designers must be very careful when quoting prices, to ensure that costs are recovered adequately and allow for a profit. When purchasing design services, remember that each designer possesses a unique talent that may be priceless to your particular event. This perception of value may, in your estimation, overrule the pricing formulas already described.

Themed Events

The theme party or theme event originated from the masquerade, where guests dressed in elaborate costumes to hide their identity. From these masquerade events a variety of themes were born. Today, it is typical to attend western-, Asian, European, or South and Central American–themed events, as themes are often derived from destinations or regions of the country or world. Robin Kring, author of *Party Creations: A Book of Theme Design* (1993), says that "theme development and implementation are really very easy. Themes can be built on just about any item you can think of."

Themes usually are derived from one of three sources. First, the destination will strongly influence the theme. When guests travel to San Francisco, they want to enjoy a taste of the city by the bay rather than a Texas hoedown. The second source is popular culture, including books, movies, and television. Whether the theme is popular such as from a hit movie like *Avatar* or classic (*Gone With the Wind*) or topical such as preserving the environment, the idea is usually derived from popular culture. The third and final source is historical and current events. Themes reflecting the Civil War, World War II, or the landing of a human on the moon, as well as the collapse of the Berlin Wall, have strong historical or current significance and may be used to develop themes. See the examples of themed events in Figure 3.10.

Theme	Audience	Elements
The Wild Wild West	All ages; very popular with men	*Décor:* hay bales, western-style bar, western jail set for photos, saloon with swinging doors
		Entertainment: gunslingers, lariat act, whip act, knife-throwing act, medicine-man magic show, western band, western dancers, fiddle ensemble, harmonica act, strolling guitarist, cowboy singer on live horse, steer, trainer
		Food and beverages: barbecue, hamburgers, biscuits, baked beans, rattlesnake, fowl, fresh pies
South of the Border	All ages; international guests; events held in states or areas bordering Mexico	*Décor:* small bridge over the Rio Grande; Customs officials and signs at the entrance; bright yellow lighting inside entrance; carts with vendors in Mexican attire selling novelties; cacti; colorful blankets in southwestern designs; umbrella tables with tequila logo on top
		Entertainment: mariachi musician, flamenco and folk dancers, folk artists weaving baskets and other handicrafts
		Food and beverages: tacos, fajitas, refried beans, rice, chili, tamales, guacamole, margaritas
The New Millennium	Younger guests; men and women; businesspeople; scientists; engineers; scholars	*Décor:* large video projection screens projecting star pattern at entryway, followed by a darkened tunnel with thousands of miniature lights and space-like sound effects; dance floor covered in light fog with pulsing lights; Internet stations on personal computers set throughout the room
		Entertainment: robots, actors in astronaut costumes, actors in alien costumes, high-tech band performing space-associated music

Figure 3.10 Themes from Popular Culture, History, and Current Events *(Continued)*

Theme	Audience	Elements
		Food and beverages: space food preset at each setting with freeze-dried ice cream and jellybeans representing various vitamins
Mardi Gras	Younger guests; especially appropriate for New Orleans events	*Décor:* two large papier-mâché heads or floats framing the entrance; one doubloon given to each guest to exchange for a drink; purple, green, and gold balloons; exterior facades of Bourbon Street landmarks
		Entertainment: quick-sketch artists; jazz band, including second-line parade; Mardi Gras revelers throwing beads
		Food and beverages: muffaleta sandwiches; seafood, including crawfish and oysters; gumbos; red beans and rice; shrimp Creole, biscuits; po'boy sandwiches; snowball; king cakes; hurricane-style drinks
Riverboat	All ages, especially older audiences	*Décor:* small gangplank bridge leading to doorway; life preserver over doorway with name of event displayed; inside main function room is casino, theater, long bar, colorful pennants, and flags
		Entertainment: Dixieland jazz band, banjo players, close-up magicians masquerading as gamblers
		Food and beverages: Southern cuisine, including ribs, pork, fried chicken, grits, mint juleps, bourbon served in souvenir shot glasses
Paris Nights	All ages, especially younger audiences	*Décor:* entryway marquee with chaser lights representing a Paris nightclub; in the center of the room, a three-dimensional replica of the Eiffel Tower outlined in miniature lights; ficus trees on the perimeter with miniature lights; backdrops or sets of typical Parisian facades, including the Louvre, the Folies Bergère, and the Comédie Française
		Entertainment: quick-sketch artists, cancan dancers, café orchestra, chanteuse
		Food and beverages: crepes, cheeses, pastries, wines, champagne
Hooray for Hollywood	All ages	*Décor:* sign announcing "The Hollywood Palladium"; red carpet with rope and stanchion on either side; follow spotlights sweeping the carpet; inside the function room, film props such as directors' chairs, cameras, lights, backdrops, a wind machine

Figure 3.10 *(Continued)*

Theme	Audience	Elements
		Entertainment: a team of young male and female fans screaming as the guests arrive; a recording studio for instant sing-alongs; improvisational movie-set area with instant replay; photo area with guests wearing wardrobe items from famous movies *Food and beverages:* menu items from Hollywood
Broadway Bash	All ages	*Décor:* large entrance sign proclaiming "Opening Night Starring [the name of the guests]"; fake ticket booth distributing programs; guests enter through stage door and actually walk onto the stage *Entertainment:* actors portraying ticket sellers, ticket takers, stage doormen, actors; Broadway orchestra in pit performing selections from top Broadway shows; musical-comedy performers performing popular Broadway songs; photos taken with Broadway look-alikes *Food and beverages:* New York cuisine, including Coney Island frankfurters, New York strip steak, Manhattan clam chowder
Rock Around the Clock	Younger audiences; baby boomers	*Décor:* giant jukebox facade serves as entranceway; interior transformed into gymnasium complete with basketball hoops at each end of dance floor and school name and logo on dance floor; bright ribbon in the school colors swagged from the ceiling; mirror ball for lighting effect *Entertainment:* 1950s, 1960s, 1970s rock 'n' roll; hula-hoop contest; servers on roller blades; a phone booth–stuffing contest; a '57 Chevy for photos *Food and beverages:* beer, pizza, hot dogs, hamburgers, malts, French fries, cherry Cokes
Dickens of a Christmas	All ages	*Décor:* entryway with Covent Garden design; fake snow scattered throughout; cemetery area with the tombstones of Marley and famous British writers; facades of London landmarks, including the Tower of London, Big Ben, and Parliament *Entertainment:* a team of strolling urchins sings for their supper; a Salvation Army worker plays harp; Father Christmas poses for photos; a woman strolls by selling live geese in cages *Food and beverages:* cider, ale, beer, wassail, holiday punch

Figure 3.10 *(Continued)*

Theme	Audience	Elements
Rave Party	Generation X; teenagers	*Décor:* fencing, salvage, industrial equipment *Entertainment:* punk-rock band; DJ with lighting effects *Food and beverages:* fast food
Dancing with the Stars	All ages	*Food and beverages:* Champagne, chocolate fountain and fresh strawberries. *Décor:* A historic theater or a dance studio with the draperies dramatically swagged.
Big Brother	All ages	*Food and beverages:* Peanut butter and jelly sandwiches, beer, wine, subway sandwiches. *Decor:* An abandoned house or a public building that may be outfitted to look like several rooms. Pipe and drape may be used to divide the rooms.

Figure 3.10 *(Continued)*

An important consideration when planning theme parties is to understand the history of the group. Themes can be overused, and it is important that you rotate themes to maintain the element of surprise. When planning theme parties, ask your client these questions:

- What is the history of your theme parties? What did you do last year?
- What is the purpose or reason for this event?
- Is there a specific theme you wish to communicate?
- To convey the theme, is food and beverage, décor, or entertainment most important for your group's tasks?
- Remembering that first and last impressions are most important, what do you want the guests to most remember from this event?

The answers to these questions will provide you with ample instructions to begin your planning of a terrific themed event. The list of themes in Figure 3.10 is by no means exhaustive. However, it does reflect a sample of the top themes currently in use in American events. When selecting a theme, make sure you are certain that the theme can be communicated easily and effectively through décor, entertainment, food and beverage, and of course, invitation and program design.

John P. Tempest is a funeral director in Leeds, England, who notes that, while fashions come and go when planning "the ultimate final tribute," tradition governs the format of most funeral rites. For example, Tempest notes that, in Great Britain, many families engage a funeral director to arrange for the burial of their deceased family member. The services Tempest provides include providing essential staff, preparing all official documentation and liaison with the proper authorities, making and receiving all necessary telephone calls, arranging for the attendance of the minister for the funeral service, placing obituary notices in newspapers, and making the necessary disbursement payments on behalf of the family. In addition, his firm will supply a traditional coffin with fittings for cremation (more frequently selected as a burial option in Great Britain than in the United States), vehicles, and professional fees for the director.

When planning this important final event, Tempest suggests that most families select a traditional service rather than deviate from the norm. After the funerals of public figures, such as Princess Diana, Tempest noted that, for a short time, certain new customs are adopted, such as the use of white flowers, in an effort to emulate the funeral rites of the departed celebrity. However, these are the exceptions to the rule, in a country where hundreds of years of tradition and precedent govern most decisions.

Tempest states that the total cost for these services is approximately $3,000. Deviation from tradition resulting in further customization will increase the costs. Event Leaders may elect to use the formula of basic pricing for standard services that is customary in the funeral industry to create standard packages and improve efficiency when providing price quotations. Although every event represents the unique tastes and sensitivities of the host/purchaser, many standard steps can be priced well in advance to ensure consistent profit when providing individual quotations.

Big Theme Success with Small Budgets

Even the slightest budget can enjoy big results through a carefully planned theme event. First, you must decide what elements are most important, because it is not likely that you will be able to fund equally everything you desire. If your guests are gourmets, the largest percentage of the budget will be dedicated to food and beverage. However, if they are creative, fun-loving people who are only slightly interested in the menu, you will want to shift your expenditure to décor and entertainment. Make certain that the first impression (entrance area) is well decorated, as this not only sets the tone for an event but is often the most photographed area. Next, include a series of surprises, such as a dessert parade or the arrival of a guest celebrity as your auctioneer, to keep guests on the edges of their seats.

Finally, share your resources with others. Check with the director of catering at the hotel and find out if other groups are meeting in the hotel before, during, or following your stay. Ask for permission to contact their Event Leader and determine if you can produce the same event and split the costs for décor and entertainment. You will find that you can afford 50 percent more by allocating your scarce resources in this manner.

Trends in Theme Events

Interactive events are transforming couch potatoes into fully participatory guests. David Peters of Absolute Amusements in Orlando, Florida, and Las Vegas, Nevada, annually produces hundreds of interactive events, ranging from corporate celebrations social events. He provides interactive equipment such as sumo wrestling (where participants wear giant foam rubber suits), the Velcro wall (where the participants wear Velcro-covered jumpsuits and jump and land in various positions on a large wall covered with Velcro), and virtual surfing (where surfers stand on boards attached to electronic terminals and see themselves on a large video monitor as they roll, slide, and sometimes tumble into the virtual ocean). When designing interactive events, keep in mind the safety of the participants.

One of his most recent inventions is a product called PopNoggins® (www.popnoggins.com). PopNoggins allows guests to have a personalized video made of themselves dancing to a popular song. Their faces appear on the video but their bodies are replaced by voluptuous dancing torsos.

Alcohol will, of course, increase the margin of risk for a guest when participating in a interactive activity such as faux sumo wrestling. Some Event Leaders require guests to sign hold-harmless waivers to acknowledge the risk involved with the activity.

Your event environment is the opportunity to explore dozens of opportunities in décor, entertainment, and other elements to make every moment unique and memorable. Every Event Leader has essentially this same opportunity. By understanding how the various pieces fit together to solve the puzzle that is the event environment, you provide a finished picture that will be remembered by your guests for years to come. Your ability to design, balance, and mold this collage will be rewarded by the guests' total immersion in the environment, leaving an indelible impression for many years. Especially in the new world of Event Leadership, you must be sensitive to the cultural, political, and other unique factors represented by your event guests. Remember, this is one reason why you are so valuable. You are the artist and scientist; use your experience, sensitivity, good taste, and talent to create and plan this unique moment in time.

Sustainable Event Leadership: Conserving the Environment

When I addressed the Nature Conservancy, a major U.S. environmental research and educational organization that focuses on environmental issues, I was impressed with how these leaders use events to communicate the important message of conservation. You can use every event as an opportunity to stress environmental sensitivity. Whether implementing a recycling plan or selecting products that do not harm the ecosystem, the Event Leader has an implied responsibility to produce events that are environmentally sensitive. In the chapter entitled Greener Events, Sam Goldblatt explores this topic in greater detail so that you may design a more sustainable special event in the future.

Environmental Ecological Sensitivity

Environmental and ecological sensitivity are important for two major reasons. First, they are the right thing to do. When allocating scarce resources for an event, remember that no resource is as scarce as the environment in which we live, work, and play. Second, clients are increasingly requesting that every event meet or exceed certain environmental standards. Major corporations have been criticized by their customers for not demonstrating enough sensitivity to the environment. Therefore, when these corporations retain you to manage an event, they want you to reflect their renewed commitment to environmental concerns.

The best way to accomplish this is to clearly define the organization's environmental policy and then incorporate these policies into your event environment design and operations. Event sponsors who practice recycling in all likelihood will want recycling bins at an event they sponsor. Event sponsors who do not use foam products for disposable serving utensils will not want you to specify these items in your catering orders. Meet with the key environmental policy person for the organization sponsoring your event and determine, with his or her help, how to incorporate such policies within the event environment.

Why not create your own policies? To ensure that events enjoy sustainable growth, it is important for you to establish your own environmental policies that will demonstrate to prospective event sponsors your knowledge and sensitivity regarding these issues. These policies need not be repressive. However, they must be consistent. Do not alter your policies merely to satisfy the budget considerations for the event. Instead, seek creative solutions, such as finding a sponsor for the recycling station, to make certain that your environmental ideals are well protected at every event.

Recycle your Success

In the exposition event field, a growing trend is the recycling to local schools of leftover materials such as paper, pens, pencils, and other reusable supplies. Usually these items end up in the dumpster when, only a few blocks from the venue, there may be a school with children who cannot afford these basic supplies. You may wish to incorporate this program in your agreements to inform your sponsor of your policy of recycling your success to help others.

Many event sponsors recycle leftover food products to local homeless shelters or food distribution agencies. Doing this assures your guests that you are committed to sharing the success of your banquet with those less fortunate. Some venues require the recipients to sign a hold-harmless form; however, regardless of the legal technicality, this opportunity to feed others should be seized for every event.

Still another way to recycle your success is to build into your event a project to benefit a local organization. Some event organizers schedule a day before or after the event for attendees to use their skills to clean up a local playground, paint a school, or perform some other community service. To arrange this activity, contact the volunteer center in the local community. The office of the mayor is a good place to start to locate the local volunteer coordinating organization. Tell the office what resources you are bringing to their destination and then apply your success to help others.

Inspiration and Perspiration

The inventor Thomas Alva Edison reportedly once stated that success is 10 percent inspiration and 90 percent perspiration. Although the design phase provides inspiration, it also expands and tests the limits of research. At the conclusion of the design phase, the Event Leader should have a clear idea of the needs and desires of event stakeholders. The goals and objectives that were identified in the research phase represent the skeletal structure in the anatomy of an event, and the flexible elements identified in the design phase represent the musculature needed to move event research forward. Now it is time to add the cardiovascular system to give and sustain life for the event. This is the beginning of the event's life, and the primary organ that will sustain this life is the event strategic plan.

Event Strategic Planning

The event strategic plan (ESP) provides the definition for event stakeholders of the steps, people, time frame, and other critical elements needed to ensure that an event reaches a successful outcome. Your ESP can be compared to the tracks driving a locomotive. Without tracks, the train cannot reach its destination. Without a workable plan, an event cannot achieve the optimum outcome and arrive at the destination that you and the stakeholders desire.

The planning phase is a direct result of the data collected during research and the color, luster, and texture mixed into the process during design. The plan must be reasonable (as confirmed during the research phase) and match the expectations of the stakeholders (as identified during the design phase). The planning phase involves the key informants or leading stakeholders who will manage the event. During the planning meeting, it is important to involve those people who not only have the responsibility but also the authority to make decisions. The plan will reflect those decisions, and these important stakeholders must be included to ensure that they take ownership in the creation of the plan. These key informants should be involved in the planning process:

- Admissions coordinator
- Advertising coordinator
- Assistant Event Leader
- Audiovisual coordinator
- Caterer
- Decorator
- Entertainment coordinator
- Environmental / ecological sustainability coordinator
- Event coordinators
- Event Leader
- Exposition coordinator
- Facility manager
- Fire department
- Food and beverage coordinator
- Insurance coordinator
- Legal advisor
- Lighting, sound, and technical production coordinator
- Logistics coordinator

- Marketing coordinator
- Medical coordinator
- Municipal, state, and federal officials
- Police/public safety
- Public relations coordinator
- Registration coordinator
- Risk management coordinator
- Safety coordinator
- Security coordinator
- Sponsorship coordinator
- Transportation coordinator
- Ushering coordinator/house manager
- Volunteer coordinators
- Weather and meteorological experts and officials

Planning to Plan

Tom Kaiser, author of *Mining Group Gold* (1995), suggests that, prior to any meeting the participants should be assigned prework to prepare them to participate actively in the meeting. The scope and level of the prework is determined by the Event Leader based on the skills and responsibilities of the planning team members. The planning team members should, however, be prepared to contribute empirical information in addition to their opinions as a result of their preparation.

The planning process begins with the announcement of the planning meeting. This announcement should include a time and date for the meeting that is convenient for the planning team members. One of the most common mistakes is to schedule this meeting without consulting with the participants in advance. An effective planning meeting requires that the planning team members be fully committed to the process. This commitment requires advance approval of the date, time, location, and format. Another common mistake is not allowing sufficient time for the first meeting. Prior to scheduling the first meeting, you should assemble a small group of senior members of the team to actually plan the planning process. This planning to plan (or preplanning) is a critical part of the ESP process.

Most Event Leaders require several planning meetings to establish the final timeline and thorough event plan. During the preplanning meeting, you should reach consensus on how many planning meetings will be needed and when and where they should be scheduled. The location and length of the planning meeting will have a direct impact on the efficiency you achieve. It is important to locate a site for the meeting that is convenient for the participants yet free of distraction. It is also important to remind stakeholders that they will need to leave beepers, cell phones, and other personal distractions outside the meeting.

The length of the meeting will ultimately influence the productivity. The maxim "less is more" is appropriate for planning meetings. Limit meetings to 90 minutes maximum. If the meeting must last longer than 90 minutes, schedule frequent breaks. The agenda for the ESP meeting will guide the team toward their eventual goal: the production of a workable and sustainable plan. Therefore, the agenda should be developed during the preplanning process and distributed to the full team in advance of the first planning meeting. A typical agenda for the ESP meeting follows:

I. Welcome and introduction of team members
II. Review of goals and objectives of event
III. Review of critical dates for event
IV. Reports from team members from prework
V. Discussion of event preproduction schedule
VI. Consensus regarding event preproduction schedule
VII. Discussion of production schedule
VIII. Consensus regarding production schedule
IX. Final review of plan to check for any illogical elements, gaps, oversights, or other
X. Adjournment

Confirming Validity, Reliability, and Security

After the planning meeting or meetings are concluded, the Event Leader must make certain that the event plan is valid, reliable, and easily communicated to a wider group of stakeholders. Prior to distribution of the plan, make certain that your event plan passes the "grandmother test." Show the plan to those stakeholders who were not directly involved in the planning process. Ask these stakeholders pointed questions, such as: "Is this logical? What is missing? Does the plan support the goals and objectives of the event?"

Once the plan is validated and prior to distribution to a wider group of stakeholders, make certain that there are no security implications of this release. For example, if a very important person (VIP), such as a high-ranking elected official or celebrity, is included in the plan, you may wish to assign the individual a pseudonym or limit the distribution of the plan to preserve the security of your event.

Timeline

The tracks that your event train will travel to reach its successful destination are reflected in the instrument known as the event timeline. The event timeline literally reduces to writing the major decisions that will be included in the event from the beginning of research through the final tasks involved in evaluation.

Often I am asked, "When does the event timeline begin?" After many years of experience and literally thousands of event experiences, I can state that it must begin with the first inquiry about the potential or prospective event. For example, the first telephone call from a prospective client researching your availability to manage an event or from an Event Leader who is researching information about your catering services may quickly lead to design, planning, coordination, and, finally, evaluation.

Therefore, I suggest that you begin the construction of the timeline when you first hear that unmistakable sound that telegraphs curiosity and enthusiasm or that twinkle in the eye that immediately and firmly announces that a potential spectacular is hiding just around the corner (from research and design). In fact, the only distance between you and the ultimate realization of the event may be a few hours, days, weeks, or months. To best control this period, it is essential that you construct a realistic time frame.

One reason that many events fail is due to an insufficient time frame to effectively research, design, plan, coordinate, and evaluate them. When time is not sufficient to research an event properly, you may end up paying more later, due to insufficient or incorrect information. When time is not sufficient to design an event, you may overlook some of the more creative elements that will provide you with the resources to make the event magical and, therefore, memorable.

Each Event Leader should construct a timeline that begins with the research phase and concludes with the evaluation phase. The timeline should cover each aspect and component of the event. It should include the start and ending times for each activity or task. It must be comprehensive and incorporate the individual timelines established by auxiliary organizations, such as vendors and government regulations. The Event Leader should carefully collect individual timelines from all vendors and other service providers. The timeline should detail the elements or components that appear in other people's timelines. This process of purging and merging the various timelines into one master production instrument is essential for communication between all parties.

Prior to distribution of the final copy, the Event Leader should seek consensus among all stakeholders before codifying the final results. The timeline must be acceptable to all stakeholders. One way to ensure the careful review and approval of each critical stakeholder is to require that they initial their acceptance on the final document. The final timeline should be distributed to all stakeholders as well as appropriate external officials (i.e., police, fire, media) to ensure timely service and provide effective damage control. By providing media and other external stakeholders with accurate information in a timely manner, you may avoid problems with innuendo and hearsay that cause erroneous reporting of your event planning process.

The way you depict your timeline ultimately will determine its effectiveness in communication to the broadest possible number of event stakeholders. Figure 3.11 shows a typical event timeline in summary form. Although the information in the figure is presented in summary form, it demonstrates that the timeline must be a comprehensive instrument that provides a separate column for each task, list of participants, and start and end dates and time. For example, in the evaluation phase, only the quantitative survey evaluation is listed as the task to be performed. In fact, as you will discover later in the book, evaluation is a comprehensive process, and in this phase you will also evaluate factors ranging from finance to timing. Each of these factors will be listed on a separate task line with specific participants assigned to supervise this process.

The timeline provides the Event Leader and event stakeholders with a precise tool for managing the event. It is the comprehensive map that results from the event planning process. Just as with any map, there may be shortcuts; however, you must depict the entire map to ensure accuracy to provide the traveler with the best choices for gaining efficiency during the journey. The same may be said of the timeline. Once you have created this master planning document, in subsequent meetings you may adjust the timeline to gain

Phase	Task(s)	Participants in Event and Responsible Persons	Start Date and Time	End Date and Time
Research	Collect and analyze three years of event history or review comparable events	Key stakeholders and informants: Event Manager, financial manager, marketing manager, and volunteer coordinator	June 1, 9 a.m.	June 14, 5 p.m.
Design	Collect ideas from similar events; brainstorm with key informants and vendors	Event Manager, key informants, vendors, creative staff	June 15, 12 noon (luncheon)	June 16, 5 p.m.
Planning	Preplan planning meetings, announce/schedule planning meeting, assign prework, facilitate planning meeting, develop timeline	Event Manager, key informants, critical stakeholders, key advisors	June 18, 9 a.m.	June 29, 5 p.m.
Coordination	Identify prospective vendors, contract vendors, develop final production schedule, implement production schedule	Event Manager, event coordinators, vendors, key external stakeholders	July 1, 9 a.m.	August 1, 5 p.m.
Evaluation	Prepare and distribute surveys, collect data, tabulate data, analyze data, prepare report of findings and recommendations, submit final report	Event Manager, evaluation team, client representative	Sept. 1, 9 a.m.	Sept. 30, 5 p.m.

Figure 3.11 Event Timeline Summary

speed and save time and money, ensuring that you will also ultimately reach your destination in order to achieve your goals and objectives.

The process of planning—from preplanning through the essential corrective planning during the coordination phase—forces the Event Leader and his or her team to logically assemble the best ideas to produce added value for the client. In addition, the planning process must result in a document or instrument that will guide and memorialize the journey of the stakeholders. From a legal standpoint, the timeline, organizational chart, and production schedule can be used to show illogical planning or, even worse, gaps in the planning process. As an expert witness in numerous trials involving negligence by event professionals, I often see attorneys use these three documents to prove that the Event Leader and his or her organization did not meet or adhere to the standard of care generally accepted in the modern profession of event planning.

As the modern profession of event planning transforms into the twenty-first-century global marketplace, Event Leaders must not only meet and exceed the standard of care that is generally accepted in developed countries but also use these instruments to begin to communicate a global standard for the worldwide event industry. Through standardized planning instruments and processes, event planning will join other well-developed professions, such as medicine and engineering, in establishing protocols that will lead to better communication, increased safety, and higher-quality performance wherever Event Leaders research, design, plan, coordinate, and evaluate professional events.

Career-Advancement Connections

Corporate Social Responsibility Connection

Describe how your planned event supports sustainability and corporate social responsibility. How is the natural environment improved as a result of your event being conducted? How has your social event promoted social cohesion in the community where it was conducted? Are there health and education benefits that accrue as a result of your event? How will you measure these sustainable outcomes?

Global Connection

When planning events in countries outside North America, these considerations must be incorporated to ensure a smooth planning process:

- Some countries and cultures have a more rigid planning framework. Ask experienced event organizers in the country where you are working to offer their insights as to the best way to organize and lead your planning team.
- In many countries, event planners hold the title of professional congress organizer (PCO). This person is usually responsible for multiple functions, including

financing the event as well as marketing the overall program. When working with a PCO, determine in advance the range of his or her responsibilities regarding the planning phase. Some PCOs adhere to the requirements identified by the International Association of Professional Congress Organizers (IAPCO). For more information about IAPCO, visit its Web site at www.iapco.org.

Technology Connection

Although planning software is increasingly global in configuration, nuances in languages can lead to critical oversights and even errors. Therefore, it is important

The Protégé: Anders Müller, Meeting Architect, Imagine Group, Stockholm, Sweden

The event wizard of Scandinavia, Anders Müller has been a leading light in the Scandinavian events industry for over two decades. His offices are located on a boat that is docked in the city center of Stockholm, Sweden. From this lovely vessel, he is able to promote creativity and expertly navigate to solve his clients' marketing and education challenges. According to Anders, he has been in love with the event profession ever since he was enrolled in kindergarten. Müller states that "Ever since kindergarten, I enjoy producing. To design a meeting or a show has been something I always loved. From the first theater play in first grade, to the fashion shows and night club acts as a 19-year-old, to the full-blown productions at Ericsson Globe Arena or Stockholm City Hall for clients, I love to see the audience react the way I hoped and worked for."

He realized that he was in the right field when he first appreciated the importance of getting people in the right mood. By being in this business, he says he can do it all the time. This is an instinctive feeling, according to Anders: "I just feel it. I started in the advertising business, but left at 26 to start my first business in the Event Marketing field. I just love to make brands go live."

Müller has a number of personal mentors and individuals that he admires; however, as he was a pioneer in this field, professional mentors were few and far between. He recalls that "Since the business was young in Sweden during the eighties, there were not any particular persons I could turn to as a mentor. My father was an inspiration as a graphic designer. But the person I admire most is the award-winning film director Tim Burton (the director of the films *Edward Scissorhands* and *Batman,* among many others), who designed his own world in his movies. He is one of the best storytellers ever. I also admire Steve Jobs for fighting the PC-business with his vision of computing should look and be like. And

for you to appoint a local technology consultant to assist you with technology planning in the country where your event will be held. These suggestions will further expedite your technology connections in the global event marketplace:

- Use the World Wide Web to research, confirm, and communicate inexpensively prior to your first site inspection. For more information about useful Web sites, see the Web directory lists available online for this book.
- Visit www.MeetingMatrix.com to explore how you may quickly and easily source thousands of venues for your event and design using advanced computer and assisted design technology a floor plan for your program.

I am inspired by the musical artist Prince for being able to create music from scratch, play all instruments, record it, and even distribute the music on his own. Finally, the artistic director and founder of Circe de Soleil, Guy Laliberté, is also a person that I greatly admire."

Storytelling is a major influence and theme in Müller's career. He says, "I admire Burton, Prince and Laliberté because they bring stories to the people. They create dreams. They have visions."

Müller has held a front-row seat in the events industry for many years. He has noted a 180-degree turn in the business. He notes, "We have seen big changes in the business. Especially when it comes to use of events as media. Events is no longer the young, funny brother who just likes to have fun. Events is now serious business."

The catalyst for these major changes he describes is technology and the compelling need to do things differently to gain attention.

He envisions that the future of events will represent mature media that use storytelling and all our senses, along with clever technology, to educate, sell, or just make people happy. His vision is one that springs forth from observing his own children. "My children are never watching television, so the commercials do not have any effect on them. They don't read paper magazines, so the ads are of no use. The next generations will not be interested in ads, they want to look, feel and experience a brand or an organization. Or a holiday. Or a story. We are in the experience business."

Anders Müller has been successful throughout his career because he says he listens to the customer and the customer's customer. He finds out what they really want. He says, "The key to the right event is always within the company or the organization. It just has to be found. Never invent stuff just for fun. A great event is better than just fun. It's something you never forget."

He cites Marshall McLuhan as a major influence in his thinking and recalls that McLuhan once said, "Everybody experiences far more than he understands. And it is experience, rather than understanding that influences behavior."

Müller's ability to continually innovate and explore new experiences in Scandinavia and beyond has resulted in his preeminent position as one of the world's most respected meeting and special-event architects. He certainly understands and expands McLuhan's concept of experience through his remarkable and influential events that greatly influence the positive behavior of his guests. His pioneering efforts have also inspired and challenged legions of future event leaders both in Scandinavia and throughout the world.

The Protégé: Kari Felicia Nestande, Norwegian Cancer Society, Oslo, Norway

Not quite a protégé, really more of a pioneer in many regards, Kari Felicia Nestande earned her Master of Tourism Administration degree with a concentration in Event Management from The George Washington University in the 1990s. Kari was one of the first individuals in the world to attain a graduate degree in events management. She states that her career first began in the hotel industry after hotel management studies in Canada—"I guess inspired by people who meant I had talent for hospitality and an eye for bringing people and things together. Since I have a curious mind, I have always wondered about why and how things are done. Since I primarily worked with meeting and events in the hotel, I moved into meeting planning, event marketing and subsequently communication."

Her interest in events began as a child when she loved bringing people together. She was later able to combine this passion with her talent for organizing and found it quite rewarding. She says, " I enjoy my work because I see that the events I plan have an impact on people."

Although she has been fortunate to be inspired by many event leaders, her primary mentor is Sissi P. Solberg, who was the first professional event and meeting planner in Norway and was a client of the hotel where Kari was working. The events Solberg planned were demanding, and she was a stickler for details. Kari greatly admired her professionalism and was fortunate to work with her a few years later. Kari recalls of that experience: "She taught me so much about people and what it takes to make an event with impact."

Kari sees meetings and events as communication tools. Therefore, she believes that increased

- Visit www.meetingmetrics.com to see how you may use technology to quickly, easily and efficiently evaluate your events.
- Make certain that your planning process includes a thorough review of the technological capability of the venue and destination where the event will be held. Not all phone systems are created equal. In many developing countries, you may have difficulty with sending and receiving large files due to bandwidth limitations. Consult with local technology experts to plan in advance to overcome these challenges.
- The technological infrastructure of many event venues in countries outside North America is superior to systems in place in the United States and Canada. When planning the meeting site, keep in mind the critical importance of technology and select the site based on the technological capabilities to support your event.
- Plan to use technology to create a 24-hour, seven-day time band for your event. Your event can easily begin with online marketing and registration; this can lead

focus will be placed on integrating meetings and events into marketing and communication strategies. This will require the development of new skills for the next generation of meeting and event planners.

She also sees technology as an important tool to enhance communication of meetings and ensure cost effectiveness of meeting organization. However, she states firmly, "I believe that it will be important to ensure that meetings and events are people-driven—and not technology driven."

The meeting and events industry is changing dramatically due to the development of professionalism, and Kari believes this will one of the key success factors of the future. This professionalization of the field will be driven by the customers' demand for integration of meetings and events into other strategies, quality, and value for money. She further believes that niche businesses and specialties will develop as well.

She is confident about the growth of the industry because globalization will open new markets and increase the use of meetings and events as business and communication tools. As the field grows, she is convinced that the next generation will benefit from advice she was given much earlier in her career.

"One of the key success factors for any meeting and event is to focus on the needs of the key stakeholders you want the event to impact. You need to know why you are holding this meeting and what you want to achieve through the meeting. To me, everything else is packaging. If you lose focus on the primary stakeholders, you have lost the whole point of the event or meeting. It may end in disaster if you do it too often! I apply this in everything I do, actually, and definitely in all the meetings and events that I organize."

Kari Felicia Nestande is both a pioneer and a protégé in the field of meetings and events. As a pioneer, she was one of the first in the world to see the advantage and value of earning a graduate degree in this area of study. As a protégé, she is continually learning through her involvement in professional associations such as Meeting Professionals Association. In Norway and throughout Scandinavia, Kari is widely considered a thought leader in the field of meetings and events. As a result of her innovative approach to evaluation of events and meetings, the industry has greatly advance not only in Scandinavia but throughout the world.

to chat rooms prior to the event, and be followed after the event with new online chat rooms. Furthermore, you can create a password-protected site for people to log into your event when they cannot be there in person. You can also develop this site as an electronic commerce area and sell products, services, and access to information to create new revenue streams for your event budget.

Resource Connection

To identify resources for the planning phase, remember these key points:

- Review the hundreds of comparable events described in the Wiley Event Management series of books to identify models that may assist you in your development.
- If you need models of comparable events, such as the complete planning guide for the National Football League Super Bowl or the Goodwill Games Opening

Ceremony, visit The George Washington University Gelman Library Event Management and Marketing Archives (www.gwu.edu/gelman/spec).

- If you use software to create a planning matrix like a PERT chart (www.criticaltools.com) or a Gantt chart, make certain that you select the model that will be easiest to communicate to each of your stakeholders.
- The Convention Industry Council (www.conventionindustry.org), through its Accepted Practices Exchange (APEX), provides 200 planning templates for meeting, convention, exhibition, and event-planning purposes in a software package called APEX Meeting and Event Toolbox by Office Ready.

Learning Connection

Answer these questions and complete the activities.

1. Who are some of the key informants for your event, and why should they be included in the planning meeting?
2. What information should you send to the key informants prior to the first planning meeting?
3. How can you make certain that the planning meeting includes the input and consensus of all participants?
4. Write a memorandum to announce the first ESP meeting and assign prework to the participants.
5. Create a schedule for the planning process and show the linkages between the planning steps and the goals and objectives of the event.

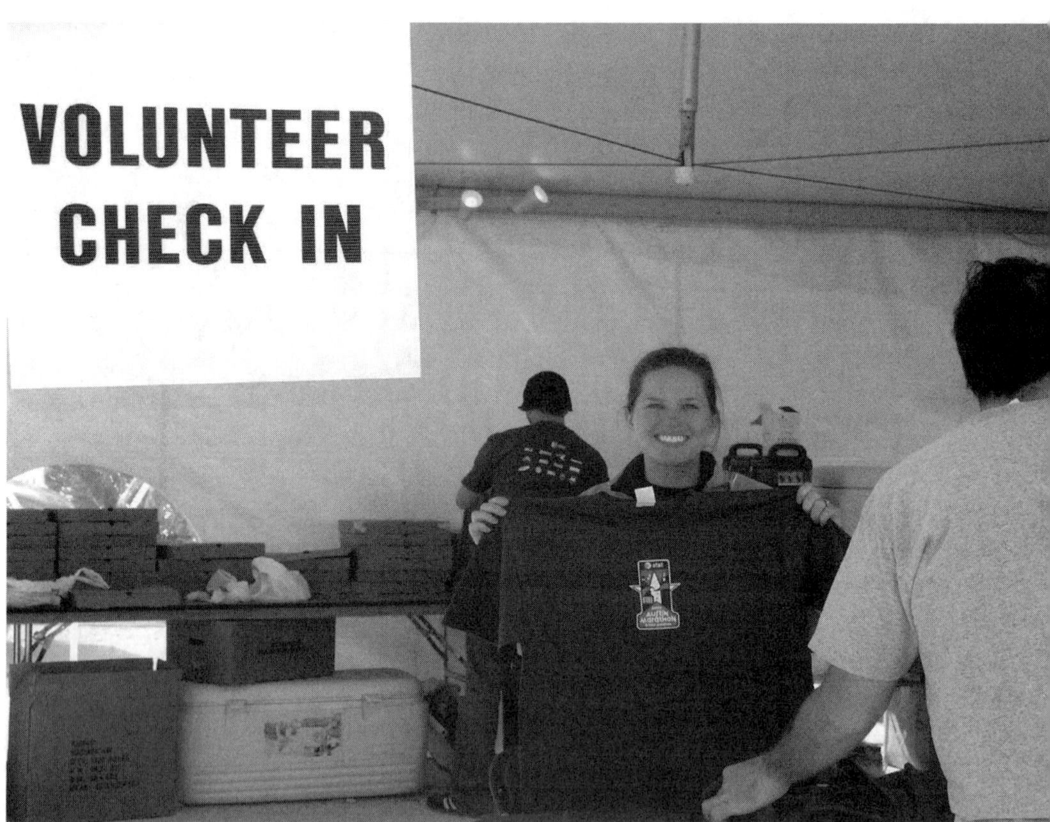

The Austin, Texas, Marathon provides an efficient way for its volunteers to check in and receive their tee shirts and credentials for this event.

CHAPTER 4

Event Leadership Through Human Resource and Time Management

In this chapter you will learn how to:

- Identify leadership characteristics in an Event Planner and in yourself
- Make critical decisions and act decisively
- Solve problems
- Overcome communication challenges
- Improve human resource management
- Recruit excellent staff and volunteers
- Orient, train, inform, educate, motivate, and inspire staff and volunteers
- Establish an effective recruitment and promotion plan
- Create effective organizational charts
- Develop policies, procedures, and practices
- Improve time management
- Benefit from diversifying your staff

Professional event management is truly a leadership process. Linda Higgison (1947–2007), former chair and chief executive officer (CEO) of the TCI Companies and curriculum designer for the Temple University Event Leadership Executive Certificate Program, described the leadership process this way: "The global Event Leader must be a leader and he or she must wear many hats in various leadership roles. One role is the creator, another is the communicator, another is the visionary, and still another is the problem solver. The successful Event Leader must not only wear these hats and many more but must also become adept at continually changing hats (roles) to achieve the goals and objectives of the event." Higgison was correct in her assumption that the event planner must, indeed, play many roles. However, historically, management has been a command-and-control approach rather than a collaborative process. How much command and control should the event planner relinquish if he or she is to become an effective Event Leader?

Julia Rutherford Silvers, author of *Professional Event Coordination* (2003), states: "Leadership requires trust, and trust depends on integrity, competence, and confidence. Managers analyze information, make inferences, and make decisions. They allocate resources to solve problems, assign tasks, and make schedules. Leaders influence and inspire others to achieve a goal. Leaders motivate. Leaders evaluate decisions, imagine consequences, and build contingencies."

Leadership Styles

When teaching, I often use a leadership exercise to dramatically convey the three different leadership styles found among event planners. I divide the class into three groups and give each team a set of popsicle sticks. I then instruct each group to construct an event site using the sticks. One group will do this using a democratic approach, the other with autocratic principles, and the third will use a laissez-faire approach.

The democratic group arranges the popsicle sticks easily and efficiently in a pleasing formation, and their conversations, discussions, and decision making flow smoothly. The arrangement of the sticks is a dramatic representation of the effectiveness of their process.

The autocratic group can barely decide how to place their popsicle sticks, due to dissension and arguments regarding turf. This group is too busy battling among themselves to accomplish the goals required by the event.

The laissez-faire group constantly arranges and rearranges their popsicle sticks, as without clear direction or facilitation they have trouble achieving consensus; their popsicle sticks demonstrate this confusion.

Each of these styles has an important role to play in the Event Leadership process. Your ability to navigate among these styles and use the one that is appropriate at the right time is essential to achieving success.

Democratic Style

Typically, the democratic leadership style, which involves considering the thoughts of all members of a group and coming to a collaborative decision about how to proceed, is used during the early stages of the event process. It is an excellent approach for facilitating discussions, conducting focus groups, and building consensus as you assemble your stakeholders. It is also effective as you move from the design phase into the coordination phase. Before you can coordinate your team members' efforts, you must demonstrate that you are willing to listen and that you are able to function as a good facilitator. These two skills—listening and facilitation—are hallmarks of democratic Event Leadership.

Autocratic Style

When the fire marshal tells you to evacuate an event site, you should not use the democratic approach. The democratic Event Leadership style has one major drawback: It takes time to reach consensus. When an emergency evacuation is required, there is no time or any reason to try and reach consensus. Instead, you must use the autocratic approach and give the order to evacuate. Then you must supervise carefully to make certain that your instructions are being followed. The autocratic approach should be used sparingly. It is impossible, for example, to force volunteers and increasing staff members to do things they do not wish to do. Therefore, the autocratic approach should be used only when time is of the essence.

Laissez-faire Style

The laissez-faire approach of individuals working toward a common goal, as opposed to a team working together toward a common goal, is least used in event management because it requires a team whose members have skills that are equal in level; therefore, the Event Leader does not have to facilitate to ensure that goals are being achieved. It is rare that an event organization has a team with skills at a similar level. Most event organizations are composed of many people with a variety of different skills and even commitment levels. Therefore, it is impossible for the event planner to sit back and let the group decide for itself how to proceed. Beware the laissez-faire event planner. He or she may be unskilled and trying to transfer his or her incompetence to the entire event team.

When you are faced with this scenario, move quickly to empower others on the team to assist this person with decision making to ensure that the event goals and objectives are being met. The most common way to reduce large amounts of complex information about an event to a manageable communications process is through published policies and procedures. All events of substance have such a document, and it helps drive the event's decision making.

Leadership Characteristics

Throughout ancient and modern human history, a number of people have been identified by historians as effective leaders. Some of these people became leaders due to a defining moment or event in their lives, while others sought leadership opportunities to cause positive change. In Figure 4.1, the general traits associated with effective leaders are compared to those specialized characteristics that Higgison and Rutherford Silvers have identified within successful event planners. Although some will argue with this list and

Traditional Leaders	Event Leaders
1. Communication skills	1. Integrity
2. Confidence	2. Confidence and persistence
3. Courage	3. Collaborative decision making
4. Decision making	4. Problem solving
5. Enthusiasm	5. Communication skills
6. Integrity	6. Vision
7. Persistence	7. Focus upon sustainable events
8. Planning	8. Corporate Social Responsibility (CSR) as a core value for every event
9. Problem solving	

Figure 4.1 Leadership Characteristics

ranking, I am firmly convinced, based on my observation of literally thousands of event planners throughout the world, that the eight characteristics listed in the right column of the figure generally define the qualities of the top Event Leadership leaders. These qualities or characteristics are ranked in this order for a specific purpose. It is important for event planners to understand that not all leadership characteristics are equal; however, integrity is paramount. Integrity is the value that determines the external perception by others.

In addition to traditional characteristics, event planners demonstrate the traits listed in Figure 4.1 and described as follows.

Integrity

The event planner must set the standard for integrity. If he or she does not exemplify integrity in performance and decision making, event stakeholders will soon lose faith not only in the Event Leader but also in the event organization. For example, if an event planner reminds his or her staff that it is inappropriate to accept gifts from vendors and then is seen by subordinates receiving a substantial gift from a vendor, the credibility of the person, as well as that of the organization, may be shattered. The event planner who exhibits high integrity will not only refuse the gift but will effectively communicate to his or her colleagues that the gift has been refused and why it would be inappropriate to accept this gift. Figure 4.2 demonstrates perceptions of high and low integrity by event stakeholders.

Confidence and Persistence

When your back is against the wall, will you have the confidence and persistence to forge ahead? Typically, most events have a reality check where funds are low, morale is even

Perception of	Perception of	High Integrity Evidence	Low Integrity Evidence
Consistency	Punctuality	Tardiness	Communications
Inclusiveness	Participation	Absenteeism	Intolerance
Participation	Consistency	Inconsistency	Participation
Tolerance	Inclusiveness	Exclusiveness/favoritism	Exclusiveness
Punctuality	Tolerance	Intolerance	Inconsistency

Figure 4.2 Integrity Quotient

lower, and impending disaster seems just around the corner. During these times of trial and tribulation, all eyes will be on the event planner. Your ability to stay the course, maintain the original vision, and triumph is what is expected by your event stakeholders.

Let us suppose that you are responsible for acquiring sponsors for your event. Only a few weeks before the event, your biggest sponsor backs out. There is no time to replace the sponsor. In addition, the neighbors whose houses are near your event venue are starting to make rumblings in the media about noise, traffic, and other disruptions that they believe will result from your event. A traditional manager would collect all the necessary information and perhaps assign each problem to an appropriate subordinate after making a decision as to the best course of action. An event planner, however, will use these challenges as opportunities for the event organization to learn and grow. The event planner may ask members of the board as well as staff for recommendations on how to replace or at least mitigate the damage that could be caused by the missing sponsor. Furthermore, the event planner will meet with the neighbors or their association and work collaboratively with his or her staff to offer the assurances they need to provide new and long-term support for the event. Event planners use their confidence and persistence as teaching tools to influence other event stakeholders.

Event planners must work effectively with cross-functional teams. One definition of effective leadership is to occasionally look behind you and see if anyone is actually following you. A great leader must be supported by an even greater team. In 2006, when the Temple University Event Leadership Executive Certificate Program was selected by the International Festival and Events Association to receive the Haas & Wilkerson Gold Pinnacle Award for Best Certificate Program in Events Education, I immediately notified and acknowledged the team that achieved this success. However, despite camaraderie that may result from effective teams, challenges do occur and must be anticipated and addressed by the Event Leader.

Collaborative Decision Making

Since Frederick Winslow Taylor (1856–1915) created the management methods used to propel industrialized America, most management theory has focused on achieving efficiency to maximize profits. As workers began to organize into labor unions, they challenged this approach and sought an equal share in the decision-making process regarding not only the type of work they do but how they do it. Event organizations are not linear organizations like factories. Instead, they are pulsating organizations that may start with a small staff, swell to a large part-time and volunteer organization as an event grows near, and then rapidly deflate to the original small staff as the event winds down. This type of organization requires close collaboration between the event planners and those who will actually deliver the services that provide the final perception of the event by the guests.

Collaborative organizations or quality teams have been used for the past three decades by numerous for-profit and not-for-profit organizations to achieve high quality and, consequently, better financial results. Event Leaders should always perceive their associates (permanent and part-time staff), volunteers, and others as collaborators who share a mutual goal of producing a successful event. Therefore, all decisions should be preceded by close collaboration among the stakeholders. However, there are also times when the event planner must lead by making timely decisions without consulting all affected stakeholders. For example, when the event planner is notified of an unsafe, illegal, or unethical activity taking place, he or she must intercede swiftly. Following the decision to act, the event planner must make certain that he or she has used The event planner must notify the affected stakeholders that he or she has taken an action, then seek their input in case a similar decision has to be made in the future.

Problem Solving

A colleague of mine once said that she counted thousands of potential problems during the development of an event and, therefore, concluded that events consist of a series of problems whose solutions determine the level of success achieved by event stakeholders. I prefer to see a problem as a challenge that temporarily tests the skills of the event planner and his or her stakeholders. Few event planners continue in the field unless they are comfortable with their ability to solve problems. Therefore, it is understood that event planners who are experienced and trained possess the skills not only to analyze problems but also to provide a solution or solutions that will improve the outcome of the event. This five-step list provides a framework for event planners to understand, analyze, and solve event problems:

1. Make certain that you thoroughly understand the size, scope, and time sensitivity of the problem.
2. Identify the key informants and stakeholders affected by the problem.
3. Determine if there is a model or comparable problem whose solution could be used for this problem.
4. Test the potential solution by seeking the collaborative input of those affected by the problem. If the problem is urgent and requires an immediate response, use a precedent or other model to frame your response.
5. Once a decision has been made, monitor the impact to determine if anything further must be done to mitigate future problems resulting from your decision.

Here is an example of how this model would work during an actual event. A prominent Texas university had a tradition of allowing students to construct a giant bonfire before the major football game of the year. This tradition stretched back several decades and had become a hallowed ritual/rite for students and alumni. Unfortunately, one year the bonfire materials collapsed, killing several students and critically injuring many others. University officials then had to decide whether to allow the bonfire to be rebuilt the following year. The framework just given may be applied to this problem to produce an outcome that can be accepted by a majority of stakeholders.

First, the president of the university and other administrators had to hold a thorough investigation to make certain that they had all the facts concerning the scope, size, and time sensitivity of the problem. Next, they had to make certain that their empirical information represented input from key stakeholders (those most seriously affected by the problem). Then they had to conduct further research to determine if there had been a similar problem and solution that may be used as a model for this incident. By researching academic journals, conducting interviews with administrators at other schools, and seeking anecdotal information from other institutions, the administrators can identify responses that may guide them to an appropriate solution.

The institution must first test the potential solutions with key informants and other critical stakeholders to make certain that their response is accurate, thorough, and appropriate. The input that will be received from other stakeholders will further refine not only the strategic solution but also the implementation tactics. Due to the gravity of this problem, university administrators decided immediately to cancel further bonfire structures for the next 12 months, pending an official investigation and analysis of the problem. This decision was made to prevent other groups, including off-campus organizations, from continuing the tradition.

Finally, the solution to the problem (canceling the bonfire for a period of years) must be monitored to determine if other challenges occur as a result of the solution. Indeed, as soon as the cancellation was announced, an off-campus alumni organization announced that it wanted to build a bonfire to continue the tradition. University administrators strongly discouraged this activity and promoted their concern to media to go on record opposing this activity.

Most event problems are not of the magnitude of the university bonfire tragedy. However, unless problems are solved efficiently and appropriately, they can easily escalate to a level that may threaten the reputation of the event. Once the reputation is injured or ruined, it may be difficult to sustain the future of the event. That is why it is critical that the Event Leader design and promote a carefully crafted internal communications strategy.

Communication Skills

Although communication is a critical component of the entire event process, it is also the single largest culprit when it comes to problems that may arise. How many times has a lack of communication or, more often, miscommunication, resulted in a missed opportunity, an error, an oversight, or even a dangerous situation? Although an event planner need not be particularly articulate or even eloquent, he or she must be an excellent communicator. Communication is a continuous process that involves both sending (transmitting) and receiving information. This information may be verbal, written, or even abstract symbols, such as body language. The event planner must be able to receive and transmit complex information to multiple stakeholders throughout the event process. The glue that literally binds the various disparate components of the event plan together is the communications process. Therefore, the event planner must lead through excellent communications from research through evaluation. Following are the most common communications problems that may affect the planning process in planned events and how to correct them:

- Communication is not received by stakeholders: Confirm receipt.
- Communication is misunderstood by stakeholders: Ask questions.
- Communication is blocked among stakeholders: Promote open communications.

Without open and continuous communication, event stakeholders cannot form the collaborative team needed to achieve common objectives. To promote open communications, the event planner must listen, analyze, and act. To listen effectively, an event manager must be intuitive, set specific criteria for the analysis of facts, and, when necessary, act quickly and decisively to unblock communications among stakeholders.

Julia Rutherford Silvers recognizes that coordinating events requires a complex set of skills, including effective communication. She states in *Professional Event Coordination* (2003), "Creating and producing events is an exhilarating and sometimes exhausting occupation, but it is always rewarding emotionally, spiritually, and often economically. The professional event coordinator must be flexible, energetic, well organized, detail-oriented, and a quick thinker. As a professional event coordinator you must understand the integrated processes, plans, and possibilities specific to each event you coordinate so that you will be a better planner, producer, purchaser, and partner in delivering the special event experience that exceeds expectations." One important communications strategy is the event planners presentation of the vision of the event to his or her team.

Vision

The professional event planner must clearly demonstrate that he or she has a vision of the event's outcome. During early meetings with the stakeholders, the event planner must describe in a visual manner the outcome that will result from the event. For example, the event planner may state: "On the opening day, thousands of guests will line up to buy tickets and, once inside, they will smile, participate, and have a good time, all due to your efforts." Furthermore, the event planner must "lead" the stakeholders toward that vision of the event by asking leading questions, such as, "Can you see this happening? Are you prepared to help me make it happen? What will you do to help us achieve this goal?"

Achieving the goals and objectives of the event is the ultimate challenge for every event leader and his or her team. Six unique factors promote the rapid and complete achievement of your event goals.

Event Leadership Factors

These six leadership factors ultimately result in an event planner who has the skills, experience, and intuition to form the best judgment and act appropriately to advance the goals of the event organization. This is no small task. It requires continuous monitoring by stakeholders to ensure that the event planner is doing his or her best to lead the team. Event Leadership requires constant vigilance and continuing education to ensure that the power that is entrusted to the event planner is used wisely, judiciously, and thoughtfully.

Finally, it is important to note that event planning is neither charisma nor control, the ability to command nor the talent to inspire. Rather, it is that rare commodity, like good taste, that one recognizes when one sees it. Every event planner should aspire to become the kind that others will not only recognize but will follow to see where he or she leads them. Ultimately, the best event planners become ones whom other event stakeholders not only admire but also emulate as they seek to develop their own leadership potential. Through this admiration and emulation, these event stakeholders will soon become leaders themselves, producing even greater events in the twenty-first century.

Challenges of Teamwork

If you have ever served on a committee, marched in a band, sung in a choir, or played on a team, you know the challenges of developing successful teams. The most frequent challenges that Event Leaders face when developing teams are (1) communications, (2) self-interest, (3) dependability, (4) trust, and (5) collaboration.

Communications

Excellent event coordination is the result of continuous, consistent, high- quality communications between the event stakeholders. The event planner is responsible for developing and sustaining the event communications to ensure that all stakeholders are informed, in touch, and involved in each of the phases of managing the event. Several methods that you may use to establish and/or improve a high-quality communications network for your event follow.

- Conduct a communications audit and find out how your event stakeholders best send and receive information.
- Avoid communications that are blocked by noise, visual distraction, or other interference.
- Include an "Action Required" statement on all written communications to confirm that communications have been received and understood.
- Use nontraditional communications such as audio- and videotapes to increase impact, retention, and action.

- Use written change orders to record changes during your event. Make certain the client or other responsible person signs the change order to authorize the addition, deletion, or substitution of services or products.

Self-Interest

Many committees are composed of people who essentially bring their personal views, biases, and agendas to the event planning process. It is the responsibility of the event planner to persuade each person to forgo personal interest for the sake of group interest. Only through a strong group effort can an event achieve a successful outcome. You may wish to invite an expert in team building or conduct team-building exercises yourself to develop trust, congeniality, and a common purpose among the team members. One way to begin this process is through an informal series of events such as social functions where the event stakeholders get to know, like, and trust one another before they sit down to deliberate (plan) an event. During this social period the event planner may observe the participants to begin to identify those who naturally work best in teams and those who will need more coaching or persuasion to feel comfortable working on a group project.

Dependability

One of the biggest management problems in working with volunteers is time and attendance. Because volunteers are not compensated for their efforts, many do not feel the obligation to arrive on time or even to show up at all. To compensate for the serious problem of attrition at events, many Event Leaders actually schedule between 25 and 50 percent more volunteers than will be needed.

The Sydney Organizing Committee for the Olympic Games (SOCOG) developed a unique passport system for the 60,000 volunteers who helped coordinate the 2000 Summer Olympic Games. Each volunteer was issued a personal passport and asked to have it stamped each day by his or her supervisor. When the passport was completely stamped, the volunteer would be entered in a drawing to win a wide range of valuable prizes.

Jason Quinn, a professional theatrical stage manager In New York City, states that most vendors do not want to be late when purveying an event. Therefore, for the first infraction he waits for a calm moment and asks, "What happened?" Later he may state: "Let me know if there is anything I can do to help you with your scheduling, because we are depending on you being on time to ensure a successful event."

Of course, the easiest way to ensure dependability is to recruit dependable people. Keep accurate records of time and attendance, and use the records to determine who to engage for future events. During the interviewing or recruiting process, check references carefully to make sure that your stakeholders have a pattern of punctuality that can be shared with your event.

In the Event Leadership profession, the correct definition of being on time is to "arrive early." Because of the numerous variables that can occur before, during, and after an event, it is essential that all event stakeholders arrive at an event site early enough to be able to spot potential challenges and overcome them before the guests or other vendors arrive. When interviewing potential event coordination staff, I often ask: "If the event setup time is at 8 A.M., what time do you believe is the best time for you to arrive at the venue?" Those who answer between 7 and 7:30 A.M. are most likely to receive final consideration for employment. This is because I have often arrived at an event venue to coordinate the setup, only to find that it takes up to one hour to open the locked parking lot, contact security to gain entrance to the building, and locate engineering to turn on the lights in order to be ready for the vendors' arrival.

Trust

Trust must be earned by the event planner. Trust is the result of the event planner's sustained effort to develop an atmosphere and environment wherein the event stakeholders invest their trust in his or her behavior and judgments. Trust, in fact, is the net result of a pattern of positive behaviors exhibited by the event planner. When the event planner's behaviors are erratic or quixotic, the trust factor begins to diminish. To develop, establish, and sustain trust, the event planner must earn it and ask for it from his or her stakeholders.

Event stakeholders cannot blindly trust every event planner. Rather, they must use their best judgment to determine when and how to invest their trust. Trust should not be invested without question or careful analysis by the stakeholders. However, an event organization that is not firmly rooted in trust between the event planner and his or her stakeholders is one that is precarious and cannot achieve the level of success required to meet the expectations of all the stakeholders.

Collaboration

The final quality of effective event coordinators is the ability to develop close collaboration between all the stakeholders. This is extremely difficult, due to the disparity between the personalities, skills, and experiences of each stakeholder. Imagine a pre-event conference with all the stakeholders. You may have at the same table persons with a wide variety of formal education, an even wider range of skill and experience level, diverse ethnic backgrounds, and completely different technical abilities.

How does the event planner inspire and encourage close collaboration between such a varied group of stakeholders? The key to collaboration is purpose. The event planner must clearly articulate the purpose of the event and convince each stakeholder that he or she must work with others to achieve or exceed the expectations of the guests.

The distinguished anthropologist Margaret Mead (1901–1978) once wrote: "Never doubt that a small group of thoughtful, committed citizens can change the world; indeed, it's the only thing that ever has." Your world or universe is the event you are responsible for managing. Therefore, you must firmly remind the stakeholders that self-interest must be left out of the event environment. The purpose of the event team is to cooperate and collaborate to achieve the goals and objectives of the event, and the event planner is the leader of this effort.

Human Resource Management

The event management industry is primarily a service industry. Therefore, its vital function often consists of intangible things such as customer service. You cannot touch it or smell it, but it exists, and moreover, it can make your events a disaster or a complete success. You are being paid for creating memorable positive experiences, and you and your staff are the critical resource that makes a guest's experience memorable. Issues such as your human resource organization, training, and employee retention are vital if you are to remain competitive.

For example, most event planning organizations offer similar services, but it is their people that make the difference. Members of your association are not very likely to attend next year's convention if they had a bad experience this year, and without trained and experienced people, the event cannot succeed. That is why you should always remember that you and your colleagues are the most important asset of any Event Leadership organization.

You are the locomotive that makes the event train move forward. The human resources (HR) for your event represent the fuel that will drive the successful outcomes for your program. This fuel represents scarce resources that must be conserved and carefully deployed to achieve maximum benefit for your events organization. Southwest Airlines refers to its HR department simply as the "people" department. And in fact, the event industry's most important resource is people.

The global human resource sector endured major changes during the past several years. With the rapid growth of the global economy, the employee turnover in many fields, including the event planning field, increased tremendously. An average of five-year employee retention decreased to less than a year and a half per employee. This high turnover became a constant challenge to human resource and department managers. Under these circumstances, it is more important than ever to motivate your employees and offer various soft benefits in addition to monetary rewards. Benefits such as travel, employee meals, subsidized parking in big cities, employee-appreciation events, employee-performance awards, training, and company-paid memberships in industry associations are no longer a rarity. In many cases, you can encourage your employees greatly by creating growth and learning opportunities, supporting promotions, and creating valuable titles.

Celebrate Your Success

The effective event planner looks for opportunities to celebrate the individual and the success experienced by your organization. Is registration way ahead of last year? Break out the champagne! Mary confirmed that $10,000 sponsorship? Blow up the balloons and cut the cake that reads "Way to go, Mary!" Your team has won an award for your recent event? Celebrate with dinner and dancing for the entire team. Your team will readily recognize that every good deed can be rewarded if you take the time to notice and mark the occasion.

You may wish to appoint one person from your organization as the internal event specialist in charge of these celebrations so that you can readily delegate these tasks and be assured that each one is handled by a capable person. Too often, event employees are like the shoemakers' children in that their managers plan wonderful events for others but scrimp on their own behalf. Your internal events should be models for all external events, and your team should feel proud not only to be part of your celebration but to have made a positive contribution to the event. This is especially true of volunteers who work long hours for no financial remuneration.

Diversify Your Staff

It is extremely important to diversify staff to better represent your guests, as well as to provide new, creative viewpoints to develop your events. This will help the Event Leadership profession to grow and develop successfully. Currently, female representation in the profession is much higher than male. However, this may change in the future to better represent parity between men and women. More minorities in the United States will also join the exciting field of Event Leadership and bring their magnificent ethnic ceremonial traditions from African, Asian, Hispanic, and other cultures. The fusion of diverse cultures can weave a beautiful and strong tapestry to best display the potential of global Event Leadership.

One excellent suggestion for promoting diversity within organizations was offered by Judith McHale, president of Discovery Communications. In cases where managers are slow to recognize the importance of promoting women and others who are underrepresented in management, McHale recommends that diversity goals be made part of their bonus package. "That, at the end of the day, has a pretty positive impact," suggests McHale (2001).

Volunteer Coordination

Volunteers are the lifeblood of many events. Without volunteers, these events would cease to exist. In fact, the vast majority of events are entirely volunteer driven. The profile of the volunteer has changed dramatically during the past three decades, and it is important that the event planner recognize this change.

The emergence of the two-income family has resulted in the fact that half of the volunteer force in the United States (women) is no longer available to work as full-time volunteers. Furthermore, since many people have more than one job and must carefully balance school, children's activities, and other commitments with their volunteer responsibilities, it is increasingly difficult to attract volunteers to assist with events.

According to the Institute for Volunteer Research (www.ivr.org.uk), although there are more volunteers than ever before, there is a net deficit in the number of volunteer hours due to the time pressures that all workers are facing today. Therefore, event planner must be highly creative and persistent when recruiting, training, and rewarding their future volunteer resources.

Effectively recruiting, training, coordinating, and rewarding volunteers is a vital part of many Event Leadership operations. Although challenging, the recommendations that follow will help you streamline this critical function.

Julia Rutherford Silvers, CSEP, in *Professional Event Coordination* (2003), describes how using "reverse scheduling" assists event planner with realistic scheduling of human resources. According to Rutherford Silvers, "When estimating the time required for each task defined, you must consider all constraints, assumptions, capabilities, historical information, and mandatory dependencies (the tasks that must be completed before another task can begin)."

Recruitment

Many event planner are now turning to corporate America to recruit legions of volunteers for their events. First, the corporation is asked to serve as an event sponsor, and as part of its sponsorship, the corporation may provide key executives to give advice and counsel or a team of 100 or more volunteers to manage the beverage booths, games, or other aspects of the event. A good source for volunteer leadership through corporations is the office of public affairs, public relations, or human resources. Toni McMahon, former executive director of the Arts Council of Fairfax County and producer of the International Children's Festival, goes right to the top. "I start with the chief executive officer. If I can get this person to buy into the event, others will surely follow," McMahon says. Her track record speaks for itself, with literally dozens of major corporations providing hundreds of volunteers for this annual event.

Other sources for volunteers are civic and fraternal organizations. Part of the mission of these organizations is community service, so they will be receptive to your needs. A related organization is that of schools, both public and private. In many school districts across the United States, high school students are required to complete a minimum number of community service hours in order to graduate. And do not overlook colleges and universities. Many institutions of higher learning have dozens of student organizations that also have a service mission and may be willing to participate in your event.

Social consumer generated media such as Facebook, Twitter, and MySpace has become critical to the recruitment process. Encourage your current employees and family as well as friends to post on these sites about opportunities to work with your event. These sites now reach a wide range of diverse stakeholders whose talents may be well used for your upcoming event.

The key to attracting these groups is the WIFM ("What's in it for me?") principle. When you contact these organizations, learn a little bit about their needs and then use the objectives of your event to help them fulfill their needs. The service aspect is a natural. Ron Thomas, former CEO of the Tennessee Walking Horse National Celebration, coordinated dozens of community organizations, such as the Kiwanis Club, who provide concessions for his equestrian events. Their activity is the major fund-raising aspect of the organization each year. Jeff Parks, president of ArtsQuest, the producer of the Bethlehem, Pennsylvania, award-winning MusikFest, also works with numerous community groups to produce everything from good and beverage stands to maintaining the porta-johns and, in turn, each group raises thousands of dollars to support the good work for their not-for-profit organization. These groups know exactly what's in it for them: cash. This cash enables them to do good work all year long. Determine what's in it for them and you will quickly find volunteers standing in line to help your event succeed.

Training

All volunteers must be trained. This training need not be time-consuming, but it must be comprehensive. One way to reduce the amount of time required is to publish a handbook for volunteers that summarizes event policies and procedures. Training may take the form of a social gathering, such as an orientation, or it can be formalized instruction in the field at the actual event site. It does not matter how you deliver this training, as every group of volunteers will require a different method in order to help them learn. However, what is important is that you test for mastery to make certain that they are learning and applying the skills you are imparting. Testing for mastery can be done through a written exam, observation, or a combination of both.

Coordination

The on-site management of volunteers entails coordinating their job performance to ensure that you are accomplishing the goals of the events. Depending on the skill level of the volunteers, you must assign team leaders or supervisors in sufficient number to oversee their performance. Remember that the coordination of volunteers involves coaching and mentoring. Make certain that your team leaders or supervisors are skilled in these areas.

Rewarding Excellent, High-Quality Performance

Don't wait until the end of the event to say "thank you." Some organizations publish volunteer newsletters; others host holiday parties to thank the volunteers for their help during the annual summer festival. Giving volunteers early, frequent, and constant recognition is a critical component in developing a strong and loyal volunteer team. You may wish to create an annual contest for Volunteer of the Year or some such recognition to encourage good-natured competition among your team members. Make certain that you carefully research with your volunteers how to effectively recognize and reward their service to the event.

Contract Temporary Employees

You may incorporate cost-efficient human resource management with cost control by contracting temporary employees for peak seasons. This will allow you to keep in place only those employees whom you need all year long. This will also help you to retain your permanent staff longer, since you will be in a better position to extend your resources to a smaller number of permanent staff. The biggest downside of this strategy is the challenge of attracting qualified personnel for short-term assignments. You can minimize the risk of having to deal with unprofessional behavior by hiring hospitality and event students from your local colleges and universities or by establishing long-term trusting relationships with a specialized staffing agency. Your collaboration with local schools can be based on offering shorter- and longer-term professional internships. Such programs can also be helpful for screening your potential future employees.

One of the scarcest resources within any event organization is time. In fact, some event leaders describe their time as their only real resource. Therefore, it is important that every event leader become a master of time management.

Careers in Special Events

The highly recommended companion book to the sixth edition of *Special Events* is the first comprehensive guide to careers in special events by Gene Columbus. Gene served in a wide variety of managerial positions for Walt Disney World for nearly 40 years. During this time period, he was instrumental in interviewing, hiring, coaching, and mentoring thousands of event planners and professionals in other fields. His experience, expertise, advice, and wise counsel is priceless, and I recommend that you review this book for more information about your own human resource development and career development.

Time Management

Your return on your event investment is in direct proportion to your ability to manage your time efficiently and meet various deadlines. This is so important that it bears further explanation. If you have only 8 hours to produce an event that normally requires 12 or more hours, you can either lose money or make money by how you plan and use the available time. For example, you may ask yourself what resources can be consolidated, what meetings combined, and what tasks delegated to allow you to remain focused on your 8-hour deadline. You can hire extra labor, purchase additional resources, schedule more meetings, and try to handle all the details yourself. The choice is yours.

These principles of time management are first applied in your daily life. How you spend your time performing everyday activities directly influences how you achieve your goals during your Event Leadership career. The ability to manage your time does not decrease as the number of assignments and tasks that you are involved in increases. The opposite is true. The busier you get and the more things you have planned, the more efficient you are in your time management and the more projects you manage to complete. It simply proves the famous Parkinson rule, which states that "a task can be accomplished within the amount of time assigned for its accomplishment"; getting a time extension on a project would normally push back the time of its accomplishment. Although in many situations this rule is true, you should, however, be careful and not overestimate your capacity. Always remember that it is better to underpromise event expectations and overdeliver final event perceptions.

Organizational Chart

Although not all Event Leadership organizations have their organizational charts in document form, all organizations have an internal structure that determines important things such as promotion and growth and that simply regulates everyday operations. Even if you have never seen an organizational chart, you know to whom you report, who reports to you, and at what level of responsibility and authority you are at a certain point in time.

However, it is important to be able to evaluate organizational charts from the employer and employee standpoints. Figure 4.3 represents a typical "flat" organizational structure with little opportunity for growth and significant power in two managers' hands. Although these structures exist, it is important to realize that employee retention under this structure is likely to be low, since most people would like to see a potential for growth and promotion within their organization. If they do not find it, they will soon start looking for other opportunities elsewhere. The few managers in such organizations share high power and probably will keep their positions for a lengthy time period.

In some cases, the organization structure cannot be changed; therefore, you may develop loyalty in your employees by creating incentive programs, improving the work environment, and increasing compensation. Figure 4.4 represents a more dynamic and complex organizational structure that offers its employees better growth potential, higher titles, and more focused work assignments. In this kind of organization, you can offer your employees cross-training opportunities that will add to their professional growth. You can clearly see identifiable departments, which will make it easier to form teams.

Less frequently, you can find other types of organization structures (see Figures 4.5 and 4.6). For example, some organizations have one subordinate reporting to three supervisors. This kind of situation rarely works out successfully and often leads to frustration

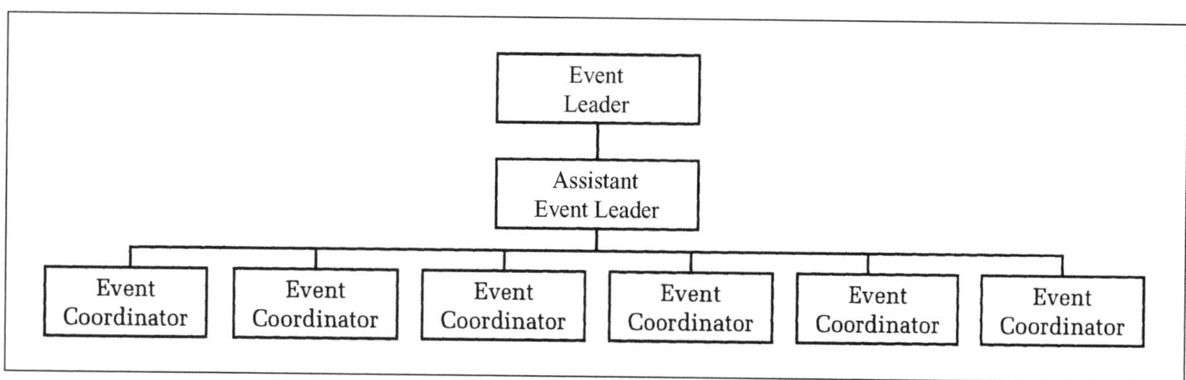

Figure 4.3 Flat Traditional Organizational Structure

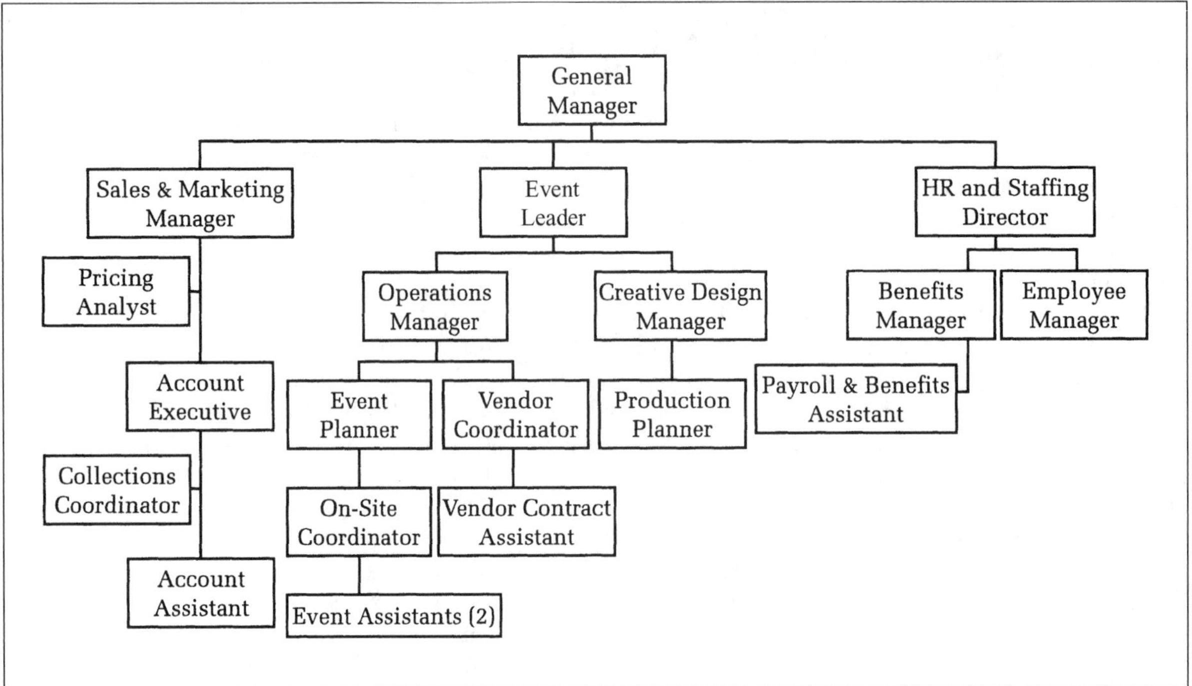

Figure 4.4 Dynamic Organizational Structure

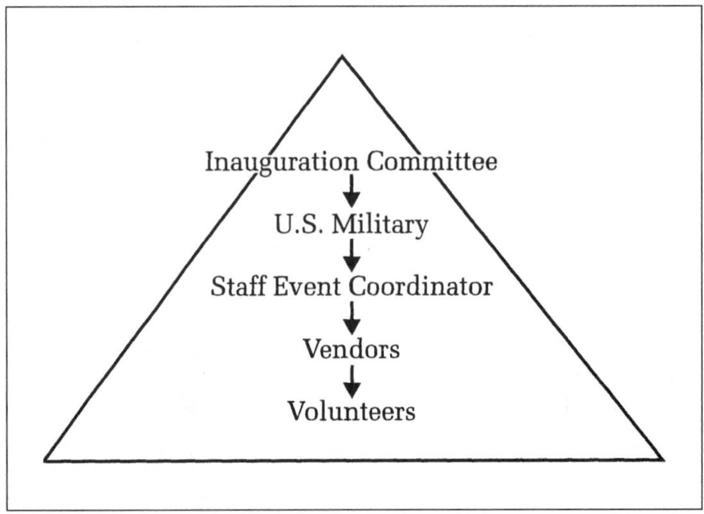

Figure 4.5 Top-Down Organization

Figure 4.6 Bottom-Up Organization

Baby Boomers	Generation Y
Compensation (salary and benefits)	The values of the organization are aligned with those of the worker
Title (position name)	Flexible hours
Promotion opportunities	Travel opportunities Education Compensation Career advancement

Figure 4.7 Motivations for Special Event Human Resources

for both employee and manager. Many small event organizations run into difficulties when they hire very few people to complete a vast variety of tasks due to limited financial resources. If the relationship is built on trust and mutual cooperation, such alliances can be beneficial for either party for a limited period of time. However, when the company gains more business, the situation needs to be changed. If an employee is overscheduled with work and is not physically able to complete it due to the lack of help, this employee will probably quit and look for another job. You have to remember that valuing your employees, investing in their development, and building their loyalty will be more financially rewarding to you in the long run than saving money on employee incentives and generating extra costs for recruiting and training.

Although the baby boomers were primarily motivated by compensation packages, generation Y employees are motivated by different incentives. Figure 4.7 demonstrate the similarities and vast differences in motivation between the baby boomers and generation Y.

As Figure 4.7 demonstrates, the motivations for the generation Y worker are vastly more complex than the baby boomers. It is likely you will be supervising both baby boomers and generation Y so it is important to understand the motivations of both types of workers so that you may address these issues through recruitment and meet their expectations to Insure retention. For further Information about generation Y visit www.generationwhy.com.

Developing Policies, Procedures, and Practices

The best organizational chart will not completely communicate to your stakeholders the precise actions they should take in specific situations before, during, and following the event. This is why it is important that you carefully develop policies, procedures, and practices that reflect the culture of your event organization.

Everyone benefits from well-written policies and procedures. First, the internal stakeholders benefit from having a clear process through which to make decisions. Second, the external stakeholders benefit from using a tool to help them understand the organization and the decision-making process of the event team. Finally, the guests themselves benefit. Although they may never see a copy of the policies and procedures, in the event of a life-threatening emergency, thanks to this document, lives may be saved.

This document is used in a variety of ways. It may be given to all full-time staff and volunteers as a reference tool. It may be distributed to members of the board of directors to guide the development of future policies. Most important, it may be used by the Event Leader to implement the board's policies through carefully developed procedures.

Policies are conceived and approved by the sponsoring organization's trustees. Typically, the trustees are the owners of the event, such as a private businessperson, a corporate board of directors, or the trustees of a not-for-profit group. The policies that are developed and approved reflect the vision and mission of the organization as well as comply with local, state, provincial, and federal laws.

Procedures are the implementation tactics for policy. Policy may be broad, overarching rules of conduct, whereas procedures are the regulations that administrators or Event Leaders use to implement policy. Both policies and procedures are essential to produce and sustain successful events.

Many events have well-crafted policies and procedures that can serve as a model for an organization. Contact another event organization of similar size and scope, and ask it to share a copy of its policies and procedures. In addition, ask the company how it most effectively communicates these policies and procedures to its stakeholders.

Carefully review your vision and mission statement, and use your event strategic plan as a litmus test for every policy and procedure you create. Appoint experts in a variety of event fields, including volunteer coordination, risk management, sponsorship, and others to help you review and create the final draft of your policies and procedures.

Convene a focus group composed of typical event stakeholders to make certain that what you have written can be implemented easily and effectively. Next, survey a wider group to sample their opinions. This group should include external stakeholders, such as government, police, fire, and other officials.

Make certain that your policies and procedures are fully in compliance with local, state, provincial, and federal laws. Retain an attorney to review your document to ensure compliance. Your document may be beautifully written, but unless it is in full compliance with all laws, it will be of no value.

Finally, regularly evaluate and revise your policies and procedures. Laws change, events mature, and other changes require that your policies, procedures, and practices document be revisited annually to look for gaps and provide updates to close these gaps. One example of this is the massive revisions that were required after the implementation of the U.S. Americans with Disabilities Act. A typical event policy and procedure can be outlined as follows:

- I. Media conferences. Media conferences will be held prior to the annual event and at other times as required. (Policy)
  - A. The Event Manager will schedule the media conference with staff. (Procedure)
    - 1. The public relations coordinator will implement the media conference. (Practice)
  - B. Participants will include but not be limited to credentialed members of the media, members of the board of trustees, and invited guests.
    - 1. The public relations coordinator will issue these credentials.
  - C. The chair of the board of trustees will serve as the official spokesperson for the event organization at all media conferences. In the absence of the chair, the Event Leader will serve in this position.
    - 1. The official spokesperson will prepare in advance copies of his or her written remarks and distribute the copies for comment to the board.
    - 2. An audio recording will be made of each media conference.
    - 3. The public relations coordinator will be responsible for recording the media conference and providing a written transcription.

Event Leaders are only as effective as the teams that support them. By creating a culture of professionalism, quality, and yes, fun, you will not only educate and inform but even occasionally inspire your event team to exceed the expectations of their guests. Two examples of successful Event Leaders who have led their teams to continually exceed expectations and positively transform their organizations at the same time follow.

Career-Advancement Connections

Corporate Social Responsibility Connection

Identify ways in which you may demonstrate Corporate Social Responsibility in your recruitment and training of staff and volunteers. Does your recruitment plan include identifying individuals in marginalized communities to apply for your positions? Does your training program include cultural sensitivity, ecological sustainability, and does it promote inclusion? Does your organization have a *first promote from within* strategy? Look into the corporate soul of your special events organization and ask yourself and your colleagues, are we promoting corporate social responsibility through our most important resource, the people who represent us to the world?

Global Connection

Appoint people from different cultural and ethnic backgrounds who will contribute to the success of your event. You can learn more about other national traditions and how to incorporate them into your theme by researching the Center for Popular Culture at Bowling Green State University (www.bgsu.edu/departments/popc/center.html). However, diversity also presents potential challenges, and you should encourage training, orientation, and other employee assistance to support mutual respect and understanding.

Technology Connection

- As technology becomes more affordable, one of the growing trends is to use tele- and videoconferencing for group projects and team-building activities. In many cases, this helps to save money on travel expenses and improve
- productivity. One excellent (and free) online resource for this form of communication is Skype (www.skype.com).
- Use the Internet to improve communications among all stakeholders through real-time online conversations.
- Maintain the vision of your event by designing a Web site for your event staff and volunteers that is password-protected.
- Provide your staff and volunteers with a downloadable screen saver of your event logo to remind them constantly of the mission, vision, goals, and objectives that you share as an event organization.

Resource Connection

- Use the Microsoft Organization Chart to practice constructing a top-down or bottom-up event organization chart.

- Visit the American Society for Training and Development (ASTD) Web site (www.astd.org) for additional resources.

Learning Connection

- Draft an organizational chart of your event organization or another event organization with which you are familiar. Evaluate this chart from a long-term perspective, and answer these four questions:
    1. Based on this chart, what are the educational, promotional, and growth opportunities for employees?
    2. How can this chart be modified to increase employee retention?
    3. What kind of cross-training programs can be incorporated in the organization to make employees more valuable and at the same time create additional learning opportunities for them?
    4. Based on the chart, what teams can be formed within the organization?
- Improve your personal leadership skills by training and actual practice offered through organizations such as the International Special Events Society (www.ises.com), Meeting Professionals International (www.mpiweb.org), and Professional Convention Management Association (www.pcma.org).
- Complete these activities to advance your growth in the area of Event Leadership:
    1. What are the five most important qualities of twenty-first-century Event Leadership leaders?
    2. How do these qualities differ from those in other fields, such as politics, education, and others?
    3. What are the best methods for improving communications among event stakeholders?
    4. Use a Microsoft Word organizational chart to construct an organizational chart for your event. What is the "best fit" for the Event Leader within the organizational chart?
    5. Analyze and discuss this case study by incorporating the principles included in this chapter: A small-event organization has an annual music festival, and each year for the past five years the number of volunteers has decreased. This decrease can be attributed to a perception by potential volunteers that the organization is too exclusive and does not really value new ideas and opinions. How will you increase the number of volunteers for the next festival without seriously jeopardizing the relationship that you have with other volunteers who have been with the organization for many years?
    6. Write a one-page description of the type of leader you believe your staff and volunteers perceive you to be, and then describe the type of leader you can become with proper training and practice (experience).social responsibility through each event they produce."

The Pioneer: Dianne Budion-Devitt, CMP, President, Dianne Devitt presents!, Adjunct Professor of Special Events, New York University, New York, New York

Dianne Budion-Devitt is a visionary and inspiring educator at New York University and Big Apple Hall Award Winner whose university students greatly benefit from her extensive experience in the meetings and events industry. She states, "In 1984, we planned events without realizing at the time we were building a business. As a theater graduate in design and developmental drama, I was looking for something that combined both business and theatre with a creative component that would ultimately positively affect people's lives, and that became events."

She sees events and meetings as opportunities to identify a clear objective and develop a vision and then produce an experience that is brought to life through the program. She further states that "The fulfillment of the creative process, enthusiasm, and satisfaction to witness emotional change continues to this day to fill my passion for the industry."

Although Dianne has had many mentors, her first were her mother and father. "They encouraged my creative thinking," she says. Her parents also taught her how to fix, take anything and make something of it. Later, her first boss, Richard Butler, encouraged her to go to college. While a student at Hunter College, her early mentors were CUNY professors, specifically Patricia Sternberg. Sternberg gave her a budget of US$300 to design and build 30 costumes for a show. Dianne recalls that "Although she had never seen my sketches, she had faith in my ability and that gave me greater confidence."

When considering the significant changes that have occurred in the industry since Dianne first began her career she states, "What existed? We were the human resources and that was it. She laughs and says, "Our technology was a pencil, budgets were designed to include us as creators, we did it all. I remember my boss once admonishing us for using rush overnight delivery because a client wanted things too fast. When faxes and computers first appeared in our offices, six people shared one machine!"

However, today, according to Dianne, things are markedly different. She is enthusiastic about the opportunities for young people in the field today. "Design is so exciting today and will continue in its evolution, always. As I learned, there are no new ideas, just new interpretations of old concepts. With today's choices and the specialization from candy bon-bons to balloons to ballroom dancers, the designer has unlimited choices in her toolbox to choose which applications work best to create a specific environment or enhance an existing one. The technological advancements with computer effects and lighting are taking us to another dimension of the live experience. There are no boundaries to the vision, and the choices come in all budget levels to the talented professional. I grew up in a time where 'greening' was part of life. We were always conscious of waste, excess and how to make more of less. Because we collectively have grown and events and meetings involve large groups of people at once, our industry has (and is taking) the opportunity to be a leader in environmental issues."

These opportunities have arisen, according to Dianne, because of a new awareness of the power of the meeting and event to positively affect business. She believes, "As more and more universities offer courses in meeting and event management and cross train between business schools and the industry, we will continue to grow with the awareness of the event and meeting as a communication tool. Educating the next generation with the tools needed to work as a communication specialist did not exist 20 years ago and will continue to mature as the correlation and relationship to advertising and public relations becomes more and more evident."

Finally, Dianne is extremely optimistic about the future of the meetings and events industry worldwide.

Dianne see positive changes ahead: "Future event professionals will become more specialized in their respective fields as the buyer, the meeting professionals mature in their roles as account executives. Like advertising, there will be outsourced agencies for planning and strategy and separate agencies specializing in creative application. These exist today in some meeting production companies but the integration of all disciplines (meetings/events/production) will continue to develop where meeting *design* becomes the recognizable force behind the message and purpose of the event." She is confident of these changes and further states that "I know this will happen based on continuing involvement with education, trade associations, and having a cross-discipline understanding of the various niches in the industry. As other communication fields matured (i.e, advertising and public relations), new services were generated. Event professionals have developed independently and are recognized as a service where, not too long ago, there wasn't a designation or recognition from the government."

When asked what is the best advice she has received during her distinguished career, she quotes the Pulitzer prize–winning author Maya Angelou, who wrote, "People will forget what you said. People will forget what you did. But people will never forget how you made them feel."

Dianne Budion-Devitt's remarkable career is a sterling role model for the next generation of Event Leaders as she exemplifies the importance of training, experience, and mentoring future leaders through her teaching at New York University. She reminds us, "Regardless of how sensational a venue, décor and design are, or how well executed an event is, the response to the smallest surprise detail that emotes a personal connection or response is the true responsibility of the event and the event professional. We bring visions to life; let people be the inspiration to create these visions. Regardless of the size of the budget, the location, a given set of circumstances, creating an experience, an environment, an emotional response is all about the people involved and that above all, we come together because we matter to each other."

The Protégé: Liz Glover Wilson, CSEP, Event Planner and Producer / VP Corporate Events, Innovative Creative Events / iStar Financial

Rather than choose a career, according to Liz Glover Wilson, past president of the New York City chapter of the International Special Events Society, the profession of special events, chose her. Her aspiration was originally fashion, believe it or not, and she had gone to fashion school in New York city to pursue that career path. However, after one short year, she became somewhat disappointed in that "world" and started to rethink her career route. She then made the decision to go find a "stable" job as an assistant. She never in her wildest dreams imagined that her stable job would provide the opportunity to launch into the creative and innovative world of events.

Liz is an artist, and she says, "Event planning gave me the forum in which to exercise my creativity and paint a picture. As a communicator, the event industry was a place in which I could use my voice to inspire, create, and move mountains. As a visionary, the special events world gave me the ability to develop memorable experiences. As a business-minded person, it gave me the understanding of the power of event marketing. Finally, as a philanthropic spirit, event production presented itself as a powerful tool to educate the world on important matters."

According to Liz, one of her most incredible mentors is Dianne Budion-Devitt. She recalls, "When I was very new to the industry, I had a lot of instinct, strong instinct for that matter, but no real guidance and no one to validate my instinct or guide me in the right direction. I signed up for a course at New York University and met Dianne Budion-Devitt. Her dedication to educating newcomers like me was remarkable. Here was the amazingly talented woman who ran her own busy event company, and yet she took the time to teach us the basics, to push us to limits and to challenge us. It was in her class that I was able to fine-tune my instinct and launch my passion for special events."

When choosing a professional mentor, Liz advises that it is important to find the right match. She says, "I most admire those who truly influence; the hardworking, the educators, and those who are willing to go the extra mile for their profession. I never based my selection on popularity alone, but instead always watched for those who were really making it happen. I admire those who work tirelessly to change policy or fight for the rights of our industry. I admire those who take their job seriously, respect other, respect our industry, and are ethical in their business practice."

During her career she has seen many changes, including the very real financial crisis now affecting New York and the rest of the world. As a result of the economic recession she sees an immediate impact on the special events industry as many companies and government agencies are trying to do away with event marketing techniques as they are viewing them as extraneous. With this threat of extinction looming, she is witnessing the resilience of the events industry as its members are rising up, and fighting for the importance of event products and services. With technology advancements on the rise, the events industry is learning to utilize tools such as Facebook, webcasts, and other viral marketing techniques to bring them together as an industry. Liz says, "I believe this time of struggle is going to push us to the next level of refinement as an industry. I do believe that it will result in tighter policies, higher ethics, stronger business practices and a push for more education options. I believe that we will gain more respect as an industry and a discipline and be able to implement more accredited coursework throughout the U.S. and abroad. The next ten years will be tough in some ways, but ultimately will be the exercise we needed to make us stronger than ever."

Despite the tough economic times, Liz is hopeful about the future. She remembers that her mother always described her as a woman who, if you wanted her to do something, just tell her she cannot. Liz passionately states that "I believe that the special events industry is being told no right now. We are being told no by the government. We are being told no by the media. It is the no that is pushing us to say yes and fight for what we believe is the true quality of what we do and offer. This will give us the strength to make the changes we need to make and grow."

As Liz envisions the future of her industry, she is confident about the days ahead. "I will be moving through a more educated, technically savvy special event industry. As technical aspects become more sophisticated, we will see production move to the next level. Equally, I believe there will be a push for some "back to the basics" techniques as a result of our current recession, which has happened because of excess. I also believe that as a result of the current times, there will be many collaborative projects that will bloom into some of the most influential event industry resources in the next ten years. I am excited by what lies ahead of us."

She believes the events industry will grow stronger but not necessarily larger. In fact, she believes it needs refinement or a "makeover," as the events marketplace has become saturated with too many unqualified candidates. Liz states, "We need to have a better validation system for newcomers and a stronger offering for education and certification. In the future, I believe that there should be certain qualifications required to start a special events company and one unified code of ethics and practices by which all adhere to. We are a multi-billion dollar industry and should represent ourselves as such."

She says that the best single piece of advice she has received during her career is, "Stay true to yourself!" To be a leader and innovator in this industry, she believes you need to respect others and be true to yourself. It is a fast-paced industry, with lots of creative energy flowing, and if you do not hold on to your own identity, it is easy to get caught up in a journey that is not truly yours.

Liz Glover Wilson exemplifies the leadership that the modern special events industry must identify to ensure a successful future. Her hopes for the future are strong but she is also realistic about the present and the need to continually improve professional practice. Similar to her mentor, Liz is using her creativity and talent for event design to not only create beautiful and memorable events but, perhaps even more importantly, to redesign the events industry in a more positive and sustainable manner for those who will then follow her into what will certainly be a even more exciting future.

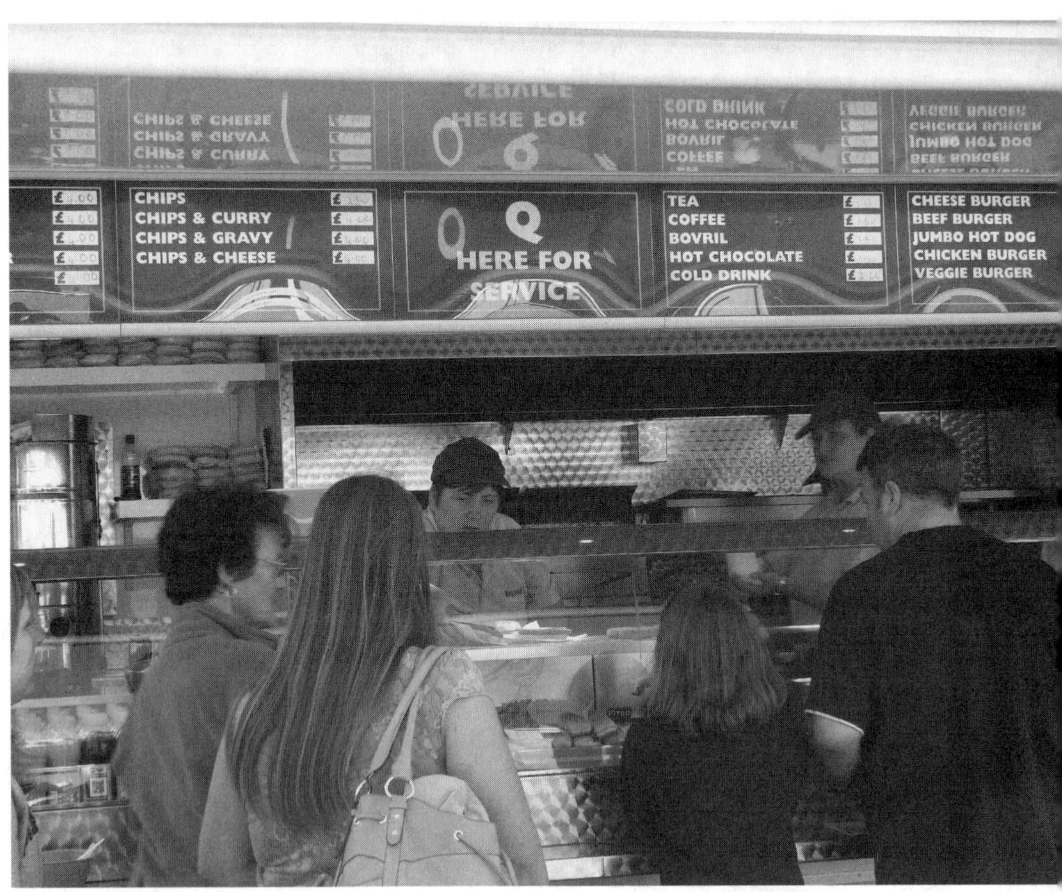

The Gathering 2009 food stall generates significant financial income for this event.

CHAPTER 5

Financial Administration

In this chapter you will learn how to:

- Understand basic Event Leadership financial and accounting terminology
- Maintain event financial records
- Understand and interpret the event balance sheet and income statement
- Calculate the break-even point and profit margin for your event
- Forecast projected revenues and expenses for your event
- Estimate reliable budget goals for your event
- Identify sustainable funding for your event
- Manage your event during turbulent economic times
- Plan and allocate your event budget

The most common deficiency I have identified in many event planners relates to the area of financial management. Event planners by nature rely on the right side of the brain and often ignore the important logical thinking abilities that help ensure long-term success. Whether you use the services of a professional bookkeeper and/or accountant or not, knowledge of financial management is essential to the practice of modern event planning. This knowledge is not difficult to master. With modern software systems, it is actually simple and, many say, fun to practice. Whether you enjoy financial management is not the issue. Few people enjoy studying for and taking their driver's license exams. However, can you imagine what the streets would be like without this baseline of knowledge? Accidents, death, and destruction everywhere might result from this lack of rigor. Financial ignorance can just as easily wreck a creative, successful event planning business and destroy your reputation, as well as have serious legal ramifications. This chapter is essential if you are planning not only to make money but to keep it. Additionally, as your business ages along with you, this chapter will help you learn how to work a little less and earn a little more.

Budgeting

The budget represents an action plan that each successful event plan must carefully develop. Budget preparation is probably the most challenging part of financial management since the entire preparation is usually based on limited information or assumptions. To complete the budget preparation, you should come up with estimates based on assumptions.

The event budget is the most important tool you will use to manage the financial decisions within your event planning business. Each event represents a separate budget. All individual budgets are combined into an annual budget. Your daily business operations also require an annual budget to reflect your earnings and expenses. Event planners should use the expression "staying within the budget" every day and for every project.

Each budget represents the financial philosophy of the event. Since different events are designed for different purposes, they may fall into one of three categories:

1. *Profit-oriented events.* In this type of event, revenue exceeds expenses. Typical examples are events produced by corporations for the purpose of generating new sales.
2. *Break-even events.* In this type of event, revenue is equal to expense. A good example is an association conference. In this case, event professionals should budget the event, keeping the break-even assumption in mind. Admission fees should be calculated at the rate that will cover all expenses and break even.
3. *Loss leaders or hosted events.* These events are designed from the very beginning to lose money. Good examples of such events are university graduations or governmental celebrations. These events usually are organized for the purpose of promoting a cause or agenda and not designed to break even or generate a profit.

If your event is a charitable endeavor, your financial philosophy will be markedly different from that of a commercial venture. First, determine what is the financial philosophy of your event before you begin the budget process. A budget represents the income and expenses of your organization or the individual event. An event budget is based on five factors:

1. Marketing projections and estimates
2. The general history of previous identical or similar events
3. The general economy and your forecast for the future

4. The net profit or excess you reasonably believe you can expect with the resources available (return on investment)
5. The type of financing that you choose to use to finance your event (borrowed funds, prepayments, existing funds)

Financial History

The best financial history is that which occurs over a three-year period. In some cases, it is not possible to construct a precise history, and the event planner must rely on estimates or on what is known at the time the budget is prepared. In still other cases, the event planner will have to rely on events of similar size and scope to develop the budget because his or her event is a first-time venture and no history exists. Not only is it important to base your budget on history, it is equally important that you develop controls to begin collecting financial data on the event budget you are currently preparing. These data will become the next event's historic information and help you construct a better budget.

The longer you are in the planned events industry, the more accurate your estimates will be. A good technique used for developing income projections is high–low. The logic is that an Event Leader compares two scenarios: the best and the worst. Next, the Event Leader decides whether the losses that may occur under the worst-case scenario are bearable. If so, the project is accepted. If not, the project is refused. This method is especially beneficial to small and mid-size planned events businesses that operate under financial constraints and do not have much margin for error.

General Economy

As 2009 closed, the world economy was chaotic, unpredictable, in recession and, some economists would add, on the verge of depression. You, however, must not be a victim of these predictions. Instead, you must use general economic data to assist you with the development of your budget. Reams of secondary data are available about the local, state, and national economy from offices of economic development as well as the U.S. Department of Commerce. No event takes place in a vacuum. Whether you are managing the International Special Olympics in New Haven, Connecticut, or the local food and wine festival, your event's success will be affected by the general economy. Indicators of strong economic health usually include low unemployment, a steady rate of inflation, and healthy retail sales. Other indicators include new home building activity, new industry, and capital investments by local, state, or federal government. Before locking in your final budget, consult with an economist from a local college or university, a representative from the local office of economic development, or the editor of the business section of your local newspaper and ask for his or her opinion on the health of the economy.

Reasonable Projected Income

The Greek word *logos* (or logic) means to "act reasonably." A budget based on certain logical assumptions of projections of income is one that is within reason. To logically project revenue based on the resources available, you must consider market research as well as a general knowledge of the economy. For example, if your city festival is being held this year on the local payday from the area's largest industry, does that mean you can reasonably expect that spending will be increased for your event? The only way to test this theory is with research. You may wish to contact other events of similar size and scope and evaluate their experience with similar circumstances. Furthermore, you may wish to survey some of the workers to determine if they are more likely to attend the event this year and, if so, if they will be inclined to increase their spending due to the coincidence of their payday and the event date. Making reasonable assumptions about projected revenue is one of the most important decisions that you must handle as you begin the budgeting process. Gather all the facts, seek objective opinions and counsel, and then conservatively project the revenue you hope to achieve.

Sustainable Funding

Kuan-wen Lin, MBA student at Queen Margaret University, studied the budgets and financial reports of the major festivals in Edinburgh, Scotland, over a ten-year period. His study found there was no correlation between public funding for events and a successful financial outcome for the organization. Rather, his study found that the more mature the event, the more likely the financial outcome would be successful. Using Mr. Lin's study as a base, Dr. Rebecca Finkel and I interviewed public leaders in both Glasgow and Edinburgh, Scotland, to identify potential alternative sustainable funding for their cultural events including festivals. The majority of persons we interviewed supported voluntary donations from individuals at the time of ticket purchase (such as an optional £1.00 per ticket) or an optional donation at the time of purchase of a product or service that directly benefits from the cultural event (restaurant meal, hotel room night or other business whose income may be somewhat derived from the events). The public officials stated that redirecting the tax that is already collected from these businesses would not be as successful.

Furthermore, the overall reaction by most officials in both Glasgow and Edinburgh was that future public funding for the cultural sector will be less than in the past. It will also be erratic as it will reflect the current turbulence in the general economy. Therefore, finding alternative funding is critically important. Sustainable funding for your events should come from a variety of streams including the public purse, corporate sponsorship, philanthropy, and earned income from ticket sales, merchandise, food and beverage, and other sources. The greater the diversity of your funding the less likely you will be strapped for cash if one of your streams dries up.

Typical Income Categories

Due to the wide range of events represented by the subfields within the Event Leadership profession, it is difficult to list categorize every type of income. However, there are some general items that most budgets include:

- Advertising revenues
- Concession sales

- Donations
- Exhibit or exposition booth rental fees
- Gifts in kind (actual fair market financial value)
- Grants and contracts
- Interest income from investments
- Merchandise sales
- Registration fees
- Special events ticket sales
- Sponsorship fees
- Vendor commissions (hotels)

Expenses

When preparing your budget, the first thing you will note under the expense category is how many more items are listed as compared to income. My late father-in-law, a successful businessman, once told me, "The income comes in through one or two doors, but the expenses can leak out of many doors." In the strange economic times of the mid-1990s, organizations placed greater emphasis on monitoring expenses because it was easier to control costs than to project revenue. My father-in-law also reminded me that Benjamin Franklin observed some 200 years ago, "A penny saved is a penny earned." Developing solid, predictable expense categories is critical to sound financial management. These expense items often come from historical data or comparing your event to others of similar size and scope. The actual amount budgeted for each expense line item is what you and your advisors believe to be reasonable based on the information known at the time the budget is prepared. Therefore, the more you know, the more precisely you can budget for expenses. This is another reason why record keeping is so vital to the success of your financial management operations. The general expense categories for most events are:

- Accounting
- Advertising
- Advertising specialties
- Audiovisual equipment rental
- Audiovisual labor
- Automobile mileage reimbursements
- Automobile rental
- Awards and recognition
- Bonds
- Brochure and other collateral design
- Brochure and other collateral mailing
- Brochure and other collateral mechanical preparation
- Brochure and other collateral printing
- Complimentary registrations or admission
- Consultants
- Corporate Social Responsibility (social, economic, environmental)

- Décor
- Ecological sustainability
- Entertainment
- Evaluations
- Food and beverage
- Gratuities
- Guest transportation
- Insurance
- Legal counsel
- Licenses
- Lighting equipment rental
- Lighting labor
- Local, state, provincial, and federal taxes
- Materials shipping/freight fees
- Miscellaneous or other
- Percentage of administrative overhead
- Permits
- Photocopying
- Photography
- Postage
- Proceedings editing, design, and printing
- Public relations
- Registration contract labor
- Registration materials
- Report preparation and publishing
- Research
- Risk management corrections
- Signs
- Site office furniture rental
- Site office supplies
- Site rental
- Site telephone expense
- Sound equipment rental
- Sound labor
- Speakers' fees and/or honoraria
- Speakers' travel
- Staff travel
- Taxes (federal, state, local)
- Videography
- Volunteer appreciation activities and gifts

Structuring Account Codes

Each income or expense item must have a corresponding account code. Accounts are those general budget categories where items of similar type and impact on the overall budget are grouped together for more efficient analysis. For example, in the administration category, these items would appear:

- Décor
- Insurance
- Site telephone expenses

Under the account category "staff/volunteers," these items would be grouped together:

- Staff accommodations
- Volunteer accommodations
- Volunteer appreciation activities and gifts

Each account code has a numerical listing to make it easy to find individual entries. The general categories start with the 100 series. For example, administration would be 100, marketing would be 500, and so on. Each item would have a separate sequential numerical listing:

100 Administrative
500 Marketing
501 Advertising
502 Advertising specialties
503 Brochure and other collateral design
504 Brochure and other collateral mechanical preparation
505 Brochure and other collateral mailing
506 Brochure and other collateral printing
507 Public relations

Finding and Supervising an Accountant

Contact your local chamber of commerce or local business association to obtain a referral for an accountant who may be familiar with event budgets or service businesses. Once you have prepared a draft budget, seek the counsel of the accountant to review your budget and help you with establishing the various line items and account codes. Your accountant will be able to interpret the tax codes for you to make certain that your accounts match the terms and requirements for the local, state, provincial, and federal tax authorities.

Make certain that you discuss billing and fees with your accountant. You may retain the accountant to handle specific operations or to coordinate all of your financial procedures. Obviously, the cost will fluctuate greatly based on the number of tasks you ask the accountant to perform. Using accounting software may help you reduce your costs and provide you with better, faster information.

Accounting Software

Since the invention of the spreadsheet program for computers, accounting has never been the same. Commercial software packages such as Quicken have allowed small-business owners to record their journal entries quickly, accurately, and cost-effectively. What once required many hours with a pencil and eraser has, thanks to modern computer science, been reduced to a fraction of the time. Microsoft Excel is also very useful in budgeting and creating financial projections. I encourage you to spend some time familiarizing yourself at least with basic functions of this software.

Although using commercial software is time-efficient, it does require certain additional safeguards. First, make certain you always back up your data on a disc and store this information in a safe, fireproof location. Next, regularly send a copy of your data to your accountant so that he or she can prepare your monthly, quarterly, and annual financial reports. Consult with your certified professional accountant to determine the best type of software to invest in because, to a large extent, you will be partners, and you should be using software that will allow you to communicate effectively on a regular basis.

Producing Profit

The financial purpose of every for-profit business is to produce a fair net profit. The term *profit* means the earnings over and above all expenses.

$$\text{Profit} = \text{Revenue} - \text{Expenses}$$

Not-for-profit organizations do not, for obvious reasons, use the term *profit*. Instead, they refer to this excess of income over expenses as *retained earnings*. In fact, the earnings are not retained for long, as the organizations are required by the tax code to reinvest the earnings in their business operations rather than distribute them to shareholders, as some for-profit businesses do.

Producing a fair net profit is challenging but possible for Event Leadership businesses. The challenge is that Event Leaders must work with a wide range of clients, and it is difficult to budget for each event carefully to ensure a net profit. There are too many variables to ensure that this happens every time. However, if the business is to remain healthy at year-end, the business activities must result in a net profit.

Although there is no average for net profit, let us consider, for the purposes of discussion, that your financial goal is to achieve an annual net profit of 15 percent. To do this, you must guard all fixed overhead expenses carefully. All expenses can be divided into two major categories: (1) fixed overhead expenses and (2) variable expenses. Although both of these categories are expenses, the methods you use to manage and control them are different. To understand how you can minimize your expenses, you should be able to make a distinction between these two categories.

Fixed Overhead Expenses

Fixed overhead expenses of an organization are those predictable items such as rent, salaries, insurance, telephone, and other standard operating expenses required to support the Event Leadership business. The better you are able to achieve a lower cost of sale, the greater net profit you will achieve. To lower your cost of operations, it is imperative that you try to reduce your fixed overhead expenses. Many Event Leadership firms have suffered great losses or have even gone out of business entirely because they tried to expand too rapidly. Expansion brings increased cost of sales, and increased cost of sales means that you must produce much greater income. As we discussed earlier, due to the volatility of the world economy, this is not always possible. Once you have cut your fixed overhead expenses to a level that allows you to maintain quality but at the same time produce a fair net profit, you must return your attention to variable, or direct, expenses.

Fixed expenses of an individual event do not depend on the number of participants. For example, rent is a fixed expense. Rent expense usually does not vary when the number of participants increases or decreases slightly. The expense of live music is similar. If an event planner contracts a local band to entertain guests, the cost of this entertainment is fixed. Variable costs are the costs that depend on the attendance (e.g., food and beverages). Food and beverage expenses for 100 people will be approximately twice as large as if only 50 people attend the event.

This example will help you to understand the difference. The event planner of a mid-size corporation has to budget expenses for a reception. He or she is not sure about the exact number of guests; however, the minimum and the maximum number of guests are known. The minimum number is 200 guests and the maximum is 400. The catering company has provided the Event Leader with its price quote of $25 per person for food and $15 per person for beverages. The event planner creates the expense calculation shown in Figure 5.1.

Variable Expenses

Variable expenses are more difficult to predict because often they relate to items that are purchased at the last minute from vendors, and the prices may fluctuate. Variable, or direct, expenses include audiovisual rentals and labor, registration materials, proceedings design and printing, and other items with a total cost that relies on the final number ordered and your ability to negotiate a fair price. Due to last-minute registrations and an increase in walk-up guests for a variety of events, it is extremely difficult to wait until the last minute to order certain items. Printing, as well as advance notice for audiovisual

Number of people	200	400	
Food $25 per person	$5,000	$10,000	Variable
Beverages $15 per person	3,000	6,000	Expenses
Rent expense	2,000	2,000	Fixed
Entertainment expense	1,000	1,000	Expenses
Total expenses	$11,000	$19,000	

Figure 5.1 Fixed and Variable Expenses

equipment rental and labor, requires a sufficient window of time to deliver a quality product. This means that your ability to use historical data to project the volume of items you will need or to order less with an option to obtain additional supplies rapidly will greatly help you reduce your variable or direct expenses. In addition, your ability to negotiate the best deal for your event organization will have tremendous impact on these items.

Net Profit versus Gross Profit

Event Leaders endeavor to produce a fair net profit. The difference between net profit and gross profit is the percentage of fixed overhead expenses that was dedicated to producing a specific event. Fixed overhead expenses dedicated to the individual event include a percentage of staff salaries and benefits, a percentage of the office expense, and other shared expenses. This percentage will fluctuate, but by using time sheets you can easily calculate the staff time directed to the event. The other expenses, such as rent, insurance, and telephone, may be given a percentage based on the time recorded from the time sheets.

Break-even Point

To understand the break-even calculation, you have to understand one more term: contributional margin, the difference between the revenue received from a single person and the variable costs incurred for one person. For example, if an Event Leadership company receives revenue of $50 per person but the total variable cost for one person is $40 ($25 food and $15 beverages), the contributional margin is $10 per person:

$$\text{Contributional margin} = \text{Revenue per person} - \text{Variable cost per person}$$

The final step to calculate the break-even point is to divide the total fixed costs by the contributional margin:

$$\text{Break-even point} = \frac{\text{Total fixed costs}}{\text{Contributional margin}}$$

For example, if the total fixed costs are $3,000 and the contributional margin is $10, the break-even point is 300 people:

$$300 = \frac{\$3{,}000}{\$10}$$

or

$$300 \times \$50 = \$15{,}000$$

If fewer than 300 people attend the event, it loses money. It turns profitable once the attendance exceeds 300 people. Therefore, the break-even point is achieved when you collect $15,000 in revenue. Figure 5.2 demonstrates the break-even analysis.

A street celebration in Singapore exemplifies the Asian cultural traditions that span over a millennia. Parades and festivals are held in public locations to unite their society through ceremony and ritual. ***Courtesy PhotoDisc, Inc.***

Event Solutions Hall of Fame member Doron Gazit, founder of Air Dimensional Design, has revolutionized design within the modern events industry. At this event, Gazit and his team have transformed a huge room within an art center into a magnificent kaleidoscopic environment through his unique sculptures. *Photo courtesy of Air Dimensional Design*

The entrance for The Gathering 2009, a major event for Scottish Homecoming 2009. The greeting is in both English and Gaelic to provide an authentic welcome for all guests.

Sports events such as this swimming race are attracting thousands of participants. They not only enjoy the health benefits and the spirit of competition, but also the communal feeling that comes from participating in an event that benefits others through raising funds for good causes.

The Asakusa market in Tokyo, Japan, dates back hundreds of years. It features the annual Sensoji Festival in May that attracts tens of thousands of participants who carry giant shrines throughout this festive location. ***Courtesy Corbis Digital Stock***

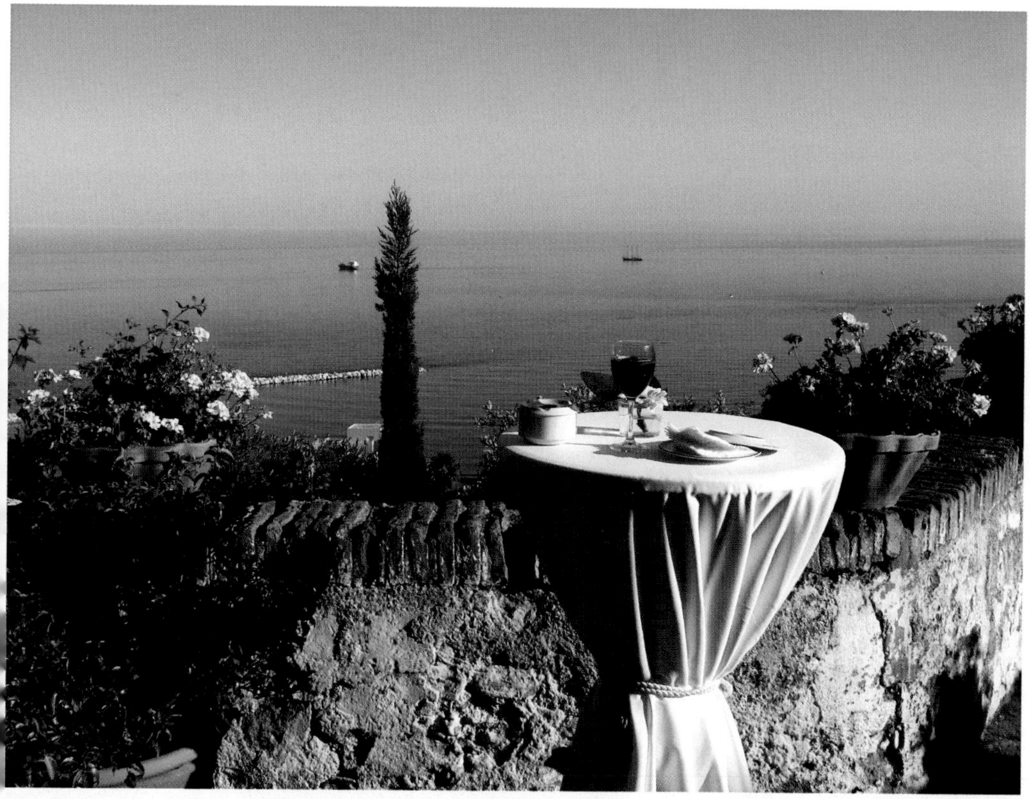

The International Congress and Convention Association held its annual marketing research conference in Malaga, Spain. This romantic castle served as the perfect venue for a warm and inviting welcome dinner.

Weddings are a major industry around the world as brides and grooms are older and have more disposable income to contribute to these important social milestones. This cake from a wedding in Frankfurt, Germany, provides one example of the lavishness of these celebrations.

Throughout the world, millions of people sing Robert Burns's nostalgic song *Auld Lang Syne* to celebrate times gone by and express their hope for better tomorrows. Some destinations, such as New York City and Edinburgh, Scotland, turn their annual New Year's celebrations into major hallmark events attracting hundreds of thousands of visitors.

Fear No Ice, a team of professional ice carvers, creates a chilly and exciting opening for the Event Solutions conference in Miami, Florida. Using contemporary music, dramatic lighting, and a cast of expert ice carving professionals, a set is created before the audience's eyes.

Two actors wearing colorful, hand-made masks, created earlier, entertain children at the SUNOCO Welcome America Festival in Philadelphia, Pennsylvania.

	Loss	Break-even	Profit
Number of people	290	300	310
Revenue:			
$50 per person	$14,500	$15,000	$15,500
Expenses:			
Variable expenses:			
Food $25 per person	7,250	7,500	7,750
Beverages $15 per person	4,350	4,500	4,650
Fixed expenses:			
Rent expense	2,000	2,000	2,000
Entertainment expense	1,000	1,000	1,000
Total expenses:	$14,600	$15,000	$15,400
Profit (revenue − expenses)	$(100)	$—	$100

Figure 5.2 Break-even Analysis

Cutting Costs

As an event planner, your ability to cut costs rapidly to ensure consistent profits is one that will serve you well throughout your career. To decide which costs may be cut without sacrificing the integrity of the entire event, you must begin with the budgeting process by prioritizing expenses. Seek counsel from your stakeholders and honestly determine what, in the worst-case scenario, they would like to preserve and what they could give up to ensure a profit. Although this is a difficult decision process, it is wise to make such decisions free from internal and external pressures during the final phases of the event planning process. Typically, these costs are associated with variable or direct expenses. Therefore, the expenditure is not made until later in the event planning process. Cutting your event's costs is one way to help improve your cash flow.

Ensuring Positive Event Cash Flow

It is not enough to just have profitable operations. Many event planning companies were unsuccessful because they were always out of cash. These companies showed profit on their books but had an empty checking account. This situation is called *insolvency*. The best way to avoid insolvency is to execute sound cash-flow management.

Cash flow is the liquidity that allows you to pay your bills, including salaries, in a timely manner. When this liquidity is gone, your reputation may not be far behind. To ensure a positive event cash flow, two measures are necessary. First, you must prearrange with your vendors payment terms and conditions that will allow you to collect revenues adequate to honor these obligations. Second, you must diligently collect those funds that are due and payable to you in a timely manner in order to meet your obligations to your vendors.

Payables are those financial accounts that you have established with vendors. These are funds that are due according to the agreements you have arranged with individual vendors. Receivables are those funds due to your event organization by a certain date. Aging receivables are simply those funds that were not collected at the time they were due. Five simple techniques for collecting Event Leadership receivables follow.

1. Log on your calendar the day the receivable is due.
2. Telephone early in the morning to ask when your payment will be processed.
3. If possible, arrange to pick it up.
4. If it is not possible to pick it up, offer to provide an overnight mail service.
5. Courteously but firmly request payment until it is received.

One of the challenges with the value of event planning services is that there is often rapid depreciation as soon as the curtain rises. Consider this scenario. Your client has invested $50,000 with your firm to produce a gala awards dinner. Midway through the dinner, the client's spouse notices a cigarette burn in the tablecloth. Later, he or she comments on "skimpy" floral arrangements. Finally, he or she complains loudly about the inferior music and food. Before long, the client locates you and wants to discuss the bill. Ironically, only three hours earlier, the client walked through the ballroom and event planning Leadership services and products are not usually experts in your profession. That is why they have retained you. Because the purchase of event planning services and products is sometimes an emotional decision, the buyer may easily be influenced by others. The only leverage you have as the professional provider of these services is to collect your full fee as soon as possible, because otherwise the value of your performance will deflate rapidly. As in medicine and other established professions, the old maxim "people only value what they pay for" is absolutely true in this profession.

Effective management of accounts receivable is only half of the equation needed for solid cash flow. The second half requires that you become knowledgeable about typical accounts-payable agreements and learn to negotiate for the best possible payment terms. The best policy is to collect cash as fast as possible but pay off your bills on the last day allowed by the contract.

Accounts Payable: Finding the Best Terms

When establishing relationships with vendors, it is important that you learn as much as possible about the size, scope, and nature of their business. You will want to know if they own or lease their equipment. You will also want to know when they may have periods of slow business. Their off-season can produce favorable terms and perhaps discounts for your event. You will also want to know if a vendor could benefit from exposure through your event. Some Event Leaders have a stringent rule about not letting vendors promote themselves directly to their clients. However, it is my belief that these hard-and-fast rules may prevent you from providing your client with the products and services your vendor may be able to offer. In one example, a video production company telephoned me after a major corporate event and asked permission to contact the corporate headquarters to provide services directly. Not only did I encourage the company to do so, I wrote letters to my client and others on the company's behalf. As a result of this courtesy and flexibility, this firm will work with me on price in the future for other clients whom I may serve. Therefore, beware the dangerous word *always,* as it may cause you to provide less service than possible.

The key to negotiating excellent terms with vendors is first to establish professional friendships and conduct business in an atmosphere of mutual respect. The more you know about your professional partners (vendors) and the more they know about you, the easier it is to do business. There are typical accounts-payable customs and traditions in the Event Leadership profession; however, your ability to make friends and provide assistance to your vendors will alter these customs to your benefit.

Typical Accounts-Payable Customs

One accounts-payable custom is for the vendor to require a deposit of 50 percent of the final contracted cost as a deposit and receive the full balance plus any additional agreed-upon charges immediately following the event. Entertainment vendors, especially those representing major celebrities, are even more stringent. They may require full payment in the form of a certified check prior to the first performance as a guarantee.

Another accounts-payable custom is for the vendor to require a small deposit (as low as 10 percent) and then invoice you for the balance due net 10 or 30 days after the event. Still another custom allows you to pay your balance on account. In this custom, typically you are a regular good customer of the vendor, and the company allows you to pay off the balance monthly or within a reasonable amount of time without interest, late charges, or other penalties. Sometimes vendors even provide small discounts if you pay off your balance faster than required. There is a special terminology for this situation. For example, if a vendor offers you a 3 percent discount if you pay off your balance within the first 10 days, you may hear this formula: "3/10, net 30." This means that if you pay off the balance within 10 days, you receive 3 percent off your total bill; otherwise, you have to pay the entire balance within the next 30 days.

The final custom is for the vendor to extend credit to your organization, allowing you to authorize purchases and be invoiced by the vendor at a later date. This is the best scenario, as you are able to negotiate credit terms well in advance. Although most accounts are due within 30 days of the date of the invoice, I have heard of some arrangements where the vendor will extend credit for 60 or even 90 days to maintain the account. It is up to you to negotiate the best possible terms.

Negotiating Accounts Payable

Always negotiate from a position of strength. Strength in the area of accounts payable means that you have collected as much information as possible about the vendor with whom you need to negotiate. The answers to six questions will enable you to negotiate favorable terms for your accounts payable:

1. How important is your business to this vendor?
2. During what time period is your business most needed?
3. Are your clients the types of organizations your vendor would like to do business with? How well funded/capitalized is your vendor?
4. How does your vendor market his or her services and products? How sophisticated are your vendor's business operations?
5. What are your vendor's standard and customary accounts-payable terms?
6. Most important, can you speak with other clients of this vendor to determine what types of terms they are receiving?

Once you have the answers to these questions, it is time to ask your vendor for more favorable terms. To do this, you will need to provide your vendor with documentation about your own business health. Testimonials from recent clients, a list of accounts receivable, and other financial data will also help you create a favorable impression. Once you have established your credibility with the vendor, ask for the most favorable terms. You might ask for credit and 90 days. The vendor may counter with 30 days, and you then agree on 60 days. Do not play hardball. Remember, this vendor will be servicing your clients, and maintaining their goodwill is of supreme importance. However, you have a responsibility to your event organization to negotiate the most favorable terms and must remain firm in your pursuit of what you believe to be a fair agreement.

Your vendor may ask for a trial period, after which he or she may extend better terms once you have demonstrated your ability to meet your obligations consistently and provide the benefits your vendor expects. I cannot emphasize enough how important your relationships with your vendors are in the full spectrum of your event operations.

Controlling Purchases

The most common device for approving purchases is the purchase order (PO). No purchase should be authorized without an approved purchase order. This form specifies the product or service approved for purchase, the number of units, the price per unit, and the total amount due, including taxes and deliveries. The type of shipping and date and time of arrival should also be clearly specified. The PO should also state the payment terms. Instruct all your vendors by letter that you will be responsible only for purchases preceded by a valid purchase order. Include this statement on each purchase order: "Vendor may not substitute or alter this order without the written permission of the purchaser."

This statement helps you avoid the creative vendor who is out of red tablecloths and believes that you will accept blue instead at the same price.

Finally, the purchase order must have a signature line that grants approval and the date of the approval. The PO is the most important tool you have to control your purchases and, therefore, monitor those numerous doors where expenses leak and potentially drain your event economic engine. Since your PO is a very important financial document that can hold you or your company liable, it is important to ensure a safe procedure for issuing and approving all purchase orders. All your vendors should be informed as to who in your company is authorized to sign purchase orders. A PO signed by the authorized person should be mailed to a vendor at the beginning of the transaction. This PO procedure is very important, and it can help save you money when you compose the final invoice.

Barter

As the general economy tightened in 2008 and 2009, many event planning firms turned to the ancient practice of bartering to help increase their cash flow and remain profitable. Bartering simply means that you trade services with a supplier. For example, you may agree to provide event planning services for a corporation in exchange for the products you need (lighting, sound, audio visual, décor) to produce a future event. Although cash is not exchanged there may still be some tax implications related to the value of the goods you barter. Therefore, check with your accountant to determine how you report these exchanges to avoid any surprises at tax time.

Common Event Financial Challenges and Solutions

The planned events profession is a business. As in other businesses, there are common problems and solutions. When planned events business owners assemble for annual meetings and conferences, they can be heard discussing many of the same challenges year after year. As one wag said, "The problems don't change, the solutions only become more difficult." Perhaps by reviewing the examples that follow you will be able to anticipate some of these challenges and thereby take measures to avoid them entirely.

- **Challenge**: Negotiating employees' salaries and benefits.
  Solution: Collect information from the Event Solutions Black Book (www.event-solutions.com), Salaries.com (www.salaries.com), or from firms in similar market areas. Use this information to determine a market basket figure from which you can negotiate up or down based on the potential value of the employee to your firm.

- **Challenge**: Proper compensation for Event Leadership salespeople.
  Solution: Three methods are customary. First and most prevalent is the draw against commission. This approach requires that you provide the salesperson with a small stipend until his or her commissions have equaled this amount. After he or she has equaled the amount of the draw, the stipend stops and the salesperson receives only sales commissions. The second approach is straight commission. In this case, usually the salesperson has existing accounts and is earning commissions immediately. Typical commissions range from 3 to 7 percent of the gross sale. Therefore, a salesperson who produces $500,000 in gross revenue will earn $35,000. The final custom is to offer the salesperson a salary plus bonuses based on sales productivity. This bonus is typically awarded after the salesperson reaches a certain threshold in sales, such as $1 million. A typical bonus is 1 or 2 percent of sales. A salesperson earning a salary of $50,000 could earn an additional $20,000 based on a 2 percent bonus on $1 million in sales.

Straight salary as compensation is the least desirable because it provides no financial incentive, and salespeople typically are driven by financial incentives. Whatever arrangement you agree on, do not change it for one year. You will need one year of financial data on which to base your review and future course of action.

- **Challenge**: Client is slow to pay balance of account.
  Solution: Inquire how you can help expedite payment. Can you pick up the check? Is there a problem, and could the client pay the largest portion now and the rest later? Are other vendors being paid? Does the client have a history of slow payment? What leverage do you have? Can you suspend services until the balance is paid or payment on account is made? Can you speak with one of the owners or principals and solve this problem? Can you find a creative solution, such as the one that Andy Stefanovich of Opus Event Marketing, Richmond, Virginia, found? Andy had his dog send a collection notice, complete with begging for food and a paw print.
- **Challenge**: Out of cash.
  Solution: With prudent management of accounts payable and receivable, this problem should not occur. Assuming that a business emergency has caused this unfortunate situation, you must contact vendors immediately and notify them of your intent to pay. Then notify all past-due accounts receivable and accelerate collection. Reduce or stop spending with regard to fixed overhead. Next, contact your lenders to access a line of credit based on your receivables until you have sufficient cash to meet your expenses.
- **Challenge**: Vendor promotes himself or herself to your client directly.
  Solution: Do you have written policies and procedures outlining what is and what is not permissible by your vendors? Realistically, how will this promotion injure your business? Can you negotiate with your vendor to receive a commission from any future sales to this client since you were the first contact?
- **Challenge**: Employee is terminated, starts own business, and takes your clients.

Solution: Does the employment agreement forbid this practice? Assuming that it does, you can have your attorney send a cease-and-desist letter. This rarely helps because clients have no constraints on whom they do business with. Either way you lose. Instead, suggest to the former employee that he or she may wish to provide you with a commission on the first sale he or she makes with your former client, as a courtesy for providing the first introduction. This way you can release the client and also receive some compensation for your effort in first identifying the account. If former employees refuse to provide you with a commission, chances are that their bad business ethics will eventually alienate them from enough industry colleagues that it will limit the amount of sales that they are able to achieve and reduce significantly the level of services they receive from vendors suspicious of their behavior.

These common challenges and typical solutions should serve as a guide or framework to guide your decision making. Although most of the solutions in modern business still rely on common sense, I have noticed that there is nothing as uncommon in today's business environment as common sense. You will want to test each of these solutions with your business advisors (attorney, accountant, mentor) before implementing it to make certain that it addresses your particular problem and provides the most logical solution. There is no such thing as a general solution for a specific problem. All business problems are specific in nature, and you must seek a solution that addresses your precise problem.

Foreign Exchange Rates

It is important in this global world that you understand exchange rates, their fluctuations, and the differences that international exposure brings to your financial operations. Remember that although large international Event Leadership companies depend greatly on global changes that occur regularly in various countries, mid-size and small Event Leadership companies are also affected by these changes. Event Leadership today is a global economic enterprise. Food and beverages that you purchase in the United States or elsewhere are often produced outside of the country in which they are sold. Payments that your organization makes or receives from overseas can be conducted in either local or foreign currency.

The foreign exchange rate is the price of one currency expressed in another currency. For example, EUR 0.6896/1 USD means that for 1 U.S. dollar (USD), the market requires 0.6896 euro; USD 1.448/EUR means that for 1 euro, the market requires $1.448. The currency exchange rates vary in the same way that stocks do. Changes are usually not significant for small and mid-size businesses and affect mainly large banks and investment companies. Exchange rates generally are affected by market conditions and government policy and also by national disasters (especially for small countries).

Market Conditions

The general rule is that currencies of countries with strong economies are in greater demand than currencies of countries with weak economies. If the economy of country A is getting stronger and stronger but the economy of country B is getting weaker and weaker, the exchange rate between the currencies of these countries will favor the currency of country A.

Government Policy

The currency of countries with strong governments that have predictable policies is always preferred over the currencies of countries whose governments have unpredictable policies. Even during the close 2000 U.S. presidential election between George W. Bush and Al Gore, the U.S. dollar exchange rate was not greatly affected because the United States is known for its predictable domestic and foreign policy. Major financial newspapers, such as the *Financial Times* and *Wall Street Journal,* contain daily information about currency exchange rates and projections. You should monitor journals to forecast the economic conditions in countries where you will be doing business.

Changes in exchange rates affect all companies. Large businesses are affected directly; small businesses are affected indirectly. In one example, a large Event Leadership company based in the United States signs a contract with a U.K.-based corporation to produce a large event in London. The U.S. Event Leadership company is paid in pounds sterling (£). The total cost of the contract is £400,000. The contract is signed on June 1 and the event is to be held on December 21. The contract says that the U.K. company must make a 50 percent advance payment in June with the balance payable on the day of the event. On June 1, the British pound was worth $1.658. If the exchange rate between the pound and the dollar stays unchanged until December 21, the income statement of the event would appear as shown in Figure 5.3. Note that since the Event Leadership company is U.S.-based, all expenses that it incurs are in U.S. dollars and total $500,000.

	U.K. Pound	U.S. Dollar
Revenue		
50% advance on June 10	£200,000.00	$331,600.00
50% payment on December 20	200,000.00	331,600.00
Total	400,000.00	663,200.00
Total expenses	n/a	(500,000.00)
Gross profit	n/a	$163,200.00

Figure 5.3 Income Statement: No Exchange Rate Fluctuation

	U.K. Pound	U.S. Dollar
Revenue		
50% advance on June 10	£200,000.00	$331,600.00
50% payment on December 20	200,000.00	300,000.00
Total	400,000.00	631,600.00
Total expenses	n/a	(500,000.00)
Gross profit	n/a	$131,600.00

Figure 5.4 Income Statement: With Exchange Rate Fluctuation

The gross profit is calculated to be $163,200. This represents a 25 percent profit margin ($163,200/$663,200). Obviously, the project looks very attractive. The question is how attractive the project would be if the exchange rate were to change by December 20. Suppose that, due to the strong economy in the United States, you predict that the U.S. dollar will appreciate (its value will increase). Now suppose that the exchange rate in December will be $1.5 for £1. Figure 5.4 shows how this change could dramatically reduce your margin of profit. Due to the exchange rate change in December, £200,000 will be worth only $300,000 but total expenses are still $500,000 (since they occurred in U.S. dollars). Therefore, the gross profit dropped to $131,000 and the profit margin dropped to 20 percent.

The more expensive the U.S. dollar becomes, the less profit the U.S. organization makes from its overseas events that are paid in foreign currency. This means that the U.S. organization can purchase fewer dollars for the amount of foreign currency earned. To attain the same level of profitability, the organization should start charging more for its service event; however, if it does so, it becomes less competitive. Alternatively, when the U.S. dollar depreciates, services provided by U.S. Event Leadership organizations overseas become less expensive, hence more competitive.

Typical Events Budgets

Your budget is a general guide to the income and expense projected for your event. It may be adjusted as necessary, provided that you can justify these changes and receive approval from the stakeholders. For example, if your revenue projections are way ahead of schedule, your variable costs will also increase proportionately. Use the budget as a valuable tool that may be sharpened as needed to improve your percentage of retained earnings.

The sample budgets shown in Figure 5.5 will serve as a guide as you develop your financial plans for various events. Each budget has the same structure; however,

AWARDS BANQUET

Income		
100	Registrations	
101	Preregistrations	$ 25,000
102	Regular registrations	50,000
103	Door sales	5,000
	Subtotal	$ 80,000
200	Marketing	
201	Sponsorships	$ 15,000
202	Advertising	10,000
203	Merchandise	5,000
	Subtotal	$ 30,000
300	Investments	
301	Interest income	1,000
	Subtotal	$ 1,000
400	Donations	
401	Grants	$ 5,000
402	Individual gifts	10,000
403	Corporate gifts	25,000
	Subtotal	$ 40,000
	Total income	$151,000
Expenses		
500	Administration (fixed expense)	
501	Site office furniture rental	$ 1,000
502	Site office supplies	1,000
503	Site rental	3,000
504	Site telephone expense	1,000
	Subtotal	$ 6,000
600	Printing (fixed expense)	
601	Design	$ 3,000
602	Printing	5,000
603	Binding	1,000
	Subtotal	$ 9,000
700	Entertainment (fixed expense)	
701	Talent fees	$ 10,000
702	Travel and accommodations	1,000

Figure 5.5 Sample Budgets *(Continued)*

703	Sound	2,000
704	Lights	2,000
	Subtotal	$ 15,000
800	Food and beverages (variable expense)	
801	300 dinners @ $50	$ 15,000*
802	Open bar for one hour	3,000*
803	Ice sculpture	500
	Subtotal	$ 18,500
	*Include taxes and gratuities.	
900	Transportation (variable expense)	
901	Staff travel	$ 1,000
902	Valet parking	750
	Subtotal	$ 1,750
1000	Insurance (fixed expense)	
1001	Cancellation	$ 1,000
1002	Host liability	500
	Subtotal	$ 1,500
	Total expenses	$ 51,750
	Total variable expense	$ 29,250
	Total projected income	$151,000
	Total projected expense	51,750
	Gross retained earnings	$ 99,250
	Percentage of fixed overhead	25,000
	Net retained earnings (reinvestment)	$ 74,250

MUSIC FESTIVAL

Income		
100	Ticket sales	
101	Regular advance	$ 50,000
102	Student advance	25,000
103	Regular door sales	100,000
104	Student door sales	50,000
105	Group sales	25,000
	Subtotal	$250,000
200	Marketing	
201	Sponsorships	$ 50,000

Figure 5.5 *(Continued)*

202 Advertising	25,000
203 Merchandise	30,000
Subtotal	$105,000
300 Investments	
301 Interest income	3,000
Subtotal	$ 3,000
400 Donations	
401 Grants	$ 10,000
402 Individual gifts	0
403 Corporate gifts	25,000
Subtotal	$ 35,000
Total income	$393,000
Expenses	
500 Administration (fixed expense)	
501 Site office furniture rental	$ 500
502 Site office supplies	500
503 Site rental	10,000
504 Site telephone expense	1,500
Subtotal	$ 12,500
600 Printing (fixed expense)	
601 Design	$ 1,000
602 Printing	5,000
Subtotal	$ 6,000
700 Entertainment (fixed expense)	
701 Talent fees	$ 50,000
702 Travel and accommodations	5,000
703 Sound	5,000
704 Lights	5,000
Subtotal	$ 65,000
800 Transportation and parking (variable expense)	
801 Staff travel	$ 500
802 Parking lot rental	3,000
Subtotal	$ 3,500
900 Insurance (fixed expense)	
901 Cancellation	$ 1,000

Figure 5.5 *(Continued)*

902 Host liability	500
903 Comprehensive general liability	2,000
904 Pyrotechnics rider	1,000
Subtotal	$ 4,500
Total expenses	$ 51,750
Total variable expense	$ 29,250
Total projected income	$393,000
Total projected expense	91,500
Gross retained earnings	$301,500
Percentage of fixed overhead	150,000
Net retained earnings (reinvestment)	$151,500
CONFERENCE AND EXPOSITION	
Income	
100 Registration	
101 Early-bird discount	$100,000
102 Regular	50,000
103 On site	25,000
104 Spouse/partner	10,000
105 Special events	15,000
Subtotal	$200,000
200 Marketing	
201 Sponsorships	10,000
202 Advertising	15,000
203 Merchandise	10,000
Subtotal	$ 35,000
300 Investments	
301 Interest income	$ 1,000
Subtotal	$ 1,000
400 Donations	
401 Grants	$ 5,000
Subtotal	$ 5,000
500 Exposition	
501 200 booths @ $1,500	$300,000
502 50 tabletops @ $500	25,000
Subtotal	$325,000
Total income	$566,000

Figure 5.5 *(Continued)*

Expenses		
600	Administration (fixed expense)	
601	Site office furniture rental	$ 1,500
602	Site office supplies	500
603	Site rental	30,000
604	Site telephone expense	1,500
	Subtotal	$ 33,500
700	Printing (fixed expense)	
701	Design	$ 2,000
702	Printing	10,000
	Subtotal	$ 12,000
800	Postage (fixed expense)	
801	Hold this date	$ 1,000
802	Brochure	5,000
803	Miscellaneous	500
	Subtotal	$ 6,500
900	Entertainment (fixed expense)	
901	Talent fees	$ 5,000
902	Travel and accommodations	500
903	Sound	0
904	Lights	0
	Subtotal	$ 5,500
1000	Transportation and accommodations	
1001	Staff travel	$ 1,500
1002	Staff accommodations	1,500
	Subtotal	$ 3,000
1100	Insurance (fixed expense)	
1101	Cancellation	$ 3,000
1103	Comprehensive general liability	2,000
	Subtotal	$ 5,000
1200	Speakers (variable expense)	
1201	Honoraria	$ 10,000
1202	Travel	3,000
1203	Accommodations	1,000

Figure 5.5 *(Continued)*

1204	Complimentary registrations	3,000
1205	Per diem	1,000
	Subtotal	$ 18,000
1300	Audiovisual (variable expense)	
1301	Rentals (general sessions)	$ 25,000
1302	Labor (general sessions)	10,000
1303	Rentals (breakouts)	2,000
1304	Labor (breakouts)	1,000
1305	Prerecorded modules	5,000
	Subtotal	$ 43,000
1400	Exposition (variable expense)	
1401	Pipe and drape	$ 10,000
1402	Aisle carpet	20,000
1403	Signs	5,000
	Subtotal	$ 35,000
	Total projected income	$566,000
	Total projected expense	161,500
	Gross retained earnings	$404,500
	Percentage of fixed overhead	199,000
	Net retained earnings (reinvestment)	$205,500

Figure 5.5 *(Continued)*

you will note that in the case of not-for-profit organizations, the term retained earnings has been substituted for the term profit. Use these budgets as a model as you endeavor to create consistently effective financial management systems for your organization.

Although most Event Leaders find that financial matters are the least interesting aspect of their role and scope of their jobs, you now understand that to sustain long-term success, it is critical that you firmly control this important management area. The better you become at watching the bottom line, the more resources will become available to you for other more creative activities.

Julia Rutherford Silvers, CSEP, believes that financial goals, objectives, and tactics must be considered when evaluating the event elements being deployed. In *Professional Event Coordination* (2003), Rutherford Silvers puts this concept into perspective by offering this example. "Suppose you are coordinating a conference for your professional

Pioneer: Ira Rosen, President, Entertainment on Location and Director, Temple University Event Leadership Executive Certificate Program

Ira Rosen, a member of the International Festivals and Events Association Hall of Fame recognized very early during his college career at Montclair State University in New Jersey how much he enjoyed working on events. Then, according to Ira, "It was just a matter of determining how I was going to make a career in an industry that at the time did not really exist."

From his first event, Ira knew this was the right field for him because he enjoyed seeing the excitement and anticipation in the people who were attending the events. "The excitement was addictive," notes Ira.

He has had many outstanding mentors during his long and successful career. While working in university events, he learned a tremendous amount from the Director of Student Activities at the time, Tom Stepnowski.

He states that his first two bosses, Edith Frank at Fairleigh Dickinson University and Barbara Milne at William Paterson University, were influential mentors. When he left university events to go to Radio City Music Hall, he continued to be mentored by leaders such as his boss Ray Brennan, Esq., the legendary producer Bob Jani, and award-winning event luminaries Barnett Lipton and

association. The costs to a delegate may include a registration fee of $600, an airline ticket at $500, a hotel room at $600 (four nights at $150 per night), and meals, business center services, and other incidentals that may add up to $400. Add to that $900 for a week away from work (a factor too many organizers ignore), and the cost to the delegate is $3,000. To achieve a positive return on his or her investment, the delegate will have to come away from the conference with a $3,000 idea."

Jerry Edwards, CPCE, is the owner of Chef's Expressions and the immediate past president of the National Association of Catering Executives (NACE). Edwards has observed significant changes in spending since the September 11, 2001, attacks. "Although September 11 marked the beginning of significant cutbacks in two major lines of catering business (conventions and corporate events), social business has become all the more important. Clients desire a very classic look that reflects high quality instead of ostentatiousness. Therefore, our catering budgets must reflect these changing tastes."

Frank Supovitz. As his career advanced and he started his own business, his circle of mentors expanded to include industry figures such as Jean McFaddin, Steve Schmader, CFEE, and Dr. Joe Goldblatt, CSEP. From all of these mentors he says he learned the value of trust and the inherent goodness in people.

According to Ira, during his career he has seen many dramatic changes. He said, "Technology has been one of the biggest changes. The Internet and electronic access to data have increased our ability to be creative and cost-conscious at the same time. Budgets are always challenging even in the best of circumstances, and with the global economic downturn, this has been even more challenging. Environmental considerations will continue to present us with both challenges and opportunities as the demand for green and carbon neutral events continues to grow."

The primary catalyst for these changes, Rosen believes, has been globalization. He observes that "anyone who watched the opening ceremonies for the 2008 Beijing Summer Olympics has to recognize how high the bar has been raised now for mega-events."

His optimism for the future is strong. "As someone who started in this industry before it really existed as a definable entity, I am encouraged by the fact that we are training a group of professionals who will leave us in the dust when it comes to creativity. The young professionals are learning from those of us who have gone before, avoiding our pitfalls and building new and exciting opportunities for the world."

Ira continues to make a positive contribution to this industry from his contributions as an event consultant, producer, leader and most recently university professor. It is admirable that Ira Rosen, who began his events career while in college being mentored by his professors is now mentoring the next generation through his teaching at Temple University and helping them reach the next frontier.

How to Manage Your Finances During Turbulent Economic Times

The first quarter of 2009 was one of the bleakest in modern economic times. As a result, many event businesses trimmed their projections for the new year, cut costs, or even considered closing their doors if they could not find sufficient investment to support their overhead.

The fundamental rule for surviving and thriving during turbulent economic times is to first ensure you have enough liquid assets to support your business for at least 12 months. A bank loan should not be considered a liquid asset as the bank may call it at any time. Further, it may be difficult to find a reasonable loan during a turbulent time. Therefore, having access to cash is the best plan.

The second rule for ensuring you will thrive during a difficult time is to renegotiate all payments with your subcontractors and vendors. During a difficult economic climate hotels, caterers and others may be more amenable to lowering their costs and being more flexible with their payment terms.

Third and finally, do not panic. A recessed economy may be just the right time to actually grow your business through savvy investing. There will be fewer people advertising, and that means lower rates and less competition. Use this time to go out and market your business aggressively.

Protoge: Cynthia Reantaso-Bernabe, Event Specialist, Wish Works Event Management, Manila, the Philippines

When Cynthia Reantaso-Bernabe graduated from the Temple University Event Leadership Executive Certificate Program in Philadelphia, Pennsylvania, the air of respect for this dedicated event professional was well acknowledged. Cynthia, a native of the Philippines, had commuted thousands of miles between her country and Philadelphia to complete her course and achieve her dream. During her remarks, she said, "I would have traveled anywhere in the world to advance my career and receive the level of training I received from this program."

Cynthia's career began as an administrative relations officer, and part of her job was to organize activities for the marketing department of her company. She was part of a team that planned and coordinated incentive travel, product launches, exhibits, conventions, conferences, seminars and trainings, award ceremonies, birthday, and anniversary parties. Her main job was to prepare weekly and monthly bulletins and sales reports, prepare recruitment ads, source vendors and suppliers, and deliver motivational talks. Of all these tasks, she enjoyed the ones that involved celebrating the most. In fact, she wished that this would be her primary job.

She left the company to begin a family. As a young mother of small children, she organized many birthday and other celebrations for her children and family members. According to Cynthia, this is what she most enjoyed, the charm that comes from designing, creating, and producing unique celebrations.

Before starting her own firm, she went to work for the Philippine Stock Exchange. Cynthia recalls that she quickly learned that this was not her destiny. "I was hired because I am an economics major and I was a former training director. This job entailed analyzing the stock market. I was in front of a computer practically the whole day. I was scheduled to

During the Great Depression of 1929, many businesses failed due to panic. Those that thrived were the ones that steered their ship with a steady hand on both receivables and payables. Further, they were the ones who knew that the customer is king and queen and that this is a good time to get closer to them and find more ways throughout your unlimited talents to fill their needs.

It is an old maxim, but it is true: tough times do not last, but tough people do. I would add that in addition to being tough, being prudent with your investments, flexible with your vendors, and devoted to your customers will pay even bigger dividends in the future.

go to Singapore to get further training for about four months so I may train a newly formed group when I get back to the Philippines. The compensation package was very good, but I resigned after only two weeks of being in the company. That experience further confirmed I was not meant to be in front of a machine the whole day and deal with numbers and graphs. I knew the celebrations industry is the right field for me because I love being a participant and a witness to celebrations by being the planner and organizer. I love helping people and organizations realize their dream celebrations."

When Cynthia launched her business, Wish Works Event Management, she knew she was doing something right when suddenly she had many imitators. Her business achieved rapid success, and when asked to describe the mentors who had encouraged her, she named her teachers. "I greatly admire educators and believe that within every event professional there is a future educator. One event leader I truly admire, among others, is Dessislava Boshkanova of Sofia, Bulgaria." When Cynthia read about her in the book *Special Events: The Roots and Wings of Celebration* (2008), she confirmed the importance of education in the events industry. Like the other leaders mentioned, she is also a teacher.

Her forecast for the events industry is positive, and believes that the field will increase in the years to come. However, she also states that "despite globalization, the special events industry will further preserve customs, traditions, ceremonies and rituals because of the consciousness of its divinity."

Cynthia is firmly committed to continuing education in special events and regularly purchases books to keep her informed on the latest trends and developments. Although the special events industry in the Philippines is relatively young as a formalized field of study, she said, "In my country, there is so much room for growth. We are beginning to adapt to the globalization of the industry. Each year, I notice an expansion in the number of event companies, party planning businesses, event venues and event practitioners. I also discovered an increase in the number of people shifting from the traditional jobs to a job in event planning."

Cynthia Reantaso-Bernabe exemplifies how hard work, dedication, and a commitment to continuing education may help a protégé soon become a pioneer. She, like one of her mentors Desslislava Boshnakova, is rapidly helping her developing economy achieve greater stability and strength through a very old tradition and new and rapidly growing industry, the art and science of celebration.

Career-Advancement Connections

Corporate Social Responsibility Connection

Are your purchases being made from local suppliers to first support the local economy where the event is being held? Are your suppliers providing Fair Trade products? Are your Investments supporting microeconomic enterprises as well as macro ones? The economic opportunity you have through your event is significant, and if you plan carefully, your efforts will result in not only a successful event but also a better society.

Global Connection

The role that international finance plays in the Event Leadership industry was highlighted by the changes that occurred within the industry from the moment the North American Free Trade Agreement (NAFTA) was implemented. The entire economy of the United States, including the Event Leadership industry, has undergone major changes. Major labor-intensive industries were moved to Mexico because of cost savings in the labor force. At the same time, more knowledge-intensive industries were concentrated in the United States and Canada. Today the term outsource no longer means hiring domestic freelancers; rather, it refers to employing workers in countries where wages and, therefore, costs are lower.

Technology Connection

To learn more about financial management and financial markets, I encourage you to visit these Web sites:

- www.ft.com; Financial Times
- www.wsj.com; Wall Street Journal
- www.sec.gov; Securities and Exchange Commission
- www.freeedgar.com; EDGAR (Electronic Data Gathering, Analysis, and Retrieval) database, which contains information about financial performance of all companies, including Event Leadership, whose stocks are traded publicly
- www.rubicon.com/passport/currency/currency.html for easy, fast currency exchange-rate data

Resource Connection

The best strategy for understanding event financial management is practice. Excellent textbooks to assist you further include: *Analysis for Financial Management, Sixth Edition*, by Robert C. Higgins (McGraw-Hill, 2000); *Financial Management: Theory and Practice,* by Eugene F. Brigham and Louis C. Gapenski (South-Western

Educational Publishing, 1998); and *Financial Analysis with Microsoft Excel,* by Timothy Mayes (South-Western Educational Publishing, 1996).

Learning Connection

Your Event Leadership organization is seeking a contract with a large corporation. It is a promotional event that will be organized to promote a new service. In order to make a final decision on whether you want to accept the project, you have to conduct financial calculations and a break-even analysis. Your Event Leadership organization is willing to accept the project if the total gross profit for the event is more than $5,000. Your client estimates that there will be somewhere between 100 and 300 guests. The company pays $100 per person, with a minimum of $10,000. You know that your variable costs (food and beverage) total $30 per person. The total fixed costs are $4,000. Now calculate the maximum and the minimum gross profit that you can achieve for this event.

The recycling bins at the Fiddles and Drams event at Winton House in East Lothian demonstrate the organizers' commitment to producing greener events.

CHAPTER 6

Greener Events

In this chapter you will learn how to:

- Produce sustainable events
- Reduce your carbon footprint
- Precycle
- Conserve natural resources and save money
- Minimize waste
- Employ environmentally friendly practices
- Reduce use of paper
- Implement energy efficiency
- Utilize renewable energy
- Market your greener event
- Create a sustainable bond with local cultures and local economies
- Partner with greener suppliers, vendors, and hotels

Former Vice President Al Gore's film *An Inconvenient Truth* demonstrates that the excessive burning of coal, gas, and oil has overpowered the Earth's atmosphere with greenhouse gases such as carbon dioxide (CO_2). Mass deforestation has limited the environment's ability to absorb these greenhouse gases, allowing them to pollute the atmosphere.

Authored by Sam Goldblatt, MA, Queen Margaret University, Edinburgh

This pollution causes increased temperatures, known as global warming, and abnormal weather patterns, known as climate change, and, according to *National Geographic*, the symptoms are as follows:

- The last two decades of the twentieth century were the hottest on record in 400 years.
- Montana's Glacier National Park, which had 150 glaciers in 1910, now has only 27.
- By the end of the twenty-first century, sea level may rise between 7 and 23 inches. Rises of just 4 inches could flood many South Seas islands and large parts of Southeast Asia.
- More than a million species face extinction (*National Geographic* 2009).

Gore has championed the environment in public debate, but aside from his role as a political leader, he is also a greener Events Leader. His now-famous 2007 Live Earth concert series featured mega-concerts on seven continents, and was broadcast around the world to teach an estimated 2 billion people about climate change (Live Earth 2009). Gore also organized 2009's most notable greener event, the Green Ball celebrating the inauguration of President Barack Obama. In many ways, the Green Ball, which featured email invites (to avoid paper waste), a green carpet made from recycled materials, and organic food sourced from local farms, was a model greener event (BizBash 2009).

The global events industry is following Gore's example. The 2007 Event Solutions Magazine Forecast of the events industry found that, of the over 1,350 events professionals surveyed, "green meetings" rated the third-most anticipated trend, higher than "risk management" and "performance metrics" (Baragona 2007, p. 4). The Web site of *Special Events* magazine now features an entire section on greener events (specialevents.com/green_events). Event leaders now have three green associations to choose from in the Green Meetings Industry Council (GMIC, www.greenmeetings.info), Convene Green Alliance (CGA, www.convenegreen.com), and the Association of Green Meetings & Events (AGME, www.agmeinc.org), and the United States Environmental Protection Agency (EPA) has established the Green Meetings/Conference Initiative to promote environmentally friendly practices in the events sector (Golding 2008; U.S. EPA 2009, www.epa.gov/oppt/greenmeetings).

We can learn from Gore's example. As world leaders create green policies and industry leaders set green initiatives, so too will Event Leaders need to pioneer the new field of greener events.

Defining "Greener"

To stay in touch with the current public discourse and communicate effectively with stakeholders, familiarize yourself with the following terms:

- *Global warming*: the increase in the Earth's average temperature since the mid-twentieth century and its projected continuation.
- *Climate change*: abnormal deviations in the weather and other meteorological factors.
- *Greenhouse gases*: water vapor, carbon dioxide (CO_2), methane, nitrous oxide and other gases. The excessive use of greenhouse gases contributes to global warming and climate change.
- *Carbon footprint*: the total combined CO_2 emissions of your event.
- *Carbon offsetting*: financial investment towards CO_2-reducing projects like renewable energy or forestry. One offset = one metric ton of CO_2.
- *Renewable energy*: energy generated from recurring natural resources such as sun (solar), wind, and water (hydro).
- *Organic*: foods or natural products made without the use of pesticides or other artificial or chemical agents.
- *Environmentally friendly practice (EFP)*: an action designed to minimize negative impact and/or promote positive impact on the environment.

Defining "Greener Events"

As Thomas Friedman argues in *Hot, Flat and Crowded*, rising oil prices and war in the Middle East have fed a geopolitical energy crisis, thus contributing to a growing public focus on alternative energy solutions, a focus sharpened by President Barack Obama, who promises to invest heavily in green technologies as part of a new vision for America (2008). As diverse businesses seek to apply eco-friendly strategies to their industry practices, many predict a green boom similar to the 1990s Web boom (Esty 2006). In recognition of this major societal shift, tourism, the sister industry of events, established *ecotourism* as a unique and thriving subsector in the 1990s, but an authoritative, academic definition of greener events has not yet been published—until now.

Greener events can be defined as special events that continually endeavor to provide superior experiences through environmentally friendly strategies.

In accordance with this definition, greener events promote three core values: innovation, conservation, and education.

1. *Innovation*: creatively harnessing emerging strategies and green technology for increased energy efficiency and environmentalism
2. *Conservation*: responsible use of the earth's natural resources and waste minimization
3. *Education*: promoting ethical behavior towards energy and the environment by creating memorable event experiences

You should create your own image of a greener event by the end of this chapter. Your definition should include environmental strategies and technologies, harnessed to provide unique experiences. It should imply a symbiotic, mutually beneficial relationship between Event Leader and the natural biosphere. It should include the three core values of innovation, conservation, and education. Above all, it must describe and aspire to sustainability.

Sustainability

Sustainability derives from the theory of sustainable development created by the United Nations during the 1980s to encourage development that "meets the needs of the present without compromising the ability of future generations to meet their own needs," as stated in the UN document *Our Common Future* (2009). Air and land pollution of an outdoor event site directly compromises the ability of future Event Leaders to produce events on that site. Indirectly, careless wasting of resources such as paper or gasoline compromises future generations' special events.

Although the concept of sustainability allows environmentalists to communicate their green concerns in the language of strategic planning, sustainable development does not necessarily imply environmental activism. Affixing the words "green" or "eco" to the start of a term (i.e., Green Energy, EcoTechnology) more clearly reflects a concerted effort to reduce environmental impact and conserve natural resources, beyond the definition of sustainable development. Responsible Event Leaders will always pursue sustainability in their long-term business plans. This chapter is titled "Greener Events," and not "Sustainable Events," in reflection of the emerging environmental trends that new, imaginative events utilize. I encourage you to consider the specific ways in which green technology and environmental initiatives can sustain and improve your long-term business plans.

Ecotourism

The tourism industry, with its market for recreational air travel, is one of the world's largest gas consumers and polluters. Perhaps this is why tourism experts were quick to apply the principles of sustainable development to their field. David Fennell (2007, p. 24) defines ecotourism, or environmentalist tourism, as:

> *A sustainable, non-invasive form of nature-based tourism that focuses primarily on learning about nature first-hand, and which is ethically managed to be low-impact, non-consumptive, and locally oriented (control, benefits and scale). It typically occurs in natural areas, and should contribute to the conservation of such areas.*

Greener events pioneers can glean much from this definition of ecotourism. Certainly, Event Leaders recognize the value of sustainability in long-term business growth, but is this sustainability nature-based? No man is an island, and no event is disconnected from its natural resources and environment; think of sustaining not just your business but your event site, your resources, your energy. Similarly, all events impact the culture of their locations, and greener events must therefore be "locally oriented" to maintain meaningful and beneficial relationships with local culture. Lastly, Event Leaders can use corporate social responsibility (CSR) to "ethically" manage greener events.

What about "low-impact" and "nonconsumptive"? Should not the best events always be high-impact, offering guests a lavish feast to consume? Actually, greener events can deliver a huge, spectacular impact on patron experience, complete with sights, sounds, and foods to consume. Japan's Fuji Rock Festival (www.smash-uk.com), known anecdotally as the world's cleanest music festival, annually presents major bands like the Red Hot Chili Peppers and The Cure in a huge outdoor environment that encompasses 10 different stages for performance, vendors offering outstanding local cuisines, sustainable campgrounds, and other attractions such as a Japanese *onsen* spa and a cable-car ride. Through rigorous recycling procedures, responsible land maintenance, and consumer education, Fuji Rock Festival gives consumers a high-impact festival experience like none other through sustainable, green practices that minimize environmental impact.

You, too, can make a big impact on your patrons without making a big impact on natural resources. Fennell's definition of ecotourism presents a goal for greener events pioneers to meet, a beacon of sophistication for you to labor towards. Not all events may be certified greener events, and very few events will achieve a zero-carbon footprint, but all events may aspire to be a shade greener each time they are created and produced.

Fair Trade

One of the more visible trends to emerge from sustainable development is the Fair Trade movement, created to counteract unfair Third-World labor practices. As defined by the Fairtrade Foundation (www.fairtrade.org), a "fair trade" between manager and laborer means:

- Fair pay
- Investing in projects that enhance workers' quality of life
- Partnership
- Mutually beneficial long-term relationships
- Social, economic, and environmental responsibility (2008).

Event Leaders know firsthand the importance of customer service: The greatest food on earth is garbage when delivered by a grumpy waiter. Keep your staff committed to the cause and dedicated to excellence by treating them as partners in your enterprise. Offer them discounts. Keep them informed of company news. Encourage employee culture. Consider an annual employee thank-you event. The Oxfam Charity runs a hugely popular program for volunteers to serve as stewards at UK music festivals, picking up litter or directing crowds in exchange for free admission to concerts. The music festivals gain a free, enthusiastic work force and the volunteers gain inspirational work and affordable recreation. Instead of seeing a sharp divide between staff and patron, try blurring these boundaries to create a festive atmosphere that celebrates fair trade and equality. If the service staff is having fun, chances are, the patrons will, too.

Outgreening & CSR

Corporate social responsibility (CSR) features strongly in this book as a charitable value for for-profit companies, and, indeed, CSR serves as motivation for many environmental initiatives. However, a growing number of forward-thinking companies are environmentally motivated by sheer profit incentive and competitive advantage. Friedman describes how green initiatives saved money and improved performance of New York City taxicabs, and how solar power gave the U.S. Army a tactical advantage in the Iraq War. He calls these strategies "outgreening," and calls for companies to not just settle for being "carbon neutral," but to seek a "carbon advantage," for increased profitability and heightened performance (2008, p. 126). He makes this same argument, but in a political context, earlier in the book, quoting energy expert David Rothkopf (2008, p. 23):

> *Green is not simply a new form of generating electric power. It is a new form of generating national power—period.*

Similarly, green is a new form of generating business power—period. Before even mentioning the ethical justification, Live Earth's Environmental Guidelines lists six tactical advantages of greener events:

- Attract and partner with artists (at Live Earth, more than 200 acts joined the environmental cause on a pro-bono basis).
- Be a responsible citizen and a visible environmental leader in your community.
- Appeal to the audience that, although its members may not recycle, likes to know others are contributing to the good of the world.
- A marketing and PR advantage over the competition.
- Doing your part—and knowing you and your employees make a difference every day.
- Financial savings (2007, p. 14).

Financial savings come not just from fewer expenses but also from government grants, which green companies are increasingly eligible for. As an event leader, you will know the iconic, unsurpassed value of a Steinway piano, but did you know that Steinways run on solar? Steinway's New York factory has the largest solar rooftop of its kind in the world, for which it received a $588,000 grant from the New York State Energy Research and Development Authority, and for which it expects to claim $266,000 in federal solar-energy tax credits. As Steinway's Vice President for Manufacturing Andrew Horbachevsky explains, "We kind of backed into the ecological thing. Green is also the color of money" (Barron 2008).

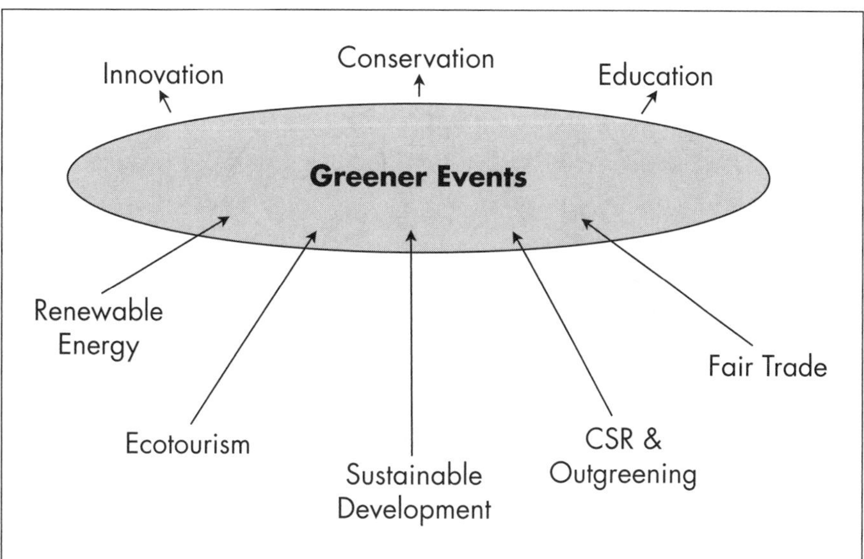

Figure 6.1 S. Goldblatt Theory of Greener Events. Greener Events draw upon inputs of Ecotourism, Sustainable Development, Fair Trade, Renewable Energy, CSR, and Outgreening. Three Defining Outputs of Greener Events are Innovation, Conservation, and Education.

Green is certainly the color of money for billionaire media mogul Ted Turner, America's largest land-owner, a committed environmentalist, and creator of the cartoon show *Captain Planet,* about an environmental superhero. At a fundraiser for the Captain Planet Foundation, the *New Yorker* quotes a conversation that Turner's daughter recalls having with her environmental father (Widdocombe 2008, p. 31):

> *He reminds me constantly, "Do you know who Captain Planet is?" I'm like, "No, Dad, who is he?" And he's like, "It's me!"*

As Friedman predicts, tomorrow's captains of industry may all be Captain Planets. Green business strategies of CSR and outgreening are two important aspects of emerging greener events. Figure 6.1 shows that these strategies, along with ecotourism, sustainable development, fair trade, and renewable energy (discussed later) help to define greener events. These diverse inputs form the modern definition of greener events, and generate the three core outputs of innovation, conservation, and education.

Event Pollution

The 1999 Woodstock festival generated approximately 1,200 tons of landfill waste, the recycling of which would have meant the conservation of 5,100 trees, 2.1 million

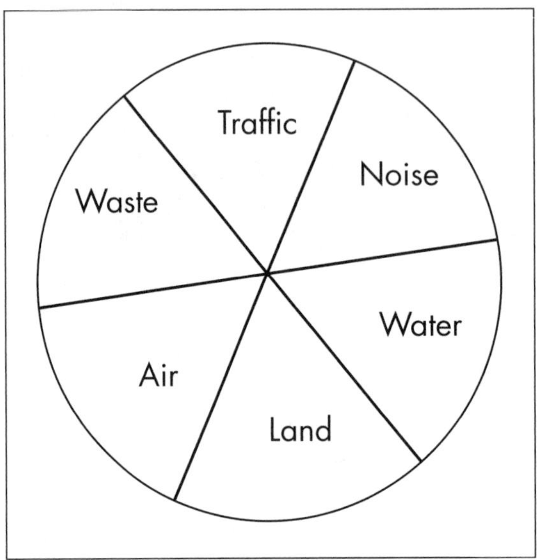

Figure 6.2 Event Pollution. Air, Land, and Water Damage have Direct, Visible Effects upon the Event Site. Waste and Traffic Pollution Contribute to the Global Warming and the Energy Crisis, while Noise Pollution Disrupts Cultural Sustainability.

gallons of water, and 1.2 million kWh of electricity (Live Earth 2007, p. 14). Peace and love, huh? The current trends in the events industry are unsustainable for the Earth's natural resources. Many events follow patterns of careless consumption handed down through society since the Industrial Revolution. As celebrities such as Al Gore create awareness of impending threats from global warming and President Obama supports green technologies, we have the opportunity to reassess our pollutive patterns. Events often pollute the environment in five basic ways: waste, traffic, air pollution, land use, and noise.

Waste

Modern events are built around waste. Every Styrofoam plate, plastic spoon, confetti blast, helium balloon, and paper tablecloth that is not reused is essentially wasted. Not only are high waste levels unsustainable, they degrade patron experience. Claire O'Neill's study of UK music festivals, A Greener Festival, available at www.agreenerfestival.com, surveyed 649 festival patrons and found that 71 percent agreed that waste was a negative environmental impact of festivals. Disposable items make for disposable events; don't let your event's greatest outcome be an overflowing dumpster. Make *Waste Minimization*, the process of reducing waste, a priority for your event. Figure 6.3 shows a hierarchy of waste-disposal methods. Note that prevention, minimization, and reuse are all preferred

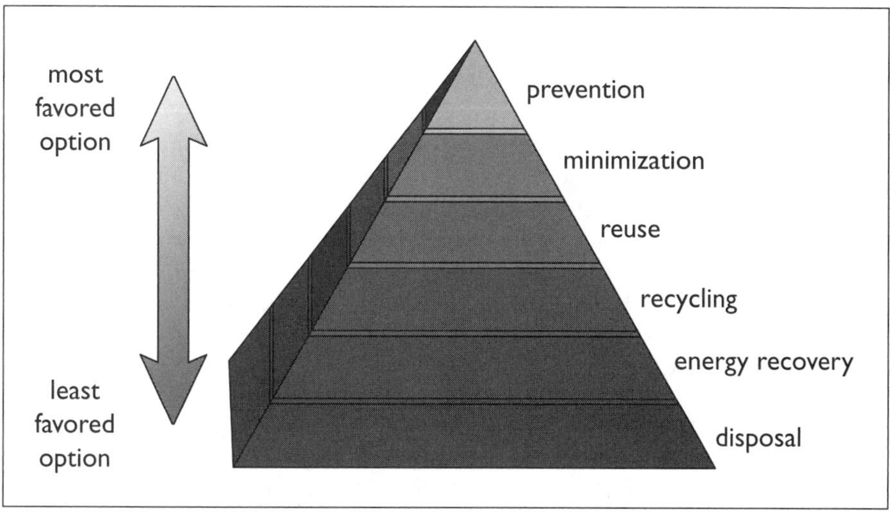

Figure 6.3 Waste Disposal Hierarchy. The Absolutely Best Way to Minimize Waste is to Prevent it through Precycling before it occurs. If it Cannot be Minimized or Reused, Waste should at least be Recycled, instead of Sent Straight to a Landfill for Potential Energy Recovery.

over recycling, although recycling beats disposal. The first step in waste minimization is avoidance through precycling, discussed later in this Chapter, but no event can avoid waste completely. Event waste comes in three forms: standard, recyclable, and biodegradable, each of which can be closely managed.

Standard Waste

Standard garbage receptacles must be available throughout any event site, in accordance with health and safety regulations and common sense. Trash cans need to fit in with the atmosphere and decor as much as possible so as not to denigrate the event. At the same time, they must be widely available and clearly labeled. Obvious high-traffic areas necessitate trash cans, but try to predict the more unusual areas that patrons may require receptacles. Monitor all receptacles during the event, making adjustments or additions as needed in a manner unobtrusive to the event experience. After the event, record the locations that collect litter so that you can add receptacles to these locations in future events.

Limiting the number of trash receptacles will not decrease trash, it will only increase litter, and the only thing worse than excessive trash is excessive litter. Litter degrades the atmosphere of an event, spoils patron experience, and creates unnecessary work for event staff. It's also bad for the environment. One cigarette butt contaminates a square meter of land and takes between 18 months and 500 years to decompose. That's why Ashcan, a small aluminum tube that functions as a receptacle for cigarette butts, was invented. Ashcans, which fit inside a pack of cigarettes, give smokers a safe, clean way to extinguish and store their cigarettes no matter where they are. Some greener events pioneers distribute Ashcans (others improvise their own out of used plastic film canisters) to smokers at outdoor events. This shows the way that effective waste minimization requires "thinking outside the bin." Oxfam stewards dress up like green fairies and teach patrons waste management skills. A growing number of events encourage patrons to create group-art sculptures out of aluminum cans as a public celebration of recycling. Figure 6.4 shows several ways that greener events pioneers can "think outside the bin."

Recyclable Waste

Greener events place recycling bins next to every trash can. Glass and plastic bottles, aluminum cans, and paper are just some of the many materials that can be recycled for later use. The key to effective recycling management is communication with your collection agency. Contact your local authority's waste management office and find out the exact date, time, location and manner in which your event's waste and recyclables will be collected and processed. The two key issues for collection are what to contain recyclables in (government-issued bins? paper sacks?) and how to separate recyclables. The Washington, D.C., Department of Public Works offers "single stream" recycling, in which residents combine all recyclable materials in government-issued blue bins for the recycling plant to separate the various materials into plastic, glass, and so on. The City of Edinburgh Council requires residents to separate their own recycling. Get to know your local waste officers to ensure that your recyclables are processed correctly. Recycling stations are one of the most visible ways to market your event's environmental ethics, so make them look good!

- Appoint staff stewards to creatively interact with and educate guests on waste minimization.
- Give guests portable waste disposal units such as Ashcans or used film canisters for cigarettes or gum.
- Design creative and eye-catching waste receptacles.
- Up-Cycle: give waste a higher purpose by having guests create group sculptures with aluminum cans.
- Cup Deposit Scheme: guests pay an extra fee for cups, which is refunded on return of the cup.
- Print instructions for disposal on the labels of disposable items.
- Give guests party favors in reusable bags.

Figure 6.4 Think Outside the Bin. Several Ways to be Creative in your Approach to Waste Minimization

Biodegradable Waste

Much of your standard waste, such as solid and liquid food waste, need not ever see the plastic lining of a garbage bag. More adventurous greener events pioneers can explore *composting*, the process by which biodegradable organic matter is decomposed into fertilizer. Composting has never been easier since the advent of indoor composting tools like Nature Mill, available at www.naturemill.com, an easy-to-use electric composter that fits under your kitchen sink. Simply scrape your dishes into the Nature Mill and let it decompose the food matter into tidy plant soil, which you can remove and use in your garden. Outdoor composting sites need to be created in coordination with local government and event site managers, and generally require more cost and effort than standard waste collection. Still, they are an impressive and noble boon to any greener event, and more sustainable than standard landfill systems. If creating a compost heap is out of your event's reach, consider collecting your biodegradable waste anyway and donating it to a local farm for their composting.

Australia's Peats Ridge Sustainable Arts and Music Festival (www.peatsridgefestival.com.au) proved the feasibility of composting when it initiated 100 percent composting toilets. According to Peats Ridge, the toilets are "waterless, very pleasant to use, odor free, and six months after the festival, the bi-product will be fantastic soil conditioner for our festival site" (Peats Ridge 2009). Australian company Natural Events, which supplies these composting toilets, serves a growing demand for ecological waste management, and has recently seen its business soar. Hamish Skermer, of Live Earth Sydney, explains how its waterless toilets (critical for a water-poor nation like Australia) work, saying, "By adding the sawdust, what you're doing is creating a carbon-nitrogen-oxygen balance that's really appropriate for composting. There's a very large decrease in the amount of material that needs to be removed from site. We don't use any water at all" (*Greening Live Earth* 2007).

Share Your Surplus

Sadly, many events allow the mass disposal of perfectly good, brand-new items and untouched foods. Tradeshows may donate unused pencils, pens, notepads, and other supplies to local schools. Untouched box lunches can be sent to local homeless shelters. Even plastic fencing, temporary staging, and signage can be contributed as raw materials to a local festival or theater (Figure 6.5). Contact charities in your area and create meaningful partnerships with them to ensure that your event does not gratuitously waste useful items. By creating strategic partnerships with charities, you will enhance your public image and please your patrons.

Traffic

Together with waste, traffic is one of the biggest negative impacts of events. Excessive traffic not only pollutes the air with CO_2 emissions, it disrupts natural terrain, clogs streets and denigrates event experience. A Greener Festival found that 70 percent of

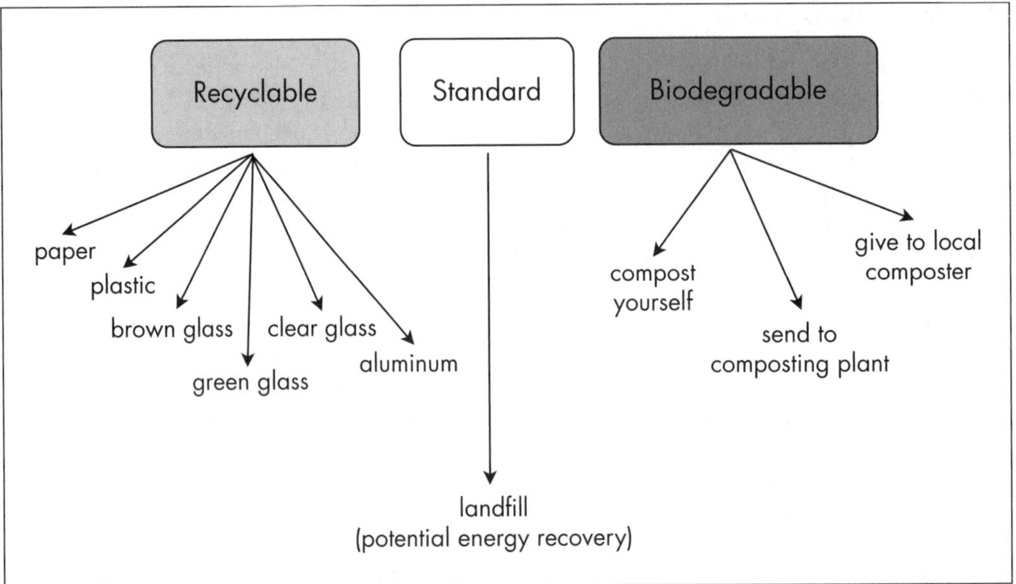

Figure 6.5 Event Waste. This Diagram Shows the Possible Outcomes of Event Waste. Recyclable Waste can be Separated and Reprocessed; Biodegradable Waste can be Composted; Standard Waste goes to a Landfill, where the only Potential Benefit is that it can be Decomposed to Generate Heat or Electricity.

music festival patrons found traffic to be a negative event outcome. Greener events pioneers will take their cue from ecotourism in minimizing traffic congestion and promoting sustainable travel alternatives. The first and best solution is mass transport. The widespread benefits of mass transit at destination events are summarized in Figure 6.6. When booking tickets for the 2008 Connect Music Festival in Argyle, Scotland (www.connectmusicfestival.com), patrons were strongly encouraged to also book a ticket on 1 of 35 buses running from various locations around Scotland directly to the festival site. The benefits of this scheme were huge: patrons could eat, drink, relax, and socialize, while a driver navigated difficult winding highland roads. Not only was the bus ticket cheaper than the gas required for the car journey, the bus also delivered patrons closer to the event site. The event organization also benefited, with less disruptive traffic to manage, fewer parking lots to maintain, and increased insurance against car accidents.

Even more eco-friendly than a bus is a train, and it may surprise you to find that some of the greenest events occur in urban areas where the least amount of transport is required. Paul Tollett, who founded Cochella Music Festival in the Southern California desert, produced All Points West in 2008 as an urban variant of the Cochella model (www.apwfestival.com). Featuring major bands like The Roots and Animal Collective, All Points West occurred in Liberty State Park, just across the Hudson from Lower Manhattan,

	Cost Savings	Freedom	Experience	Safety	Environment
For Event Organizers	Fewer parking lots to create, adjust, supervise, and maintain Fewer event parking and traffic crew	Less traffic congestion and parking allows for more usable space on event site	Fewer parking lots to maintain Cleaner event site Less land reconstruction needed	Increased insurance against car accidents	Fewer CO_2 emissions Less air pollution Less land destruction
For Guests	Mass transit is often cheaper than the price of gas required for the drive Carpooling and car-sharing initiatives save costs	Ability to eat, drink, and relax on journey without worrying about driving	Stress-free journey No event traffic/ parking lot congestion Arrive closer to the entrance area Increased socializing and networking, especially in carpools	Professional, insured driver No need to follow directions to unfamiliar event locations	Environmental self-esteem Less mud Preserved, cleaner event site

Figure 6.6 Benefits of Mass Transportation at Events. Greener Events Pioneers can Reap the Benefits of Promoting Public Transit Options and/or Organizing their Own Mass Transport Initiatives.

easily accessible to thousands of local residents by using the New York subway and New Jersey transit. Urban events provide much greener transportation options.

Traffic doesn't stop with the patrons, either. Staff and artists are a huge part of a greener event's transportation plan. John Rego, environmental director of Live Earth, explains how the complex travel plans of all the famous music stars are coordinated, saying, "We help them figure out what's the most sustainable way they can actually get to the event. A lot of them are taking turbo props, which lowers the emissions of the flight, or taking commercial flights, taking public transportation to the events" (Greening Live Earth 2007).

The best way to cut down on transportation is to cut it out completely. Thanks to new Web technology, videoconferencing has never been easier and can save Event Leaders an expensive drive or flight for business meetings. *Webinars*, or seminars delivered and experienced on the Internet, continue to evolve as competition to live events. Greener events pioneers will need to assess the value of webinars and online meeting technology in order to reevaluate the role of face-to-face conferences. As technology continues to deliver more isolated communication options, the demand for real-life human interaction increases.

Similarly, the increasingly prohibitive financial and environmental costs of air travel may force greener events pioneers to reassess the value of destination events. Does the Kansas City Rotary Club really need to hold their annual meeting on Lake Michigan, or can they do it right there in Kansas City, putting the cost savings from travel toward other local event amenities? Research where your patrons are located, and search for venues convenient to them. Don't make your patrons drive an hour both ways to attend an event at an arbitrary location. Events that require multiple venues, like a hotel and a conference center, can use venues within walking distance of each other. Amy Spatrisano, principal with Meeting Strategies Worldwide is clear-headed about the ethics of event tourism, saying, "It doesn't mean we don't meet anymore. But how, when, and where may look a little different. What our industry needs right now is to be proactive, rather than reactive" (Golding 2008, p. 136).

Air Pollution

The main environmental reason to cut transportation is to cut CO_2 emissions that pollute the air and contribute to global warming. Whether it powers a car, bus, an outdoor kitchen, or a high-tech sound and light system, any engine or generator powered by gasoline emits hazardous and unpleasant greenhouse gases. These emissions can be minimized through alternative energy solutions, which are discussed later in this chapter.

Land Use

Remember the U.S. Boy Scout pledge to "Leave No Trace." A Greener Festival recommends the following strategies to minimize land damage:

- Use portable tracking and roadway to keep cars off the grass and out of the mud.
- Where possible, enhance the environment by planting trees and preserving nature.
- Research the local wildlife and consider ways to support it.
- Liaise with local environmental and wildlife charities and organizations to create a plan for sustaining the event site ecology.
- A percentage of income could be donated or invested into local environmental/wildlife projects. Check out www.groundwork.org (2009).

Noise Pollution

It may not produce CO_2 emissions or waste natural resources, but excessive noise pollution certainly disrupts the event site. Greener events need to respect both the event site and its human inhabitants. Washington, D.C.,'s Fort Reno Concert Series, which features local punk bands such as Fugazi, enforces a strict 9:30 P.M. curfew out of respect for local residents. Even when the Santa Barbara Bowl presented Radiohead, they were still legally bound to end the concert by 10 P.M.

Your First Five Steps

Once you have analyzed the various kinds of pollution your event is likely to generate, it is time to create your plan of attack. A greener event's weapons against waste are known as *Environmentally Friendly Practices* (EFPs), strategies that include everything from alternative energy to recycling. But Rome wasn't built in a day, and neither can events immediately turn green. Before we tackle the big EFPs, here are five little EFPs that you can employ right this minute in your home or office to drastically cut waste and conserve energy.

1. Go Paperless

Nearly all work is e-mail-based today. Think before you print: Do you really need to see it on paper? Consider the many documents distributed to clients, staff, patrons, and stakeholders that could be e-mailed instead of mailed. Make e-mail your first option, with a snail-mail alternative for those who request it. Instead of keeping paper files for everything, burn digital files onto discs or portable hard drives. Of course, you will need hard-copy originals of all signed legal documents, as well as sentimental documents. The Capital Fringe Festival in Washington, D.C., annually outfits the office walls with an enormous festival calendar made from butcher paper and thousands of sticky notes, a process that encourages transparency and community within the organization. The official calendar, however, is digital, and they have recently taken the cost- and time-saving measure of going paperless with all artist applications (www.capfringe.org). Remember that unimportant documents can be printed on junk paper, and other documents can be printed double-sided. Double-sided printing cuts your paper bill in half!

2. Turn Off the Lights

How many electronic devices are plugged in around you right now that are not in use? Stereos on standby, computers on screensaver mode, and fully charged cell phones that are plugged into electrical sockets are using electricity for no good reason. Turn off the stereo and computer, and unplug your fully charged cell phone. Most importantly, turn off all lights not in use. These cost-saving measures for office and home are directly applicable to your greener event. All electronic devices and technical equipment need to be tested before the event, but, once tested and fully charged, they should be turned off until the pre-event phase. Video projectors, sound boards, spotlights, and PA systems can waste enormous amounts of electricity when left on standby. Turn it off and marvel at how low your next electricity bill is.

3. Turn Down the Heat

Insulate your building and your body. Winter is cold for a reason; if you have to wear a parka outside you shouldn't get away with a t-shirt in the office. Outdoor heating units are increasingly popular but huge energy wasters. Instead of fighting against cold weather, capitalize on it! The 2009 London Ice Sculpting Festival brought thousands of people to the grounds of the National History Museum in chilly January 2009 with a little help from Icebox, the United Kingdom's leading ice-art specialist (www.londonicesculptingfestival.co.uk; www.theicebox.com). Challenge your patrons to embrace the cold with imaginative winter event themes. For indoor environments, double- or triple-glaze all windows and invest in better wall insulation. Germany has recently developed green buildings that are so insulated that they stay warm in the winter without any internal heating at all. How does "zero" sound for your next heating bill?

4. Buy Greener

Energy-efficient light bulbs are slightly more expensive in the short term and vastly more cost-effective in the long term. Green cleaning products are competitively priced and much more pleasant to use and to smell. You can find consumer shopping guides on everything from green shoes to green furniture on Tree Hugger, a green lifestyle Web-magazine at www.treehugger.com.

5. Use Silverware

Get rid of those plastic spoons and paper cups and treat yourself to real food and drink served with real silverware and dishes. Think about how much money you spend on Starbucks coffee, and then consider the savings of brewing your own coffee and encouraging staff to bring in their own mugs and thermoses. If you provide coffee for event crew, consider encouraging them beforehand to bring in their own thermoses. Giving your staff opportunities to do their bit for the planet may just keep them motivated.

Three Cycles

Like the Earth, the world of greener events is circular. The event cycle of research, design, planning, coordination and evaluation described at the start of Chapter 2 shows how events come full circle. Greener events pioneers see their event as a unified whole: the staff, patrons, stakeholders, technology, and natural resources all part of a cohesive sphere. Greener event sites must come full circle, looking the same after an event as they do beforehand. Many EFPs are cycles as well, and here are three of the most important cycles of greener events.

Precycle

Before you recycle, precycle. *Precycling* is an emerging strategy that promotes buying used, recycled, or recyclable products. Bringing your own canvas tote to the supermarket instead of wasting plastic bags is precycling. So is bringing your own thermos to work.

The perfect precycled event might resemble a gorgeous dinner party where the food is made from your own backyard garden, served with silver flatware, porcelain plates, and cloth napkins, and everyone licks their plates clean. There is no trash. Disposable materials are necessary for many events, but unnecessary for far more. Any item that is manufactured to be used just once before going straight to an ever-expanding landfill represents a tremendous misuse of human labor and natural resources. Consider the long-term benefits of reusable materials: How much do you annually spend on purchasing and disposing of plastic spoons? Would it be cheaper to own your own steel spoons? Would it improve patron experience?

Many events necessitate disposable materials by their very nature. They didn't hand me a glass of water at the twenty-fifth mile of the Austin Marathon—it came in a paper cup that could be easily dropped without breaking stride. For these situations, consider buying recycled materials. Visitors love the recycled wooden spoons used at the cafe in London's Science Museum, and they will love them at your event, too: Biodegradable cutlery and food containers are widely available from companies like Vegware (www.vegware.us). Live Earth recommends buying PVC-free fencing, and ensuring that all fencing and other temporary staging materials be reused after the event or else donated to a local group. Likewise, signage can be made from recycled paper and using organic vegetable-based inks. Recycled materials are available today which look every bit as stunning as standard materials. But buying precycled doesn't always mean buying reprocessed or biodegradable items—it could mean buying vintage. Precycling can mean impressing your patrons with an antique popcorn machine instead of a ugly modern one. The 2008 Edinburgh International Book Festival used antique church pews for seating instead of new chairs. Instead of buying a bland modern podium, take the time to find a funky vintage—one that will make your event stand out from every other event.

A key component of precycling is minimizing packaging. Greener events pioneers will avoid individually wrapped items in favor of goods either unwrapped or packaged in bulk. The perfect example here is the water bottle. Although Event Leaders can purchase water bottles made from recycled and recyclable plastic, it is much greener to use water coolers and water jugs and to give patrons reusable cups. Not only does the recycling of water bottles waste energy, many patrons will leave their bottles half-full, wasting water. Greener events pioneers will provide either water coolers, or, if sanitary, water from the tap, to both patrons and event crew. Nothing cheapens an event more than tiny packets of ketchup or butter; buying ketchup or butter in bulk and serving them in real dishes will actually be cheaper and look nicer. Many event suppliers can cut down on packaging if asked. Just as you bring your own canvas bag to the supermarket, you can bring your vases straight to the florist to avoid unnecessary plastic wrapping. Current greener Event Leaders already recognize precycling as one of the most effective EFPs for Greener Events. As John Rego, Environmental Director of Live Earth says, "With all the three aspects we go through—energy, waste and transportation—it really comes down to reducing first. That's the key. It's been the mantra of sustainability for decades, and we've really tried to incorporate that as our first step to greening Live Earth" (*Greening Live Earth* 2007). Figure 6.7 shows five ways to reduce waste in a greener event budget.

Buy Retro	Buy Real	Buy Recycled	Buy Bulk	Biodegradable
Antique furniture gives classical style. Retro arcade games give vintage fun. Everyone loves remembering his or her youth. Give event patrons a flashback with real design elements from their heyday: Baby Boomers = 1960s; Gen X = 1970s; Gen Y = 1980s.	Disposable items make for disposable events: avoid one-use-only products. Invest in reusable products such as silverware for long-term cost savings. Hand out reusable thermoses with your event logo on them.	Recycled paper now comes in every color of the rainbow. You can use it for not just invitations, but also streamers, banners, signage, tablecloths, napkins, and confetti! Tradeshow handouts should be made of recycled goods.	Ask suppliers to minimize packaging. Bulk buys are often cheaper. Bulk foods can be arranged in real dishes for elegant looks; nothing is tackier than a pile of ketchup packets. Avoid water bottles; use water coolers or tap water.	Containers for food and drink, cutlery, dishes, and other food items are all available in biodegradable forms for mass purchase. Buy green cleaning products instead of chemicals-they smell nicer!

Figure 6.7 Five Precycled Buys

Once seen as the ultimate EFP, recycling (the reprocessing of used products into new products) is now acknowledged to be less desirable than precycling because of the energy required to reprocess recycled materials. Prevention, minimization, and reuse of potential waste all sit above recycling on the Waste Management Hierarchy pictured in Figure 6.3. That being said, recycling is greener than standard waste disposal, in high public demand, and a critical aspect of any greener event. It is also typically the most visible and well-noticed EFP of any greener event. Greener events pioneers will deliver a broad portfolio of recycling strategies, which may include:

- Omnipresent recycling stations
- Clearly labeled and attractive receptacles
- Volunteers and staff dedicated to recycling maintenance
- Educating patrons on how and why to recycle
- Incentives for patrons who recycle
- Thinking outside the bin: distribute Ashcans and other portable receptacles
- Providing catering staff with separate receptacles for recycling
- "Up-cycling:" using recyclable products to create art, such as having patrons stack aluminum cans as a sculpture.
- Tax on recyclable items, which gets refunded when items are returned

This last strategy has proved hugely successful for UK events. For every purchase of a pint of beer in a plastic cup, patrons pay an extra £2, which is refunded upon the return of the plastic cup. Nearly all patrons will return the cup for their refund, a second sales interaction that often results in another pint purchased. There are no littered plastic cups to be seen anywhere on the event grounds, as savvy patrons are happy to recycle them for £2. In the German Market at Edinburgh's Winter Festival grounds, patrons pay an extra £2 for every mug of mulled wine, money that is refunded upon return of the mug. Many patrons choose to keep the souvenir mugs, thus effectively making a second purchase. This is called a *Cup Deposit Scheme.* It's good for the environment and good for business. Matt Grant, Director of Peats Ridge, describes the vastly enhanced atmosphere instilled by a cup deposit scheme:

> *The psychology of putting a value on a piece of waste can change behavior. If a can is worth one dollar, then someone will pick it up. There are no cans on the floor, and so that creates a psychology as well: there are no cigarette butts on the floor and people generally litter less. If anyone doesn't care, then they pay a dollar for not caring.*

Education, innovation, and conservation are all inherent aspects of a cup deposit scheme.

Bicycle

This cycle uses two wheels and can carry greener events pioneers to new and exciting places. Bicycling is good for the environment and good for your health. The Mayor of London Boris Johnson is famous for bicycling between downtown meetings instead of wasting the taxpayer fuel and money on a taxi. You, too, can make a statement by biking to meetings. Many events employ expensive transportation devices such as Segways or golf carts when a simple bicycle will do. *Pedicabs* are just simple rickshaws pulled by bicycles, but they offer passengers a thrilling, new, and eco-friendly travel experience. When liquor conglomerate Diageo threw the 200th birthday party for Johnnie Walker Scotch Whisky in New York City, they hired pedicabs from Manhattan Rickshaw Company (www.manhattanrickshaw.com) to elegantly take tipsy patrons home. (BizBash 2005) New York's Revolution Rickshaws even offers cargo pedicabs, which can transport 500 pounds of materials through Manhattan streets faster than a taxicab (www.revolutionrickshaws.com). In our zest for innovation, humankind has forgotten that the complex automobile is often less convenient and useful than our most ancient of inventions, the wheel. As with all new transportation methods, a comprehensive risk assessment must be undertaken when using bicycles and pedicabs at your event.

Greener Energy

Not only do bicycles conserve resources and promote exercise, they can also be used to generate energy. The 2008 Super Bowl, which was 100 percent powered by renewable energy, hosted a four-day stationary-bike ride event that powered 30 minutes of the pre-game show solely by pedal power. You can purchase Pedal-A-Watt bicycles from www.econvergence.net to power your event while giving your event patrons an exciting, competitive activity. Engineers have powered long-lasting electric lighters from the mere click of a finger for years, using the *Piezolectric Effect*, or the ability for certain materials to generate energy from simple friction (i.e., rubbing tiny crystals together). Pioneering engineers are looking to apply this technique to cell phones, using the motor energy generated from fingers when sending text messages to charge the phone battery. It is now possible to buy portable clocks, radios, flashlights, and electrical generators that are powered solely by winding a crank. Perhaps most spectacular of all is the Sustainable Dance Floor, available from www.sustainabledanceclub.com, which powers a full nightclub LED lighting system from the energy of feet dancing on an energy-sensor dance floor. Like the automobile, in our pursuit of new sources of energy, we forget the most obvious source: human energy.

For those not inclined to exercise, an even easier energy source can be discovered by simply basking in the sun, riding a wave, or enjoying a cool breeze. Solar, water, and wind power all provide free, renewable sources of energy if you can harness them. *Renewable Energy* use means sustainably harvesting those of earth's natural resources which we have an unlimited supply of. Additionally, Friedman differentiates between coal and oil, which comes from underground, and sun, water, and wind, which come from above. He calls coal and oil "Fuels From Hell." By comparison, sun, water, and wind are "Fuels From Heaven."

Switching to renewable energy may be as simple as calling the electric company; the U.S. Department of Energy (DOE) lists more than 750 U.S. electricity suppliers that already offer alternative energy plans, which you can switch to at http://apps3.eere.energy.gov/greenpower/buying/buying_power.shtml, 2009. The 2008 Super Bowl simply contracted the Salt River Project, a provider in Arizona, to get 100 percent renewable energy from solar, hydro, and wind power. Many events without access to an alternative energy supplier may consider designing their own alternative energy solutions. While such endeavors can make a spectacular impact, they need to be carefully coordinated with event suppliers, independent experts, and local authorities. Much of the technology discussed here is available for purchase from altE at store.altenergy.com or ABS Alaskan at www.absak.com, and Appendix 18 has a complete list of renewable energy suppliers.

Biofuels

Events that are unable to simply plug into a renewable energy provider will need local energy generators. Greener events pioneers can seek generators that run on *biofuel*, or farm-grown fuel made out of agriculture such as corn or vegetable oil. Like coal and oil, biofuels emit CO_2. Unlike coal and oil, biofuels come from renewable agricultural sources, which, in their raw form (e.g., wheat or corn), also absorb CO_2. However, because very few automobiles can run on pure *biomass* (pure organic matter), most biofuels are *biodiesel*: a combination of regular diesel and biomass. All diesel engines can run on a biodiesel mix that uses 10 percent biomass, and many can run on much more. Biodiesel is labeled according to its percentage of biomass; B20 biodiesel contains 20 percent biomass and 80 percent diesel. With the right car, you can actually take the *Waste Vegetable Oil* (WVO) straight out of your local fast-food joint's deep fryer, filter it through a sifter, and put it straight into your gas tank. How's that for free gas? Biodiesel is popular with environmentally conscious touring music acts. The eccentric and ecocentric Willie Nelson sells his own biodiesel from a truck stop in Texas called Carl's Corner. Many other famous entertainment acts such as Bon Jovi and Incubus travel in biofuel-powered buses.

Solar Power

Every summer, the Croissant Neuf Solar Tent is booked at major festivals and private events in the United Kingdom to present music in its lively 1,000-seat tent with a full light and sound rig. What is remarkable is that Croissant Neuf's entire operation is solar powered, in a country known for rainy weather. Solar power is an increasingly feasible energy source for events. As with all energy sources (and all other aspects of events), a backup is required. Many companies make solar paneling and generators that collect solar power and convert it into electricity—this technique is known as *active solar power.* Try www.solarhome.org or www.wholesalesolar.com for active solar power distributors. *Passive solar power* is much simpler; it involves using raw sunlight for light or heat. The design of an event's architecture can be altered to maximize passive solar power and minimize electric light: Using a tent with transparent walls can give patrons natural light and a beautiful vista. Many of the most innovative new green buildings employ passive solar power with window shades that allow warm sunlight in the winter and keep it out in the summer. Passive solar power can also be used to cook things like sun tea: just put a jar of water outside in hot weather with a teabag in it. Best of all, passive solar power requires no technology whatsoever.

Hydropower

Hydropower is the harnessing of naturally flowing water sources to generate hydroelectricity, and it is already a critical part of the Earth's energy supply. As of 2005, hydroelectricity accounted for 19 percent of the Earth's electricity. The nation of Norway runs on 98 percent hydroelectricity, and has the sixth greatest capacity of all nations for generating hydroelectricity. The United States has the fourth greatest capacity, with immense untapped potential hydropower ("Binge and Purge" 2009). Many hydroplants offer scenic locations with breathtaking views, making them ideal event venues. Smaller refurbished mills offer cozy meeting rooms, while larger civic dams can support major outdoor events. Events held at or near hydroplants may save energy costs by using hydroelectricity. Other events may investigate designing their own *microhydropower*, simple technology that can harness local water sources for specific event use. Try www.canyonhydro.com or www.utilityfree.com for microhydropower solutions.

Wind Power

In the past few years, the United States has skyrocketed to become the world's leading generator of wind power, thanks to initiatives in California and Texas. Wind power is generated from *turbines*, or windmills placed either on land or offshore that convert kinetic wind movement into electricity. Small-scale wind power can be not only feasible but profitable; citizens of the Danish island of Samso have generated enough wind power from both large municipal turbines and small personal turbines to both power the entire island and sell remaining energy at a profit (Kolbert 2008). As with microhydropower technology, greener events pioneers can investigate small-scale wind power for events. Try www.bergey.com or www.aerostarwind.comfor wind power solutions.

Wood

An old-fashioned wood-burning fireplace is often more carbon efficient than gas heating. Although mass deforestation is wholly unacceptable, energy experts are generating interest in the sustainable harvesting of trees for wood fuel as an alternative to coal and oil. It's not renewable, but clean wood fuel combustion is cheaper than oil and generates only about 10 percent of the CO_2 emissions. If a wood stove is too old-fashioned, try a modern *pellet stove*, which burns small wood pellets that are easier to handle and emits less CO_2 than raw wood.

Energy Efficiency

Remember Rego's mantra of reducing first. Before investing in renewable energy, make sure you are getting the maximum use out of your existing energy. Two of your first five

Human	Solar	Wind	Hydro	Biofuel
Pedal-A-Watt bicycles generate electricity. Staff can commute via bicycle. Bicycle couriers. Pedicabs offer patrons a new, renewable transport option.	Let the sunshine in! Create skylights and windows to use passive solar power to light and heat a room or tent. Consider solar power panels and generators for active solar power.	Wind turbines can provide site-specific wind energy. Turbines make a striking, powerful look on an outdoor event site. Many local energy companies offer wind power already.	Hydroplants make for scenic and unique venues for events run on renewable energy. Look into micro-hydropower solutions from either running water or rainwater.	Filtered Waste Vegetable Oil (WVO) from deep fryers can power your car Find out what percentage Biomass your car can handle, and switch to that grade of Biodiesel. Work with your local generator rental company to find generators that can run on biodiesel.

Figure 6.8 Renewable Energy Sources for Events

steps are to turn out the lights and turn down the heat; take these steps further to realize companywide savings. Turn in your stage lights for compact fluorescent or *Light Emitting Diode* (LED) lights, which are two thirds more efficient and can last up to 10 times longer than standard lights. LED lights are available from Color Kinetics at www.colorkinetics.com. The LED lights used at the 2009 Super Bowl required only 290 watts per fixture, compared to the 1,600 watts a standard fixture requires (Klingler 2009). Greener events pioneers will remember to cut lighting costs by utilizing passive solar power, and, if that is not an option, mirrors. Decorative mirrors can brighten and expand an event environment while increasing the efficiency of your lighting system.

Cultural Sustainability

Part of greening your event is making a meaningful connection with your event site in order to ensure the preservation of its natural environment. The same goes for the inhabitants of that environment. Greener events pioneers will find new and exciting ways to support *cultural sustainability*, an important principle of ecotourism wherein the host culture is incorporated respectfully and meaningfully into the event design. Greener events can partner with host cultures in two direct ways: culturally and economically.

Local Cultures

High in the North Sea, between Scotland and Norway, sit the Shetland Isles, the northernmost islands in the United Kingdom. Isolated from the mainland by a 12-hour ferry ride, Shetland's stunning, treeless landscape contains an exceptional culture that combines rich nautical traditions evolved from whaling to fishing and oil-rigs, with Scottish and Viking heritage. This culture is celebrated and reinforced by Up Helly Aa, a uniquely Shetland event celebrated on the last Tuesday of every January (www.uphellyaa.org). Originally a disorganized riot of marauding men firing guns and dragging flaming barrels of tar through the city streets, the event was institutionalized into a safer community heritage event around the end of the nineteenth century. Like New Orleans' Mardi Gras and the Philadelphia Mummers Parade, Up Helly Aa consists of more than 40 different squads of men dressed in flamboyant costumes based on different themes. These "guizers" parade through city streets in a torchlight ceremony, which culminates in the bonfire of a Viking longboat. They then spend the following 12 hours, from 8 P.M. to 8 A.M., visiting 12 separate town halls where they regale local audiences with a brief skit or song, engage in a Scottish country dance or two and taste the local food and drink. Although the Shetland Hotel serves as the unofficial town hall for tourists, tourism is not a core goal of Up Helly Aa. Many of the guizers' skits revolve around obscure local issues, and unlike tourist-friendly "ceilidhs" (traditional Scottish folk-dancing parties), there is no instruction on how to perform the complex group dances. This spectacular event is meticulously organized by Shetlanders, for Shetlanders, with the explicit purpose of sustaining Shetland heritage, culture, and community.

Greener events pioneers will hold up this rich Viking pageant as a model of cultural sustainability. If your annual conference can connect with the Association of Dental Hygienists in just 1 percent of the meaningful cultural way that Up Helly Aa connects with Shetlanders, your event will succeed. Before arbitrarily imposing an event theme, research your patrons and discover their passions and dreams. Find unique ways to create meaningful connections between patrons. Similarly, respect the host culture of your event site location. You can win favor with the local authority by partnering with local organizations or inviting prominent local figures to attend your event. Perhaps the Association of Dental Hygienists can donate surplus toothbrushes to a local hospital, or invite students from a local dental college to attend the conference.

Local Economies

A local authority's greatest concern when reviewing an event proposal is often the potential economic impact. Destination event patrons want to experience local culture and consume local goods and services. By partnering with local businesses, you can satisfy both local stakeholders and patrons. Connect Music Festival features diverse food stalls and bars operated by a wide variety of UK vendors. The best location and most spacious tent, however, is reserved for local distillery Loch Fyne Whisky and local seafood merchant Loch Fyne Oyster Bar. By featuring these emblematic local delicacies, Connect stands out from all other music festivals, offering patrons a uniquely Scottish Highlands experience. This also supports the local economy, ensuring a stable political and economic environment for future festivals. What about the environment? By favoring local suppliers, greener events cut down on supplier transportation, and therefore CO_2 emissions.

Marketing Your Greener Event

Marketing is one of the most important aspects of greener events, not only because it sells the event as contemporary and ethical, but also because it educates patrons. Greener events pioneers should endeavor to leave every patron educated and inspired to pursue sustainability in his or her life and work. Creativity is key. When the University of Colorado initiated a recycling program at football games, they periodically lit up the scoreboard with an "environmental savings report" to the cheers of 50,000 screaming fans (*It's Easy Being Green!* 1996). Greener events can target various niche markets: are you attracting a wild, free-spirit hippy crowd who seek spiritual connection with nature, or are you serving ethical professionals who require modern amenities with elite environmental standards? The first group may thrill for composting toilets, while the second group might prefer the finest locally-sourced, organic, gourmet cuisine. Regardless, events with an explicit environmental theme should publicly catalog every green initiative and strategy employed, distributing well-rounded information online, at the event, and in the press. Other events may employ more subtle themes, making artful use of the color green and employing smaller, more elegant informational signage.

Information and signage must be readily available. The same customer who complains about a *cup deposit scheme* may be thrilled to find that he is actually helping the environment. As Rego explains, "The challenge of really greening a venue is that a lot of it happens behind the scenes. What people see is the lights going on. They don't see the power that's going in from the windmills. They don't see the power from the biodiesel sitting out back behind the stage that's going into the generators" (Greening Live Earth 2007). Publicize your windmill. Highlight your biodiesel. Encourage public discourse about greener events.

Greenwash is false or misleading marketing that promotes an organization unfaithfully as environmentally responsible, and allegations of it can destroy a public image. As a slogan, "green" continues to serve marketers around the world as a cheap and easy way to suggest ethics or instill consumer trust, but this marketing godsend does not come without a price: "green" claims must be supported by hard evidence and real actions. If you want to talk the talk, you have to walk the walk.

Plan and Partners

This chapter has presented EFPs as diverse as precycling, mass transit, waste minimization, renewable energy, and pedal power. Which EFPs are right for your event? This questions is much the same as deciding what to plant in a garden. A good gardener analyzes the soil, climate, and environment before planting; Greener events pioneers will analyze the context, goals, culture, and resources of an event in order to create an environmental plan and choose the best EFPs. Base your plan on careful situational analysis, but don't be afraid to take risks; the future of greener events lies in innovative pioneers. Until they saw the golden leaves rising high above the fence, our neighbors didn't believe that my father could grow Iowa sweet-corn in his Chevy Chase, Maryland, garden. Until they see the flashing lights and hear the blasting speakers, patrons don't believe that a concert venue in rainy old England can run on solar power.

Gardeners

A larger event's commitment to the environment begins with hiring or nominating an *environmental manager*. On the level of a production manager or a marketing manager, an environmental manager holds significant overarching responsibility for a greener event. Environmental managers will research, plan, and implement areas including EFPs, energy efficiency, waste minimization, precycling, and cultural sustainability. They will coordinate these initiatives in conjunction with other managers, and maintain direct communication with all staff and crew to ensure organizational continuity regarding EFPs. Smaller events that cannot hire an environmental manager can delegate environmental responsibilities among current managers. Assign your marketing team to find affordable recycled paper; challenge your catering manager to find local food vendors.

Environmental Audits

One way to begin is to have an outside firm or consultant analyze your environmental impact and measure your carbon footprint. As part of such an environmental audit, the world's largest tradeshow, Consumer Electronics Show (CES) has ambitiously decided to track its 2009 carbon footprint and minimize it through energy efficiency and carbon offsetting (www.cesweb.org). When considering research, find consultants that understand your event and work with them to establish goals for enhancement. Once you have oriented them to your institutional values, allow these consultants to research and analyze the environmental impact of your event. Make sure that they provide detailed, specific action items for you to implement towards a greener event. The presence of an environmental auditor at an event can be used in publicity to show your commitment to greener events.

Greener Partners

Grant enjoys recalling the many event suppliers that Peats Ridge has convinced to go green over the past few years:

> *There was no one in Australia that would do biodiesel. It was an uphill battle talking to companies. Finally, we found a company that would give it a go. They took a punt and ran the whole festival on biodiesel. According to their information it was a huge risk, but it was completely fine. They tripled in size the year they converted to biodiesel. Now they do forty to fifty events, and they only do biodiesel. They have opened up another two stores throughout Australia. (Author Interview)*

Some event suppliers might present you with innovative green solutions, but more often than not, it is the greener events pioneer who will have to press suppliers towards innovation. See Appendix 18 for a complete list of suppliers and other organizations that can enhance your event with greener products and services. Because of the newness involved in greener events, always maintain constant and explicit communication with greener event suppliers. When possible, do a comparative analysis of competing suppliers, and consult experts or greener Event Leaders. Try to shop locally, and challenge suppliers to develop greener products if they want your business. If you cannot find what you are looking for, consider the feasibility and risk involved with building it yourself.

Greener Hotels

As with tourism, the hotel industry has succeeded in applying theories of sustainable development toward enhancing their sector. The greener hotels movement has produced many notable EFPs, topmost among which is minimizing excessive laundering. The "Green" Hotels Association (www.greenhotels.com) offers simple cards to hang on towel racks asking guests to consider using towels more than once in order to ethically conserve water. At least 70 percent of guests participate. Greener events pioneers will look for the following characteristics in greener hotels:

- Variety of recycling programs: reuse, precycling, composting, etc.
- Guests are asked to reuse linens
- Low-flow toilets and showers which conserve water
- Energy efficient lighting
- Thickly insulated walls and windows to conserve heat
- Located near public transportation
- Bicycle rental program
- Sustainable swimming pool
- Pesticide-free gardening
- Careful maintenance of grounds
- Renewable energy sources
- Locally owned, operated, and staffed
- Locally-produced items in gift shop
- Local foods served
- Visible signage and information on EFPs
- Guests encouraged to participate in EFPs

Ask potential hotel partners about these aspects of their business. If the hotel does not have an environmental policy in place, work with them to create some simple EFPs for your guests, such as allowing guests to reuse linens. For a thorough directory of green lodging, check out "It's a Green Green World" at www.itsagreengreenworld.com.

Greener Food

Together with recycling stations, catering is one of the most visible aspects of a greener event, with potentially the biggest audience impact. A greener menu is often the best way to showcase your commitment to the environment, and greener menus will feature foods with four fundamental qualities:

1. *Natural: Organic*, or pesticide-free food, celebrates natural resources instead of chemicals.
2. *Seasonal*: Strawberries in September? Get real. Only foods grown and harvested during their natural seasons reflect sustainable farming. They also taste a lot better. Go to www.eattheseasons.com for a complete guide to seasonal foods.
3. *Local*: Regional produce supports the local economy while reducing the CO_2 emissions of long-distance food import. More to the point, Destination Event guests want to sample the local foods. Impress your guests at the Orlando Conference Center with fresh Florida oranges.
4. *Ethical*: Foreign goods such as coffee or bananas often cannot be sourced locally. In these situations, buy certified Fair Trade goods, which guarantee fair pay and human rights for the third-world workers supplying these goods. Also, consider animal rights by purchasing free-range chicken and eggs.

Greener caterers will put these ingredients together using traditional local recipes. In searching for the ideal greener caterers, many of the criteria for greener hotels apply: They should be locally owned, operated, and staffed, making efficient use of renewable energy sources, and using green cleaning products. The ideal greener caterers will source ingredients from local farms, conserve cleaning water, and compost all food waste.

Carbon Offsetting

After considering the many environmental impacts of special events, one might conclude that the greenest event is the one that doesn't happen. Ultimately, no event can completely avoid generating waste, misusing natural resources, or having an environmental impact. Green services that acknowledge their unavoidable debt to the environment sometimes offer *carbon offsetting*, or charitable investment in environmental causes as a way to balance their CO_2 emissions. Many airlines offer this option, and events like Connect Music Festival do as well. Carbon offsetting is sometimes criticized as greenwash, used as a free pass to pollute the environment. Grant believes in minimizing CO_2 first, and offsetting it second, and explains the psychological problems of offsetting: "People should buy their own carbon. If you offset your patrons' carbon then you are saying it's okay to not take responsibility for your actions." (Author Interview) Carbon offsetting is, however, a charitable act which is popular with consumers. Greener events pioneers should seek meaningful and relevant offsetting projects, and should not use offsetting to forgive event pollution.

Ingredients	Yes	No
Natural	Pesticide-free produce Chemical-free goods	Chemical fertilizers Pesticides Genetically modified foods Chemically enhanced foods
Seasonal	Strawberries in June Apples in August	Strawberries in September Apples in January
Local	Florida oranges in Orlando Valencia onions in Atlanta	Florida oranges in Toronto Valencia onions in Seattle
Ethical	Fair Trade coffee Free-range eggs	Products made in sweatshops Third-world labor without human rights Cage-raised poultry

Figure 6.9 Greener Ingredients

Toward a Greener Tomorrow

If the greenest event is the one that doesn't happen, why do we celebrate events? Why, for that matter, do we allow ourselves air travel when we know that the CO_2 emissions are corrupting the atmosphere? To be completely carbon neutral, must we live in thatched huts and sustain ourselves through local farming and hunting? Envisioning a completely green lifestyle can be quite scary, and too much to ask of any modern man or woman. However, thanks to constantly emerging technology and human ingenuity, carbon efficiency is becoming attainable within our contemporary lifestyle, and for every sacrifice, there are new opportunities. Trading in your Segway for a pedicab, for example, can be viewed as either a reluctant sacrifice or an exciting opportunity. As a greener events pioneer, it is your job to harness new technologies and ideas to create your own imaginative portfolio of sustainable initiatives. These initiatives will grow a healthy business by growing a healthy environment. While you need not switch to 100 percent composting toilets, switching to energy-efficient light bulbs will save you time and money. Remember that not all events can become completely green, but all events can become greener.

One of my most memorable event experiences comes from my hometown of Washington, D.C., where I attended the U.S. Department of Energy's biannual Solar Decathlon. The Decathlon is a competition between 20 universities around the world, each of which design a sustainable, solar-powered home of the future and then construct the home, from scratch, at the National Mall. The spectacularly innovative houses feature recycled industrial materials, modular-assembly designs, agriculture organically interwoven with architecture, and, of course, complex solar, hydro and wind power-generating technologies. The houses are stunningly beautiful, remarkable in their innovative technologies, and designed for average middle-class Americans. During this period of mortgage crisis and home foreclosures, the Solar Decathlon presents a bright future for sustainable homeownership. Greener events pioneers who see their own sustainable, rewarding, and environmentally responsible futures in these homes are not alone. We have a friend. In a November 17, 2008, speech to the Global Climate Summit, President Obama ushered in a new era of government-supported environmental initiatives. He had this to say of climate change:

> *The science is beyond dispute and the facts are clear. Sea levels are rising. Coastlines are shrinking. Climate change and our dependence on foreign oil, if left unaddressed, will continue to weaken our economy and threaten our national security. We will invest 15 billion dollars each year to catalyze private sector efforts to build a clean energy future. We will invest in solar power, wind power and next-generation biofuels. I promise you this. Any company that is willing to invest in clean energy will have an ally in Washington (change.gov 2008).*

Like the university students creating tomorrow's homes, greener events pioneers will create tomorrow's meetings, conferences, and events. And like these homes, greener events will conserve energy, save money, improve experience, protect resources and assets, and create a beautiful, safe, twenty-first century environment for life and celebration.

All references from this chapter, along with a complete reference guide to greener events, including green suppliers, can be found in Appendix 18.

The Pioneer: Joan L. Eisenstodt, CEO, Eisenstodt Associates, LLC, Washington, DC

A true meetings industry icon and thought leader, Joan Eisenstodt has been largely responsible for much of the professional development and many of the innovations within the meetings industry in the past three decades. Like many in her generation, she says she fell into this field. Joan says, "As a young person I produced events at my grade and high schools, and then, as a young adult, volunteered with numerous organizations around the United States to organize meetings. I then worked as a volunteer coordinator at an art museum where I was responsible for citywide events held in the museum. All along, I never knew I had a profession brewing! When I decided to leave my home state of Ohio and received some career counseling, I learned more about the meetings industry and only really understood it when I moved to Washington, D.C., and got my first job."

From the beginning of her career, Joan knew this was the right career for her. She recalls, "It felt right—and at the time, I thought I was a detail-oriented person. It was only later that I realized how much I hated details. However, I was good at details for a time. I can use my left-brain skills when needed and even enjoy some details now and then. The overall field of meetings and the entire hospitality industry are what truly interest me. The home that I found in this industry was largely because there are so many opportunities for growth and learning."

Joan has served as mentor to thousands of newcomers to the meetings industry, however she has many mentors who are from outside the industry. She says, "Looking back, I see that those who mentored me and provided guidance did so in the areas that ultimately became my focus. My teachers in high school created different learning environments and opportunities. For risk management, with a particular focus on contracts, Jeff King, Esq., taught me early on that it doesn't matter if you are right or wrong; you can still be sued. People I admire tend to come from far outside the industry, such as the civil rights pioneer Rosa Parks, the human rights leader and author, Elie Wiesel, the iconic leader Martin Luther King Jr., and all others who are seeking and bringing justice. My belief is that I can be in this industry and promote justice issues, since our industry is about bringing people together."

When considering the changes in the meetings industry during her long and distinguished career, she notes says that "I fear it has not changed much at all. We are using technology, but we do not see it as an enhancement for

Career-Advancement Connections

 Corporate Social Responsibility Connection

Consider the greener values of innovation, conservation, and education. How may you employ these three values in your greener events? Write down one practical

learning. Budgets ebb and flow with the times and right now the cycle is horrific because of the downward world-wide economic trends. We have not really looked at why people meet or when we do, we don't capitalize on it nor do we work to make meetings interesting to a variety of participants. We are also focused now on green issues without getting beyond the basic idea of not providing paper handouts at meetings. We seem to take things on the surface and then let them go when they are not trendy. Still another example is that having a Certified Meeting Professional (CMP) or other designation is a good thing and human resource departments now advertise for Certified Meeting Professionals as preferred or required. Yet there is still not a hard look at the expertise one has as long as there are letters signifying professional after one's name."

She recalls that the more things change, the more they stay the same. According to Joan, "Even contracts are not that different. I have one from 1944 that my grandparents signed for my parents' wedding and it's pretty much the same front and back banquet event order (BEO) that is used in the industry today!"

Joan believes that the meetings industry needs a wakeup call, and not just a economic one. She says, "The industry just began to show why meetings are valuable and it took an assault on our industry to do so. We are still reactive rather than proactive."

Following her long experience in the modern meetings industry, Joan is cautious about the future. She says, "We have changed much of what we are handing over and we are not demanding that the next gen be taught differently. We are handing over an industry that has yet to really incorporate concept of strategy into how it operates and only now really talking about it. When one asks what the term *strategic* means there is often a blank look. We need to regroup and look at what Maarten Vanneste is doing with his theory of Meeting Architecture™ and what others are demanding we do to make it better and have more research conducted to see what trends will impact meetings, meeting attendance, even travel to determine what next."

Joan passes on some sage advice for the next generation when she reminds newcomers in the meeting industry to "Be curious and be inquisitive. Ask why, how, when, and what before you do more and keep digging deeper when an answer is given. It is only when we ask questions that we get to better answers."

Joan L. Eisenstodt has asked the tough questions during her career that have provoked, prodded, and ultimately helped form the modern meetings industry, one now recognized as a legitimate profession for thousands of young people throughout the world. Her creativity and innovation have not only informed and helped educate the next generation but most importantly have given them a new aspiration to become curious and ask the important questions that will further advance the profession that Joan Eisenstodt helped give birth to.

The Protégé: Astrid Schrier, Meeting Coordinator, Association Headquarters, Inc.

Astrid Schrier served as the president of the Professional Convention Management Association student chapter at Temple University, and her leadership skills have taken her to Toronto, Canada, Seattle, Washington, and even Taiwan. She chose the meetings and events industry as her career because she wanted every day to be different. Astrid says, "The events industry allows me to meet a wide array of people and to see a project from inception to the actual product."

From the very beginning, she knew that this was the right field for her because it allows her to work with people on a constant basis and to be hands-on throughout the entire process of designing and delivering the event. She reflects that "I always knew that I would never be able to handle having a 9 to 5 desk job and while I know there is some desk work involved with the meetings and events industry, I will not be tied to a desk constantly."

Although still in the formative stages of her career, she has relied on a strong mentoring network to help her succeed. She describes two mentors who especially have strongly influenced her career development.

"Dave Buckley, CSEP, has truly taken me under his wing to teach me about the special events industry and to keep me involved in it. From joining committees to attending conferences, Dave has always placed me in the right direction to succeed.

Eva Matyskiela, CMP, taught me all I know about meetings and convention planning as I interned under her for two summers. Eva was one of my first bosses to entrust a great amount of responsibility to me and give me a certain amount of freedom to complete projects and tasks. "

Without using a crystal ball, Astrid thinks it is difficult to predict how the special events industry will change in the future. One of the reasons for this trepidation is the weakened U.S. economy. "The United States, is being impacted drastically by the economic crisis that is taking place, and I am unsure how and when we will bounce back from it. I do, however, see some trends that will continue

action item that you could feasibly implement in your event for each value. Think about how you can implement this, how it reflects the greener value of your event, and how it reflects your own events' organizational values. Combining your action items, the three greener values, and your own organizational values, now draft a mission statement with an environmental commitment that will appeal to your stakeholders.

to grow, such as the green movement and the use of the Internet for things such as communications and marketing. Also, the industry will have an influx of students who have bachelor's degrees in the field, like me, as well as more professionals with certifications because of the more competitive job market that is being created by the economy."

She believes that there will be two main catalysts or causes for these changes. "I think the economy will play a drastic part in changes that will be made within this industry, both positive and negative. I believe the other catalyst will be how the members of the special events industry and the hospitality industry as a whole react to the economic crisis and the negativity surrounding planning events during a crisis."

Although the meetings and events industry is hitting some rough patches right now, Astrid believes it will restore itself and begin to grow again. She predicts that "the special events industry that I will inherit in the next ten years will be environmentally conscious, technologically savvy and much larger than it currently is. I think that even though there are pressures from the government, major corporations, the media and the general public to cut back on things like travel, meetings, conferences, and special events because of the economy, the members of the meetings and events industry are working hard to show the great economic impact that this industry has on the United States and how if this industry were to decline, many other industries would be negatively impacted."

Astrid says that the best single piece of advice she ever received from a mentor was to join a professional organization and begin networking. She selected this piece of advice because of the impact that it has made on her life in the academic, professional and personal sense. Through joining PCMA and ISES, she has had the opportunity to, according to Astrid, "meet amazing people from across the United States and around the world, further my education in the meetings and events industry, gain internships and job opportunities, and travel to different areas for conferences and conventions. I believe that it is these associations that will ultimately led me to achieve my goals with my career."

During the early days of her career, Astrid Schrier has demonstrated that through hard work, a professional network of strong and well-connected mentors, and by becoming engaged in the leadership of professional societies, success may be accelerated in the meetings and events industry. Her success has taken her far already, both from an experience level as well as through her travels to the Far East. He future is truly boundless as she continues to expand her professional network and mentor the next generation of meeting and event professionals, who will most certainly emulate her fine example.

Global Connection

Greener events are a global phenomenon, and many nations are already steps ahead of the US in some regards. The United Kingdom made a giant leap when the British Standards Institute (BSI), one of the world's most reputable authorities of industry standards, released BS8901, the British Standard for Greener Events. BS8901 is available at an inordinately expensive price from BSI at www.bsi-global.com, but the UK government also provides a free guide for managing greener events at: www.defra.gov.uk/sustainable/government/advice. Click on "Sustainable Events Guide," to download a useful PDF document. To see EFPs in action, check out Australian Peats Ridge Festival's best practices at www.peatsridge-festival.com.au by clicking on "Sustainability." Greener event pioneers will analyze global trends in order to innovate local markets and stay ahead of the competition.

Technology Connection

Create an action plan for cutting down on paper waste. Turn documents into PDFs using a scanner and Adobe Acrobat Reader and then e-mail these documents instead of mailing them. Any documents requiring a signature need to be hard copies, but countless others can be digitized. To minimize any potential affront, put a small sentence at the bottom of your e-mail signature that says something along the lines of, "This e-mail is part of my environmental initiative to cut down on paper waste." I put a similar line in my signature, and within the week the entire office had adopted it in their e-mails as well. With the money saved on massive cases of paper, you can buy recycled stationary for those hard-copy letters that need a personal touch.

Resource Connection

Watch Al Gore's *An Inconvenient Truth* for an introduction to global warming. For an analysis of the sociopolitical undercurrents of the energy crisis, I can recommend no better than Friedman's *Hot, Flat, and Crowded. Green to Gold* by Daniel Esty and Andrew Winston offers practical business advice on greening your business. Take a look at Appendix 18 for a complete list of organizations and suppliers that can deliver goods and services toward your greener events. Are these goods and services available in your area? If not, perhaps there is a gap in the local market that you can fill.

PART THREE

Event Coordination

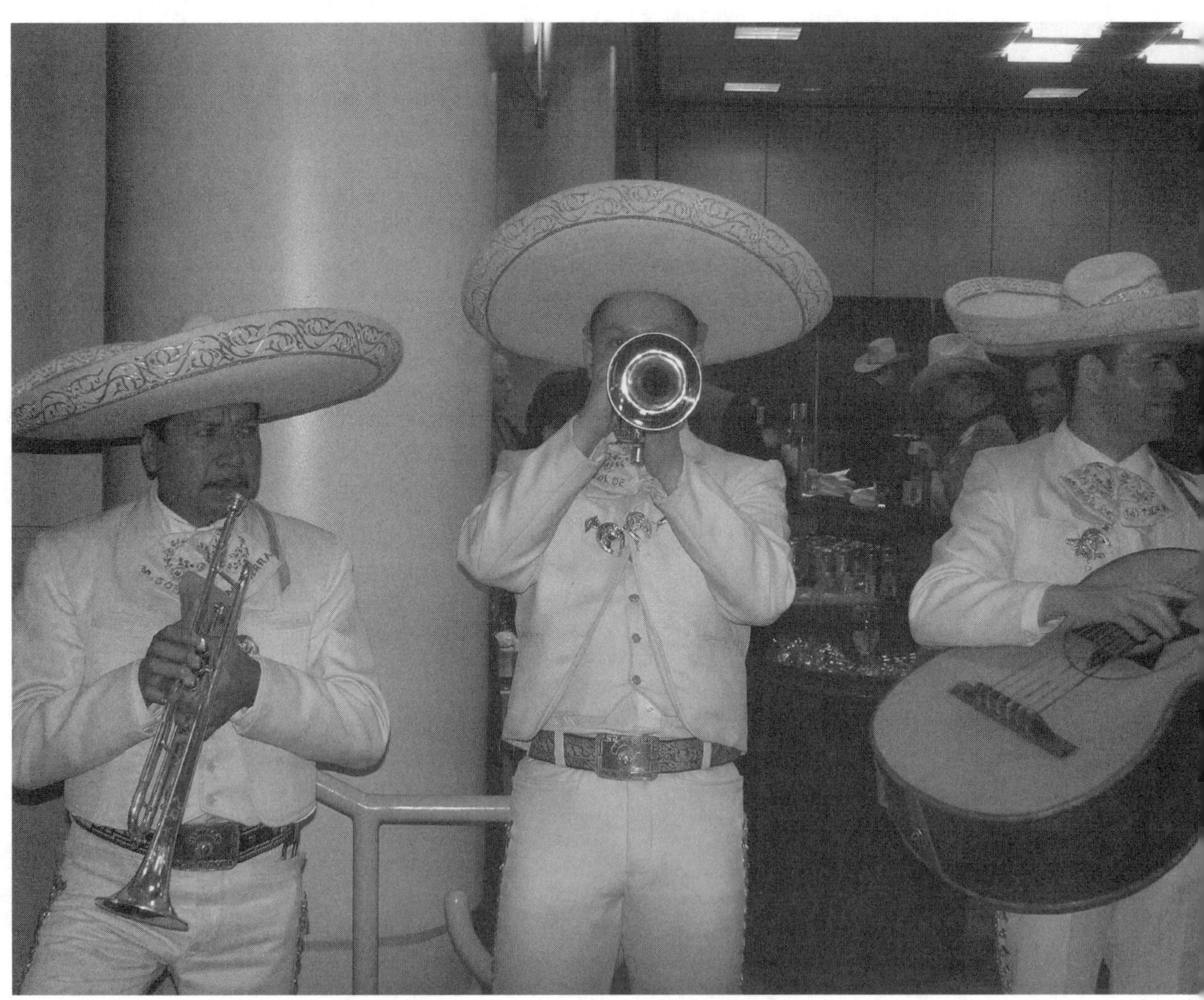

Managing vendor contracts may include entertainers such as these musicians.

CHAPTER 7

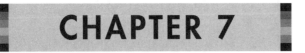

Managing Vendor Contracts

In this chapter you will learn how to:

- Develop and implement the design for your event
- Develop appropriate resources
- Coordinate catering operations
- Use trends in event catering
- Coordinate technical resources, including lighting, sound, and special effects
- Conduct and analyze the site inspection
- Develop and construct the production schedule
- Anticipate and resolve operational conflicts

The International Special Events Society (ISES) annually awards several Esprit prizes for excellence in the spirit (esprit) of teamwork. This is the only awards program that I am aware of in the hospitality, meeting planning, and related industries that salutes achievement through high-quality teamwork. No single person is honored; rather, the awards are bestowed to teams that are responsible for innovative, excellent event production. ISES members understand that great events are the result of great people working together to achieve a common goal.

Creating and Implementing the Design for Your Event

Once the design has been developed and the plan finalized, the two must be merged to begin the implementation process. During the coordination phase, we arrive at the intersection of research, design, and planning, and through the convergence of these three places begin to operationalize the event itself. The coordination phase provides us with the opportunity to see the results of our early labors in research, design, and planning. It is also the opportunity to ensure that we preserve the integrity of our early efforts. Too often, changes are made during the coordination phase that negatively affect the outcome of the event because they do not preserve the integrity of the design and planning process. One technique for ensuring that you continually preserve the integrity of your event design is to appoint one person to monitor the coordination and make certain that there is an obvious relationship between the design, the plan, and the final version of the event. Another method is to develop a series of written or graphic cues, such as design renderings or goals and objectives to make certain the stakeholders hold fast to the early vision of the event.

Developing Appropriate Resources

Event resources generally include people, time, finances, technology, and physical assets. Although each is important, each is also extremely scarce. Occasionally, someone will tell me that he has unlimited resources for his event. I am skeptical about this because of the economic theory, which states that you must learn to allocate scarce resources to achieve maximum benefit. No matter how many resources you have, the fact is that they are always limited. The way you stretch your resources is through careful and creative allocation.

The Event Leader must first identify appropriate resources for his or her event during the proposal stage. It is not unlikely that you will receive a telephone call one morning at 9 and be told that you need to deliver a proposal by 12 noon to be eligible to earn the right to produce the event. Given this short time frame, the event planner must be able to identify appropriate resources quickly and accurately. Figure 7.1 provides a general guide to where to find these important resources.

The event planner must be able to identify quickly the most appropriate resources for the event. Furthermore, the event planner has to attest that these resources are reliable. This is not always possible, due to time constraints. Therefore, after every effort is made to verify the quality of an event resource such as entertainment or catering or venue, the event planner may wish to include this statement in the proposal to reduce his or her liability: "The information contained herein is deemed to be reliable but not guaranteed." It is impossible to verify and confirm every resource within the brief time constraints imposed by most events. Therefore, the event planner should do what is reasonable and

Category	Examples	Sources
Money	Starting capital, contingency funds	Investors, credit, vendors, sponsors
People	Volunteers, staff, vendors	Convention and visitors' bureaus, destination management companies, schools, colleges, organizations, public relations, event alumni, advertising
Physical	Transportation, venue, catering	Destination management companies, school assets districts, caterers, convention and visitors' bureaus
Technology	Software, hardware	Internet, industry organizations
Time	Scheduling, organization,	Scheduling software and delegation strategies management, expanded time and tactics

Figure 7.1 Event Resources and Where to Find Them

inform the client of the status of the level of reliability of the information that he or she is providing. The most common method for identifying appropriate resources consists of 10 steps:

1. Conduct a needs assessment.
2. Determine the budget.
3. Develop the request for proposal document and evaluation criteria.
4. Identify appropriate firms or individuals to submit proposals.
5. Distribute a request for proposal.
6. Review the proposals.
7. Select the suppliers.
8. Negotiate with the suppliers.
9. Develop and execute contracts with the suppliers.
10. Monitor contract performance.

Steps 1 and 2 are critical in order to proceed to develop an effective request for proposal (RFP). They may be conducted during the research phase and will include using historical as well as comparable data. The RFP must include the history of the event and/or the goals and objectives, as well as the budget parameters. You may wish to establish a broad list of qualified organizations or individuals to receive the RFP. These lists can come from the resources shown in Figure 7.1 or through historical or comparable information. Regardless of how you acquire these lists, it is wise to qualify them further by calling each potential proposer to ask if he or she would like to receive the RFP. The initial list of proposers may be lengthy; however, the final list should not include more than five organizations or individuals. Typically, no more than three proposers receive the RFP.

Event title:	Med-Eth Conference and Exposition
Sponsoring organization:	International Medical Ethics Society
Description of organization:	Med-Eth is the world's largest professional society in the field of medical ethics
Tax status:	Med-Eth is a 501(c)(3) U.S. tax-exempt membership organization
Description of attendees:	Medical doctors, medical administrators, suppliers to the medical ethics profession
Event date(s):	June 6–11, 2010
Event location:	Washington, DC, Convention Center
Service(s)/product(s) to be proposed:	Audiovisual equipment and labor
Total budget not to exceed:	$5,000

Technical specifications:

1. Equipment and labor for video magnification and sound for two general sessions with 1,000 persons using rear projection.
2. Equipment and labor for seven breakout sessions with an assortment of equipment, including slide projectors, video projectors, personal computers with PowerPoint, front projection screens, microphones, flip charts (pads and markers), and laser pointers. Average audience size is 55 persons. Audience size will range from 30 to 75 persons.

Submission requirements:	All proposers must follow these guidelines to be considered for this assignment:

1. Company/organization profile and history, including names of owners or principals as well as persons assigned to coordinate the event
2. Itemized list of equipment and labor that will be provided, including redundant (backup) equipment
3. Complete listing of all costs, including taxes if applicable
4. Evidence of insurance company and evidence of commercial general liability with minimum limits of $2 million per occurrence

Deadline for submission:	5 P.M. EST May 30, 2010
Submission instructions:	Proposals may be submitted electronically to Ms. Jane Doe via e-mail to: jdoe@med-eth.com or by mail to: Attn: Jane Doe Med-Eth 6000 Massachusetts Avenue, N.W. Washington, DC 20039

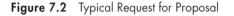

Figure 7.2 Typical Request for Proposal

The average event planner responsible for a large event such as the one described in Figure 7.2 may have as many as 50 or 60 proposals to receive and review. Therefore, it is important that you develop a methodology or system for receiving, reviewing, and responding to these proposals. Figure 7.3 provides an example of how to manage this process. Coordinating the flow of documents is the first step in this phase in managing a successful event. The system shown in this figure will help you track these important documents and evaluate the qualifications and value of each proposer. This system will also help you develop a historical profile for each vendor so you can plan more efficiently in the future.

The Convention Industry Council through its APEX initiative has developed several standard request for proposal forms for the meetings and events industry, all of which are available for download at http://conventionindustry.org/apex/panels/RFPs.htm.

William O'Toole and Phyllis Mikolaitis report in *Corporate Event Project Management* (2002) that the ideal situation for contracting goods and services is with the use of the black-box view system. The black-box view dictates that the way in which the vendor accomplishes the deliverable is usually of no interest to the Event Leader. According to O'Toole and Mikolaitis, "Only the results matter." Using the black-box approach, the inputs include the event charter, the design specifications, the performance specifications, and the contract additions. These requirements are given to the vendors who process these components into outputs or deliverables, which are the event goods and services. In order for this process to be successful, you must first clearly and accurately communicate to your vendors the requirements for your event.

Event name: Med-Eth Conference and Exposition
Service(s)/product(s) required: audiovisual products and labor
Proposal due date: May 30, 2010

Proposer	Date & Time Received	Qualifications	Value Ranking	Total Score
3 Sound and Pictures, Inc.	May 15, 2010, 4 P.M.	4	2	6
1 Techno Services	May 17, 2010, 10 A.M.	5	4	9
2 Light and Sound, Inc.	May 25, 2010, 2 P.M.	5	2	7
4 Microphones, etc.	May 27, 2010, 5 P.M.	3	2	5
5 Video, Inc.	May 29, 2010, 4 P.M.	2	2	4

Scoring matrix: 1, poor; 2, fair; 3, acceptable; 4, good; 5, excellent

Figure 7.3 Proposal Tracking System

Working with Suppliers and Vendors

Your ability to work with your vendors to satisfy the needs of your guests will ultimately help determine the level of success you achieve as an Event Leader. There are innumerable vendors; for example:

- Advertising agencies
- Advertising specialty providers
- Amusement-games providers
- Animal providers
- Audiovisual providers
- Balloons
- Caterers
- Clowns
- Décor specialists
- Destination management companies
- Environmental specialist
- Entertainment providers
- Envelope addressers
- First-aid providers
- Flag providers
- Florists
- Government agencies
- Hotels
- Insurance brokers and underwriters
- Invitation designers
- Legal counsel
- Lighting providers
- Magicians
- Printers
- Public relations counselors
- Puppeteers
- Pyrotechnic designers
- Security providers
- Simultaneous interpreters
- Special effects providers
- Translation providers
- Valet parking providers
- Venue lessors and operators

In this chapter, we explore two of the more frequently used resources: caterers and technical production specialists.

1. Equipment and labor for video magnification and sound for two general sessions with 1,000 persons using rear projection.

2. Equipment and labor for seven breakout sessions with an assortment of equipment, including slide projectors, video projectors, personal computers with PowerPoint, front projection screens, microphones, flip charts (pads and markers), and laser pointers. Average audience size is 55 persons. Audience size will range from 30 to 75 persons.

Submission requirements. All proposers must follow these guidelines to be considered for this assignment:

1. Company/organization profile and history, including names of owners or principals as well as persons assigned to coordinate the event.
2. Itemized list of equipment and labor that will be provided, including redundant (backup) equipment.
3. Complete listing of all costs, including taxes if applicable.
4. Evidence of insurance company and evidence of commercial general liability with minimum limits of $2 million per occurrence.

Catering Management

Historically, events have been associated with food and beverages. Here we examine how to ensure that the catering elements of an event are well coordinated.

Event caterers are usually one of three business types, and each is defined by location. First is the institutional caterer, commonly described as an in-house or on-premises caterer, who may or may not have permanent kitchens and offices at the event venue. This caterer may limit the choices for the Event Leader but can provide greater security by being familiar with the idiosyncrasies of the venue.

The second business type is the traditional off-premises caterer, whose clients engage him or her to cater meals at a temporary location. The location or venue may or may not have permanent kitchen facilities. However, the off-premises caterer is responsible for providing the necessary equipment and services to create an atmosphere of permanence in this temporary locale.

The third and final type of event caterer is the concessionaire. This person may use a mobile kitchen or concession trailer to dispense his or her product or may work in a fixed venue from a permanent or temporary concession area. In some venues, the in-house catering operation operates all concession activities simultaneously as well.

Obviously, there is significant variation in these event-catering business operations. Generally, however, when contracting caterers, the three types will be on-premises, off-premises, and concessions. A growing trend in an effort to boost revenues is for on-premises caterers to begin catering off-premises in private homes and even other venues.

Although the on-premises caterer provides the lion's share of major event-catering operations, the off-premises caterer may actually feed the broadest possible constituency. The off-premises caterer must have the ability to establish a temporary kitchen in a tent, in an aircraft hangar, or even in a jewelry store. This type of caterer works closely with party rental specialists to ensure that he or she can provide the appropriate equipment on a moment's notice. Furthermore, the off-premises caterer must establish adequate resources for utilities, deliveries, waste disposal, and other critical elements of any catering operation. Finally, the off-premises caterer must stay abreast of local health and sanitation regulations to ensure that he or she is in compliance, regardless of an event's location.

In actuality, although many off-premises caterers may boast of their ability to provide their services uniformly in any location in most major metropolitan areas, relatively few are able to do so. When you add multiple events on the same date, this number shrinks dramatically.

As the on-premises caterer continues to expand off-premises, he or she is learning that the rigor of the temporary location is much greater than the fixed or permanent venue. Some on-premises caterers have ceased off-premises operations for this very reason. They quickly discover that on- and off-premises are two very different catering skills and that, when trying to conquer both worlds, one inevitably suffers.

Location, Location, Location

Of the five Ws in event planning, "where" is perhaps the most critical to the on- and off-premises caterer, for a variety of reasons. First, the caterer must comply with specific health department codes and regulations that will govern where he or she may operate. Second, food and beverage preparation is time-dependent, and the distance between the food preparation area and the serving location can determine an entire range of quality and service issues. What happens if hot food becomes cool or even cold during transit? How will the guests feel about slow food delivery? Finally, what utilities, equipment, and other resources are available to the caterer to prepare, serve, remove, and clean up successfully?

The location of the event is, therefore, a critical consideration for the off-premises caterer. However, the on-premises caterer must also be sensitive to these issues, as even the most routine event can suffer from logistical problems. As one example, what happens in the convention center when the caterer must serve 1,000 guests on the ground floor, the kitchen is located on the second floor, and the elevator stops working? Or perhaps the Event Leader has asked the caterer to serve the meal in an unusual location, such as in a tent in the parking lot. Does the caterer have the necessary equipment and additional labor to accomplish this task successfully? These questions and many more must be considered well in advance of establishing the location for the catered meal.

Equipment

Obviously, tables, chairs, china, silver, and other standard equipment will be required to serve a high-quality meal. However, the Event Leader must ensure that the caterer has access to the appropriate style and quantity to match the needs of the event. Some caterers own a sufficient inventory of rental equipment, while others have close relationships with party and general rental dealers to provide these items. The Event Leader must inspect the equipment to ensure that the caterer not only has sufficient quantity but that the quality is appropriate for the event.

When considering quantity, remember that the caterer may have multiple events on the same date. Make certain that additional inventory is available in case your guest list increases at the last moment. Furthermore, make certain that if the quantity of items is increased, the inventory will remain high quality.

Beyond china and silver, some caterers also maintain a healthy inventory of tables, chairs, linens, and other serving utensils (cutlery), such as chafing dishes, props, and other elements that will provide you with a cohesive look. Some caterers stock unusual items from a specific historic period or feature items that reflect their style of catering. A caterer who primarily services the social life-cycle market may provide latticework props and gingham linens, while the caterer who works in the corporate event market may provide white linens and more traditional china and silver. The Event Leader must select a caterer who has equipment and experience that matches the goals and objectives of the specific event.

Utilities

As the caterer plugs in the coffee urn, the music from the band suddenly comes to a screeching halt. The guests on the dance floor look confused, but both the Event Leader and catering director know what has happened: an overloaded circuit caused by the coffee urn. The Event Leader must audit the caterer's utility needs as well as those of the other vendors to determine if the venue can support these requirements.

In addition to electricity, the caterer will require water. The proximity of the water will also be an important factor, as costs may increase if water must be transported from a great distance. The third and final requirement for all catering operations is waste management. The caterer must have a system for disposing of waste materials. The Event Leader must ensure that the caterer has the necessary resources to perform professionally.

Time Constraints

Time is of the essence in most catering operations, for a variety of reasons. First, the caterer must prepare and deliver his or her product within a reasonable amount of time to ensure freshness and quality. Second, the caterer must carefully orchestrate the delivery of his or her product within a complex setting in which multiple activities are being staged. For example, a dinner dance may require that the caterer serve various courses between dance sets. At some events the caterer must provide the entire service within a short time frame to ensure that all servers are out of the function room in time for speeches or other aspects of the program.

Service Styles

The term *service* refers to the method used for serving a catered meal. In the United States, the three most popular forms of service are the seated banquet, the standing or seated buffet, and the standing reception, where servers pass food items to guests. Each

Event	Service Style
Brief networking breakfast	Standing buffet
Breakfast with speaker	Seated buffet
Breakfast with speaker, program	Seated banquet
Brief networking luncheon	Standing buffet
Luncheon with speaker	Seated buffet
Luncheon with speaker, program	Seated banquet
Brief cocktail reception	Passed items
Extended cocktail reception	Standing buffet or individual stations
Brief dinner	Standing buffet or individual stations
Dinner with speaker, program	Seated banquet
Formal dinner	French service

Figure 7.4 Event Catering Service Styles and When to Use Them

of these service types helps satisfy specific goals and objectives. Figure 7.4 provides a simple guide on when to employ a specific type of service.

In addition to these service styles, the exposition is an important venue for effective catering. Exposition managers know that food and beverages serve as a strong attraction and increase traffic greatly in an exposition hall. One of the more popular methods is to provide guests with an apron (usually donated by a sponsor and imprinted with their logo) and then distribute pocket sandwiches. With this technique the guests can walk, talk, shop, and eat. It is a very efficient way to provide food service for guests at an exposition and resembles a giant walking picnic.

Picnic style is also a popular technique for corporate and reunion events. Although this style is difficult in terms of service, it is extremely popular among guests who want to sit together as one large group. This style is also popular with Oktoberfest events, as it resembles a German beer hall.

English and Russian services, although not very popular in the United States, are two styles that may be implemented for the right occasion. English style involves serving each table from a moving cart. In Russian service, the server uses silver platters from which he or she places each course onto a guest's plate. Both styles of service may be requested, but the caterer must be equipped and schooled properly to produce an effective result.

Logistic Considerations

Proper and efficient guest flow as well as effective methods for ensuring timely delivery of food and beverages are essential considerations for a catered event. The event caterer may have substantial experience working in a permanent venue, but when asked to provide services off-premises, he or she may not be aware of the additional rigor required to survive in the jungle. To survive and thrive, one must know these basic laws of the event jungle:

- Determine in advance the goals and objectives of the catered event and match the logistical requirements to these objectives. For example, a brief networking event should use fewer chairs and tables, to allow guests time to mix and mingle.
- Determine the ages and types of guests and match the requirements to their needs. For example, for older guests, more chairs may be needed to provide additional comfort during an extended reception.
- Identify the food preparation and other staging areas and ensure that there is a clear passageway to the consumption area. Check the floors to make sure that they are free of debris and allow the service staff to move quickly.
- Whenever possible, use a double-buffet style for this type of service. The double buffet not only serves twice as many guests but also allows guests to interact with one another as they receive their food.
- Do not place food stations in areas that are difficult to replenish. Large crowds of guests may prevent service personnel from replenishing food stations efficiently.
- When passing food items, place a few servers at the entryway so that guests notice that food is available. This technique ensures that most guests will see and consume at least one of the food items being offered.
- Use lighting to highlight buffets, carving, and other stations. Soft, well-focused lighting directs guests' eyes to the food and makes it easier to find as well as more appetizing.
- Use servers at the entryway to pass drinks rapidly to guests as they enter, or open the bars farthest from the entrance first. For smaller events with ample time, passing drinks may be preferable; however, for larger events where the guests must be served quickly, staggering bar opening may be beneficial. Once the distant bars begin to experience lines of 10 or more persons, succeeding bars are opened, working back toward the entryway.
- Instruct the bar captain to close all bars promptly at the appointed time. Use servers to line up at the entryway to assist in directing guests into the main function room.
- Provide return tables to accept glassware as guests go to the next event. Staff these areas to avoid too many glasses accumulating.
- Request that servers distribute welcome gifts or programs during the setup period and be staged in each dining station to assist with seating. Servers should be requested to offer chairs to guests without hesitation, to expedite seating.
- Use an invocation, moment of silence, or a simple "bon appétit" to signal the beginning of the meal.
- These service times typically should be used for catered events:
    - Cocktail reception: 30 minutes to 1 hour
    - Seated banquet: 1 to 2 hours
    - Preset salad consumption and clearing: 15 to 20 minutes

  - Entrée delivery, consumption, and clearing: 20 to 40 minutes
  - Dessert delivery, consumption, and clearing: 15 to 20 minutes
  - Coffee and tea service: 10 to 15 minutes
- Make certain that all service personnel have exited the function room prior to the program or speeches. If this is not possible, make certain that front tables have been served and that servers continue service as quietly as possible in back of the function area.
- Request that servers stand at exit doors and bid guests good-bye and distribute any parting gifts from the host or hostess.

Your catering event professional will suggest other ideas to help you accomplish your goals and objectives. However, remember that you must prioritize the event's goals and objectives, and catering may or may not be high on the list. Therefore, it is important to maintain balance as you decide where to focus during specific periods of the event.

Once you have identified the event's goals and objectives, you choose the service style to make certain that your guests' needs are satisfied. After basic needs are satisfied, it is time to add some magic to turn an ordinary catered affair into an extraordinary special event.

Coordinating Catering Operations

As caterers assume increased responsibilities in the Event Leadership profession, other members of the professional team will need to adjust their marketing and operations strategies to cope with this new phenomenon. "Can and will caterers charge for event planning services beyond the cost of food and service?" and "Will all future catered events place significant emphasis on food and beverage at the risk of ignoring other elements and producing a more balanced event?" are but two of numerous questions that will be raised.

Earlier, I stated that, historically, caterers have provided event planning services. Now the question becomes: Will caterers develop these services further to reflect full depth and breadth of resources available within the planned events industry? If they choose to broaden their education, their impact can have substantial implications within the industry. The future of Event Leadership may include both good food and beverages, as well as equally excellent services managed by the caterer. This consolidation will be welcomed by some clients who desire one-stop shopping and rejected by others who may, for a variety of reasons, prefer to entrust their event to another event planner. Regardless, the future force in catering will include offering many diversified services carefully combined into a nutritious, filling, and satisfying buffet. At the center of the bountiful buffet of these diversified services may be Event Leadership.

Global event leaders must also recognize that trends are typically regional and then national in scope. For example, recently I have noticed a trend that involves the elaborate design and construction of full-scale ice martini bars. These bars are constructed entirely of ice; fiber-optic lights illuminate them internally. The bartenders dispense hundreds of martinis, which are well received by baby boomers who want to relive the classic moments from the 1930s and 1940s enjoyed by their parents. The same is true of cigars, which are very popular in many parts of the United States. In other countries, cigars and martinis are usual and customary; in North America, they are often reserved for special occasions.

To best utilize the trends in event catering, I recommend that you first review all event literature to be sure that you are incorporating a trend that is on an upward trajectory. Next, make certain that you test the trend idea with a focus panel of your event guests and others to make certain that it is appropriate and can be implemented with high quality. Finally, remember the difference between fads and trends. Fads are often short-lived. You may purchase 5,000 pairs of Croc knock-offs as part of your fun Ausie-themed mega-event, only to discover that they went out of vogue six months ago. Cautiously incorporate trends into your event design to enhance your plan.

Catering Ideas

Living Buffet

Effect

As guests browse along a seemingly normal buffet table, they are startled as the head of lettuce suddenly starts talking to the cauliflower and the cauliflower turns to the guest for advice on how to handle the unruly lettuce.

Method

Using a standard buffet table, cut two 24-inch holes in the top. The holes should be located approximately 12 to 18 inches apart and away from the front edge of the table. Place two actors, in headpieces that resemble lettuce and cauliflower, under the table with their heads penetrating the hole. It is best if the headpiece covers the eyes or they keep their heads slightly bowed until time to speak. Elaborately garnish all the area around the fake lettuce and cauliflower. Use theatrical lighting to soften the light on this area of the buffet.

Reaction

Guests will shriek with delight, and the talking lettuce and cauliflower will become one of the best memories of your catered event.

Bonus

Write a brief script between the lettuce and cauliflower in which they engage in a heated discussion about health and nutrition. Have the actors turn to the guests to ask their opinions.

Human Buffet Table

Effect

A person supports an entire buffet on his or her garment.

Method

Place a male or female actor in the center of two buffet tables. The buffet should be slightly elevated on platforms so that the edge of the table is at eye level. Construct a costume that appears to support the entire buffet. A woman may wear a long dress and the skirt may be supported with matching fabric used to skirt swag the front edge of the buffet table (see Figure 7.5), or a male may wear a colorful tailcoat with the tails extended with matching fabric to drape the tables. Place bright light on the actors in colors to complement their costumes and slightly softer light on the buffet tables. Match the lighting for the actor's wardrobe with softer lighting in matching colors on the buffet skirting.

Reaction

Guests will ooh and ah as your elegant actors wave and invite them to dine.

Bonus

Direct the actors to freeze and come to life periodically. This will create an ongoing activity for the guests to observe and enjoy.

Resource

Roberts Event Group (www.robertseventgroup.com) offers this attraction and many other innovative entertainment ideas.

Figure 7.5 Roberts Events Group of Jenkintown, Pennsylvania, Rewards their Many Satisfied Clients with a Living Martini Bar at the Benjamin Franklin Institute in Philadelphia, Pennsylvania.

Old Black Magic

Effect

Thirty servers enter once the guests are seated. Each server is carrying a silver tray with two top hats. Suddenly the entire room begins to glow in the dark.

Method

Purchase 60 black-plastic top hats. Fill each top hat with 20 glow-in-the-dark bracelets and sticks. Line the waiters up outside the room service entrance of the function. Dim all the lights and instruct the servers to enter as you play music such as "Old Black Magic" or "Magic to Do." As the servers arrive at the tables and place their hats in the center, quickly turn off the lights. Instruct the servers to place their trays under their arms, clap their hands, and distribute the glow-in-the-dark pieces from inside the hats to the guests.

Reaction

Your guests may first wonder why there are no centerpieces for this elaborate catered event. However, once the glow-in-the-dark gifts are distributed, the guests will applaud as they become the room décor and you produce magic at a fraction of the cost of traditional décor.

Bonus

Purchase white gloves for the servers and color them with glow-in-the-dark dye. As the lights go dim, have the servers wave their hands above their heads and then clap them before producing the glow-in-the-dark gifts.

Resource

The Oriental Trading Company, Inc. catalog (www.orientaltrading.com) offers hundreds of inexpensive party supplies.

Dessert Parade

Effect

Your guests receive a unique dessert that has been created for them as your team of servers parades the dessert to their tables.

Method

Use glow-in-the-dark swizzle sticks or other items to decorate the dessert trays. Play a lively march or theme music that reflects the style of the catered event as the servers march forward. Stage the servers so that they enter at the rear of the room and march through the tables holding the trays high above their heads. Lower the lights and use follow spotlights to sweep the room to create additional excitement. Prior to their entrance, announce: "The chef has prepared a once-in-a-lifetime dessert creation to celebrate this momentous occasion. Please welcome your servers!" The servers march (or dance) to each table and serve dessert.

Reaction

Your guests will respond with spontaneous applause followed by clapping rhythmically to the music as your servers deliver dessert.

Bonus

At the conclusion of the dessert parade line, have the servers line up in front of the stage and gesture to the left or right as the pastry chef appears for a brief bow. Make certain that the pastry chef is dressed in all white with a traditional chef's hat so that he or she is easily recognized. This will cause an additional ovation, perhaps a standing one.

Resource

The Culinary Institute of America (www.ciachef.edu) or Johnson & Wales University College of Culinary Arts (www.jwu.edu) can refer you to their graduates throughout the world who are among the leading pastry chefs working in the modern food and beverage industry.

Incredible Edible Centerpiece

Effect

Your guests will notice that their centerpiece is both beautiful and edible. They will see and smell as well as taste this delicious work of art.

Method

Engage a chocolatier to carve a centerpiece out of chocolate for your guests to enjoy. The carving may represent the symbol of the event or the logo of the organization sponsoring the program. Use a pin light to illuminate each sculpture independently. Make certain the sculpture is on a raised platform, such as a gold or silver epergne. Include fresh fruit in your display to add color to your final design. One excellent subject is a large chocolate cornucopia filled with fresh red strawberries.

Reaction

Your guests will soon notice the work of art gracing their table and engage in lively conversation about its origin. Some guests will take photos, and others may try to nibble.

Resource

Belvedere Chocolates (www.belvederechocolates.com) and Forget Me Knot.com (www.forgetmeknot.com) have standard chocolate sculptures, such as a signature Bonsai Tree or magician's top hat, or they can create original designs for your event.

Ice-Cold Logo

Effect

As your guests arrive for the cocktail reception, they observe an ice carver putting the finishing touches on an elaborate sculpture.

Method

Your caterer can refer a professional ice carver who will pre-carve from a large block of ice your organization's logo, image, name, or other important and valued symbol of your group. Place the carver on a raised platform, and use rope and stanchion to provide ample working room and keep your guests from being hit by flying chips of ice. Make certain that the ice carver completes his or her work of art at the very moment your main function is to begin. Upon completion, stage several photos of your key leaders with the new work of art and then announce that the main function will begin.

Reaction

Your guests will crowd around the carver and begin intense discussions with one another about the creation. At the conclusion of the carving, they will erupt into applause and begin taking numerous photos.

Bonus

Ask the ice carver to use an electric chain saw, as this creates noise and excitement. In addition, the use of flame (fire and ice) is another dramatic touch that your ice carver may wish to incorporate into the final design (e.g., a dragon breathing fire).

Resource

An excellent and creative resource for this type of production is called Fear No Ice (www.fearnoice.com). A multimedia, performance art team of professional ice carvers creates masterpieces in ice, including corporate logos, while performing to high-energy music.

Selecting the Best Caterer

The best caterer is the organization best equipped with experience, knowledge, creativity, personnel, and resources (human and actual equipment) to achieve your goals and objectives. In each community, there may be several full-service off-premises caterers with excellent reputations. However, you can narrow the list to one, two, or perhaps three by using these 20 criteria:

1. Find out how many years the company has been in business and the size of events it has catered.
2. Ensure that caterer has health and occupancy permits (and all other necessary permits).
3. If serving alcohol, make sure that caterer has on- and off-premises alcoholic beverage permits.
4. If permits are in order, make sure that caterer has liquor liability insurance.
5. Ask to see references and/or client letters.
6. Ask to see pictures of past events—look for professionalism and setup of kitchen/staging area.
7. Identify past and present events that caterer has handled and find out maximum and minimum sizes.

8. Check to see if site meets Americans with Disabilities Act requirements and complies with laws.
9. Find out policies on client tastings.
10. Review printed materials—menu descriptions will tell about level of professionalism.
11. Ask to see design equipment and/or in-house rentals—look for innovation and cleanliness.
12. Leave messages with company receptionist—see how long it takes to return calls.
13. If on-premises, make sure that any electronic or live music complies with Broadcast Music, Inc. (BMI) or American Society of Composers, Authors, and Publishers (ASCAP) regulations.
14. Check for membership in professional organizations (i.e., National Association of Catering Executives [NACE] and ISES).
15. Find out where executive chef received training.
16. Find out how waiters are attired for different levels of services.
17. Find out if servers are proficient in French service, modified French service, or plated service.
18. Find out deposit requirements and terms.
19. Review and analyze contracts and cancellation agreements.
20. Call the local party-equipment rental company and find out about its working relationship with the caterer.

Catering Coordination

The Event Leader must closely coordinate all event activities with the director of catering or other catering team leader. Within the catering team, each member has particular responsibilities:

- Director of catering: Senior catering official who coordinates sales and operations
- Catering manager: Coordinates individual catered events, including sales and operations
- Banquet manager: Manages specific catered functions; servers report to banquet manager
- Server: Person responsible for serving the guests
- Bartender: Person responsible for mixing, pouring, and serving alcoholic and non-alcoholic beverages

To ensure that you are coordinating each element effectively with your catering team, make certain that you hold a series of telephone or in-person meetings to review the various elements that will be included in your event. The first meeting should be used to review the proposal and answer any questions you may have about the food, beverage, equipment, or service and terms of payment. The next meeting will be held prior to signing the contract to negotiate any final terms, such as the inclusion of a complimentary food tasting. Some caterers prefer that you attend a comparable event and taste similar items that will be served at your event. However, if your event is introducing new cuisine, it is essential that you insist on a separate food tasting to ensure the quality of each item prior to serving your guests. In some instances, there will be a charge for this service; you should confirm this prior to signing the contract. The final meeting should include a thorough review of all elements, including the schedule, equipment, and service levels, and answer any final questions the caterer may have regarding delivery, utilities, or other important issues.

Reviewing Proposals

Most caterers will provide a complete proposal, including the type of cuisine, number of servers, schedule, equipment rentals, payment terms, and other pertinent information. Using the next checklist will ensure that all important information is included in the catering proposal:

- History of the catering organization, including other clients of similar size and scope they have served.
- Letters of reference from other clients of similar size and scope.
- Complete description of cuisine.
- Complete description of style of service, including the number of servers/bartenders that will be provided.
- Complete description of equipment that will be provided by the caterer. Equipment may include tables, chairs, and serving utensils as well as other items. Make certain that each is described and that quantity is included.
- List of additional services to be provided by the caterer. This might include floral, entertainment, or other special requirements.
- Complete description of payment terms, including date of guarantee, taxes, gratuities, deposits, balance payments, and percentage of overage provided by the caterer.
- All schedule information concerning deliveries, setup, service, and removal of equipment through load-out.
- Insurance, bonding, and other information pertinent to managing the risk of your event.
- Any additional requirements. This might include utilities such as water, electric power, and so on.

Negotiating with the caterer is an important step in the process of selecting the best caterer. In smaller Event Leadership markets, where competition is not as great as in larger markets, negotiation may be more difficult. Still, regardless of size, five areas often can be negotiated:

1. *Ask to pay the lowest deposit in advance or to pay a series of smaller deposits spread evenly over a period of months.* Even better, if your organization has a good credit record, ask to pay net 30 days after your event.
2. *Ask for a discount for prepayment.* You may receive up to a 5 percent discount if you pay your entire bill in advance.

3. *Ask for a discount if you are a not-for-profit organization.* Although all not-for-profit organizations ask for this concession, you may be successful if you can convince the caterer that your guests may bring him or her additional new business. Offer to actively promote the presence of the caterer at the event to ensure high visibility.
4. *Ask for a complimentary service.* Some caterers will provide services ranging from a complimentary ice sculpture to a pre- or post-event reception.
5. *Ask for a complimentary food tasting for yourself and your key decision makers.* This should not take the form of an additional event; rather, it is a business activity for the purpose of inspecting the food presentation, taste, and other important elements of the event.

Final Step

The final meeting should be held in person. Often it is held in conjunction with the food tasting or final walk-through. This important meeting is your final opportunity to review the critical details regarding the caterer's contribution to your event. Five major points must be covered during this meeting:

1. Confirm the day, date, time, location, parking, and other critical information with the caterer.
2. Carefully coordinate all catering deliveries and access to the loading entrance with other vendors.
3. Review the times for the service, and instruct the caterer regarding the other elements of the program and how he or she will interface with these aspects.
4. Review the caterer's alcohol management program. Ask the caterer if his or her staff has received training and how they will handle guests who are obviously inebriated.
5. Review all payment terms and any elements you are required to provide as part of your agreement.

Cost-Saving Measures

Increasingly, both clients and their Event Leaders are concerned with cost. In some corporate circles, it is not the actual cost but the perception of a high-priced event that is of greater concern. Use this list to avoid these concerns and lower your overall catering costs:

- Carefully analyze the meals that must be provided. Some meals may be taken by guests on their own, such as at networking dinners, where all guests pay their individual bills. You may also wish to substitute concessions for some meal functions. An individually priced buffet line may be a good alternative for some meal functions.
- Use buffets and boxed lunches instead of seated banquet service. Reducing labor cost may reduce expense.

- Price food items by the lowest possible unit (cup, piece, or dozen) rather than by the tray or gallon. Order only the amount of food you will require based on the history of your event.
- Secure sponsors for meal functions. In a recent study, we learned that sponsors are very much interested in providing funding for meals that are related to educational programs.
- Secure in-kind sponsorships from bottlers and others in the food and beverage industry.
- Reduce or eliminate alcohol from your event. Many events are becoming beer-and-wine functions in place of full-open-bar affairs. This change is happening not only due to concerns about health but also because of the perceived association between heavy drinking and drunk driving.
- Serve a signature drink to everyone. A signature drink is an original drink that your bar manager creates for consumption by the entire group. At a catered function, the first need of most guests is to occupy their hands with a drink. Offer your signature drink at the entrance to your event and solve this need while reducing your budget by controlling consumption.
- Allow guests to serve themselves. This is especially popular with children's events. Make Your Own Sundae bars and the making of a five-foot-long submarine sandwich are not only entertaining but may also result in cost savings.

Catering Trends

A trend is a pattern of behavior that is likely to be sustained over time. Although the event catering profession is susceptible to shifting tastes and is certainly affected by the state of the economy, several trends are emerging. These trends are well worth noting, as they will certainly influence many of the decisions you will make.

Nutritious and organic foods have become as much a health issue as they have an ethical one. Since Eric Schlosser's 2001 landmark *Fast Food Nation* exposed the perilous, unsustainable fast food industry, the organic food market has taken off running. One direct result has been the Slow Food Movement (www.slowfood.com), which promotes using organic, locally grown, seasonal ingredients in traditional recipes. Event guests increasingly want to know the ingredients in their food and beverages to make wise decisions regarding menu items. Therefore, caterers will want to make available the ingredients and may even wish to list these items in a menu on signs posted near the food items. As noted in Chapter 6, organic (free of pesticides), locally grown, and seasonal foods should take priority. As the world's population ages (especially in the United States), guests will be more and more concerned with good health and will turn to nutritious foods as a primary means of promoting this lifestyle. Furthermore, caterers will continue the practice of promoting heart-healthy menu items, as offering these items will provide a popular alternative but also differentiate the caterer from competitors because of this attention to low cholesterol.

A second trend is the shift away from beer and wine in the 1990s to the increased popularity in the twenty-first-century of martinis that are now being featured at many event

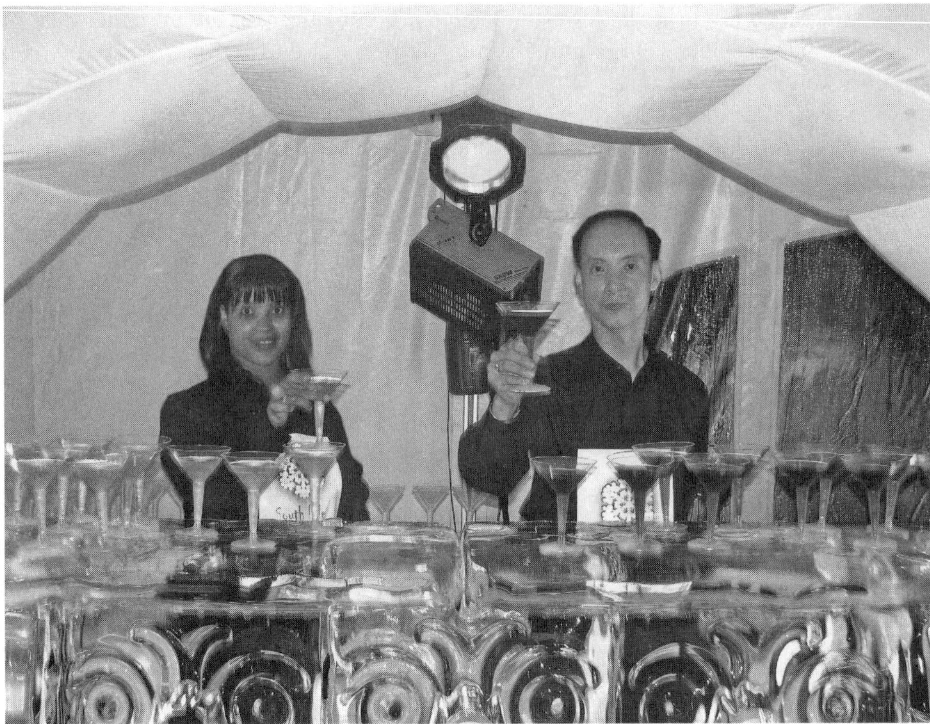

Figure 7.6 The 2005 Event Solutions Off-premise Party Titled Southern Exposure, Produced at the Magnificent Flint Hill Mansion (www.flinthill.com) by Kendall Collier, CSEP, and Teresa Day of MMinc Catering & Special Events and Tim Lundy, CSEP, of Rosewood Market/Distinctive Design Events (www.distinctiveevents.com). It Featured a Martini Bar made Entirely of Ice that Served as a Cool Refuge.

bars. In fact, some bars only feature martinis. The martini was probably derived from the sweeter drink called the Martinez and invented in California in the 1870s. Whether the popularity of the James Bond films or the nostalgia craze being experienced and promoted by the baby boomers, more and more events are featuring this classic drink. Figure 7.6 depicts a modern martini bar constructed entirely of ice.

The third trend relates to the second trend in that, increasingly, caterers are seeking additional revenue streams and some are even moving from strictly food and beverage operations into full Event Leadership services. This change comes with great challenge as well as potentially great opportunity. Historically, caterers have been involved in all aspects of Event Leadership. Caterers, especially in the social life-cycle event market, have been responsible for providing or recommending the services of florists, musicians, decorators, invitation designers, and other allied professionals. Today's trend merely quantifies this historic business opportunity and repositions the caterer as an Event Leader who specializes in catering services. However, to take full advantage of this trend, the catering professional must be willing to round out his or her education with a rigorous course of study in Event Leadership. In every profession, eventually, superior quality combined with good value can conquer fierce competition. Event Leadership is no different from other professions in this regard. If catering professionals are to expand their services to include those of Event Leadership, they must be willing to acquire the new skills that will complement their existing talents to improve their quality and provide them with the tools to compete effectively in the event marketplace.

Therefore, these three trends—nutritious and organic menus, a wider range in alcohol service, and the expansion of the caterer's services to include those of an Event Leader—may be viewed as economic opportunities provided that education and commitment to quality is implemented consistently.

Coordinating Technical Resources

The Event Leadership profession has seen perhaps the greatest paradigm shift in the live production sector of this industry. Live production is also what differentiates events from other entertainment or creative products. Although one may argue that television specials are billed as "special events," in most instances these events are filmed or taped before a live audience. Productions ranging from the National Football League Super Bowl halftime show to the Three Tenors concert combine live production with various audiovisual, lighting, sound, special effects, and video resources to produce a well-crafted event that ultimately is viewed by millions via television. The modern Event Leader cannot ignore this major shift and must understand as well as implement these resources when appropriate.

Why = What

In Chapter 2, I described that, prior to selecting the most effective resources for your event, you must establish clear goals and objectives by asking why this event is necessary. Due to the myriad new technologies now offered, this question is more important than ever before. The inexperienced Event Leader may decide to mix and match a wide array of new technology to impress his or her guests during the event. In fact, this mixture becomes a collage of inappropriate resources that results in confusion to the guests. An award-winning designer reportedly cautioned his young apprentices that "less is indeed more." The Event Leader must also use caution when selecting appropriate resources to support or enhance the event to make certain that each device is well integrated rather than extraneous. The list that follows can be used as a primary coordination tool for selecting and engaging these resources:

- *Identify the purpose of event technology for your program.* Will the event technology be used to attract attention or to improve communications?
- *Determine the size of the live audience.* The technology you select for the audience will be determined by the number of guests.

- *Identify the age, culture, and learning style of your guests.* Some guests are visual learners, while others are more attuned to audio influences. Still other audiences, due to their age, may prefer a louder or quieter sound level.
- *Inspect the venue and inventory assets.* This includes preexisting light (natural and artificial), in-house audiovisual equipment, utilities, the experience of local technical labor, and any other elements that will interact with your event.
- Sit in a guest's chair or stand in the guest's place and try to envision the event through his or her eyes and ears. Check for obstructed views and other distractions. Identify potential solutions to develop optimum enjoyment through the entire event.

Purposes of Event Technology

Whether the purpose of your event is to educate or entertain or, perhaps, both, the technology that you select will help you best achieve your goals and objectives. In the conference event field, you may select slide projectors, overhead projectors, a Teleprompter, or perhaps one microphone to improve communications between the presenter and the participant. The entertainment field may require theatrical lighting and special effects, such as fog, laser, or strobe lights. Other fields will require different technologies; however, ultimately the purpose of the event will determine the final selection and coordination of the event technology. Figure 7.7 provides a guide for general use in selecting equipment for the event style and purpose.

Audiovisual Effects

The term *audiovisual* was probably first coined in the 1950s, when schools and, later, businesses and then associations used slide and overhead projectors and sound recordings for instructional purposes. During the 1970s, this technology expanded rapidly with more sophisticated audio tools as well as video enhancement due to the invention

Style	Purpose	Technology
Civic	Attract attention	Special effect: pyrotechnics
Conference	Communicate	Audiovisual: video magnification
	Focus	Lighting: key lighting of lectern
Education	Build retention	Audiovisual: interactive CD
Entertainment	Attract	Sound and lights: announce and chase
Exposition	Educate	Video: product description
Festival	Communicate	Sound: public address
Reunion	Excite	Audiovisual: slide show of guests

Figure 7.7 Matching Technology to Style and Purpose

of video-projection systems. Indeed, today dozens of audiovisual tools are available for use by Event Leaders. However, I concentrate on those 10 tools used most often in the production of civic, entertainment, exposition, festival, and conference events. These tools are readily available in most event markets or may be obtained from nearby larger markets.

Audiovisual projection is divided primarily into two projection fields: visual and audio. The tool and its power depend on the factors described in the checklist in Figure 7.8. Audience size, distance, and the age and type of attendee are critical considerations when

Amenities:

1. Ability to display banner in prominent location
2. Limousines for very important persons (VIPs)
3. Upgrades to suites available
4. Concierge on VIP floors
5. Room deliveries for entire group upon request
6. In-room television service for special announcements
7. Personal letter from venue manager delivered to room
8. Complimentary parking for staff or VIPs
9. Complimentary coffee in lobby
10. Complimentary office services, such as photocopying for staff

Americans with Disabilities Act

1. Venue has been modified and is in compliance
2. New venue built in compliance with act
3. Modifications are publicized and well communicated

Capacity

1. Fire marshal approved capacity of venue for seating
2. Capacity of venue for parking
3. Capacity for exposition booths
4. Capacity for storage
5. Capacity for truck and vehicle marshaling
6. Capacity for pre-event functions such as receptions
7. Capacity for other functions
8. Capacity for public areas of venue such as lobbies
9. Size and number of men's and women's restrooms

Catering

1. Full-service, venue-specific catering operation
2. Twenty-four-hour room service
3. Variety of food outlets
4. Concession capability
5. Creative, tasteful food presentation

Figure 7.8 Event Site-Inspection Checklist Criteria *(Continued)*

Equipment
1. Amount of rope (running feet) and stanchions available
2. Height, width, and colors available for inventory of pipe and drape
3. Height, width, and skirting colors available for platforms for staging
4. Regulations for use and lift availability for aerial work
5. Adequate number of tables, chairs, stairs, and other equipment

Financial Considerations
1. Complimentary room ratio
2. Guarantee policy
3. Daily review of folio
4. Complimentary reception or other services to increase value
5. Function-room complimentary rental policy

Location/Proximity
1. Location of venue from nearest airport
2. Distance to nearest trauma facility
3. Distance to nearest fire/rescue facility
4. Distance to shopping
5. Distance to recreational activities

Medical Assistance/First Aid
1. Number of staff trained in CPR, Heimlich maneuver, and other first aid
2. Designated first-aid area
3. Ambulance service

Portals
1. Size and number of exterior portals
2. Size and number of interior portals, including elevators
3. Ingress and egress to portals

Registration
1. Sufficient well-trained personnel for check-in
2. Ability to provide express check-in for VIPs
3. Ability to distribute event materials at check-in
4. Ability to display group event name on badges or buttons to promote recognition
5. Effective directory or other signs for easy recognition

Regulations Public Assembly and Fire
1. Designation of a civil defense venue to be used in emergencies (earthquake, hurricane, flood, etc.)
2. Preexisting prohibitive substance regulations
3. Other regulations that impede your ability to do business
4. Fire-code requirements with regard to material composition for scenery and other decoration
5. State/local fire officials' requirements for permission to use open flame

Figure 7.8 *(Continued)*

6. Requirement regarding the use of live gasoline-powered motors
7. Policy regarding live trained animals

Safety and Security

1. Well-lit exterior and interior walkways
2. Venue has full-time security team
3. Communications system in elevators in working order
4. Positive relationship between venue and law-enforcement agencies
5. Positive relationship between venue and private security agencies
6. Fire sprinklers controlled per zone or building-wide; individual zone can be shut off, with a fire marshal in attendance, for a brief effect such as pyrotechnics
7. Alarm system, initially silent or announcing a fire emergency immediately
8. Condition of all floors (including the dance floors)

Sleeping Rooms

1. Sufficient number of singles, doubles, suites, and other required inventory
2. Rooms in safe, clean, working order
3. Amenities such as coffeemakers and hair dryers available upon request
4. Well-publicized fire emergency plan
5. Balcony or exterior doors secured properly

Utilities

1. Electrical power capacity
2. Power distribution
3. Working on-site reserve generator (and a backup) for use in the event of a power failure
4. Responsible person for operation of electrical apparatus
5. Sources for water
6. Alternative water source in case of disruption of service
7. Separate billing for electricity or water

Weight

1. Pounds per square foot (meter) for which venue is rated
2. Elevator weight capacity
3. Stress weight for items that are suspended, such as lighting, scenic, projection, and audio devices

Figure 7.8 *(Continued)*

selecting a tool. The right tool will make your task easier and the event more enjoyable for your guests; the improper tool will cause you frustration and irritate your guests. Therefore, when selecting audiovisual tools for an event, refer to the checklist to check and balance your decision.

Digital images have replaced traditional photography in the Event Leadership production industry. Yesterday's slide projector has been replaced by the notebook computer loaded or the universal serial bus (USB) storage device with hundreds of slides and entire educational programs, including music and video. Monitor industry publications such as Sound and Video Contractor (www.svc.online.com) and Digital Content Producer (www.digitalcontentproducer.com) to stay current with the latest technological advancements in the audiovisual field.

Conducting and Analyzing the Site Inspection

Site inspection occurs during both the planning and coordination phase. During the planning phase, potential sites are inspected to identify those that should receive requests for proposals. Increasingly, this task is conducted using the Internet. However, I caution you whenever possible to visit the site yourself or send a representative to inspect the physical assets. Even using three-dimensional technology on the Internet will not allow you to view every nook and cranny of the venue. Therefore, a physical inspection is essential to confirm and verify the quality of the physical space.

It is particularly important that you schedule a site inspection during the coordination phase to reconfirm that there have been no changes to the site since the planning period. I recommend that you visit the site no less than 30 days prior to the event to reinspect and make certain that you will be able to conduct the event effectively within the venue. If there have been dramatic changes, this type of lead time will give you sufficient time to rework your event design or even, if necessary, change venues. Figure 7.8 is a good beginning for you to be able to develop a customized site inspection checklist.

Site Inspection

Perhaps the most important activity involving space is the site inspection. Using a comprehensive, customized checklist will make this task efficient and thorough. It will also allow you to delegate this task to others if you are not able to travel to the site yourself.

MeetingMatrix (www.meetingmatrix.com) has greatly expedited this process through their development of a Web-based program that lists thousands of venues throughout the world. Their service also includes certified diagrams to further ensure the accuracy of your event design. Finally, once you locate the appropriate venue, using their exclusive computer assisted design and drawing program, you may create original designs using tables, chairs, lecterns, drape, ice sculptures, and even the organization logo to completely outfit the room where the event will be held.

When conducting the in-person site inspection always carry a laser measure, a digital still or video camera, notepad, and pencil. Upon arrival, note the ingress to the parking facilities for up to one mile away. What will be the estimated travel time in heavy to moderate traffic, and are there alternative routes if the main artery is blocked by an accident or construction? Determine where the parking area will be for your official and VIP vehicles. Find out if special identification is required for those vehicles to park in these preapproved areas. Measure the height of the loading dock (if available) from the driveway to make certain that your vehicles can deliver directly onto the dock. This knowledge alone may save you thousands of dollars in additional labor charges.

Ask the venue officials to show you the entrance door for your personnel and the walking route to the pre-event waiting area (dressing rooms, green rooms, and briefing rooms). Write down these instructions and read them back to the official. Note who supplied these instructions, as they will later be given to your personnel, and should there be a problem, you must be able to refer back to your original source for clarification.

Measure the square footage of the waiting area and determine how many persons can be accommodated when official furnishings are included. Locate the restrooms and note if they are adequate or require upgrading (e.g., bringing in nicer amenities, such as specialty soaps, toiletries, perfumes, full-length mirrors, and fresh flowers).

Ask the venue official to lead you from the waiting area to the location of the actual event. Thoroughly examine the event site from the perspective of the spectator or participant. Most important, can the spectator see and hear comfortably? Sit in the seat of the spectator farthest from the staging area. Determine how the person with the most obstructed view can best see and hear.

When possible, ask the venue official to supply you with their most recent floor plan or diagram of the site. Use this site diagram as a general blueprint and then confirm and verify by using your measuring device to measure random locations. Note any variances for later adjustment on the final diagram.

Finally, before you leave the venue, sit for a minimum of 15 minutes in one of the chairs your spectator will occupy. Determine if it is comfortable for your guests. If not, ask if alternate seating is available, and at what cost.

Developing the Diagram

At one time transferring the results of the site inspection to a final, carefully produced diagram was a major labor-consuming operation. Using computer tools such as computer-assisted design and drawing (CADD) systems, this task has been simplified and automated. For those Event Leaders who are uncomfortable with computers, a manual system has been developed involving scale cutouts of magnets that correspond to the typical inventory of most venues (chairs, tables, platforms, pianos, etc.). Once assembled, the final product can be photocopied for distribution. A resource called Room Viewer™, using a CADD system, may be found at www.timesaversoftware.com.

Before beginning the process of developing the diagram, audit all internal and external stakeholders and create a list of every element that must be depicted on the diagram. These elements may range from décor to catering tents and from first-aid centers to parking locations. You will later use this checklist to cross-check the diagram and make certain that every element has been included.

After the first draft diagram has been developed, it must be distributed to stakeholders for a first review. Ask the stakeholders to review the diagram for accuracy and return it within a fixed amount of time with any additions, deletions, or changes.

After you have received comprehensive input from the stakeholders, prepare a final copy for review by officials who must grant final approval for the event. These officials may include the fire marshal, transportation authorities, or others responsible for enforcing laws and regulations.

Once you have constructed a final, approved diagram, you have made the giant step forward from dream to idea to final plan. Event Leadership planning requires that you consistently implement your plan effectively.

Determining the Production Schedule

The production schedule is the primary instrument (other than the event diagram) that is used during the coordination phase. During this phase, the Event Leader must implement a minute-by-minute plan and monitor the tasks that lead to the ultimate conclusion of the event itself. The production schedule ensures that you will be able to achieve this goal efficiently. Figure 7.9 is an example of a typical production schedule. Note how it is different from the timeline shown in Figure 3.11.

As Figure 7.9 suggests, the production schedule begins with load-in and concludes with load-out. The first line in the production schedule generally is "inspect venue" and the last line is "reinspect venue" to review and return the venue to the best condition. You will note that the production schedule is much more precise than the timeline and includes minute-by-minute precision. Typically, the Event Leader will include the production schedule in the timeline in the coordination phase and then provide a full version on-site at the event for the event coordination staff to manage the minute-by-minute operations.

The Convention Industry Council has adopted the term *Event Specification Guide* as the official standardized term for the previously used résumé or production schedule. The function schedule in this document is similar to the production schedule. To view a template of the Event Specification Guide, visit www.conventionindustry.org, click APEX, and then click Accepted Practices.

Anticipating and Resolving Operational Conflicts

During the coordination phase, numerous operational conflicts will develop. The key is for the Event Leader to anticipate and resolve these problems quickly by practicing what is often referred to as damage control. Some of the typical operational conflicts that arise and how you can resolve them quickly follow:

- *Late-arriving vendors.* Maintain cell-phone numbers and contact late-arriving vendors to determine their location.
- *Multiple vendors arriving simultaneously.* Sequence arrivals in logical order of installation.

Task	Start Time	Stop Time	Details	Person(s) Responsible	Notes
Inspect venue	7 A.M.	7:45 A.M.	Check for preexisting damages, problems	Event Leader	
Lighting and sound company loads in	8 A.M.	9 A.M.	Arrivals and load-in	Event coordinator	
Lighting and sound company installs	9 A.M.	12 noon	Set up, hang, focus, test	Event coordinator	
Lunch break	12 noon	1 P.M.	Lunch for 10 stage hands	Caterer	
Florist loads in and installs	1 P.M.	3 P.M.	Decorate stage and prepare centerpieces	Florist	
Rental company loads in and sets tables, chairs, and cloths	1 P.M.	3 P.M.	Place tables and chairs and clothe the tables	Rental company	
Place centerpieces on table	3 P.M.	4 P.M.	Position centerpieces	Volunteers	
Caterer loads in and sets up preparation area	3 P.M.	4 P.M.	Set up staging area for food preparation	Caterer	
Caterer sets tables	4 P.M.	5 P.M.	Final setting of tables	Caterer	
Inspection of tables, décor, lighting, sound by Event Leader	5 P.M.	5:30 P.M.	Final review	Event Leader	
Sound check and rehearsal with band	5:30 P.M.	6:30 P.M.	Final sound check	Event Leader and talent and technicians	
Waiters in position to open doors	6:45 P.M.	7 P.M.	Workers ready to open doors for guests	Event coordinator	
Open doors	7 P.M.	7:15 P.M.	Guests enter and are seated by waiters	Event coordinator	Doors opened early (7:10 P.M.)
Invocation	7:15 P.M.	7:17 P.M.	Minister delivers invocation	Stage manager	

Figure 7.9 Typical Production Schedule

(Continued)

Task	Start Time	Stop Time	Details	Person(s) Responsible	Notes
Salad course	7:17 P.M.	7:30 P.M.	Salad served	Caterer	
Salad removed, entrée served	7:30 P.M.	7:50 P.M.	Entrée served	Caterer	
Entrée removed, dessert served	7:50 P.M.	8:10 P.M.	Dessert served	Caterer	
Coffee and candies served	8:10 P.M.	8:20 P.M.	Coffee and candies passed	Caterer	
Welcome speech and introduction of entertainment	8:20 P.M.	8:30 P.M.	All waiters out of room; speeches	Stage manager	
Entertainment	8:30 P.M.	9:00 P.M.	Band	Stage manager	Entertainment started late (8:40 P.M.)
Dancing	9:00 P.M.	12 midnight	Dancing	Stagemanager	
Close bars	11:45 P.M.	12 midnight	Stop serving	Caterer	
End of event	12 midnight	12 midnight	Lights up full	Event Leader	
Dismantle and load-out	12:30 A.M.	6 A.M.	All equipment dismantled and removed from venue	Event coordinator	
Reinspect venue	7 A.M.	8 A.M.	Venue checked for any damages or losses caused by event	Event Leader, event coordinator, venue official	

Figure 7.9 *(Continued)*

- *Caterer running late in food delivery.* Monitor service carefully and use distractions such as dancing to cover long delays.
- *Speaker or entertainer cancels.* Use prerecorded music or video to cover.
- *Guests arrive too early.* Prepare for this and have appropriate staff greet and serve them.
- *Medical emergency.* Use standard operating procedures and work closely with venue to resolve.

As you can see, that wise Event Leader Murphy was prophetic when he wrote: "What can go wrong will go wrong." His cousin, O'Goldblatt, however, was perhaps even more prophetic when some years later he wrote: "Murphy is an optimist."

As a professional Event Leader, the coordination phase is the most exciting and often most grueling time during the event process. However, because you care deeply to achieve a high-quality outcome for the event, your ability to research, design, plan, and lead your team will smooth even the roughest edges during coordination of the event. The intersection of coordination can be crossed easily and safely because you are prepared, programmed, and ultimately polished in your ability to make the most difficult and intricate tasks appear easy and seamless.

Finally, during those maddening moments before guests arrive, you may wish to add one additional ritual to your arsenal of coordination tools. A colleague once told me that before she opens the doors to receive her guests, she closes her eyes for a few seconds and silently repeats three times: "This event is going to be easy, fun, and successful." Although events are rarely easy, in fact your event may be more fun and successful if you are relaxed in your approach to receiving the guests. Now, relax, and let's go on-site to begin coordinating the details that will produce your next successful event.

Career-Advancement Connections

Corporate Social Responsibility Connection

Each time you work with a vendor you have an opportunity to promote socially responsible events through sourcing and contracting. When possible, ask your vendors about their corporate social responsibility practices. Do they promote reuse, recycling, and reduction in their products? Are they purchasing their supplies locally and using fair-trade vendors? How do they treat their own employees in terms of equal pay, equal opportunity, health, and other social benefits? Most importantly, is your contracting process representative of best practices in social, economic, and environmental responsibility? You can monitor your CSR with the assistance of www.BSDglobal.com.

Global Connection

Moving events from city to city, state to state, or even country to country, is a complicated task with a number of challenges. One of the more important parts is transportation. Although many professionals are available to assist you in accommodating transportation needs, it is important for event professionals to have some basic knowledge of the issue. Transportation within one country involves mostly negotiations with a transport agency. A transportation agency usually provides services such as packing, loading, moving, unloading, and sometimes even unpacking as part of a contract. Event professionals should also remember about insurance. Usually, transportation companies provide basic insurance on their services; however, it is important to confirm that the amount of insurance is sufficient to cover not

The Pioneer: Rebecca Finkel, PhD, Program Leader and Lecturer in Event Management, Queen Margaret University, Edinburgh, Scotland

Dr. Rebecca Finkel brings a unique background to the field of modern events management. As a historian and cultural geographer, she is interested in the ways in which people celebrate their lives. According to Rebecca, "Festivals provide wonderful insights into a society, as their beliefs and values are on display during these convivial times. Learning more about festivals is key to learning about our own or other people's cultures and heritage. I believe this can precipitate social change by helping communities to develop better understanding and tolerance."

Her intellectual curiosity about other peoples' lives perhaps began with her own family. Her mother, Dr. Madelyn Finkel, has been her main mentor. Rebecca states, "I admire the work she has done in the public health field. Her strength, resolve and good nature are characteristics I try to emulate in my own life." When it comes to mentors, she says, "I am inspired by people such as my mother who overcome challenges and are not afraid to put themselves out there and try to make the world a better place."

She has noted that the field of events management is maturing similar to other disciplines. "I think events management, and certainly events management education, is being taken more seriously today. Perhaps driven by economic rationales, festival management is now viewed as a serious profession rather than a hobby. The development of such structure and benchmarks can only help the

only physical damage and/or loss of equipment but also potential losses that may occur due to event cancellation.

International transportation is more complicated than domestic. When conducting business internationally, event professionals should work with a much larger number of government and private institutions than for local events. Moving equipment to or from overseas venues often involves payment of import or export duties, various excise duties, various fees, and other payments. Before planning any international event activity, event professionals are strongly encouraged to consult international trade and tax professionals, who often will be affiliated with your international transport agency. An excellent reference for this task is *Global Meetings and Exhibitions* (Krugman and Wright 2006).

industry to grow from strength to strength in the future."

She believes that this maturing of the field and industry is the result of an increasing recognition of the social, economic, and political benefits of events by communities and various levels of government. Rebecca notes, "The role of the media in aiding this paradigm shift in how events are perceived also should not be underestimated."

According to Rebecca, "The future of the events industry will be a much more structured, target-driven industry. Like most changes, this is both positive and negative. In many respects, it can be seen as a positive progression because events will be more strategic and therefore more sustainable in the future. They have the potential to reach broader groups of people this way. On the other hand, events could also become less spontaneous and more polished due managerial changes, thus sanitizing their traditional carnivalesque roots."

Rebecca sees that one of the key signs of this change is the increased emphasis on the economic in all aspects of our world. The events industry already is becoming more and more involved in issues of financial accountability and cross-cutting agendas. She further notes, "This is especially true when public funding is involved as it is throughout Europe."

When advising the next generation of event professionals, Dr. Finkel states that the best piece of advice she ever received was "Although you can tick all the boxes, you have to have passion for your career. Don't forget to plan from the heart."

When asked to explain her reason for selecting this piece of advice, she further explains that "events by their very nature are emotional, meaningful and filled with symbolic value. They can only come alive and reach people if they embody the kind of energy that is fueled by love."

Dr. Rebecca Finkel has a love of people that is combined with a natural intellectual curiosity. This has helped form her career and will greatly influence the field of events in the future throughout her scholarship. Her students may benefit from her historical knowledge but they will grow infinitely wiser from her passion for both producing and understanding events that are fueled with love.

Technology Connection

Use a Microsoft Excel spreadsheet or other software to track all vendor agreements. Utilize event planning software such as Meeting Pro, Event Manager, Day to Day Event Manager, EVENTS, Special Event Management, and other products to efficiently organize and document your event planning operations.

For a more extensive list of event software, see Appendix 9. Software such as Microsoft Outlook will allow you to use the calendar function to set up appointments, reminders, and other date- and time-specific operations to ensure more accurate planning.

Resources Connection

Contact industry associations and local convention and visitors' bureaus for key contact information. Comprehensive listings may be found at the Convention Industry Council (www.cic.org), the Destination Marketing Association International (www.iacvb.org), the International Congress and Convention Association (www.icca.nl), or www.ises.com. These organizations will assist you in identifying qualified vendors to support your event. Interview prospective and current

The Protégé: Alicia Brett, PhD, in Planned Events Student, Queen Margaret University

Alicia Brett decided to pursue her PhD in Events at Queen Margaret University after receiving high marks during her undergraduate studies. When asked why she decided to pursue the arduous path to her doctorate she says, "Since I can remember, I have always loved attending parties, concerts, and local arts festivals. However, I must admit I would always come away from these events wondering what I would have done to make it better." When it came to choosing what career she would pursue after leaving school, planning events wasn't so much a career choice as more of a natural progression. She recalls, "Whatever other paths I chose to pursue, I would somehow find myself researching the next event to attend or planning the next Christmas party and I realized that rather than doing these things alongside my studies, perhaps I should study them."

She finds that the growing political intervention in the events industry is a fascinating area of study, and therefore, her research is both stimulating and satisfying. She observes, "I guess when you can go home at night and feel satisfied and fulfilled about your job, that's how you know it is right for you."

Alicia grew up in a small town in Ireland, where there were very few public events. She is still inspired by her childhood dance teacher, who instigated the production of many concerts, musicals and plays which allowed many young people in the town the opportunity to take part in something meaningful. "My teacher's determination to fundraise and give our town much needed entertainment has shown me that the determination and passion

vendors and determine what systems they are using to manage events. This will help you ensure that your systems are congruent.

 Learning Connection

Use the Event Specification Guide template to detail the arrangements for a association event for 1,000 persons with 100 exhibitors. The event's duration is three days and includes one opening reception, two luncheons, and one gala awards dinner.

of just one person can make a difference in this world as it did in my little town."

She recognizes that the growth of the events industry has been unprecedented in the past decade and firmly believes that it will continue to grow: "Events have been utilized more and more by cities, towns, and regions to address public agendas such as economic, cultural, social, and environmental policy. This only illustrates the growing significance and importance of the industry. The greater political interest in events is starting to bring about greater regulation to the industry. This regulation may affect the number and variety of smaller events being produced due to their insufficient ability to address public policy."

She believes that a number of factors have promoted this change. "It seems to have been the recent global consensus by communities and various levels of government that hosting events may be a panacea for attracting tourism whilst simultaneously bringing social, economic and political benefits to a place. Events are becoming more accessible, appealing, and known as a result of new forms of media such as the Internet. If the communication media are well exploited by event organizers, an event has the potential to sell its host on the global stage."

Looking toward her future in the Events Industry, she hypothesizes that "in this current period of economic decline, it may prove difficult for many events to prove their economic worth in post-event evaluation reports. It is also proving very difficult to measure the less tangible social and cultural impacts of events. This may see public funding that events are presently receiving withdrawn. Event managers will be under more pressure to evaluate their events and provide evidence of both the tangible and intangible benefits of these events if they are to secure funding to produce these events."

Throughout her life, she has been guided by the sage advice that you need to believe in yourself. "In the events industry, you are not always going always agree with everyone else. But everyone will have something unique to bring to the event. If you believe in yourself and your ideas enough, you can show the passion, drive, and commitment needed to persuade others. Creativity is a fantastic trait, but without passion and self-belief, it can be more difficult to convey this to others."

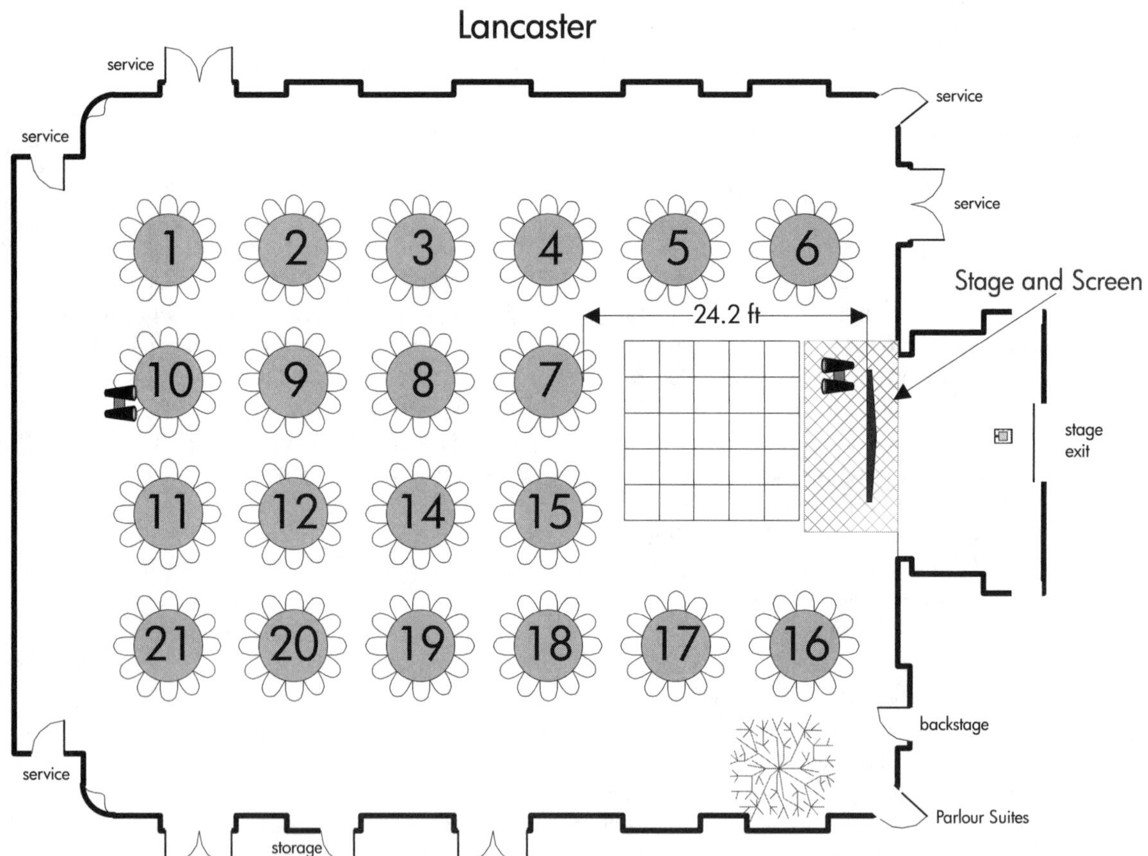

MeetingMatrix International (www.meetingmatrix.com) provides a simple, easy-to-use computer-assisted drawing system, along with thousands of certified floor plans, to make the development of an on-site production accurate, efficient, and creative for your event.

CHAPTER 8

On-Site Event Production

In this chapter you will learn how to:

- Understand the differences between the timeline, productions schedule, résumé, and Event Specification Guide (ESG)
- Integrate new technologies in production operations
- Reduce cost and increase quality with new technology
- Develop and implement event contingency plans
- Monitor each element of an event during event operations
- Establish and manage efficient registration operations
- Coordinate industry and professional speakers
- Identify and utilize appropriate amenities
- Identify, create, and post informative signs
- Develop an awareness of lighting, sound, and video for live events.
- Use visualization software for events planners and organizers

Once the event has been thoroughly designed and planned, the elements are now ready to be implemented through on-site production. One of the leading experts in this field is Stuart Green, senior lecturer in Lighting and Live Event Technology at The University of Glamorgan in the United Kingdom. Stuart continues to practice as a lighting designer and programmer for live events, theater, and dance and has worked on productions in both the United Kingdom and the European continent. He has extensive experience within the events industry, as a lighting designer and visualization expert; He has also designed the lighting for productions in many major venues in the United Kingdom, including the West End. Working as an assistant lighting designer, production electrician and programmer Stuart has worked for companies such as the Royal National Theatre, Sadler's Wells, Essential Lighting, and renowned lighting designers Rick Fisher and Paul Pyant.

Stuart has a close working relationship with Cast Software, which in 2006 saw him claim the Wysiwyg Trainer (AWT) status from Cast Lighting. He is now one of only five certified Wysiwig trainers in the United Kingdom, and the only Authorized Trainer at a university in the United Kingdom. *Wysiwyg* is a computer acronym for ***W**hat **Y**ou **S**ee **I**s **W**hat **Y**ou **G**et*, and is used in computing to describe a computer system in which content displayed during editing appears very similar to the final output. In the events industry, *wysiwyg* is used extensively to plan and prepare the lighting for events, which, when used alongside Vivien (virtual event designer), enables event planners to take their clients' ideas from computer to reality. As a recognized authority in his field, Stuart has made significant contributions to the updating of this chapter to ensure that the most recent technological innovations for special events are included.

As we have learned in previous chapters, policies and procedures provide a rationale and regulation for day-to-day event decision making. However, the timeline and production schedule serve as the road maps that ensure you will arrive safely at your destination. The policies, procedures, and practices are the rules of the road, but without the production schedule, you may never find the right road or might navigate so poorly that your event is lost before you even begin.

Timeline

The timeline is the sequential listing of all tasks and duties associated with the event project. It is divided by the five phases of the event process: research, design, planning, coordination, and evaluation. Within each of these tasks, the Event Leader lists every action that is required to develop and execute the event. These actions represent units of time or, as described by project managers, *work packages,* that may be measured in hours or days. Therefore, the timeline is listed in calendar order by days, weeks, or months. The first task is reviewing previous data from preceding events, and the final task is to conduct a comprehensive evaluation and to create and transmit a thorough final report to promote sustainability.

Production Schedule

The production schedule is one of the major series of tasks and duties within the timeline. In the coordination phase of the timeline, the Event Leader coordinates the logistics of the event that has been planned. The first task in the production schedule is to inspect the venue prior to moving in any equipment. The final task in the timeline is to reinspect the venue at the conclusion of the event after removing all equipment. This enables the Event

Leader to observe and note any physical changes to the venue as a result of the event activity. The production schedule lists minute by minute (or, in the case of television production, second by second) each activity that is performed in sequential order. For example, the Event Leader would want to make certain the lighting company precedes the catering company when installing equipment. Lighting must be raised into place and requires a clear floor area. Therefore, tables may not be dropped and decorated until the major lighting has been hung and generally focused.

Résumé

Historically, meeting professionals have used the term *résumé* to describe all of the components for the meeting or function room. The résumé will not only list the time for each function, but also the equipment, food, and beverages required. This document serves as a major communications tool for all stakeholders, including the hotel or convention center as well as individual vendors. A typical résumé is shown in Figure 8.1.

Event Specification Guide

Recently, the Convention Industry Council (CIC) has adopted the term and format of an Event Specification Guide (ESG) through its successful APEX initiative. The ESG takes the production schedule and résumé to a higher level by providing a series of integrated components and, for the first time, encouraging universal adoption by all stakeholders in the meetings and events industry. The ESG, if widely adopted, has the potential for saving time and therefore saving money by promoting easier and better communication among event stakeholders. The ESG is available in a software package through the Convention Industry Council at www.conventionindustry.org.

Improving Event Performance

Hundreds or perhaps thousands of elements must be coordinated to produce a flawless event. Just as a coach writes down plays and shares these plans with the team, the Event

Date	Time	Function	Location	Setup	Attendance	Catering	A/V
Friday	10 A.M.–12 P.M.	Board meeting	Room 102	Hollow square	20	Coffee, juice	Overhead

Figure 8.1 Typical Résumé

Leader must reduce his or her plans to writing and communicate these details with the event stakeholders. Using the timeline–production schedule will improve your event performance in many ways. A few of these are listed next to enable you to better understand the benefits of this planning tool:

- A production schedule requires the Event Leader to schedule every element involved in an event systematically and logically.
- It provides a unique comprehensive communications tool for the use of other team members.
- It enables external stakeholders, such as police, fire, security, and medical personnel, to stay informed regarding event operations.
- It can be easily distributed to internal and external stakeholders via e-mail for quick updates.
- It provides an accurate historical accounting of the entire event.

Many of the competencies we have discussed in previous chapters, including history, communication, and logical and reasonable thinking, are incorporated in the production schedule process. However, the most important reason for implementing the timeline–production schedule into your planning process is that it absolutely improves event performance. This is accomplished through improved communications. Every member of your event team is able to refer to the timeline–production schedule and determine quickly and efficiently what is supposed to happen at what time. For this reason alone, it is a very valuable tool and should be used from the research period through the final evaluation.

Improving Financial Effectiveness

One area that governs all other areas of an event is financial management. The production schedule allows you to see, in spreadsheet fashion, how you are allocating your scarce event resources in the most efficient manner. Once you have assembled all the details in logical sequence, you can review them carefully to see if there are any duplications or ways in which resources may be reallocated for greater cost savings. For example, if you notice that the installation is scheduled for Sunday at 7:00 A.M. and that will result in paying "time-and-a-half" to your crews, you can try to rearrange your Friday activities to schedule the setup within the straight-time rate.

Improving Quality and Reducing Costs

Every element on the production schedule affects your event financially. Therefore, when using this schedule, you should look constantly for ways to best allocate your event resources in the most cost-effective manner. Three ways to accomplish this task include making certain that you only schedule labour when it is needed. Carefully review the work that is to be performed and make certain that you have scheduled labour just for these hours. Next, whenever possible, share equipment and other resources with other groups, including the venue itself. By using in-house resources, you may save significant funds, as you will not have to pay for travel, per diems, or other costs from outside contractors. Third and finally, reduce, reuse, and recycle equipment to promote environmental sustainability and reduce your overall costs.

Production Schedule

Creating the Schedule

The production schedule is the minute-by-minute (or in the case of television, second-by-second) running order for your event. It differs from the timeline in that it only reflects the time period from move-in (referred to in Europe and Asia as "load in" or "get in") to move-out (referred to in Europe and Asia as "get out" or "strike") for your event. It does not include the research, design, planning, or evaluation phases of the event. These phases, as well as the coordination phase, are included in the event timeline.

The first task in the production schedule is to inspect the venue, and the final task is to inspect the venue. These inspections are critical because they allow the Event Leader to identify any physical or other challenges with the venue prior to the official move in and also to note any change in the condition of the venue prior to the conclusion of the move out.

There are three important resources to incorporate when creating your draft document. First, you must check with key informants to make certain that you have incorporated all critical information. Second, you will want to explain the production schedule at an upcoming group meeting to receive feedback from the entire group. Finally, you must recheck the timing, function, and assignment to check for gaps and make certain that your production schedule is logical.

Key Informants

Ask the senior members of your team to assist you with constructing the draft production schedule. Instruct each team member to create an individualized production schedule reflecting the operations of the individual departments. After you have received all the schedules, combine them into one integrated document. Then distribute the draft document to the same key informants and ask them to check your work for accuracy and see if there are additions, deletions, or changes. Typical key informants assisting you in preparing and reviewing the production schedule are:

- Admissions coordinator
- Advertising coordinator

- Assistant Event Leader
- Audiovisual coordinator
- Box office coordinator
- Caterer
- Corporate social responsibility monitor
- Decorator
- Entertainment coordinator
- Environmental coordinator
- Exposition coordinator
- Facility management
- Fire department
- Food and beverage coordinator
- Legal advisor
- Lighting designer / coordinator
- Medical coordinator
- Police
- Public relations
- Registration coordinator
- Rentals coordinator
- Risk management coordinator
- Safety coordinator
- Security coordinator
- Sound designer/coordinator
- Ticket coordinator
- Transportation coordinator
- Ushering coordinator

Group Meetings

Transfer the production schedule to a slide and use the next team meeting as an opportunity to explain this document. Walk through each step of the schedule slowly and carefully, pausing occasionally to ask if there are any questions. Solicit feedback from the group on how best to depict the schedule as well as ways to consolidate operations and improve efficiency.

Testing, Timing, Function, and Assignment

The production schedule is a table with six columns. These columns allow you to enter the various key components or elements of the event in logical sequence. It is critical that you test your production schedule by seeking input from critical friends who have produced similar events of the same size and scope. Similar to a budget, the timeline–production schedule is a projection of how things should happen based on the knowledge available to you at this time. Figure 8.2 shows a typical event production schedule table. You may

Task	Start Time	Stop Time	Details	Person(s) Responsible	Notes
Inspect venue	7:00 A.M.	7:45 A.M.	Check for preexisting damages, problems	Event planner	
Lighting and sound company get in	8:00 A.M.	9:00 A.M.	Arrivals and load-in	Event coordinator/ Production manager	
Lighting and sound company installs	9:00 A.M.	12 noon	Set up, hang, focus, test	Event coordinator/ Production manager	
Lunch break	12 noon	1:00 P.M.	Lunch for crew	Caterer	
Florist loads in and installs	1:00 P.M.	3:00 P.M.	Decorate stage and prepare centrepieces	Florist	
Rental company loads in and sets tables, chairs, and cloths	1:00 P.M.	3:00 P.M.	Place tables and chairs and clothe the tables	Rental Company	
Place centerpieces on table	3:00 P.M.	4:00 P.M.	Position centerpieces	Volunteers	
Catererloads in and sets up preparation area	3:00 P.M.	4:00 P.M.	Set up staging area for food preparation	Caterer	
Caterer sets tables	4:00 P.M.	5:00 P.M.	Final setting of tables	Caterer	
Inspect tables, décor, lighting, sound by Event Leader	5:00 P.M.	5:30 P.M.	Final review	Event planner	
Sound check and rehearsal with band	5:30 P.M.	6:30 P.M.	Final sound check	Event Leader, talent, technicians	

Figure 8.2 Typical Production Schedule *(Continued)*

Task	Start Time	Stop Time	Details	Person(s) Responsible	Notes
Waiters in position to open doors	6:45 P.M.	7:00 P.M.	Workers ready to open doors for guests	Event coordinator	
Open doors	7:00 P.M.	7:15 P.M.	Guests enter and are seated by waiters	Event coordinator	Doors opened early (7:10 P.M.)
Invocation	7:15 P.M.	7:17 P.M.	Minister delivers invocation	Stage manager	
Salad course	7:17 P.M.	7:30 P.M.	Salad served	Caterer	
Salad removed, entree served	7:30 P.M.	7:50 P.M.	Entree served	Caterer	
Entree removed, dessert served	7:50 P.M.	8:10 P.M.	Dessert served	Caterer	
Coffee and candies served	8:10 P.M.	8:20 P.M.	Coffee and candies passed	Caterer	
Welcome speech and introduction of entertainment	8:20 P.M.	8:30 P.M.	All waiters out of room; speeches	Stage manager	
Entertainment	8:30 P.M.	9:00 P.M.	Band	Stage manager	Entertainment started late (8:40 P.M.)
Dancing	9:00 P.M.	12 midnight	Dancing	Stage manager	
Close bars	11:45 P.M.	12 midnight	Stop serving	Caterer	
End of event	12 midnight	12 midnight	Lights up full	Event planner	
Dismantle and load-out	12:30 A.M.	6:00 A.M.	All equipment dismantled and removed from venue	Event coordinator/ Production manager	
Reinspect venue	7:00 A.M.	8:00 A.M.	Venue checked for any damages or losses caused by event	Event planner, event coordinator, venue official	

Figure 8.2 *(Continued)*

adapt this model for your own needs. Make certain the timeline–production schedule includes the five phases of event planning: research, design, planning, coordination, and evaluation.

Implementing the Schedule

After you have completed the production schedule, you must circulate a series of drafts to key constituents to ensure that approvals are received before issuing the final document. Always attach a cover memorandum instruction for each reader on how to analyze the production schedule and describe the kind of input you are seeking. For example, you may ask one reader to proof for typographical errors while another concentrates on validating the timing for the various activities. Each key constituent should have a specific role to play relevant to his or her level of expertise. However, each constituent should review the entire plan to check for overall gaps as well as his or her own particular area of expertise.

Monitoring the Schedule

Appoint several capable people to serve as monitors and oversee various stages of implementation of the production schedule. They should have a copy of the schedule and should, in the notes section, list any variances from the schedule published. If, for example, the event is late in starting, this should be noted with the actual start time. If the event runs overtime, this should also be noted with the actual stop time. This kind of information is extremely important when planning future events and budgeting adequate time to the various elements you will use.

The monitor should turn in his or her copy of the production schedule with the notes included immediately after completing his or her assignment. Figure 8.2 demonstrates typical notes that your monitor may insert.

Handling Changes

About the only thing you can count on today is that things will change, and sometimes far too rapidly to update the production schedule. When a change must be made quickly, use a printed bulletin headlined "CHANGE NOTICE" to ensure that every member of your team is aware and able to adjust his or her schedule to accept this change. Figure 8.3 depicts a typical change notice.

Using the Timeline–Production Schedule to Manage Change

One of the most useful aspects of the production schedule is its ability to assist you in managing change. As literally hundreds of decisions must be made on a daily basis, the production schedule provides a solid framework for decision making.

Perhaps your celebrity has been delayed in another city and will be arriving late for your function. A quick glance at the production schedule allows you to make the nec-

CHANGE NOTICE
Distribution: All event staff and volunteers

Change: The opening ceremony previously scheduled to start at 10:00 A.M. on May 15, 2010, has been changed. **The new start time is 10:15 A.M.** The reason for this change is that the television feed has been moved and the new time is the actual start of the broadcast.

Summary: Note time changes for opening ceremony.

Previous Time: May 15, 10:00 A.M.

New time: May 15, 10:15 A.M.

Figure 8.3 Typical Change Notice

essary adjustments and see how these adjustments are affecting other elements of the event. In addition, by sharing a common document with your team members, you can solicit their input before making the adjustments, to ensure that you are in concert with one another.

Using integrated system design network (ISDN) technology, you will be able to send the most complex production schedule using fiber optics and involve as many people as necessary in your review and decision-making process. As each of you sits in front of a computer sharing the same document, you will be able to make minute or major changes and immediately see and discuss the ramifications of your decisions. In a world fraught with accelerated change, this will be a major advancement in the Event Leadership process.

The deficiencies in the résumé shown in Figure 8.1 include the absence of a contact person or person responsible for this function and a cell for notes regarding the actual start and stop times for the event. Although the résumé is widely used in the meeting Event Leadership field, it has some gaps. When deciding which tool to use for your event, first share your template or model with the venue that will be responsible for handling most of the meeting event logistics. Confirm and verify that the tool you propose to use will be accepted and used by the venue's staff prior to implementation.

Evaluating the Schedule

The best way to evaluate the use of the production schedule is to ask the key stakeholders if the process was effective: "Did the schedule help you understand the big and little picture of the event? Was the production schedule useful in keeping track of start and stop times? Were there any deficiencies in the timeline–production schedule? How could the schedule be improved next time?"

A quantitative way to monitor the use of the schedule is to review the notes section and look for wide gaps between the scheduled start and stop times and the actual times. Carefully study those elements of the event where the gaps were inordinately wide, and seek solutions in planning your next event.

Remember that the production schedule is similar to a budget in that it is a broad project management tool with a history that may be used to improve the overall planning process. Make certain you are diligent about reviewing the final schedule and comparing your projected elements with the final event. From this process, improvements will be made and your production scheduling process will become more scientific in the future.

Audiovisual Effects Management

Audiovisual, lighting, sound, special effects, and video are growing in importance with emerging techniques, lower costs, and improved quality.

Standard Audiovisual Equipment

Liquid Crystal Display Projector

Technology

The liquid crystal display (LCD) projector is used in conjunction with a computer to project graphic text and video onto a screen. This technology, which allows a presenter to have maximum flexibility when preparing and showing slides.

Use

An LCD projector may be used to present complex charts and graphs, photographs, text, Internet Web sites, graphics, and video as well as other images in a lively format similar to that of television production incorporating wipes, crawls, rolls, and other moving images. With additional technology, it is possible to incorporate video and audio to create an attention-grabbing presentation and liven up even the most tedious conference. Be careful not to allow your content to become buried under too much technological wizardry. Content must supersede presentation to maintain the integrity of your message. However, make certain you limit your text to three or four lines per screen to keep your presentation bright, brilliant, and above all, brief. The PowerPoint presentation must never replace or upstage the live presenter. Rather, it must always be used as a visual enhancement to support and reinforce the live message.

Light Emitting Diode Screen

Technology

Light-emitting diodes (LEDs) are essentially little colored light bulbs.

Use

Use an LED screen in large outdoor and especially daylight situations where the brightest possible projection is required. LED screens are often used in large stadiums or in locations with high pedestrian and vehicle traffic, such as New York's Times Square or London's Piccadilly Circus. LED lights greatly reduce power consumption because they last longer than traditional incandescent light bulbs.

Flat Screen Technology

Technology

The flat-panel screen uses liquid crystal display technology (LCD) (see earlier LCD description).

Use

The most common use is in computer screens and flat-panel TVs. In the meetings and events industry, the flat-panel screen is often used in smaller events to magnify the speaker or live onstage activity. It may also be used as an alternative for the traditional teleprompter. Increasingly the flat-panel screen is used in public buildings as a directional device to provide instant messages and direct delegates to the correct room for their meeting.

Microphone

Technology

The lectern microphone is perhaps the most common technology in use in conference events. Two primary types of microphones are available for use by Event Leaders. The unidirectional microphone is ideal for the individual speaker, and the omnidirectional microphone is designed for occasions when several people share the lectern.

In addition to the lectern microphone, a head microphone (one with a small frame that fits over the head or around the ear and positions the microphone near the mouth), a halo rig (a small microphone that is attached to a loop that fits on the top of the head, similar to a angel's halo with the microphone resting on the forehead), and the traditional lavaliere or clip-on microphone (sometimes the names are used interchangeably) allow a presenter to be mobile and move around the stage or room.

Although sometimes more expensive, the wireless handheld, head, halo rig or lavaliere microphone provides greater freedom, as no cable is attached. Using a transmitter and receiver, the audio signal is patched directly into the audio system and produces high-quality sound.

Use

When using a halo rig, head, or clip-on microphone, placement of the microphone head is extremely important. It is wise to have a wired microphone as a backup should problems arise with the wireless system.

Projection Screens

Technology

Event Leaders use both rear and front projection screens for different reasons and different venues. A front projection screen generally provides brighter illumination; however, a rear projection screen makes it possible to hide the projection equipment from audience view. Typically, two types of screens are used. A tripod screen is supported by a metal tripod, and a fastfold screen is supported by a metal frame and may be either supported on legs or hung from above. Projection screens generally range in size from 6 feet high by 8 feet wide to 15 feet high by 20 feet wide.

According to Da-Lite, a provider of professional projections screens, the following formula (Figure 8.4) may be used in determining the dimensions of the screen you will require for your event.

These screens accept slides produced in horizontal formats. In addition to the screen, most audiovisual suppliers will provide a dress kit for the fast-fold screen. This kit consists of a skirt, valance, and perhaps side drapes for masking. You may also wish to use other pipes and drapes to run off to the side of the room to further mask the backstage area. In addition to traditional screens, increasingly Event Leaders use a wider range of surfaces for front and rear projection. One such projection surface is a product known as Transformit™ (www.transformitdesign.com).

Use

Screens may be used for laser, slide, or video projection. Typically, screens are underutilized at conferences. Consider using the screen surface to project the names of your event's sponsor or other information in addition to the educational content of the conference. Avoid leaving screens blank by using a title-slide to cover periods when no video or slides are required. In case of an emergency, to create an instant title-slide without the expense of a slide projector, use the video camera to shoot the lectern sign that usually features the organization's logo or name. This shot will then be projected onto the screens as if it were a title-slide.

1. Screen height should be approximately one-sixth the distance from the screen to the last row of seats, allowing text to be read and for detail to be seen. For example, if the last row of your audience is located 60 feet from the location of the screen, the screen should be 10 feet high.
2. The bottom of the screen should be a minimum of four feet above the audience floor, allowing those seated near the rear of the audience to see the bottom of the screen. This may require additional screen drop (skirting) for ceiling-hung screens.

Source: Da-Lite (www.da-lite.com, 2009)

Figure 8.4 Sizing Your Projection Screen for Your Audience

Water Projection Screens and Curtains

Technology

A pipe with hundreds of holes projects water from the top of the stage to a catch pan and drain below. A video projector and lighting is projected on the water curtain to create various images from text to graphics to elaborate lighting effects.

Use

The water curtain may be used to reveal a person or a new product by transitioning from the video or lighting projection to turning off the water and revealing the person or product behind the screen.

Cost

In addition to rental and labor costs you will need to provide continuous water and an open drain. Furthermore, you may need to provide additional upkeep for the surrounding area if the water spray causes any damage to floor, walls, or ceiling.

Cost-Saving Measures

When renting audiovisual equipment, remember that this business, like many in the meetings and conference field, is somewhat seasonal. Therefore, the prices for the equipment may be negotiable. The price for labor is typically not negotiable. When bidding on audiovisual equipment, make certain that you list every possible application and amount of time required for labour so that the bidders may evaluate the total value of your event. You may be able to receive discounts on equipment by adjusting the dates of your event to reflect periods when equipment is more readily available.

Still another way to save money is to find multiple uses for your audiovisual equipment during the same 24-hour period. Too often, Event Leaders use a video projector for one hour when, in actuality, the rental is factored on a 24-hour period. Preplan the use of this equipment to maximize the value. For example, can the projector be moved to a different room instead of renting a separate piece of equipment?

Finally, look for ways to share costs on audiovisual equipment with other groups. Perhaps there is another organization meeting in the same venue at the same time as your organization. Can you co-rent equipment with them to save costs?

Lighting

When, according to the Old Testament of the Bible, the Almighty proclaimed "Let there be light," it may have been the first time in recorded history that a lighting cue was called. Since that fateful day, lighting has come to symbolize safety, mood, atmosphere, and transition, as well as time of day and location. In almost every event environment, lighting improves the atmosphere. It may be used to focus attention on the speaker and to enhance the look of décor and food as well as to change the mood dramatically from one scene to another.

Miniaturization has affected the lighting field in major ways. Only a few years ago, a lighting control system would require enough space to fill a small bedroom. Today, the lighting for your event can be controlled from a laptop computer. This major reduction in size has made lighting more flexible and available than ever before.

Driven by market and economic pressures lighting technology is constantly being improved and developed. At present, LEDs are the emerging lighting technology of choice by event planners and designersfor effect lighting. LEDs provide lower cost, power consumption, and offer greater flexibility. The recent explosion in LED products now offers event planners and designers new possibilities, from the ability to change the color of your projection screen or backdrop through dance floors, cocktail bars, table centers and even banquet tables.

Lighting Control

Technology

A lighting controller allows the lighting designer to fade, black out, and perform other lighting changes. Many modern lighting controllers are computer-driven, allowing the operator to store the cues once recorded for easy recall.

Use

The lighting controller allows the lighting designer to designate specific output levels to any dimmer (and therefore lanterns), thereby creating a lighting state. It then allows for accurate altering of this information (cue) over a period of time. Cues may range from blackouts to slow fades to everything in between. Modern lighting controllers come in all shapes, sizes, and levels of complexity. Most modern lighting controllers have an effects engine for execution of lighting chases, for example. The lighting controller can also be used to control the house lights.

Ellipsoidal Reflector Spotlight

Technology

The major difference between the ellipsoidal reflector spotlight (ERS), also known as Leko in the United States (Profile in Europe) and other luminaries discussed later, is the ability to focus light selectively and to use a gobo for projecting specific images such as company logos.

Use

Using shutters, the ellipsoidal reflector spotlight allows the Event Leader to focus light to highlight specific areas in a cylindrical, horizontal, or vertical format. Additionally, these instruments can accept a metal, glass, or transparency gobos. The gobo uses a design that can be projected on a surface such as a curtain, wall, floor, or other area. These designs may be mixed and matched to create a variety of effects. Using a scrim curtain, you can project an image such as a window, and using a rear light source, an actor may actually appear to raise the window by adding a second gobo of an open window. Gobos may also be used to project text such as sponsor names. This is a quick and inexpensive way to add sponsor recognition to an event.

Follow Spot

Technology

Follow spots in their simplest form are basically profile spots mounted on a floor stand, with the addition of an iris, color magazine and blackout card. A follow spot is a manually operated (although automated luminaires are sometimes used as follow spots), focusable spotlight with the ability to change colour through the use of gels. A follow spot can be used to highlight and follow speakers, actors, or other persons as they perform. To achieve the intensity required, most follow spots use discharge lamps.

Use

Follow spots focuses attention on a principal performer, prop, or other important item.

Fresnels

The Fresnel spot takes its name from the Frenchman who originally designed the lens for use in lighthouses. This luminaire provides a soft-edged beam, which can be varied in size by moving the lamp and reflector toward or further from the lens, as with a PC.

Fresnels are ideal for lighting adjacent areas, because the soft-edged beam means there will be no hard edges where the beams merge. Typical beam angle ranges from 8 to 60 degrees.

Par Can

The Parabolic Aluminized Reflector, or PAR, is a sealed beam lamp like a car headlight. It consists of a lamp that has both a lens and a reflector built into it. The luminaire shell is used to support the lamp and to keep flare to a minimum. Pars are perfect for strong lighting effects. A Par Can is an invaluable source of strong key light. The most commonly used type of PAR is the Par 64. The lamps in a Par 64 are generally 1000 watts, available in three beam widths; (9×12, 10×14, 11×24). Other variants are available, including the Par 56, Par 36, and Par 16. Typical beam angle ranges from 5 to 20 degrees. Energy efficient LED versions of the traditional Par are now widely available and offer a wide range of benefits to the events industry.

Pin Spot

The pin spot is a version of the Par Can that can be used to provide a narrow, focused beam of light on a table centerpiece. This low-wattage instrument is extremely effective for lighting a specific area, such as a centerpiece or in conjunction with a mirror ball.

Floods

As the name implies, floodlights are used to cover as large an area as possible. They consist simply of a lamp and a reflector, and are supplied with 150-, 500-, and 1000-watt lamps. By using several of these units together, it becomes possible to light large backcloths or cycloramas. A cyclorama is a curved or straight backcloth hung at the rear of a stage. It may be used as a sky or background, painted and lit as required.

There are three types of floodlighting. The first provides an even distribution of light. The second provides more light at the bottom of the beam than at any other point. This is achieved by shaping the reflector in a complex way and using an epitaxial lamp, which is very long with a filament that travels its whole length. These are excellent for lighting backcloths where the luminaire is rigged near to the top of the cloth, and when even illumination is needed from top to bottom. The third type is on a batten. Several units are fixed together in a section on the stage floor. Used like this, they are called ground rows, and when used on the front edge of the stage, they are called floats or footlights. Typical beam angle ranges from 80 to 90 degrees.

Automated Luminaires

Automated luminaires offer the ability to change focus, location, color, beam size, and gobo and perform other maneuvers. Automated lights can be used on events for lighting effects, or for subtle changes of atmosphere, color, or visual focus, and can save space in a crowded lighting rig by taking the place of several 'specials'.

As with generic luminaires, automated lights are available in spot or wash light variants with discharge, tungsten, or LED light sources. Automated luminaires work on the principle of controlling various "attributes" of the luminaire by assigning them to channels of control in a lighting console. Automated luminaires typically take between 8 and 32 attributes, requiring a similar number of control channels.

Digital Lighting

Bridging the gap between lighting and video, digital lighting technology is increasingly being used on events from the smallest conference to spectaculars such and the Olympic Games. Digital lighting is essentially projection, whether through the use of a projector in a cage, housed in an auto-yoke or through an LED array. Digital lighting involves the use of 'content' sent from a media server. The content used on your event could be 'stock' footage of abstract imagery, the output from a live camera or documentary footage. Using the latest in digital light technology gives the Event Leader a powerful visual graphics tool that can meet the expectations of today's sophisticated audiences, while also offering many creative and labour-saving possibilities.

Fiber-Optic Drop or Curtain

Technology

Thousands of microthin fibers carry light from a remote source and create changing colours or chase effects. Fibre optics can be either end or side emitting and have a multitude of uses.

Use

In the events industry fibre-optic technology is most commonly used within a backdrop for a stage set and may also be used in a theme event to create the illusion of a galaxy of stars. Other uses include set dressing, tread markers and lectern illumination Fibre Optics are a good choice when heat output is a primary concern

Strobe Light

Technology

This rapidly flashing light creates the illusion of slow or fast motion when used with movement. It is available in a variety of sizes, including small egg-shape products that, when used in combination with other instruments, produce a starlight effect.

Use

Strobe lights may be used for a range of effects from the reveal of a new product or to highlight a building though simulation of someone moving in slow-motion.

Caution

Strobe lighting may cause discomfort or even injury to guests with disabilities, such as hearing loss or epilepsy. When using these devices, you should arrange for a sign to be posted at the entrance stating that strobe lighting will be used during the event.

Ultraviolet (UV) or Black Light

Technology

Popular during the 1960s, ultraviolet (UV) or black light technology has improved tremendously. Originally available only in tube format, its major drawback was the limited throw distance. In recent years, manufacturers have invented new technology that allows longer throw distance and focusable light to create fantastic new effects.

Use

This technology may be used to create a dark and haunting atmosphere or a space-age thrill. When used in conjunction with UV treated scenery or costumes, images or graphics that would not normally be visible to the human eye can be unveiled.

Lighting Opportunities

When planning an event, lighting should be thought of as an integral part of the event, not a luxury. There are many areas in which professionally designed lighting can enhance your event. Look to engage a designer from the outset. They will then be able to work with you throughout the planning process often guiding and offering ideas to maximize the impact of your event. By utilizing the services of a lighting designer, you can enhance the overall look and effect of your event. Lighting can help to create mood, atmosphere, direct your audience and even promote your client's brand.

Cost-Saving Measures

The easiest way to save money on lighting equipment and labour is to select a venue that has lighting equipment permanently installed in its facility. Sometimes the venue will include in the rental fee the use of some or all lighting equipment. You may also wish to share the costs of equipment rentals with other groups in the same venue.

When you must rent lighting equipment, make certain that you solicit bids. When possible, ask bidders to inspect the venue with you, as they may be able to offer additional ideas that you may not have thought of previously.

Finally, remember that costs escalate rapidly when work is performed outside normal business hours or you are utilising the latest technology. Find the time frame for straight time and work within this window. Sometimes this will require renting the venue on a weekday to prepare for a weekend event. Compare the labour cost savings to the rental charges and determine which is better. Schedule labour carefully to avoid overtime charges.

Sound

The level of complexity and purpose of the event determines the level of audio support that is required. In most event environments, audio is used for simple reinforcement and playback. However, as the size of the audience increases or the complexity of the production rises, simple audio must be replaced by the services provided by a production sound company.

Sound reinforcement is used for public address, entertainment, to project speakers, to transmit sound from video or film as well as numerous other applications. Figure 8.5 describes some of these applications and the type of equipment that may be required.

Sound Equipment	Application
Audio mixer and rack	Full-sound production capability, including playback and recording.
Boom attachment	Television, film, recording, specific sound source, and large groups.
Compact disc player	Playback of instrumental music and other sound, including effects.
Delay speaker	Used to project sound to areas that are a greater distance from the original sound source. In a stage setting, the delay speakers may be mounted halfway over the audience. The signal received by these speakers is delayed to avoid an echolike quality.
Digital audiotape (DAT) machine	Synchronized music.
Fill speaker	A speaker used to send sound signals to dead spots such as the front center of an audience

Figure 8.5 Applications for Sound Equipment *(Continued)*

Mixer	Used for blending sound sources through one central unit.
Omnidirectional microphone	Chorus.
Perimeter zone microphone	Chorus, singers, and piano. (PZM)
Speaker	Used for projecting sound to either a specific area or a wide distribution.
Speaker cluster	A group of speakers clustered together to project a wide distribution of sound.
Speaker tripod	A speaker mounted on a tripod.
Stage or ear monitor	Playback from other instruments and vocalists.
Unidirectional microphone	Solo speaker.

Figure 8.5 *(Continued)*

Mixer

Technology

A mixer is the hub of any audio system. All mixing desks are designed to make operation as simple as possible. In simple systems of perhaps three or four inputs it allows smooth transitions between each input or a mix of each input to produce a combined effect. The number of inputs may vary from four to dozens. Traditionally audio mixers utilized analogue technology; however it is now increasingly common to see sound designers using digital mixing desks.

Use

Instrumental musicians and multiple vocalists as well as event programs that feature both live and recorded sound sources will require the services of a mixing unit.

Equalizer

Technology

The range between treble and bass is equalized using this valuable technology.

Use

A professional sound engineer is required to equalize the range between treble and bass. He or she will use either your prerecorded sound source or the live performance to equalize the sound to provide a full range of audio dynamics.

Compact Disc Player

Technology

A compact disc (CD) player produces high-quality audio and video signals and provides enduring quality. Unlike its predecessor, the audiocassette player, the CD player allows for instant cueing and random access to specific audio or video segments. Data storage is an important use of this technology.

Use

Instrumental music and/or video/slides may be retrieved instantaneously with this technology. CD players can be used for background or specific audio musical cues, as well as to project photos or video images. They are ideal for instrumental music for background music, fanfares, or dancing.

MP3

Event Leaders are increasingly using MP3 and MP4 devices such as the iPod from Apple for playback in place of the traditional compact disc (CD) due to their size and versatility. The audio quality of an MP3 and MP4/4 player is comparable to a CD and enables the event planner to quickly download music from the Internet to satisfy the immediate need of a specific event.

When downloading music, it is critically important to ascertain who owns the rights to the material that is being downloaded. For example, some music may be downloaded for personal use only, such as iTunes music from Apple™ (www.itunes.com). If you wish to use the same material for commercial purposes or to synchronize the music with another media, such as video, you may need to negotiate additional rights with the music licensor.

Technology

This device is rapidly replacing the traditional compact disc as a storage medium for prerecorded audio files (music, sound effects and other files) for live events.

Use

Music for pre- or post-event, cues for walk music for an awards program or special effects may be prerecorded onto a flash drive (also called a jump or thumb drive) and then integrated with the computer and amplifier to play the effect at the desired time during the event.

Common Microphones

There are two primary types of microphone used for sound reinforcement: *dynamic* and *condenser.*

Dynamic Microphones

Dynamic microphones are typically robust and relatively inexpensive, and they don't need a power supply or batteries to make them operate. This, coupled with their high gain before feedback, makes them ideal for on-stage use. A commonly found dynamic microphone is the SM58 by Shure www.shure.com.

Condenser Microphones

Spanning the range from inexpensive to high-fidelity recording microphones, condenser microphones are often seen as the more refined cousins of dynamic microphones, and traditionally they were more expensive than dynamic microphones. They generally produce a high-quality audio signal and are the popular choice for studio-recording applications, though for some recording jobs such as drums, dynamic mics are hard to beat.

Perimeter Zone Microphone (PZM)

Technology

The perimeter zone microphone (PZM) is a flat microphone that picks up sounds in a 180-degree radius. It is used inside a piano, on the floor of a stage, to record choirs or large musical ensembles, and other applications where sound may originate from more than one point.

Use

Place the PZM inside the piano lid, on the center of a table for a group discussion, or on the floor of a stage to record or broadcast sound from multiple sources.

Wireless Microphone

Technology

There is a multitude of wireless microphones available to the event professional. The most commonly found types are the head, handheld and clip-on wireless microphones. Through utilizing wireless technology, you can enable your speaker to move freely before and among the audience.

Use

When conducting a presentation featuring audience questions and answers, the wireless microphone is ideal. It is also the instrument of choice for speakers who move randomly on the stage and among the audience. It is still advisable to have a wired microphone available in case the wireless microphone should fail. For a static presentation or debate, a *lavalier microphone* is often chosen. These small microphones are worn on the body and held in place either with a lanyard, worn around the neck or a clip fastened to clothing. The cord may be hidden by clothes and either run to an RF transmitter in a pocket or clipped to a belt (for mobile use), or run directly to the mixer (for stationary applications).

Stage or Ear Monitor

Technology

The stage monitor (sometimes referred to as a wedge due to its wedgelike shape) is used to monitor sounds from other instruments in a musical group, including vocals, as well as to monitor the sound level as the audience experiences it. The ear monitor is popular among entertainers. This small hearing-aid type of device is custom-fitted to the ear and allows for monitoring of sound as well as cueing and synchronizing when singing or performing to a prerecorded track.

Use

Singers and musicians use stage monitors to communicate with one another and to review their sound as the audience hears it. Singers, television performers, and others use ear monitors to receive cues from the director and monitor their vocal performance.

Sound Opportunities

There are generally three periods when sound equipment is utilized:

1. Prior to the event, audio products such as sound tracks or fanfares are prepared for the live performance.
2. During the actual event, it is needed for broadcasting both to the live audience attending the event and to those listening by radio, television, and the Internet.
3. A postproduction session may follow, in which the recorded event is processed to create a documentary, marketing tool, or other media product.

Preproduction

The preproduction period generally occurs during the design, planning, and coordination phases. Preproduction may include the design and production of specific audio elements for the event. These elements will vary, depending on the complexity of the event. Your task could be as simple as selecting appropriate instrumental music tracks or as complex as mixing an entire symphony orchestra to provide recorded accompaniment for a major mega-event, such as the opening or closing ceremony of the Olympic Games. The preproduction period must be planned carefully, as others may need to review the finished product before use in the actual event. Therefore, allow sufficient time to identify the appropriate resources, produce the product, and receive feedback from your important event stakeholders. When budgeting this time, allow 25 to 50 percent more time than estimated to handle last-minute changes and requests.

Production

During this period, the Event Leader coordinates the live, simulcast, delayed broadcast, or archival recording of sound from the actual event. Depending on the size and complexity of the event, the Event Leader may wish to assign a specific person from his or her staff to monitor the sound production. In most cases, a competent and capable sound technician will handle the myriad of details required for this function. However, in those circumstances when the event is new or highly specialized, it is wise to have one person supervise the sound department to ensure that this element of production is consistent with expectations. Too often, event planners assign too low a budget for production sound. Do not fall victim to this error. Make certain that you have budgeted carefully for the level of quality required. One way to do this is to be certain that you have retained a sound console operator as well as a stage sound technician. Speakers, actors, singers, musicians, and others who are using sound equipment will benefit from the knowledge that a qualified sound technician is nearby to help prevent or correct problems. A simple mistake, such as failing to turn on the wireless microphone, can easily be prevented by investing in a professional sound technician to monitor these important details.

Postproduction

Once the event has ended, the sound responsibilities may continue. More and more events are being recorded for both documentary, archival, Internet download, and marketing purposes. Therefore, during the design, planning, and coordination process of the event, careful attention must be paid as to how you may use the sound product after the live event has ended. Although the two most common uses are documentation and recording, it is also possible to use the sound portion of your event for communications, as well as risk management purposes. For example, a well-edited sound version of your event may be an effective way to communicate with your volunteers. You may duplicate this program on CDs and distribute them to volunteers to enjoy during their drive time to and from work. Should your organization become involved in a lawsuit resulting from a risk management incident, the sound recording may provide evidence that you practiced a standard of care acceptable in your area. For example, a recording of the evacuation announcement may provide you with evidence that you conducted this important activity with a reasonable degree of care to prevent injury. Throughout the research and design process, the Event Leader must carefully consider how he or she will later use the sound product created during the event.

Soundscaping

Sound Designer for the Olympic Games and the Super Bowl, and Event Solutions Hall of Fame Member Bob Estrin, president of Creative Event Technology in Orange County, California, may have been the first person of his generation to actually soundscape a room. The soundscaper works very much like the landscape artist or architect in that he or she designs specific areas of the event venue to reflect the form and function of the event theme. Estrin has used miniature speakers to transform a themed environment into a symphony of sound effects that subtly transports the guest into a total experience.

Sound Ideas

There are no limits to the possibilities for exciting sound production for your event. However, implementing these ideas requires careful planning and well-executed coordination. Here are a few examples of how you may use sound to create an event that will be listened to and well remembered.

Invisible Actors

The president of a corporation wanted to reward his senior staff with a series of bonuses. To introduce this announcement dramatically, the president agreed to dress as Ebenezer Scrooge and meet the ghosts of Christmas past, present, and future. However, due to budget constraints, there were no funds to hire or wardrobe actors to play the ghosts. One solution to this problem is by prerecording the voice of one actor playing all three ghosts. Then when the ghosts appear, utilize fog and lighting effects to create the illusion of a ghost. The president, impersonating Scrooge, can then speak to this area of the stage and the ghost will appear to answer him.

Sound Quality

The Event Leader must recognize that, today, many people have high-quality stereophonic sound systems in their homes and automobiles. Because of this new sophistication, your guests are extremely discriminating when it comes to the quality of sound used at your event. Make certain that you determine in advance the level of sophistication of your listeners and then allocate your resources effectively to satisfy their needs, wants, and desires.

Cost-Saving Measures

Wireless products are significantly more expensive than wired ones. Unless the production requires wireless products, avoid this costly equipment. In some cases, you will still pay for wired equipment, because you will want to have redundant equipment, as described earlier.

Labor can be a major cost in installing heavy-duty sound equipment. Consult with your sound rental expert and determine if small units can be used to avoid the rental of lifts and riggers required for the larger equipment. Bid sound equipment carefully to make certain that the experience of the operators and condition of the equipment will ensure that you meet the goals and objectives of your event. For example, in the Washington, D.C., area, only three or four sound companies have the capabilities to handle the large-scale sound requirements for major demonstrations and marches. Using an inferior company can incur much greater costs than selecting the most qualified and perhaps higher bidder.

Special Effects

It is a little-known fact that most special effects reflect variations in the weather of the planet. Effects such as fog, rain, thunder, lightning, and even pyrotechnics (fireworks) immediately conjure images of dramatic changes in the climatic conditions. Weather is perhaps the most talked-about subject in the world. As so much depends on it, including one's mood, it is natural that special effects have come to play an important role in the development of event planning.

Event planners use special effects to attract attention, generate excitement, and sustain interest as well as startle, shock, and even amuse. The key to proper integration of special effects into an event scheme is to determine, during the design process, how special effects will support or enhance an event's goal and objectives. The most common error made by event planners when using special effects is to add too many different components and thereby confuse the guests. Instead, special effects should be viewed as a natural and necessary part of the entire event strategy.

Figure 8.6 lists the most common special effects used in event planning. However, it is important to remember that some event technicians also use the term *special effects* to describe a variety of specialty lighting devices, such as black or strobe lights.

Fog

Technology

Fog is usually dispensed from a small box using a chemical ingredient (glycol or mineral oil solution) and heat. Chemical fog rises and may set off smoke sensors. It is available

Effect	Application
Air-propelled confetti cannons	Showers of paper or mylar rectangles, ovals or streamers flutter over and on guests as part of finale of entertainment.
Balloon drop	Hundreds of balloons drop onto the heads of the audience from a net or bag suspended above.
Dry ice	Low-level fog for ground cover to create a spooky effect.
Flash pot/box	Explosion to attract attention or distract the audience.
Flying	Aerial effects such as outer space or illusions.
Fog	Ghost, magic, laser-beam projection, explosion, and outer space.
Haze	A fine mist that can be used to enhance light beams.
Hologram	Illusion, attraction, and communication.
Laser	Communication, entertainment, focus attention, and reveal product.
Pyrotechnics (indoor)	Reveal new product and finale of production.
Pyrotechnics (outdoor)	Capture attention and finale of sport or other event.
Wind machine	Create effect of blowing, billowing trees, flags, and other fabric.

Figure 8.6 Applications for Special Effects

in a variety of scents or in an odorless form from numerous manufacturers and theatrical rental / hire equipment providers.

Use

From creating an eerie graveyard scene at a theme party to establishing a cone shape for a laser beam to highlight in producing a Star Trek "Beam me up, Scotty" effect, fog has become an indispensable part of many events. When using this device, post a sign at the entrance stating that atmospheric effects are being used at this event.

Cautionary Note

Once I used the "Beam me up, Scotty" effect to introduce the president of a large company. Prior to his entrance, he was seated in a warm room backstage for quite some time. When he walked into the laser device and the fog began, he waved at the audience as the key light illuminated him. However, when he walked from stage right to center stage to speak behind the lectern, a long trail of fog continued to pour out from the seat of his pants. At first the audience thought his pants were on fire, and then they laughed uproariously. The lesson here is that chemical fog will stick to warm surfaces. Keep your participant "cool" prior to their "Beam me up, Scotty" introduction, or you may later get beamed yourself by an unhappy client.

Dry Ice

Technology

Dry ice, when combined with water between 38°C and 93°C, produces a thick, low-lying blanket of fog typically associated with dream sequences. Many other kinds of machines are now available that will produce this effect, although dry ice machines remain popular.

Use

A remote moat, graveyard, or lagoon at a theme party, as well as a snowy winter wonderland, can be established easily with this effect.

Dry ice effects should only be conducted by professionals to avoid injury to the event participants, technicians, and audience.

Haze

Technology

Haze is a subtle atmospheric effect that is almost invisible to the audience or camera until beams of light shine through it.

Use

Haze makes the volume of a space visible, and it should be imperceptible except for the effect it has on the light in the space. Often used to make the beams of light from automated luminaires visible, used in film to add a subtle diffusion to the scene, lighten shadows, and reduce contrast.

Indoor Pyrotechnics

Technology

Indoor pyrotechnics are small devices that emit little smoke and create sparks, flame, or other indoor effects.

Use

Over an ice rink at the conclusion of an opening ceremony a shower of sparks falls from the ceiling or on the front of a stage, or flames appear to leap from the footlights.

Cautionary Note

Pyrotechnic effects are EXPLOSIVES as defined and classified by the United Nations (UN) and should only be operated by a trained professional following a thorough risk assessment.

It is important to establish at the earliest possible stage what the client/director is trying to achieve and to assess how appropriate the effect required is for the event and for the venue. This is incredibly important, as pyrotechnics are usually the last thing in a production to be thought about and the first thing to be cut (budget constraints). This usually means that very little time is available for the planning process to take place.

Flash Pot

Technology

A small amount of gunpowder and flash paper combined with a small electric charge creates a flash, followed by a small amount of smoke.

Use

The appearance of a genie, ghost, or other magical moment is appropriate for this startling effect.

Cautionary Note

Make certain you introduce a flash pot through careful rehearsal to the persons who will be affected by the device to avoid a backstage blowup that could detract from your event in the future.

Confetti Cannon

Technology

Air-propelled cannons range from small to huge and can propel large pieces of confetti 100 feet or more.

Use

A confetti cannon provides a fitting conclusion to an important meeting or conference or an effective way to attract attention through the introduction of a new product.

Outdoor Pyrotechnics

Technology

Outdoor pyrotechnics are large shells ranging in size from 3 to 12 inches that propel up into the night sky and burst, creating patterns and other colorful effects.

Use

Many professional sport events conclude with an aerial fireworks display, and some organizations use fireworks as a way of celebrating the culmination of a historic meeting or holiday, such as Independence Day in the United States.

Cautionary Note

Whilst producing the Nashville, Tennessee, Summer Lights Festival, the chief pyrotechnician notified me that 50 automobiles were parked near the launch site. He further advised that when the shells exploded, the debris (burning ash) would fall on the cars and damage them, as well as harm anyone in the area. This notice only came a few minutes before the pyrotechnics show was scheduled to begin. I instructed the event volunteers to dismantle some of the tents and cover the automobiles with the fabric and to rope off the area and assign security to keep people away. We fired the show and, fortunately, no cars or people were injured. However, remember, what goes up comes down. Always make certain the fall-out area for your pyrotechnics show is completely clear or well-protected from falling debris.

Pyrotechnic Set Piece

Technology

A pyrotechnic set piece is a large sign that is illuminated with pyrotechnics. Sometimes it includes movable pieces that spin, rotate, rise, and fall.

Use

A pyrotechnic set piece can be used to announce a new idea or product or celebrate a historic occasion or holiday. Sometimes it is used in combination with indoor or outdoor pyrotechnics.

Laser

Technology

A laser is a high-powered light source cooled by either water or air. The water-cooled laser projects beams many hundreds of feet.

Use

From creating a graphic image on the side of a large skyscraper to the linking of several monuments throughout a local destination, lasers can dynamically animate and focus the activities of an event. Using graphics, the laser beams can create logos and animation to tell a story or set the tone for an event.

Cautionary Note

In the United States, lasers are regulated by the U.S. Department of Radiological Health. Make certain your laser production providers have all required permits to display these devices.

Balloon Drop

Technology

A bag or net suspended above the heads of the audience opens and releases hundreds of balloons.

Use

Traditionally used on New Year's Eve as well as at the conclusion of U.S. political party conventions, this technology is always appropriate as a capstone or finale element for a significant event. In some instances, prizes or slips of paper announcing gifts may be placed in the balloons.

Flying

Technology

Individuals, props, or both can appear to float effortlessly over the stage and sometimes over the heads of the audience.

Use

Flying is appropriate for a space-age illusion or theme incorporating magic. May be used to levitate individuals or new props being introduced to the audience. Two of the largest event flying specialists are Fly By Foy (www.flybyfoy.com) and Zfx (www.zfxflying.com), both of which are based in Las Vegas, Nevada.

Wind Machine

Technology

A wind machine is a large, high-powered fan mounted on a secure floor base.

Use

A wind machine can be used to blow curtains, flags, or other scenery or costumes to create the illusion of movement by wind.

Cost-Saving Measures

When using special effects, there are usually ancillary costs, such as site preparation and cleanup as well as additional security. Make certain that you factor in all costs before you blast the confetti cannon and later realize that a cleanup fee of must be paid to the venue.

Some lighting and production companies will include special effects devices in the total bid for equipment. Consult with lighting and production vendors to determine what equipment they own and then include these items in your specifications.

Finally, use special effects only if they support the overall goals and objectives of the event. Special effects may be the first area of a budget that can be trimmed unless the added value is justified.

Video

Due to the growth of television and the rapid acquisition of digital video disc (DVD) players, video has become an integral part of many live events. Video is used to enhance the live image of the speaker or performer so that a person seated in the far reaches of a venue may see his or her facial reactions. Video is also used to document the entire event for future use, such as for historical or marketing purposes, or both.

The expansion of this field has placed the video camera in the hands of large numbers of the public, and as a result, guests are more sophisticated with regard to video production. Because of supply and demand, even editing equipment is now available to consumers, allowing them to perform simple editing functions for home-video features.

Figure 8.7 identifies the most common uses for video at an event and the types of equipment required for these purposes.

Use	Equipment
Audience interaction event	Multiple cameras and video switcher
Complex special-effects editing	Online editing equipment
Corporate communications	Animated character
Image magnification	Camcorder and projector
Simple cuts-only editing	Off-line editing equipment
Film roll	DVD player and projector

Figure 8.7 Video Uses and Typical Equipment

Character Generator

Technology

A character generator (CG) is an electronic device used to create titles and project text on the video image.

Use

It may be used to identify speakers, project messages to the audience, or create other communications through video production.

Off-line Editing

Technology

Off-line editing is designed primarily for simple edits, such as cuts only. During off-line editing the video product is refined further prior to the more expensive online editing session.

Use

Simple video products may be prepared during the off-line session or may be used to prepare the product for the online session.

Online Editing

Technology

Sophisticated, complex special effects may be achieved using online editing equipment.

Use

During online editing, complex digital effects are included to produce exciting transitions, sweeten the music, and add other technical elements to complete the production. At one time, the cost of this process was exorbitant because of the need to hire a professional editor and editing studio. However, today there is a plethora of video editing software available for Mac as well as PC platforms. These programs include Apple iMovie and many others.

Switcher

Technology

A switcher enables the video operator to switch electronically between two or more cameras and also to cue prerecorded video products.

Use

Complex event production that requires two or more cameras and use of prerecorded video products must be programmed through a switching system.

Video Animation

Technology

An operator uses a mechanical device similar to a finger puppet and creates a dancing, talking electronic figure video-projected on a screen.

Use

Video animation can be used to establish a new image or character, interact with the main presenter at the meeting, improve corporate communications, or improve other communications. When Xerox introduced its new logo—the digitized X—I retained Interactive Personalities of Minneapolis, Minnesota, to create an animated character we named Chip. He immediately brought the new symbol to life for the guests and even endeared himself to them, as they literally became friends during this conference.

Camcorder

Technology

Consumer as well as broadcast-quality cameras are available for rental from most audiovisual production firms. Cameras are now available in High Definition (HD), Digital Video (DV) and removable hard drive format. HD-DV cameras are top-quality, but for simple events where editing will not be required, more affordable consumer equipment may be acceptable.

Use

Either live coverage for video magnification or live and recorded for future use, the video camera is the primary tool in video production. One drawback with regard to video production at live events is the presence of the video camera, tripod, and sometimes a platform to elevate the equipment. This complex setup may interfere with the audience's view of an event's live performance. Bob Johnson of Corporate Video Communications has overcome this challenge with the invention of robotic cameras designed for event production. In the Video Bob system, each of the 12 broadcast-quality robotic cameras is placed on a thin metal rod and is operated electronically by one operator. This saves both labor and space. One experienced operator may be able to control up to eight different cameras simultaneously.

DVD Player

Technology

A digital video disc (DVD) stores video/audio media. A DVD shares the same overall dimensions of a CD, but has significantly higher capacity—holding from 4 to 28 times as much data. Single-sided DVDs can store 4.7GB for single-layer and 8.5GB for dual-layer disks.

Use

This player reads digital video files and may be precisely cued for a specific start/stop point.

Fragrance Systems and Other Trends

Bob Estrin has been creating technical innovations for special events for over three decades. Most recently, he saw the technical fulfillment of a prediction he made some 15 years ago. He explained, "When you first interviewed me for your book, I predicted that smell would become one of the most important and dominant of all the senses in event production. Now, through the new Envirodine Studios (www.envirodine.com) EnviroScents fragrance system, we are able to make this prediction a reality."

Estrin states that the fragrance system is a gel that creates powerful smells such as Grandma's kitchen, Christmas morning, and even a barbecue. These smells create moods and feelings among event attendees that revive memories and help develop their attitude during the event. He has used this new system to overcome negative smells in event facilities and also to stimulate the imagination of his guests through sense memory. According to Estrin, "You only have to fool a couple of the senses to develop the illusion of reality, and smell is one of the most powerful ways to do this effectively."

Estrin says that the biggest change in event technology is the development of virtual systems through computer projection. Once again, he predicted nearly a decade ago that this would be a simple and cost-effective way to create atmosphere. Now the technology finally exists to be able to do this reliably and cost-effectively.

New and/or aspiring Event Leaders must be extremely computer-literate, says Estrin. "Today, most events are programmed through computer show control systems where all technologies are controlled through a single powerful computer. Event Leaders must understand the significance of this change and be prepared to integrate all systems."

Bob Estrin also notes that, due to changing demographics and psychographics, sound will be louder and many, if not all, events will feature assisted-listening devices. "The most exciting change is that the cost is dropping for many of these technologies, which allow more widespread use. For example, an outdoor television screen that once would have cost $180,000 and required several days to set up is now only $4,000 and is usually working in a few hours."

Estrin cautions that safety for special events must become an everyday concern. Event Leaders must realize that safety is something that must be integrated throughout the entire event process if you are to reduce error and prevent harm. He points to the

Rhode Island Station nightclub fire as one example of how a tragic event has affected the event industry throughout the world, with greater legislation and scrutiny concerning pyrotechnics.

Cost-Saving Measures

Contact a local university or college and determine if its events, production, radio, television, or film department can provide you with equipment or services for event. Significant savings may be available through use of these facilities.

When using video, keep in mind that the better you plan your shots, the less time may be required in postproduction. Shoot any video with editing firmly in mind. Some video directors shoot in a style that requires very little postproduction by matching shots carefully and maintaining continuity.

Plan your postproduction schedule carefully. The majority of time should be devoted to off-line editing, as this costs less. The more you can accomplish in off-line editing, the greater the overall savings. Check with the postproduction editing facility to find out if you can use off-peak times to complete your project. Avoiding normal business hours may result in significant savings.

Retain an experienced crew that can handle multiple functions. For example, the shooter or cameraperson may also be able to coordinate the audio feed, and this will eliminate additional labour costs. Video crews' daily rate can vary, depending on the type and quantity of equipment and labour required. Always solicit bids for these services and ask to see a demonstration reel of the crews' work.

Use robotic cameras for simple meeting and conference event production and include an option (with the permission of the speakers and entertainers) to sell tapes to the attendees. By selling the tapes, you may not only recover all video production costs but also generate additional net proceeds for your sponsoring organization.

Synergy of Audiovisual Effects

Carefully integrate audiovisual, lighting, sound, special effects, and video to ensure a smooth and seamless event. Avoid overproducing your event merely to demonstrate the latest high-tech wonders. Most production personnel will state that their work is designed to support and enhance, never to dominate. In fact, these technologies should be so well incorporated into event planning and coordination that they are invisible to guests. However, as a result of their combined power, a positive enduring effect should result.

The key elements of many events include musicians and other entertainers. Coordinating and presenting these artists is both an art and a science. The Event Leader must plan with precision and also incorporate sensitivity and thoughtfulness to achieve the desired outcome through their performances. Veteran entertainment producer Jack Morton once told me, "I always asked the performer to let me know how to help them succeed. After, all, every performer wants to be successful and my job is simply to help them."

Music and Entertainment Management

Mark Sonder, CSEP, author of *The Complete Guide to Event Entertainment and Production* (2004) observes, "A person who enjoys a certain event entertainment experience can be associated with a particular lifestyle, interest group, attitude, educational level, buying behavior, voting habits, and even a set of beliefs." Sonder notes throughout his book that event entertainment is a critical consideration when designing the mood, the atmosphere, and the outcome of many events.

Deciding whether to use music and entertainment at your event or not can mark the difference between captivating your audience and confusing them. Next we discuss the major issues that involve event entertainment.

Although most events benefit from music and entertainment, not every event needs to incur this expense. The Event Leader must assess the needs of his or her guests carefully and determine whether music and entertainment are appropriate for each event. For example, the groundbreaking of a historic battlefield site may require speeches, but it would be inappropriate to engage a Dixieland jazz band. Too often, music and entertainment are engaged based on the personal tastes and desires of the organizers with little regard for the appropriateness of the event or the interests of guests. To avoid making this mistake, use this checklist to conduct some preliminary research:

- Research the history of the event to determine if music and/or entertainment were used in the past.
- Interview the event stakeholders through a formal focus group or informally to ascertain their individual and collective tastes.
- Determine how music and/or entertainment will be used to further the goals of the event.
- Analyze the event budget to determine available resources for music and/or entertainment.
- Review the time frame for planning and production to determine if sufficient time is available for incorporating these elements into the event.

Identifying the Resources

Once you have conducted the research to identify the need, the next step is to identify the most appropriate and cost-effective resources for your event. Fortunately, in the postmodern entertainment era, there are many more choices.

In most communities, literally dozens of resources are available for music and live entertainment. Many resources are available for both professional and amateur music and entertainment (see Figure 8.8).

Matching the best music and entertainment resource to the needs, wants, and desires of your guests, as well as the goals and objectives of your event, is a complex task. The first step is to comprehend the various musical and entertainment options that are available

1. Players Directory, a list of television and film stars (www.playersdirectory.com)
2. Actor's Equity Association, the union of professional stage actors and actresses (www.actorsequity.org)
3. Agents (responsible agents) who represent a variety of acts
4. American Federation of Musicians (www.afm.org)
5. American Federation of Television and Radio Artists, the union of television and radio artists (www.aftra.org)
6. American Guild of Musical Artists, the union of professional chorus, opera and dance artists. (www.musicalartists.org)
7. American Guild of Variety Artists, the union of live-entertainment artists, such as circus performers and the Radio City Music Hall Rockettes (212–675–1003)
8. Amusement parks and permanent attractions, such as zoos (www.iaapa.org)
9. Arts advocacy societies and commissions
10. Bars, nightclubs, restaurants, and taverns
11. Churches (www.rcma.org)
12. Circus Report, a magazine for circus enthusiasts (www.lionden.com/circus_report.htm)
13. Clubs, including fraternal organizations (www.cmaa.org)
14. Dance clubs, groups, and dance advocacy organizations (www.aahperd.org)
15. Educational institutions, including public, private, primary, middle, and secondary schools, as well as colleges and universities
16. Event Solutions magazine (www.event-solutions.com)
17. Special Events magazine (www.specialevents.com)
18. Fraternal organizations, such as the Shriners (www.shrinershq.org)
19. Historical reenactment organizations (www.livinghistoryassn.org)
20. Institutions, such as museums that may provide lecturers (www.aam-us.org)
21. Instrumental music organizations (www.americanorchestras.org)
22. Musical contractors (www.afm.org)
23. Native American organizations (www.nmai.si.edu)
24. Newspaper critics familiar with local arts organizations (www.americantheatrecritics.org)

Figure 8.8 Resources for Music and Entertainment *(Continued)*

25. Parks and recreation organizations that offer dance, music, and other arts programs (www.nrpa.org)
26. Producers of radio, television, or live-entertainment programs (www.aftra.org)
27. Radio disc jockeys who are familiar with local bands and who may provide DJ services (www.aftra.org)
28. Religious organizations other than churches, mosques, and synagogues
29. Schools, colleges, and university music and theater departments (www.edta.org)
30. Screen Actors Guild, the union of film actors and actresses (www.sag.org)
31. Shopping centers that feature live music and entertainment (www.icsc.org)
32. Synagogues (www.naase.org)
33. Theatrical organizations from professional to community or amateur groups (www.aact.org)
34. Travel agents familiar with local entertainment resources (www.asta.org)
35. Very Special Arts, an organization representing disabled people who are artists (www.vsarts.org)
36. Zoological parks and aquariums (www.aza.org)

Figure 8.8 *(Continued)*

(see Figure 8.8). Although descriptions of music and entertainment are largely composed of industry jargon and may vary according to location, the terms are considered standard and customary in these fields. See Figure 8.9 for a list of music and entertainment terms. For further definitions, refer to *The International Dictionary of Event Management* (2000) or the APEX glossary of terms (www.conventionindustry.org).

Music for Mood, Atmosphere, Animation, and Transitions

According to a well respected orchestra leader, the late Gene Donati (1930–2004) of Washington, D.C., who conducted dozens of U.S. Presidential Inaugural ball orchestras, music is used to create the proper mood, sustain the atmosphere, and, most importantly, to "animate" the room. Donati stated, "The music should begin before the doors open, to draw people into the room. Up-tempo songs should be used to energize this segment of the party." Like Donati, his successors, Phil McCusker and Bill Barrick (www.mccuskerandbarrick.com), conduct not just the music but also the guests, using music to animate the guests' actions. Figure 8.8 describes a wide variety of organizations and resources for live entertainment to animate your event.

Music and entertainment has a specific vocabulary and language that is used to contract, direct and control the outcome of your event. Becoming familiar with the terms in

Act: a self-contained, rehearsed performance of one or more persons.
Agent: a person who represents various acts or artists and receives a commission from the buyer for coordinating a booking.
Amateur: a musician or entertainer who does not charge for his or her services, usually due to lack of professional experience.
Arrangements: musical compositions arranged for musicians.
Band: a group of musicians who perform contemporary music, such as rock 'n' roll, jazz, or big band.
Booking: a firm commitment by a buyer of entertainment to hire an actor artist for a specific engagement.
Combo: a musical ensemble featuring combined instruments (usually, piano, bass, and drums)
Commission: the percentage received by an agent when booking an act or artist.
Conductor: a person responsible for directing/conducting the rehearsal and performance by musicians.
Contractor: a person or organization that contracts musicians and other entertainers. The contractor handles all the agreements, payroll, taxes, and other employment tasks.
Cover song: a tune popularized by another artist performed by a different artist or group.
Doubler: a musician who plays two or more instruments during a performance.
Downbeat: the cue given by a conductor for musicians to begin playing.
Drum riser: a small platform used to elevate a drummer above the other musicians.
Drum roll: a rolling percussive sound used for announcements and to create a suspenseful atmosphere.
Duo: an act with two persons. Also known as a double.
Fanfare: a musical interlude used to signal announcements of awards or introductions. Usually includes horns, but not always.
Fife and drum corp: a small or larger musical ensemble featuring fifes and drums playing music from the eighteenth century.
Horn section: a group of musicians that specializes in wind instruments and is usually part of a larger ensemble.
Leader: a person who organizes and conducts a musical or entertainment group.
Manager: a person who provides management services to an artist, act, or several artists and acts. The manager normally handles all logistics, including travel, and negotiates on behalf of the artist or act. The manager is paid by the act or artist from fees that are earned through performing.
Marching band: a musical ensemble of persons who play and march simultaneously. It usually includes percussion, horns, woodwinds, and other instruments.
Minimum: the minimum number of hours for which musicians must be paid.
Octet: a musical ensemble comprised of eight musicians.
Overture: the music performed before actors or entertainers enter the stage. Also known as preshow music.
Professional: a musician or entertainer paid for his or her services.
Quartet: a musical ensemble comprised of four persons.
Quintet: a musical ensemble comprised of five persons.
Road manager: a person who travels with an act or artist to handle all logistical arrangements.

Figure 8.9 Music and Entertainment Terms *(Continued)*

Sextet: a musical ensemble comprised of six persons.
Sideman/men: musicians within a musical ensemble who accompany an artist.
Single: an act with one person.
Soloist: a single performer.
Stage manager: a person who coordinates the technical elements for the act or artist, cues the performer, and provides other services to support the performance.
Stand: the music stand used to hold sheet music.
Top Forty: the top 40 musical compositions/recordings selected by Billboard magazine. A Top Forty band is able to perform these selections.
Trio: a musical ensemble comprised of three persons.
Walk-in, walk-out music: live or recorded music played at the start and end of an event as guests enter or leave a venue.
Walk music: live or recorded music played as award presenters, speakers, and recipients enter or exit the stage area.
Windjammers: the slang name for circus musicians (mostly horn players).

Figure 8.9 *(Continued)*

Figure 8.9 will help you improve your communications skills with musicians and other live performers.

Alice Conway, CSEP, director of the Event Management Program at Stratford University (www.stratford.edu), recommends that her event clients close their eyes and describe what they see their guests doing as the music plays. Music may also be used as a transition to create punctuation marks in the order of a program. One of the best examples is the awards event. Using music associated with the presenters or award recipients helps the audience remain interested and focused on the program. Some typical tunes for awards programs are shown in Figure 8.10. It is important to remember that the music you select may be copyrighted and therefore you must purchase the rights from the appropriate licensing agency prior to use.

Use awards music to introduce the presenters by sequencing the music in this manner. First, cue the drummer to perform a drum roll. Next, have your offstage announcer introduce the presenter using this text: "Ladies and gentlemen, please welcome the president of XYZ Corporation, from New Orleans, Louisiana, Ms. Jane Smith!" As the presenter's name is announced, the rest of the musicians should play a lively Dixieland jazz melody and conclude promptly when Ms. Smith reaches the microphone. This will help accelerate the action for the event and keep things running on time.

As Ms. Smith introduces the award recipient, the musicians should begin to play as soon as the name is called. Because musicians need a warning before they begin to play, I recommend that you give the cue to play as the first name is announced so that, as the surname is announced, the tune has begun. Here is an example:

Ms. Smith: "And now welcome our award winner, from New York City, Mr. (cue conductor) John Doe (music begins)."

Occasion	Music
Person from California	*The O.C.* theme or "California Dreamin'" by the Mamas and the Papas
Person from New York	*New York, New York* theme or Billy Joel's "New York State of Mind"
Sports-related award	"Eye of the Tiger" by Survivor, or *Chariots of Fire* theme
Championship award	*Rocky* theme or "Simply the Best" by Tina Turner
Chapter of the year	"We Will Rock You" by Queen or "Best of You" by the Foo Fighters
Person of the year	"Hot, Hot, Hot" by The Cure or *The Bodyguard* theme
Volunteer of the year	"You've Got a Friend" by James Taylor or "Don't Stop Believing" by Journey
Leadership award	*Masterpiece Theatre* theme or "You're the Top" by Cole Porter

Figure 8.10 Typical Music for Audience Entrance, Stage Walk On and Off and Audience Exit

The music should continue until Mr. Doe reaches Ms. Smith and then conclude with a brief fanfare as the award is presented. A generic walk-off melody may be played as Mr. Doe exits the stage.

Properly sequenced and timed, music can ensure that your event runs on time. Even Old Blue Eyes himself, Frank Sinatra, learned at the Grammy Awards that unless you sustain the interest of the audience, the music will abruptly change the mood, ending one segment and cueing another.

Musical Formulas for Success

Legendary society band leader Lester Lanin (1907–2004), who conducted orchestras for bar mitzvahs and weddings well into his nineties, recommended that Event Leaders carefully consider the number and type of guests who will be attending an event prior to the selection of musical performers. Lanin stated that, while at one time both opera and classical music were commonly used for social life-cycle events, today it is not uncommon to incorporate contemporary music.

Rabbi Arnold Saltzman of Washington, D.C., cautions people involved in religious events to work closely with their clergy to select appropriate music that is in accordance with the traditions and customs of the religious denomination. As one example, a bride asked Rabbi Saltzman for permission to use the theme from Star Wars as the processional music. Since the event was a secular occasion, no policies were set by the location. However, Rabbi Saltzman correctly counseled the bride and groom that if this music was used for the processional, the guests might be distracted by this departure from tradition and the rest of the ceremony could suffer as a result.

Number of Guests	Minimum Number of Musicians
125	5–7
250	7
500	12
750	12, plus strings if budget allows
1,000	15–20

Figure 8.11 Attendance and Minimum Musicians Required as Recommended by Lester Lanin (1907–2004)

Lanin performed before millions of people during his long career. He recommends a minimum number of musicians be used for each event to ensure the look of the event is achieved as well as the sound. Although a 30-member orchestra might have been standard fare for special events a few years ago, in today's cost-conscious times, Lanin's formulas are more likely to be used as a general guide and often, a small ensemble will be engaged and supplemented with electronic synthesizers. Figure 8.11 describes Lanin's formulas.

Electronic Music

Miniaturization in lighting and sound has also found its way into the orchestra. Many modern musicians use electronic instruments to perform the sounds of dozens of instruments. It is not unusual today to see four musicians performing music that once required a 100-member symphony orchestra. However, certain liabilities, such as losing the visual appeal of having live musicians, result from this economically driven change.

Managing Musicians

Musicians, as well as other personnel, require careful management to be able to deliver an optimum performance. Musical artists require the Event Leader to provide support systems that allow them to do what they do best: deliver a quality musical performance. The 15 most common considerations for effectively managing musicians include those shown in Figure 8.12.

Union Requirements

Whether contracting union musicians or other entertainers affiliated with labour unions, it is important that the Event Leader study union contracts carefully and complies with the responsibilities that apply to the event sponsor. For example, union musicians must be compensated separately if their performance is audio- or videotaped. Failure to provide additional compensation can result in severe penalties for the event organizer. In addition, union members must be given a certain number of breaks during each performance

1. Provide clear, written instructions regarding date, time, and location.
2. Communicate a profile of the guests so that appropriate music may be selected.
3. Provide an event schedule, and supply the leader of the musical group with a summary of the musical activities.
4. Arrange for parking for the musicians and notify them of the locations authorized.
5. Identify and communicate to the musicians where equipment may be loaded into a venue.
6. Select and notify the musicians of a room where their cases may be stored during a performance.
7. Provide adequate dressing rooms for breaks.
8. Adhere carefully to required breaks.
9. Arrange for and provide food and beverage service if required by contract.
10. Assign a key contact person to serve as principal liaison to the leader of the musical group.
11. Locate adequate electric power.
12. Provide ample performance space, as required by contract.
13. Adhere to schedule specified by contract.
14. Notify musicians if overtime is required.
15. Assist musicians with load-out/departure and offer thanks.

Figure 8.12 Recommended Methods for Managing Musicians

or be paid additionally for performing continuously without the prescribed number of breaks. Therefore, it is important that the Event Leader work closely with his or her music contractor when engaging union musicians. Certain union locals have established trust funds that will provide some money for musicians to perform for worthwhile causes at no cost to the sponsor. If based in the USA, check with your local American Federation of Musicians (www.afm.org) to determine if your event may qualify for this support.

Electronic Music

During the 1970s, as recording quality improved, disc jockeys became popular at many events. Indeed, in some situations electronic or recorded music is more appropriate than live music, for three reasons.

1. Electronic music may be easily controlled. Unlike live music, it may be faded, stopped, started, and refocused through different speakers.
2. It is usually less expensive than the engagement of live musicians.
3. Perhaps most important, for those events with space restrictions, electronic music solves important logistical problems.

Today, disc jockeys can provide not only music but entire party production services, including lights, effects such as fog, and interactive games. In addition to providing music for dancing and background atmosphere, electronic music may serve other purposes as well.

In lieu of using a live orchestra, many professional entertainers and industrial productions use prerecorded tracks to supplement their live performances. When using these systems, it is critical that the Event Leader use redundant equipment in case of failure. In other situations, live musicians actually play along with the recorded tracks, creating a combination of live and recorded sound. In still other situations, the orchestra will perform some music live and pantomime to the prerecorded sound in other numbers.

When music is synchronized to video or film, separate rights must be negotiated and obtained. Usually these rights include a clause limiting use to certain mediums and time periods. Ultimately, someone will pay for the use of privately owned music each time it is used. Therefore, the Event Leader must budget for this expense.

Music Licensing

In the early 1990s, the two major music-licensing firms in the United States decided to enforce their rights to collect fees from sponsors of meetings, conventions, and expositions as well as other events. Prior to this date, the American Society of Composers, Authors, and Publishers (ASCAP) (www.ascap.com) and its competitor, Broadcast Music, Inc. (BMI) (www.bmi.com), collected fees from restaurants, nightclubs, hotels, and even rollerskating rinks. However, perhaps recognizing the enormous possibility for revenue from the meeting, convention, exposition, and event industry, these organizations made it clear that they planned to require sponsors of these events to pay for the use of live or recorded music they licensed.

The first organization to sign a separate agreement with ASCAP and BMI was the International Association for Exposition Management, now known as the International Association for Exhibition and Events (www.iaee.com), and soon the American Society of Association Executives (ASAE) convened a task force to study this issue. As a member of this task force, I asked both organizations to assign the responsibility for payment to either the musical contractors or the professional producers of these events. Both organizations rejected this request, and today there continues to be acrimony regarding who pays what to whom and why.

The official sponsor or organizer of an event, the entity that bears the financial responsibility for the event, is responsible for obtaining a license for the use of protected music from either or both ASCAP or BMI or other rights-licensing organizations. The only exception to paying these fees is for events that are small gatherings of people who are known to you. This usually means social life-cycle events, such as weddings, bar and bas mitzvahs, birthday parties, and other events attended by family and friends.

ASCAP and BMI each have separate licensing agreements that require careful consideration by Event Leaders. Both electronic and live music is covered in these agreements. According to ASCAP, the majority of popular music is licensed through its organization. However, most Event Leaders obtain, on behalf of their sponsors, agreements with both

ASCAP and BMI for obvious reasons. Among these reasons is the problem associated with the live dance band and the guest who requests a tune from the band leader, only to have the band leader decline because the rights are assigned to BMI and the license is with ASCAP.

For most events, the costs associated with music licensing are minimal, and the filing of the license agreement is merely another part of the long paper trail that is a natural part of Event Leadership. However, in the field of expositions, especially the larger ones that attract tens of thousands of persons, the costs can quickly mount. How are these fees assessed?

Both ASCAP and BMI assess fees based on the daily attendance at each event. The fees are, therefore, charged daily and are factored using separate formulas for recorded and live music. If both recorded (electronic) and live music are used, the costs are higher.

To enforce these licenses, both ASCAP and BMI use spotters who visit event venues randomly and investigate organizations that are using their licensed works unlawfully. The penalties for this illegal activity are substantial.

Legal actions concerning expositions have somewhat weakened the position of ASCAP and BMI to require that sponsors of expositions assume responsibility for their individual exhibitors with regard to the use of music. However, ASAE continues to investigate the entire music licensing issue, with the major concerns relating to potential monopolies by ASCAP and BMI, which control the majority of all musical composition.

What music is covered? Literally any musical work licensed by ASCAP and BMI, and this includes "Happy Birthday." Even classical compositions may be covered if they have recently had a new, authored arrangement.

Alternatives to paying music licensing fees are limited. The Event Leader may, of course, elect to not use music at all. Or the Event Leader may commission an original work of music and purchase the song or selections for use at the event. Another option is for the Event Leader to purchase commercial music produced by a private firm. Commercial music may be obtained from recording studios or other private organizations and usually includes some sound-alike tunes that are appropriate for use at awards programs and events other than those where popular tunes may be requested. Still larger organizations may negotiate individually with ASCAP, BMI, or other rights-licensing organizations and seek to create a separate agreement. In some cases, licensing fees may be waived. However, this is a rare occurrence.

In order to play, you must pay. Failing to do so may adversely affect your event sponsor and your reputation. Therefore, it is the responsibility of the event organizer to fully comprehend the requirements for music licensing and allow sufficient planning and coordination time to attend to these important details.

Entertainment Options from A to Z

Figure 8.7 presents a variety of resources for music and entertainment. However, now it is time to consider entertainment as a separate resource. The most commonly used entertainers for live events include those shown in Figure 8.13.

- Acrobats (Cirque-like performers as first introduced by Cirque De Soleil)
- Animal acts
- Artists (working on large canvasses and accompanied by music)
- Balloon sculptors
- Ballroom dancers
- Bands
- Break dancers
- Cancan dancers
- Caricaturists
- Carnival games
- Carnival rides
- Chinese dragon dancers
- Circus performers
- Clowns
- Comedians
- Contortionists
- Dancers
- Disc jockeys
- Dixieland bands
- Escape artists
- Female impersonators
- Flamenco dancers
- Folk dancers
- Fortune tellers
- German oompah bands
- Giant heads and giant puppets
- Hat designers such as Party Hats™
- Horseshoes
- Hula hoop performers
- Humorists
- Hypnotists
- Ice skaters
- Ice carvers
- Illusionists
- Japanese koto musicians
- Jazz bands
- Jugglers
- Klezmer bands
- Limbo dancers
- Magicians
- Marching bands
- Marionettes
- Mentalists
- Mimes
- Modern dancers
- Muralists
- Opera singers
- Organ grinders
- Organists
- Portrait Painters
- Palm readers
- Pep bands
- Photo booths
- Puppeteers
- Rap artists
- Reggae musicians
- Robots
- Roller skaters
- Sand dancers
- Sand painters (working on an opaque projector and accompanied by music)
- Singers/vocalists/gospel groups
- Spaceships
- Sport games
- Square dancers
- Stilt walkers
- Tap dancers
- Tattoo artists
- T-shirt designers
- Tight-wire walkers
- Trapeze artists
- Ventriloquists
- Wax hand artists
- World music

Figure 8.13 Typical Entertainment Options for Planned Events

Inexpensive Options for Live Entertainment

The term *amateur* implies one who has not yet begun to charge for his or her services. However, the term literally means "what one does for love." Every community is filled with hundreds and perhaps thousands of people whose vocational interests include performing. From barbershop and sweet Adeline singing groups to entire community orchestras, with a little detective work, you can identify a great deal of entertainment at low cost.

When using amateur performers or technical support, make certain that you supplement their performance with those elements that will achieve the level of sophistication required for your event. This may mean the addition of professional costuming, lighting, or other elements. In some cases, you will need to assign a professional producer to develop the amateur performers' act further to fit the needs of your event.

Amateurs will require more time in advance, immediately preceding, and during the production. Therefore, although you will save significantly by using nonprofessionals, you may often find yourself allocating additional resources and allowing more time for to accommodate them.

Professionals may be obtained directly by contacting them or via their managers, through agents, or in the case of performers, by holding auditions. When contracting professionals, first identify all the tasks you wish them to handle during your event. List these tasks and then prioritize them so that if you find you cannot afford everything you want, you will be able to identify quickly the most important elements that must be preserved.

One way to save lots of money when using professional performers is to block-book the act or artists with other organizations. Block-booking entails contacting other organizations in your city or area that may also be able to use the services of the act or artists. By offering performers a series of engagements closely connected by time and location, you may be able to save as much as 50 percent of the cost.

Another way to save is to work with companies that are locally based. Major production and events companies may be able to accommodate your event through intricate knowledge of your event venue. Often, performers will participate in additional events for the same basic fee. Therefore, determine well in advance what other activities, such as book signings, media conferences, and hospitality events, that you want the performer to participate in and incorporate these into the agreement.

Travel expenses can often be a significant part of an event cost, especially for those that require a large production. To save money on travel, first determine if the act and production company will travel on public transport versus private means. Next, aim to negotiate inclusive contracts so that hidden expenses do not appear at a latter date. Finally, although people like to have flexibility, arrange the travel as far as possible in advance to take advantage of lower fares.

Whether contracting amateur or professional personnel, the Event Leader is ultimately responsible for the final performance. To ensure the satisfaction of your client and guests, invite the client to attend the sound check and lighting rehearsal so that he or she can meet the performer/s in advance of the event. Furthermore, make certain that the performer mentions the name of the sponsoring organization during his or her act. To facilitate this, write this information in large block letters on an index card and hand it to the performer during rehearsal. A second copy is given to the performer before he or she walks on stage for the final performance, in case the first copy was misplaced or lost.

Sourcing, contracting, and managing live entertainment carefully will further ensure the financial and artistic success of your event. When you make the decision to include live entertainment as an important element of your event, you have assumed a considerable and complex responsibility. Make certain that you devote the proper time and resources to fulfill this important responsibility effectively.

Celebrities and Speakers

The National Speakers Association in Tempe, Arizona (www.nsaspeaker.org), reports that its association represents over 3,000 people who earn some or all of their living by giving speeches, conducting seminars, or presenting workshops. Their topics may range from anthropology to zero population growth. However, as members of this association, they are committed to improving their performance on the public platform.

Previously, the professional speaker was an accomplished person whose credits from another field produced demand for public appearances and speeches. Consequently, people such as film and television stars, politicians, and leading religious figures delivered speeches to their devotees. According to most futurists, continuing education will be the major growth industry of the new millennium. As a result, there is greater demand than ever before for sales trainers, motivators, and other experts in both content and performance.

When contracting a professional speaker for an event, first identify the needs, wants, and desires of your audience. Next, identify how you will use the speaker from a marketing perspective. Will the speaker's name or subject matter help increase attendance? Finally, and perhaps most importantly, determine what you expect to happen as a result of the speaker's appearance. The outcome of the event is paramount to every other decision.

Matching the speaker type to the outcome is the most important task facing the Event Leader who has decided to use a professional speaker. Although speaking fees may range from a few hundred dollars to tens of thousands of dollars, the most important consideration is what value will be derived from this investment. For example, if the sales trainer's fee is $10,000 and there is the potential of generating $100,000 in sales as a result of his or her appearance, the outcome is well worth the investment.

Figure 8.14 lists the most popular types of speakers and the audience locations that may benefit from their content.

In addition to professional speakers, most organizations can provide you with outstanding lay speakers whose industry expertise qualifies them to speak to your audience. However,

Speaker	Plenary or General Session	Luncheon	Spouse or Partner Program	Evening Banquet
Author	X	X	X	X
Celebrity	X			
Futurist	X			X
News person	X	X		X
Humorist		X	X	X
Hypnotist				X
Magician		X		X
Motivational speaker	X	X	X	X
Psychologist	X	X	X	
Sales trainer	X	X		
Seminar leader		X	X	
Workshop leader		X	X	

Figure 8.14 Speakers and Their Audiences

it is important to consider that the failure rate for lay speakers is extremely high. Therefore, plan to provide them with coaching or support equal to their stature on the program. For example, if the lay speaker is your plenary keynoter, you may wish to provide a speech coach to assist the speaker with his or her talk. However, if the speaker is presenting a workshop, it may be sufficient to work with him or her via telephone to fine-tune content and presentation techniques.

All speakers require an investment of time, and time is money. To maximize your investment, communicate clearly and often to the speakers what you want them to accomplish. Determine if they can perform other functions at your event (such as serving as emcee for the banquet) and perhaps author an article in advance for your newsletter or magazine. Finally, ask if there is a discount for multiple engagements in one day or week. You may be able to save substantial dollars by block-booking your speaker as you would an entertainer.

Finding the appropriate speaker involves finding the right resources, auditioning the speaker either in person or using videotape, and then confirming your assumption by speaking directly with the speaker. Possible resources for locating the appropriate speaker for your event include those shown in Figure 8.15.

Negotiating with Celebrities and Speakers

Most personal appearances require some degree of negotiation prior to signing a contract. The success of the negotiation ultimately will depend on both parties' desire to complete the deal. The greater the desire from both parties, the more quickly the deal will come to fruition.

Remember that you are in search of a win-win-win outcome. In this scenario, the guest, the celebrity or speaker, and the Event Leader win because of hard work and persistence. Do your homework to determine the history of fees for celebrities or speakers. Also find out what other income they have generated from the sale of books, tapes, and

- Agents and bureaus that represent professional speakers, International Association of Speakers Bureaus (www.igab.org)
- Churches (www.rcma.org)
- Colleges and universities (www.case.org)
- Issue-based speakers (www.ecospeakers.com)
- Industry speakers (www.asaenet.org)
- Mosques (www.mosques.co.uk)
- National Speakers Association "Who's Who in Professional Speaking" (www.nsaspeaker.org)
- Synagogues (www.naase.org)
- Volunteer speakers bureaus (Contact local media such as television and radio stations and also local charitable organizations such as Toastmasters International (www.toastmasters.org)

Figure 8.15 Typical Sources for Celebrities and Speakers for Planned Events

Harith Productions won multiple awards for this event that utilized environmentally friendly products to demonstrate how to produce a greener event.

Gymnastics is one of many sports that has benefited from the worldwide television coverage of the International Summer Olympic Games. As a result of this exposure, thousands of young people have enrolled in gymnastics classes throughout the world. This is one example of the many social benefits from planned events. *Courtesy PhotoDisc, Inc.*

An artist creates parade floats at Blaine Kerns Mardi Gras World in New Orleans, Louisiana.

Food events have expanded in recent years to encompass eating competitions ranging from the consumption of hot dogs to pies and other popular food items. *Courtesy PhotoDisc/Getty Images*

This Motor Cross event provides an example of the growing popularity in extreme sports in North America and beyond. *Courtesy Corbis Digital Stock*

A participant in the Edinburgh Hogmanay torch procession joins 5,000 revelers as they climb Calton Hill to welcome the New Year. Fire festivals are among the oldest known types of celebration in recorded history.

The Edinburgh Jazz and Blues Festival is launched with an annual parade similar to the Mardi Gras parades in New Orleans, Louisiana, featuring musicians and dancers.

Crowds in stadiums and arenas provide special risk challenges for event organizers as they cheer for their favorite national teams. However, many stadium and arena officials restrict or even ban the use of large banners and poles to reduce the chances of possible injury to fans, officials, and athletes. ***Courtesy Digital Vision***

Large concert audiences provide new challenges for event organizers to ensure that they enjoy the entertainment and also have a comfortable and safe experience as fans. *Courtesy Digital Vision*

Traditional celebratory objects provide evidence that every celebration may include symbols of ritual that invoke magic, mystery, and promote positive memories and outcomes. *Courtesy Purestock*

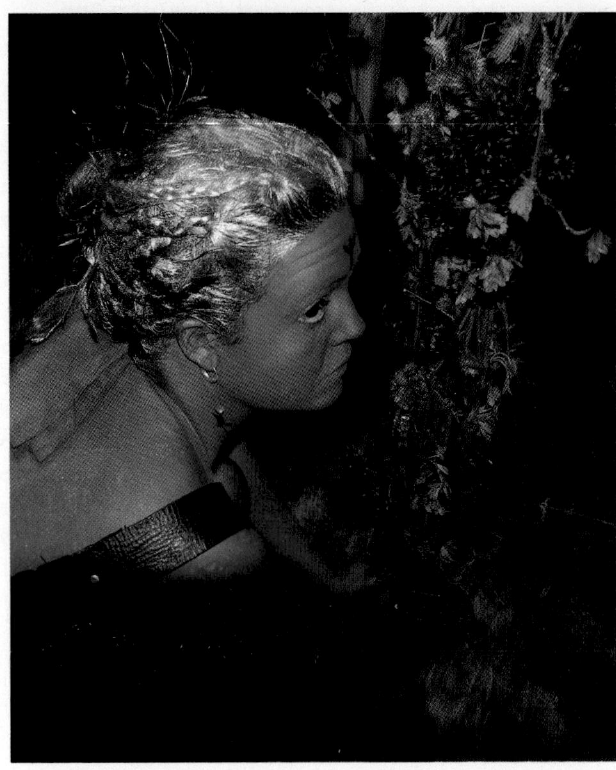

A performer at the Beltane Festival on May 1 in Edinburgh, Scotland. Volunteer performers reenact sacred Celtic rites and rituals to celebrate the coming of Spring.

The Pageant is a theatrical production produced by The Gathering 2009 upon the Edinburgh Castle Esplanade. It concludes its spectacle of light, sound, music, and drama before 7,000 guests with this memorable final moment of a Scottish family moving triumphantly forward, once again, toward their future.

other products. Next, explain to the celebrity or speaker, or his or her representative, your desire to book the person. Describe in detail the role the celebrity or speaker will play at your event. Explain the outcome you desire from his or her involvement. Then, and only then, ask him or her to quote a fee. Say that you would like to have a few days to consider this fee and then thank the person for his or her time. At this point, two things may happen: The celebrity or speaker or representative may call you back and offer a better deal, or the person may accept another engagement.

To prevent the latter, you can ask the person to put a tentative hold on this date for a specified period of time. A tentative hold implies that the person will contact you prior to accepting another engagement on the same date as your engagement. If another client calls the celebrity or speaker, he or she will tell the other client that he or she is tentatively holding the date for you and then will check with you first before accepting the other engagement.

After a few days, call the speaker, celebrity, or representative back, and ask him or her to reserve a time to discuss the engagement with you when he or she will not be interrupted. During the discussion/negotiation, offer other incentives in lieu of the full fee. For example, if you are projecting the speaker's image on a large screen to magnify his or her image, you could offer to provide the speaker with a professional video of his or her speech (estimated value of $3,000), or you could allow the speaker to sell books, tapes, and other products before, during, and after the engagement. Another valuable concession is to offer the speaker your mailing list or offer to promote his or her services to your guests. After determining the value of these concessions, ask the speaker to work with you on the fee so that you may complete the contract. Once you make your request, ask for his or her reaction. Tell the speaker to take his or her time to think about your offer, but set up a time frame to complete the agreement. When the person calls you back within the specified period of time, ask for his or her answer. Now you have the first news. It may not be the best news, but it is sufficient for you to provide a counteroffer. Make certain that you are prepared to make a counteroffer, such as shifting the date, shortening the responsibilities, or increasing the fee. When you use these techniques, step by step, you and your negotiating partners will move closer to closure.

If for any reason you fail to reach closure, always thank your negotiating partners for their time and interest and tell them you will recommend their services to others but are not able to work with them at this time. Do not be surprised if the other party calls you in a few days with a very attractive offer to use his or her services.

Contracting with Celebrities and Speakers

A letter of agreement, a contract, or a contract with rider must be prepared and/or executed by the Event Leader to engage a celebrity or speaker. In some cases, the celebrity or speaker will provide his or her own contract, and in others the Event Leader will be responsible for drafting the agreement.

The rider is the attachment on the contract that spells out the special conditions under which the celebrity or speaker will perform. The rider may specify lighting, sound, transportation, food, beverage, and other conditions. To make certain that you are providing only necessary items in the rider, contact previous clients and find out what they provided. In some instances, the rider may be used to incorporate everything, including the kitchen sink. You cannot allow the celebrity or entertainers to use the rider as a tool to abuse your limited resources.

Trends in Music and Entertainment

The music and entertainment field has undergone tremendous change during the past several decades since Lester Lanin organized his first orchestra. However, changes in the last decade of the twentieth century have far surpassed all of the previous changes.

During the 1990s, many musicians were replaced by electronic instruments. The electronic synthesizer, the musical instrument digital interface (MIDI), and the development of additional computer software for composing have revolutionized the music field. Entertainment, too, has experienced great change. Perhaps the most significant change has been the incorporation of technology such as video and computers within the context of a live performance. This blend of live and electronic media is known as interactive media.

Interactive Media

The interactivity inherent in interactive media is supplied by online users, who provide both proactive and reactive techniques for event purposes. For example, a general session at an association meeting may require that a vote be taken by hundreds of delegates to settle an important issue. Instead of requiring a manual show of hands, a large screen flashes the command "Vote Now," and each delegate presses green for yes, red for no, or yellow for abstain. Their votes are recorded and tallied electronically, and in seconds the results are shown on the screen both numerically and graphically.

Another example of interactive media involves live performers interacting with electronic media. This engagement may be live action combined with prerecord. In one such occasion, I produced a film of a car racing down a track, and suddenly the car came to a screeching halt. The film was shown using rear production on the back of a screen. The screen had a small door cut into the exact location where the driver would later emerge. When the car stopped, the door opened and the president of the corporation walked right through the screen. This is but one of many examples of live and electronic media interacting with one another.

It is in the field of education that the potential for interactive media may be the greatest. Using technologies such as high-speed media, networking, and powerful personal computers, tomorrow's event may look something like this: First, the guest enters the venue and is greeted by a robotic registrar who requests that the guest insert his or her credit card in the "Welcome" station. Upon reading the card, the machine welcomes the guest to the meeting and issues a smart card, which contains all critical information about the guest, including medical data, to ensure a safe and productive visit. The same card may be used to gain access to his or her sleeping room.

Next, the guest reports to his or her first meeting and uses the smart card to receive a complimentary computer disc from the Communications Center, a multistation machine that provides workspaces for telecommuting with the home office. The computer disc will be used to record the lecture to be delivered by the keynote speaker.

Finally, the guest is seated in an ergonomically correct chair, fastens his or her seatbelt, and "experiences" the opening ceremony. Such experience includes not only a visual and auditory presentation, but also sensory experiences, such as smell, taste, and touch. The visual images are delivered three-dimensionally as the guest wears glasses provided by a commercial sponsor. The chair moves hydraulically, controlled by dozens of levers and pumps as the visual images unfold on the 10-foot-high-definition screen. The audio portion of the program is enhanced with over 100 miniature speakers positioned throughout the venue to create a total surround-sound effect. At the conclusion of the opening ceremony, the guest is invited to vote using his or her smart card to gain access to the ballot box. He or she will vote to select the topics the electronic speaker will address. Instead of merely receiving what the motivation speaker delivers, the guest will become an interactive learner, selecting those topics that are most useful at this time. Once the selection has been made, the prerecorded speaker will instantly process the choices and provide state-of-the-industry knowledge that the guest most requires. This is recorded directly onto a disc that is inserted in a DVD writer within the chair where the guest is sitting.

Have no fear. All of this new technology will not decrease the demand for in-person events. Instead, it will create even greater demand as people meet online and seek other opportunities and venues within which to interact in person. People who participate in list-serves or other bulletin board–type communications technologies such as the meetings industry forum mega site (www.mimegasite.com) will discover new organizations and new groups where they want to affiliate in person to improve their skills or simply enhance their lives. These technologies will serve as the catalyst for bigger and better events.

Event Planning Software

All successful events, big or small, depend on accurate and timely communication. Perhaps one of the most startling and certainly most effective event design and planning tools in recent years has been event planning software such as *Vivien Virtual Event Designer* by Cast Software (www.castsoftware.com). In an ever-demanding society, clients often know what they want, and they demand to see more and more detail before committing their money.

Virtual reality software such as Vivien enables the Event Planner to orchestrate the entire production, from concept to delivery. Though the use of full-color 3D virtual views and photorealistic renderings, you can impress your clients and sell ideas that have been tailored to reflect your client's unique brand and image. While planning your event using virtual reality software, your event resources can be dynamically tracked, enabling easy communication with all service departments.

Teleconferencing: Up-Link, Down-Link, and Fiber Optic

Increasingly, meetings and conferences as well as other event fields are being linked using both satellite and fiber-optic technologies. In the case of video, the satellite technology is less expensive and more reliable. However, data transmission is more cost-effective via fiber-optic technology. This may change as economies of scale prevail in the telecommunications industry.

When assessing the need for a teleconferencing or data-transmission component for your event, first determine what resources currently exist and then review the added value of using these technologies. If the added value provides significant advantages, the added cost may provide sufficient return on the investment.However, some event planners succumb to these technologies without careful thought regarding the need, the added value, and the return on the investment.

To select a firm to assist you with teleconferencing, first discuss your needs with the venue directors to find out what vendors they recommend. The venue is usually your best reference because the recommended vendors have probably transmitted or received communications successfully for a previous organization. In some instances, modern conference and congress centers have this technology in place and can purvey this service directly through their staff audiovisual or communications personnel.

Next, meet with those who will provide this service or those who will submit bids. Provide them with a list of transmission dates, times, content, purpose, locations, and other pertinent data. Seek their recommendations for reducing costs and improving quality.

Finally, put a contingency plan in place. Weather, power blackouts, and other unforeseen problems can affect your transmission or reception. Determine in advance how you will cover for an interruption in the signal. In some instances, it may be appropriate to ask the audience to adjourn and reconvene. In other cases, you may wish to have a local moderator lead a discussion and generate additional questions to be used when the teleconference continues. Regardless of what you decide, it is important to have an alternative plan or program firmly in place.

Webinar

The webinar is a video, audio, or slide-based communications medium delivered through the Internet. It is typically used for short courses to deliver information to learners at a distance from the physical site of the organization such as a university, college or association. Online systems such as Elluminate (www.elluminate.com) or Microsoft Live Meeting (office.microsoft.com/en-us/livemeeting) enhance the ability for interactivity between learning and online facilitator by providing live two-way video and audio, white board for drawing, and a chat function to enable sending messages. These programs are most effective if they are visual, provide highly targeted content, and are brief in duration.

That's Edutainment!

The term *edutainment* may have been coined during the early 1970s, when a large number of corporations began to combine entertainment with education to motivate their human resources. Edutainment is simply the use of live or recorded entertainment to promote learning.

Edutainment productions may range from a group of actors who present short skits about sales, customer service, or negotiation, to an elaborate interactive multimedia program involving video, slides, teleconferencing, and live entertainment to motivate customers to invest in a new product. When designing edutainment programs for your event, start with behavioral objectives in mind. Focus carefully on what you want to happen as a result of your edutainment activities.

Perhaps the best example of edutainment is the murder mystery phenomenon, which became very popular during the mid-1980s. During this period, largely due to popular television programs such as *Murder She Wrote,* murder mystery companies began popping up all over the United States and other countries. In Harrogate, England, the Old Swan Hotel (where Agatha Christie was found mysteriously in 1926 after having been missing for several days) stages a popular murder mystery weekend. During the opening reception, the guests witness a murder. The next morning a real coroner/medical examiner delivers the autopsy results as the "detectives" take exhaustive notes. By Sunday evening, the mystery is solved and everyone goes home satisfied that they participated in finding the murderer.

Andy Craven is a theatrical director who has produced murder mysteries at the Old Swan Hotel. Craven states that there are probably over 100 murder mystery companies actively performing in Great Britain. In fact, there are now 10 to 15 companies in the immediate area of Harrogate. When I interviewed the murder mystery director at the Old Swan for the first edition of the book, his troupe was the only one performing in Harrogate. Craven says that to differentiate his product now, he must carefully customize each performance. To remain competitive, he continually strives to offer greater value for the money that is expended rather than to lower his prices. Craven suggests that Event Leaders must at all times have a passion for their work and for trying new things. Prior to producing murder mysteries, Craven was a computer programmer; he sees the organization and creativity required for theatrical production as similar to the skills he needed for developing award-winning computer programs.

Corporations and associations in the United States as well as other organizations may use the murder mystery premise as a way of delivering important messages about sales, customer relations, membership development, ethics, and other principles. To use this medium as your message, first interview several murder mystery directors and select the one who will carefully customize his or her script to meet your goals and objectives. Next, make certain that you see his or her troupe in performance before you make engagement plans. While a videotape is a convenient audition device, it is far better to see them in person and determine how they handle the important audience participation segments of their production.

Whether you use a murder mystery, a musical production, or a tightly scripted three-act play, it is critical that the message be simple, repeated, and well produced. Too often, Event Leaders develop a complex message that requires too much explanation to make sense to the guests. In other instances, the message is used once and never repeated. This denies the guests the opportunity to review and have the message reinforced. Retention requires repetition. Finally, regardless of what budget is assigned to this production, make certain that it is produced with high-quality ingredients. The message will suffer if the packaging is not of sufficient quality.

Event Leader as Producer

The modern Event Leader is both consultant and producer. He or she must not only research, design, and plan, but also coordinate all the event elements, as a producer does with a play, film, television show, or other theatrical presentation. While the music and entertainment will ultimately reflect the tastes of your clients and their guests, you must never allow your own taste to be compromised. Remember that your signature is part and

The Pioneer: Kathleen B. Nelson, PhD, CSEP, CMP Assistant Professor, Tourism and Convention Administration Department, University of Nevada Las Vegas

Dr. Kathy Nelson entered the Special Events industry in 1987 after touring as a road manager for a show band and revue for over 15 years. Some of her duties on the road included scheduling rehearsals, taking performance notes, designing and constructing costumes, bookkeeping and payroll, working with the press, contract negotiations with artists, and coordinating with managers and agents. While performing in a Las Vegas lounge, the venue manager asked if the act was interested in performing a "one-nighter" at a convention on their night off. In that performance she discovered a new industry, *special events*. With her husband Dan, she opened a business in 1987 that is still producing and consulting in the events industry two decades later.

Although she learned from the "school of hard knocks," there were still gaps that needed to be filled and she decided to seek her bachelor of science degree at the University of Nevada Las Vegas in the William F. Harrah College of Hotel Administration. She recalls, "While I was in my junior year at UNLV, I joined the student chapter of the Professional Convention Management Association (PCMA) as a charter member. There were only five of us. Our faculty advisor was Patti Shock, the Tourism and Convention Administration Department Chair." Also at that time, she enrolled in a special topics class titled "Special Events Management," which was taught by an adjunct professor who owned a local Destination Management Company (DMC). The textbook used for the class was *Special Events: The Art & Science of Celebration* (1990) by Joe Goldblatt.

Later, she approached Professor Shock and asked her what she would have to do to become a teacher of entertainment and events at UNLV in the Tourism and Convention Administration Department. Shock answered, "Well, first you would need to get a master's degree." She was running a business with her husband and raising a toddler and so it all seemed overwhelming. However, her husband was supportive and she took the leap and earned her M.S. in Hotel Administration. During her last semester, her professor informed her that the Department was advertising a position for someone to teach the "Business of Entertainment." She applied for the position and was hired. She says, "At the time I was hired, my 25 years of experience and an M.S. degree equaled a terminal degree in the eyes of the University and College and I was told that a Ph.D. would not be necessary. Therefore, I was qualified to apply and accept the position."

Kathy immediately knew that teaching was the right field for her because it combined her love for the entertainment industry with her entrepreneurial spirit. During her career, Kathy has had many strong mentors, including her husband, Dan, as well as Patti Shock, CPCE director of distance learning at the William F. Harrah College of Hotel Administration, and John T. Bowen, Ph.D., Dean and Baron Hilton Distinguished Chair of the Conrad N. Hilton College of Hotel & Restautant Management in Houston, Texas. From her husband she learned about the technical and business elements of entertainment. Patti Shock encouraged her graduate studies and introduced her to key leaders in the events and hospitality industry. Dean John Bowen, according to Kathy, "epitomized a scholar. He is one of the most student-centered professors I ever encountered. When I had an idea for a new program, he would always say, 'How will this benefit the student?'"

Kathy has noted many changes in the special events industry since the days of touring with her husband. She says, "When I managed tour groups on the road, you couldn't send or receive an overnight letter; fax machines didn't exist; neither did ATM machines. We were paid in cash at the end of the week. And, of course, mobile phones that plugged into your car had not been invented, much less cell phones. I used adding machines, not a calculator. There was no such thing as a personal computer. Technology is changing at such a rapid pace today that it is difficult for most of us to keep up with the new technology products that would enable us to organize our lives, and businesses, and enhancing the teaching of our classes, because the market is becoming over-saturated.

She notes, "Education has changed as much as technology. The growth of education programs internationally has had a huge influence on our entire industry; probably the greatest influence. Whether formal, at universities, or informal, through continuing education, professional development programs and earning designations such as certifications, it is education that has the greatest impact."

Other changes are perhaps more difficult to work with. "Today, our industry is dealing with tremendous budget challenges due to the economic crisis we are currently facing. And, after September 11, 2001, in the United States, our company lost every piece of business we had booked for the next three years because clients overreacted to the degree of appropriateness it might be to ever celebrate again."

Dr. Nelson firmly believes, "Greening is a very important issue, however, I hope that the next generation of event professionals will inherit a sense of responsibility toward economic and social sustainability issues as well. I hope they will feel a duty to leave the event space in which they created the 'magic' a little bit better than they found it. I hope they will have heart for the people in the communities where the events take place and realize the opportunities they have to actually change lives in a positive sense through the events they are producing." One of the ways she has brought this theory into practice is by working with students and others to produce an event for homeless teens benefiting the De-stigmatizing and Understanding Street Kids (DUSK) project.

The Protégé: Robin Holt
Event Manager, Sharon Sacks Productions, Inc.
Graduate, University of Nevada at Las Vegas William F. Harrah College of Hotel Administration

Robin was going to school to become a lawyer when, one summer while home from college, she had the opportunity to work at either an event planning company or a dental office. She remembers that "My choice was 'parties,' as that seemed like a fun way to spend my summer. I did return to college, however, with a brand new career path. Event planning was a natural fit for me, and I looked forward to going to work every day, though it never seemed like work. I enjoyed it so much that I couldn't believe this could be an actual career. With inspiration from my boss at the time, Sharon Sacks, I sought a higher degree and attended the graduate program at the University of Nevada Las Vegas, where I earned my master's degree. I thoroughly enjoyed the collaboration of logistics, planning, creativity, and intellect. Each event seemed as though I was putting together a puzzle."

Robin's goal was to choose a career that she not only excelled in, but that she also enjoyed doing every day. "Within a week of interning for my first special event company, it was, without a shadow of a doubt, the answer to what I should be doing. Being able to use my passion for organization, planning, scheduling, designing as well as utilizing both a logistical and creative side all wrapped up into one job was what convinced

parcel of every production. Your next opportunity to produce an event is tied directly to the one you produce today. Quality, and only quality, must prevail if you are to have the opportunity to produce future events. Therefore, see every Event Leadership opportunity as your personal and professional challenge to produce the very finest music and entertainment with the time, logistical, and financial resources that may be allocated.

Career-Advancement Connections

Corporate Social Responsibility Connection

The use of production elements will enhance the communications ability of your event, however, as the Canadian scholar Marshall McLuhan (1911–1980)

me that I wanted to be an event planner. While doing my research for my graduate thesis, I was offered a job at an event company in Los Angeles, and I knew that it was my ticket to a successful career."

Robin describes two women who have served as exceptional mentors for her career. Dr. Kathy Nelson, CSEP, CMP opened her eyes to the endless possibilities to obtain future success in the special events industry. She recalls, "Dr. Nelson emphasized the importance of education and taught me how to apply what I was taught in graduate school to real-life situations. She also taught me that education is an endless open book that continues to be updated with new means, methods, and strategies for planning events. She also taught me that life and special events are not always going to be easy, but with careful thought and application of what was learned in her classroom you can achieve success."

Her other mentor is also responsible for her position today. "Sharon Sacks encouraged me to go to graduate school. Once I had my degree I worked in the field for two years before going back to work for her, and that is when she took me back under her wing. The most important thing she has done for me has been allowing me to make mistakes and giving me guidance on how to fix each situation. In my opinion, the best event planners are those that know how to overcome every hurdle, and there certainly will be hurdles with every event!"

She cautions those who are seeking future careers in the special events industry by noting that "the competition for success will be more demanding, and challenging economic times will help weed out the best from the mediocre. This will cause people to rethink and more carefully plan out their businesses. The need for higher degrees will increase, and those that receive them will earn a greater respect."

The best advice Robin has received is, "If you don't have the right answer, don't just make one up. Respond by saying, 'Let me do some research and get back to you with the correct answer.' I have been in this situation countless times and have learned from my mistakes. Honesty, confidence and trust are elements of a successful career. Clients appreciate having all the facts, and much prefer a planner who will be straight with them. I have gained respect and consideration from some of the most successful people in the entertainment business by listening to this advice that I was given."

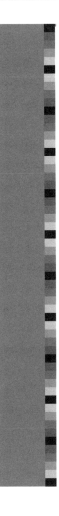

observed, "The medium is the message." It is important that you incorporate CSR in every element of your production whenever possible. For example, when purchasing or hiring / renting lighting, sound and video equipment for your event, whenever possible, use local vendors and suppliers to reduce the carbon footprint of transportation and to reduce economic leakages. Furthermore, whenever possible, conserve electricity by reducing the use of lighting or using newer energy-efficient light sources and other equipment in use for rehearsal and production. Finally, consider using local students to perform in your events to promote education and social cohesion in your community.

Global Connection

Do your homework to be certain that you are aware of the subtle but important language and cultural differences when conducting on-site management. For example, in the

United States, if you request shag, the vendor will deliver carpeting. However, in Great Britain, the vendor may give you a curious look because the term shag refers to sexual favors. Furthermore, body language has significant cultural implications. In North America, the index finger curled to join the thumb signifies that everything at your event is "OK." However, in Brazil, this gesture is an insult that could erupt into a fistfight. Therefore, it is important that you review books such as *Gestures: The Do's and Taboos of Body Language Around the World* (Axtell 1997).

Event Communications

Clear communication between all parties is as important throughout your planning and preparation as it is during the event. Invest in communication devices such as two-way radios to enable all departments and critical stakeholders to communicate effectively during an event. Assign appropriate codes for emergencies, such as first aid, evacuation, criminal activity, and other issues, that may develop during the event. Test all communications equipment carefully prior to the start of the event to ensure stability. If you are using simultaneous interpretation systems, rehearse with speakers and interpreters to ensure that the rate, language ability, and other critical factors are synchronized to provide consistently excellent communications for your participants.

Resource Connection

Read *Professional Event Coordination* (Silvers 2003). See also the *APEX Industry Glossary* (www.conventionindustry.org/glossary) for additional techniques to improve on-site operations.

Learning Connection

- Create a sample Event Specification Guide (www.conventionindustry.org/apex/acceptedpractices/ESG/eventspecifications.htm) for your event. Once you have completed the Event Specification Guide, adjust the times by 15 minutes to allow for last-minute changes.
- How will this change affect the financial, operational, and other outcomes of your event?
- Now you must also teleconference or videoconference this event to another country. How will the production schedule be affected by the different time zones?

PART FOUR

Event Marketing

The Green
Fashion Even

THURSDAY, 26TH MARCH '

@ QUEEN MARGARET UNIVERSITY

FOOD FOR THOUGHT AREA

7PM - 10.15PM

• fashion show competition

(for staff and students of QMU), entrants must design and create a fashionable item from material purchased from a charity shops and other recyclable materials and the final designs w be showcased on the runway.

FREE DRINK ON ARRIVAL, BUFFET AND RAFFLE PRIZES UP FOR GRABS.

• live performances b

THE DEBUTS.

& DANCE SOCIETY SELECT

Tickets are £7 or £5 for students...
this will include 1 complimentary drink and a finger buffet.
Proceeds will go to Friends of the Earth charity

To purchase tickets please contact Arlene Rush 07894236402 or Rebecca Jones 0781452746

Advertising for your event may include posters such as this one, a Web site, and newspaper, television or radio ads. Successful event marketers use strategic multiple channels to reach their potential guests.

CHAPTER 9

Advertising, Public Relations, Promotions, and Sponsorships

In this chapter you will learn how to:

- Conduct event-marketing research
- Develop an integrated marketing program
- Use the five Ps of event marketing
- Incorporate both internal and external marketing programs
- Develop retail marketing events
- Promote fairs and festivals
- Launch new products
- Develop, design, and execute print, electronic, and other advertising programs
- Develop comprehensive public relations programs
- Organize street promotions and creative stunts
- Develop and manage effective sponsorship programs
- Create and conduct successful cause/event-related marketing programs

- Integrate the Internet into the event-marketing strategy
- Weigh the pros and cons of online event marketing as compared to traditional channels
- Comprehensively evaluate event-marketing programs and measure return on event

---

The international television programs *American Idol* and *Britain Loves Talent,* as well as Eurovision, were described in the media as "event television," and the Broadway musical version of *Saturday Night Fever* was labeled "event theater" by *The Wall Street Journal* because the audience is encouraged to dance in the aisles at the conclusion of each show. It seems that, everywhere you look, someone is marketing events and events are being used to market products and services.

The first step in the event planning process—research—is mirrored in the marketing process. Without valid and reliable research, you may waste scarce time and resources. Therefore, the first step in the event-marketing process must be careful, thoughtful, and comprehensive research. The outcome of this research must result in the identification of measurable goals and objectives for your event-marketing campaign or program.

A campaign is usually an extended series of marketing activities designed to market an event, cause, product, or service, whereas a program may include many campaigns targeted at a wide variety of different market segments. For example, regional shopping centers design and implement annual marketing programs that may include a separate campaign for each of the four seasons or for specific events, such as the expansion of the center or introduction of a new major anchor store.

Regardless of whether you are designing a campaign or an entire program of marketing activities, the resources and channels available to you are expanding rapidly. However, with this expansion, there is also greater competition than ever before. This growth and competition is well documented.

There are numerous publications now devoted almost entirely to event management, event marketing, experiential marketing, and related subjects. Increasingly, mainstream publications such as *The Wall Street Journal* and others devote considerable editorial to reporting events and their marketing value such as the National Football League Super Bowl, the International Olympic Games, and other mega and hallmark events.

The Five P's of Marketing

Traditionally, marketing students have recognized that product, promotion, price, public relations, and place, or location, are critical components in the marketing process. Each of these five P's of marketing is a catalyst for sales. Although marketing has become more sophisticated in the twenty-first century, savvy event marketers recognize that, ultimately, marketing is only a three-syllable word for sales.

The founder of *Parade* magazine, Red Motley, once wrote: "Nothing really happens until someone sells something."(University of Minnesota Arthur Motley archives) According to some marketing experts, the most efficient and cost-effective way to make sales is through events. Whether you are selling a product, service, idea, or cause, an event allows you to use all of the senses to persuade the prospect to make an investment. The components of product, promotion, price, public relations, and place directly influence the desire and decision to make this investment. However, it is important to remember that a festival, fair, wedding, meeting, exposition, or other event is a legitimate product that also must be developed and sold.

Product

Successful salespeople have both expert product knowledge and effective sales skills. Expert product knowledge is essential in today's competitive environment. The expertise the salesperson demonstrates regarding the sponsorship package or other event component will differentiate this person from the competition. More important than sales skills, demonstrated product expertise shows the client that he or she is making a purchase that has added value and helps to develop confidence as well as long-term loyalty.

Every event product combines history, quality, and value to produce a unique program. Even new events may draw from the experience or history of the organizers. This demonstration of consistent capability to produce similar events will influence prospective clients to recognize the overall quality of the event organization. Finally, every event product must convey not only perceived value, such as dollar-for-dollar worth, but also added value. The concept of added value is perhaps best described with the Cajun word *lagniappe*. This term literally means "everything one deserves and a little bit more." The little bit more may mean providing the client with the home telephone number of the key contact person, developing a unique approach to achieving the event objectives, or perhaps simply spending additional time with the client to better understand his or her needs.

Promotion

You may have the best-quality event product, but unless you have a strategic plan for promoting this product, it will remain the best-kept secret in the world. Even large, well-known mega-events such as the Super Bowl, Rose Parade, and Olympic Games require well-developed promotion strategies to achieve the success they require.

Following is a five-step list to assist you with identifying and budgeting for your event promotion:

1. Identify all event elements that require promotion, from the proposal through the final evaluation.
2. Develop strategies for allocating scarce event promotion resources with efficient methods.

3. Identify promotion partners to share costs.
4. Target your promotion carefully to those market segments that will support your event.
5. Measure and analyze your promotion efforts throughout the campaign to make corrections as required.

The promotion strategy you identify for your event requires a careful study of past or comparable efforts, expert guidance from people who have specific expertise in this field, and, most important, benchmarks for specific measurement of your individual promotion activities.

There are a variety of ways to measure promotion efforts. First, you may measure awareness by your target market. Anticipation of the event may be tantamount to ultimate participation. Next, you may measure actual attendance and the resulting investment. Finally, you may measure the post-event attitudes of the event promotional activity. Did the promotions you designed persuade the participants or guests to attend the event?

Promotion is the engine that drives the awareness of your event. Throughout event history, legendary promoters such as Bill Veck, Joe Engel, and P. T. Barnum realized that you must shamelessly promote your event product to attract the attention of the public.

Veck did this in Major League Baseball by hiring little people as players. At the time of this stunt, there was no height requirement, and Veck took advantage of this oversight to promote his Chicago team. Engel, a Minor League Baseball promoter in Chattanooga, Tennessee, staged a fake elephant hunt on the baseball diamond to generate capacity attendance for his losing team. And, of course, P. T. Barnum continually amused the public with his legendary promotions, such as the smallest man (Tom Thumb) and the biggest mammal (Jumbo).

Most event marketers use a variety of media to promote their products. However, it is essential that event planners carefully select those media outlets that will precisely target the market segments that are appropriate for their events. Targeting promotion strategies is essential to ensure the alignment of the event's attributes with the needs, wants, and desires of potential attendees.

Price

Market research will help you determine price. Part of this market research will include conducting a competitive analysis study of other organizations offering similar event products. You may initially believe that your product is uniquely different from every other event. However, when you interview potential ticket buyers or guests, you may be surprised to learn that they consider your event similar to many others. Therefore, you must carefully list all competing events and the prices being charged to help you determine the appropriate price for your event.

Typically, two factors determine price. First, the event planner must determine the financial philosophy of the event. If the event is a not-for-profit venture, the organization may not be concerned with a large commercial yield from the event. Instead, the philosophical purpose of the event may be to generate overall awareness and support. However, if the event is a commercial venture, the goal is probably to generate the greatest potential net profit. Once the philosophy is clear, the event planner will be able to determine price. The price must reflect the cost of all goods and services required to produce the event, plus a margin of profit or retained earnings.

The second factor is the perceived competition from similar events. If your event ticket costs $100 and does not offer the same perceived value as a similar event selling for $50, your prospective guests are more likely to select the latter event. Therefore, you must be price-competitive. Becoming price-competitive does not mean lowering your ticket price. Rather, it may require raising the perception of value (as discussed earlier) to justify the slightly higher price.

These two factors—the cost of doing business and the marketplace competition—certainly influence price. A third area that may also influence price is the general economic conditions, not only in your area but also in the region, your country, and, increasingly, the world. During times of recession, some events with lower ticket prices will flourish, while other upscale event products may not be as successful. Keep a close eye on market economic indicators to make certain that your price matches the purchasing power of your target market.

Public Relations

Advertising is what you say about your event, whereas public relations is what others (their perceptions) are saying about your event. Since many events require a second-party endorsement or even review to encourage people to attend, public relations is significantly more valuable and effective than traditional advertising.

In the 1930s and 1940s, public relations consisted primarily of press agents who worked diligently to convince the print media to devote editorial space to their clients. With the influence of leaders such as Edward Bernays (1891–1995), the public relations effort soon became more complex and respected. Bernays, credited as being the father of public relations, was both a blood nephew and nephew-in-law to the father of psychoanalysis, Sigmund Freud. Bernays recognized the psychological factors that govern a person's decision-making ability. Therefore, he advocated that public relations professionals first engage in research, including focus groups, to determine the values, attitudes, and lifestyles of their target markets and carefully match their messages to these important factors.

Today, in many event-marketing campaigns, public relations is at least equal to and, in many cases, even more important than traditional advertising. However, public relations involves much more than merely grinding out a short press release.

The effective event public relations campaign will involve research with event consumers as well as the media; the development of collateral materials such as media kits, fact sheets, and other tangibles; the organization and implementation of media conferences; the development of a speaker's bureau; and on-site media relations assistance at the event.

Event public relations help create the overall impression that others will develop about your event. In that regard, it is significantly more valuable than advertising because it implies greater credibility. For that reason, the Public Relations Society of America, an organization whose members include professionals in the public relations profession, states that public relations exposure is more valuable financially than advertising. For example:

- Half-page newspaper advertisement

Cost = $5,000

- Editorial about your event in the same space as the advertisement

Value = $15,000 to $35,000 (three to seven times more), depending on placement

Use the power of public relations to beat the drum loudly for your event. Carefully select those public relations tools that will most effectively and cost-efficiently help you inform and persuade others to support your event.

Place

In real estate, location is everything. In event marketing, distribution of your product may be everything as well. The location of your event often determines the channels of distribution.

If your event is located in a rural area, it may be difficult to promote the event due to limited media resources and logistical constraints. However, in the post–September 11, 2001, world, rural events are growing in number and size in the United States. This may be due to the perception of safety and security and convenience of local guests. Therefore, despite the limitations, demand has overcome these obstacles.

The place where you locate your event ultimately will determine the marketing efforts you must exert to drive sales. For example, it has been shown that those events that are close to inexpensive, safe public transportation or those events that feature closed-in reasonably priced parking will attract more guests than those that do not offer these amenities. Furthermore, those events that are connected to other nearby attractions or infrastructures (such as shopping malls) may also draw more attendees due to the time efficiency of the destination. For upscale events, the addition of valet parking may improve the chances of attracting guests to a new or nontraditional location.

The event planner must seriously consider place when designing the marketing program for the event. Place does not only imply the taste or style of the event; it also, in large part, defines the type of person that will be persuaded to invest in the event. In this regard, the event marketer must determine the place in the early stages through research and design. This is the perfect time to convene a focus group or conduct a survey to determine who is likely to attend your event when they are given a variety of location choices. Making certain you have thoughtfully analyzed this important issue will save you time and money throughout the entire event-marketing process.

A Sixth P: Positioning

According to Leonard Hoyle in his book *Event Marketing* (Hoyle 2002), there is an additional P that is critical to the marketing mix. Hoyle describes *positioning* as follows:

"Positioning is the strategy of determining through intuition, research, and evaluation those areas of consumer need that your event can fulfill." He further states that the five key considerations when positioning an event include location, attention span, competitive costs, the program, and the simplicity of the marketing plan. Hoyle states:

> *Issues of location must be continuously evaluated, because interests of the markets change constantly. Maintaining the attention of the prospective event attendee is very important because people have so many images and messages competing for their attention. Competitive costs include the critical factor of cost of admission, which further defines the market. The program must be something that no one else can offer. Finally, the most important variable of all may be the plan itself. Keep it short and sweet and easy to track. The plan should spell, as briefly as feasible, the strengths and weaknesses of your organization and event, the objectives, the needs of your potential market niche, economic considerations, and elements that make the enterprise unique from others.*

Internal versus External Event Marketing

Event planners may use an event or a series of events as one of the marketing methods to promote external events, products, or services, such as shopping malls, tourist destinations, or attractions (e.g., amusement parks or zoos), or any entity that is appropriately promoted through events.

However, in most cases, event planners use marketing forces such as advertising, public relations, promotion, advertising specialties, stunts, and other techniques to promote individual events. These traditional marketing techniques should be used to inform, attract, persuade, sustain, and retain potential customers for your event.

Increasingly, a blend of internal and external event marketing is being utilized to promote events. In some cases, event planners use miniature events as a means of promoting major events. The Sydney Organizing Committee for the Olympic Games (SOCO) staged a major fireworks display to celebrate the decision by the International Olympic Committee to stage the games in Sydney, Australia. The fireworks spectacular began the marketing process of identifying Sydney as the city of the next Olympic Games. Smaller events, such as a torch run, are used throughout the days preceding the opening ceremonies to promote this event.

On a smaller scale, fundraising organizations such as the National Symphony Orchestra use smaller focus-type events (e.g., receptions) to promote larger events (e.g., the Symphony Ball or the annual Designer's Show House). These ancillary events serve to promote the larger event to different market segments and maintain excitement about the overall event product.

Therefore, both internal and external event marketing are important strategies for your event. Figure 9.1 depicts how this process is used to market your event product. Since resources for marketing are always limited, it is important to select those internal or external elements that will reach and influence your target market most effectively.

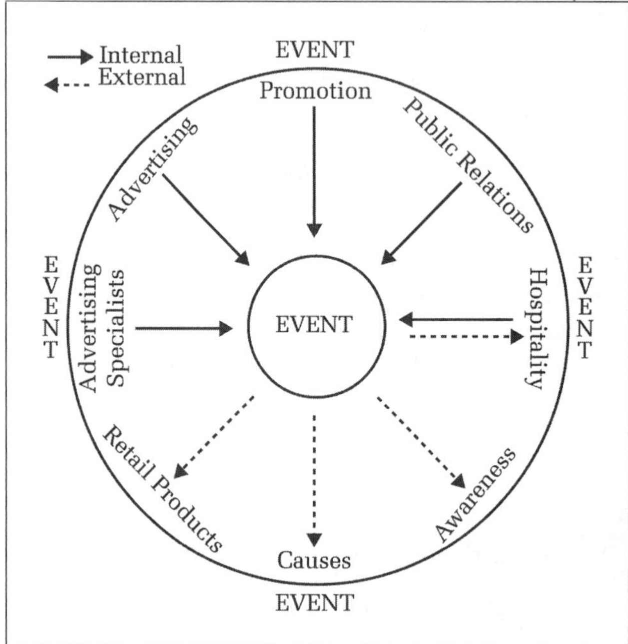

Figure 9.1 Internal and External Event-Marketing Model

External Event Marketing

Using events to market products and services is increasing. Publications such as *Advertising Age* have declared that events are now critical in the total marketing effort. Therefore, although using an event-marketing strategy may be more costly due to the additional labor required, it must be considered seriously when promoting products and services.

Retail Events

Our firm began by producing fashion shows, petting zoos, Santa Claus appearances, and other retail events. During the mid- to late 1970s, regional mega–shopping centers opened throughout the United States, and mall developers such as the Rouse Company and Homart recognized that they were the new Main Streets of America. To attract the appropriate target market, a series of events was developed and implemented to position the shopping mall as an attraction.

Using the fashion show as one example, shopping mall management could satisfy the needs of both its internal and external customers. First, the store owners and managers could showcase their goods and services to a highly targeted audience in a cost-effective manner. Second, the external customer—the shopper himself or herself—would be held captive during the 20- to 30-minute production and then directed to visit each store for special discounts immediately following the show. According to the International Council of Shopping Centers, the trade association that educates and promotes the shopping center industry, many marketing directors are earning the Certified Marketing Director (CMD) designation to develop specialized knowledge of this increasingly complex and competitive profession.

Figure 9.2 lists several retail events that have proven successful and the market to which they are best targeted. You will note that most of these events target women, as historically women have been the largest customer bases for retail businesses. However, these demographics are shifting as two-income families have emerged in the United States, and now both men and women increasingly share the responsibilities and pleasures of shopping. Therefore, successful Event Leaders will look for events that they may use to develop other markets with disposable income, such as men, teenage boys, and even senior citizens.

Timing is everything when developing and producing the retail event. To allow the consumer to devote as much time as possible to spending money, the live event should be

Event	Potential Target Markets (Gender and Age)
Arts and crafts shows	Women and senior citizens, 18–35, 36–55, 56–85
Children's entertainer	Young children, 5–9, 10–12
Circus and petting zoo	Young families, 5–9, 10–12, 13–17, 18–35, 36–55, 56–85
Computer show	Men, 18–35, 36–55, 56–85
Cooking demonstration/tasting	Women 18–35, 36–55, 56–85
Fashion show	Women and teenage girls, 13–17, 18–35, 36–55
Fine art show	Women and men, 36–55, 56–85
Health fair	Senior citizens, 56–85
Magician	Young boys and girls, 5–9, 10–12, 13–17
Model railroad show	Young boys and men, 5–9, 10–12, 13–17, 18–35, 36–54, 55–85
Puppeteer	Young children, 5–9, 10–12
Soap-opera-star appearance	Women and teenage girls, 18–35, 36–55, 56–84
Sport-celebrity appearance	Men and boys, 13–17, 18–35, 36–55
Sport-memorabilia festival	Men and teenage boys, 13–17, 18–35, 36–55

Figure 9.2 Retail Events and Their Target Markets

brief in duration (under 20 minutes) and offered frequently throughout the day to allow a variety of customers to experience the event activity. Obviously, due to the increase in working adults, weekdays during normal working hours should be avoided so that the most consumers can witness the event. Finally, many retail events are tied directly to paydays. Find out what the pay period is from large organizations such as factories, government, or other sources of large numbers of consumers, and then time your event to coincide with this window of time when there will be a large amount of expendable income available.

Fairs and Festivals

Fairs, festivals, and other public events may also serve as temporary retail locations (TRLs). These events often contract space to vendors, craftspeople, and others to demonstrate and sell their products and services. However, like their permanent retail counterparts, to be successful such events must be marketed aggressively through both internal and external event-marketing efforts.

A media preview event is an excellent way to inform the media about the size, scope, and excitement being offered at your fair or festival. Designing a ribbon-cutting event featuring prominent local citizens along with celebrities is an important way to announce "open for business." Finally, a series of ongoing ancillary events held at other public venues, such as sporting event halftime shows, is an important form of external marketing to introduce and remind other market segments of your event's importance.

Launching New Products

Perhaps one of the more important activities within the event-marketing area is that of launching new products developed by corporations. Each year in the United States and other countries, billions of dollars are invested in advertising to promote new products. Before these products are introduced to the general public, they are usually showcased to retailers or dealers. An event such as the launch of a new automobile serves several constituent groups. The trade media may be invited to promote the product to others. Then the general media (newspapers, radio, and television) may be invited to help make the general public aware of the new product benefits and features. Finally, and perhaps most important, the product launch must target those people who will either sell the item to others or purchase it themselves.

The organization and presentation of the product launch event may be one of the most important steps in the overall marketing effort. Whether introducing the latest software or an attraction such as a new hotel resort, great thought must be given to the goals, objectives, and desired outcomes to create a successful event.

The following is a 10-step list for developing and producing consistently successful product-launch events.

1. Determine the goals and objectives of the product-launch event.
2. Identify the target market(s).

3. Coordinate planning with sales promotion, public relations, human resource development, and other critical departments.
4. Conduct research to refine your general production plans.
5. Use creativity to introduce your product in a nontraditional yet attractive manner.
6. Use creativity to unveil a new product.
7. Identify who will speak, for what length of time, and why.
8. Identify ways to reach those who could not attend the event (such as through a video program or satellite presentation).
9. Measure and analyze your results by how sales are affected.
10. Develop opportunities for added value the next time you produce a similar event.

Lavish plans for product-launch events sometimes are foiled by circumstances beyond the control of the Event Leader. However, most circumstances can be controlled easily through close communication with other parties. Make certain that you contact the corporate communications or public relations department early in the process to identify their goals and incorporate them into your plans. Next, and equally important, make certain that the vice president or director of sales is closely involved in your planning, as your activities will directly affect his or her efforts. Finally, ensure that senior management, including the chief executive and operating officers, understands, supports, and is committed to your success. However, despite all this careful interaction with other stakeholders, sometimes Murphy's Law (which states that "anything that can go wrong will go wrong") is invoked and subsequently problems arise.

In 2008, in the early days of the global financial crisis in the United States and other countries, several key meeting industry organizations released recommended voluntary guidelines and standards for organizations that were conducting product launch events. The generally accepted purposes of these events as agreed upon by these organizations included "effective product launches to educate sales force, channel partners and customers." However, the same organizations recommended as well that the investment in these events, if they involved incentive travel, shall not exceed 15 percent of the total sales and marketing spend. Furthermore, the recommendations also stated that any expenditure of $75,000 or greater must have a corresponding document that the event is for a legitimate business purpose US Travel Association, February 9, 2009, http://www.ustravel.org/news/press-releases/travel-community-issues-event-guidelines-emergency-assistance-recipients.

Therefore, as a direct result of the global financial crisis experienced in 2008, corporations and other organizations are practicing greater due diligence and care when it comes to the approval of incentive travel, meetings, conferences, and product launch programs. In order to improve the chances of your product launch event being approved and fully funded, you should develop a legitimate business case demonstrating the purpose and outcome as related to the organizations return on investment (ROI, return on marketing investment (ROMI), and return on objective (ROO).

Event Promotion Techniques

Five typical or traditional techniques are used to promote events: advertising, public relations, cross promotions, street promotions, and stunts. Some events use only one of these techniques; others may use all of them to ensure that their message is received and acted on by their target market.

Advertising

Advertising includes print and electronic media, transportation media (such as bus and rail), advertising specialties (calendars, key rings, coffee mugs, and other products), and outdoor media (billboards). Larger events may use many of these media resources, while smaller events may carefully target their message to one or two media.

Print advertising is not limited to magazines and newspapers. It may also include membership directories, inserts in local newspapers, flyers (sometimes called one sheets), posters, church and synagogue newsletters, brochures, and virtually any printed media. When analyzing your print advertising needs, make certain that you test your advertising product in advance with a small distribution to test its effectiveness. Specialists in direct mail recommend that you use a split-test approach. This requires that you mail one type of advertising printed matter to one group and a different type to another to test the best response from both types. Varying items such as the color of the ink, copy, type, and weight of the paper, or other decisions may produce different results. Test your print advertising using focus groups to make certain that your event product is well positioned for success.

Classic advertising terms such as "free," "discount," "now," "sale," and "new" may help you influence the consumer to invest in your event. Clever graphics, endorsements, testimonials, and other credibility-building devices will help differentiate your event product from others.

Electronic media include radio, television, the Internet, and any form of advertising that involves electronic delivery. Radio advertising is typically used to remind the listener about the event, whereas television is used to build excitement. The Internet is an excellent means with which to reach upscale consumers and those who are interested in science, technology, and travel. Before you select electronic media as a means to advertise your event, examine all potential media outlets.

Within television media, you may elect to cast your event broadly through major networks or narrowly cast by selecting a finely targeted cable station. For example, if you are promoting an arts-related event, you may select a cable station with arts programming. Selecting the appropriate media outlet may require the assistance of experts in media buying or from an advertising agency specializing in radio or television media.

Transportation media require that you place your message on buses, subways, and other forms of transportation. Usually these media are aimed at a very wide market and have proven effective for circuses, fairs, festivals, and other events that require large attendance from diverse groups.

Advertising specialties are those items that are usually given away or offered as a premium, as an incentive to purchase a product or service. Advertising specialties include thousands of products; however, the most typical are calendars, refrigerator magnets, coffee mugs, writing instruments, and key chains. In recent years, clothing has become popular as an advertising specialty, and some event organizers give away clothing to the media and other key constituent groups and sell the rest at souvenir stands. Once again, research this purchase carefully to ensure that the recipient values the item and will use it. Prolonged use will serve as reminders of your event.

Outdoor advertising was, at one time, one of the major forms of advertising in the United States. However, during the late 1960s, many billboards were banned in a "beautify America" campaign. Still, the outdoor billboard is an excellent way to reach large numbers of potential event participants for an extended period of time.

Regardless of the type of advertising media you select, first conduct market research and follow up with tests to determine actual response. Once you have found a medium that effectively reaches your target market, use repetition to build reinforcement and retention. Finally, measure all responses to develop history and determine where your advertising dollar will pull best for each event.

Public Relations

Public relations involves informing the media and your target market about your event and persuading them to support your programs. Public relations activities for your event may include designing, printing, and distributing media kits, producing public service announcements for radio and television, producing and distributing audio and video news releases, or even producing events. In fact, according to many public relations professionals, events are the fastest-growing segment of the public relations strategy.

The media kit is typically a presentation-type folder that contains a fact sheet, request for coverage notice, media releases, and even a public service announcement (either written or recorded). This kit is distributed well in advance of the event to the print and electronic media to inform them of opportunities for coverage. In smaller markets, some media outlets may print your media releases word for word; in larger, more sophisticated markets, members of the media may use the kit for background information alone.

Leonard Hoyle Jr. suggests that press kits should include these materials:

- Press or media releases
- Photos
- Media alerts
- Requests for coverage
- Press conference announcements and invitations
- Speeches
- Background news stories
- Videotapes of the event
- CDs and DVDs of the event
- Organizational information

- Biographies of the key individuals leading the event or appearing at the event (speakers, entertainers)
- Folders, brochures, postcards
- Advertising specialty items

A public service announcement (PSA) is a written or prerecorded audio or video announcement about your event. Broadcasters in the United States are required by federal law to allot a certain amount of time for public service announcements. In some cases, the broadcaster may provide help, as a further public service, in producing these announcements. Often a local celebrity or nationally prominent person will participate at no charge, to add credibility to your announcement.

The audio or video news release, while a relatively new phenomenon, is one of the most effective ways to distribute your event message. Audio news releases (ANRs) and video news releases (VNRs) require that you prerecord a news story about your event and then, by overnight mail or use of satellite transmission, send the story to local stations that you would like to have air the story as part of their news programming. Since news programs are often the most watched segments of television programming, this type of public relations has the potential of reaching a large, well-targeted audience in a credible and cost-effective manner.

Finally, events themselves often become major public relations vehicles. To promote the effort to raise funds for Haiti relief following the January 2010 earthquake, actor George Clooney appeared on the red carpet for the Golden Globes Awards on E! TV to promote a telethon to be held the following Friday. Throughout the awards show broadcast by NBC, actors and actresses promoted the upcoming telethon and reminded people how they could contribute to the relief effort. The telethon was recorded, and further money was raised when it was offered on iTunes.

Remember that the two chief goals of public relations are to inform and persuade. Therefore, using collateral materials, public service announcements, and audio and video news releases as well as smaller events are excellent ways to accomplish these two important goals of an overall marketing campaign.

Cross Promotions

To allocate market resources in the most efficient manner, you must identify and incorporate marketing partners into your campaign. These organizations may actually contribute marketing dollars or may provide in-kind services, such as providing celebrities, tagging their ads with your event date and time, or contributing other valuable components to your campaign.

When seeking marketing partners to develop a cross-promotional strategy, study the advertising and marketing activities of compatible businesses in your area. Determine which of these activities will benefit your event. Next, develop a proposal that clearly describes the resources that you can bring to the event. Finally, present the proposal to your prospective marketing partners and answer any questions they may pose.

Tagging advertising involves your marketing partner adding a line of copy to his or her regular advertising placements that promote your event. It may read "Official supporter of XYZ event" or "Meet us at XYZ event, date and time." Tag lines may appear in both print and electronic advertising.

Make certain that you chronicle all marketing activities so that you can report to your partners after the event and describe in specific detail those placements that were successful. Cross promotions and tie-in activities are sensational ways to reach a much larger market in a cost-effective manner.

Street Promotions

This marketing activity requires that you literally take your message to the street. Street promotions may include the handing out of flyers by a clown in a high-traffic area, the appearance of a celebrity at a local mall, contests, or other promotional activities designed to draw high visibility to your event. Before leafleting (handing out flyers), make certain that this is allowed by local code. You certainly do not want to generate negative publicity by having the clown arrested for causing a disturbance. A celebrity appearance can help generate significant publicity if it is handled properly. Schedule the celebrity to include radio and television interviews, appearances at a local children's hospital or other public facility, and ceremonial events with local, state, provincial, or federal leaders. At each appearance, make certain that the celebrity is well informed about the event and articulates your event message in a consistent manner. Contests and other promotional events also require analysis to ensure that they are within the bounds of the local code and that they are appropriate for your event. For instance, selling raffle tickets at a nonprofit event may require that you file legal forms.

Stunts

During the early 1950s in the United States, advertising agencies used stunts as an important method of breaking through the clutter of traditional print and electronic advertising. Today, stunts continue to be effective but must be crafted carefully to ensure that the integrity of the event is preserved.

A stunt involves an activity designed to generate media coverage and attendance by spectators to promote a specific event or series of events. Radio stations continue to rely heavily on stunts and will often provide remote broadcasts to cover stunts involving their on-air personalities. Stunts can be tied to charitable endeavors, such as locking up prominent officials until enough donations are raised to cover their release. Other stunts may involve creating the world's largest pizza, cake, sandwich, or other product. Before you incorporate a stunt in an event-marketing program, it is important to analyze how the stunt will further your marketing objectives and to determine all associated costs. Finally, make certain that you chronicle all media coverage that results from the stunt, distribute bounce-back coupons to attendees, and track all responses resulting from the stunt.

Getz describes one type of stunt as a flash mob. The flash mob is an event that is preplanned but appears spontaneous. One example is a crowd of dozens of individuals at Grand Central Station during rush hour in New York City who suddenly freeze for one or two minutes to draw attention to their cause or to promote a product. The participants received advance instructions including the time, date, wardrobe, location, and other information by e-mail and then after assembling at the venue they are cued to begin their activity by mobile phone. If you elect to use a flash mob to draw attention to your product or cause, make certain you not only notify the media but also, to the extent possible, the venue management and other officials. It would not serve your client well if the outcome of your event were mass arrests because you and your participants were accused of disturbing the peace and disorderly conduct (Getz 2007).

Invitation

Whether your invitation is a print or electronic advertisement, a flyer, or a formal engraved document, the copy that is composed, art that is created or selected, and paper that is chosen will greatly influence the response. The six central components of all effective invitations are:

1. Name of host or event organizer
2. Date, time, and location
3. Dress requirements
4. Transportation and parking
5. Web site address (URL) that includes Google MapQuest Information for directions.
6. RSVP

Six additional components may include:

1. Purpose of the event
2. Names of honorary board or committee members
3. Names of prominent speakers
4. Frequency or historic nature of the event (second annual, 100th anniversary celebration, or biannual event)
5. Limited supply of tickets
6. VIP status

Remember that an invitation is an official offer to the consumer or guest to participate in your event. Therefore, from a legal perspective, it is important that you choose your words carefully to reflect the actual event you are promoting.

Each of these components is designed to generate a specific response from the recipient. The most important response is to build anticipation toward acceptance followed by actual attendance.

Marketing Thrust

The late Ira Westreich, noted corporate marketing expert and eloquent professional speaker, described the word *event* as an acronym that represents "Extract Value with Every New Thrust." The purpose of your event-marketing campaign is to ensure that every decision you make provides greater value for the overall event outcome. To do this, you must carefully match the objectives to the strategies, test all ideas using feedback from actual event consumers, and, perhaps most important, use creativity and innovation to differentiate your event product as a unique and valuable investment. By integrating marketing activities such as advertising, public relations, cross promotions, street promotions, and stunts, you will be able to build a strong campaign that will effectively promote your event to your target audience.

Event Sponsorship

According to the International Events Group (IEG) of Chicago, sponsorship worldwide is a $25 billion industry (IEG 2004). IEG is a recognized leader in the field of sponsorship research and education. Although the vast majority of sponsorship dollars is invested in sports-related events, there is a trend to diversify funding into festivals, fairs, and cultural events. The primary reason for this diversification of investment is due to the need of advertisers to reach more targeted demographics. Sports have generally attracted broad demographics, whereas cultural events are able to target high-income and well-educated consumers.

However, as a result of the global financial decline first experienced in 2008, many corporations chose to cut back or eliminate their sponsorship programs. Some event organizations in the United States reported loss of sponsorship of upwards of $250,000. Therefore, while sponsorship is still a critical component of most event funding schemes, event planners must work harder and be more clever in gaining sponsorship dollars in the future.

It is important to understand that the event in sponsorship language is defined as the property or sponsee. The sponsor is the organization (usually a corporation) that provides funding or in kind resources in exchange for specific marketing benefits.

Sponsorship generally becomes more valuable if the event organization is able to offer precise targeting that matches the marketing objectives of the prospective sponsor. The growth in sponsorship is due primarily to the need of advertisers to find alternative marketing channels to inform, persuade, promote, and sell their products and services. However, the number of events that require sponsorship has also grown in recent years.

Without sponsorship, many events would not be financially feasible. Other events would not be able to provide the quality expected by event participants. Still other events would not be able to achieve their specified goals and objectives. Suffice it to say that, more often than not, sponsorship provides the grease that allows the event wheel to function smoothly.

Historically, sponsorship has its earliest modern origin in professional sporting events. These events have always appealed to the widest demographics and were, therefore, perfect event products for sponsorship. Sponsorship is a uniquely American invention brought forth from the need of advertisers to reach certain markets and the need of event organizers to identify additional funding to offset costs not covered by normal revenue streams, such as ticket sales.

In recent times, there has been a noticeable shift in sponsor dollars away from sporting events and toward arts events. The reason for this shift is that sponsors are seeking more highly targeted upscale demographics and the arts' audience delivers that market segment. Therefore, those events that deliver the higher-income demographics are predicted to benefit most from sponsorship dollars in the future.

Perhaps the best example of sport sponsorship is the 1984 Summer Olympic Games in Los Angeles, California. For the first time in the history of the modern Olympic Games movement, sponsors were aggressively solicited as marketing partners for this unprecedented event. Offers were made, deals were cut, and the Los Angeles Olympic Organizing Committee received net earnings of over $200 million.

From fairs to festivals to hallmark events such as a world's fair, the role of the sponsor has earned a permanent place in the marketing lexicon of events. Following are typical types of sponsors for a variety of events:

- Fair: bottler, grocer, automotive, and bank
- Festival: department store and record store
- Sport: athletic wear manufacturer, bottler, brewery, and hospital or health-care facility
- School program: children's toy stores, children's clothing stores, and amusement park
- Meeting/conference: printer, bank, insurance broker, and associate member firms

Use this list as a guide to begin to identify sponsors for your event.

Sponsorship Needs Assessment

Although most events may benefit from sponsorship, not every event is appropriate for this component. Sponsorship is a commercial endeavor and is extremely time-consuming. Therefore, unless you are prepared to enter into a commercial relationship with other parties and have the time resources to devote to this activity, you may instead wish to solicit donations.

Many Event Leaders confuse sponsorship with benevolence. A fundraising event where donors contribute without any expectation of commercial benefit is a benevolent activity. Sponsorship, however, is a commercial transaction in which two parties agree by way of an offer and acceptance. The offer generally involves marketing services provided by the event organizer in exchange for the sponsor's cash or in-kind contribution to the event. The marketing services may range from advertising, to banner displays, to hospitality, to a full-blown marketing plan involving public relations, advertising, and promotion.

As you can see, these marketing services place new demands on the event organizer. Therefore, event resources may need to be reallocated to handle this new demand. Not every event is able to do this.

Before you give the green light to soliciting sponsorships, use the next checklist to determine if your event is appropriate for this activity:

1. Does the event require an infusion of sponsor dollars to achieve the quality required?
2. Are there sufficient internal and external resources to support this activity?
3. Is commercial sponsorship appropriate for the nature of the event?
4. Are there sufficient prospects for sponsorship sales, and is the timing appropriate to approach them?
5. Is this activity legal, ethical, and appropriate for the spirit of the event organization

These questions can save many event organizations much wasted time, energy, and heartache. Examining the internal and external resources may be one of the most important aspects of this process.

Although sponsors may provide much needed funding for your event, to help you achieve the quality that is required, sponsors also require that your own financial resources meet their objectives. They may, for example, require that you commit a certain amount of marketing dollars. They also may require minimal or substantial hospitality services that may amount to hundreds or thousands of dollars per day. If you are going to retain these sponsors, assign one or more people to monitor the activities, service these accounts, and develop long-term relationships. Yes, sponsors can provide needed funding; however, as in any commercial transaction, they must also receive a fair return on their investment. You are responsible for orchestrating this return.

Your event may benefit from additional exposure through sponsorships. Earlier, we discussed using tag lines in advertising as one way to increase your exposure inexpensively. Sponsors may also provide you with shelf space in their retail stores, or to promote your event through coupons. Your sponsors can also help you with the development of a public relations campaign or can supplement their own public relations efforts with your message. Some sponsors have celebrity athletes, television stars, and movie personalities on contract with whom they may wish to involve your event.

Perhaps one of the more important reasons event organizers align themselves with commercial sponsors is the opportunity to achieve greater credibility for the event. Securing the sponsorship of AT&T, IBM, Coca-Cola, or other Fortune 500 firms immediately positions your event as a major player and may help your event organization secure additional funding from other sources.

Developing Sponsors

The competition by event organizers for sponsors is keen at every level. Whether your event is a local event or a national one, you must first conduct a competitive analysis to identify all competing events and study their sponsorship history and current activities. Several suggestions on how to identify appropriate sponsors for your event follow:

1. Determine the financial level of sponsorship you require. Not every sponsor can make a five- or six-figure commitment.
2. Review trade journals such as *Advertising Age* and *Sponsorship Report* to track sponsor activities.
3. Review the local business tabloid in your area to search for prospective sponsors.
4. Network with advertising and public relations agency officials to find out if their clients have an interest in your event.
5. Conduct a focus group with prospective sponsors to solicit and later analyze their opinions and attitudes toward your event.
6. Make certain you link your sponsorship program directly to the business case the corporation has developed.

Once you have developed a list of prospective sponsors, the next step is to qualify them for solicitation. Do not waste your valuable resources by making endless presentations to sponsors who do not have the interest or resources to support your event financially. Instead, qualify your sponsors by contacting local organizations, such as the chamber of commerce, board of trade, banks, and other centers of commerce, to inquire about the financial viability of the prospective sponsor. Next, thoroughly review the sponsor's past marketing efforts to determine if its overall marketing plans are conducive to sponsoring your event. Finally, talk to advertising and public relations executives and attempt to forecast where your prospective sponsor may put its marketing dollars in the future. Perhaps the logical place for investment is your event.

Selling Sponsorships

Always do your homework regarding the sponsor's needs, wants, and desires prior to attempting to sell a sponsorship. To make the sale, the sponsorship offer must be an exact fit with the needs, expectations, goals, and objectives of the commercial sponsor. Customize the offer to achieve these goals and objectives prior to your presentation.

Constructing a successful proposal is equal parts of art and science. As an artist, you must design an attractive, enticing, and aesthetically pleasing product that the sponsor will want to purchase. Therefore, describe the capability of your organization and past sponsors (if any), incorporate testimonials and references from leading individuals, and package the proposal in a professional design. Avoid being clever. Remember that the sponsor will be making an important business decision and will prefer a serious business plan rather than one that demonstrates cleverness. The science part involves carefully identifying your target market and linking all sponsorship activities to sales or recognition that will benefit the sponsor. List the benefits and activities that the organization will enjoy as a sponsor of your event. For example, the sponsor might be able to provide free samples of his or her product or service and conduct marketing research. It might be able to offer its product or service for sale and measure the results. Or the sponsor may benefit from public relations exposure.

Include in the proposal sponsorship terms for payment and any requirements the sponsor may have in addition to these payments. In some events, the sponsor is allowed to provide an exhibit at its own cost. In others, the exhibit is provided as part of the sponsorship costs. Describe any additional costs or services the sponsor is required to contribute to avoid any future surprises. This list summarizes the key elements in a winning sponsorship proposal:

1. Describe the history of the event.
2. Include a capability statement about your organization's resources.
3. Incorporate testimonials and references from other sponsors.
4. Describe the benefits and features that the sponsor will receive.
5. List all financial responsibilities that the sponsor must accept.
6. Describe any additional responsibilities that the sponsor must accept.
7. Describe how you will chronicle the sponsorship activity.
8. Include a time and a date for acceptance of the offer.
9. Include a provision for renewal of the sponsorship.
10. Include an arbitration clause in case you and the sponsor disagree regarding the sponsorship activities.

One of the more effective ways to persuade sponsors to participate in an event is to organize a prospective sponsor preview program. During this program, you and your staff describe the benefits and features of your sponsorship activities to a large number of prospective sponsors. You may wish to invite a couple of previous sponsors to provide in-person testimonials about the benefits of the sponsorship. You may also wish to presell one or two sponsors so that when you ask for a reaction from those in attendance, at least two from the group will respond favorably. Their favorable response may, and usually does, influence others. Avoid trying to hard-sell during this program. Use this program to plant seeds that will be further cultivated during meetings with individual sponsors.

Overcoming Sponsor Objections

Most sponsors will want their sponsorship activities customized to achieve their specific goals and objectives. Therefore, they may have some preliminary objections after receiving your initial offer. Once you have presented the offer, ask for their reaction on each benefit and feature. Listen carefully and list these comments. Make two lists. One list is for approvals, those items that they see the value in sponsoring. The second list is for objections, those items that they cannot see the value of at this time. Your goal is to move all the items from list 2 to list 1. To do this, ask sponsors what their organization requires to overcome their objections on each point. In some cases, it might be additional exposure. In other cases, it might be the price of the sponsorship. To overcome these objections, be prepared to provide sponsors with the tools they need to make a positive decision. For example, if their objection is cost, you may be able to combine their sponsorship with others and lower their contribution. If their objection is limited exposure, you may be able to reposition their involvement inexpensively to provide them with greater and more sustained visibility. Handling objections is an integral part of the sponsorship sales process. Rehearse these discussions with your internal stakeholders to identify other common objections, and be prepared to provide the solution your sponsors need to remove these barriers.

Negotiating Your Sponsorship

Almost every sponsorship will require intense negotiations to move it to fruition. Whenever possible, conduct these negotiations in person with the decision maker. Assign a specific date and time for these negotiations and confirm that the sponsor is a feasible prospect before entering into a serious negotiation. In most negotiations, both parties desire a win-win-win outcome. In this type of negotiation, you win as the event organizer, the sponsor wins as the event funding agent, and the stakeholders of your event win from your mutual efforts to secure these dollars.

Carefully analyze what your sponsor expects from the sponsorship prior to your negotiating session. Determine in advance what additional components you may be able to offer if required. Also, list those concessions that you cannot make. Finally, list these items that may require further approval from your board or others before you agree to them. Begin the negotiation by asking the prospective sponsor to list all items that are acceptable, bundle them, and have the sponsor approve them. Now you are prepared to focus on those items that require further resolution. Ask the sponsor to describe his or her concerns about each negotiation point and take careful notes. Look at your list of concessions and decide if any item you have listed will help resolve these concerns. If it is appropriate to offer a concession, do so and ask the sponsor for his or her approval. Once the sponsor has approved, ask him or her to provide you with an additional service, usually at modest additional cost to the sponsor, to balance his or her end of the negotiation. If the sponsor is unable to provide you with an additional service or product, determine if you are able to proceed to the next point.

Do not be afraid to walk away if the sponsor asks for concessions that could sacrifice the credibility or reputation of an event or that would undermine the financial wealth of your event. Instead, thank the sponsor for its time, offer to work with the sponsor in the future under different circumstances, and leave the room as quickly as possible. In some instances, event organizers have reported that this approach has forced the prospective sponsor to reexamine its position. It is not unusual to have the sponsor call the event organizer the next day and offer a greater concession to save the sponsorship.

Closing the Sponsorship Sale

You must always ask for the order when presenting your sponsorship proposal. State at least three times that you want to develop a positive relationship with the sponsor. Start your discussions by stating that your desired outcome is to ensure that the sponsor understands all the benefits and features of your event and will desire to become a sponsor.

Throughout your presentation, ask for feedback from the sponsor and build on the sponsor's positive reactions by saying that you are pleased that it recognizes the value of your event product. Finally, at the conclusion of your presentation, ask the sponsor's spokesperson for his or her overall impression and state, once again, that you would like the sponsor's business.

Unfortunately, these techniques may not be enough to get a clear answer. In some cases, you may have to say something like "So, can we count on you to sponsor our event?" Sometimes you need to secure the answer to this question in order to plan your next step in sponsorship negotiations or to decide to move forward with the next sponsor. The word *ask* is the most powerful three-letter word in sponsorship sales. Unless you ask, you will never know. Remember to ask early, often, and before leaving to confirm the sponsorship sale.

Servicing Sponsorship Sales

Once the sponsor has accepted your offer, the next task is to service the sale in order to retain the sponsor's support in the future. One of the more common reasons that sponsors fail to renew their sponsorship is due to poor communications. In Part One of this book, we discussed in great detail the importance of open and continuous communications. Make certain that you develop methods for implementing positive communications with your sponsors. Some event organizers use newsletters to update their sponsors, others provide regular briefings, and still others offer their sponsors marketing seminars to help them design a booth or target their product or service to event guests. It is wise to assign one or more persons on your staff to service all sponsorships and communicate regularly with sponsors to make certain they remain informed, excited, and committed to the event activities.

Another reason that some sponsorships go sour is the inability of the event organizers to deliver what they promise. If you promise that the sponsor's banner will be suspended on the main stage above the head of the performing artist, you must first confirm with the artist that this is acceptable. It is unacceptable to renege later on your commitment to the sponsor. It is always best to underpromise and overdeliver when stating the benefits of sponsorship. Exceeding the sponsor's expectations is how you turn a one-year sponsorship into a five-year plan with options to renew forever.

Every sponsor has a hidden agenda. It can be as simple as the chair of the board wanting to meet his or her favorite celebrity or as complex as the sales manager's bonus and promotion decision resting on this particular sponsorship activity. Ask the sponsor's representative what else you need to know about the needs of his or her organization as you design the sponsorship measurement system. For example, if the sponsor's representative is in the public relations department, his or her interest may be in seeing lots of ink and television time devoted to the name of the sponsor. Therefore, you will want to measure these outcomes carefully to assist your sponsor. Remember that you may sign a sponsorship agreement with a large corporation or organization, but the day-to-day management of this agreement is between people. Find out what these people desire and try to provide them with these outcomes.

Although communications between you and your sponsors is critical to your success, perhaps even more important are the internal communications between the Event Leader and his or her operations personnel. You must first confirm that your personnel will be able to support sponsorship activities at the level required by the individual sponsors. Determine if you have sufficient internal resources to satisfy the requirements both in contract as well as implied to ensure the well-being of your sponsor's investment. For example, if your sponsor wants a hospitality setup arranged at the last minute, do you have a catering operation that can handle this request? One way to ensure that the sponsors' needs are handled expeditiously is to create a written system of orders, changes, and other instructions that clearly communicates those activities required by your sponsors. Prior to distribution of these forms, have the sponsor's representative sign one copy. Then have the event's representative initial approval before forwarding it to the appropriate department or team leader.

Evaluating Sponsorships

To secure multiple-year sponsorships, it is important that you develop and implement a system for measuring the sponsor's activities. First, decide what needs to be evaluated and why. The answers to these questions typically may be found in the goals and objectives of the sponsorship agreement.

To collect these data, conduct sponsorship evaluations that are comprehensive in scope. You may wish to interview the sponsors, your own staff, the sponsor's target market, and others to solicit a wide range of opinions regarding the effectiveness of the sponsorship. Furthermore, you may wish to include in the event survey-specific questions about the sponsor's participation. Finally, ask the sponsor for tracking information regarding sales that have resulted from the sponsor's participation in your event.

You may measure the sponsor's public relations benefits by measuring the number of minutes of television and/or radio time, as well as the number of inches and columns of print media, that was devoted to the sponsor's products or name. List the comparable value using the 3:1 ratio provided by the Public Relations Society of America.

Ask the sponsor how the data you have measured should be presented. Some may prefer an elaborate in-person presentation using video clips and slides; others will prefer a simple summary of the goals, objectives, and outcomes that were achieved. Make certain that you present this information in a manner that is useful to the sponsor and that you take the time to prepare this presentation professionally to address the sponsor's needs. All future sponsorship activities will come from this important activity.

Timing Is Everything

The process for identifying, soliciting, negotiating, securing, servicing, and evaluating sponsorships is a complex one. However, as is true with most things, timing is everything. Allow a minimum of 12 to 18 months to formulate and consummate a successful sponsorship program. A typical timeline for the various stages just described follows here:

18 months in advance	Conduct needs assessment and research.
16 months in advance	Identify prospective sponsors.
14 months in advance	Develop and present proposals.
12 months in advance	Negotiate proposals and sign agreements.
9 months in advance	Implement sponsorship operations plan.
6 months in advance	Audit sponsor's changes and additions.
4 months in advance	Review changes and additions with staff.
2 months in advance	Meet with sponsor to provide update on event progress.
1 month in advance	Begin sponsor public relations campaign.
1 month after event	Meet with sponsor to provide analysis of results.

Although this schedule may be effective for most event sponsorship programs, there are exceptions that should be noted. For example, macroeconomic changes, such as the recent financial crisis, provide new short-term opportunities for some event organizers to approach certain organizations (banks and financial services providers) to continue their sponsorship through the internal community relations budget rather than their traditional marketing spend. This will allow those organizations that could greatly benefit from positive public relations to continue their investment and make the decision short term, albeit for a smaller amount of money, so the event continues to benefit from support.

Some event organizers have come to see sponsorship as the goose with the golden egg. However, while specific benefits come from individual sponsorships, prior to engaging in this time-consuming and expense-laden activity, an Event Leader must audit for each event the needs, resources available, and benefits offered. When developing sponsorship activities, always start small and build a base of sponsors year by year or event by event from your ability to deliver high-quality and successful events consistently. This is the best way to make sure that your goose lays a golden egg, not a rotten one, for your event organization.

Internet Event Marketing

Not since the invention of the printing press has advertising been changed as dramatically as with the introduction of the Internet. For example, the number of Internet users in the events industry grew from 50 percent to over 80 percent between 1996 and 1998. Today, virtually every event industry worker uses the Internet to search for resources, reserve or contact vendors, and promote continuous communication. Event marketing has now fully embraced the electronic marketplace. Reggie Aggarwal, CEO of Cvent (www.cvent.com), a leading Internet event-marketing firm, told the Convention Industry Council Forum attendees that "the fastest, most precise, easiest, and most cost affordable way to reach prospective event attendees is through e-mail." According to Aggarwal, the penetration of the Internet will soon be 100 percent and will soon be equal to or even replace traditional television and radio in some segments as an electronic source for daily information and communications.

Cvent is one example of how the technological revolution is driving the Event Leadership industry. Aggarwal started the firm after he used e-mail invitations and reminders to promote registration for a local association that he directed. He soon discovered that he could increase the response rate significantly and better target his prospects using e-mail communications. For example, Cvent.com technology enables meeting and event planners not only to send e-mail messages but also to note whether they have been read. Direct-mail marketers cannot monitor whether their communications are read; they can only note when a purchase or inquiry has been received. This innovation gives Cvent a competitive edge in the event market because the firm can determine quickly whether the e-mail event invitation has been opened and read. If it has been opened, the event marketer can assume that there is interest and build on that interest with follow-up communications. This customized marketing approach is one of the many benefits of the new technologies that are being developed to assist event marketers.

When developing event marketing, Internet marketing must be considered as a central part of any strategy. For example, regardless of size, all events should have a Web presence through a dedicated Web home page, a banner on an existing Web home page, or a link to a separate page. Following are points to consider when developing a comprehensive e-marketing event strategy:

- Identify your event market segments and targets.
- Design your Web strategy to reach your target market quickly, efficiently, and precisely.
- Use a focus panel of prospective event attendees to review your plans and suggest modifications to your overall design.
- Audit and evaluate the competition to determine how your Web presence can be more effective.
- Match the color scheme and design components to your printed matter.
- Determine whether you require a separate home page for your event or a link from an existing home page to a unique page.
- Identify and establish links with all marketing partners.
- Determine whether you will need a transaction page and ensure security for your ticket buyers.
- Determine whether you, your staff, or others can build the pages and/or make changes should they be needed.
- If consultants are contracted to build your site or pages, determine how they will be maintained (frequency, speed, and reliability).
- Use viral marketing (e-mails copied to prospective attendees) to promote your event.

- Use search engines to promote your event, with careful selection and registration of your URL.
- Use e-mail reminders to increase attendance during the last two weeks of an event.
- Use online registration systems.
- Use online evaluation systems to collect survey information before, during, and after an event.
- Use online chat rooms to create discussion areas for preregistered attendees and to generate follow-up discussion post-event.
- Carefully monitor all online activity for potential data mining to determine future needs, wants, and desires of your target audience.

The Internet will continue to drive the development of the global Event Leadership industry. You must use this dynamic technology quickly and accurately to ensure that your event remains competitive throughout the twenty-first century.

Event-Marketing Evaluation

Aggarwal and I coined the term *return on event* (ROE) in 2000 to identify the percentage of earnings returned to an event organization sponsoring the event based on marketing efforts. The ROE is an important concept for all event marketers, regardless of event size. For example, if you are marketing a small event for 100 persons and you increase attendance by 25 percent due to your new e-marketing strategies, you may, in fact, not only have saved a significant amount of money but also have generated a sizable net profit that may be directly attributable to this marketing activity. Figure 9.3 outlines how this formula may be used to identify the ROE.

The income statement shows a significant increase in total revenues in Year 2 as well as a slight increase in net income. Now we measure the increase in return on marketing and see how the marketing function performed as part of the overall financial analysis (Figure 9.4). By careful monitoring, tracking, and measuring of each marketing activity, you are able to identify that, in Year 2, your event generated a 160 percent return on marketing investment as compared to Year 1, with only 39 percent. To monitor, track, and measure each of these separate marketing functions, you need to use a variety of simple but effective systems.

Coding

Make certain that you assign a unique code to each marketing response item. For example, if you allow your attendees to register by mail, phone, newspaper, radio, and Internet, each marketing channel should have a separate code. Figure 9.5 demonstrates how to code and track each response. By identifying the response ratios from each marketing channel, you are better able to adjust your marketing efforts during the promotional period prior to the event and evaluate where to place your marketing dollars in the future.

	Year 1	Year 2
Expenses		
Advertising		
Newspaper	$25,000	$35,000
Radio	$15,000	$20,000
Television	$50,000	$60,000
Direct mail		
Design and printing	$10,000	$10,000
Postage	$5,000	$5,000
Internet	$10,000	$15,000
Promotions	$5,000	$5,000
Public Relations	$5,000	$10,000
Subtotal	$120,000	$160,000
Income		
Ticket sales	$100,000	$125,000
Sponsorships	$25,000	$45,000
Subtotal	$125,000	$170,000

Figure 9.3 Measuring the Return on an Event: Income Statement for Family Festival of Fun

Expenses	Year 1	Year 2	Penetration (%)	Response (%)
Advertising				
Newspaper	$25,000	$35,000	25–40	5–10
Radio	$15,000	$20,000	10–15	1–5
Television	$50,000	$60,000	5–7	20–25
Direct mail				
Design and printing	$10,000	$10,000		
Postage	$5,000	$5,000	75–85	5–10
Internet		$15,000	0–55	1–90
Promotions	$5,000	$5,000	1–2	3–10
Public relations	$5,000	$10,000	5–7	5–10
Subtotal	$120,000	$160,000		39–160

Figure 9.4 Evaluating the Return on an Event

		Total		
Response Method	Code	Year 1	Year 2	Response (%)
Direct mail	DM99	100	200	<100
Internet	IN99	1000	3000	<200
Newspaper				
Daily Courier	DC99	1000	1200	<20
Weekly Standard	WS99	500	750	<25
Radio				
WLAC	R-WLAC	15	25	<10
WPIR	R-WPIR	10	15	<5
Television	WNEW	150	300	<100

Figure 9.5 Coding and Tracking Event-Marketing Responses

Determining the return on your event accomplishes three fundamental purposes that are critical to your future marketing success:

1. You are able to track where your responses are being generated.
2. You are able to compare investment versus actual marketing performance by each channel.
3. You are able to compare return on marketing with other economic performance indicators, such as risk management, labor, and utilities, on an annual basis and determine whether you need to increase or reduce the budget accordingly to achieve your revenue targets in future years.

Online versus Other Marketing Channels

The online marketing environment that seems to permeate most marketing decisions today must be seen as one, not the only, form of attracting, persuading and converting customers to attend your event. Too often, some event organizers solely rely on one marketing channel such as e-mail promotion to drive attendance at their event. In fact, most event attendees require multiple touch points to ensure that there is sufficient opportunity to reach the potential event attendee. Therefore, the process shown in Figure 9.1 demonstrates how to reach the event guests through multiple touch points to increase the likelihood of their participation in your event.

Other Marketing Evaluation Tools

The ROE is a quantitative system for evaluating marketing response. However, in addition to quantifying your responses, you must also qualify them. Using a focus panel to review marketing promotional campaigns, including ink colors, logo design, and copy, will help you fine-tune your visual impressions to match the tastes of your prospective event attendees.

You may also wish to use personal interviews to determine why nonattendees refuse to accept your invitation to participate in your event offer. These telephonic interviews can reveal important information that will help you in marketing your event in the future. For example, a nonattendee may reveal that he has trouble finding a babysitter. If this comment is replicated with a large enough sample, you may wish to consider offering on-site child care to increase attendance by families with young children or add more children's activities to your event programming.

The overall benefits associated with marketing should not be focused solely on the economic performance of an event. Remember, even if someone did not attend your event, he or she may have recommended it to others. Furthermore, he or she may be positively influenced to attend in the future. Following are some of the qualitative areas you may wish to measure in your marketing analysis and measuring techniques for each:

- Image improvement: survey, interviews, focus panel
- Recall of event name: interviews, focus panel
- Recall of event slogan: interviews, focus panel
- Increase in number of volunteers: survey, focus panel
- Increase in sponsorship: focus panel, survey
- Increase in gifts (philanthropy): interviews, survey
- Improved political relations: interviews
- Improved media relations: interviews, clipping, and clip monitoring
- Improved community relations: interviews, focus panel

The overall purpose of marketing analysis and evaluation is to provide you with the essential information you need to make better decisions in the future. Whether your event is one that recurs year after year or is a one-time affair, the data you collect from your marketing analysis will help you in the development of many different types of future events. Make certain that you assign a line item in the event budget for marketing evaluation. Some of the typical costs include: survey development and printing; focus panel facilitation; interviewer fees; data collection, tabulation, and analysis; and report writing. In addition, you may wish to contract with third parties, such as a clipping services firm, to track the media generated about your event. Your ability to measure the return on marketing for your event comprehensively will provide you with dividends for many years to come. Do not miss this opportunity to improve your competitiveness, your event's image, and your profitability now and in the years to come.

Leonard Hoyle Jr. suggests that the following trends will influence event marketing in the near future:

1. Through improved technological delivery, such as wireless application protocol (WAP), you will be able to better promote your event in real time through cell phones and other wireless systems.

2. Through faster technology (broadband), you will be able to send much more information to potential attendees at faster and faster speeds.
3. A wide range of new media outlets (including schools, colleges, clubs, amusement parks, and other locations) will develop where your potential target market can receive your message.
4. Your copywriters will need to develop a new vocabulary to communicate effectively with new event consumers, including generations X and Y.
5. Event marketers will be able to achieve greater success if they emphasize the health benefits associated with attending their events as the baby boomers age and generations X and Y have greater interest in health and wellness.
6. A seamless registration system, wherein the consumer can arrange transportation, registration, accommodation, tours, restaurant reservations, and much more with a visit to one Internet site, will be essential for event marketers to remain competitive.
7. As the multicultural trend continues to escalate, it is essential that event marketers use multiple languages to communicate with their constituencies.
8. Due to heightened concerns about terrorism, event marketers must focus their messages on safety and security and also emphasize the need to be there to benefit fully from the event.

In addition to Hoyle's eight points, it is increasingly important for event planners to embrace yield management in their pricing. As event tickets are perishable and individuals may have fewer dollars due to redundancies, layoffs and long-time unemployment, the event organization that offers discounts and even free tickets for certain groups may win in two big ways. First, they will increase their overall attendance which may lead to greater per capita spending, and second, they will be growing their audiences for the future because these individuals who are now receiving discounts or free admission will one day be ticket buyers and even potential future sponsors.

Career-Advancement Connections

Corporate Social Responsibility Connection

Event planners may contribute to CSR by partnering with nonprofits and charities to ensure a positive, ethical outcome from an event. Leftover food can be donated to a local homeless shelter and excess tradeshow giveaways (pencils, pens, paper) can be donated to a local schools. These charitable sponsorships show off your commitment to CSR and give guests the pride of doing good deeds. Likewise, many corporate sponsors are eager to support charitable initiatives for PR purposes. Read the business section of the newspaper to find which corporations are receiving bad press, then offer these corporations a highly

The Pioneer: Andrea Michaels President,Extraordinary Events, Sherman Oaks, California

Andrea Michaels, an inductee in the Event Solutions Event Industry Hall of Fame and recipient of multiple Special Events Magazine Gala Awards for excellence in event design and production, actually entered the special events industry by accident. According to Andrea, "While going to college I took on a part time job for a bandleader. While typing and filing for him I came to realize that in the early 1970s there really was no event industry, and I tried to imagine what it could be. Didn't know what exactly, just knew there were possibilities that were unexplored. After I left the bandleader to go out and save the world (but didn't), he called me and said he agreed that there were possibilities and if I wanted to, I should come back and explore them and develop them. I loved this challenge and accepted. The rest is history."

Early on in her career, Andrea knew this was the right path for her future life because she was able to use her creativity, her imagination, and her need to take risks. She says, "I loved seeing my dreams become realities. I loved meeting and working with creative people and dreaming up creative environments that would be "experiences" for people. There were not enough hours in the day to do all I wanted to do, and that's how I knew it was the right career for me."

During her long and successful career, Michaels has seen many changes. She observes, "I started with a typewriter and mail. Then, we purchased a fax machine. And later a mobile phone, which weighed a ton at first and it was when it was first introduced and was known as a 'car phone.' Next, computers came along and they initially terrified me, along with their programs such as Word Perfect. By contrast, today the event business is conducted in nanoseconds. Overnight mail, computers, all lead to immediate responses. I feel that all of this technology often handicaps authentic creativity that takes time and thought and cannot always happen with the immediacy that is available from technology."

Another major change she describes is in budgeting for events. "You always see ups and

visible sponsorship opportunity for a charitable, positive cause. For example, as coal-power companies lose public credibility, they will increasingly be eager to sponsor renewable energy initiatives. Get your local gas company to sponsor your solar-powered stage!

downs in budgets in the events industry," notes Andrea, and she adds, "The cost of producing a quality event product has not decreased, but the monies allocated to making an event great have decreased dramatically. Budgets are also transparent nowadays and clients are educated in terms of what things cost so there's no room to provide economic padding in budgets." Additionally, she states that event professionals are dealing with corporate procurement and/or purchasing departments who look at where the dollar sign and decimal point are placed and not at the real value, just "what does it cost" and they often base decisions on that factor alone.

On a positive note, she states that today there is a huge available work force. However, she observes that some young people want enormous salaries and feel a sense of entitlement to get them. According to Andrea, "They sometimes come to us without life experience, just theoretical learning and do not feel like they have to pay their dues. Today, generation Y values their leisure time, vacations and freedom and feel that if they want to spend half of their paid day on Facebook or surfing the Web, that's their right. It's very different from the way I was raised."

Andrea believes the environment will be a key factor in the future development of the events industry. She recalls that when she started in 1973 no one cared about the environment as it related to events. However, she still finds that people are merely paying lip service to these initiatives. According to Andrea, "A few companies want to be 'green' or socially responsible, but rarely if it costs more or interferes with a good time for their guests. I do, however, see that changing."

As Andrea looks to the future of the industry she helped to cultivate, she sees one that is more and more transparent, where less costs may be hidden, where we'll have to prove our value in everything we do, and where there will be great attention to the detail and perfection of product. However, she also believes that more and more business will be conducted virtually through online tools rather than in person. She cautions, "As clients can access information on the Web, they'll think they can design and produce events themselves. More and more people will enter our industry and competition will be fierce."

Her sage advice to newcomers entering the special events industry is the same she would offer to those entering any business endeavor. Andrea says, "Surround yourself with the best people money can buy (that includes a great lawyer and a great accountant) and treat them like gold, with honesty, integrity and generosity, because they will make you into a hero. Give back with your whole heart. Mentor others. Teach others. Share information. Always tell the truth. Treat everyone you encounter as if they and they alone were the most important person in your life. Realize that you are valuable and never discount that with clients, vendors, or associates."

Global Connection

When marketing to two or more cultures, make certain that you use focus group research to review all marketing communications. Simply translating a marketing slogan into a language other than English will not always achieve the meaning or intent you require. Furthermore, some cultures are sensitive to certain colors and

The Protégé: Orit Blatt
MTA, graduate, George Washington University Department of Tourism and Hospitality Management, Event Management Concentration
Senior Account Manager, Extraordinary Events, Sherman Oaks, California

Orit Blatt's first stop after graduating was Los Angeles. She recalls, "When I interviewed with Extraordinary Events, I really had no idea what I was getting myself into." She finally realized that she had what it takes and that this was what she wanted to do when she was part of the team that produced a conference in Barcelona, Spain in 2002. She says, "After a year of planning, every piece of the pie fell in place, every challenge was conquered, the client was thrilled, and the attendees were thanking us for an amazing experience. The sense of team, the feeling of camaraderie and the sense of accomplishment left me wanting

may not respond favorably to your design. Convene a focus panel composed of people from various cultures to review your marketing plan and designs prior to implementation.

Technology Connection

Use desktop publishing software to create simple advertisements, flyers, brochures, and other print matter. Use the Internet to distribute your media releases to targeted media. Use audio and video news releases (ANRs and VNRs) to broadcast your event news item to television and radio stations worldwide.

Resource Connection

The Public Relations Society of America (www.prsa.org) publishes the informative *PR Journal,* which documents the latest trends in public relations research and methodology. The American Advertising Federation (www.aaf.org) offers

more. It was at the end of the final night party that I recognized that I had been bitten by the bug. I didn't want this feeling to end. I longed for more."

Orit believes that in the future, being "green" won't just be a saying. She believes, "Standards will be developed, guidelines will be set and markers put in place that measure the success and positive effects being green has on the environment. This spans the entire events industry, not just using recyclables, but even into the development of biodiesel generators, organic food design and so on. The events industry will be a leader in creativity and delivery of events and messaging in the greenest way possible."

When looking to the future, she says, "People will always need to get together to meet, celebrate and recognize achievements and milestones as well as strategize during challenging times. They will however, be far more critical regarding budget allocations as well as how the money is spent. I think it would be prudent in some way to educate the public on how big the industry really is and the positive impact that we have on the economy both in revenue and job placement."

Orit says that, "As an event planner you are tasked with juggling many different elements and communicating with a number of different people. It is a fast-paced, high energy profession that requires you to not only be a good communicator but also a good listener." Orit recommends that future Event Leaders listen to what people are saying to them: "Take away the message and apply it in a way that lets them know you have understood them. I apply this advice every day. It has helped me connect with people, create long-lasting relationships, earn trust as well as a competitive edge that can't be matched."

extensive research information at the World Advertising Research Center. The International Events Group (www.sponsorship.com) offers an annual sponsorship seminar that includes informative seminars concerning how to find, recruit, and keep sponsors. The American Marketing Association (www.ama.org) *Journal of Marketing* offers an online journal that includes marketing research and many other resources. The most comprehensive book on the subject of event marketing, *Event Marketing* (Hoyle 2002), is part of the John Wiley & Sons Event Management series.

 Learning Connection

Develop a marketing plan for your event that identifies the competitive advantages, target market(s), strategies, tactics, budgets, schedule, and evaluation methodologies. Describe how you will increase your marketing performance through creative and innovative tactics, despite a significant reduction in the marketing budget.

Online and consumer-generated media, such as weblogs or social media such as Facebook, are increasing the best, most efficient, and most effective way to bring your guests to your event.

CHAPTER 10

Online Marketing and Consumer-Generated Media

In this chapter you will learn how to:

- Understand the role, scope, and potential of online consumer-generated media to advance your event
- Establish a powerful and effective event presence through online social media
- Differentiate the major advantages in online marketing
- Maximize event Internet marketing opportunities
- Determine the major types of Web sites and their characteristics
- Identify, prevent, and correct common mistakes in Web site management
- Include security and confidentiality for your URL
- Incorporate special features for your URL
- Develop and effectively utilize blogs and podcasts to promote your event
- Measure and evaluate the data collected through your online marketing activities

There is no question that the development of the Internet has become the most important communication and marketing breakthrough since the printing press in the mid-fifteenth century. It has fundamentally reshaped our understating of sales and marketing. However, because so few years have passed since the Internet became available for widespread public use, the marketing tools used in cyberspace are still works in progress. You must now take an active role in developing Internet marketing rules, standards, and benchmarks for planned events.

Role and Scope of Online Consumer-Generated Media

Some marketing theorists observe that consumers wish to be fully engaged in the product or service experience before they will recommend or advocate their positive opinion to others. Therefore, a live planned event provides a tremendous opportunity to turn your prospective and actual guests into, as marketing guru Guy Kawasaki suggests, *evangelists* who will rave to others about your event.

To expose, fully engage, and totally experience your event, you must use multiple touch-points, including online consumer-generated media, to turn your casual guest into a raving evangelist who will tell everyone about your event. Thanks to social networking Web sites such as Bebo, Facebook, Linkedin, Tagged, Twitter, and others, this has become much easier. Furthermore, as the Internet has quickly penetrated many more channels thanks to mobile technology, it is infinitely possible to stay in touch with your guest at all times.

The role of online consumer-generated media is to provide your prospective and actual guests with the opportunity to become better informed and to fully participate in your event before, during, and after the actual event experience. By creating a 360-degree online event environmental opportunity for your guests, you are literally surrounding them with opportunities to learn and grow through their own predetermined levels of participation.

Internet Marketing for Events

The Internet can be a highly efficient tool in marketing events. At the same time, it can be a major financial burden if your organization does not formulate specific goals for its Internet marketing policy. The objectives for each event-management organization may vary depending on company size, dynamics of operations, financial and staff resources, location, overall development strategy, and client base. The Web site for a small planned events startup will differ from that of a large multinational conglomerate. Major marketing concepts enhanced by online tools include brand building, direct marketing, online sales and online commerce, customer support, market research, and product or service development and testing.

Leonard Hoyle, in *Event Marketing* (2002), states that there are six advantages of Internet marketing for your event.

1. Internet marketing can help build and extend your brand.
2. Internet marketing eliminates many of the costs customarily associated with direct mail.
3. You can immediately begin making online sales in an interactive and secure environment.
4. By posting frequently asked questions (FAQs), you can provide easy access to commonly sought information.
5. Through conducting online surveys and analyzing the data from Web visits and transactions, you may acquire valuable marketing research.
6. You can use the Web to publish information that has resulted from your event (abstracts, papers, and reports).

Brand Building

Online marketing—combined with television, media, and print—is a major brand-building tool. The biggest advantage the Internet has over television and old-fashioned media is the favorable cost/benefit ratio. Events organizations can achieve a much higher return on their marketing investments in Internet promotions than in a traditional campaign. The research conducted by Millward Brown Interactive, a 20-year-old international advertising research group, found that an organization can achieve significant progress in brand recognition simply by placing its logo on banners of search engines or online databases. It is important for your organization to secure the presence of its logo on the Web. You can start simply by trading space on the banner section of your Web site with a partner organization. You place your logo on your partner's Web site and create a hyperlink from his or her Web site to yours, in exchange for placing your partner's information on your Web site. It is very important to submit your company's profile to all major search engines. A few years ago, when students were conducting a search on Yahoo! using the key words *event management*, they obtained only a few matches, whereas now there are thousands. Submitting your company's profile to most search engines is free, so there is no reason not to do it.

Use these four steps to register your Web site with a search engine:

1. Enter a search engine (Google, AltaVista, DogPile, Yahoo!, Bing, etc.).
2. Go to "register your site."
3. Carefully describe your site's profile using tag words that describe you.
4. After submitting your site, test the search engine by searching for your tag words.

Raising Your Search Engine Profile

You may purchase advertising on the search engines that best represent and reach your target markets or you may also work behind the scenes to try and move your event profile to a higher listing within a search engine. Text Link Brokers.com (www.textlinkbrokers.com) has examined thousands of Web sites to develop the best strategies for improving your overall Web site optimization. This process is known as search engine optimization, or simply SEO. The first step to improve your SEO is to conduct research. Figure 10.1 provides six steps to SEO Success for Your Event.

Although there are search engine optimization consulting firms who may be able to help you achieve your online goals, they may be beyond the budget for your individual event or event organization. However, the six tips could be a first step in optimizing your search engine performance to boost the visibility of your events Web site.

Online Marketing

According to Bruce Ryan, vice president and general manager of Media Metrix (a research firm that studies Web users' characteristics and profiles), in 2002 more than 80 percent of personal computer (PC) owners had at least one college degree. Their average household income was at that time about $50,000 per year, well above the $35,000 U.S. household average. These consumers could be a prime market niche for planned events organizations. Customers with household incomes of less than $40,000 per year often cannot afford to contract a professional event planner. By placing well-designed information and ads about your event planner services on the Internet, you gain immediate, direct contact with your target market group. In addition, on the Internet, larger competitors have no significant advantage over smaller organizations.

Online Sales and Security

An online sales concept is more applicable to companies that sell consumer goods (such as Amazon.com), not services. However, this is changing, and there are now many consulting sites online to provide event services. Planned events organizations may still benefit greatly from online, electronic commerce features. Planned events organizations conduct registration, ticket sales, and distribution of materials over the Internet. All of these are segments of event sales. By putting them online, planned events companies achieve financial savings and preserve resources that can now be reallocated.

Among the most important problems of online commerce is the problem of security. If an event planning organization conducts financial transactions over the Internet, security of clients' personal financial information is the top priority. Data that contain such information as credit card and Social Security numbers are highly sensitive. It is important to ensure that these data are protected. Since this is a critical point, it is highly recommended that you involve security professionals in this aspect of your Web site development. Many smaller and medium-sized events organizations utilize online transaction tool

1. Carefully and precisely research, profile, and identify the target audience for your Web site.
2. Pick the most effective key words to write your copy. You may wish to use tools such as Yahoo's Keyword Suggestion Tool. (www.sem.smallbusiness.yahoo.com/searchenginemarketing.com). Take your time to assemble about 200 words and check your progress in the search box. Google may be of help to you (www.adwords.google.com) in identifying key words. Once you have assembled a large number of key words you may wish to use Wordtracker (www.wordtracker.com), which will evaluate your key words and help you see which ones will be most effective in spreading your message to your target audience.
3. Now you are ready to write your Web pages. Make certain you use the fully optimized key word phrases four to nine times per page.
4. The next step is to optimize your pages. This is done by adding optimized meta tags. According to Rob Sullivan, SEO expert of Text Link Brokers.com:

   > The meta description should be a readable sentence or two with the same keywords that you wrote the page for. In other words, the same phrases should appear in the meta description as the body. They should also appear as near to the front of the tag as possible; however don't sacrifice readability for this. If the tag doesn't make sense with them at the front, then reorganize until they do make sense. Be sure to use proper punctuation as well.
   >
   > (Sullivan, Text Link Brokers.com, 2009)

5. Sullivan recommends that you write a compelling title tag for each section of your Web site. Here is an example of how to use bold typeface to raise your profile.

   key phrase in title tag **key phrase** in title tag title tag with key phrase **key phrase in title**

   According to Sullivan, the third line will stand out and be more readily recognized by Google and other search engines because the key term is in a different position from your competition. Therefore, it is important for you to carefully study the competition prior to writing your Web pages.
6. Constantly utilize tools such as Google Analytics (www.google.com/analytics) to determine how your Web site is performing and make adjustments periodically to improve its performance.

Adapted from 5 Tips to a Perfectly Optimized Web Page, Rob Sullivan, www.textlinkbrokers.com/blog.

Figure 10.1 SEO Event Success Tips

PayPal to help ensure secure transactions for their customers (www.paypal.com). PayPal uses VeriSign as its encrypted security service to protect data and transactions.

Furthermore, they, along with eBay and other major online sellers use SSL certificates (Secure Socket Layers), which allow Web site visitors and customers to further trust your security measure in three ways. First, an SSL certificate enables *encryption* of sensitive information during online transactions. Second, each SSL certificate contains unique, *authenticated* information about the certificate owner. Finally, a certificate authority *verifies* the identity of the certificate owner when it is issued. Therefore, it is critically important that when designing your events Web site that you incorporate careful pre-planning to ensure financial and data protection security for your customers.

Customer Support

Event customer support is one of the areas where the Internet can prove truly indispensable. To date, few event companies have realized the full potential of this opportunity. Industry analysts predict that, in coming years, many event companies will shift their telephone customer support services to the Web. This does not mean that telephone-based services will disappear, but they will become a secondary source that customers will use if they need to get a more detailed response or resolve a problem. The primary source will be the Internet.

The first step in shifting at least part of your customer support services online is to start a Frequently Asked Questions (FAQ) section of your Web site. Simply by adding this section to your Web site, you can achieve better customer service and improve efficiency. Before the Event Management Certificate Program at George Washington University started an FAQ Web section in 1998, a large portion of all questions that the program received from students was about the same issues: location of classes, directions, and the registration process. By posting answers to these frequently asked questions on the Web, GWU contributed greatly to customer satisfaction and enhanced the overall positive image of the program.

The next step after posting an FAQ page is to personalize online customer service. This may be accomplished by adding an interactive feature to a customer-support site. A customer is asked to type his or her question and submit an e-mail address. Then the customer receives an answer within a certain time frame via either e-mail or telephone. By adding this feature, an event organization can achieve much more personalized customer service and can also collect valuable data about its clients. Whenever possible, it should be easy and efficient for the caller to contact a live person if they have additional questions. If this is not possible through the use of existing resources, the caller should be able to receive a return telephone call from a customer service professional within a specified period of time.

Market Research

Increasingly, events organizations are recognizing the Internet potential for market research. Burke, Inc., a leading international market research firm with a history of over 65 years, conducts online focus-group meetings for its clients in addition to face-to-face interviews and telephone surveys. Using Internet technology, the company was able to bring together participants from different parts of the world for small, real-time chat sessions. Clients can observe these chat sessions from anywhere in the world. Software such as Aptex, Autonomy, Adforce, and Accrue can monitor users' behavior constantly. This information can then be used to improve the site or services or to personalize content for users.

Your Web site can be used to conduct market research by surveying visitors. This information can be effective if the process is well-planned. Unfortunately, many websites require users to complete online registration forms without providing incentives. As a result, users often submit incorrect information or simply ignore the forms. This behavior may be explained by the desire of users to guard their privacy online and fear that their e-mail addresses will be sold to third parties. The best way to overcome this constraint is to build a sense of trust between the event organization and clients or to compensate users for submitting their data. One excellent example of online polling is used by www.event-solutions.com.

Product or Service Development and Testing

The Internet is an ideal place for event companies to test new products and services before they are launched. An event organization can post information about a conference that it is planning to organize online and monitor the interest that users express toward the conference. By doing this, the organization can see a market's reaction to the conference before it invests large amounts in actual planning. This testing refers to the first stage of successful events, event research. One of the biggest advantages that the Internet has over other marketing tools is real-time contact. Marketing professionals use a number of special technical features to leverage this point. Chat rooms, live broadcasting, and time-sensitive promotions are only a small part. The Internet allows marketing professionals to change and update content in almost no time, ensuring that customers have the most recent information.

Web Design and Management

Event marketing specialists today speak about second and third generations of Web sites. The best definition I have heard of all three types of online marketing development comes from Jupiter Communication, a leading Internet research firm based in New York. The company's analysts describe three types of Web sites, from least to most effective from the Internet marketing point of view:

1. *Brochureware* is the name for the first and least developed type of Web site. This type of Internet material has long been recognized as primitive and boring. Web sites of this type are static and contain basic information about an organization, including its address and services. The site reflects a paper brochure placed on the Web. These kinds of sites miss the entire idea of marketing on the Web, and their effectiveness today is not very high.
2. *Show-biz* is the name for the second group of Web sites. These sites try to amuse visitors through interactive features, flashing pictures, news reports, or press reviews. Although these features can serve the purpose of making an organization's Web site more attractive, often they are not appropriate for the content and only distract the viewer's attention.

3. *Utilitarian* is the last and most developed type of Web site. These sites offer viewers a unique and balanced interactive service that is both highly informative and helpful in building brand recognition and loyalty. A classic example mentioned by Rick E. Bruner in *Net Results: Web Marketing That Works* (1998) is FedEx online services. The company's Web site does not contain a lot of flashy effects, is easy to navigate, and contains useful features, such as shipment tracking and customer address books. The result of such a high-performing online marketing strategy is that, today, about two-thirds of all FedEx customer contacts are conducted electronically. In addition to offering great customer service via the Internet, the company's Web site saves millions of dollars a year in regular customer support costs and marketing expenses.

Blogs and Podcasts

The relatively new phenomena of blogs and podcasts are dramatically changing the online marketing environment for special events. These new tools are the offspring of consumer-generated media (CGM) where online content is created and managed entirely by consumers. As a result of CGM, e-pinions, or online consumer opinions, are formed. The forums for these e-pinions are often blogs. A blog is a Web log of comments and opinions created, controlled, and driven directly by consumers. Obviously, in the democratic world of the Internet, these opinions can both help and harm your ability to market your event. A site for developing a blog is www.blogger.com. You may list your blog on search engines such as www.newsgator.com or www.bloglines.com. One example of using a blog to promote travel and tourism events is the Homecoming Scotland 2009 event blog at www.homecomingscotlandblog.blogspot.com.

Additional tools that are the result of CGM include podcasts and wikis. A podcast may be audio or video or both and provides brief, high-content information for consumers through streaming on the Internet. It can be used to promote entertainers or speakers who will appear at your event, as well as to provide instructions, information, and education for your participants or volunteers. The millennial generation loves podcasts because they can download them and listen to them at a later time. For a directory of podcasts, visit www.itunes.com or www.podcastalley.com.

According to experts in this field, there are about 10–20 million podcast listeners worldwide (Arbitron 2007), and this number is growing rapidly. According to Forrester research, the number of U.S. households who will listen to podcasts will increase to over 12 million by 2010 (BBC News 2006). For example, there are nearly 350 National Public Radio podcasts. Furthermore, in 2006, BRMB research stated that nearly 12 million Britains would go in search of podcasts within the next six months. In February 2006, over 1.7 million people downloaded a BBC podcast. (BBC News, 2006). Therefore, you should endeavor to have your podcast available through iTunes (www.itunes.com), which has become the most popular Internet download site.

The wiki is perhaps best exemplified by Wikipedia (www.wikipedia.org), which is the world's largest online consumer-generated encyclopedia. You may wish to list your event on a wiki site such as Wikipedia or create a wiki of your own to direct consumers to your event.

The rapidly growing online environment for promoting events will increasingly include blogs, podcasts, and RSS technology, which means Really Simple Syndication (RSS 2.0), Rich Site Summary (RSS 0.91, RSS 1.0), or RDF Site Summary (RSS 0.9 and 1.0). This is a family of Web feed formats used to transmit frequently updated digital content such as podcasts or other published materials through the Internet, as well as other advancements. You should continue to review consumer publications such as *Advertising Age* to keep abreast of these developments. The book *How to Do Everything with Podcasting* (Holtz and Hobson 2007) can also help event planners expand the footprint of their events through the Internet.

Video Streaming and YouTube™

The rapid expansion of global bandwidth within the Internet has greatly escalated the use of video streaming through platforms such as YouTube. Events organizations may use online video streaming before, during and following the event to share the highlights of their program with millions of Internet users throughout the world. Figure 10.2 provides

Before

- Conduct a competition for individuals and groups to submit a short video showing what they most love about your event. The video may then be shown on your event Web site.
- Develop a video training program to inform and train volunteers for your event and upload this to your event Web site.
- Develop a video interview with your event director announcing the highlights of your upcoming event.
- Stream videos of the speakers or entertainers who will appear at your upcoming meeting or event.
- Conduct on-the-street interviews with individuals who have attended your event and have them provide testimonials about why they will attend your event again.
- Produce a music video to promote your event and involve, if possible, celebrities providing testimonials. One excellent example is the Visit Scotland Caledonia video with actor Sir Sean Connery, Olympic Gold Medalist Sir Christopher Hoy, singer Sandi Thom, and others performing Dougie MacLean's well loved song of the same title (www.visitscotland.com).

During

- Provide daily, hourly, or simultaneous video feeds from your Web site.
- Conduct interviews with event attendees and upload their comments to your Web site.
- Conduct behind-the-scenes interviews with speakers and entertainers and upload these comments to your Web site.
- Conduct kitchen tours and interview the culinary team at your event and share these videos with your Internet visitors.

After

- Provide a highlights video of your event.
- Post testimonials from your volunteers describing how much fun it was to participate in your event.
- Promote next year's event with previews of new attractions, entertainers, and other key information.

Figure 10.2 Video Streaming Opportunities for your Event

examples of how to use Internet streaming to inform, educate, and persuade Internet users to support your event.

Often, event planners will shoot first rather than ready, aim, and then shoot. When producing videos or podcasts, however, it is critically important to secure permission in advance from the participants. This permission may be limited or very broad in scope. Regardless, you must secure, in writing, their permission to use their image in the pod or video cast for your event. If it is not possible to secure individual permissions, you may wish to post a sign at the entrance of your event that states that: "Video recording is taking place at this event. As a condition of entry, guests consent to being videotaped without compensation for future promotional purposes by the event."

For sample photo release forms in the US, visit:

http://www.asmp.org/commerce/legal/releases/custom_forms/

Or visit this site for UK sample photo release forms:

http://www.professionalphotographer.co.uk/Magazine/Downloads/Model-Release-Form

A good source for general knowledge about the legal issues affecting photographers and photography is *The Legal Handbook for Photographers, the Rights and Liabilities of Making Images* (Krages 2001).

Mobile Phone Marketing

The online environment has rapidly extended to mobile phone technology. Advertisers are regularly using mobile phone technology to market directly to consumers. Text messaging is rapidly evolving into full-motion video, and you can now send streaming video of your event directly to mobile phones. This technology has enormous potential for reaching the millennial generation. However, with every advancement in communications, there is also the increasing concern about privacy issues. Make certain you thoroughly research the laws and regulations regarding sending unsolicited advertisements through telecommunications systems prior to implementing your plan.

RFID Technology and Target Marketing

In 2006, at the fiftieth anniversary of their first convention, the Professional Convention Management Association (PCMA) launched a new service using laser registration (www.laser-registration.com) technology. This technology involves using radio frequency identification (RFID) to track the attendance of participants. A small microchip is attached to the name badge of the event participant. This microchip contains all of their critical information. In the future, this technology may be used to further target to whom you will market your event by determining levels of interest through tracking people's engagement at your event.

In addition to tracking attendance and participation (or lack of attendance and participation), this technology may also be used to segment your market to provide you with better return on marketing (ROM) investment. The ability to achieve higher return on event (ROE) will be a critical measurement tool for event organizers and marketers in the future.

The examples and models just described are applicable to many different professional services, including event planning. You can visit Web sites of various events organizations and observe how lack of proper planning or understanding of online marketing concepts results in boring Web sites, useless online questionnaires, and annoying e-mail listservs. At the same time, those events organizations that carefully plan their online activities and balance design and content succeed in achieving their Internet marketing goals.

Career-Advancement Connections

Corporate Social Responsibility Connection

You may wish to use your consumer-generated media to further inform or promote the values your event organization believes in. For example, if you have an outstanding environmental program, why not tell others through podcast, video stream, or blog? If your event organization is helping regenerate a destination through the construction of a new playground or rebuilding of homes through organizations such as Habitat for Humanity (www.habitat.org), you may not only help improve the external image for your event but also help further advance the mission you have exemplified through your event activities. Make certain you include in your podcast or blog the contact details for organizations who may benefit from your stakeholders' future support and participation.

Global Connection

Carefully evaluate the type of coding and bandwidth required for your data transmission. Remember that your ability to reach prospective event customers through the Internet depends largely on their communication infrastructure. Therefore, you must first determine if your target market can download your event e-marketing message easily and quickly. Also, be very careful to ensure that the design, color, and language are appropriate and effective for the market you are trying to influence.

Technology Connection

Familiarize yourself with these software applications: Microsoft FrontPage and Netscape Composer.

Resource Connection

Read these books about Internet marketing:

- Holtz, Shel, and Ted Demopoulos (2006). *Blogging for Business: Everything You Need to Know and Why You Should Care*. Chicago: Kaplan Publishing.

The Pioneer: Richard Aaron, CMP, CSEP, President, BizBash Media and Associate Professor, New York University's Preston Robert Tisch Center for Hospitality, Tourism and Sports Management

Richard Aaron was thrust into the field of special events from the world of Broadway Theater following a decade of acting in and directing numerous shows, both on and off Broadway in New York City. According to Richard, "Events encompassed the similar elements of staging, lights, and sound with pacing and content development and a sharper focus. I was right at home with my skill set in the world of events. I started entertaining at events and soon was working on organizing the entertainment for events. It all fell into place."

Richard recalls, "I was able to get onboard quickly with my skills and the field grew rapidly. I saw where it was all heading and expanding as a communication tool for organizations to entertain and extend their products and message in the most engaging fashion. I knew it was my future when I produced my first Roaring Twenties Casino in New York for the General Electric Company. I produced a sparkling entertainment showcase, designing an atmosphere and all the food according to a theme, which included shoot-outs in the streets of New York by costumed actors. This event was staged on four floors at the famous 21 Club in New York. From that moment, I was hooked on the excitement of this industry called Special Events."

Although Richard has had many mentors, he cites the legendary showman P.T. Barnum as a source of inspiration because, according to Richard, Barnum was the ultimate impresario. Richard states, "I read about him extensively and modeled many ideas as a promoter with his example to guide me."

- Holtz, Shel, John Havens and Lynne Johnson (2008). *Tactical Transparency: How Leaders Can Leverage Social Media to Maximize Value and Build their Brand.* San Francisco: Jossey-Bass.
- Li, Charlene and Josh Bernoff (2008). *Groundswell: Winning in a World Transformed by Social Technologies.* Boston: Harvard Business School Publishing.
- Weber, Larry (2009). *Marketing to the Social Web: How Digital Customer Communities Build Your Business.* Hoboken, NJ: John Wiley & Sons.

During his long career, he has seen many changes and he describes that the field has evolved in sophistication enormously. Richard says, "Now we have actual books on topics in a vast library covering event marketing and production and event design that did not exist previously. Strategy and tactics are now studied. Magazines provide environmental advice—such as information on LED lights for today's planners—that was unheard of when I began in this industry. Today computers, text messages, e-vites, and Internet-driven evaluation tools make event outcomes easy to analyze from attendees and make communication clear for the entire team.

He sees the future of special events as becoming a totally green event industry focused on sustainable events. Richard believes, "Organic food and flowers and resources with a low carbon footprint will be needed more and more in the future. LED lights and wireless sound and lighting will be readily available, making for an easy setup." He also envisions a dynamic series of online communities surrounding and engaged in events as they are occurring with social media employed to operate interactions at events to scale new heights.

Richard states that to be an effective, successful and outstanding event producer you must think 360 degrees at an event. Richard firmly believes, "You need to constantly survey the surroundings for the safety and comfort of your guests, monitoring the overall pacing to assure it does not fall short. Do develop keen antennae for everything in the realm of event operations to and assure they are at the highest standards possible. Do not dumb down quality or safety for any reason ever."

Richard Aaron, in addition to pioneering in the design, production, and promotion of live events, is also a great humanitarian who served as the founding chairman of the SEARCH Foundation (www.searchfoundation.org). The Search Foundation's mission since 1997 is to support special event professionals confronted with a catastrophic occurrence. It fosters, develops, and promotes educational initiatives for the advancement of the industry. Both on and off the special events stage, the enduring influence of Richard Aaron is far greater than even the legendary nineteenth-century showman Barnum could have conceived. Through his business leadership, humanitarian work, and mentoring of students, Richard has earned the respect and appreciation of thousands of people in the global events industry.

 Learning Connection

- Locate 15 event organizations randomly on the Internet using any search engine. Visit their Web sites and try to divide the sites into the three major categories described in this chapter.
- Develop a blog for your event.
- Create a podcast to inform and educate your volunteers about the policies and procedures of your event organization.

The Protégé: Robyn Jancovich-Brown, Second-year events student, former co-president of Professional Convention Management Association, Queen Margaret University, Edinburgh, Scotland

Robyn perhaps inherited her love of events from her mum, Katie Brown, who is a leader of events for the Kingdom of Fife Council in Scotland. However, Robin states that she had always enjoyed working and volunteering at events and wanted to change to a career that offered the possibility of travel, working within a "people environment," and new challenges and opportunities at every turn.

She further states, "I have always been a planner, and I love the excitement of seeing the outcome of my work visually. I definitely knew that this was the right field for me after talking with one of my lecturers about the skills that an event manager needs to possess. I realized that I not only possessed these, I enjoyed using them in day to day life."

Her mum, Katie, who is one of her mentors, has greatly influenced Robyn's career through her work on local grassroots-type festivals and events that involve hundreds of community members. In describing her mum, Robyn states, "I admire my mum as I have physically seen and been involved in a lot of the events she has organized, and each one has made me more enthusiastic about entering this field of work myself."

While she is only beginning her career in the events industry, she believes that this technology will have a big impact on the way events are produced, although she doesn't think that technology will ever be able to replicate or replace the live event. Robyn says, "Technological advances have the possibility to influence all areas of the event management process and will become an even larger issue and potential tool. I think that if the popularity of event studies continues to grow, then certification, especially in the United Kingdom and throughout Europe, could become a much more important and crucial part of working in the field."

Furthermore, Robyn believes that as the field of event studies grows and becomes more global, the need for better technology and education will push these changes. She also sees the growing trend of greener events and adds, "I also think that due to the world becoming more environmentally aware, options for physical resources (paperwork, etc.) will dwindle and become less popular and other alternatives will need to be found."

Ever confident about the future, Robyn feels that the events industry will continue to grow, as there will always be that need for physical contact and because people crave the atmosphere that can be created from special events when done right. She said, "Due to the current financial crisis, this need has been neglected, and once it starts to subside, peoples' desire for this type of contact and experience will return. I believe that this will create a sudden spike in demand. However, this should not be taken as an automatic indication of the growth of the industry."

Despite the omnipresence of social media such as Facebook, Robyn states that in order to succeed it is important to remember that "this is a people industry, and you have to be able to communicate and connect with people if you want to succeed. However, if you walk into a room full of people and feel intimidated—remember you will not be the only one."

Robyn states that after becoming more aware of how important it is to meet and know people in the events industry, the idea of networking—especially with those already established and educated in the field—was a scary thought at first. However, it helped her to remember that she is not the only person in the world who feels this way and she is no less professional for feeling nervous; it always makes it that much easier to approach people in the future.

Robyn Brown possesses the rare ability to not only see and understand her career challenges but also to overcome them by conquering her weaknesses and fears and forging ahead to connect people through events. As a leader and the co-founding president of the first chapter of the Professional Convention Management Association in Europe, Robyn also recognizes how important it is to organize groups of people around a common interest in order to help others. As a direct result of her mum's positive influence, her desire to connect people through events, as well as her confidence in meeting future challenges, her career opportunities are truly boundless in the global events industry.

PART FIVE

Legal, Ethical, and Risk Management

The Metropolitan Police prepare for a royal procession in London, England.

CHAPTER 11

Risk Management: Legal and Financial Safeguards

In this chapter you will learn how to:

- Recognize and comply with standard and customary event regulations and procedures
- Read, understand, and evaluate legal event documents
- Understand and comply with the general requirements of U.S. regulations related to the Sarbanes-Oxley Act
- Access, plan, manage, and control potential event liabilities
- Obtain necessary permits and licenses to operate events
- Develop and manage risk management procedures
- Understand and comply with environmental regulations governing events
- Comply with regulations governing sponsorship of conferences and meetings
- Maintain documentary evidence of compliance procedures

Whether you are the event planner for a wedding or the Olympic Games, according to risk management and safety expert Dr. Peter Tarlow, author of *Event Risk Management and Safety* (2002), "All events carry two risks, (1) the risk of a negative occurrence both on site and off site, and (2) the negative publicity that comes from this negative occurrence."

Tarlow, a sociologist and rabbi who has studied tourism and other types of events throughout the world, realizes that whenever we bring people together, there is an element of risk.

Most modern events have a potential for negligent activity that can lead to long and costly litigation. As the number of professionally managed events has increased, so has the concern for risk management and other legal and ethical issues. During the mid-1970s in the United States, many events were held to celebrate the 200th anniversary of American independence. During this period most events were organized by amateurs. As a result of a lack of understanding or training in risk management, there was a corresponding interest by the legal profession in bringing litigation against negligent event managers. This relationship continues today, with one notable difference. Event Leaders are becoming smarter with regard to legal, ethical, and risk management issues.

Attorney James Goldberg the author of *The Meeting Planners Legal Handbook* (http://assnlaw.com/publications.htm), addresses in this book critical issues for association meeting and event specialists such as taxation, antitrust issues, tort liability, and intellectual property challenges. In addition, Goldberg offers seminars and workshops. Courses are also being offered throughout the United States covering recent developments in the areas of legal, ethical, and risk management and Sarbanes-Oxley issues relating to Event Leadership. Perhaps the best evidence of this change has been the development of alternative dispute resolution (ADR) programs to avoid lengthy and expensive litigation. Indeed, the paradigm has shifted dramatically from an environment governed by ignorance to one where education and proactive measures may reduce the level of risk and the resulting cost to event organizers.

Sarbanes-Oxley Act

In 2002 the U.S. Congress approved and the president signed into law the Sarbanes-Oxley Act. According to the American Institute of Certified Professional Accountants (www.aicpa.org), the act, which generally applies only to publicly held companies and their auditing firms, dramatically affected these companies and the entire accounting profession. The legislation was created as a reaction to the court actions against U.S. companies such as Enron, MCI, WorldCom, and others.

As a direct result of this new legislation, there is much greater transparency in the accounting industry and within the companies they represent. For example, an auditor working for an accounting company must now report to a company's audit committee rather than only one or two executives within the firm. Furthermore, the chief executive officer of public companies must certify the auditing report; if there are errors, he or she may also face criminal prosecution.

Therefore, when you are producing events on behalf of a public company, it is important that you carefully review the Sarbanes-Oxley legislation (www.aicpa.org/info/Sarbanes-Oxley2002.asp) and seek counsel from your accountant as well as your client's accounting department regarding any specific compliance issues that may involve you as you comply with this new law.

Contracts, Permits, and Licenses

Most public events in the United States and other countries require some type of official permission to be held. The larger the event in terms of attendance or technical complexity, the more official oversight is usually required. Official review may come from local (town, city, county), state or province, or federal agencies. There are numerous reasons why an event must comply with existing laws and regulations. The four primary reasons are to protect your legal interests, to abide by ethical practices, to ensure the safety and security of your event stakeholders, and to protect your financial investment.

Protecting Your Legal Interests

Preparing proper contracts, researching the permits and licenses that are required, and complying with other legal requirements helps ensure that your event may proceed without undue interruption. Contracts or agreements may range from a simple letter or memorandum of understanding to complex multipage documents with lengthy riders (attachments). The Event Leader should utilize the services of competent legal counsel to review all standard agreements, such as hotel contracts, to ensure validity prior to execution. Furthermore, when writing new agreements, local legal counsel must make certain that the contract conforms to the code of the jurisdiction where it is written and executed (usually where the event takes place). Lawyers are admitted to the state bar in the United States and must be experts on the state code (laws). Therefore, it is important to use an attorney who is admitted to the state bar where your event is being held or where, in the case of litigation, the case may be tried.

The majority of permits and licenses will be issued by local agencies. However, some state, provincial, or federal authorities may also issue licenses for your event. Therefore, it is wise for the Event Leader to audit past and similar events carefully to identify the customary permits and licenses that are required for an event.

The permitting and licensing process may require weeks or even months to accomplish, so the Event Leader must carefully research each jurisdiction where he or she will produce an event and meet these time requirements. The cost for permits and licenses is typically nominal. However, some larger or high-risk events (such as Grand Prix auto racing) may require the posting of expensive bonds.

The major reasons why you must convince your event stakeholders of the importance of legal compliance and the need to obtain all necessary permits and licenses follow:

- Event Leaders are legally required to obtain certain permits and licenses to conduct many events. Failure to do so may result in fines, penalties, interest, or cancellation of an event.
- You have a fiduciary responsibility to event stakeholders to plan, prepare, and provide evidence of compliance. Avoiding compliance can have dire economic consequences.

- You have an ethical responsibility (as stated by various industry codes of ethics) to comply with all official regulations and to provide written agreements.
- Although an oral agreement may be binding, the written agreement usually takes precedence. Written agreements provide all parties with a clear understanding of the terms, conditions, and other important factors governing the event.
- One of the primary ultimate responsibilities of an Event Leader is to provide a safe environment in which to conduct an event.

Although developed countries have many more regulations and compliance requirements, developing countries are rapidly instituting controls to ensure the safe and legal operating of events.

Honoring Ethical Practices

One of the primary definitions of a profession is adherence to a code of ethical / professional conduct. As event planning has emerged as a modern profession, a code of ethics has been developed by professional associations such as Meeting Professionals International and the International Special Events Society. The code of ethics is different from biblical moral laws and from legal codes voted by governing bodies.

A code of ethics reflects what is standard and customary in both a profession and a geographic area. In that sense, it is somewhat elastic in that it is applied in various degrees as needed for different circumstances. For example, when a hotelier offers an event planner a complimentary lunch at the first meeting, should this be construed as a bribe by the event planner and, therefore, refused? Attorney Jeffrey King, an expert in the field of event legal procedures, states that he advises his event planner clients always to pay for their lunch when meeting with a hotelier for the first time. "This immediately lets the hotelier know that the relationship is equal and represents a business transaction," according to King. It also sets an ethical standard for future discussions and the building of a relationship.

Although many professional societies, including ISES, enforce their code of ethics with a grievance procedure, in most cases it is up to the event planner to determine what is and is not appropriate ethical behavior using the code of ethics as a guide. Robert Sivek of The Meeting House Companies, Inc., suggests that event planners use the front-page-of-the-newspaper rule. "Ask yourself if you would like to wake up and see your decision or action plastered across the front page of the newspaper," says Sivek. This may quickly determine whether your proposed action is one that is acceptable not only to you but to others in your events community. Ethics are covered in detail in Chapter 12.

Ensuring the Safety and Security of Event Stakeholders

A safe event environment implies that it is free from hazards. A secure environment is one that is protected from future harm. The event planner is responsible for constructing a safe, secure environment and sustaining it during the course of an event. Do not transfer this responsibility to others. The event planner either extends the invitation or coordinates the event at the invitation of others. You have both a legal and an ethical responsibility to event stakeholders to design and maintain a safe and secure event environment.

Protecting Your Financial Investment

The legal, ethical, and safety-security aspects of an event can affect the bottom line dramatically. Therefore, every decision you make that is proactive may reduce your risk of unforeseen financial impacts. Practicing thorough legal, ethical, and risk management proactive measures may actually help your event produce greater revenues.

Although not every contingency can be anticipated, the more adept you are at strategically planning preemptive measures to prevent contingencies, the better your balance sheet may look at the end of the event. Lapses in legal, ethical, and risk management judgment may cause not only loss of property, life, and money, but loss of your event's good name as well.

Key Components of an Event Management Agreement or Contract

The Event Leadership contract reflects the understanding and agreement between two or more parties regarding their mutual interests, as specified in the agreement. A binding contract must contain the key components described in this section.

Parties

The names of the parties must be clearly identified. The agreement must be described as being between these parties, and the names that are used in the agreement must be defined. Typical event agreements are between the event planner and his or her client or the event planner and his or her vendor. Other contracts may be between an event professional and an insurance company, an entertainment company, or a bank or other lending institution.

Offer

The offer is the service or product tendered by one party to another. The event planner may offer consulting services to a client, or a vendor may offer products to an event planner. The offer should list all services that an event professional offers to provide. Any miscommunications here may lead to costly litigation in the future.

Consideration

The consideration clause defines what one party will provide the other upon acceptance of an offer. Consideration may be either cash or in-kind products or services. Therefore, a sponsor may offer a event property complimentary products or services in addition to cash to pay for their sponsorship.

Acceptance

When both parties accept an offer, they execute (sign) the agreement confirming that they understand and agree to comply with the terms and conditions of the agreement.

Other Components

Although the key components are the parties, the offer, consideration, and acceptance, Event Leadership agreements usually include many other clauses or components. The most typical clauses are listed next.

Terms

The terms clause defines how and when the funds will be paid to the person extending the offer. If the event planner offers consulting services, he or she may request a deposit in the amount of the first and last month's retainer and then require that the client submit monthly payments of a certain amount on a certain date each month. These terms define the financial conditions under which the agreement is valid.

For some large events, payments are made during a specified period. In this case, or in case of another complicated payment arrangement, a separate payment schedule should be attached to a contract. This schedule should be treated as an essential part of the contract and signed and dated by both parties. If advance payment is mentioned in the payment term section, special attention should be paid to the provisions of how the deposit is returned in the case of event cancellation. For example, is the deposit credited toward future transactions within a specific time period, or is a cash refund offered?

Within the events industry, event professionals are increasingly concerned with reducing internal or operational risk in order to improve profitability of their enterprise. Internal risk issues include theft, slippage, and intellectual property safeguarding. Event professionals must work closely with colleagues to put in place procedures aimed to reduce internal risks.

Cancellation

Events are always subject to cancellation. Therefore, it is important to provide for this contingency legally with a detailed cancellation clause. Usually, the cancellation clause defines under what circumstances either party may cancel, how notification must be provided (usually in writing), and what penalties may be required in the event of cancellation. To view samples of various hotel contracts, please visit http://www.ieee.org/web/conferences/organizers/contracts.html.

Force Majeure (Act of God)

In the force majeure clause, both parties agree on which circumstances, deemed to be beyond their control, will permit an event to be canceled without penalty to either party. The force majeure clause must always be specified to reflect the most common or predictable occurrences. These may include hurricanes, earthquakes, floods, volcanic eruptions, tornadoes, famines, wars, or other catastrophic disasters such as terrorism.

Arbitration

It is common practice to include in event planning agreements a clause that allows both parties to use arbitration in place of a legal judgment when they fail to agree. The use of arbitration may save the parties substantial costs over traditional litigation.

Billing

Because many events involve entertainers or are theatrical events in and of themselves, the agreement must define how entertainers will be listed in advertising and in the program. Generally, a percentage, such as 100 percent, is used to describe the size of their name in relation to other text.

Time Is of the Essence

The time-is-of-the-essence clause instructs both parties that the agreement is valid only if it is signed within a prescribed period of time. This clause is usually inserted in order to protect the offerer from loss of income due to late execution by the purchaser.

Assignment

As employees have shorter and shorter tenures with organizations, it is more important than ever that agreements contain clauses indicating that the contract may not be assigned to other parties. For example, if Mary Smith leaves XYZ Company, the agreement is between XYZ Company and the offerer and may not be transferred to Smith's successor, who may or may not honor the agreement as an individual. Therefore, Mary Smith has executed the agreement on behalf of XYZ Company.

Insurance

Often agreements detail the type and limits of insurance that must be in force by both parties, as well as a requirement that each party coinsure the other. Some agreements require copies of certificates of insurance that name the other party as additional insured in advance of the event date.

Hold Harmless and Indemnification

In the event of negligence by either party, the negligent party agrees to hold the other party harmless and to defend it (indemnify) against harm. For example, if the hotel where you are conducting your event causes harm to a guest through its negligence, the hotel will be responsible for defending the event planner and his or her company from the future action. In many event agreements, the provision for hold harmless and indemnification is mutually shared by both parties.

Reputation

The production of an event is a reflection of the personal tastes of the event organization and sponsors. Therefore, some event planners include a specific clause that recognizes the importance of the purchaser's reputation and states that the event planner will use his or her best efforts to protect and preserve the reputation during management of the event.

Complete Agreement

Typically, the complete agreement is the final clause and states that the agreement constitutes the full understanding of both parties. Figure 11.1 demonstrates how a complete agreement is used in a typical event planning consulting agreement.

Agreement

1.0 This agreement is between Jane Smith Productions (otherwise known as Event Planner) and ABC Corporation (otherwise known as Purchaser).

2.0 Event Planner agrees to provide the following services:

2.1 50 hours of research regarding XYZ festival.

2.2 40 hours of design regarding XYZ festival.

2.3 30 hours of planning regarding XYZ festival.

2.4 20 hours of coordination regarding XYZ festival.

2.5 10 hours of evaluation regarding XYZ festival.

2.6 A total of 150 hours of consulting time will be provided by Event Leader.

3.0 Purchaser agrees to provide:

3.1 A total fee in the amount of $7,500.

4.0 Terms:

4.1 The Purchaser agrees to provide a nonrefundable deposit in the amount of seven hundred and fifty dollars (U.S.) ($750.00) to officially retain the services of Event Planner. The Purchaser furthermore agrees to provide monthly payments in the amount of seven hundred and fifty dollars (U.S.) ($750.00) on or before the fifteenth day of each month commencing August 15, 2010, until the balance has been paid in full.

5.0 Cancellation:

5.1 In the event of cancellation, notice must be received in writing. Should Purchaser cancel 90 days or more prior to event, Event Leader shall be entitled to retain all funds paid as of this date. Should Purchaser cancel less than 90 days prior to event, Event Leader shall receive full payment as specified in the agreement above.

Figure 11.1 Event Planning Sample Consulting Agreement *(Continued)*

6.0 Force Majeure:
- 6.1 This agreement is automatically null and void if event is canceled due to an act of God, including hurricane, earthquake, flood, volcanic eruption, tornado, famine, or war. In the event of cancellation due to an act of God, neither party shall be liable for any further payments.

7.0 Insurance:
- 7.1 Both parties shall maintain in full force one million dollars ($1 million) per occurrence comprehensive general liability insurance. Each party shall name the other as additional insured for the duration of the event. Both parties shall provide a certificate of insurance demonstrating evidence of additional insured status prior to the start of the event.

8.0 Hold Harmless and Indemnification:
- 8.1 Both parties agree that if either party is negligent, they will defend the non-negligent party and hold them harmless against future action.

9.0 Arbitration:
- 9.1 Both parties agree that if a dispute arises concerning this agreement, a professional arbitrator certified by the American Arbitration Association or the alternative dispute resolution process through the Conventional Industry Council will be used in place of normal litigation.

10.0 Reputation: Both parties agree to use their best efforts to preserve and protect each other's reputation during the conduct of this event. The Event Leader recognizes that the Purchaser has, over time, developed good standing in the business and general community and will use the best efforts available to protect and preserve his reputation from harm.
- 10.1 Billing: Because many events involve entertainers or are theatrical events in and of themselves, the agreement must define how entertainers will be listed in advertising and in the program. Generally, a percentage, such as 100 percent, is used to describe the size of their name in relation to other text.
- 10.2 The Event Leader shall be listed in the official program of the event with the following text in type the same size and style as the body copy:
- 10.3 This event managed by Jane Smith Production.
- 10.4 The Event Planner shall be listed in the official program with other staff in the following manner with text in type of the same size and style as the body copy:
- 10.5 Jane Smith, Event Planner

11.0 Time Is of the Essence:
- 11.1 This agreement must be executed by July 15, 2010. After this date this agreement must be considered null and void and a new agreement must be created:

12.0 Assignment:
- 12.1 This agreement may not be assigned to others. The persons executing this agreement have the full authority to sign this agreement on behalf of the organizations they represent.

Figure 11.1 *(Continued)*

13.0 The Full Agreement:

13.1 The agreement and any riders attached represent the full understanding between both parties. Any amendments to this agreement must be approved in writing and separately attached to this agreement.

14.0 Execution:

14.1 The signatures below confirm complete understanding and compliance with the terms and conditions described in this agreement.

______________________________	______________
ABC Corporation, Purchaser	Date
______________________________	______________
Jane Smith, Event Planner	Date

Figure 11.1 *(Continued)*

Rider

A rider is an attachment to a main agreement and usually lists the important ingredients that support the main contract. These may include sound equipment and labor, lighting equipment and labor, food and beverages, transportation, housing for artists/entertainers, or other important financial considerations other than the artist's fee (e.g., a payment schedule). The rider should be attached to the main agreement, and it should be initialed or signed separately to signify acceptance by both parties.

Eco Rider

The eco rider is a type of rider that requires that specific activities take place to reduce the carbon footprint that is created a concert or other entertainment production. The eco rider may specify that food and other supplies be locally sourced to reduce travel and fuel or that recycling, re-use and reduction policies be enacted across the entire event. An artist such as a band or speaker may specifically request a eco rider to perform at your event. For more information about eco riders visit http://liveearth.org/docs/LEGreen_Guidelines_First_edition_final.pdf.

Changes to the Agreement

Most agreements will require negotiation prior to execution, and the result of these executions will be changes. If only two or three nonsubstantial changes are made, you may choose to initial and date each change prior to returning the agreement for execution by the other party. Your initial and date signify your acceptance of the change but do not obligate you to fulfill the entire agreement until you have affixed your signature. If there are substantial changes (such as in the date, time, venue, or fees) or more than three changes, it is best to draw up a new agreement.

Terms and Sequence of Execution

First and foremost, always require that the purchaser sign the agreement prior to affixing your signature. Once both signatures are affixed, the agreement becomes official. If you sign the agreement and forward it to the other party, and the purchaser makes changes and signs it, you may be somewhat obligated for those changes. It is always wise to request the purchaser's signature before affixing your own.

Second, never use facsimiles. Should you be forced to litigate the agreement, the court will seek the "best copy," and that is usually an original. You may use a facsimile for an interim memorandum of understanding, but binding, official agreements must be originals.

Third, take the time to sign the agreement in person. Explain to the purchaser that the terms implied in the agreement are only as valid as the integrity of the persons signing the document. Offer your hand in friendship as you jointly execute this agreement.

Other Agreements

In addition to the main event consulting agreement, the event planner may be required to prepare and execute other types of agreements. Samples of the client and supplier agreements may be found in Appendices 9 and 10 which you will be able to find at www.wiley.com/college/goldblatt. Typical event planning agreements include:

- Consulting agreement: an agreement whereby one party (usually the event planner) agrees to provide consulting services for another party
- Employment agreement: an agreement whereby an employee agrees to specific terms for employment
- Exhibitor contract: an agreement between an individual exhibitor and the sponsor of an exposition to lease space for a specific booth at the exposition
- Hotel contract: an agreement between a hotel and the organization holding an event to provide rooms and function space, as well as other services (food and beverages), for a specific event or series of events
- Noncompete agreement: an agreement whereby an employee agrees not to compete within a specific jurisdiction or marketplace for a specified period of time following termination of employment

- Purchase order: an order to a vendor to provide services or products
- Sponsorship agreement: a contract between a sponsor and an event organizer in which the organizer agrees to provide specific marketing services to the sponsor for a prescribed fee and/or other consideration
- Vendor agreement: an agreement between a vendor and an event planner or client to provide specific services or products for an event

These agreements, along with many others, may be required to ensure the professional operation of an event. To identify all the agreements that may be required, check with other event organizers and local officials as well as your vendors to determine the critical documents that must be executed prior to the start of the event.

Permits

Permits are issued by local, state, provincial, or federal governmental agencies and allow you to conduct certain activities at your event. Figure 11.2 details the typical permits that may be required. Allow sufficient time to obtain the permits. A permit may be issued only after you have submitted the appropriate documentation and have paid a fee. Determine well in advance what type of documentation is required by the issuing agency and how funds are accepted.

Permit	Source
Bingo	Lottery or gaming department
Customs	Revenue and customs office of the country where the event is being conducted
Food handling	Health department
Lottery	Lottery or gaming department
Occupancy	Fire department
Parking	Transportation and parking department
Park use	Park department
Public assembly	Public safety and police department
Pyrotechnics	Fire department
Sales tax	Revenue or tax collector's office
Signs and banners	Zoning department
Street closing	Transportation and parking department
Visas	Consulate or embassy of country where entry is required

Figure 11.2 Typical Event Planning Permits and Where to Obtain Them

Remember that permits are not issued automatically. A permit reflects that an agency is permitting your event organization to conduct certain activities provided that you conform to the regulations established. Make certain that you are able to comply with these regulations prior to applying for the permit. If you are denied a permit, you may consider appealing your case. In some cases, event planners have sued an agency to obtain permission to conduct an event. However, since most event planners rely on the goodwill of local agencies to conduct an event successfully, litigation should be the absolutely final resort.

Licensing

A license is granted by a governmental institution, a private organization (as in music licensing), or a public entity to allow you to conduct a specific activity. The difference between a permit and a license may be slight in some jurisdictions. Usually the requirements for obtaining a license are much more stringent and require due diligence (evidence of worthiness) prior to issuance.

Figure 11.3 lists the more common licenses required for events and their sources. Additional licenses may be required for your event. To determine what licenses are required, make certain that you examine the event's history, check with organizers of similar events, and confirm and verify with the appropriate agencies that issue these licenses.

One of the best sources of information will be your vendors. Audit your vendors, especially in the technology field, and determine if licenses are required (as in the case of laser projection) or if the Event Leader must obtain a license.

For many events, both permits and licenses must be secured. The larger the event, the more likely the number of permits and licenses will increase. Remember that licenses and permits are the government's way of establishing a barrier to entry to protect its interests. Work closely with government agencies to understand their procedures, time frames, and

Permit	Source
Alcohol	Alcohol beverage control boards (usually at the state level in the United States)
Business	Economic development agency; recorder of deeds
Food	Local or state health department
Music	American Society of Composers, Authors, and Publishers or Broadcast Music, Inc.
Pyrotechnics	Local or state fire department/service, the U.S. Bureau of Alcohol, Tobacco, and Firearms

Figure 11.3 Typical Event Leadership Licenses and Where to Obtain Them

inspection policies. A close working relationship with the agencies that issue licenses and permits will help ensure the success of your overall event operation.

Environmental Regulations

Increasingly, local government bodies are requiring that event planners submit an environmental plan with their other required documents for the event to be approved by the government agencies. This requirement is due to citizen pressure to reduce the carbon footprint and the environmental damage caused by large-scale and hallmark events.

Therefore, event planners must be prepared to comply with all environmental regulations, including recycling, reuse, reduction, waste management, and even, where possible, on-site composting of waste matter. You might be asked to submit a separate environmental management plan for your event or might be required by a local government to provide additional funds to restore the area to its original state.

Regardless of the requirements by local authorities, it is important that you think well in advance what may be required and then put the procedures in place to minimize environmental damage as a result of your event.

Sponsorship Regulations

Since 2008, U.S. healthcare organizations have been required to only accept funds from corporate sponsors when those funds directly support the educational mission of the organization. The requirements for accepting funds have dramatically limited the capacity of some health care organizations to provide traditional hosting services for doctors, nurses, and other medical providers because the pharmaceutical companies are now severely restricted by what they may provide.

Although these regulations are not mandated by a government body, they have been widely accepted in the health care industry as a way to improve public perception of their industry and to not unduly influence doctors or others through lavish hosting as traditionally provided by the pharmaceutical companies.

According to *Medical Meetings* magazine in 2009, "The Pharmaceutical Research and Manufacturers of America's updated Code on Interactions with Healthcare Professionals, takes effect in January 2009. The new, voluntary code places a strict focus on science and education. When it comes to medical meetings, resorts and noneducational gifts are out, and the watchword for everything from venues to menus is 'appropriate.'"

The interpretation of the term *appropriate* is very difficult to understand with these new regulations. However, the responsibility for compliance is firmly in the hands of the pharmaceutical companies. Therefore, medical and health care event planners should work closely with their pharmaceutical colleagues to determine how best to appropriately position them and their financial support within the planned event.

Visas and Work Permits

Following September 11, 2001, many countries have tightened their visa procedures to ensure that only individuals who have valid reasons for entering the sovereign nation state may do so. Typically, when one country raises the threshold for entry to its country, other countries reciprocate. For example, in recent years Brazil has required that American citizens be fingerprinted upon entering Brazil as a direct response to the United States implementing the same requirement for Brazilian visitors.

Therefore, it is very important that event planners check with the consulate or embassy of the country where they will be conducting their event to determine the types of visas and work permits that will be required for their workers and guests. Generally, guests from the United States attending an education meeting may enter certain countries for a specified period of months and will not require a special visa. However, it is best to check first as these rules and policies are extremely fluid. Workers or staff who are being paid by the country wherein they will be working will be required to have a work permit or other credentials and may also be required to pay taxes upon the wages they receive.

In 2008, the British government decided to require that all performers from countries other than the United Kingdom who were engaged by festivals would be required immediately leave the United Kingdom following their final performance. The festival producers and local council officials objected to this requirement and it was relaxed in 2008 to allow the entertainers to remain as tourists in the United Kingdom for a specified time period.

In 2009, the Western Hemisphere Travel Initiative will require all U.S. citizens and others to have a valid U.S. Passport or Passport Card to enter the United States from Canada, Mexico and other countries. This includes passengers who travel by air, land or sea.

According to the U.S. Department of Homeland Security, the final documents will be required for entry.

U.S. PASSPORT AND WHTI COMPLIANT DOCUMENTS:

- *U.S. Passport*: U.S. citizens may present a valid U.S. passport to enter or re-enter the United States when traveling via air, land, or sea from Canada, Mexico, the Caribbean region, and Bermuda.
- *The U.S. Passport Card*: The passport card is only valid for re-entry into the United States at land border crossings and sea ports-of-entry from Canada, Mexico, the Caribbean region, and Bermuda.
- *WHTI-Compliant Travel Documents for U.S. citizen travel via land or sea, as of January 31, 2008:*
  - Trusted Traveler Cards (NEXUS, SENTRI, or FAST)
  - State Issued Enhanced Driver's License (when available)
  - Enhanced Tribal Cards (when available)
  - U.S. Military Identification with Military Travel Orders
  - U.S. Merchant Mariner Document when traveling in conjunction with official maritime business
  - Native American Tribal Photo Identification Card
  - Form I-872 American Indian Card

  Source: www.travel.state.gov/travel/cbpmc/cbpmc_2223.html

Therefore, as more and more events become transnational in scope, it is incumbent upon the event planner to work closely with customs and immigration officials to make certain their delegates and staff have an efficient and easy means to entering the country where the event is being conducted. Furthermore, the event planner must also work closely with departments of revenue and customs to ascertain the proper work permits for full and temporary staff that are providing services for the event while in a foreign country.

Contracts, Permits, and Licenses: A Synergistic Relationship

Professional event planners understand, and use to their advantage, the synergy between a well-written and executed contract and the acquisition of proper permits and licenses. All three instruments are essential for the professional operation of modern events. When developing an agreement, determine in advance who is responsible for obtaining and paying for specific permits and licenses and incorporate this language into the agreement. Failure to specify who is responsible for obtaining and paying for permits and licenses can lead to an interruption of your event and conflicts among the various stakeholders.

Therefore, conduct research carefully during the planning stage to identify all necessary permits and licenses and determine who will be responsible for coordinating this process. Include this information in your master event consulting agreement, as well as your vendor agreements. Since permits and licenses are unavoidable in most event situations, it behooves the event planner to practice the maxim that an ounce of prevention (or risk management) is worth a pound of cure. Use the planning phase to examine potential permit processes, and then use the coordination stage to link these two important steps within the event management process.

Contracts, permits, and licenses have legal, ethical, and risk management ramifications. To ensure that these impacts are positive, Event Leaders must understand their importance and work diligently to communicate with the required agencies, as well as to prepare and execute valid agreements.

Risk Management Procedures

"100 die in nightclub event," shouted the headlines and television newscasters in Providence, Rhode Island, immediately after the tragic 2003 Station nightclub fire. This news story became an international incident and profoundly affected the laws regarding fire and public assembly in Rhode Island. Furthermore, every year on the anniversary of this tragedy, the newspapers and televisions stations remind local citizens of this terrible loss of life, and this will probably continue for many years to come.

Governor Donald Carceri of Rhode Island appointed me as chair of a task force to determine how the new regulations that would inevitably be developed could be implemented in a manner so as not to inhibit or impede the development of the events industry. After several hearings including testimony from experts in event risk management it was determined that as a direct result of this tragic incident, the fire and public assembly regulations in Rhode

Island would need to be greatly strengthened. These changes impacted small, medium, and large business as a direct cost of millions of dollars.

Whenever human beings assemble for the purposes of entertainment, celebration, education, marketing, or reunion, there is an increased risk of loss of life or property. This has been proven many times, as similar newspaper headlines have reported accidents that have occurred at events.

With increased injuries, thefts, and other misfortunes come, of course, increased expense. This may stem from two sources: the loss of revenue resulting directly from the occurrence and increased insurance premiums when underwriters are forced to pay large settlements as a result of negligence. Perhaps the most profound loss is the loss of business opportunity that results from the bad publicity attached to such tragedies. After all, who wants to visit an event where a tent might collapse and injure people or where there is a risk of food poisoning?

Alexander Berlonghi, an expert in the field of risk assessment and risk management, has devised a method for attempting to identify and contain the many risks associated with events. Berlonghi describes the first step in the risk assessment process as that of holding a risk assessment meeting. A step-by-step guide to holding such a meeting follows. I suggest that you use it for each of your events—it could be a lifesaver.

Organizing a Risk Assessment Meeting

The first question to ask when organizing a risk assessment meeting is: Who should attend? Ideally, all key event stakeholders should be involved in this meeting, and you may wish to use a written survey to audit their opinions regarding risks associated with an event. However, for practical purposes, you must first identify those event team leaders who can bring you the best information from which to manage present and future risks associated with your events. These event team leaders should be included in the risk assessment meeting:

- Admissions manager
- Advertising manager
- Animal handler
- Box-office manager
- Broadcast manager
- Catering manager
- Comptroller
- Computer or data processing manager
- Convention center safety director
- Customs officials
- Department of Homeland Security
- Electrician
- Entertainment specialist
- Environment safety specialist
- Federal Bureau of Investigation (FBI)

- Fire department liaison
- Food and beverage manager
- Health and safety coordinator
- Hotel security director
- Human resources director
- Immigration officials
- Insurance broker
- Laser specialist
- Lighting specialist
- Office manager
- Parking specialist
- Police liaison for event
- Public relations manager
- Pyrotechnic specialist
- Security director for event
- Sound specialist
- Special-effects specialist
- Transportation specialist
- Venue safety director
- Weather and meteorological experts

Before the Meeting

Once you have identified the participants for a risk assessment meeting, it is time to put them to work. Assigning prework helps meeting participants focus on the seriousness of the meeting and will probably improve the efficiency of the meeting. Figure 11.4 demonstrates a typical risk assessment meeting announcement that you may customize for your own use.

TO:	Event Risk Assessment Team
FROM:	Event Leader
SUBJECT:	Meeting Announcement and Instructions
DATE:	May 15, 2010
ACTION REQUIRED:	Return your list of potential risks by July 15, 2010.

A risk assessment meeting will be held on July 20, 2010, at 1 P.M. for the purpose of identifying and managing the major risks associated with this event. Prior to this meeting, you should audit your area and prepare a comprehensive list of risks associated with your event responsibilities.

Interview the team members in your area and ask them to assist you in this important task. Risks may involve potential injuries, loss of life or property, or other risks.

Submit this list to me by the close of business on July 15, 2010. Thank you for your contribution to this important process.

Figure 11.4 Risk Assessment Meeting Announcement

Make sure that you follow up with meeting participants to ensure that all lists have been returned and that you understand the risks they have identified as important to their area. Once you have received responses, it is time to compile a master list of all risks that have been identified. You may list these risks in alphabetical order or subdivide them by event area.

The final step in preparing for a risk assessment meeting is to prepare a detailed agenda that may be used to conduct the meeting. Prior to the meeting, circulate the agenda and seek feedback from the participants. Figure 11.5 provides a sample agenda and premeeting announcement that you may customize for a risk assessment meeting.

Conducting the Meeting

After the agenda has been distributed, corrected, and approved, it is time to convene the risk assessment meeting. Use a hollow square seating design and prepare tent cards for each participant, listing his or her name and event area of responsibility. A flip chart displayed on an easel stand should list the agenda for the meeting, and subsequent pages should list the risks previously identified by meeting participants. In addition, participants should receive a typed copy of the agenda and the comprehensive list of risks, along with any other collateral material that will help them make the important decisions that will be required during the meeting.

As the event planner, you are also the meeting facilitator. To facilitate the participation of all, first welcome the participants and explain that the meeting will be successful only if they participate actively by offering their expert opinions and engaging in a lively discussion concerning recommendations for reducing or alleviating the risks that have been identified.

TO: Event Team Leaders
FROM: Event Leader
SUBJECT: Event Risk Assessment Meeting Agenda
DATE: July 15, 2010
ACTION REQUIRED: Return the enclosed agenda to me with your comments by July 18, 2010.

Tentative Agenda

I. Welcome and introduction
II. Explanation of purposes, event planner
III. Comprehensive risk review, all participants
IV. Additional risks not covered in listing, all participants
V. Recommendations for risk management, all participants
VI. Economic impacts of risk management, all participants, comptroller
VII. Post-meeting work assignment, event planner
VIII. Adjournment

Figure 11.5 Risk Assessment Meeting Sample Agenda/Announcement

After you have set the tone for the meeting, review the list of risks and ask the meeting participants to study them for a few moments and identify any gaps. What risks have been overlooked?

The next stage of the meeting is to begin discussions on how to reduce, control, transfer, or eliminate the risks that have been identified. This is a good time to ask the participants to form small groups that represent cross-disciplinary task forces. For example, you may ask the admissions, box office, and comptroller team members to work on reducing the risk of theft from the box office or eliminating the risk of gate crashing. Allow 15 to 30 minutes for this activity.

When you reconvene the group, ask participants to communicate their recommendations to the entire group and try to seek consensus from group members. Do not rush this process. During these discussions, important concerns may be expressed. You must make sure that you address and attempt to satisfy these concerns before moving on to the next stage.

Every risk decision will have corresponding financial impacts. This is a good time to use a Likert scale to rate the importance of each risk in terms of the overall event. For example, to identify risks that should receive the greatest consideration when considering the financial impact on your event, ask each participant to assign a number to each risk, with 1 representing least concern and 5 representing most concern. Theft from the box office might rate a 5, while rain might receive a 1. Once you have reached consensus on the level of importance of each risk, you may concentrate the discussion on risks that the group deems most important.

Documenting the Meeting's Recommendations

The final stage of a risk assessment meeting is to document your recommendations and assign post-meeting work groups to continue to address the important issues covered in the meeting. Assign one person as a scribe during the meeting and ask him or her to prepare review notes to be circulated within three business days. The notes should reflect the substance and content of the discussion and list the recommendations the group has agreed to pursue.

The work groups are responsible for conducting additional research to identify ways in which to better manage the risks that were discussed and perhaps lower the cost of the event. Their work may include interviewing external experts or brainstorming with their fellow event stakeholders to seek better solutions.

The review notes also serve the important purpose of preserving the history of the meeting. Should there be an incident at your event that requires evidence that you conducted risk assessment and management procedures to attempt to prevent this occurrence, the review notes may serve as valuable proof documenting your proactive stance.

Safety Meeting and Other Considerations

Before you allow vendors to install the various event elements, you must conduct a brief safety meeting to alert all event stakeholders to the standards your organization has established with regard to safety. Notify the event stakeholders in writing and explain that this meeting is required for participation in the event. Usually, the meeting is held prior to installation and is conducted by the Event Leader. Survey the event stakeholders to determine if they have particular expertise in event safety. You may wish to call on this expertise during the safety meeting.

Use a checklist or written agenda distributed to each participant at the meeting to remain focused on the goals and objectives of the meeting. Detail your expectations of minimum safety requirements for the event. These may include taping or ramping of exposed cables, grounding of all electric power, keeping the work areas cleared of debris, nonsmoking policies, and other important issues.

Ask those assembled if they have been trained in the Heimlich maneuver or CPR (cardiopulmonary resuscitation) during the past three years. Ask those who have been trained to serve as first responders for the event if someone requires this level of response. The Event Leader should be trained in both the Heimlich maneuver and CPR and be prepared to use these techniques to sustain or save lives, if required. Make certain that you ask each person to sign in when he or she attends the meeting. This will provide you with a record of those who participated and may be helpful if there is a later claim against the event. Conclude the meeting by reminding all participants that the overall goal of this event is zero percent tolerance of unsafe working conditions.

Inspections

Prior to opening the doors to admit guests to your event, conduct a final inspection. Walk the entire event site and note any last-minute corrections that must be made to ensure the safety of guests. Walk-throughs are best conducted by a team that includes your client, key vendors, key event team leaders, and, when possible, police, fire, and other officials.

During the walk-through, use a digital camera and/or videocamera to record corrections you have made, and post caution signs where appropriate to notify guests of possible risks.

These areas must be reviewed when conducting a walk-through prior to admitting guests to your event:

- Accreditation/credentialing systems are in working order.
- Admissions personnel are in place.
- Air walls are in working order in case of evacuation.
- Bar personnel have received alcohol management training.
- Doors are unlocked from inside the venue in case of evacuation.
- Edge of stage is marked with safety tape.
- Electric boxes are labeled with caution signs.
- Electric cables are grounded.
- Electric cables traversing public areas are taped or ramped.
- Elevators are working.
- Light level is sufficient for safe ingress and egress.
- Lighting has been properly secured with safety chains.

- Metal detectors are in place and operational for VIP appearances.
- Ramps are in place for the disabled.
- Security personnel are posted.
- Signs are visible and well secured.
- Staging has chair and handrails.
- Stairs have handrails, and individual steps are marked with safety tape to highlight the edges.
- Ushering personnel are in place.
- Final visual inspection of all areas and verbal confirmations with support staff and volunteers prior to opening doors/admitting guests.

These are but a few of the areas that must be inspected prior to admitting guests. You may wish to prepare a checklist to inspect each area systematically or simply use a small pad of paper and note areas that must be corrected prior to the event. The walk-through should be conducted one to two hours prior to the official start time of an event. This will give you time to make any minor corrections that are required.

Documentation and Due Diligence

Each of the steps included in the walk-through demonstrates to officials, and perhaps one day to a jury, that you have attempted to do what a reasonable person would be expected to do under these circumstances to ensure the safety of guests. Documenting your risk assessment, management, and prevention steps may assist you in demonstrating that you have practiced due diligence for your event. The goal is to achieve or exceed the standard of care normally associated with an event of this size and type. The steps just listed will help you move rapidly toward this goal.

Obtaining Insurance

Insurance is used by event planners to transfer the risk to a third party: the insurance underwriter. Many venues require that the event planner or event organization maintain in full force a minimum of $1 million per occurrence of comprehensive general liability insurance. Some municipalities require similar limits of insurance for events to be held in their jurisdiction. Events that are more complex and pose greater risks may be required to have higher limits of insurance.

Identifying a properly qualified insurance broker is an important first step in receiving expert advice regarding the types of insurance that may be required for your event. After checking with the venue and municipality to determine the level of insurance required, you will need a well-trained specialty insurance broker to advise you further on coverage available.

A specialty insurance broker has insurance products and services specifically relevant for the Event Leadership profession. For example, large firms such as Arthur J. Gallagher & Co. or K & K insurance provide products for clients ranging from the National Football League Super Bowl to local parades and festivals. They are experienced experts in providing advice and counsel for the unique risks associated with events.

Identifying the Appropriate Premium

After you have contacted two or more specialty insurance brokers and determined the type of insurance products that may be required for your event, you will request quotes from each broker. The brokers will ask you to complete a detailed form listing the history of the event, specific hazards that may be involved (e.g., pyrotechnics), and other critical information. The broker will submit this information to several underwriters and present you with a quote for coverage.

The most cost-effective premium is an annual policy known as comprehensive general liability insurance. Some event planners pay as little as $2,000 annually for liability coverage for a variety of risks. Other Event Leaders pay their premiums on a per-event basis. Your insurance broker will help you decide what the best system is for you.

For example, the Summer Olympic Games in Athens, Greece, reportedly paid, according to Bloomberg News Service, over $30 million for insurance coverage for the first 2004 Summer Olympic Games following the tragedy of September 11, 2001. Therefore, it is critically important for you to carefully assess your potential risks and work closely with your insurance professionals to purchase sufficient insurance coverage.

These insurance products are typically associated with events:

- Automotive liability
- Board of directors' liability
- Business interruption
- Cancellation
- Comprehensive general liability
- Disability
- Earthquake
- Errors and omissions
- Fire
- Flood
- Health
- Hurricane
- Key person
- Life
- Nonappearance
- Office contents
- Officers
- Performer no show
- Rain
- Terrorism
- Workers' compensation

Your client or others involved with your event may ask that they be named as an additional insured on your policy. The term *additional insured* means that, if for any reason there is an incident, your insurance policy will cover claims against those listed as additionally insured. Before agreeing to name the other party or parties as additional insured, check with your insurance broker to find out if there is an additional charge or if this is appropriate. You may also want to ask the other parties to name you as additional insured on their policies.

Exclusions

Every insurance policy will list certain hazards that are excluded from coverage. Make certain that you check with your broker and review your policy carefully to make sure that there are no gaps in coverage for your event. For example, if your event is using pyrotechnics and they are excluded specifically from your current coverage, you may wish to purchase additional coverage to protect your event. Oftentimes, especially during the Y2K period of 2000, a typical insurance exclusion included computer systems. Today, some policies may exclude terrorist acts. Make certain you carefully review all exclusions to eliminate any gaps in coverage.

Preexisting Coverage

Before purchasing any coverage, audit your existing coverage to check for gaps regarding your event. Your event organization may already have in force specific coverage related to the risks associated with your event. Once you have conducted this audit, your specialty insurance broker can advise you with regard to additional coverage for your event.

Risk Control

Theft Prevention

The best strategy for theft prevention is segregation of duties. All transactions that involve cash handling, returns, and deposits should have at least two employees performing that transaction.

Cash

Cash must be handled accurately. I encourage you to establish a special cash log where all cash transactions should be recorded. Even small petty cash numbers add up to a substantial amount, so if you think that $20 cash expense is not worth recording, you are wrong; $20 per week turns into $1,080 per year. Anyone who handles cash should be given occasional unscheduled vacation days to check his or her cash-handling practice. While an employee is away, a replacement is in a very good position to catch all illegal activities set up by the employee.

Inventory

One of the more important tools in preventing theft of inventory is incorporation of special procedures for inventory management. Storage facilities should be monitored; two people should be involved in storage operations. All records of inventory disbursement should be stored and checked on a random basis. In a real-time computer system, inventory should have bar codes that have to be entered into the system as soon as inventory is disbursed.

As an event planner and supervisor, you should approve all equipment breakdowns and/or replacements. Management of event planning organizations should analyze the level of breakage that is typical for their operations. Any constant abnormalities should be investigated in more depth. Physical inventory counts should be taken regularly. Shortages should be reviewed, comparing them to acceptable loss levels.

Copyright

Some Event Leadership organizations have their brand names listed separately in their assets. This is an important part of their goodwill. Any event planning organization should protect its brand. Event professionals should consult copyright and intellectual property specialists to evaluate copyright areas where an organization can have potential problems. All brand names and logos of event organizations should contain clear copyright marks and warning statements. The universal symbol for copyrighted material is ©.

Trademark, Service Mark, and Registered Mark

A trademark is a symbol to indicate that the product or service is from a unique source and to distinguish it from other entities. The symbol ™ is an unregistered mark used to promote brands or brand products. The symbol (SM) is a service mark used to promote bands or brand services. Finally, the symbol ® is a registered mark for a registered product or service. Trademark is used to protect a type of intellectual property. For example, if your event name or logo (visual identity) is unique, you may wish to register it as an official trademark to protect it from being used by others without your permission.

Terrorism and Biochemical Risk

Dr. Peter Tarlow, the author of *Event Risk Management and Safety* (2002), advises soberly, "It takes only small amounts of a biochemical substance to murder hundreds of people, including those in charge." He advises that personnel should know when to enter and when to avoid possibly contaminated areas, types of equipment to use, and what the signs of a biochemical attack might be.

Events are often considered soft targets for terrorists. A soft target is one that is easily penetrated due to many different vulnerabilities. Tarlow has identified eight reasons for the interaction between terrorism and events and why terrorists see them as soft targets:

1. Events are often close to major transportation centers.
2. Events are big business.
3. Events impact other industries, such as restaurants, hotels, and entertainment.
4. Events draw media coverage.
5. Events require tranquility or places where business can be conducted in a peaceful manner.

6. Events must deal with people who have no history; thus, risk managers often do not have databases on delegates or attendees.
7. Events are based on a constant flow of guests; thus, it is hard to know who is and who is not a terrorist.
8. Events are the point where business and relaxation converge, and, therefore, guests often let down their guard.

Managing Risk: Everyone's Responsibility

The field of event risk management has grown so rapidly that there is emerging a specialization within the profession for risk experts such as Alexander Berlonghi and others.

The Pioneer: Liam Sinclair, Director, The Edinburgh Mela, Edinburgh, Scotland

Liam Sinclair directs one of the newest and most unusual festivals in the constellation of world-renowned festivals in Edinburgh, Scotland. The Edinburgh Mela was conceived in 1995 and is the leading celebration of cultural diversity through the arts. *Mela* is a Sanskrit word that means gathering. Indeed, the Edinburgh Mela gather together each summer artists from a wide variety of cultures to provide a unique kaleidoscope of entertainment, arts, crafts, and, of course, food. When asked to describe how he came to direct this event, Liam states that he was first a keen audience member of the Mela festival who relished the chance to lead the organization and event into the future.

With a strong background in theater and the performing arts, Liam says that the festival industry is a perfect career for him because it has the right balance of challenge, intensity, and reward, along with the opportunity to work with some brilliant and talented people.

One of his most valued mentors is Faith Liddell, the director of Festivals Edinburgh. According to Liam, "The work she does in the City of Edinburgh, in terms of focusing on the joint strategic interests of Edinburgh's festivals and events is truly inspiring. She has the ideal combination of passion, tenacity, and humor and is an excellent colleague."

Liam notes that the events industry has changed significantly in terms of technology, budgets, human resources, design, education, environmental considerations and other key areas since he began his career. Liam notes, "Budgets are clearly under pressure at the moment due to the global economic situation. We all have to think smarter and more efficiently about how we spend our financial resources. That, in turn, makes us draw on our most precious resource, our talented and creative staff and colleagues. The use of technology assists us in our efficiency

Larger events, such as the Pope's visit to Colorado, may require a risk manager. However, for most events, the event manager is also the risk manager.

To improve your event operations, as the risk manager, you must assemble a risk management team that will assist you in identifying and managing risks. You must communicate to all event stakeholders that event risk management is everyone's responsibility.

Documentation, Discovery, and Disclosure

Some members of the legal profession will caution event planners about documentation of all risk procedures due to the fact that they may be subpoenaed if there is

and ability to make things happen fast! We're increasingly under the spotlight with regards to our impact on the environment. In Edinburgh this is just one area where all the major festivals are collaborating to consider and implement ways we can mitigate our impact on the environment. These sorts of collaborations are important as they allow us to draw on a wide range of experience and expertise, again making us more efficient, and ultimately more sustainable.

He thinks that these things were always in the mix, but we are now living in a world that has changed quite fundamentally due to economic conditions. He says, "In a sense we are beginning to re-invent and re-prioritize our value systems for the future, and that is both daunting and exciting at the same time."

However, despite the economic challenges he is facing, he believes that festivals and events will continue to be valued. According to Liam, "Festivals and events will always generate substantially more benefits, both culturally and economically, than the resources they require to stage. Therefore, the future will be tough, and certainly not as 'cash rich,' but it will be a future where creative and innovate festivals and events will have an important role to play in shaping our communities and societies."

When asked to provide advice for the next generation of festival and event directors, he says, "Be open to being challenged but be confident about what you believe in." This positive outlook and hopeful attitude was selected, according to Liam, because it has been central to his first 18 months as director of the Edinburgh Mela and is his own personal mantra.

Having a personal mantra, such as the one Liam Sinclair has adopted, may also serve the next generation of festival and event producers well. While the future is uncertain, Liam understands that festivals and events are extremely valuable to their stakeholders, and this value far exceeds the investment. Furthermore, he recognizes the important of using challenges and opportunities for reinvention events. Though still at an early stage in his own career, this talented pioneer is helping shape the future of the festival and event industry through his creative approach to producing one of Edinburgh's most interesting festivals. The future may be uncertain, but with Liam Sinclair's continued strong and creative leadership, it will certainly be interesting, valuable, and successful as he carefully weaves the annual colorful tapestry known as the Edinburgh Mela.

The Protégé: Raymond Bremner, Third Year Events Student, Queen Margaret University, Edinburgh, Scotland

Raymond Bremner represents the type of student in higher education that was once classified as "nontraditional." He returned to university at the age of 30 desiring to earn a business degree with the aim of moving into operations management. In his second semester of his first year, he took an events module and found it inspiring. "I realized that my years of working in hospitality had given me a grounding in this field and that I had a natural aptitude for events and that this was a career where I should be. I believe that if you find your talent you should use it." And that is exactly what Raymond is doing as he works toward earning his degree in business and events.

One of his mentors at Queen Margaret University has been Liam Sinclair. According to Raymond, "The Mela has been instrumental in breaking down boundaries in Edinburgh between all communities. The social impact of this event goes throughout Edinburgh and Liam's work on making the Mela a larger and more aware festival is true a inspiration for the future of our community."

Looking to the future of his burgeoning career, he believes that events will be used more for education and environmental issues than ever before. He says, "As governments and businesses see the value of bringing people

an act of negligence associated with the event. However, it has been my experience as an expert witness at numerous trials, where event planners are accused to negligence, that having sufficient documentation to demonstrate having met the minimum duty and standard of care will help reduce damages or even lead to a dismissal of the case.

Therefore, I recommend that event planners document and be prepared to surrender the following documents associated with the event if necessary:

1. Contracts
2. Organizational chart
3. Risk assessment procedures and risk management plans
4. Insurance policies and certificates
5. Budgets, if required, to demonstrate investment in risk management recommendations

Although you may produce sufficient documentation of your good judgment and planning as well as actions before, during, and after the event, you and your event may still be subject to litigation. Therefore, the real test you must pass is one that is quite ancient

together in events to promote social causes, this will then lead to more events of this type. Events will aim to have a lasting legacy, which can be used for a brighter future." He sees the current financial climate will greatly influence government and business to work together to best utilize their resources to improve the overall community.

Raymond envisions a more socially aware events industry. He believes that new events will not only be produced for financial value, but also to help communities and even countries develop in every way. He also feels the events industry it will grow as the need for events to bring people together will grow stronger and, as with the Edinburgh Mela, events may be used to help communities move in the same direction together for mutual positive benefit.

Although hopeful about the future, Raymond states that the best advice he ever received was to be financially realistic as well. He says, "In this day, money is not as easily available to fund events, and people do not have as much money to attend events. The social climate is such that you have to work toward making events more financially viable for all stakeholders concerned."

Although Raymond began his career as a nontraditional student, in fact, more and more older students are returning to universities throughout the world to study planned events. Students such as Raymond Bremner bring great experience, maturity, and dedication to their studies. However, Raymond brings something more. His wisdom regarding the importance of financial realism is a value that will greatly help him and those he leads throughout his future career. His future is not only based on his already-rich professional experience but also solidly grounded in understanding that events must be financially viable to ensure sustainable success, the kind that Raymond Bremner will certainly inherit in his career.

and, some would suggest, event simple. Ask yourself, did you perform your event planning duties in a manner to not cause harm to others? If the answer is honestly and confidently affirmative, then you have succeeded in helping advance your profession and industry into the future while simultaneously advancing through a new frontier that is expanding every day with newer and perhaps greater challenges.

Career Advancement Connections

Corporate Social Responsibility Connection

Does your risk management plan incorporate principles of corporate social responsibility to ensure that you are adequately protecting your staff, vendors and guests before, during and following your event? Do you have a written code of conduct for your event planning organizations, and do you comply with the code of ethics and professional conduct recommended by your industry? Corporate social responsibility fundamentally means doing the right thing for the right purpose. As you develop your risk management plans and implement them throughout your organization, ask yourself and others if you are exemplifying a model of corporate social responsibility through these procedures. You may further wish to consider including a eco rider in your consulting contracts to advise your clients of your strategic initiatives regarding environmental sustainability.

Global Connection

Create a list of written risk management policies, procedures, and practices, and ask a colleague in another country to examine these statements to determine if they are standard and customary in their country.

Technology Connection

Use a computer-assisted drawing and design (CADD) system to prepare the final diagram for review by public officials. Conduct a trademark search using the Internet to determine if your brand identity may be qualified to have a trade, service or registered mark.

Resource Connection

The American Society for Individual Security (www.asisonline.org) provides a wide range of books, articles, and videos to help you understand the many issues regarding safety, security, and risk management. The most comprehensive book in this field is *Event Risk Management* (Tarlow 2002).

The American Institute of Certified Public Accountants (www.aicpa.org) is a good source of information concerning how accounting firms should comply with Sarbanes-Oxley legislation.

Learning Connection

Design a risk management plan for an event for a publicly traded corporation. Describe how the plan will change based on various weather conditions. Explain how you will conduct, if necessary, a mass evacuation due to a catastrophic condition, such as fire or violence. List the types of insurance you must purchase to reduce your financial exposure. Describe how Sarbanes-Oxley legislation may or may not affect your event.

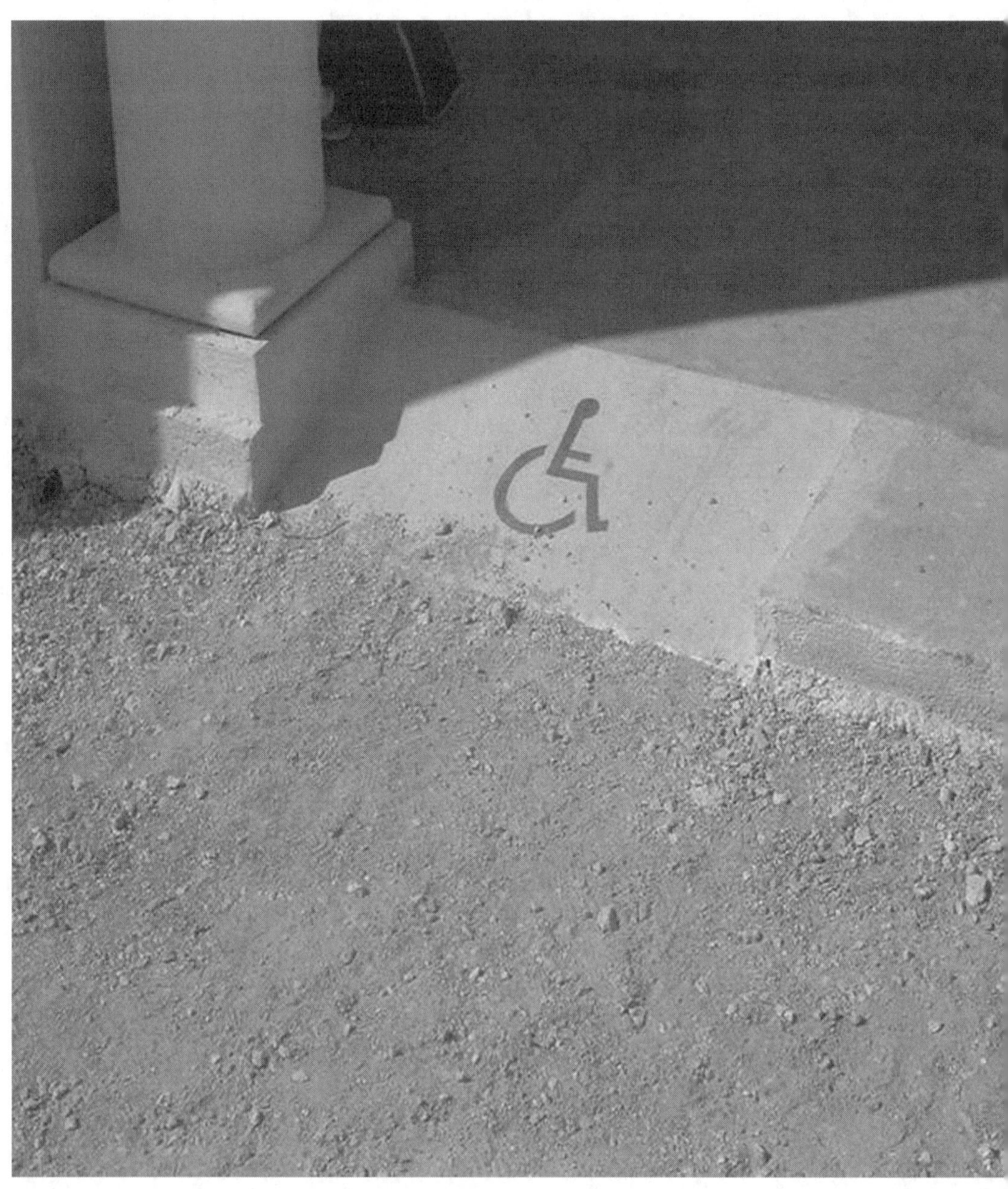

This curb cut to enable wheelchair users to have access to the event demonstrates the events commitment to inclusivity at Mexico's Yucatan Fair and Exposition.

CHAPTER 12

Inclusiveness, Morality, Law, and Ethics in Event Planning

In this chapter you will learn how to:

- Develop special events within events to satisfy the needs of all guests and perhaps increase attendance
- Organize and conduct appropriate accompanying persons programs
- Promote principles of inclusiveness throughout your event plan and production
- Comply with the U.S. Americans with Disabilities Act and other International Equal Access Regulations
- Understand the differences between morals, laws, and ethics
- Identify common ethical problems in the special events industry
- Avoid certain ethical problems
- Establish policies and procedures for ethical issues
- Identify and use industry ethical guidelines
- Appoint an "ethical brain trust" to guide your ethical decision making

Two decades ago, this chapter probably would not have appeared in this book—or any business book, for that matter. However, as businesses have grown and the events industry in particular has expanded rapidly, more and more ethical issues have appeared. Headlines screaming about AIG, the Royal Bank of Scotland, Enron, Arthur Andersen, and other major controversies in business have made all of us more aware of the potential for loss of reputation through ethical missteps. Therefore, it is essential that issues of inclusiveness, morality, ethics, and law be discussed in this book.

Only a few years ago, when I introduced a required unit on ethics in my master's degree courses, several students told me that the other business professors found this to be ironic in a business school curriculum. I have persevered and continue to include this unit, and slowly but surely more and more business schools are now requiring not only units but also entire courses in business ethics. Largely prompted by the corporate supporters that ultimately employ their graduates, business schools have come to realize that their discussion of business ethics may be the first and last time students are exposed to this important issue. Indeed, the majority of the population may never earn an advanced degree, so providing this discussion at the baccalaureate or graduate level could fill in a gap left by parents and teachers.

I often tell my colleagues that we must teach ethical decision making because, ultimately, it may affect and influence students" actions at the university and beyond. As faculty and mentors, we have a responsibility to help students make the personal and professional decisions that ethical behavior requires. I suggest that event planners also have a responsibility to themselves and those they mentor to understand the requirements for making sound ethical decisions.

Differences among Morals, Laws, and Ethics

Etymologically, the term *moral* is derived from the Latin term *moralis*, that is, related to the word *custom* or right or wrong in terms of behavior. When Moses received the original commandments, he may have also realized that if he or his followers disobeyed, there would be penalties. Morals are personal decisions that have personal consequences for right or wrong behavior. The legal system is a series of laws (many based on the Mosaic code) that are linked to specific punishments. Laws are enacted by groups, and punishment is imposed by peers (juries) or judges. Unlike morals, laws use third parties to enforce them and issue the punishment based on the degree of the violation. Professional ethics are, however, neither morals nor laws. Some argue that professional ethics incorporate both law and morals, but in actuality, ethics are the principles of conduct governing individuals or groups. These principles are based on the business culture that is accepted at the time of the action. Although ethics are personal decisions, they are guided by group behavior and group acceptance.

To better understand the interrelatedness of morals, laws, and ethics, ask yourself a series of questions. Let us start with a moral question: "Would you kill another person?" A moral person would immediately answer, "No, never." However, what if your children were being attacked by a violent person and the only way to stop the attack would be to kill the assailant? "Would you steal?" Once again most people would answer, "No." However, let us suppose that your children are starving and their very lives are threatened unless they receive some food to nourish them. Now what would you do?

"Would you attack someone?" Most of us would answer negatively. However, if your country was attacked, and you were part of the army that must defend your nation, you would answer in the affirmative or face serious punishment.

As you can see, many moral questions also have legal and ethical repercussions. Most of us will not be confronted on a daily basis with serious moral or legal decisions; however, many members of this profession regularly face serious ethical dilemmas.

Common Ethical Problems in the Special Events Industry

Ethical problems often vary according to type of industry and geographic location. In the special events industry, some ethical problems faced by hoteliers may or may not affect those in the party rental industry. The same may be said about the event planner in the country of Brazil versus the event planner in the United States. For example, in Chapter 11, you examined some risk management and legal issues associated with the consumption of alcohol. In the United States, the person who pours the alcohol may be legally responsible if a person being served overindulges and causes injury to others. In Brazil, just the opposite is true. The legal system of Brazil places the responsibility on the drinker rather than on the server. This has important ethical ramifications. If you are serving alcohol in Brazil, is it ethical to allow your guests to drink until they are inebriated and capable of causing injury to others? As you can see, the type of industry (or industry segment) and the geographic location often dictate the customs, practices, and values that are practiced by members of that community. These customs, practices, and values of the industry and local culture often drive the ethical decision making within the event organization.

Numerous typical ethical issues are addressed on a regular basis by members of the planned events industry. Figure 12.1 lists some of the ethical issues that you will encounter most often.

Avoiding or Addressing Ethical Problems

The proactive methods described in Figure 12.1 illustrate some of the simple and practical steps that you can take to avoid the pitfalls of unethical behavior. Realistically, you cannot predict every ethical dilemma that may arise. You can, however, be prepared to resolve these problems with a proven three-step process: admission, remorse, and correction.

Despite your best efforts to avoid ethical misconduct, you can always recognize the mistake and notify the person or persons who may have been affected and tell them, "I made a mistake. I'm sorry. I will try not to let it happen again." Too often, individuals

Issue	Those Affected	Proactive Measures
Breach of confidentiality	Staff members	Include a confidentiality clause in employment agreements and policies and procedures.
Gifts versus bribes	Buyer and seller	Define gifts, set limits for receipt of gifts, and establish policies and procedures.
Sexual harassment	Staff members, supervisors, clients, guests	Establish written policies and procedures in accordance with federal laws, conduct training for new staff, and notify clients of policies and procedures.
Staff members soliciting clients from previous employment at new place of employment	Staff members	Establish employment agreements that limit this exposure.
Taking credit for others' work	Staff member and organization	Clearly identify who is responsible for work produced.
Theft of ideas by clients and competitors	Clients, competitors	Insert a copyright statement on proposals, and notify others of infringement.
Vendors accepting work directly from clients	Vendors and clients	Establish written policies.

Figure 12.1 Typical Event Industry Ethical Issues

and organizations attempt to avoid confronting the problem of ethical misconduct, and the misdeed festers like a wound that never heals. From the highest office in the land to local places of worship, most of us know far too many examples of ethical violations that are swept under the rug with the supposition that they will go unnoticed. Despite the rug, these ethical infractions continue to smell, and the small lump under the rug may grow and trip others in the future unless you address the problem promptly.

There are numerous successful examples of the three-step process for handling the problem of ethical violations. This is why it is important that you and your organization develop policies, procedures, and practices to address ethical issues when they arise. One of the best examples of professional handling of a major ethical situation is the 1982 Tylenol tampering incident. Johnson & Johnson, the maker of Tylenol, immediately withdrew the product from all shelves worldwide and issued a statement describing its plans for researching the problem and improving the safety measures for its products. As a result of its response, Johnson & Johnson received plaudits from the media and customers, and sales remain strong today.

How did Johnson & Johnson know how to respond to this ethical issue? The Johnson & Johnson credo states in the first paragraph that its company exists for the purpose of providing safe products and services: "We believe that our first responsibility is to the doctors, nurses, and patients, to mothers and fathers and all others who use our products and services." You can create your own credo to guide you as you face the many ethical decisions you will encounter in your career. One of the important facets of the Johnson & Johnson credo is the statement: "We must constantly strive to reduce our costs. . . . We must be good citizens. . . ." These statements not only reflect the credo of the organization but also address the operational aspects to enable managers and other employees to make decisions on a daily basis that are congruent with the values of Johnson & Johnson. When you draft your credo, make certain that it is more than cold type on a page; instead, it should burn like a branding iron into the hearts and minds of all persons who are responsible for serving as the stewards of your organization's good name. One of the many ways that Johnson & Johnson communicated its strong ethical message was through a series of internal events produced by one of the leading firms in the industry: Jack Morton Worldwide (www.jackmorton.com).

According to Bill Morton, chairman of Jack Morton Worldwide, "We were given a very small window to develop and produce these events. However, Johnson & Johnson entrusted us with their brand because of our long relationship with them. And ultimately, we were successful, despite the short time frame for development and production." Jack Morton Worldwide also has a strong credo that is based on integrity. It is a credo first solidified by the founder Jack Morton in 1939. And this is one of many reasons why the Athens, Greece, Olympic Games Organizing Committee (ATHOC) selected Jack Morton Worldwide to produce the opening and closing ceremonies of the 2004 Summer Olympic Games.

Nearly 50 years ago, my father opened his small hardware store in Dallas, Texas. Instead of hanging a grand opening banner or blowing up balloons, he sat down and composed a simple but profound message to his customers. The message was then transformed into elegant calligraphy and displayed just inside the front door of his store, where it greeted customers for almost 50 years. As I write these lines, that message faces me, and it reads:

> *Once upon a time, I met a stranger . . . not so many years ago . . . in a distant city. When he learned that he knew my grandfather, the stranger looked at me and said, "You have a good name." He went on to explain that my grandfather held the respect and esteem of his fellow businessmen, his customers bestowed their confidence upon him, and his compassion and service for others was an inspiration to all. It is the hope of this business that we will so conduct our affairs that someday, somewhere one of our descendants will meet a stranger who will say, "You have a good name."*
>
> —*Max B. Goldblatt (1911–1995)*

As further evidence of the value of this important credo, I offer a anecdote provided by ny nephew Aaron Lahasky, Certified Registered Nurse Anthesist. Aaron had recently accepted a position in a hospital in Dallas, Texas where my father served as a city council leader during the 1970's. A patient asked Aaron if he was from Dallas and he said no, however, his grandfather was. The patient asked Aaron the name of his grandfather and when Aaron said, Max Goldblatt, the patient sat up in her bed and shouted for her husband to come and meet the grandson of Max Goldblatt! The patient then told Aaron that she had received the Max and Rosa Goldblatt Award for Community Service from the Dallas County Community Colleges. The patients warm smile reminded Aaron, that indeed, he has a good name.

Establishing Policies and Procedures for Ethical Issues

In Appendix 17, you will find the Code of Ethics of the International Special Events Society (ISES). This is one example of how an industry establishes standards for ethical behavior. Some ways to avoid or resolve many of the issues within the code of ethics follow:

- Do not accept expensive gifts. Ban or set a financial limit on gifts.
- Avoid confusion regarding a change in an agreement. Put all agreements (and changes) in writing and have both parties initial acceptance.
- Avoid improper promotion of your services. Seek written authority while working for another Event Planner.
- Avoid claiming credit for an event you produced while working for another firm. Clearly disclose the circumstances concerning the production of the event.
- Avoid submitting photos of an event as an example of your work. Clearly disclose that you helped produce your specific contributions to this event.

Inclusiveness Is an Ethical Responsibility

Perhaps one day the ISES Code of Ethics will be further amended to reflect the growing importance of promoting and achieving diversity and inclusiveness within event organizations. The statistics in the event industry reflect that females continue to outnumber males. What is not evident unless you attend industry conventions is that the percentage of minorities is relatively small as compared to the general population. While many industry organizations have made significant strides in promoting minority participation at the top level of their organizations, many minorities still prefer to form their own independent organizations that may more closely address their own needs and issues.

In the late 1990s, the Washington, DC, chapter of ISES held its annual awards event at the television studios of Black Entertainment Television. As a result of this decision, the percentage of African Americans attending this event was much greater than in previous years.

This is one example of how traditional members of this profession must rethink their locations, programming choices, and other considerations to promote and achieve diversity and inclusiveness. Without diversity and inclusiveness within our events, they and the entire profession will not be as successful and may, in fact, fail to be sustainable. Every living system requires diversity to ensure sustainability. The event industry is no different. Through active and effective programs promoting diversity and inclusiveness, you can expand your event market rapidly. To do this effectively, you must regularly look beyond your own sphere of knowledge to find out what you are missing.

For example, although in 1999, nearly 25 percent of the students in The George Washington University Event Management Program were African American females, no photographs of African American females appeared in the catalog used to promote the program. When an African American staff member brought this to my attention, I wondered what other groups might also be underrepresented.

As Gene Columbus, the longtime manager of entertainment casting for Walt Disney World (now the Executive Director of the Orlando Repertory Theater in Orlando, Florida), stated, it is time for Event Planners to ensure "places for everyone" and make certain that every possible opportunity is developed within the events industry to create a future that is both inclusive and representative of the diversity within the new world of events.

Identifying and Using Industry Ethical Guidelines

In addition to the ISES, many related industry organizations use guidelines for professional practice or ethical beliefs to guide decision making. One criterion that you may wish to use for joining a professional organization is whether it has established a strong code of ethics, along with appropriate enforcement procedures. Although these guidelines are at best guideposts rather than firm edicts, they will be useful not only to you but also to your clients as they raise the image of your profession.

Appointing an Ethical Brain Trust to Guide Your Ethical Decision Making

I have always relied on wise counselors and advisors to help me when faced with making a difficult ethical decision. Instead of assembling this brain trust at the last minute or on a case-by-case basis, I recommend that you identify people who know you well enough to provide you with critical input during times of ethical decision making.

A colleague of mine was faced with a tough ethical decision when he discovered some papers that contained highly personal information in a file left by a recently deceased relative. The papers included letters describing the circumstances of a death that took place 60 years earlier. After consulting with his immediate family members, he decided to contact his minister, who had been a friend of the family for nearly 60 years. The minister listened to the dilemma and asked a few questions relating to the medical consequences of the case. Finally, the minister offered simple but important advice that would spare much future pain to the survivors of the person who had died. "There is a reason the letters were hidden for 60 years. Burn the letters and do not discuss this with anyone." Obviously, the minister had faced this dilemma many times before and knew the framework for reaching this critical decision.

In another instance, someone's will granted lifetime use of a house for a longtime friend of the family. When told of the gift, the friend declined to live in the house and authorized sale of the property. The heirs wanted to share with the friend some of the proceeds from the sale, but a question arose as to how much would be appropriate. Once again, a brain trust was contacted. This time, three wise and experienced persons were consulted: a minister (and longtime family friend), an attorney, and a peer of the same chronological age who had recently had a similar experience. The consensus of the advisors was to use the rule of tithing and provide a gift of 10 percent of the net proceeds to the friend but to forward the funds in the form of a specific gift for past services rather than an arbitrary amount.

These are the types of complex and difficult decisions that require the collective wisdom of the community to reach an appropriate ethical conclusion. Once you reach this conclusion, you can feel confident that your judgment has been not only tested but also strengthened by the counsel of others, who in many instances are more experienced than you yourself. Therefore, once you make the decision, do not look back. Instead, look forward to the next ethical decision you will face, because you will use the experience of all your past decisions to make future ones.

According to the *Washington Post*, the Washington, DC, Millennium-Bicentennial Celebration in 2000 resulted in $290,500 in unpaid bills. The *Post* also reported that there were questions of ethics violations. The District of Columbia established a not-for-profit organization for the purpose of raising funds to plan and coordinate the millennium and bicentennial celebrations for the District. However, there were questions about whether the organization used DC government employees to raise money for the event.

Polly A. Rich, the ethics counselor in the District of Columbia corporation counsel's office, wrote in a memo that city employees should not raise money for nonprofits or solicit contributions from companies and individuals who do business in the District. Anthony W. Williams, mayor of the District of Columbia, responded to the criticism by stating: "Clearly, the lesson from the millennium-bicentennial events and the loss of a substantial amount of money from a lot of this nonprofit fund-raising is: 'What is the proper mechanism to do it?'" The question of appropriateness is not solely moral or legal but also an ethical dilemma that every Event Planner must address.

Furthermore, the Event Planner must realize that his or her event is only as good as its ability to include everyone in the process. Therefore, it is critically important that Event Planners carefully analyze their board, planning committee, volunteers, and staff to ensure that they have attempted to include as many diverse opinions and groups as possible.

Including Everyone: Arranging and Organizing Activities

Many events use tours and other off-site visits to expand the educational value of the program. Other events regularly incorporate tours of the destination and its attractions to provide guests with added value. Finally, some event organizers incorporate tours to offer diversions for accompanying persons, such as spouses, partners, friends, or young people attending with their parents. Regardless of the reason, increasingly, the arrangement and organization of tours is a critical component of most conferences, conventions, reunions, and even weddings.

There are three steps to consider when planning and coordinating tours for your event:

1. *You must conduct an audit of the destination to determine if there are attractions or activities that are of interest to your guests.* You can obtain this information from the local convention and visitors' association or from the chamber of commerce. Make certain that you ask the providers of this information what programs are most appropriate for specific market segments (females, males, children, mature guests, etc.).
2. *Use this research to begin to assess the interest levels of your prospective guests with a brief survey of their interests.* If you can match their strong interests with the best attractions and activities in the destination, you are well on your way to finding a winning combination guaranteed to increase attendance and produce excellent-quality reviews.
3. *Find a price point that will be acceptable to your guests and perhaps provide excess revenues for your organization.* To do this, you will need to obtain bids from local providers. In many destinations, a for-profit organization known as a Destination Management Company (DMC) provides tour services. These services are generally priced on a per-person basis and require a minimum number of participants to operate the program successfully.

In addition to tours, the DMC can provide services such as planning and coordinating local transportation, receptions, parties, and other events within your large event, as well as a wide range of other services. Outside the United States, the term *Professional Congress Organizer* (PCO) is often used to refer to DMCs. The PCO generally provides an even greater range of services than the DMC. In addition to tours and events, the PCO may provide travel bookings, marketing of the event, and registration services, among many other services.

Two organizations represent the top DMC and PCO organizations. In the United States, the Association of Destination Management Executives (ADME) (www.admoe.org) represents the leading destination management companies, and in Europe, the International Association of Professional Congress Organizers (IAPCO) (www.iapco.org) represents the most respected PCO firms.

Developing Special Events within Events

The event professional is often required to organize numerous individual events within a larger special event. In fact, this is so prevalent that the certified special events professional programs require that candidates understand and be able to coordinate accompanying person events, tours, and other auxiliary programs related to special event management. Typical activities that often help form the context of a larger special event include:

- Accompanying person programs
- Arts and crafts displays and/or sales

- Auctions (live and silent)
- Book signings
- Carnivals
- Children's activities
- Coffeehouses
- Cyber Internet café(s) areas
- Dance lessons or parties
- Educational programs
- Etiquette seminars
- Exercise classes such as Pilates, aerobics or others
- Exhibitions
- Fashion shows
- Festivals
- Films
- Formal dinners
- Golf tournaments
- Health lectures
- Hospitality rooms
- Hot-air ballooning
- Lifestyle lectures
- Museum tours
- Personal finance programs
- Races, runs, and marathons
- Sports activities or programs
- Tea ceremonies
- Team-building activities
- Tennis tournaments
- Tours (city, scenic, historic, cultural, walking)
- Yoga
- Youth programs featuring motivational speakers
- Zoological programs and tours

The Event Planner must assess, through research, how the internal or external events will support the overall goals and objectives of the total event. These events should be seen as the frame of a large umbrella. Each spoke or event must carefully support the individual objectives of the overall event. If any one event is poorly planned or weakly coordinated, the entire structure may weaken. Therefore, the Event Planner should conduct an audit of typical event guests, as well as those who are atypical and nonattendees, to determine their interests, needs, wants, and desires. This data can be very helpful in determining which events to offer and during which times they will be most popular.

Once the audit is completed, the Event Planner will usually contact a third party, such as an entertainment, production, or other professional company, to obtain proposals to present the type of event or attraction that is required. Make certain that you encourage the proposers to use their creativity to develop your event ideas further. For example, a game show requested by a major corporation became an "event" when the game company supplier suggested a hostess who was a *Wheel of Fortune* Vanna White look-alike and a set that reflected the popular game show *Wheel of Fortune*. The creativity of others can quickly embellish your event design and bring added value without additional cost.

The final consideration when selecting the events that will comprise your larger event is to confirm the reliability of the vendors. Too often, event organizations driven by committees will develop extraordinary ideas with ordinary budgets and resources. It is much better to select those event elements that will bring high quality and consistent excellence to your event than to stretch the event to the breaking point. To confirm the reliability of individual vendors, it is best to inspect the event during operation before a similar group of guests or to seek references from organizers of events that are similar to the one you are producing.

Organizing and Conducting Spouse and Partner Programs

One of the key competencies in the coordination knowledge domain of the certified special events professional program is the organization and coordination of spouse and partner programs. The term *spouse* is actually somewhat antiquated and has been replaced with the term *accompanying person* to reflect the broader spectrum of persons who are attending an event with the invited guest. The actual taxonomy of the guest list is:

1. Delegate or principal invitee or guest
2. Guest of principal invitee or accompanying person
3. Observer

The accompanying person may have a wide range of interests that must be satisfied during the overall event experience. Typically, the accompanying person will be invited to all social events with the principal invitee, delegate, or guest. In addition, special programming as discussed earlier may be organized to provide diversions while the delegate, principal invitee, or guest is involved in official functions, such as education, governance (debate, discussion, elections), or other similar activities that generally are not of interest to the accompanying person.

The event planner must strike a balance between diverting the accompanying person and totally disengaging him or her from the basic goals and objectives of the overall event. To ensure that the accompanying person is fully engaged and recognized, the person should be identified through credentials as a guest, accompanying person, or observer. In addition, an orientation program should be organized at the beginning of a conference or other multiday event to help accompanying persons to understand the opportunities available during the larger event, as well as to make them feel welcome and answer any pertinent questions.

The accompanying person very often influences the principal guest or delegate to return to an event year after year, so it is critically important that the person has an excellent experience that is equal although different from that of the person he or she is accompanying. To monitor the experience, it is important that accompanying persons be surveyed or surveyed through a focus group to thoroughly analyze their event experience, to allow you to improve your practice continually in the future.

Complying with the Americans with Disabilities Act and Similar International Laws and Regulations

It is projected that the number of persons in North America with disabilities will grow exponentially in the next several years as the baby boomers show the natural signs of the aging process. As a result, the large number of persons with visual, auditory, and physical disabilities will significantly affect the research, planning, design, and coordination phases of twenty-first-century event planning.

During the research phase, the event planner must assess the types of disabilities that are most likely to be reflected by event participants. These important data may be obtained through historical information or through a survey of potential guests. Research will include learning about individual disabilities in order to best prepare and serve the population that will be attending your event.

The design phase enables the event planner to work closely with the disabled community to determine the services and accommodations that must be implemented to ensure the comfort and satisfaction of all guests. During the design phase, many creative solutions may be suggested by members of the disabled population to help the event organizer satisfy his or her needs with little or no additional investment.

During the planning and coordination phases, the Event Planner fine-tunes the recommendations proposed by the disabled community and works with event vendors and staff to implement the best ideas to achieve the best outcomes for the overall event. These two phases should include the identification of contingency plans for serving disabled individuals who were not identified previously but must be accommodated once they arrive at the event.

Event Sensitivity

At one time, the term *handicapped* was used to describe individuals with limited abilities. In recent years, the disabled community has asked that this term be replaced with the term *disabled*. When conducting staff and volunteer training, I prefer to use the term *different abilities* because in my experience, every human being has different abilities with which to enjoy your event. Your job is to find these abilities and, through the event plan and practice, satisfy the needs, wants, and desires of all guests regardless of their individual abilities.

There is a fine line between attending to the needs of guests with special needs and interfering with their personal space. According to the International Association of Amusement Parks and Attractions video resource titled *Disability Etiquette*, (www.iaapa.org) here are some key methods for helping rather than intruding.

Visually Challenged Guests

When approaching guests who have visual challenges, first speak and offer to assist them. Do not touch them first, as this may startle them; rather, use a soft voice and offer your help by saying, "May I help you?" Consider providing additional services including Braille programs, Braille signs, and infrared technology that will verbally alert guests when there is a step up or step down or turn.

Physically Challenged Guests

When speaking to persons in wheelchairs, bend down to their level so you are making face-to-face contact. The chair is a physical extension of the individual; therefore, ask

Total Number of Parking Spaces Provided (per lot)	(Column A) Total Minimum Number of Accessible Parking Spaces (60″ & 96″ aisles)	Van-Accessible Parking Spaces with Min. 96″ Wide Access Aisle	Accessible Parking Spaces with Min. 60″ Wide Access Aisle
1 to 25	1	1	0
26 to 50	2	1	1
51 to 75	3	1	2
76 to 100	4	1	3
101 to 150	5	1	4
151 to 200	6	1	5
201 to 300	7	1	6
301 to 400	8	1	7
401 to 500	9	2	7
501 to 1000	2% of total parking provided in each lot	1/8 of Column A*	7/8 of Column A**
1001 and over	20 plus 1 for each 100 over 1000	1/8 of Column A*	7/8 of Column A**

*One out of every eight accessible spaces.
**Seven out of every eight accessible parking spaces.

Figure 12.2 ADA Standards for Accessible Design of Parking Lots 4.1.2(5)
Source: U.S. Department of Justice, ADA Business Brief, "Re-striping Parking Lots," http://www.ada.gov/restribr.htm.

before touching it. According to the U.S. Department of Justice, parking is a critical issue for persons who are physically challenged. Event Planners therefore are required to make certain that they provide sufficient accessible parking for their physically disabled guests. Furthermore, the Americans with Disabilities Act (ADA) requires that van parking spaces provide three additional features: a wider access aisle (96 inches) to accommodate a wheelchair lift; vertical clearance to accommodate van height at the van parking space, the adjacent access aisle, and on the vehicular route to and from the van-accessible space; and an additional sign that identifies the parking spaces as "van accessible." Figure 12.2 lists the minimum requirements for accessible parking spaces according to the U.S. Department of Justice.

Guests with Auditory Challenges

Make eye contact with your guest so he or she may be able to read your lips as you speak. Do not raise your voice; rather, speak slowly and carefully enunciate. Keep a pad of paper nearby and write down your communications, if necessary. If possible, seek help from an American Sign Language (ASL) interpreter to help with communications. The U.S. Department of Justice provides an excellence business connection Web page to help individual businesses better comply with the standards and guidelines of the ADA act. Visit http://www.ada.gov/business.html for additional ideas on how to better serve this population.

You can contact American Sign Language qualified interpreters at the Registry of Interpreters for the deaf, www.rid.org. In Great Britain, contact the National Registers of Communication Professionals working with Deaf and Deafblind People, at www.nrcpd.org.uk.

Providing for Special Needs of Your Guests

Once you have gathered all the quantitative data from the site inspection, it is time to analyze your findings and determine what implications emerge for your event environment design. Most important considerations include the legal, regulatory, and risk management issues that are uncovered during site inspection.

If the venue is not in full compliance with the Americans with Disabilities Act (signed into law in 1992), you may need to modify your design. For example, a large quasi-government corporation asked me to create a tropical theme, including a small bridge at the entrance where guests would stroll over a pond containing live goldfish. In creating this design, we factored in the need to provide full and equal access for disabled guests and ramped both ends of the bridge to satisfy this need.

The statute states:

> *Title III-Sec. 302 a) General rule. No individual shall be discriminated against on the basis of disability in the full and equal enjoyment of the goods, services, facilities, privileges, advantages, or accommodations of any place of public accommodation.*

As a result of this historic legislation, wheelchair ramps, Braille menus and signs, sign-language interpreters, and other elements have become commonplace at events. Event planners are responsible for complying with this law, which affects nearly 50 million Americans.

A comprehensive checklist for incorporating the Americans with Disabilities Act into an event environmental design follows:

- Survey your guests in advance of the event to determine what accommodations will be required.
- Include the following language on all brochures or other offerings: "If you require special accommodations, please describe below."
- Survey the venue to determine what gaps must be closed prior to your event.
- Establish wheelchair seating positions.
- Maintain a clear line of sight for guests who will be using sign-language interpreters.
- Work with speakers with disabilities to provide access to the podium.
- Provide audio headsets for the hard of hearing.
- Provide audio-description services of the stage action for the visually disabled.
- Provide "touch tours" for the visually impaired, allowing them to visit the site before the event and touch the sets, props, costumes, and other objects while an expert describes the visual environment so that they will better enjoy the event.
- Provide American Sign Language (ASL) interpreters to translate spoken words.
- Select venues with, or provide, handrails for guests with physical infirmities.
- Provide tables with appropriate height for wheelchair users.
- Contact the U.S. Department of Justice or in other countries your central government or local council if you have additional questions about designing an event environment that meets compliance regulations. In the United States, you may telephone the free ADA information line at (800) 514-0301.
- Train your staff to better meet the needs of people with disabilities.

Edinburgh's Festival Theatre (www.eft.co.uk) goes above and beyond to welcome persons of all abilities through its doors. At least one performance of every touring show features a sign-language interpreter as well scrolling LED screens that display all spoken words in a performance. The Festival Theatre also provides "touch tours" for guests, inviting them on a guided tour backstage before the performance to touch the sets, props, and costumes while an actor or director describes the visual elements of the production. Headsets that amplify the performance sound are available for every performance, and are checked regularly by the Front of House team. Most importantly, all entrances are ramped, and disabled patrons are greeted by a designated usher who will welcome them in and escort them to their seat.

After seeking written feedback from your prospective guests regarding their special needs, it is important to take one additional step to meet their expectations fully. You may wish to invite people with special needs to conduct their own site inspection of your proposed venue and become part of the planning team. People in wheelchairs, older guests with limited mobility, and visually and hearing-impaired persons can provide you with important information to improve the total event environment. Local organizations, such as Easter Seals or the Muscular Dystrophy Association, can refer you to people who will volunteer to offer their advice and counsel during the planning stage. Listen carefully to their suggestions and incorporate them where feasible. Your goal is to produce an event environment that is accessible and effective for everyone.

Every guest has special needs. Abraham Maslow recognized these needs with his hierarchy of needs, which ranged from basic needs to ephemeral requirements such as the need to be loved. The professional event planner may not be able to forecast or satisfy every need his or her guests bring to an event. However, guests must sense that the Event Planner or host is genuinely concerned with their welfare and will work diligently to attempt to anticipate, identify, and satisfy their needs to provide them with a total high-quality event experience. When this occurs, the guest experience rises to a heightened level, as defined by Maslow.When guests begin to feel appreciated or even loved, this ultimately defines in an intangible but powerful way their enduring memories and experiences from your event.

Career Advancement Connections

Corporate Social Responsibility Connection

Why not appoint an advisory task force composed of individuals from the disabled community to advise you in advance with regards to your event planning? Why not survey your board members and ask them to refer you to members from the disabled community who perhaps should be elected members of your governing body for your event? When planning activities for spouses and partners, are you being sensitive to often-marginalized groups such as members of the gay, lesbian, bisexual, and transgender community? Are you providing services for members of religious groups such as the Muslim community so that they have a proper location for their daily prayers while attending your event? Practicing CSR means looking for opportunities to find a place for everyone to feel comfortable, safe, and successful while participating in or attending your event.

Global Connection

Working with multicultural organizations can be challenging unless the Event Leader does his or her homework. For example, many events held outside the United States suggest that guests wear formal attire or national dress or costume to a formal dinner. It is appropriate to further define national costume as "that which reflects the culture, ethnicity, or national pride of the country where the guest has sworn national allegiance."

Once you have created a list of written ethical policies, procedures, and practices, ask a colleague in another country to examine these statements to determine if they are acceptable in that culture. To avoid committing an offense, use advisors in other countries to guide you in your ethical practices.

Technology Connection

The Internet has numerous sites that provide valuable information concerning disabilities as well as the Americans with Disabilities Act. The U.S. Department of Justice administers the act and may be contacted at www.ada.gov.

Use appropriate etiquette when using the Internet. Avoid spamming (marketing without permission), flaming (using all capital letters, exclamation points, and harsh language), or inappropriate language that may offend the reader. Visit the MPI Web site (www.mpi-web.org) and other industry sites to review their codes of ethics.

Resource Connection

- The Ethics Resource Center (www.ethics.org) in Washington, DC, provides a wide range of books, articles, and videos to help you understand the many issues affecting ethical decision making.
- The International Association of Amusement Parks and Attractions has an excellent video-training tool titled Disability Etiquette (www.iaapa.org).
- For comprehensive information on the Americans with Disabilities Act, visit www.ada.gov.

Learning Connection

- You have been offered an expensive gift from a vendor in exchange for your business. Is there any situation or circumstance in which it would be acceptable to accept this gift? How do you know this? Where will you get the information? How will you make the decision? How could the decision be different if this occurred in another culture, where the giving and receiving of expensive gifts is accepted, usual, and customary?
- One of your event guests complains to you about inappropriate behavior from one of your vendors. Although the vendor is not your employee, do you have an ethical responsibility to intervene on behalf of your event guest? How do you know what to do? Where will you get the information? What steps will you take to make the decision?
- You have been asked to bid on a future event. You are asked by your prospective client to show examples of your past work. Some of the work you have completed was when you were in the employ of others. Do you explain to your prospective client that some of this work was completed while you worked for another firm, or do you simply ignore this fact and present the work to the

client as if you were responsible as an individual? How do you know what to do? Where will you get the information to make the proper ethical judgment? How do you know that this judgment is correct?

- To improve your professional Event Leadership skills, practice completing this exercise: Describe how you will provide relevant and appropriate programming for each of the following groups who will be accompanying your guests to a three-day medical conference: youth, young children, Jews, Muslims, Christians,

The Pioneer: Rai Shacklock, Head of the UK Centre for Events Management, University Teacher Fellow, Leeds Metropolitan University, Leeds, England

Leeds Metropolitan University was one of the first institutions of higher education in the world to develop a comprehensive program in events management. The early program development was led by Rai Shacklock and others at the end of the twentieth century and today is one of the largest event management programs in the world. Rai Shacklock has been honored for her achievements in higher education by the Council of Hospitality, Restaurants and Institutional Education (I-CHRIE) and served as its international president and the European president of this prestigious organization. However, she may forever be remembered most admiringly as one of the most seminal figures in the development of events management education in the United Kingdom and throughout the world.

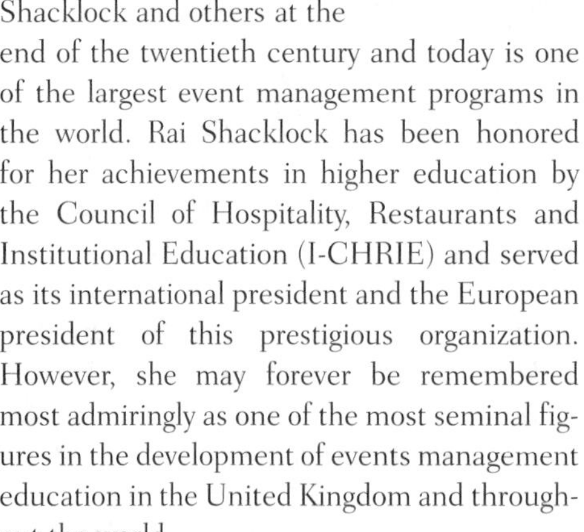

As did many of her peers, Rai Shacklock entered the special events industry purely by accident. Rai says that she simply thought at the time that "it was an industry that I thought would be exciting and challenging and have a wide appeal to develop into an educational discipline."

She knew that event management was exciting to teach and offered many opportunities for a wide range of instruction, learning, and assessment opportunities that were relevant to the needs of the industry. According to Rai, "The students that enrolled in the events management program were motivated and excited to study the program and to work in the events industry."

Rai recalls that her mentors during her long and highly productive career have included Professor Donald Getz of the University of Calgary in Alberta, Canada, who was one of the early educational pioneers of the subject area, and Randle Stonier, chief executive of Adding Value Events Agency, who was a early strong supporter of events education, as well as a great ambassador for the profession. Stonier continues today as a highly respected industry advisor of the UK Centre for Events Management.

During her distinguished career, the field of events management has been formalized and transformed. Rai states, "Technology has changed the processes for stakeholders beyond recognition; the Web has made the

heterosexuals, and homosexuals. The conference is taking place during the Muslim period of Ramadan. Twenty-five percent or more of your delegates have visual, auditory, or physical-mobility disabilities. Describe how you will accommodate each of these delegates, as well as all of them as one community. Finally, describe how you will evaluate your performance for serving each of these populations to ensure continual quality improvement at your event.

industry so much more accessible. A greater awareness of the environment, legislation, and risk has led to many changes. Innovation and creativity have become the cornerstones to developing events as a marketing tool and the development of the events curriculum at leading educational institutions. The efficient and effective use of resources, our opportunity costs, the available sources of funding, and budget planning remain the reserve of the successful organizations."

The catalyst for these sweeping changes in a relatively short period of time has been largely due to the advancements in education, according to Rai. "I believe that events education has been the catalyst for many of the changes that we have seen in the industry. As our graduates have been employed in the industry they have helped to professionalize it. We now see advertisements for events managers who have educational qualifications rather than just experience alone. To pull yourself up by your boot straps is not enough in this world of litigation and professional events management. Success and vision demands research and strategic thinking, and this is where graduates can lead."

Her view regarding the future for graduates is tempered by the current climate of economic uncertainty. However, she hopes that the knowledge, skills, and the reputation that the Leeds Metropolitan University UK Centre for Events Management has for events management will stand them in good stead. "The transferable skills that they have gained while studying at one of the top universities for Events Management education will allow them to work somewhere—perhaps even everywhere—in this very diverse and exciting industry."

One way that Rai and her colleagues support their graduates is by encouraging them to keep in contact with their University throughout their careers. Rai proudly states, "Our graduates come back to speak to students as guest speakers, they take our students on placement and some come back and teach full time. They are becoming the future leaders." The best single piece of advice she would offer to newcomers in the field of event management is to get an education. According to Rai, "An education in events management enables you to work creatively, be visionary, and to think strategically, which allows the questioning of decisions that are made."

The hundreds of graduates that Rai Shacklock and her colleagues have educated and mentored at Leeds Metropolitan University are testaments to the vibrancy and future capacity for high quality in the global events industry. As a direct result of her pioneering vision and continuous devotion to teaching and learning in events management education, the field has greatly advanced. Perhaps one day, one of Rai's graduates will also state that the best single piece of advice for newcomers is, indeed, to get an education—one that is as valuable and high quality as the one they received at Leeds Metropolitan University from the pioneering Rai Shacklock and her remarkable colleagues.

The Protégé: Sharon McElhinney, Senior Lecturer, Leeds Metropolitan University, Leeds, England

Sharon, a graduate of Leeds Metropolitan University and a former student of Rai Shaclock, had originally chosen another course at university, but just knew something was not right with her doing it. She says, "I just didn't click with the subject. So when it came time to make the decision to change courses, I found a new course in Events Management at the university and just had an instinct that it was the career path for me. It chose me!"

During her long career in the meetings and events industry, both in the United Kingdom and the United States, she has identified mentors in many of the people she has worked with. Rather than select one or two mentors, she says, "I instead have always tried to take things from each person I have worked with. I always think that everyone has a strength that you can draw from in order to make your own performance better."

She believes that the industry will become even more professional in the future, especially as the numbers of graduates and events management courses continue to increase. She says that "The increases in technology will also continue to have a big effect, especially in the meetings and conference industry with regards to registration processes and ways in which we can evaluate events. Sustainability within the industry will continue to be talked about and changes made, but I think that is something that will be a natural progression. As people become more environmentally aware they will want their events to also be considering this area."

Today, Sharon has combined her extensive professional experience with her devotion to teaching to lead modules in managing an event organization and optimizing the event space. Although she has received much sage advice during her event and academic career, the most important counsel has been, "To not be scared of any challenge put to me. Trust my creativity!" She says that she chose this advice from all others because normally she is known more for being logistical and tends to shy away from anything too creative. "I have tried to apply it, how successfully I am not sure. I will let others be the judge!"

Indeed, her students and colleagues have already judged Sharon McElhinney as a key part of the future development of teaching and learning in academic centers of excellence such as the UK Centre for Event Management. Benefiting from her strong professional credentials, the students at Leeds Metropolitan University are indeed fortunate to benefit from a scholar who informs and inspires her students and who has found a profession that indeed chose her to benefit others in the future.

Queen Margaret University event students participate in Hospitality Helping Hands at the Professional Convention Management Association (PCMA) convention in New Orleans, Louisiana. The students are cleaning up one of the historic cemeteries that was damaged by Hurricane Katrina.

CHAPTER 13

Doing the Right Thing: Corporate Social Responsibility (CSR)

In this chapter you will learn how to:

- Define CSR within the special events industry
- Contribute to the history and evolution of CSR with your future events
- Monitor changing social expectations to ensure your events are meeting or exceeding their responsibility requirements
- Increase affluence by promoting a fairer economy through socially responsible events
- Use the Internet to expand your event's social influence throughout the world
- Secure the commitment of your clients, vendors, and sponsors to promote socially responsible events
- Identify and liaise with your CSR counterparts in government, nongovernmental and other organizations
- Ensure that your CSR influence is felt both internally as well as externally
- Measure and evaluate your event's social responsibility index

- Create socially responsible programs for conventions, festivals, meetings, and other events
- Conduct social responsibility orientation and training programs for your event staff and volunteers
- Promote your socially responsible outcomes to others
- Find additional resources to continually improve your social responsibility commitment through events

What Is a Socially Responsible Special Event?

In 2009, six event management students from Queen Margaret University in Edinburgh, Scotland, traveled to New Orleans, Louisiana, to attend the Professional Convention Management Association (PCMA) annual conference. The students, with financial support from VisitScotland, the national tourism agency, agreed to help rebuild and renovate one of the historic cemeteries in New Orleans that had been badly damaged by Hurricane Katrina.

Although the students arrived at midnight the previous evening, they promptly reported for duty at 8 A.M. to help restore the cemetery. Their duties included sanding and repainting the historic and ornate gates to this sacred burial ground. During their work, several local residents approached them and offered them local coffee and drinks to thank them for the efforts they we expending to help rebuild their city.

Why did the students decide to do this work? The simple answer is their personal and collective sense of responsibility. However, in fact they were part of a group of several hundred PCMA volunteers that annually provide assistance to the destinations where their annual convention is held. The PCMA Hospitality Helping Hands, a Network for the Needy program, began in 1990 as a simple program to donate food left over from conventions to needy individuals. In the past two decades, the program has expanded to include projects such as the one that greatly benefited the city of New Orleans.

When asked why the students chose personally to participate, they said that after seeing the devastation that resulted from Hurricane Katrina, they felt like they must do something to help. For many of the students, it was their first trip to the United States. This opportunity to volunteer not only made a great impression on the students, but their work was featured in the local newspaper and on television as well as in business industry reports.

The concept of CSR actually may have been first defined by the Scottish philosopher Adam Smith in the eighteenth century, when he stated in his classic work *The Wealth of Nations* that work, if performed ethically, would result in personal and collective gain. He further stated that the person conducting the work was a steward of the organization and of society as well.

1. Satisfy customers with goods and services of real value.
2. Earn a fair return on the funds entrusted to the corporation by its investors.
3. Create new wealth, which can accrue to nonprofit institutions that own shares of publicly held companies and help lift the poor out of poverty as their wages rise.
4. Create and maintain new jobs.
5. Defeat envy though generating upward mobility and giving people the sense that their economic conditions can improve.
6. Promote innovation.
7. Diversify the economic interests of citizens so as to prevent the tyranny of the majority.

Figure 13.1 Seven Economic Duties of CSR for Managers
Source: Lantos, Geoffrey P. (2001) "The Boundaries of Strategic CSR," *Journal of Consumer Marketing,* 18 (7).

Geoffrey P. Lantos states in Figure 13.1 that there are seven critical economic duties of CSR for managers.

However, Lantos and others further recognize that, since the industrial revolution, although business has been focused on economic generation, its responsibilities have expanded to serve the other interests of greater society. Prior to the 1960s in North America and other parts of the world, ethics was not widely discussed in the business literature. In the 1960s and 1970s, society began, especially through human resources and consumer action, to place greater responsibilities on corporations to become stewards of greater society.

Despite these pressures, and the resulting changes that brought about mission, vision, and values statements from thousands of corporations, many businesses continued to suffer from public distrust. The business literature is filled with tragic case studies of once formidable and well-respected corporate citizens such as Arthur Andersen LLC, Enron, Lehman Brothers, and many others whose public statements regarding CSR did not accurately reflect their private actions.

Therefore, you may ask, how does a special events organization for the next generation and new frontier ensure that these mistakes of the past are not repeated? One way to do this is to establish a strong credo for your organization and then let this credo serve as your guide for strategic planning as well as day-to-day decision making.

Johnson & Johnson, the global health care products company, created the credo shown in Figure 13.2 over 60 years ago, and it is still used today to ensure that the company does not veer from its original values.

According to Johnson & Johnson officials, the credo serves as a strong moral compass. It was crafted by the former chairman of their firm, Robert Wood Johnson, in 1943, before the company went public and before the term *CSR* entered the business lexicon. Does your special events organization have a credo?

Our Credo

We believe our first responsibility is to the doctors, nurses, and patients, to mothers and fathers and all others who use our products and services.

In meeting their needs everything we do must be of high quality.

We must constantly strive to reduce our costs in order to maintain reasonable prices.

Customers' orders must be serviced promptly and accurately.

Our suppliers and distributors must have an opportunity to make a fair profit.

We are responsible to our employees, the men and women who work with us throughout the world.

Everyone must be considered as an individual.

We must respect their dignity and recognize their merit.

They must have a sense of security in their jobs.

Compensation must be fair and adequate, and working conditions clean, orderly and safe.

We must be mindful of ways to help our employees fulfill their family responsibilities.

Employees must feel free to make suggestions and complaints.

There must be equal opportunity for employment, development and advancement for those qualified.

We must provide competent management, and their actions must be just and ethical.

We are responsible to the communities in which we live and work and to the world community as well.

We must be good citizens—support good works and charities and bear our fair share of taxes.

We must encourage civic improvements and better health and education.

We must maintain in good order the property we are privileged to use, protecting the environment and natural resources.

Our final responsibility is to our stockholders.

Business must make a sound profit.

We must experiment with new ideas.

Research must be carried on, innovative programs developed and mistakes paid for.

New equipment must be purchased, new facilities provided and new products launched.

Reserves must be created to provide for adverse times.

When we operate according to these principles, the stockholders should realize a fair return.

Figure 13.2 Johnson & Johnson Credo
Source: www.ethiconinc.com

Why Is CSR Important in the Special Events Industry?

According to the *CSR Monitor,* in wealthy countries, individuals make their purchasing decisions based upon their perception of the level of CSR exhibited by corporations. This report also states that, in North America alone, 42 percent of individuals who do not practice CSR will be punished by customers who will take their business elsewhere. In North America, customers who support corporations with strong social responsibility programs are called *conventional activists,* and in Europe they are referred to as *demanding disgruntleds* (www.bsdglobal.com).

It may be argued that since the first traders crossed the great trade routes of Europe, practicing strong CSR behavior may not only be good for society but also good for business as well. In fact, that has long been the argument within certain business sectors. Many business leaders and philosophers such as Adam Smith agree that a business that does not look out for the greater good of society cannot expect society to look out for them.

How You May Contribute to the History and Evolution of CSR with Your Future Events

According to Silberhorn and Warren, CSR is a comprehensive business strategy, arising mainly from performance considerations and stakeholder pressure. Companies focus on how they interact with stakeholders and how business activities impact society. Therefore, all CSR efforts must be ultimately focused on performance (Silberhorn and Warren 2007).

One example of how disconnects between plan and performance often develop within business sectors is the information technology (IT) sector. According to Citizens Online, only one in six IT firms based in the United Kingdom support Internet activities for the disadvantaged. Furthermore, the same group identified in a study of over 200 UK IT firms that although many firms criticize the poor philanthropy record of IT firms, most consider it fair to cut charitable giving if there is a downturn in turnover profits (Citizens Online 2001).

This is why you must recognize your core responsibilities as a member of the special events sector with regards to CSR. Sustainable development, responsible stewardship, and legacy building are key indicators for you to demonstrate not only your commitment but also your performance in each of these important areas.

Sustainable development is a term that describes development that meets the needs of the present without compromising the ability of future generations to meet their own needs. For example, when conducting a festival in a pasture, you may wish to re-seed the grass at the end of the event to sustain growth in the future. In the area of human resources, you may wish to develop succession plans to ensure the special events organization will continue to operate even more efficiently in the future.

Responsible stewardship requires that you serve as a responsible custodian of the scarce resources you are using to produce your event. For example, from a environmental standpoint, ask yourself how you may reduce waste through the use of recycling systems. Conserving water, energy, electricity and paper are all basic ways to promote responsible stewardship of your resources.

Legacy building is critically important for many destinations in the bidding process for events. London 2012 won the bid to host the International Olympic Games by presenting a strong legacy strategy to improve the social cohesion, health, sports participation and other key performance indicators of the people who live in the neighborhoods where the 2012 Olympic Games will be conducted. While other destinations focused upon their infrastructure, their natural beauty, and even the celebrities that endorsed their bids, London trumped all of them by focusing on the legacy of the Olympic Games. What is the legacy for your event? Will you improve the community as exemplified by PCMA's Helping Hands project in New Orleans?

Monitor Changing Social Expectations

The expectations of generations Y and X are far different from those of the baby boomers. Do you have a plan for monitoring these changing expectations? The use of social media networking sites such as Twitter, Facebook, and others can provide you with macro social inputs. By developing a pre-event blog for your event, you can monitor in a very specific way what is in the hearts and minds of your future guests and then adapt your CSR plan to meet their expectations and needs. Rarely does a CSR plan succeed without the central buy-in of those who will be most invested. Therefore, it is important to continually monitor your core stakeholders to design and deliver programs that they are passionate about. For example, the city of Copenhagen, Denmark, has a series of programs designed to bring awareness about the plight of the homeless in their city and other destinations throughout Europe. Through sponsoring events such as a homeless football match and a homeless sculpture tour, they are not only raising funds but also awareness to address the problem of homelessness in their city and others as well. Can your next event not only entertain but also engage your publics in helping mitigate or even eliminate some of society's greatest social problems, such as homelessness?

Increase Affluence by Promoting a Fairer Economy

The Scottish government promotes several objectives, including a fairer distribution of wealth throughout Scotland. Their goal is not only to increase the overall wealth within the country but to make certain it is fairly distributed. To do this, they are staging the Commonwealth Games in Glasgow, Scotland, in 2014. As a result of this event the Scottish government plans to develop the future workforce by transmitting new and valuable skills to the thousands volunteers who participate in the games so they may be more employable in the future (Scottish Government 2009).

Use the Internet to Expand Your Event's Global Social Influence

Generations X and Y are often characterized as the first completely wired workforce of tomorrow. In fact, these generations are wireless. Many cities throughout the world, including Philadelphia, Pennsylvania, are investing in wifi systems to enable wireless Internet access from almost any location throughout the city. This mobility may provide you and your staff and volunteers with new and unique opportunities to influence millions of others throughout the world. Figure 13.3 lists 10 ways to use the Internet to promote CSR through your event.

1. Include in your Web site links to charitable organizations that your event is supporting. Require the charitable organizations to track the hits they receive through your Web site so you may inform your board, your volunteers, the media, and other stakeholders of the influence of your Web site on these charitable web Web sites.
2. Build a donation financial transaction system into your Web site so that participants may make donations directly to your cause online.
3. Develop a weblog to encourage the development of ideas for furthering the socially responsible activities you have begun with your event. Transfer the best ideas to your event's main Web site.
4. Conduct a global webcast with reports from around the world from individuals who are connected to your event. This could include video or audio streaming of messages as well as text.
5. Invite celebrities who support your socially responsible causes and activities to provide testimonials and endorsements to encourage others to participate. These messages may be video, audio, text, or all three.
6. Show the progress of your socially responsible activities by publishing an online barometer or report card to show in real time the progress you are making toward your goal.
7. Establish a volunteer recognition page as well as a referral form online to celebrate your volunteers, but also to have them refer (by supplying e-mail addresses) others to your event organization.
8. Establish Facebook and Twitter groups and encourage your event stakeholders (staff, volunteers, participants and guests) to tell others about their activities with your event and the importance of its socially responsible activities.
9. Publish an annual report of your socially responsible programs and link this report to your various social media sites.
10. Promote engagement in your event by encouraging your stakeholders to provide instant updates about the impacts of your socially responsible activities before, during, and following the event. Establish wireless hot spot locations at your event for this purpose.

Figure 13.3 Ten Ways to Expand Your Events Reach in a Wireless World

Secure the Commitment of Your Clients, Vendors, and Sponsors to Promote Socially Responsible Events

The anthropologist Margaret Meade once remarked, "Never doubt that a small group of thoughtful, committed citizens can change the world: Indeed, it's the only thing that ever has." Your small group of clients, vendors, and sponsors should join you in aligning their activities with your CSR program. Figure 13.4 depicts how to link others to strategically support your event's CSR mission.

Identify and Liaise with CSR Counterparts in Government, Nongovernmental, and Other Organizations

Throughout government and nongovernmental organizations, you will find numerous individuals and entire departments that could support your CSR program. Figure 13.5 depicts these important linkages.

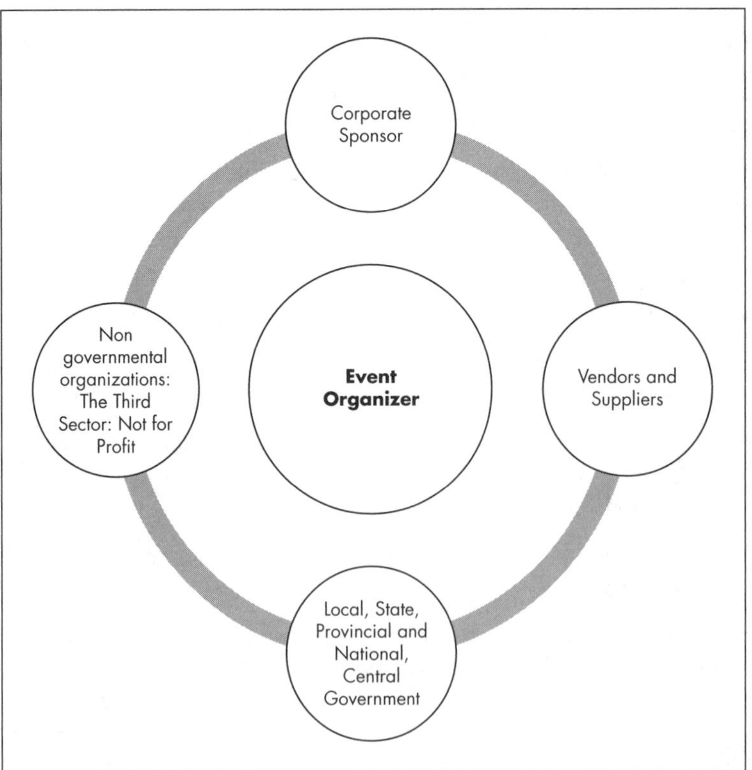

Figure 13.4 Engaging Others in Your CSR Activities

The more stakeholders you have involved in your event, the more likely you are to achieve your specified outcomes. When involving others, remember the key success factors listed in Figure 13.6.

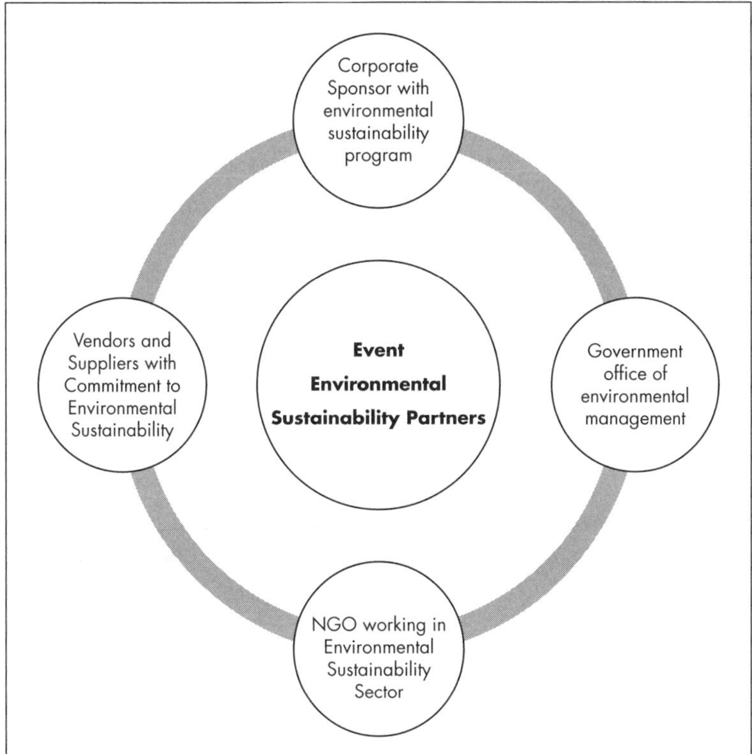

Figure 13.5 CSR Linkages with Government and Nongovernmental Organizations

1. Involve others in the development of these programs and make certain your final plan matches their needs and receives their firm support.
2. Conduct research to find the natural linkages between what you want to accomplish and what others are already doing. Do not duplicate—rather, improve efficiency and reach by partnering with others.
3. Establish a system for mutually communicating your messages to all publics.
4. Establish an evaluation plan to let your partners and others know how you achieved success through your CSR program.
5. Share your success with others. Prepare a brief post-event report case study describing how you created your CSR program and activities and how these could be improved in the future.

Figure 13.6 Five Key Success Factors for Involving Others in Your CSR Programs

Ensure That Your CSR Influence Is Felt Both Internally as Well as Externally

One of the major mistakes many of the corporations made in the twenty-first century is that they failed to share with their own employees, vendors, and other stakeholders the influence of the CSR programs and activities. Unless those inside as well as outside of your organization are aware of your aims, objectives, and outcomes, participation may be lacking. You may wish to develop an internal and external strategy to involve stakeholders—or in small organizations, your goals may be satisfied by combining these strategies.

First, it is important that you have support and strong buy-in at the top of your event organization. Make certain your CEO (chief event officer), board chairman, board members, and other stewards of your organizations support your approach and activities. Next, turn your attention to key sponsors and vendors and solicit not only their endorsement but also their support. Your sponsors may be delighted to raise their community relations profile through participating in your CSR program. Furthermore, your vendors may already be involved in a CSR program and may offer you invaluable advice and support.

Second, consider reducing your discussion to a formal written treatise, such as a manifesto that is signed by all parties to formalize your partnership. Finally, and most importantly, regularly update your internal and external partners regarding your plans, activities, and progress. This may be done through e-mail, a Web page, or even informal, periodic in-person meetings.

Measure and Evaluate Your Event's Social Responsibility Index

In order to manage your corporate responsibility performance, you must constantly measure your activities and your results. Measuring CSR may be simple, such as measuring the volume of recycling you have achieved from year to year at your event, or complex, such as measuring how your employees, volunteers and others feel about their role in your program. Regardless of how you choose to measure your results, it is important that you set general or specific *key performance indicators* (KPI) for each area of your CSR program and then select the appropriate tools to measure these outcomes. Figure 13.7 lists the five most common areas to measure in CSR programs and the tools you may use to provide valid and reliable results for wider distribution.

Measuring your CSR performance through a comprehensive index not only allows you to see where improvement is required but also lets you track from year to year the success you are achieving and to share this good news with external stakeholders such as the media to further improve the profile of your event.

Create Socially Responsible Programs for Conventions, Festivals, Meetings, and Other Events

Although the special events industry comprises many sectors, many would agree that conventions, festivals, and meetings represent three of the largest in terms of total

Outcomes	Measurement
Environmental: Recycling	Measure volume increase.
Social: Cohesion	Measure post-event increase in online community activity.
Education: New skills	Measure increase in job performance.
Health: Wellness activity participation	Measure increased physical fitness activities.
Economic: Fairness	Measure increase in dispersion of economic influence of your event throughout various sectors and communities.

Figure 13.7 Special Event CSR Outcomes and Measurement Strategies

attendance. Figure 13.8 lists examples of best practices in CSR in each of these sectors.

Conduct Social Responsibility Orientation and Training Programs for Your Event Staff and Volunteers

To fully engage your staff and volunteers in your CSR programs they must first be informed then understand, become better educated and then become committed to the ideals of your program. The information and understanding phase begins with a comprehensive orientation program that may include first an online e-mail message that links to a Web site. This could later be followed up with an in-person meeting where you show a video of the benefiting organization. Finally, training should be provided to educate your staff and volunteers. This could also be provided through the Internet or in person and there should also be a assessment component to let your participants know that they are able to fully benefit from their engagement in your program.

Promote Your Socially Responsible Outcomes to Others

Although it seems that the news media only desires to report negative stories to the general public, in fact, most news outlets allot time for feature stories such as your good news resulting from the CSR program. One way to help ensure this future coverage is to identify a media partner or partners who will help you develop public service announcements and provide free advertising space to promote your activities.

The consumer media is just one of many outlets you may use to promote your activities. You should also consider providing photos to your event stakeholders, a short fact sheet and a link to the charity benefiting from your activities so they may promote your

Conventions

1. Arrange in advance for volunteers to clean up or build a playground in the community where your event is being conducted.
2. Donate leftover food to homeless shelters.
3. Donate leftover paper, pencils, pens, and other items to local schools.
4. Invite disadvantaged individuals to stuff your convention packets prior to the meeting and be compensated for their efforts.
5. Provide a cash gift for a local school, library or other organization from funds raised during your convention.

Festivals

1. Re-seed the ground where your outdoor festival is being held and provide additional money for beautification and landscaping projects.
2. Employ disadvantaged people to serve as stewards, ushers, or help with waste management at your event.
3. Engage a not-for-profit organization to provide hospitality services for the portable toilets area for your event. This may include providing a sealed sanitary hand wipe when the person exits the portable toilet so they may wash their hands.
4. Provide free exhibit space for not-for-profit organizations to promote their causes.
5. Invite the electronic media to operate a remote radio or television studio from your festival site and interview participants and film your CSR programs.

Meetings

1. Eliminate as much paper as possible by transferring all documents to the Internet.
2. Use growing plants rather than cut flowers to recycle these plants to hospitals and care homes after the event where they will bring pleasure to others.
3. Source your food locally to reduce the carbon footprint.
4. Invite local college students or others to serve as observers at your meeting to learn about your industry.
5. Establish an electronic mentoring program with local young people where your members serve as online tutors and mentors to disadvantaged youngsters.

Figure 13.8 Best Practices in CSR

event to their friends, family and business associates. It is not unlikely that each of your 1,000 event volunteers, vendors, or sponsors has 200 friends and family that they may contact through e-mail. Therefore, if you give them the good news to share with others, they may reach over two million people!

Finally, it is important that you develop a comprehensive post-event communications plan for your CSR program to inform, educate, and persuade multiple publics about your activities. This type of publicity is indeed priceless, although it may be measured through comparable advertising valuation.

Find Additional Resources to Continually Improve Your Social Responsibility Commitment Through Events

One thing is for certain: There will be no shortage of environmental, social, and economic problems that your event may help address in the future. Therefore, it is important that you regularly monitor the media and also ask your event stakeholders to let your organization know about the needs within your community or throughout the world. Your event may not be able to solve these problems; however, every event may address a problem or problems through a well-developed, well-executed, and well-documented CSR program.

Historically, the hospitality and performing arts industries have been extremely generous with providing service and products to help those in need. Now, through a formal CSR program, the modern special events industry may build on the prior success of other sectors and through special events help repair the world, one event at a time.

Career Advancement Connections

Corporate Social Responsibility Connection

Appoint an advisory committee of individuals from the social services, public, and commercial sectors to advise your event on how you may expand your efforts to produce not only fun but also a focused approach to helping prevent or cure some of society's most pressing problems. This group could meet annually or more frequently if needed, and the purpose and outcome should be highly focused upon specific, measurable, attainable, realistic, and time-based (SMART).

Global Connection

Consider working with an intergovernmental agency such as the United Nations Education, Scientific, and Cultural Organization (UNESCO) to address global problems through your local event. One good example is the charity UNICEF, which raises funds for children in developing countries.

Technology Connection

Make certain you fully engage your technology arsenal to provide opportunities for nonevent attendees to donate online to financially support the cause you are featuring during your event.

Resource Connection

The U.S.-based Association of Fund Raising Professionals may be able to recommend individuals or organizations to help you connect your event to a successful CSR program (www.afpnet.org).

The Pioneer: Karen E. Silva-Sabitoni, EdD, CHE, Department Chairperson, The Center for Sports, Entertainment and Event Management, Johnson & Wales University, Providence, Rhode Island

Professor Karen Silva has enjoyed great success in higher education, but according to Karen, her career actually started by accident. She started in this industry by accident while working at Collette Vacations in Rhode Island where she was responsible for planning group leader luncheons and familiarization tours. When she moved on to The Travel Institute, part of her job involved the travel industry trade shows and, often, even impromptu local events.

The transition from travel professional to teacher was natural for Karen. She remembers, "Growing up, I always knew that I wanted to teach. The opportunity to combine my love of teaching with my love of events has been an ideal career for me."

Throughout her life she has had numerous mentors, including her beloved father, who was the quintessential professor and inspired her love for teaching and love for life. While at Collette Travel, Dan Sullivan Jr. taught her to have passion for excellence at work. Finally, Leah Powers-McGarr, her former department chair, exemplified the characteristics of a true leader within a constantly changing environment.

Karen has noticed that seeping changes have taken place in the events industry since she began her career. She states, "Certainly the industry adapts on a daily basis to changes in the external environment with an increased emphasis on return on investment for events (ROI). Technology has made this job both easier in terms of speed and information access,

Learning Connection

Learn more about CSR within the events industry by visiting www.searchfoundation.org. The Search Foundation is the official fundraising organization within the special events industry. You may also wish to visit Hospitality Helping Hands and Network for the Needy at www.pcma.org to learn more about how the hospitality, meetings, and events industry provides support for those in need through meetings and conventions and exhibition.

yet more difficult in terms of competition. The theme of going green has been the focus of numerous recent seminars and conferences, with hotels, restaurants, and conference centers alike rushing to stay ahead of the latest curve. Perhaps, what all of these elements have in common is that they make us more aware of the responsibilities we all share as members of this industry and inhabitants of this planet."

She believes that it is easy to say "the economy" or "the technology" when postulating about what is causing change within the events industry, but it truly is a much deeper construct. "As the industry has evolved, roles within it have changed. However, the basic needs of guests or customers have not changed. They still expect to be treated as special and it is our job as representatives of this industry to be sure that this tradition continues and these expectations are not only met, but surpassed."

She further observes that although the industry itself may change, the human touch or service element will never be replaced. Brides will still want to sample food, have an expert assist with wine pairing, and have a friendly face meet their guests. Corporate planners may look for better deals, but not at the expense of personalized service. Karen firmly believes that if she can instill in the next generation this understanding, they will continue the tradition of being genuine ambassadors of hospitality and events.

Professor Silva-Sabitoni believes that today's generation is the brightest, most tech-savvy, and best educated of any age. She further believes that if they can take this foundation and build upon it, they will break down barriers and far surpass the expectations of previous generations.

Throughout her distinguished career she has received much sage advice. However, the one she most uses is to recognize that this industry is not just a job, not just a career. Rather, it is truly a lifestyle choice. If you love it, you will not only be successful, but you will thrive as well. She says, "This is the mantra I repeat in classes frequently and have heard it echoed and reinforced by numerous guest lecturers and industry professionals."

Karen Silva-Sabitoni has mentored thousands of students in her long career in higher education. These students will carry Professor Silva-Sabitoni's mantra with them throughout their entire careers. And if they do, they will thrive, just as their professor has demonstrated during her career in travel and higher education.

The Protégé: Liane Boucher, Banquet Sales Representative/ Event Coordinator, Quidnessett Country Club, North Kingstown, Rhode Island, and Graduate assistant to Dr. Karen Silva-Sabitoni of Johnson & Wales University, Providence, Rhode Island

Liane Boucher may be best described as destined for the meetings and events industry since birth. While she was growing up, she really enjoyed planning family birthdays and get-togethers. She says, "I actually attained the nickname "The Planner" from family and friends. When the time came to start thinking about my future, I knew I did not want a career that would require me to sit behind a desk all day. I thought about what I liked and wanted to do in life, and planning events was what I concluded. Prior to investing in the college education for this dream, I first wanted to see if I really liked it."

Later in life, she called the general manager at Kirkbrae Country Club and explained that she would like to come in and see what this job entails. He allowed her to follow the sales manager, the banquet manager, and the event coordinators for a week. "I loved the fast-paced environment, and definitely wanted to pursue my education in this field. I thoroughly enjoyed my classes at Johnson & Wales University, which led me to believe I would love working in the events industry."

Liane believes that you are in the right career if you look forward to going to work every day. She states, "It is such a great feeling to know you were part of a Bride and Groom's special day or a part in a fundraiser's success." She often quotes Lorraine Kane, executive sales representative at Quidnessett Country Club where she works, "When you don't cry at wedding ceremonies anymore, it is time to leave the industry." She admits that she still sheds tears at every ceremony, which reminds her why she still cares about her job and loves what she does every day.

She has had many mentors during her career, however, she describes one in particular whom she both admires and respects. According to Liane, "Christine Perakslis taught me everything she knew, and wanted to help me succeed. Anytime I had a question about my portfolio, needed advice, or just wanted to talk, she took the time to sit down with me. When I was unsure if I should follow my dreams, she gave me the drive and confidence to do so. I thank her for where I am today because she believed in me at my young age and knew I would do well in such an important position."

Liane sees many changes on the horizon in the ever-growing meetings and events industry. One of these critical areas of change will be technology. She predicts, "We will see more webinars, broadcasts, and podcasts be taking place rather than actual in person seminars, meetings, or presentations. Communications will be even more Internet-oriented than they already are. Printed invitations may become obsolete, as they are already not as formal as years ago. E-mail and Internet marketing will prevail, and will also pinpoint potential clients by keeping logs of what types of Web sites they gravitate toward. The industry will also shift to be greener: less or no mailings; no more wrapped gifts at events; and environmentally friendly ways of running their business. Clients will stick to budgets a little closer, but budgets for businesses will decline. This is due to many costly items disappearing, such as postage, fax machines, landline telephone bills, and marketing materials. Labor costs will also be reduced because many things will become automated, which, in turn, creates fewer jobs for humans."

However, Liane also recognizes that the special events industry is a people-oriented industry, and making it more automated will only lead to a less-personal experience for both the business and the client. Even learning about the industry she feels will be different. "We went to school to gain information about managing and planning events, but you will need to be certified in the next few years besides having experience and knowledge."

She predicts, "The next decade will bring about big changes regarding special events. Potential clients will want to experience a virtual wedding online before booking. A wedding guest that cannot attend the celebration will just need to go on the Internet for a live online broadcast. I will be organizing webinars instead of planning meetings with pads, pencils, and chairs. In 10 more years, I will still be in the special events industry, but personal interaction may not."

She is also hopeful about the growth of the industry in the future. She further predicts, "Weddings, mitzvahs, and milestone celebrations will continue to take place, leading the social events aspect within the global events to be able prevail despite a decline in other areas." She believes that the meetings segment of the industry will neither grow nor decline. Instead, meetings and seminars will move to a new platform, and inevitably many will take place via the Internet, videophone, and podcasts.

Her mentor Christine Perakslis, assistant professor at Johnson & Wales University, always started her class with this: "Never miss an opportunity to network." She believes it could be the motto for the global events industry. She explains, "Not only does it help when looking for a job, but also in gaining clients once you have that job. Repeat business is one of the most lucrative types of business you can have. The public tends to gravitate toward people and places they know, so by having more contacts in different areas of your life, the more potential clients you will have. One specific example in my career is the Miss Rhode Island USA pageant. I had never participated in anything like that before, but I had just graduated college and I thought it would be a good experience. Though I did not even make it to the Top 10, I made many new friends. We all belong to a Facebook Group now, and we keep in touch. These women will all get married someday, and they will perhaps look for a wedding planner. They will not need to look too far because I will be in the back of their minds from networking at the Miss Rhode Island USA pageant from years before. Sometimes, the last place you think you will expand your contact list is the best place."

Liane Boucher may have been born into the profession of special events; however, through her commitment to education and dedication to professional networking, her future soon bring even greater credit to her alma mater, Johnson & Wales University. Her family and professors now recognize that the young woman whose family affectionately referred to as "The Planner" has used her planning skills to develop a professional career in meetings and events that is indeed truly boundless.

PART SIX

Technology for Professional Development

Technology is a major trend in the planning and execution of modern events as shown here in Stavanger, Norway as a concert moves into the convention center.

CHAPTER 14

Technology and Modern Event Planning

In this chapter you will learn how to:

- Understand the role and scope of emerging technology within the event industry
- Find resources for efficient technological solutions
- Use mobile technology to notify, inform, and confirm your guests
- Establish online transactional platforms for your event
- Differentiate data processing systems
- Apply technological solutions to solve problems
- Establish a 360-degree event experience

The major task of the technology and information system in modern planned events is to research, plan, design, collect, store, evaluate, and provide critical data to the different levels of users. The comparative advantages of technology over manual systems are:

- Opportunities to use data in a more efficient and timely manner
- Greater reliability; reduce the potential of human error
- Consistency of operations through standardization
- Improved data security
- Real-time analysis and review

The current trend of many event planning organizations is to move toward a more paperless office, where a company relies fully on software collection, storage, and retrieval of data and continuous use of the Internet for research, communications, and transfer of knowledge. Many types of computer technology systems are currently in use. These systems are distinguished by the method they use to process information, by the type of filing systems used for data storage and retrieving, and by hardware configuration.

Data Processing

There are three major types of event data processing systems: (1) batch processing, (2) online real-time processing, and (3) time sharing and service bureaus.

Batch Data Processing

In batch-processing systems, event transactions are accumulated and processed in groups. All revenues and invoices for a day are viewed as batch transactions, to be processed as a group. For example, sales divisions of an event planning company see all sales for a single day as one "day sale" and are entered into a computer system as one batch. Simplicity and reliability distinguish this system. The general rule in technology is that the more complicated the system, the greater the potential for mistakes. The biggest advantage of batch-processing systems is their cost. Since the systems do not require networks, instant backup, and training of the entire staff, they are relatively cheap. However, a batch-processing system does not allow the quick processing of transactions. Therefore, event planners do not always have the ability to retrieve current information. Because of their characteristics, batch-processing systems are rarely used in large event planning companies. They are more common for small and mid-sized event planning companies.

Real-Time Data Processing

In a real-time processing system, transactions are entered as they occur. Given the continuous updating of the database as transactions are entered, the status of all major accounts—such as admission revenue, sales revenue, and inventory—can be determined at any moment. Data-processing systems of several event planning subsidiaries can be connected to the main office's processing unit. The main office can process the data either in real time or using the batch-processing principle. Event planners may have different levels of access to the central data-processing unit. Middle-level managers can be authorized to retrieve all the data from all units or may be limited in their ability to browse through the data.

The system tracks all activities through an event planning company. It allows event planners to set their activities schedule in the most beneficial manner. The system provides event planners with a great tool for inventory control and for control over collection of revenue and of comparison data. Since this system requires real-time transactions and networking, it is more expensive than batch processing. Real-time systems are common for mid-size event planning companies with diverse operations and/or for large event planning companies.

Time Sharing and Service Bureaus

Time sharing occurs when a system services more than one branch of an event planning company at the same time. A service bureau is a company that processes transactions for other entities. Many small and mid-size event planning companies hire bureau companies to handle small operations (e.g., payroll and collection of receivables). In this case, the event company's internal data-processing system can be either linked or not linked to the bureau company's data-processing system.

Hardware Configuration

Three basic types of hardware configuration are common in the event planning industry: (1) online systems, (2) personal computer (PC) systems, and (3) distributed data processing.

Online Systems

Online systems are unique in that each transaction is entered via a communication device connected to a computer. Magnetic cards are a good example for such systems. Online systems may or may not be real-time systems, depending on whether transactions are processed and updated immediately as they happened.

Electronic data interchange (EDI) is currently being adopted by an increasing number of large event companies. EDI is a computer-to-computer exchange of intercompany information and data in a public standard form. In an EDI system, documents such as purchase orders, invoices, attendance projections, and checks are converted into standard form, permitting other companies to read and accept them. There are two methods available for implementing EDI: direct and indirect. The direct method links the computer system of an event planning company with a major client or a supplier, such as a major beverage supplier (see Figure 14.1). When an event planning company makes adjustments to its attendance numbers, the system informs the supplier, which helps to eliminate inventory shortages.

The indirect method utilizes a network of various companies' computers and companies, and provides a "mailbox" for use by all (see Figure 14.2). The network transforms senders' messages into the format preferred by receivers. The advantage of this method is that the sender can transmit documents to several receivers without changing the format each time. For example, an event planning company submits all information about a forthcoming event (e.g., attendance menu, list of beverages,

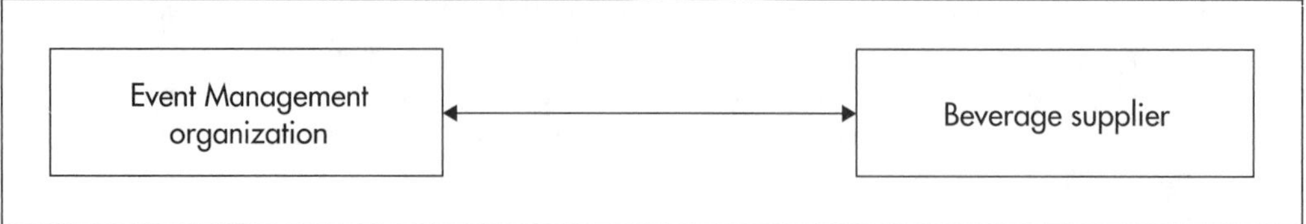

Figure 14.1 Direct Method for Implementing EDI

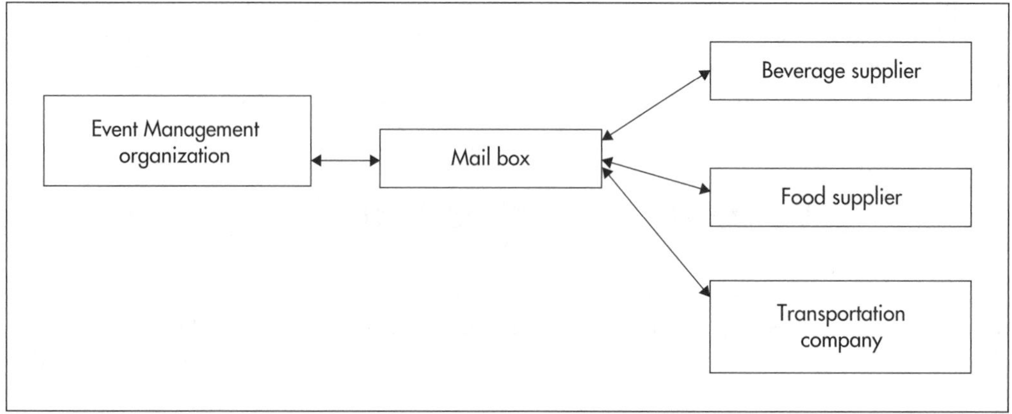

Figure 14.2 Indirect Method for Implementing EDI

setup requirements) to the mailbox. Then suppliers visit the mailbox and submit offers matching the requirements.

PC Systems

PC systems may consist of stand-alone computers used by a single event planner or event worker, or they may be connected to one another and/or to mainframe computers through a form of networking.

Distributed Data Processing

Many large event planning companies use PCs extensively for both data processing and analysis. Event planning companies with branches in various locations frequently use networks to process each branch's transactions and transmit them to the major office via communications links. At the same time, local event planners may use a PC for various kinds of analyses. Distributed data-processing systems are usually connected to a

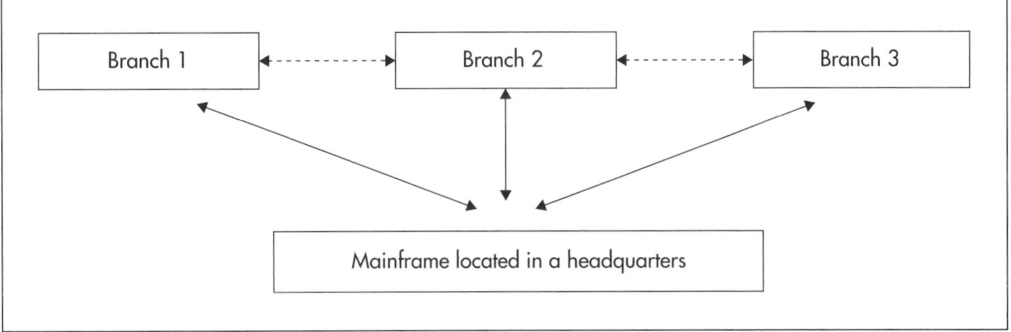

Figure 14.3 Distributed Data Processing System

mainframe computer located at the headquarters office of an event planning company (see Figure 14.3). Additionally, they can be linked to one another through a networking system, such as a local area network (LAN) or a wide area network (WAN). Networks are used to enable PCs to communicate with one another and share workloads.

Access Control

To prevent unauthorized use and alteration of files and data, access must be limited to authorized individuals. In an online, integrated file system and EDI, access limitation is archived through control over passwords, codes used to access various parts of a database. Some passwords allow only examination and retrieval of data; others allow data alteration. Database control includes voiding and changing passwords. However, it is important to ensure that at least two people have master access to a database so that if a person with master access is unavailable, the company's operations will not suffer.

Interactive Web

Development of the Internet was one of the most significant events of the last decade. At first, it was available only to academia and the military, but very soon it became an integrated part of the business environment. As the technology becomes more affordable, more companies are entering cyberspace. As a starting point, companies set up Web sites. At the beginning, sites may be viewed as simply an informative tool. Small event management companies usually start Web sites to post basic information about their services, employees, history, and information on how to contact them. However, the effect of posting the information is similar to listing your company in the yellow pages. The moment an event planning company develops a Web site, it starts to create ways to attract potential customers to the site. All the information becomes immediately available to the general public and, if presented correctly, can serve as a great marketing tool.

Companies attract potential customers in several ways using their Web sites. As a starting point, new sites should create general visitor traffic. This can be accomplished by registering the site with various search programs, such as AltaVista, Dogpile, Google, HotBot, and Yahoo, among others. Once you register a Web site with all major search engines, you may be reasonably sure that it will be available to a potential client who is conducting a search. Usually a search is conducted using keywords, such as "event planning," "event leadership New York," or just "event." The more general the keywords, the more potential matches a search program generates.

A Web site is an excellent marketing tool that can be either used or misused. A site can provide these advantages to an event planning company:

- Wide market reach
- Ability to update information quickly and easily
- Ability to track and collect data about potential clients
- Ability to cut marketing expenses

The internet is a great equalizer. Small and mid-size event planning companies have the same opportunities as industry giants to reach potential customers. Although larger companies have more technical resources to invest in the development of Web sites, the difference usually comes down to having more cookies or action. Web sites that are too complicated and contain much flashier but unnecessary effects may be annoying and make the information difficult to read. In my experience, user-friendly, well-developed, well-designed Web sites are often those of smaller and mid-size event planning companies or even individual event professionals. At the end of the day, all companies have the same opportunity to reach clients.

If you think that you must be a programmer to operate a Web site, you are wrong. In the early days, you had to know one or even several programming languages (e.g., HTML, Java) to make simple changes in a Web site. Today, many computer applications, including Microsoft FrontPage and Netscape Composer, allow users to change sites without learning the coding. Working with your site using these software applications is similar to writing a letter using Microsoft Word. The program automatically transforms the changes you want to make into HTML format. The most difficult part is posting the contents you have created to the World Wide Web, but you can learn to do this in a one-time professional consultation. After your site is designed and launched (which usually requires professional assistance), you can maintain it yourself.

A Web site can be an excellent tool for collecting information about existing and potential clients. Often, event planning companies ask their site visitors to register. Usually visitors are asked to provide their e-mail address, area of interest, basic geographic data, and other material. This information turns into a customized database of clients that you can use later. If a person visited your site and registered, it means that this person is interested, or at least potentially interested, in your services. By collecting and analyzing these data, you can optimize your marketing expenses. You can use your Web site as a tool for customizing services. Major site-development software applications provide site owners with an opportunity to monitor traffic in general and also to obtain more detailed information about what parts of the site generate the most clicks and who is doing the clicking. If, for example, your site contains information about two major services that your company offers—private banquet services and corporate events—and the corporate event service generates much more traffic, this should send you a strong signal about current and future market needs.

Planned Event Databases

The event planning industry is growing rapidly. Although there are several large event planning companies in the market, new players enter every day. A major challenge that companies face in every fast-growing industry is the problem of keeping a database up to date. How often do you dial a number that you found in a catalog, only to find that the number has been changed? It happens to me all the time. Almost every catalog is outdated the moment it leaves the print shop. The accuracy of documents decreases dramatically over time. Getting online is one way of ameliorating this problem. Internet databases are the most reliable in the event industry. One event association executive told me that within a few days of allowing members to update their online records, over 200 persons made changes to the electronic directory.

Two major criteria distinguish a database. The first is its resources. The more resources that a database has, the more valuable it is. Because resources are collected over time, young databases usually contain less data than older ones. The second criterion relates to search features. You can search a database in a number of ways: alphabetically, by region, by service offered, by price, and by age. The more criteria a database has, the more valuable it is. Search criteria should be user-friendly and easy to customize. Even users with moderate database-search experience should be able to find necessary data quickly. Some databases make their search engines overly complicated and the search process becomes very confusing.

Development of the Internet has provided new opportunities for event planners, such as real-time information databases, interactive databases, and commercial databases. Content can be updated online, and users have access at any time. You can receive catering quotes immediately after answering required questions and can book event facilities all over the world. Search criteria can be customized and changed much easier than in a paper version. The search itself can be customized to an unbelievable extent. In electronic databases, users can enter keywords and the database will conduct a global search based on these words.

Event Research Technology

In addition to using Internet search engines, many professional event organizations, as well as convention and visitor bureaus, provide a rich array of resources to help you identify the resources required to plan your next event. For example, the International Special Events Society (www.ises.com) has over 6,000 resources for events in their Finder database and they are filed by city, by ISES chapter, as well as the type of resource required. The use of a specific search engine, such as the one provided by ISES, is an example of a micro-site where highly specific information may be located quickly and efficiently.

Another example of a powerful micro-site is MeetingMatrix International (www.meetingmatrix.com). This site lists thousands of certified diagrams from event and meeting venues all over the world. In addition, the site provides event planners with a fully automated computer-assisted drawing and design (CADD) tool to enable event planners to create customized event plans and renderings.

Event Design Technology

In addition to MeetingMatrix International, Vivien—Virtual Event Designer (www.viviendesign.com) provides a different set of tools to provide CADD for various events, with specific resources to focus lighting. The Vivien system was originally created as part of a tool set to provide theatrical lighting designers with software to create lighting plots and designs for theatre. Now, these tools are available for the global events industry.

Event Planning Technology

The Accepted Practices Exchange (APEX) (www.conventionindustry.org) program developed by the Convention Industry Council provides a wide variety of Microsoft™ compatible tools to assist you with event planning. The purpose of APEX Is to find common platforms of communications and procedures to increase efficiency with the meetings industry. More information about APEX may be found in Appendix Four. Additional examples of meeting and event software may be found in Appendix 8. You may also be able to locate meetings and events related freeware on the internet. Freeware is a term coined by Andrew Fluegelman when he wanted to sell his communications program named PC-Talk. Freeware may or may not be free; however, the concept is to share software through the Internet. Shareware, by contrast, a term coined before freeware, generally requires the user to pay a fee after a prescribed trial period of use.

Event Coordination Technology

One of the pioneers in the event coordination technology realm was a company called Catermate. Their software products were first developed by Ronald Provus as tools to help on- and off-premise caters coordinate their events. The software was rapidly adopted by the broader field of event management. In 1998, Catermate was purchase by CBORD, Inc. (www.cbord.com) and today they offer a wide range of event software, including EventMaster Plus! and Food Service Suite.

Event Evaluation Technology

Evaluation is the most critical component of the event planning process, and it still does not receive the focus or resources that are required to promote continuous improvement through each and every event. One firm, MeetingMetrics (www.meetingmetrics.com), has pioneered the development of online survey research in the meetings and events industry. Their Internet program allows meeting and event planners to upload thousands of e-mail addresses from Excel into the MeetingMetrics database, and then conduct online surveys. According to MeetingMetrics founder Ira Kerns, they receive a 40 percent response from their requests for survey data from event and meeting participants. More importantly, MeetingMetrics is a fully automated system that has thousands of prewritten survey questions and produces charts, graphs, and other communications tools to share results with key stakeholders after the meeting or event.

Researchers at the Massachusetts Institute of Technology (MIT) are studying a field known as sociometrics. They are exploring the rapidly emerging field in which sensors collect detailed data during social interactions and use sophisticated software to analyze these interactions. For example, during an event, some early evidence shows that individuals who see their own social patterns are more likely to become more social if they are having more limited interactions than they realized. By using radio frequency identification (RFID) technology to monitor and report the interactions of their guests, tomorrow's event planners may promote greater socialization throughout different venues (*Supply Chain Digest* 2008).

New developments in technology are rapidly driving changes in how event planners research, design, plan, coordinate and evaluate events. The Luddites of nineteenth-century Britain, who protested new technologies in weaving by destroying the mechanical looms, would be overwhelmed at the emerging technologies that are influencing, and in many ways improving, the modern events industry.

As new technologies develop, the focus must constantly be placed on both usability and practicality to ensure a good fit between high-tech and high-touch. Technology must be used to bring us closer together, to promote creativity and innovation, and, perhaps most importantly, to help us achieve, Victor Turner's concept of *communitas* through every planned event.

Technology Trends

Twenty years ago, technology was a luxury for small and mid-size companies. The situation is different now. It is hard to imagine any event planning office without a computer, internet access, or e-mail. Although it is hard to predict what will happen with technology in 10 years, there are recognizable trends. Technology will become more customized. Several years ago, small and mid-size event planning applications did not have a lot of options, as the number of major software packages was limited. Software programming services were not very affordable. But the situation has changed. There is much more technology and many more software development companies today than existed even a few years ago. Development of the Internet has allowed software development start-ups to sell their products directly to customers. As a result, the software development market has become more competitive, services are more user-friendly, and prices are more affordable. People who, a short time ago, did not know how to create a document are now getting more and more comfortable with computers. With this in mind, we can talk about the growth of virtual offices and the amount of online business and overall globalization of event management services.

One of the most important innovations in the global high-technology revolution is the development of the wireless application protocol (WAP). WAP was developed within the wireless industry, from companies such as Phone.com, Nokia, and Ericsson. The WAP standard is to provide internet content and services to wireless clients using WAP devices such as mobile phones and terminals. The opportunities for use of WAP-driven products in the Event Leadership field is significant. According to *The Profile of Event Management* (International Special Events Society 1999), over 90 percent of event professionals regularly use cellular technology. Due to the mobility of the event planning field, the cell phone is an indispensable tool. However, what about the potential use for event guests?

In Japan, event planning firms are testing the use of WAP technologies to improve networking among guests attending events. By having the event organizer, or guests themselves, preprogram the guests' cell phones with vital demographic information, WAP technology enables event guests to quickly identify others with similar interests within a few feet of the venue space. Imagine walking into a reception, and as you approach a guest, your cell phone vibrates. You glance quickly at the cell phone screen and see the message "buyer" and can connect instantaneously as seller and buyer. Furthermore, all critical buying information is downloaded via the Internet to the expanded computer memory within your cell phone.

Indeed, WAP technology is going to make connecting with others locally and globally easier, faster, more cost-efficient, with greater interoperability and ultimately more profitable. One excellent source for WAP information is www.openmobilealliance.org.

360-Degree Event Experiences

Planned events will soon become 360-degree experiences that originate with an e-mail or text message to your mobile device, continue through communications at your desktop and culminate with an in-person meeting or event. During the in-person meeting or event, you will be able to rapidly find individuals of similar interests and business potential using WAP technology as well as radio frequency identification (RFID). And this is only the beginning. Following the in-person meeting or event you continue to communicate, negotiate and consummate your relationships through text messaging, video conference through Skype (www.skype.com), as well as more traditional e-mail communications.

Through the increased use of mobile technologies, event planners and their guests will construct a 360-degree experience that includes pre-event, live event, and post-event communications. These communications will be fast, frequent, and highly focused, due to the ability to carefully segment your communications to those individuals who are within your network.

The use of social media such as Facebook (www.facebook.com), Linkedin (www.linkedin.com), Twitter (www.twitter.com), and Xing (www.xing.com) has greatly influenced communications within the planned events field. I predict that these communications tools will not only grow, but also become highly specialized, as individual communities of practice, such as event planning, form for more specialized discussions in the future.

Career-Advancement Connections

Corporate Social Responsibility Connection

Modern technology may reduce the carbon footprint through the reduction of paper, but perhaps more importantly, it may be used as a communications tool to link millions of people together for a common cause to repair many of the world's problems. For example, the Walk the Walk (www.walkthewalk.org) charity raises millions of pounds to fight breast cancer by allowing thousands of individuals to make on line donations through its Web site. Your next event is an opportunity to connect the host organization with a cause, and the connection may be greatly improved and advanced through the use of modern technology. Technology, if not managed well, can also be intrusive, invasive and threaten individual privacy. Therefore, event planners must seek to use technology to advance event experiences without creating undue violations of privacy and reducing personal comfort.

Global Connection

Developments in technology are rapidly erasing geographical borders in the global event industry. Event companies conduct registration, planning, control, and supervision over the Internet. An event manager located in the United States can produce an event in Germany, and vice versa, without physically relocating staff and/or setting up an office. As the event industry becomes more competitive, the development of technology will further amplify and accelerate competitive factors.

Technology Connection

In using technology, especially the Internet and other networks, it is important to remember that all processes should be available for all participants. If one of your partners has a very slow Internet connection, the entire network should be designed around this limitation to ensure that the user with the slow connection can receive the same services as others can.

Resource Connection

Cvent.com provides online event marketing, regulations, and data analysis services (www.cvent.com). An excellent reference book is *Internet World: Essential Business Tactic for the Net*, by Larry Chase and Eileen Shulock (1998).

Learning Connection

Your event planning organization is about to acquire a small event planning company with inadequate technology resources. You are assigned to manage the technology transition. Prepare a checklist describing possible high-risk areas in technological integration that your organization might face during and after the acquisition.

The Pioneer: Steven Wood Schmader, CFEE

In the 1980s, singer-songwriter Neil Diamond's hit song "Heading for the Future" could easily have served as a battle cry for Steven Wood Schmader, president of the International Festival and Events Association. Schmader has helped lead us into the future of the festival and special events industry for the past quarter of a century.

As a member of the cast of the international touring company "Up With People" in the mid-1970s, Schmader realized the power and influence of live events. He transitioned from cast member to promotion manager in the late 1970s, and then was promoted to director of special events. As director, he was responsible for major projects, such as the involvement of the company in Macy's Thanksgiving Day Parade, the NFL Super Bowl Halftime Spectacular, and the inauguration of President George H. W. Bush.

As a leader in the events industry, Schmader, along with Robert Jackson, wrote one of the first books in the field, *Special Events Inside & Out* (1990). This early work continues to profoundly influence the events industry today.

Jackson was asked to conduct a feasibility study for the city of Boise, Idaho, to determine how to develop a festival or major event for the city. After Jackson issued his recommendations, the city conducted a national search and chose Steven Wood Schmader to serve as the first leader and founder of the Boise River Festival. This event, which began with a modest budget of $310,000, grew to require a budget of over $1.6 million with a staff of five employees and 4,000 volunteers, lasting four days, and featuring 400 events. The aggregate attendance at this event was over 1 million people, and it was named one of the top 100 events in North America by the American Bus Association.

When asked what the motivating force that propels his leadership abilities is, Schmader quickly answers, "You must love the unknown." According to Schmader, to advance in this profession, you must use your leadership skills effectively at every level. By using his leadership skills throughout his career, he was able to become the leading spokesperson for the festival and special events industry as president of the International Festival and Events Association (IFEA).

"I saw IFEA as an event," says Schmader, "exciting, fresh, an opportunity to learn, to get better, and, yes, to dream about the future of our industry." When asked to describe a defining moment during his leadership of IFEA, he carefully considered the question and then thoughtfully responded, "I suppose it was at the very beginning. I proposed to move the offices from Port Angeles, Washington, to Boise, Idaho, and demonstrated how this would not only create greater efficiencies but also provide new resources for the organization. Immediately following our move, September 11, 2001, occurred and we were forced to postpone and relocate our annual convention." Schmader emphasizes that he recommended they "go on with the show" rather than cancel the convention because the industry, his members, needed to get together to continue to move the industry into the future.

Since assuming the presidency of IFEA, Schmader has faced numerous challenges including most recently the global economic recession. However, he has also been able to advance many important new ideas, including redeveloping the Certified Festival Executive (CFE) program, reformatting and renaming the association publication from *Festivals* magazine to *International Events* (*IE*), and using technology to improve and accelerate communications with members. "We must continually look for better and faster ways to communicate with our members and other constituencies, and IFEA plans to be at the forefront of this important area," says Schmader.

According to Schmader, there are three important propellants of leadership that he continues to use to head for the future:

1. Relationships are critical to a leader's success because they enable leaders to build a network, to nourish friendships, and to treat all people with the highest respect and esteem.
2. A leader must be committed to doing whatever it takes to accomplish his or her goals. There should be no limits to a leader's ability to achieve successful outcomes.
3. It is critically important never to forget what business you are in.

He believes we are first and foremost in the people business. Events change people's lives. Through events we can impact millions of lives in a positive way every day. Schmader says we must embrace this responsibility and use our leadership abilities to continually advance toward future success.

From performer, to producer, to president of one of the industry's leading associations, Steven Wood Schmader's illustrious career demonstrates how relationships, commitment, and respect for people can be carefully woven together to create a strong and beautiful tapestry that, similar to a magic carpet, will carry the special events industry into a future of which we may all be extremely proud.

The Protégé: Arlene Rush, Third Year Student, Queen Margaret University, Producer, First Green Fashion Show

Arlene Rush and her Queen Margaret University events colleagues were the first students to ever win the National Event Award for best small event in Scotland. Their design and production of a green fashion show using recycled materials for the fashions created national and international publicity for the University and the students. However, her interest in event planning started while she was in high school. Arlene says that she became extremely interested in business management. She had her eyes set on becoming a business manager because she was very organized and took the lead on most things that she was involved in.

According to Arlene, "One night at a pop concert I was so intrigued by the production and art of the event that I became curious about who could organize such a fantastic event and take the risk of creating a live event to entertain thousands of people. It was at that time that I began my research in events and found how huge and creative this industry was. I wanted to work in the events industry and had the ambition to become a manager in this particular field. I also wanted to have my own events management company one day."

Arlene knew that this was the right profession for her because at every event she attended—ranging from fashion shows, concerts, training weekends to weddings—she would watch every detail of the event. She closely observed each event to notice the mistakes that most of the guests would be oblivious to. Arlene says that "I was looking for the mistakes, so I enjoyed watching the organizers follow through with their contingency plans. I loved observing events and was trying to not take control, because, after all, I was a guest. However, I just such a strong desire to become more involved.

Arlene and her fellow students decided to develop the first Green Fashion show at Queen Margaret University because their course of study required them to design and produce a real event. The process for creating the Green Fashion Show, according to Arlene, involved coming up with many ideas. However, when Gill Kelly, the University's Green Travel Sustainability coordinator, came and presented an idea of a green fashion event to encourage sustainability and recycling, they became excited at the possibilities. Arlene said, "This type of event would open my eyes to many possibilities. A fellow student used the term, 'too challenging for our first event,' but I was craving a challenge. Why not challenge yourself? The Green Fashion Event was such an amazing experience, from the high to the lows and all the obstacles. It was a success, a very good success, and I was so proud of this accomplishment. I also loved reflecting on the mistakes and the errors, which I knew would make me so much stronger to move forward for the next event."

Following the Green Fashion Event, all she could think of was the next possible event that would challenge her creativity. When asked why she is always looking forward to the next event, Arlene said, "The excitement and adrenaline I get from the events industry makes me seek more and want to exceed even further."

Arlene has learned a great deal from her many mentors, both good and bad. She recalls that "I have had many managers and many of them not as managerial or organized as you would expect. It was just a job for them instead of a life ambition or career. I guess I learned from their mistakes by comparing their performance to what I would have done better. However, on a positive note many people have influenced and me and provided inspiration—certainly, my lecturers Professor Joe Goldblatt and Dr. Rebecca Finkel, Gill Kelly, the Travel Sustainability Coordinator at Queen Margaret University, Edinburgh, Sarah Whigham, Events Manager of Queen Margaret University and Linda Bruce, Events and Conference Centre Manager.

Arlene sees a bright future for the modern events industry. She asks rhetorically, "Where would we be without events? Events are a fundamental part of our lives, the economy, the environment, and a part of each of us. It will never be an industry that will collapse. The future will bring bigger and better events in my eyes. Many things will influence the way the events industry will move forward, some making it move slower but others making it move faster."

She believes that the environment is a huge catalyst and issue for events in today's society. Arlene strongly believes, "It will become a normal way for many events to have only recyclable resources being used. However, the damage to the environment could be made worse due to some events failing to make a change and wasting the resources we have limited amounts of. Currently, the economy is in a crisis where less people have sufficient disposable income and this is a huge disadvantage to the events industry. Some businesses can no longer afford an events management service, and some people do not have the income to attend events. However, the industry is still standing strong, but once the economy improves, I feel the events industry will be bigger and better than it has been."

This national award winner in events has huge ambitions for the future. She says enthusiastically, "First, I want to have a taste of every different section in the events industry; experiencing as much as possible is essential to me. Next, I would like to work in at least one event in each field, being a leader or just a key team player. However, I currently want to produce educational and entertainment events. "

One of the many lessons Arlene has learned during her University education in events is to never say *hope*. Rather, use the word *do* to show confidence and stand out from the crowd. Arlene says, "Hope is a wish, and everyone has wish." I think of hope in a way as hoping to win the lottery. There is no way of making this happen, you can improve your chances by buying lots of tickets and playing it more frequently. I choose not to hope for things I know I can make happen; instead, I go out and do it. Becoming a successful events manager is something I will do and will make sure I do the things to make me get to where I want to be. "

Already, Arlene and her event team members have won a prestigious national award. By continuing to "do" those things that are essential for achieving future success in events, she will further demonstrate that while hope is not a strategy, her dreams are in fact coming true through her hard work and continuous desire to learn and grow.

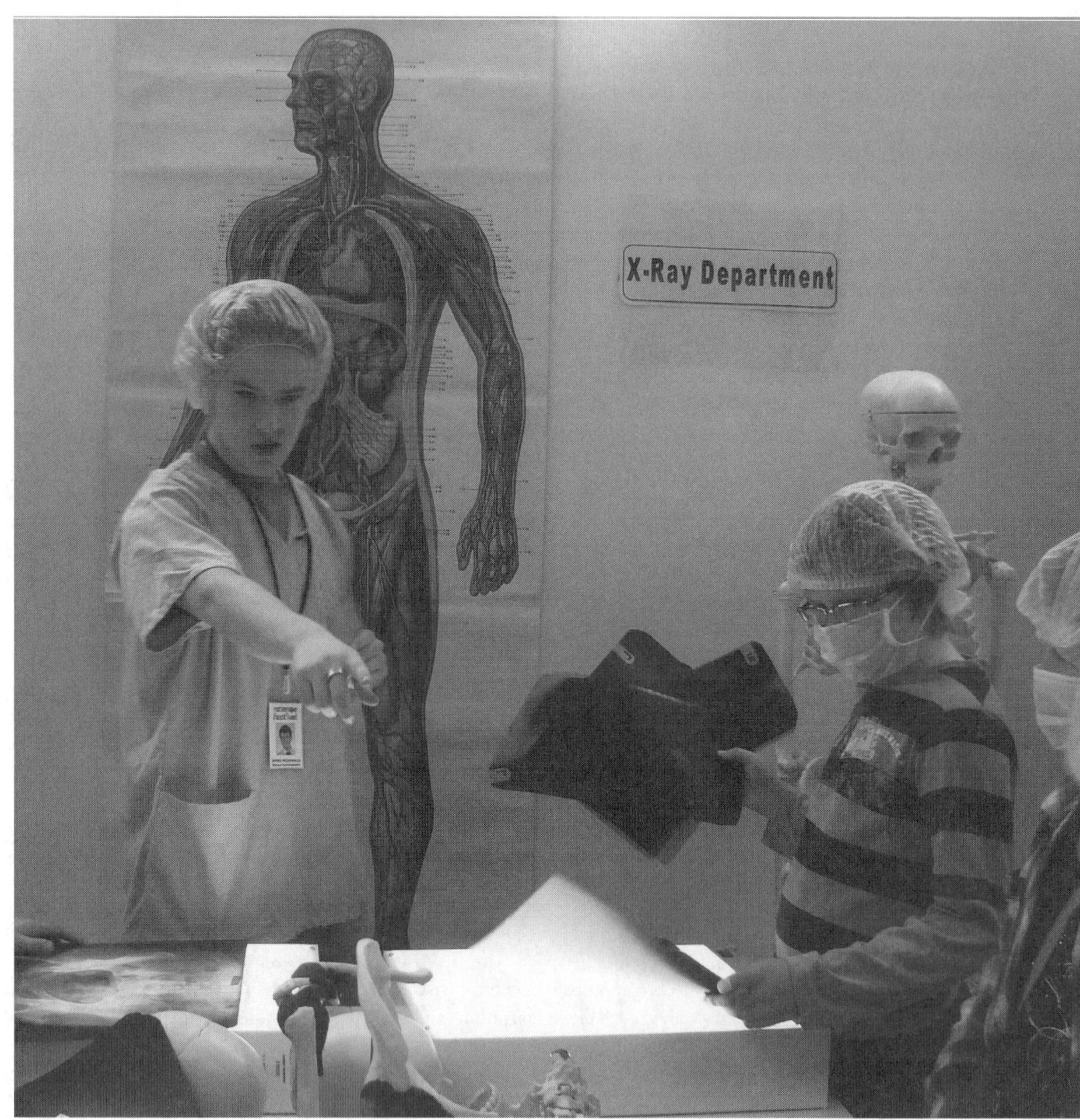

Event planners and doctors have much in common. Both are diagnosticians who provide advice and counsel and often promote wellness through their skill, experience, and talent. The young people in this photo are attending the Edinburgh International Science Festival. Thanks to a talented Queen Margaret University event planner, they are discovering the magic and mystery of possibly a future career in medicine.

CHAPTER 15

Career Development, Advancement, and Sustainable Success

In this chapter you will learn how to:

- Advance your Event Leadership career through formal and informal education
- Gain more professional experience to build your résumé
- Become a Certified Special Event Professional (CSEP)
- Earn the credentials you need for employment, promotion, and long-term success
- Build both a life and a career

Despite the uncertainty of the current economy, several factors are, in fact, very certain. First, the world population is aging. In the United States alone, nearly 70 million people will have turned 50 by 2010. As individuals age, so do their institutions and organizations. Therefore, the need to hold more life-cycle celebrations (birthdays, anniversaries, bar and bat mitzvahs) grows accordingly. Second, experiential marketing has become the marketing channel of choice for many if not most sellers of services and markets. As one example, *Sports Illustrated* magazine invested several million dollars in 2003 to promote its publication with a series of events produced by Jack Morton Worldwide. Third and finally, the rapid expansion of technology has actually resulted in the development of more live events as individuals of common interest meet on the Internet and then seek to meet in person to conduct business. As a result of these and many other positive signs, job growth in the hospitality, tourism, and event sectors is expected to increase rapidly. In fact, many economists believe that this field will be one of most demanded in the future.

In order to benefit from this future growth, event planners must continually develop their skill sets and gain as much related experience as possible. Fortunately, there are innumerable opportunities to do this.

Education

Only a few years ago, education was considered to be a minor requirement for employment as an event planning professional. I remember participating in the first meeting designed to develop questions for the Certified Special Events Professional (CSEP) examination. I argued that the questions should be more rigorous. The professional educators attending this meeting reminded me that, because there was so little formal education in the field at that time, it might be difficult for even experienced Event Leaders to pass the test.

A few months later, a brave group of industry veterans sat for the first CSEP examination. They literally trembled as they walked into the examination room. Although combined they represented hundreds of years of professional experience, none had the benefit of formal education in the special events field. Today, the landscape is dramatically different. According to studies conducted by Temple University, 172 colleges and universities throughout the world offer curriculum, certificates, and/or degrees in the planned events related fields. A partial listing of these institutions is listed in the on line resource that accompanies this book.). These courses include:

- Advertising
- Anthropology
- Art
- Beverage management
- Business administration
- Catering
- Communications
- Culinary
- Design
- Education
- Floral
- Folklore
- Hospitality
- Hotel
- Information systems and information technology

- Law
- Museum studies
- Music
- Political science
- Public relations
- Recreation
- Sport management
- Television
- Theater
- Tourism
- Travel
- Web design and management

In addition to these related fields of studies, many colleges and universities offer specific programs in the field of event planning. Leeds Metropolitan University, Queen Margaret University, Temple University, The George Washington University, the University of Nevada at Las Vegas, and dozens of other universities offer concentrations in special events, entertainment, and meetings and expositions. Northeastern State University in Tahlequah, Oklahoma, may have been the first college in the United States to offer specialization in the field of meeting planning and destination management. In addition, several colleges and universities throughout the world have adopted The George Washington University Certificate Program, so it is now possible to receive standardized training in this field in many different parts of the world as well as the United States. In 2005, Temple University, School of Tourism launched the Executive Certificate in Event Leadership, a comprehensive industry certificate program linked to six interrelated event fields. In 2010, Queen Margaret University will offer the world's first Executive Master of International Planned Events (MPE) degree to provide new and advanced training for global event leaders.

This growth in formal education for event planners may be compared to the related field of information technology. In both areas of expertise, specific skills are required to ensure that high-quality performance is achieved consistently over time. However, unlike information technology, Event Leaders must also master the critical human resource skills essential for working effectively in teams. This dimension adds challenge and opportunity for educators as they work to develop a standardized field of study similar to that of medicine, law, accounting, or public relations.

According to a 1994 study, over 60 percent of event professionals had earned a bachelor's degree and nearly 10 percent had a postgraduate degree. The percentage of event professionals with qualifications has continually increased and today it is essential to have a certificate, a degree or a professional certification for employment in planned events. Therefore, it may be assumed that professionals in this field are highly educated compared to the general working population in the United States. This means that those entering this competitive profession should expect to have a formal education plus experience in order to succeed. Increasingly, a major part of this formal education is specialized in the area of planned events studies.

A Body of Knowledge

Organizations such as the Convention Industry Council, the International Association for Exhibitions and Events, and the International Special Events Industry have identified specific bodies of knowledge within their industry sector. This knowledge is encapsulated in the certification programs that each organization has developed. While the body of knowledge varies according to the organization, generally each of these fields includes knowledge in these domains:

- Administration
  - Communications
  - Financial planning, management, and analysis
  - Information technology
  - Organizational development
  - Scheduling
  - Tax liabilities and regulations
  - Time management
    - Strategic planning
- Coordination
  - Amenities
  - Advertising
  - Awards
  - Catering
  - Décor
  - Entertainment
  - Etiquette
  - Human resource management
    - Conflict resolution
    - Staff recruiting, training, supervision, and reward
    - Volunteer recruiting, training, supervision, and reward
  - International customs
  - Lighting
  - Parking
  - Prizes
  - Protocol
  - Sound
  - Speakers
  - Strategic management
  - Transportation
  - Venues
- Marketing
  - Advertising
  - Analysis
  - Assessment

    - Conflict resolution
    - Evaluation
    - Negotiation
    - Planning
    - Promotion
    - Proposal development and writing
    - Public relations
    - Sales
    - Sponsorship
    - Strategic marketing
    - Stunts
- Risk management
    - Assessment
    - Compliance
    - Contracts
    - Financial impacts
    - Insurance
    - Licensing
    - Management
    - Permits
    - Planning
    - Safety
    - Security

In addition to these broad categories, each specialized field emphasizes additional requirements, such as exhibit planning and management, hotel and convention center negotiation, and catering. However, through consolidation, perhaps there will soon be an era of unprecedented collaboration among the various industry subfields. Event planners should, in my opinion, adopt the model generated by medicine many years ago. Event Leaders should be trained as general practitioners (such as the CSEP program), then earn additional certifications as specialists in individual fields. With this model, clients and employers worldwide will be able to use a global standard for event planning training and identify specialists who have advanced training in certain areas.

Education and Your Career In Planned Events

Obviously, it is important for you to obtain a strong general studies education at the undergraduate and perhaps graduate levels. In addition to general studies, you may wish to focus your education in areas where the majority of event planners have earned degrees (business administration, education, and tourism, in that order).

Increasingly, event planning professionals are earning advanced credentials, such as professional certificates in events, meetings, expositions, and related fields. The professional certificate is often more valued by industry employers because it represents a specialized body of knowledge that is immediately useful to organizations that employ event professionals. Therefore, to be successful, it is important for event planners to understand both the theory and practice of Event Leadership. To sustain your career, you should carefully design an educational blueprint from which to construct your future career. This blueprint should include a thorough understanding of the history and theory of the profession, skill training, and practical observation and application. A model blueprint for developing your event planning education follows.

- General studies education: arts and sciences, business administration (observation/internship)
- Postgraduate education: business administration, tourism, Event Leadership (practical training/externship)
- Executive development: certificate in event planning, meetings, expositions, or related field (observation/externship)
- Certification: CSEP, Certified Meeting Professional, or other respected industry certification program (practical training)
- Continuing industry education: through professional associations, such as the International Special Events Society (ISES), Meeting Professionals International, and others (observation/practice)

In addition to this formal education, successful event planners combine classroom experience with extensive practical training. Our students at Queen Margaret University have greatly benefited from student work experience and internships and externships ranging from small event planning consulting organizations to the International Olympic Games. They have coordinated expositions for up to 40,000 people and have observed small social events. Every opportunity has provided a rich learning experience for these professionals. I strongly suggest that you invest a minimum of 15 to 30 hours per year observing or practicing under the aegis of another event organization. By observing the best (and sometimes worst) practices of others, you will find that the educational theory and skills you studied earlier will synthesize into a new foundation for future success.

Professional Experience

Finding a worthwhile internship or externship can be a daunting task, especially for a newcomer to the industry. First, it is important to understand the difference between internship and externship. Generally, internship is used to describe a supervised experience that an undergraduate or graduate student affiliated with a college or university receives while earning academic credit. *Externship* refers to the practical experience that a senior professional employed in the event planning industry receives in an organization other than his or her own.

Internships and externships should both include a blend of observation and practice. One of the earliest descriptions of formal education is that provided by the philosopher

Socrates, who described the educational process as including observation and questioning. Using the Socratic method, you should find outstanding organizations or individuals or both, observe them, ask lots of questions, and then draw your own conclusions from this experience. In the best scenario, your industry teachers or mentors will simultaneously question and challenge you (just as Socrates did with his protégés in ancient Greece).

Finding an Internship or Externship

One of the easier ways to identify a high-quality practical training opportunity is through a formal institution of learning, such as a college or university. Another way is through professional networking in an industry organization. Using the auspices of a college or university may provide you with additional credibility for obtaining a high-quality practicum experience. In fact, a professor of planned event studies can help you open doors that were closed to you heretofore. Many planned events employers may even be suspicious of persons who wish to engage in a practicum for fear that this is merely a ploy to steal ideas for use in their own companies. Therefore, the intervention of a college professor or mentor can provide an employer with reassurance that the practicum experience is required for graduation and that students will be supervised to ensure proper ethical behavior.

Once you have identified an appropriate practical experience, you should send the potential supervisor a one-page brief description of the observations, experiences, and outcomes you desire from this experience. Figure 15.1 is an example of such a document.

Some internships are paid, others include a small stipend, a few provide living expenses, and still others provide no compensation or expenses. You must determine the best setting for your needs and whether compensation is required. If you are an event planner who is providing a practical training opportunity, it is important to remember that U.S. labor laws prohibit displacing a paid employee with an unpaid intern. Therefore, event planners and other employers may use interns to support staff but should not utilize them as a means of displacing current employees to reduce expenses.

During the internship or externship, you should exhibit good work habits (e.g., attendance, punctuality, dress) and conduct yourself in a highly ethical manner. For example, it is important to ask your supervisor about proprietary information and then to abide absolutely by his or her requests for confidentiality. Finally, remember that you are there primarily to learn from these people, who are more experienced than you. Therefore, refrain from offering unsolicited advice. Instead, carefully write down instructions, observations, and other notes in a journal to help you document what you are learning. At the same time, note any questions and then ask for time with your supervisor to probe him or her with questions concerning any areas of the practicum where you need further clarification.

At the end of the practicum experience, both you and your supervisor should have a debriefing session to evaluate the practicum. The supervisor should complete forms describing your attendance, punctuality, performance, and learning capacity, as well as write a letter of recommendation for use with future employers. You should

Date

Dear Employer, Supervisor, etc.:

Your organization is one of the most respected in the special events industry and, therefore, I am requesting the opportunity to receive a practical training experience under your auspices. The training will require the following commitment from your organization:

1. Five to ten hours per week on-site at your place of business, observing your operations
2. Participation in practical experiences you design for me to enhance my learning experience
3. Your supervision of my practical training
4. Completion of a brief form evaluating my performance at the end of my practical training
5. Submission by your firm of a letter of recommendation for me (if appropriate) to assist me in career development

I will be contacting you in a few days to discuss this opportunity, and I thank you in advance for your consideration of this request.

Sincerely,

Jane Event Manager

cc: Dr. Joe Goldblatt, CSEP, Professor and Executive Director, The International Centre for the Study of Planned Events, Queen Margaret University, Edinburgh, Scotland

Figure 15.1 Proposal for Practical Experience Opportunity

promptly write a thank-you letter to the supervisor expressing your appreciation for this unique opportunity.

A good practicum experience requires the commitment of both a generous supervisor and a curious and loyal student. When you plan this experience carefully, you will find that you have not only established a rich learning opportunity but built a lifelong connection with mentors who will encourage your success.

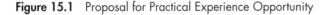

Certification

Professional certification is the sign of professions that have matured and seek a uniform standard to ensure consistent levels of excellence. Most professional certification programs, such as Certified Public Accountant (CPA), were developed early in the twentieth century.

One of the reasons for the development of industry standards and certification was to limit the role of government in licensing emerging professions. The event planning industry has followed this historic pattern.

The International Special Events Society established the Certified Special Events Professional (CSEP) certification program, which was originally based on the empirical studies conducted by the Canadian government. ISES elected to consolidate the Event Manager and Event Coordinator into one comprehensive vocation titled Event Manager or Special Event Professional.

According to the Canadian government and the ISES certification committee, the vocation of Event Leadership requires competence in four knowledge domains. These represent the body of knowledge in the field of Event Leadership and, therefore, require a high degree of competence in administration, coordination, marketing, and risk management. ISES further ratified the findings of the Canadians by stating that the critical path for the production of a professional event required administration, followed by coordination, succeeded by marketing, and then finally reduction of exposure through well-developed risk management.

Today, more than 100 persons worldwide hold the title of Certified Special Events Professional (CSEP). To obtain this difficult and challenging designation, they must exhibit a high degree of professional experience, formal education, and service to the industry and must pass a two-part examination process. The CSEP is considered by many as one of the most rigorous assessments in the event planning industry, and those who earn this designation are considered to be the preeminent practitioners in the industry. You should aspire to join their growing ranks. Their exam is fully automated and you may take the examination at various locations throughout the world. For more the most updated information about the CSEP, visit www.ises.com.

I often point to the example of doctors as one reason why it is so important to ensure that professional event planners function at a consistently high level. Doctors have the ability to save lives but also lose lives one person at a time. Event Leaders, by contrast, can save or lose hundreds or thousands of lives at one event, depending on their level of training, experience, and that illusive quality called judgment. Therefore, the event planner, in my opinion, has an even higher degree of responsibility than doctors. In addition, event planners often organize seminars or educational programs that train current and future doctors, so our responsibility extends into their profession, as well.

Recertification

Many certification programs require that certified leaders be recertified every few years to ensure that they are currently engaged in the industry and that they remain knowledgeable about developments in the field. The process for recertification typically requires documentation of education, experience, and service to the industry. The CSEP program requires recertification every five years after the initial certification has been granted. Recertification is based on continuing education and continuous employment in the planned events industry.

Credentials

I am often asked by prospective students to quantify the value of a master's degree versus a certificate. Typically, the questioner asks: "What do I need to be successful in the field of planned events—a undergraduate degree, a professional certificate, a professional certification, or a master's degree?" The question automatically assumes that credentials or third-party validation is important to success in the special events industry. This is a correct assumption. Although it has not always been the case, the facts clearly indicate that, in the U.S. economy, those who have credentials earn more, are promoted more often, and enjoy more economic and career opportunities than those who do not have appropriate credentials.

The type of credential you earn depends largely on which sector of the events industry you decide to enter. For example, in the government and education sectors, it is generally known that the education you attain affects the promotion or appointment by salary grade, whereas in the association sector, although education is important, it is also acceptable to obtain certification to demonstrate your training, competence, and experience level. However, in the corporate sector, increasingly, it is not unusual to find MBAs who are responsible for coordinating major events.

Bill Morton, former chairman and chief executive officer of Jack Morton Worldwide, one of the world's largest experience marketing and planned events firm, once told me that his firm actively recruited MBA students from leading business schools for senior management positions. He explained that the blend of strategic thinking skills, marketing analysis and execution, and financial management training and experience helped his firm ensure that strong management leaders would sustain and advance the mission of the 60-year-old firm.

It is interesting that Morton did not specifically mention the need for experience in planned events as a prerequisite for appointment as a leader in his firm. In fact, planned events experience, although important, is not essential to succeed in many organizations today. What is essential is proof or evidence that you are competent to advance the goals and objectives of your employer. Increasingly, employers are turning to third-party organizations, such as colleges, universities, and certification organizations, to vouch for this competence.

When I give references for students enrolled in planned events academic programs, potential employers ask the typical questions about persistence, punctuality, and intellectual capacity. However, ever more frequently, they ask questions about the ability of the candidate to work in a team, to communicate, and to lead an organization to accomplish specific goals and objectives. Although it is difficult to quantify, much less rate, these abilities, employers count on them to determine if the person they will hire will succeed quickly after he or she is appointed. This is another reason why it is important to obtain a credential. Behind every credential are people who tested, assessed, and can vouch for the integrity, persistence, communications, and leadership abilities of the person holding the credential. Whether they are former professors, industry certifiers, or even internship supervisors, each one has had a prolonged, intimate, and objective opportunity to evaluate the candidate. For this reason alone, it is important to earn a credential; with it comes references and contacts that will help you gain employment and promotion.

So you may ask what credential is most valuable. The simple answer is: all of them. I recommend that you determine what your industry sector demands in terms of a credential and, as soon as you earn it, begin exploring how you can earn the next credential. In today's competitive global business environment, you must demonstrate your competence continually. Whether you are in Asia, the Americas, Europe, Australia, or Africa, governments as well as nongovernmental organizations are developing higher standards for event planners. For example, the governments of Great Britain, South Africa, and Australia have joined Canada in developing standards for event planning professionals. These standards require high levels of professional education, as well as experience. Therefore, to compete in the global planned events industry, you must continually seek the credentials that future employers demand to ensure your long-term success in this growing field.

Power Tools

Once you have mapped your journey, you need transportation tools to ensure that you arrive speedily at your destination. Historically, the most powerful tools have been the résumé and cover letter. I recommend that you follow these 10 steps to best apply these tools:

1. Create a preliminary list of employers who have (or are likely to have) open positions in your field.
2. From this short list of 25 to 50 people, create a computer database using Access, Excel, Filemaker Pro, or a similar contact management software program.
3. Send a cover letter to each contact, as shown in Figure 15.2. Customize the letter for each organization based on the homework you have completed to learn about the person and the organization's strengths.
4. Wait two weeks after the letter has been mailed, and then call each contact between 7 and 9 A.M. or between 5 and 7 P.M. These are the best times to reach your contact directly without interception by an administrative assistant.
5. When you reach the contact, reintroduce yourself and assume that the person has received your letter. ("I am calling about the letter I sent you requesting a personal interview.")
6. Ask for an interview at one or two specific times. ("Could we meet in person or by telephone on Tuesday at 10 A.M. or Thursday at 4 P.M.?")
7. If the contact agrees to meet with you in person or by telephone, thank the person immediately and reconfirm in writing via e-mail or other correspondence.
8. If the person refuses to see you, ask if there are others whom you should see or other organizations that could benefit from your skills to which the person can refer you. Get at least three to five referrals. Add these names to your database.

9. If you confirmed the meeting in person or by telephone, conduct further research about the organization so that you are prepared to ask pertinent questions.
10. During the personal interview session, do not offer your résumé unless requested. Instead, show your portfolio of an event or events that you have produced. Conclude the session by asking directly: "What would be necessary for me to earn the opportunity to work for your outstanding organization?" Do not speak again until the contact tells you specifically what is necessary to earn the job.

Date

Name

Title

Organization name

Address

City, state, postal code

Dear (Ms., Mr., Dr.),

Professor Joe Goldblatt, CSEP (or other person whose name will be immediately recognized by the employer), referred me to you to request a personal interview about your outstanding organization. Your organization is one of the leading organizations in this field, and I would like to learn more about your unique attributes in this rapidly growing field. (Use research to customize this paragraph with a concluding sentence such as "For over _____ years, your organization has provided ____________ to clients, and I am impressed with your excellent reputation in the industry.)

I am currently completing my (degree, certificate, or other credential) in the planned events field (or I have been employed as a professional Event Leader for over _____ years) and am confident that my training, experience, and contacts can be of great benefit to your organization. Therefore, I am requesting a personal interview to explore future opportunities in this profession.

This interview may be conducted in person at your office or by telephone at a time that is convenient to you. In that regard, I will telephone you in the next week to determine the best date and time for you to conduct this interview. Thank you for your interest, and I look forward to speaking with you soon.

Sincerely,

Jane Event Manager

P.S. Professor Joe Goldblatt, CSEP (or other referral) sends his best regards. I look forward to speaking with you soon and sincerely appreciate your time and interest.

Figure 15.2 Model Cover Letter

Finding a great job in this field is a combination of timing, persistence, and talent. Timing is the most elusive part of the equation, because rarely is a job created specifically for you. Instead, you have to wait until a position needs to be filled. This is why persistence is important. You may wish to create a postcard that has your photograph and a few lines about your experience, skills, and credentials, and mail this to your contact list on the same date each month as a reminder of your interest in working for them. Personalize the card with a handwritten note that says: "I am writing further to indicate my interest in working for your outstanding organization. Please let me know if there is an opportunity to work with you in the near future."

The postcard technique has been highly effective with my students for the last decade, as the tenure of employees in an organization has shrunk from two and one-half years to less than one year. During a period of full employment, employers are constantly on the lookout for capable people able to start work immediately. Your postcard may arrive at just the right moment and, instead of conducting a formal search for candidates, the employer may telephone you to interview for the job. You have already shown interest, enthusiasm, organization, and persistence, and these are qualities that employers value. You have also made the company's job easier by helping it find you quickly.

The two critical tools, the résumé and the cover letter, must be consistent with the standards used traditionally in the Event Leadership field. Figures 15.2 and 15.3 provide models for you to use in the future.

Résumé
Jane Event Manager, CSEP
1234 Main Street
Celebration, Florida
Telephone: (304) 544–1234
E-mail: jem@eventsrus.net

Career Objective

To assist a leading event organization to achieve high quality and rapid growth through my contributions as an Event Leadership professional.

Professional Experience

- Managed a 2,000-person health-care exposition with a budget of $150,000 in March 2010
- Coordinated a 500-person legal conference with a budget of $50,000 in September 2009
- Developed and managed a 50-person executive education retreat with a budget of $19,000 in July 2009

Related Experience

- Conceived and coordinated a 1,000-person community festival with a budget (including in-kind contributions) of $50,000 in spring 2009
- Led a 25-person event planning workshop/retreat with a budget of $1,000 for the purpose of organizing an annual conference for a community-services organization

Figure 15.3 Model Résumé *(Continued)*

Note: Résumé should not exceed one page.

Volunteer Experience

- Founded a 500-person bazaar with 50 exhibitors and a budget of $500 for Holy Name Church
- Created and managed a 250-person banquet for Cub Scout Awards with a budget of $1,200
- Organized and managed a 100-person fundraising walking event for AIDS prevention with a budget of $3,000

Education and Training

- Candidate to receive the George Washington University Professional Certificate in Event Management (May 2011)
- Recipient of the George Washington University Master of Tourism Administration, Concentration in Event Management, degree (May 2010)
- Certified Special Event Professional (2004, recertified 2010)

Awards and Recognition

- International Special Events Society Volunteer of the Year, 2009
- Dean's List, Johnson Wales University, 2009
- Employee of the Month, Regent Hotel, May 2007

Technology Skills

Access, computer-assisted drawing, Excel, Word, World Wide Web, Web design (HTML)

Languages

Spanish (high verbal and written)
Portuguese (moderate verbal and written)
French (low to moderate verbal)

References

Available upon request

Figure 15.3 *(Continued)*

The purpose of the résumé and the cover letter is to reduce to writing the impression you will make in person. These important tools rarely help you obtain a job unless they are supported by a good reference, your homework about the organization, and, most important, the impression you make in person. I strongly suggest that you work with a career coach through a local university or college or someone in private practice to help you optimize your abilities when you are ready to make that all-important first impression.

Gene Columbus, a veteran leader for over three decades in human resources for the Walt Disney Company, has written what I consider to be the definitive resource in career planning for event professionals and aspiring professionals including students. This book, published by John Wiley in 2010, has hundreds of additional resources to help you launch or sustain your career. I recommend that you acquire *The Complete Guide to Careers in Special Events: Step Toward Success!* by Gene Columbus.

Life and Career

Too often, Event Leadership professionals build a successful career and at the same time risk ruining their personal lives. Although mental and physical stress are not unique to the events industry, the constant demand for creativity, innovation, and the increasing speed of delivery can cause event planning professionals to literally burn the candle at both ends until exhaustion and illness require professional intervention.

Recently, a leader in the festival industry grew irritated with me when I explained that many of the generation described by demographers as cuspers or busters do not want to work a traditional workweek of five eight-hour days. Instead, according to research, many prefer to work a shorter workweek with longer workdays. The reason for this major paradigm shift is the recognition that the seven-day workweek of preceding generations ultimately led to rapid burnout. In protest, the cuspers and busters choose to work a shorter number of days and a longer number of hours per day. This schedule permits them to separate work and leisure activity and grants them longer weekends (three days as opposed to one). Furthermore, they prefer to separate work from leisure in order to fully enjoy recreation, culture, and other activities.

Perhaps there is a lesson to be learned here—or several lessons. In an age defined by technology, it is often difficult to escape from the world of work. Therefore, to find a life in addition to a career, one must be ever vigilant about understanding the difference between these two values. Experts in leisure study define work as the absence of leisure. However, for work to be enjoyable, it must be rewarding and fulfilling. Therefore, to sustain life and career, it is important to understand the nuances that define the difference between each of these two similar but different states of being.

Because the special events industry is perceived by guests as "a fun business," practitioners often forget that, in fact, this is the business of fun. As a business it requires hard work, persistence, and talent. Each of these tasks is bound to deplete your energy. You must replenish this expenditure of energy with a healthy lifestyle that includes proper exercise, nutrition, and spiritual nourishment. This replenishment is essential if you are going to experience both the joy of work and the joie de vivre (joy of life).

From Invention to Reinvention

To achieve long-term career success, it is important to develop a historical perspective of careers in this field. Compared to other more established professions, such as medicine and law, the relatively new profession of Event Leadership is better positioned as a career for long-term sustainability and growth. At the turn of the twentieth century, Event Leaders were unknown despite the fact that many events, including world's fairs and expositions, were produced in abundance. Like many modern professions, Planned events first began as a craft that was learned through an informal apprentice system. However, in the 1930s, pioneers such as Jack Morton and Howard Lanin used their organizational skills in music and personnel management to conduct successful social and later corporate events. As events grew in size in the 1960s (Woodstock, Hemisphere in San Antonio), there developed a need for specialists to plan and manage these large-scale events. Specialists with experience in film, television, writing, music, and public relations/communications, such as the late Robert Jani, Tommy Walker, and David Wolper, used their skills to produce many of the marquee events of the twentieth century. These events included the opening and closing ceremonies of the Los Angeles Olympic Games in 1984, the Knoxville and New Orleans World's Fairs, the 100th Anniversary of the Statue of Liberty, the inauguration of President Ronald Reagan, and the ubiquitous Super Bowl halftime spectaculars throughout the 1980s.

David Wolper's autobiography, *Producer* (2003), summarizes the newness of this field. Peter Ueborroth, president of the Los Angeles Olympic Games Organizing Committee, invited Wolper to lunch and asked him to produce the opening and closing ceremonies of the 1984 Olympic Games. Wolper discussed it with his wife and she asked, "Do you know how to do something like that?" Although he had attended three previous Olympics and had received numerous awards for television and film production, he had not produced events of the magnitude of the Olympic Games opening and closing ceremonies. He spent the night convincing himself, and the next day he accepted the job.

As the twentieth century came to a close, the demand for trained, experienced event planners grew, largely due to the need for professionals who could fill the positions that were being created in this new field. For example, in the early 1990s, there were few classified ads listed under the heading of Event Manager, Event Coordinator, or Director of Special Events. However, by the end of the century, several ads appeared under these headings on a daily basis.

Through the development of formal education programs such as Queen Margaret University's Executive Master's in International Planned Events Management, Temple University's School of Tourism Event Leadership Executive Certificate Program, The George Washington University Event Management Certificate and Master's Degree Program (and their licensees throughout the world), Leeds Metropolitan University Diploma in Events Management and Great Britain Center for Events Management, Northeastern Oklahoma University's Destination and Meeting Management Program, the University of Nevada at Las Vegas Tourism and Convention Administration Program, The University of Technology, Sydney, Australian Center for Event Management, and, most recently, Johnson & Wales University's Master of Business Administration (MBA) degree concentration in Event Leadership, thousands of students throughout the world are learning prescribed systems for leading events toward success.

As a result of the rapid development of this field, many of the early pioneers may shake their heads in amazement at how far the profession has come. While the first generation of event leaders (Jani, Morton, Walker, Wolper, and others) might be amazed at the progress the field has made in such a short time, the current generation of educators is hopeful that, through formal education, the profession will become better respected by the general public and will encourage sustainable careers.

I characterize three periods of economic growth of this profession: First was the era of the practitioners (those who learned by doing), which was roughly from 1930 to 1980. Next came the age of the educators (those who have learned through a combination of formal education coupled with guided experience in the field), which covers the period of 1980 to the present day. However, now as we are on the cusp of the second 50 years of this young profession, we are entering the age that will be dominated by future Event Leaders.

In the first edition of *Special Events*, I interviewed David L. Wolper and asked him how he was able to motivate 100,000 people during the closing ceremonies of the Los Angeles Olympic Games in 1984 to spontaneously join hands and sing "Reach Out and Touch (Somebody's Hand)" (Ashford & Simpson with vocals by Diana Ross), and he told me that a producer must "know how to use special events to produce specific emotions in people. As a producer, I know how to invoke laughter, tears, joy, and, of course, love."

Nearly 15 years after that interview, Wolper wrote his biography, which charts his successful career as one of the preeminent producers of the twentieth century. According to Wolper, "The producer is the man or woman with the dream." Wolper examines his many successes as a producer from television's *Roots*, to the 100th anniversary of the Statue of Liberty, through Liberty Weekend, to hundreds of other television spectaculars and special events. In fact, Wolper's work created the term *special event television*. In his own words:

> *I have been successful as a producer primarily because I had the natural ability to recognize a good idea, whether it came from my mind, or someone else's. I could sell the idea: I worked as hard as I asked anyone working for me to work to bring it to fruition. I was not afraid to take risks to achieve quality, and maybe just as important, I hired good people and gave them all the responsibility they could handle. I was always there in the background. I was never afraid to dive in and get dirty, but I had the good fortune to find great people and recognize their talent. And with my banking experience, I knew finance, so I could build a company. I was the orchestra conductor who picked the music. I was the cook who mixed the ingredients. And I was the judge who made the decisions. I picked the people who worked from my documentary company. I picked the right people when I created the ceremonies for the Olympics (1984 Los Angeles Olympic Games). I picked the right people to make* Roots. *I suspect that not one of the hundreds of people who worked for a Wolper company would state that I was an easy person to work for; I wasn't. I demanded quality.*

Future planned event leaders must now embrace the traditions and educational opportunities of the past 50 years while simultaneously using their strategic planning skills to chart a course for the future of the profession. This merger of practice, theory, and the ability to balance life and career will be essential as Event Leaders address the many new and unknown challenges in the new world.

As future planned event leaders, it is important that we lead, but also record, remember, and celebrate the triumphs, joys, and even sorrows of our lives. You are responsible for leading this effort. You are a modern pioneer destined to explore, expand, and improve the global event management industry in the twenty-first century. The global technological revolution we have created can hollow us or hallow us, depending on how we embrace it. I prefer to use the metaphor that the twentieth-century scientist Albert Einstein envisioned when describing his theory of relativity. Einstein wrote that "science without religion is lame and religion without science is blind." He envisioned that, one day, he would be able to ride a laser beam of light into the twenty-first century; indeed, his theories and ideas continue to challenge and illuminate us today. Einstein continues to ride into the future, taking us along with him, as our dreams become realities, just as his theories became scientific fact.

Sometimes a lamplighter must turn his or her light toward dark places to provide greater illumination or all. Mandla Mentoor is one example of this practice with the work he is doing in Soweto, South Africa. Mentoor, a community activist, has taken one of the most impoverished areas in South Africa and helped transform it into a tourism destination by using events featuring local artisans and performers to attract economic development. Describing himself as the founder, member, and director of the Soweto Mountain of Hope, Mentoor has proven that lives and places may be transformed through events. However, numerous other lamplighters in many of the dark corners of our world are also bringing illumination through events.

Professor Anthony Cohen, CBE, is the author of *The Symbolic Construction of Community* (1985) as well as many other books and scholarly articles. He is a distinguished academic leader in Great Britain who most recently served as the principal and vice chancellor of Queen Margaret University in Scotland. Professor Cohen is eminently respected for his scholarship in anthropology, as well as his leadership roles at the University of Edinburgh and Queen Margaret University. Indeed, he is a lamplighter in anthropology and higher education.

According to Professor Cohen, Victor Turner's theory of communitas very specifically requires a heightened emotional state that is experienced by multiple persons during a ritual, rite or event. One example he cites is the crowd behavior that is exemplified at a sports event with group of spectators who collectively participate in a state of excitement, perhaps euphoria, and which entails the suspension of self. Further, Cohen believes that Turner understood this state to be an involuntary suspension or subordination of individual consciousness. Cohen argues that Turner presents *communitas* as a transcendent collective experience. Communitas is perhaps further defined as a liminal (from the Latin word *limen* meaning a threshold) moment where ones sense of identity dissolves to some extent promoting a feeling of disorientation.

Therefore, one may wonder, where does the concept of teaching and research in planned events to promote communitas in society fit within the current or future structure of programs in higher education? Professor Cohen recognizes and greatly respects the importance of traditional disciplines within higher education. However, he also believes that interdisciplinary fields such as planned events both enhance and enlarge the world view of scholars within the academy. As an anthropologist and long-time higher education administrative leader, he also recognizes that the opportunity for communitas is present in every academic setting.

After reviewing Professor Cohen's remarks, I believe that perhaps, one day, university and college students may be offered a general studies or core course that will provide the strong underpinning of theory and philosophy through planned events. This course could help them in organizing and delivering the many milestone events in their lifetime (personal as well as professional) while achieving that rare and valuable experience of communitas.

Furthermore, these planned events organized or experienced by future graduates may find additional linkages to traditional disciplines such as mathematics and anthropology to help students become better citizens that one day. Not all graduates of higher education events programs will produce events on a professional basis. However, many will perhaps as a member of a local council perhaps, vote to fund local events or as a corporate leader they may provide financial support through approving a sponsorship budget. And every graduate will most certainly attend planned events and perhaps benefit from a richer experience because of exposure to the potential discovery of communitas during his or her formal academic studies. Perhaps as a result, more lamplighters, such as Professor Cohen, will emerge from our universities and colleges.

Why Are Special Events Important to the Next Generation and the New Frontier?

Whether in Edinburgh, Scotland, or Edmonton, Alberta, Canada, Stavanger, Norway, or Seattle, Washington, Alice Springs, Australia, or Almaty, Kazakhstan, there is a common purpose for perpetuating and growing these celebrations. In my studies with the Batwa Pygmies of Uganda, the aboriginal tribes of Uluru, and other indigenous people throughout the world, I have identified five common motivations for celebration. According to my research findings, human beings celebrate to remember their ancestors, promote kinship within their tribe, demonstrate pride in their culture, and transmit rituals to future generations. However, according to the aboriginal elders I interviewed and whose commentary I researched at the Strehlow Research Center in Ayres Rock, Australia, there is a fifth motivation that may surpass all of the others in terms of power. The aboriginal elders told me that I would perhaps never really understand why these rituals, traditions, and celebrations were so important because, indeed, they were motivated and invested with magic and mystery. As one of the elders looked penetratingly into my eyes and revealed this belief to me, I reacted in a suspicious and typically skeptical manner. Although my reaction was motivated by the requirements of scientific inquiry, for the first time in my research, I realized something more important was being revealed to me than mere opinion.

For literally thousands of years, traditional people throughout the world have preserved and transmitted their celebrations for a common purpose. There is obviously a reason for this cultivation and transmission of the cultural symbols of celebration. And the reason, I have concluded, is that these celebrations imbue their very lives with meaning. In fact, without these celebrations, people lack reasons for life itself. Anthropologists and sociologists who study linguistics have learned that when a common language is removed from a tribe, the roots of civilization are also destroyed. Celebrations are a common language that is perpetuated and expanded by all people to illuminate their lives.

Perhaps our greatest challenge as future Event Leaders is not merely to light the lamps for those who will follow us in this growing industry, but also to shine our lamps into the darker corners of the world and on those who will most benefit from our talents. As you find new places to shine your light in the future, I raise my glass in a celebratory toast to you as you begin or continue your journey in the field of eventology. The celebratory toasts that follow indicate the many global opportunities ahead of you as a future Event Leader. May your celebratory roots grow stronger and your wings beat faster as they take you and others further to rapidly advance the global celebrations industry!

- Afya!/Vifijo! (Swahili)
- Apki Lambi Umar Ke Liye (Hindi)
- À votre santé!/Santé! (French)
- Ba'sal'a'ma'ti! (Farsi)
- Cheers! (Great Britain)
- Chook-die!/Sawasdi! (Thai)
- Egészségedre! (Hungarian)
- Fee sihetak! (Egyptian)
- Fi sahik! (Arabic)
- Gan bei! (Mandarin)
- Gesondheid! (Afrikaans)
- Gia'sou (Greek)
- Hipahipa! (Hawaiian)
- Kampai! (Japanese)
- Kippis! (Finnish)
- Konbe! (Korean)
- Kong chien! (Chinese)
- Le'chaim! (Hebrew)
- Mabuhay! (Tagalog)
- Minum! (Malaysian)
- Na zdorov'ya! (Ukranian)
- Na zdrowie! (Polish)
- Nazdrave! (Bulgarian)
- Noroc! (Romanian)
- Nqa! (Sesotho)

- Oogy wawa! (Zulu)
- Prieka! (Latvian)
- Prost! (German)
- Prost!/Zum Wohl! (Austrian)
- Proost! (Dutch)
- Saha wa'afiab (Moroccan)
- Salud! (Creole, Spanish)
- Sanda bashi (Pakistani)
- Saúde! (Brazilian, Portuguese)
- Salute!/Cin cin! (Italian)
- Serefe! (Turkish)
- Skål! (Danish, Norwegian, Swedish)
- Sláinte! (Irish Gaelic)
- Slangevar (Scottish Gaelic)
- Vashe zdorovie! (Russian)
- Zivjeli! (Bosnian)
- Zivjeli!/U zdravlje! (Croatian, Serbian)

Note: For more toasts, visit www.awa.dk/glosary/slainte.htm.

Career-Advancement Connections

Corporate Social Responsibility Connection

A wise person once suggested that a truly satisfied individual builds not just a brilliant career but also a successful life as well. When focusing upon your career goals, why not ask yourself if one day upon looking back at the work you have completed, you will experience a sense of pride, satisfaction and happiness. Perhaps your next career plan or decision may be predicated with this type of reverse planning to ensure that your career burns bright and that you do not burn out. Rather, you have built a career of which you are proud because you have been of service to others and you have lived a life that has had meaning for others as you helped, one event at a time, to repair and improve the world.

Global Connection

There are infinite opportunities for global event careers. From multinational corporations to international associations, the opportunities are rich for travel, transnational experiences, and multicultural stimulation. To identify international career opportunities, you need to network through international organizations such as

The Pioneer: Professor Joe Goldblatt, CSEP; Professor and Executive Director, International Centre for the Study of Planned Events, Queen Margaret University, Edinburgh, Scotland

When Professor Goldblatt was a young boy in Dallas, Texas, he began to organize backyard carnivals for his neighborhood friends. Later, in college, he was active with staging university programs. Upon graduation from college, he went to Washington, DC, and used his theatrical and business skills to create The Wonder Company, a special event production firm, with his wife, Nancy.

The Wonder Company produced events at the White House, the opening of the Nashville Convention Center and the opening of the Donald Trump Taj Mahal, among many other hundreds of events throughout the world. Reflecting upon his long career, Goldblatt says, "I suppose from the time I was a young child I wanted to connect people, ideas, and emotions through the magic and mystery of special events."

Goldblatt knew he had made the right choice when he produced a Chanukah celebration as a senior student at his undergraduate college, St. Edward's University in Austin, Texas. He recalls, "We did not inform the students that we would be celebrating Chanukah during their regular dinner time. Hundreds of college students entered the dining hall, participated with the campus Catholic Priest in the lighting of the first candle of Chanukah, enjoyed traditional foods, and danced to Israeli music. At the end of the evening they were different, and so was I."

Goldblatt's mentors are his father and mother, Max and Rosa Goldblatt, who first taught their son Joe how to celebrate and why celebrations are important. "My mother was a talented hostess and fabulous Cajun cook and our kitchen was always filled with family and friends," says Professor Goldblatt. "She made entertaining appear easy and natural."

Although his father owned a small hardware store, he was a natural showman. When Joe was only six or seven, his father took him on a delivery with him one day. They delivered Bavarian hats and decorations to a man's home. "The man had erected a large tent and was organizing an Oktoberfest celebration," Goldblatt remembers. "Papa provided the costumes and decorations. I will always remember seeing my first professional event evolve through the eyes and talents of my Papa."

University professors, professional colleagues and, interestingly, his own students

MPI Europe or the International Congress and Convention Association (ICCA). ICCA represents professionals in the meetings and events industry in over 100 countries around the world. The ICCA membership list is available at www.icca.nl. Click on "Membership" and then search in the category "Professional congress organizers."

have also inspired Goldblatt over the years. "Over the years, my students have become my mentors by introducing me to new trends and customs enjoyed by their generation," he says. "My students are a source of continuous inspiration as they seek to find new ways to reinvent and revitalize the special events industry."

When he began in the meeting and event industry, all convention nametags were typed on an electric typewriter. Now, they are of course, produced by computers. "Technology, especially computers and the Internet, have transformed the special events industry into a more efficient and, I believe, more high-touch opportunity for personal interaction through developments such as social media networking sites." In addition to technological improvements, Professor Goldblatt believes, "Today's special events workers are better educated, more desirous of training and certification, and certainly more concerned about environmental sustainability. This gives me great hope for the future of the profession."

Professor Goldblatt believes that the next generation will inherit a special events industry that requires experience, talent, skill, and the ability to take scarce resources and produce greater value through events. He adds, "I hope that the next generation will inherit our work ethic, our pride in our profession, our commitment to ethical practices and, perhaps most importantly, our curiosity about how to continually improve this field for future generations."

One of the early indicators of this is the number of students throughout the world enrolled in special events–related courses. "They want to learn, and they realize that, through colleges and universities, the doors will swing wide open for future opportunities in this field." He adds, "Furthermore, I admire their commitment to environmental sustainability and their ethical decisions regarding recycling, reduction, and reuse to minimize the negative impacts from their events. Whilst some members of my generation may have been concerned with how much they could take (such as their income), the next generation is more concerned with what they may make (the new, improved opportunities they will create for the events industry and society in general)."

When asked what single piece of advice to give the next generation, Joe replies, "Education and experience are the tools that turn your dreams into plans that will produce a fulfilling life." He explains that throughout his life and career, he has noticed that individuals who are informally or formally educated and are keen to continually gain experience in a field, and are the ones that are the most successful and satisfied. "On the other hand, people who are arrogant often are also ignorant and therefore miss opportunities that may result in them eventually becoming obsolescent."

Professor Goldblatt says the best advice he can offer to the next generation is to gain as much professional experience as possible and always keep learning. "Learning and professional experience are the positive propellants that promote boundless success and infinite satisfaction throughout your life."

Technology Connection

The breadth and depth of online education has grown dramatically in the past decade. This growth reflects the overall growth of the Internet itself. Leading providers of distance-learning programs in planned events related studies include

The Protégé: Sam Goldblatt, MA; Environmental Officer, Capital Fringe Festival; Edinburgh Producer, 48 Hour Film Project; Senior Editor, *Special Events: A New Frontier for the Next Generation, Sixth Edition* (John Wiley & Sons, 2010)

Sam Goldblatt, a recent graduate of the master's degree program in festival management at Queen Margaret University, has always believed in the power of positive events to change people's perceptions and offer them sublime moments of escape or self-actualization.

Early in his burgeoning career he recognized the potential of events through his work at the Capital Fringe Festival in Washington, DC. According to Sam, "In 2007 I created a preview night for the Capital Fringe Festival, called the Fringe Preview. Not only did many performers come to promote their shows, audience members came from all over the DC area to enjoy a free night of previews. I organized the event at a circus sideshow bar called The Palace of Wonders, which has a tiny cabaret stage. As I introduced the acts and saw magicians, jugglers, and sword swallowers interacting with the audience, I realized that I could inspire people through events."

Sam described his mentors as his parents and the founders of the Capital Fringe Festival. "My mother and father are constant sources of inspiration. Not many people know that they began as humble street mimes in Washington, DC. Papa saw Mom performing in whiteface makeup in a dance studio and fell in love immediately. They spent the next several years performing together as happy bohemians, and since then they have each had prestigious and varied careers. I admire my parents' love for diversity in life and work. They have lived in Dallas, Des Moines, DC, Tennessee, Rhode Island, Philadelphia, and now Scotland. They have each been performers, run their own events business, managed events and fundraising for the Smithsonian, gone back to school to earn higher degrees while raising a family, become professors, and taught two-year-olds how to juggle.

"My other mentors are Scot McKenzie and Julianne Brienza, who created the bohemian wonderland that is the Capital Fringe Festival. Through their perseverance and creativity they have permanently altered the cultural landscape in DC. Scot and Julianne are two of the bravest arts producers that I know. They take on major risks in order to constantly push the cultural agenda and give patrons a wild and inspiring experience."

Sam is passionate about the development of environmentally sustainable events. He says, "Environmental sustainability is a major issue and will continue to expand. Event producers will realize that environmentalism doesn't have to be about global warming. It's as simple as minimizing waste and conserving energy, two obvious best practices for any event. I foresee, and desire, a sharp decline in plastic fork and Styrofoam plate sales and an increase in solar panel technology. I predict, and sincerely hope, that future events will generate fewer dumpsters full of waste."

Sam says that these major changes are the result of common sense. "Disposable forks make for disposable events. Event producers will realize the beauty of silverware, of glassware, of things that are real and have lasting value. Sustainability is about thinking 100 years from now. A plastic fork has value for two minutes, and then it spends the rest of its life in a landfill. A steel fork, on the other hand, has integrity as a reusable item. Event producers are beginning to realize that minimizing waste greatly enhances the event experience."

He has a positive vision for the future of the special events industry. According to Sam, "In the next ten years, events will run entirely on solar, wind and hydro power. People will peddle bicycles to generate energy to run jumbotron televisions. Events will have their own gardens where the food is grown, and patrons may even slaughter their own meat at some festivals, as people begin to want to relearn where their food actually comes from. There will be nothing disposable, as everyone will bring their own cups and canvas bags."

However, Sam cautions that we must not take this growth for granted. He says, "Because the events industry seems to be reaching a saturation point, events and festivals will have to show that they have unique value and are different from others. Sustainable events that minimize waste, conserve energy, and contribute to a happier, healthier life, will flourish. Events that rely on disposable items and fail to connect with patrons on a meaningful level will decline."

When asked about the best advice he has received, he uses the metaphor of construction. "Scot McKenzie is both a festival producer and a master carpenter whom I have had the pleasure of building several art projects with. He reminds me to 'Use the right tool for the job.' This applies to carpentry, event management systems, and life in general. In carpentry, you wouldn't use a wrench to hammer nails. In events, you will always want to find the perfect tablecloth, lighting design, box office system, or food menu, that satisfies the needs, wants, and desires of your patrons, best uses your resources, and contributes to the spirit of the event. Never settle for second best in life. Decide what the perfect tool, perfect job, or perfect life is, and grab it by the horns."

Sam has successfully combined professional experience and formal education to forge a career that he finds most satisfying. His commitment to environmental sustainability through special events will further ensure his continued success in the future. He is, in fact, helping lead the way for a new frontier and the next generation through his commitment to sustainable events and his first book, *Greener Meetings and Events* will be published by John Wiley & Sons, Inc. in 2011.

the Queen Margaret University Executive Masters of International Planned Events (www.qmu.ac.uk), The George Washington University Event Management Program (www.gwu.edu), the University of Nevada at Las Vegas (www.unlv.edu), the American Society of Association Executives (www.asaecenter.org), and Meeting Professionals International (www.mpiweb.org).

Resource Connection

The American Society of Association Executives publishes a newsletter listing hundreds of jobs in the not-for-profit sector. The newsletter is available by subscription. Contact ASAE at www.asaecenter.org. The International Special Events Society also lists jobs on its Web page at www.ises.org. The International Association of Assembly Managers (IAAM) lists jobs on its Web site for persons who wish to work in auditoriums, arenas, stadiums and other places of public assemble. (www.iaam.org) You may also wish to visit www.monster.com and use keywords such as special events, event management, meeting planning, and exposition management. When I checked this listing, there were over 1,000 part- and full-time positions being advertised in the event-related categories just listed. See *The Complete Guide to Careers in Special Events: Step Toward Success!* (Columbus 2011).

Learning Connection

Develop and write a new résumé that includes the skills and abilities you have mastered as a result of studying this book. Include in this résumé lifetime experiences that are relevant to the Event Leadership profession. Invite an experienced Event Leadership professional to review your résumé and provide you with honest feedback. Just as the growth in online programs has been dramatic in the past decade, the same growth has been experienced in the classroom. Over 140 universities and colleges throughout the world offer courses, curriculum, degrees, or certificates in event-related studies. Each year institutions of higher education expand their event studies–related course offerings. Visit www.qmu.ac.uk and click on The International Centre for the Study of Planned Events to receive a list of hundreds of education providers throughout the world.

CHAPTER 16

The New Best Practices in Planned Events

The term *best practice* is defined by different industries and different organizations in numerous ways. Fletcher Petroleum defines a best practice as "management practices and work processes that lead to world-class superior performance." (HyperMedia, http://www.walden3d.com/best_practices/bp_FCP_definition.html) Industries and government agencies ranging from information technology to project management to social services utilize different definitions to achieve the same purpose. The overarching purpose of a best practice in the field of planned events is to establish a benchmark or leading example that may positively influence your ability to lead future events.

I define a best practice in the field of planned events as an event organization that demonstrates one or more of six key attributes:

1. Best practice event organizations continually, over time, advance their mission through consistent performance improvement.
2. They continually innovate to improve and enlarge their body of knowledge.
3. They create new opportunities for the expansion of the profession.
4. They seek to promote positive global impacts through their individual contributions.
5. They promote sustainability through each event.
6. They demonstrate the highest level possible of corporate social responsibility throughout their organization and with every event they design and produce.

In this sixth edition of *Special Events* I have subjectively selected only two event organizations that, in my opinion, best emulate this definition. There are perhaps thousands of best-practice event case studies to choose from each year; however, these selections represent, in my own personal and professional judgment, those that deserve recognition and meet the criteria just identified.

The choices are strategic. One event demonstrates not only advancements in technology but also the potential transformation of a people through events. The second event demonstrates how challenges may be overcome to unite people for a common purpose and, in so doing, transform a nation state. In both cases, these events provide rich examples of how events are powerful change agents for the lands where they occur and how their impacts are felt far beyond their geographic borders. Despite these two vastly different examples, both of them share a common outcome as they are advancing, innovating, and promoting the future of the special events industry through their events.

In future editions I will continue to search the world for best-practice event planning organizations, and I welcome your recommendations. Only through careful scrutiny and evaluation of these and future best practices will we continually improve our profession.

The Best Practice in International Planned Events: The Opening Ceremonies of the Beijing, China 2008 Summer Olympic Games

The opening ceremonies of the 2008 Summer Olympic Games in Beijing demonstrated perhaps the greatest advances in technology, pyrotechnic design and display, thematic interpretation, and organization of human resources in the history of the modern Olympic Games movement. The result was described by veteran Olympic Games media observers such as Dick Ebersol, executive producer of the NBC television coverage, as "the richest in terms of texture, color, and imagination that really resonated on American television." Ebersol should know, having served as producer of numerous Olympic Games broadcasts and having executive produced every Olympic Games since Barcelona, Spain, in 1992.

Conceived and led by Zhang Yimou, arguably China's most famous film director, the Beijing opening ceremonies elegantly and seamlessly incorporated thousands of years of Chinese history and culture to carefully weave a visual story that entranced 90,000 people in the Birds Eye Stadium, and two billion more viewing the event on television.

The most remarkable accomplishment of Yimou and his team was to enable the event to seamlessly blend elements of high tech and high touch to engage the worldwide audience. From the opening sequence with hundreds of heavenly drums to the lighting of the Olympic Games flame by China's most honored athlete, the program of displays provided both a technological marvel and an intensely human story that would promote long-term memories for the performers, the media, and, of course, the audience.

Whilst some have argued that the Chinese government's policy of instrumentalism with regard to sports and culture may have negatively impacted the final performance, I believe that those who participated may emerge with a wider appreciation for the international community as a direct result of their participation in these highly successful events.

The estimated 15,000 technicians, designers, and performers may have been conscripted by their government to rehearse and perform in this great pageant; however, each of the participants was simultaneously introduced to the experience of communitas through their engagement. Perhaps this introduction to communitas and the opportunity to begin to rise from a historically repressed society to one that in the future may value individuals and even welcomes other ideas and innovations, is the best of all long-term potential outcomes from this remarkable event. One cannot help but hope that the thousands of participants, who invested many years in perfecting their performance to entertain others will have also helped build a more perfect nation as a result of their efforts. Regardless, the Opening Ceremonies of the 2008 Summer Olympic Games will be remembered as both awe-inspiring for the viewer and transformative for the participants and the nation where they continue to live and work. Therefore, the Opening Ceremonies in Beijing may demonstrate that the grandness of the performance of events may be exceeded by the ultimate release and rise of human spirit. The type of release that results from this type of massive undertaking and achievement is normal and natural. It is also a potential opportunity for every event to unleash the human spirit, as was achieved in China during their groundbreaking opening ceremonies.

Producer: Beijing Organizing Committee for the Olympic Games (BOCOG)
Opening Ceremonies Artistic Director: Zhang Yimou

The Best Practice in National Planned Events: Homecoming Scotland 2009

The Scottish government's first minister from 2001–2007, Jack McConnell, MSP approved a general policy to use the celebration in 2009 of the 250th anniversary of Burns' birth as one means to encourage Scots worldwide to return to Scotland. This policy commitment was to evolve into Homecoming Scotland 2009. This general policy was later driven forward and funded by McConnell's successor government leader, First Minister Alex Salmond, MSP. Organized by the national events agency, EventScotland in partnership with VisitScotland, Homecoming Scotland was scheduled from the weekend around Burn's birthday (25 January 2009) to Scotland's national day, St. Andrew's Day, (30 November 2009) to promote opportunities for five million Scottish citizens, millions of other Scots living throughout the world and those with a love of Scotland to return to celebrate history, culture, and their pride in Scotland.

Marie Christie project director of EventScotland and her colleagues at Homecoming Scotland 2009 facilitated the support and co-ordination of over 400 events throughout the country and generated a significant positive economic impact through tourism. These events ranged from Scotland's biggest ever Burns celebration featuring major parades, fire and light shows, music events, exhibitions and a focal Burns supper presided over by Scotland's First Minister Alex Salmond to the finale weekend which was Scotland's most extensive St Andrew's Day celebration yet. Featuring more than 40 events, it included a celebration of the Saltire (Scotland's flag) in the region of Scotland where it was first discovered, East Lothian.

As part of the evaluation programme, Ekos Ltd was contracted by EventScotland to evaluate the economic impacts of this programme. In November 2009 they produced an interim report that analyses information from just under a quarter of all funded events. The report does not include any impacts derived from 'partner' events or the wider benefits of the marketing campaign. However, the early reports are excellent and confirm why this series of events was a best practice in national events.

The four core aims of the Homecoming Scotland 2009 programme were to:

1. deliver additional tourism visits and revenue for Scotland;
2. engage and mobilise the Scottish Diaspora, who in this context are identified as those with ancestral links to Scotland and Scots living abroad;
3. promote pride in Scots at home and abroad; and
4. celebrate Scotland's outstanding contributions to the world.

According to the Ekos report, a total of 66% of visitors to the events were aware of Homecoming 2009 whilst a total of 43% were aware that the event they were attending was part of Homecoming 2009 prior to their attendance at the event.

The proportion of event visitors from outside Scotland who visited Scotland specifically due to Homecoming was 19%. By contrast, most international destinations projected and experienced a down turn in 2009 in international visitors due to the global recession. Therefore, Homecoming Scotland 2009's performance from a international tourism arrivals perspective was significantly positive.

The majority (97%) of the Homecoming Scotland 2009 events were rated as 'very good' or 'good' by attendees. Many of these events were first time ever programmes and therefore to achieve such a high satisfaction rating is quite remarkable and attests to the creativity and professionalism of the organizers and the support provided by the Homecoming Scotland 2009 team.

Ekos further reported that there were a total of 714,533 visits to the 25 events that they studied with 70% being day visitors and 30% overnight. Once again, to achieve such a high level of overnight guests is commendable because this provides additional economic injection for the destination hosting the local events.

With regards to return on investment, the preliminary report demonstrates that Homecoming Scotland 2009 was ahead of its projections. According to Ekos, a total of £711,237 of Homecoming Scotland 2009 funding was provided to the 25 events they studied. In addition, they allocated a pro rata proportion of the marketing and overheads to this amount giving a total of £1,303,935. In return this has generated net additional expenditure of £19.1m to give a return on investment of 1:14.7. The target for Homecoming Scotland 2009 was a return of 1:8 so at this stage it appears to be well ahead of target. One of the major events of Homecoming Scotland 2009 was a unique two day program entitled, The Gathering. Following many years of planning, Lord Jamie Sempill and veteran event producer Jenny Gilmour conceived a major event that would serve as a centerpiece for the year-long homecoming celebrations. Sempill and Gilmour, along with their colleague Lucy-Rose Walker, envisioned in *The Gathering 2009,* an event that would reunite the traditional clan network of Scotland in one weekend. This had last been attempted in 1822, when His Majesty King George IV led a few clans up Edinburgh's Royal Mile.

Lord Sempill and his colleagues realized that reuniting the clan chieftains with their members would be problematic due to decades of rivalry, miscommunication, and a general wariness by Scots about this type of event. However, they first committed their personal funds to launching this event, and then were joined with contributions from the Scottish government as well as commercial sponsors.

The big question was whether the over 100 clan chiefs would agree to participate in the event. The tenacity, talent, and tolerance exhibited by The Gathering 2009 team resulted in attracting the full participation of 125 clans, as well as over 50,000 persons to the two-day event held in Edinburgh, Scotland's beautiful Holyrood Park. As a result of their efforts, thousands of clan members, led by their chiefs, marched up the Royal Mile on July 25, 2009, recreating and greatly expanding King George IV's historic march of 190 years earlier.

Fifteen students from Queen Margaret University's 2009 International Festival Experience Study Tour (I-FEST) conducted ethnographic research during the two days of The Gathering 2009 festivities. These students, who traveled from St. Edward's University in Austin, Texas, to study at QMU and experience Edinburgh's Festivals, observed and noted external characteristics such as applause levels and length, smile factors, and audience physical engagement, and then they recorded the memories that participants verbally dictated that they would retain from this event in the years to come.

The preliminary findings from the ethnographic research confirmed that The Gathering 2009 was a huge success in terms of guest experiences and positive memories, overcoming almost constant major media cynicism that had besieged the program for many months. The students noted that participants in The Gathering 2009 greatly appreciated the opportunity to reconnect with their clan, to experience a wide range of Scottish culture and history, and for many, to transmit these important values to their children. When asked about their memories, many stated that seeing the clans all together in one location was something that they would remember for the rest of their lives. Others mentioned that participating in the clan parade on the royal mile was something they would tell future generations about, as they were now part of the history of Scotland.

The Gathering 2009 was a private commercial venture that cost about 2.4 million pounds to stage. The majority of the funding was from private sources, with about 20 percent of funding from various government agencies. This is a unusual funding practice for such a large event in Europe, as most major events are primarily funded through government sources. However, this event, despite its huge popular success and that it brought in an estimated £10.4M in economic impact to Scotland suffered a significant financial loss after the event ended and the holding company was forced into administration to try and settle their debts. Efforts were made by the local council and Scottish government to further support the event company financially, but in the end they were not successful and the event and its organization was ultimately tarnished by the financial failure. Despite the financial failure of The Gathering, the majority of Homecoming events reported strong results and many exceeded their attendance targets.

As a direct result of Homecoming Scotland 2009 a potential groundbreaking business model has been developed for future national events throughout the world. Whether Australia or America, Canada or Cambodia, New Zealand or Norway, every culture has the need and desire to reconnect with their cultural, ethnic and familial roots. Therefore,

Homecoming Scotland 2009 may have discovered the holy grail of future national celebrations by creating a program of events that provides the opportunity to return home and celebrate as a community once again.

EventScotland, the national events agency in partnership with VisitScotland, the national tourism agency succeeded in large part due to the identification of a good idea and the support many events received from these organizations. The popular success these events enjoyed was a direct result of the organizers willingness to listen, learn, and inevitably lead others to rediscover why Scotland is cherished by Scots throughout the world and all others those who simply love Scottish history, ideas, design, and culture. Homecoming Scotland 2009 further convinced the citizens of Scotland that their land is indeed loved by people throughout the world so that they may, as a direct result of these best practice events, develop a greater appreciation and renewed pride in their homeland. The potential dawning of a second enlightenment in Scotland could not be more timely. As a direct result of Homecoming Scotland's positive international media coverage, those who love Scotland and Scottish culture will soon be grasping their strand within the amazing new cultural tartan that was first woven so well by Marie Christie and her extraordinary team, committed partners and creative and professional event organizers.

Visit Scotland CEO:	Phillip Riddle
Event Scotland CEO:	Paul Bush, OBE
Homecoming Scotland 2009 Project Director	Marie Christie

CHAPTER 17

New Frontiers in Twenty-First-Century Planned Events

The following case studies represent actual and theoretical planned events. Each case study is based on five key assumptions. First, the fixed date and time of the planned event. Second, the estimated number of participants. Third, the average budget or turnover for the event. Fourth, goals and objectives (outcomes) desired from the event versus the actual results. Fifth and finally, the corporate social responsibility (CSR) strategy employed by each event planner to promote sustainability.

These case studies may be used as examples of the actual planned event process and further researched through additional sources. More importantly, each case study is an ideal opportunity to trigger a more in-depth discussion and debate regarding the how to improve the event planning process. At the conclusion of each case study there several discussion questions as well as a debate topic that may be used to further examine, explore and expand the knowledge imbedded in each example.

Advertising and Marketing: Strike Out the Elephants!

The legendary sports event marketing guru Joe Engel needed to rapidly increase attendance for his baseball team, the Chattanooga Lookouts, based near Lookout Mountain, Tennessee. Engels decided to use elephants to introduce the players to the fans. To promote this event, he used advertising and public relations to announce there would be a elephant stampede at the start of the game! He knew that in the rural area where his stadium was located, elephants would be a major attraction. The event took place during the regular baseball summer season in the late afternoon. Approximately 10,000 fans purchased tickets to witness the stampede. While the budget is unknown, Engel probably traded advertising with a local circus or elephant trainer to borrow the animals for this onetime event. The goals from the event included to increase ticket sales, general advance buzz in the local media (newspapers and radio) and entertain the fans with a memorable experience. Although corporate social responsibility was not directly involved in this event, Engel may have offered the elephant's manure to local gardeners as a additional incentive to come to the ball park.

Discussion Questions

1. What else could Engel have done, other than a elephant stampede, to generate pre-event buzz and increase attendance?
2. How could you prevent or mitigate controversy from animal rights groups for conducting a stunt using animals?
3. How would you measure the return on marketing investment or return on objectives of this type of event?

Debate Topic

Resolved: The use of live animals at a special event is not worth the potential negative publicity the event organizations may receive.

Attractions: Let's Play!

When European Cities Marketing held its annual meeting in Gothenburg, Sweden, in the summer, it was directly across the street from a popular amusement park. The event planners for European Cities Marketing decided to use this strategic location to their advantage and conduct one of their social events at the park. The event began in the early evening with a dinner in one of the park's restaurants. At the conclusion of the dinner for approximately 200 persons, the organizers announced that at each table there was a team captain and that he or she would wear a funny head dress and lead the other guests at their table on an adventure through the park. The first team to actually complete all the assignments listed on a card that was distributed would win a prize. The assignments included riding various rides, playing carnival games, and other typical activities within the park. The organizer announced, "Ready, set, and go!" and the race was on. The sound of laughter and excitement was deafening as the teams began to fan out throughout the park. The goals of the event were to promote networking and encourage relaxation after a long day of meetings. In addition, it was hoped that a spirit of competition would develop and this rivalry would further increase the bonding among the various teams. It is estimated the cost per person for this event could have been around $100, or $20,000 total. The goals for this event were to promote networking and encourage physical participation. The amusement park promoted CSR through recycling and reuse and encouraged greener travel by being accessible by frequent public transportation. The event planners reduced the carbon footprint for the event by eliminating travel by motor coach and instead instructing the participants to walk to the park, as it was directly across the street from their hotel.

Discussion Questions

1. How would you have improved the outcomes from this event to further include educational benefits (learning) during the various activities?
2. How would you assess, analyze, plan, manage, and control the risks associated with this sort of event?
3. What additional CSR tactics could be employed in the future?

Debate Topic

Resolved: The energy used by participants at this type of event could be better deployed in a community service activity such as cleaning up a public park, rebuilding a children's playground or planting a flower garden at a care home.

Catering: Endless Appetizers

The Malaga tourism team decided to impress the International Congress and Convention Association (ICCA) Research and Marketing Conference, in Malaga, Spain, in midsummer. The closing night event was held high atop their beautiful city at the botanical gardens. As the guests walked from the coaches to the event site they passed three different bridal parties taking romantic photographs in this magical setting. Finally, upon arrival at the party site, there was a large marquee (tent) with a small dance floor.

During the cocktail hour, the servers slowly entered from the catering kitchen, and each one offered different types of tempting appetizers. This continued over one dozen times, and each time the servers appeared, the presentation and size of the appetizers improved and expanded. Finally, the guests were invited to a sumptuous three-course dinner followed by a mojito bar and dancing.

Discussion Questions

1. Why did the appearance of the bridal parties add value and meaning to the event?
2. What role did the progressive size and volume of the appetizers add to the pacing and surprise element of the event?
3. What could you have done differently in place of the mojito bar if alcohol had been an issue?

Debate Topic

Resolved: Alcohol at special events should not be allowed because it leads to inebriation and strange behavior.

Conventions: Fly Me Away to the Board Reception

Twenty board members and approximately 15 special guests were invited to the home of the association executive director on the final night of the annual convention in the autumn. The executive director and his wife and son greeted each guest individually as they arrived at their home. Guests were offered a glass or wine, beer, or cocktail of their choice and then invited to tour the private gardens, which the executive director had cultivated over many years. Following the tour, a buffet dinner was served. Toward the end of the dinner, a hot air balloon was inflated in the garden and guests were invited to hop aboard for a controlled ride into the stratosphere. Next, guests were invited to watch a demonstration of how to create the perfect Irish coffee by one of the board members from Ireland. Finally, the executive director thanked everyone for coming and the guests returned to their hotels with warm memories of this highly personal, surprising, and educational reception. The goal of this event was to provide the board with a casual evening that would allow the executive director to express his thanks for their leadership and support. It is estimated the cost per person could have been $50 per person, or a total of around $2,000. The event promoted corporate social responsibility by bussing the board in one shuttle to provide an alternative to individuals' automobiles and also allowed the executive director to introduce the guests to his garden to further demonstrate how he and his family are cultivating the earth's natural resources.

Discussion Questions

1. How did the executive director and his family provide a high-touch experience at low cost?
2. How could you promote further examples of CSR through this type of event?
3. Why was it important to offer the guests the opportunity to tour the garden, ride in the hot air balloon and participate in the making of Irish coffee throughout the evening?

Debate Topic

Resolved: In lieu of a private social event, the board of director's and volunteers should invest the same funds in creating scholarships for the organization's members.

Corporate Social Responsibility: Transforming the City

When the Professional Convention Management Association (PCMA) scheduled its annual convention in New Orleans, Louisiana, the organizers decided to invite members to participate in a community service activity prior to the official start of the program. Approximately 400 persons helped restore local cemeteries and neighborhoods that had been badly damaged by Hurricane Katrina. Each person paid approximately $75 to participate in these activities, and these fees covered transportation, materials, administration and other aspects of the program's operation. The event received widespread positive publicity and city residents actually approached the participants and thanked them for their help in restoring the Crescent City. The goals of this program were to provide participants with an opportunity to repair, improve and restore the host destination through corporate social responsibility. The CSR effort was obvious not only to the participants but also to all citizens through the positive publicity as seen on local television news programs, radio stations, and in newspapers.

Discussion Questions

1. What else could the convention organizers have done during and after the convention to promote corporate social responsibility?
2. How would you have prepared the participants in advance for the roles they would play in this community service project?
3. What other goals and objectives would you identify if you were to plan a program such as this in the future?

Debate Topic

Resolved: Corporate social responsibility should only be included in events where there is a pronounced cause or reason why this is needed, such as generating positive publicity for the sponsoring organization.

Entertainment: Men on Ice

Immediately prior to the commencement of the closing general session on a mid week morning in August, three men dressed in jump suits ascended the stage and began carving huge blocks of ice using electric chain saws. As the ice chips flew on the stage and even into the audience of approximately 2,000 persons, the men began stacking the ice blocks along the back wall of the stage. The ice soon formed the logo of the organization sponsoring the event. Using dramatic blue lighting the ice was soon transformed into a multisensorial image as the audience began to feel the coolness from the rising logo design. Finally, the ice designers took the remaining blocks of ice and fashioned a standing lectern in front of the giant logo. Rock and roll music accompanied this dramatic and highly artistic performance that would perhaps cost about $5,000 to $10,000 plus transportation for the artists as well as the cost of the ice used in the performance. The event's goals were to gain the focus and interest of the audience prior to the speech being provided by a luminary in the events industry. Corporate social responsibility was demonstrated by using a natural product that could be recycled (ice and later water).

Discussion Questions

1. Why did the organizers schedule this performance as a preshow immediately preceding the speaker?
2. How could the event planner have reduced risk when staging an event using electric chain saws and flying ice chips?
3. What would you have done to add additional drama to this event through potential audience participation?

Debate Topic

Resolved: Every program requires a preshow element to focus the audience's attention and build excitement for the main event.

Environmental Sustainability: The Free Store Fosters Environmental Freedom

The Capital Fringe Festival in Washington, DC, offers a free store where individuals may take a free item of clothing or other commodity by replacing it with a donation they provide for the store. The free store was open during the month of July in Washington, DC, and was visited by thousands of persons. The goal of this activity was to encourage recycling both at the event as well as throughout the larger community. The cost of this event was negligible, as all items were donated. The CSR elements included recycling awareness by both the participants and the larger community as a whole. The event drew widespread publicity in print and electronic media and generated pride, loyalty and advocacy among the event participants and volunteers.

Discussion Questions

1. Why should every event appoint an environmental officer to ensure it is promoting sustainability throughout the entire event?

2. How do you measure and evaluate the success of a free store in terms of sustainability?
3. How do you encourage participation in a free store to guarantee continued success?

Debate Topic

Resolved: the free store should be limited to only items that appeal to a middle- and upper-class markets to ensure the best quality of goods.

Expositions and Exhibitions: Take My Pencils and Pens, Please!

An annual trade show that attracts 5,000 persons and is held in October of each year asked its 500 exhibitors to list those items that are usually and customarily left behind following the exhibition. Then, the trade show organizers contacted the local school district where the show was taking place and asked if the teachers and students would benefit from these items. Once the need had been confirmed, the trade-show organizer asked the exhibitors to complete a donation form pledging to donate certain leftover goods to the local school district. The first year this project was initiated, 1,500 pencils and 500 ballpoint pens were donated to local schoolchildren and their teachers. Throughout the five-year history of this program, it is estimated that over 7,000 pencils and 2,000 ballpoint pens have been donated to benefit local school districts. The total value of these donations is estimated to be in excess of $5,000. The goal of this project is to recycle what would typically be waste or eliminate the need to reship these items at the end of the program. The materials are always picked up by the school district at the exhibit hall so the show organizer does not have any further costs. The goal of this project is to promote recycling and at the same time emphasize the value that the association brings to the local community. Another goal is to provide the exhibitors with an alternative to repacking and reshipping their leftover materials. The CSR element from this event is use of recycling to provide much needed equipment for local school districts. The show organizer asks the school district to have the children and teachers who directly benefit to write personal letters to the exhibitors who have provided the donations and this is always greatly appreciated.

Discussion Questions

1. How would you expand this program in the future to include vendors (suppliers) to the show?
2. How could you create a photo opportunity for this annual donation to provide additional publicity for the donors?
3. Are there any risk issues associated with this program, and if so, how would you mitigate them?

Debate Topic

Resolved: Every item left over from a trade show should be donated to local organizations.

Festivals: Tickets Please!

Upon entering the festival box office, it was apparent that there was a ticketing problem. Long lines formed at the box office and individuals were obviously very upset and angry that their tickets, ordered through the Internet, were not available at the box office. The annual festival held in August sells over one million tickets annually. A new box office system had been purchased and regrettably, was not working efficiently during the early weeks of the festivals ticket sales. The goals of this festival are to provide a wide range of programming featuring all types of artistic forms in over 200 venues. Therefore, ticketing is critically important to the festival and its affiliated artists and promoters. The festival in recent years has begun to promote environmental sustainability through recycling bins. However, there are few efforts beyond this that promote sustainability. The main problem has been the inefficiency of the box office. In addition to long delays in retrieving tickets, many online ticket buyers were concerned that their personal information, including credit card numbers, may have to be shared with others. Ultimately, the festival was required to conduct an in-depth investigation into the overall management of the events that led to the box office fiasco.

Discussion Questions

1. How could the festival improve its box office performance in the future?
2. How could the festival increase its environmental sustainability programs?
3. How would you use public relations to promote a new box office system and address the complaints of ticket buyers to restore their confidence in the future?

Debate Topic

Resolved: A new box office system should have a trial period of testing prior to going live with the public to ensure stability and consistency of performance over time.

Fundraising: When Green Is the New Black

The Green Fashion Show was held at a university to raise money for a local charity. Nearly 200 persons attended the show, and the total budget was under \$500. The tickets were priced at regular admission £7.00 and student tickets at £5.00. Various designers used recycled products to design and construct clothing that was featured in the fashion show. The judges included a department store executive as well as the leaders of various student associations. The event's goals were to demonstrate and promote the overall concept of sustainability in clothing as well as to raise money for a good cause that was directly related to environmental sustainability in the area where the event was conducted. The organizers promoted CSR by using recycled materials and reusable equipment for the reception that preceded the fashion show. Furthermore, the fashion show succeeded in its goal of raising several hundred pounds for environmental causes.

Discussion Questions

1. How would you improve the fundraising potential for the Green Fashion Show in the future?
2. How would you expand the publicity for the Green Fashion Show next time?
3. What could be done to recycle the clothing used in the Green Fashion Show to promote reuse?

Debate Topic

Resolved: Green is the new black, and therefore, every fashion show should adopt an environmental mission.

Government: Coming Home

A national government adopted a heritage theme to promote tourism in their country. Hundreds of local events were organized and some funded through government, private, and other sources. One of the major events attracted upward of 75,000 persons, and there were long lines at the food and beverage as well as merchandise stands. As a result of these long lines, many of the guests were inconvenienced. The goal of this event was to connect individuals with their heritage, history, and culture in an entertaining, family-friendly setting. Although recycling was available at this event, it was not prominently featured. The overall budget for this event was over $3 million.

Discussion Questions

1. How could the organizers ha\ve better planned for the long lines to avoid disappointing their guests?
2. How could the recycling for this event be prominently featured, and how can the organizers better publicize their environmental efforts in the future?
3. If the goal of this event was to connect the guests with their heritage and history, how could the organizers measure and evaluate their success in achieving this goal?

Debate Topic

Resolved: Connecting individuals to their heritage and history is a valid reason to develop a multimillion-dollar event that receives private, public, and other support.

Hotel: A Five-Star Welcome

A prominent four-star hotel in a Caribbean tourist resort hosted an event to welcome an internationally renowned speaker to the resort. Invitees included local members of the travel and tourism industry. The event was held on the hotel's rooftop terrace, overlooking the entire city that sparkled in the full moonlight. A lavish buffet, featuring local seafood and lamb dishes, was served to the approximately 50 guests. The program included a welcome from the hotel general manager, greetings from the national tourism leader, and brief remarks from the guest speaker. It is estimated that the budget for this event was between $3,000 and $5,000. The goal of the event was to welcome the prominent speaker, to promote networking among the members of the travel and tourism industry and to promote the host hotel. To accomplish the latter, a video presentation about the hotel was projected on a large screen. A few weeks prior to this event, President Barack Obama had spoken in the same location. When the general manager introduced the speaker, he mentioned that the hotel and entire community were delighted to welcome another great leader to their destination.

Discussion Questions

1. How could the menu for this event have been tailored to promote the latest trends in nutritious cuisine and also satisfy the needs of vegetarians?
2. What special memory could the hosts have created for the guests to promote a further sustainable meaning from this event?
3. Who else should have been invited to this event to further promote the hotel for future business opportunities?

Debate Topic

Resolved: When events are hosted to promote business interests, the hosts should refrain from overly promoting the hotel to avoid a conflict of interest.

Incentives: Luxury or Necessity?

Fifty salespeople from throughout the world qualified to participate in a five-day incentive holiday to Hawaii. Spouses and partners were not eligible to participate. The estimated budget for this event was $100,000, including transportation, hotel, meals and various entertainment activities. On the final night of the incentive event, a gala dinner was held on the beach to recognize the achievement of each member of the group. The corporate vice president of sales and marketing made the presentations by placing golden floral lei on each sales winner. Throughout the week-long celebration, the group participated in hula dancing classes, para-sailing, and a cruise to a neighboring island, and at the conclusion they were invited to enjoy several spa treatments at an exclusive resort. The goals and objectives of this incentive program were to encourage word–of-mouth promotion by the participants to promote the event to future salespeople and raise sales throughout the corporation. The second goal was to ensure the participants had a leisurely time in a relaxing destination.

Discussion Questions

1. How could the organizers have included the spouses and partners of the qualifying participants without jeopardizing the goals and objectives of the event?
2. How could the corporation redesign the event to achieve the same goals and objectives without risking undue scrutiny from the media because of the luxurious elements included in the program?
3. Who should this event be promoted to in the future to include greater participation and help further advance sales throughout the corporation?

Debate Topic

Resolved: Due to the AIG effect that has discouraged lavish spending by corporations, incentives should be limited to only providing tangible awards, such as trophies, to qualifying persons.

Information Technology: Lost and Found

A large government department scheduled a two-day workshop for 100 of its employees. The budget for the two-day meeting was approximately $50,000. The budget included meals, local transportation, and one night of hotel accommodation. The workshop was to include high-level training in sensitive areas, such as profiling terrorist suspects at airport security areas. Scheduled activities included a welcome reception, two full days of speakers and seminars, two breakfasts, two luncheons, and a closing dinner. The goals and objectives of this program were to deliver high-level training in a short time period to change and improve the behavior of the employees. The second goal of the program was to allow time for discussion that would lead to further opportunities to continually improve their practices regarding airport security. However, the event planner accidentally left a laptop computer containing confidential data about the event's intended participants on the subway, and it was subsequently stolen.

Discussion Questions

1. What should the meeting planner have done immediately after discovering the loss of the computer?
2. How could the loss of this technology be prevented in the future?
3. Should the program organizers have raised the security level for this meeting due to the missing data that could compromise the security of the participants?

Debate Topic

Resolved: Every element of information technology used in the management of an event must have minimum safeguards to ensure the protection of those persons whose information is contained within the technology.

Meetings: Meeting or No Meeting?

A board meeting with 25 persons was scheduled for an airport hotel near Rome, Italy. Shortly before the meeting was to be held, a major earthquake took place in a city 100 miles from the airport hotel. The event planner checked with various government officials and confirmed that it was highly unlikely the earthquake would reoccur and stated that the hotel and destination were safe to hold the meeting. However, the event planner received e-mails and telephone calls from over half of the board members who stated their hesitancy about attending the upcoming meeting. The event planner's budget for this meeting was \$15,000, and over \$10,000 had already been expended and was nonrefundable. The goals and objectives of this event included the review of the financial operations and passage of the annual budget, the review of the annual convention program and finally, interviews with candidates to lead the organization in the future.

Discussion Questions

1. Should the event planner cancel the meeting, postpone, and reschedule, or go ahead with those members who may attend?
2. How can the event planner reassure her board members that they will be safe and encourage them to attend the meeting?
3. How could this meeting be conducted virtually to satisfy the goals and objectives listed above?

Debate Topic

Resolved: Force majeure (Act of God) is sufficient reason to cancel or postpone any event.

Social Event (Wedding): I Feel Faint

The bride was feeling faint as she prepared to walk down the aisle with her father. The air temperature was nearly 100°F; however, nearly 250 guests assembled outdoors for this wedding at a lavish hotel in Beverly Hills, California. The budget for the entire wedding was over $150,000. The first goal and objective of the event was to provide a romantic, once-in-a-lifetime experience for the bride and groom and their guests. The second goal and objective was to provide a religious context for this ceremony within a naturally beautiful outdoor setting. During the ceremony, the bride began to feel fainter and suddenly fainted. The minister performing the ceremony and the groom helped lift the bride to her feet. The minister then resumed the ceremony, and once more the bride fainted. Finally, the minister said a quick prayer of thanksgiving, the guests said "Amen!" and the reception began.

Discussion Questions

1. Should the minister have continued the ceremony after the bride fainted?
2. How could the wedding planner have been better prepared for the fainting bride?
3. What should the minister and wedding planner have done after the bride fainted the second time?

Debate Topic

Resolved: A medical emergency during an event is cause to stop the event and treat the inured immediately.

Sports: When the Audience Vanished

A sports event producer invited a magician to develop a magic show to entertain the fans during the football match halftime period. The magician developed a series of illusions that would mystify and amaze the 50,000 fans in the stadium. When the second quarter ended, nearly half of the spectators rose from their seats and headed to the bathroom or to fetch another beer. The magician wondered what made the audience disappear when he had been rehearsing for this moment for nearly two years. With a budget of over $500,000 at stake, the show proceeded, despite the missing audience. The goals and objectives of this event were to engage the audience through magic and to provide family-friendly entertainment during the halftime show. The audience applauded loudly throughout the show, and the hundreds of dancers and magicians performed brilliantly, despite the missing audience.

Discussion Questions

1. How could the magician and sports event producer have kept the audience in their seats for the start of the show?
2. Which goal and objective is missing from those stated in the modern age of mass media?
3. How could the show have been enhanced to attracted greater television viewership in the future?

Debate Topic

Resolved: The size of the audience does not determine the quality of the final production or the effort required to achieve this quality.

APPENDICES

APPENDIX 1

References

Professional speaker Charles "Tremendous" Jones, CPAE, passed away in October 2008, but during his long career he is credited with originating the simple philosophy that, many years from now, most of us will be exactly the same person we are today except for two things: *the books we read and the people we meet along the way*. Indeed, just as Tremendous Jones philosophy will live forever through his books and speeches, similarly, your career will be sustained through your devotion to life long learning.

I encourage you to develop the rigor of reading one new book per week and surveying other written resources daily, such as magazines and newsletters. This will help ensure that you stay current in your profession and will provide you with many new ideas to accelerate the growth of your career.

I am often asked, "Where do you get all your ideas?" The questioner assumes that I reach into Pandora's fabled box and divine new wonders of creation. Usually I reply to this question by stating: "Plato, Aristotle, Shakespeare, Keats, Browning, Hemingway, Dickinson, Stein, Eyre, Barrett, Seurat, Beethoven, Bach, Brahms, Picasso, Vermeer, and other renowned writers, painters, and composers."

The following resources have guided my career and will further ensure your professional success.

Books Specifically for Event Leaders

Adcock, E., D. Buono, and B. McGee (2009). *Premium, Incentive, and Travel Buyers.* Virginia: Briefings Media Group, LLC. Available from: www.douglaspublications.com.

Allen, J. (2009). *Event Planning: The Ultimate Guide to Successful Meetings, Corporate Events, Fundraising Galas, Conferences, Conventions, Incentives, and Other Special Events.* Ontario: John Wiley & Sons.

Association of National Advertisers Event Marketing Committee (2009). *Bring your Brand to Life with Event Marketing.* New York: ANA.

Astroff, M. T., and J. R. Abbey (2006). *Convention Sales and Services.* Educational Institute of the American Hotel.

Baines, P., J. Egan, and F. Jefkins (2004). *Public Relations: Contemporary Issues and Techniques.* Oxford: Butterworth-Heinemann.

Baldridge, L. (1993). *Letitia Baldridge's New Complete Guide to Executive Manners.* New York: Rawson Associates, Maxwell Macmillan International.

Batterberry, A. R. (1976). *Bloomingdale's Book of Entertaining.* New York: Random House.

Berlonghi, A. E. (1990). *The Special Event Risk Management Manual.* Dana Point, CA: Author.

Berrige, G. (2007). *Events Design and Experience.* London: Butterworth-Heinemann.

Bienvenu, S. (2006). *The Presentation Skills Workshop: Helping People Create and Deliver Great Presentations.* New York: AMACOM.

Boehme, A. J. (1998). *Planning Successful Meetings and Events: A Take-Charge Assistant Book.* New York: AMACOM.

Bowdin, G., J. Allen, W. O'Toole, R. Harris, and I. McDonnell (2006). *Events Management*, 2nd ed. London: Butterworth-Heinemann.

Bray, I. (2000). *Effective Fundraising for Nonprofits: Real-World Strategies That Work*, 2nd ed. Berkeley, CA: Margaret Livingston.

Brotherton, B., ed. (2003). *The International Hospitality Industry: Structure, Characteristics and Issues.* Oxford: Butterworth Heinemann.

Brown, D. R. (2005). *The Food Service Managers Guide to Creative Cost Cutting and Cost Control: Over 2001 Innovative and Simple Ways to Save Your Food Service Operation Thousands by Reducing Expenses.* Ocala, FL: Atlantic Publishing Group.

Brown, R., and M. Marsden (1994). *The Cultures of Celebrations.* Bowling Green, OH: Bowling Green State University Popular Press.

Browne, R. (1981). *Rituals and Ceremonies in Popular Culture.* Bowling Green, OH: Bowling Green State University Popular Press.

Breuilly, E., J. O'Brien, M. Palmer, and M. Marty (2002). *Festivals of the World: The Illustrated Guide to Celebrations, Customs, Events, and Holidays.* New York: Checkmark Books.

Cartmell, R. (1987). *The Incredible Scream Machine: A History of the Roller Coaster.* Bowling Green, OH: Bowling Green State University Popular Press.

Catherwood, D. W., and R. L. Van Kirk (1992). *The Complete Guide to Special Event Management: Business Insights, Financial Advice, and Successful Strategies from Ernst & Young, Advisors to the Olympics, the Emmy Awards and the PGA Tour.* New York: John Wiley & Sons.

Crichton, J. (1998). *Family Reunion.* New York: Workman Publishing Company.

Church, B. R., and B. E. Bultman (1998). *The Joys of Entertaining.* New York: Abbeville Press.

Clynes, Tom (1995). *Wild Planet: 1,001 Extraordinary Events for the Inspired Traveler.* Detroit, MI: Visible Ink Press.

Cole, H. (2003). *Jumping the Broom: The African-American Wedding Planner*, 2nd ed. New York: Henry Holt.

Conetsco, C., and A. Hart (2009). *Service Etiquette*, 5th ed. Annapolis, MD: Naval Institute Press.

Cournoyer, Norman, Anthony Marshall, and Karen Morris (2007). *Hotel, Restaurant, and Travel Law: A preventive Approach*, 6th ed. New York: Delmar Learning.

Dance, J. (1992). *How to Get the Most Out of Sales Meetings.* Lincolnwood, IL: NTC Business Books.

Davidson, R. (2003). *Business Travel: Conferences, Incentive Travel, Exhibitions, Corporate Hospitality, and Corporate Travel.* Pearson Education.

Davidson, R., and T. Rogers (2006). *Marketing Destinations and Venues for Conferences, Conventions and Business Events.* London: Butterworth-Heinemann.

Deal, T. E., and A. A. Kennedy (2000). *Corporate Cultures.* New York: Perseus Publishing.

De Lys, C. (1948). *8,414 Strange and Fascinating Superstitions.* Castle Books.

Deuschl, D. (2005). *Travel and Tourism Public Relations: An Introductory Guide for Hospitality Managers.* Oxford: Butterworth-Heinemann.

Devney, D. C. (2001). *Organizing Special Events and Conferences: A Practical Guide for Busy Volunteers and Staff.* Sarasota, FL: Pineapple Press.

Dlugosch, S. E. (1980). *Folding Table Napkins: A New Look at a Traditional Craft*, 9th ed. St. Paul, MN: Brighton Publications.

Fall, C. (2003). *Family Reunion Planning Kit for Dummies.* New York: Hungry Minds.

Fenich, G. (2007). *Meetings, Expositions, Events and Conventions*, 2nd ed. New York: Prentice Hall.

Fields, D., and A. Fields (2008). *Bridal Bargains: Secrets to Throwing a Fantastic Wedding on a Realistic Budget*, 9th ed. Boulder, CO: Windsor Peak Press.

Freedman, H. A., and K. F. Smith (2007). *Black Tie Optional: A Complete Special Events Resource for Nonprofit Organizations.* Hoboken, NJ: John Wiley & Sons.

Getz, D. (2007). Event *Studies: A Multi-Disciplinary Approach.* London: Butterworth-Heinemann.

Gilbert, E. (2004). *The Complete Wedding Planner.* Frederick Fell.

Goldblatt, J., and F. Supovitz. (1999). *Dollars & Events: How to Succeed in the Special Events Business.* New York: John Wiley & Sons.

Goldblatt, J., and K. S. Nelson (2001). *The International Dictionary of Event Management.* Hoboken, NJ: John Wiley & Sons.

Graham, P. (2006) *Public Assembly Facility Management: Principles and Practices.* International Association of Assembly Managers (IAAM). Available from: www.iaam.org.

Graham, S., J. Goldblatt, and L. Neirotti (2001). *The Ultimate Guide to Sport Event Management and Marketing.* New York: McGraw-Hill Trade.

Guerard, T. (2006). *Southern Weddings; New Looks from the Old South.* Layton, UT: Wyrick & Company.

Hall, C. M. (1992). *Hallmark Tourist Events: Impacts, Management and Planning.* New York: Belhaven Press.

Hall, S. J. (1992). *Ethics in Hospitality Management: A Book of Readings.* East Lansing, MI: Educational Institute of the American Hotel and Motel Association.

Hansen, B. (2005). *Off-Premise Catering Management.* Hoboken, NJ: John Wiley & Sons.

Harris, A. L. (2005). *Academic Ceremonies: A Handbook or Ceremonies and Protocol.* Washington, DC: Council for Advancement and Support of Education.

Harroch, Richard (2000). *Business Contracts Kit for Dummies.* New York: Hungry Minds, Inc.

Heath, A. (2001). *Windows on the World: Multicultural Festivals for Schools and Libraries.* Metuchen, NJ: Scarecrow Press.

Henkel, S., and M. Lujanac (2007). *Successful Meetings: How to Plan, Prepare, and Execute Top-Notch Business Meetings.* Ocala, FL: Atlantic Publishing Group.

Hayes, G. D. (2003). *Zambelli: The First Family of Fireworks.* Middlebury, VT: Paul S. Eriksson.

Howe, J., and H. M. Schaffer (2000). *Keeping in Step with Music Licensing.* Dallas: Meeting Professionals International.

Howe, T. H. (1996). *U.S. Meetings and Taxes*, 3rd ed. Dallas: Meeting Professionals International.

Hoyle, L. (2002). *Event Marketing.* Hoboken, NJ: John Wiley & Sons.

Hoyle, L. H., D. C. Dorf, and T. J. A. Jones (1989). *Managing Conventions and Group Business.* East Lansing, MI: Educational Institute of the American Hotel and Motel Association.

International Events Group (2009). *ROS: Return on Sponsorship.* Chicago: IEG. Available from: www.sponsorship.com.

International Events Group (2009). *IEG's Guide to Sponsorship.* Chicago: IEG. Available from: www.sponsorship.com.

Irwin, L., and R. McClay (2008). *The Essential Guide to Training Global Audiences: Your Planning Resource of Useful Tips and Techniques.* San Francisco: Pfeiffer.

Jackson, I. (ed.) (2002). *Great Festivals of the World.* London: Pilot Guides.

Jarrow, J., and C. Park. (1992). *Accessible Meetings and Conventions.* Columbus, OH: Association on Higher Education and Disability.

Jolles, R. L. (2005). *How to Run Seminars and Workshops: Presentation Skills for Consultants, Trainers and Teachers*, 3rd ed. Hoboken, NJ: John Wiley & Sons.

Karasik, P. (2004). *How to Make It Big in the Seminar Business*, 2nd ed. New York: McGraw-Hill.

Kerzner, H. (2005). *Project Management: A Systems Approach to Planning, Scheduling, and Controlling*, 9th ed. Hoboken, NJ: John Wiley & Sons.

Krugman, C., and R. Wright (2006). *Global Meetings and Expositions.* Hoboken, NJ: John Wiley & Sons.

Levitan, J. (2000). *Proven Ways to Generate Thousands of Hidden Dollars from Your Trade Show, Conference and Convention.* Vernon Hill, IL: Conference and Exhibition Publisher.

Lippincott, C. (1999). *Meetings: Do's, Don'ts and Donuts: The Complete Handbook for Successful Meetings.* Pittsburgh, PA: Lighthouse Point Press.

MacCannell, D. (1999). *The Tourist: A New Theory of the Leisure Class.* Berkeley, CA: University of California Press.

Mack, W. P., and W. Connell (2004). *Naval Ceremonies, Customs and Traditions*, 6th ed. Annapolis, MD: Naval Institute Press.

Mackenzie, J. K. (1990). *It's Show Time! How to Plan and Hold Successful Sales Meetings.* Homewood, IL: Dow Jones-Irwin.

Malouf, L. (1999). *Behind the Scenes at Special Events: Flowers, Props and Design.* New York: John Wiley & Sons.

Mangels, W. F. (1952). *The Outdoor Amusement Industry, From Earliest Times to the Present.* New York: Vantage Press.

Marsh, V. (1994). *Paper-Cutting Stories for Holidays and Special Events.* Atkinson, WI: Highsmith Press.

Martin, P. (2008). *Made Possible By: Succeeding with Sponsorship.* San Francisco: Jossey-Bass.

Masciangelio, W. R., and T. Ninkovich (1991). *Military Reunion Handbook: A Guide for Reunion Planners.* San Francisco, CA: Reunion Research.

Masterman, G. (2004). *Strategic Sports Event Management: An International Approach.* London: Butterworth-Heinemann.

McDonnell, I., J. Allen, and W. O'Toole (2008). *Festival and Special Event Management*, 4th ed. Australia: John Wiley & Sons.

McGinnis, C. (1994). *202 Tips Even the Best Business Travelers May Not Know.* New York: McGraw-Hill Trade.

Meeting Professionals International. *Meeting Planners and the Law.* Available from: www.mpiweb.org. Dallas, TX: MPI.

Meeting Professionals International and Canadian Council and the Government of Canada, The Department of Human Resources Development (2006). *MPI's Planning Guide: A Source for Meetings and Conventions.* Dallas, TX: MPI.

Mikolaitis, P., and W. O'Toole (2002). *Corporate Event Project Management.* Hoboken, NJ: John Wiley & Sons.

Mitchell, S., and L. Mitchell (2009). *How To Haunt Your House.* Pensacola, FL: Rabbit Hole Productions.

Miller, S. (2000). *How to Get the Most Out of Trade Shows.* New York: McGraw-Hill Trade.

Montgomery, R. J., and S. K. Strick (2002). *Meetings, Conventions, and Expositions: An Introduction to the Industry.* New York: Van Nostrand Reinhold.

Monroe, James (2006). *The Art of the Event.* Hoboken, NJ: John Wiley & Sons.

Morgan, G. (2001). *Your Family Reunion: How to Plan It, Organize It, and Enjoy It.* Utah: Ancestry Publishing.

Morrisey, G. C. (1996). *Morrisey on Planning, Vols. I-III.* San Francisco: Jossey-Bass.

Morton, J. (1985). *The Jack Morton (Who's He?) Story.* New York: Vantage Press.

Morton, J. (1993). *The Poor Man's Philosopher.* Washington, DC: Jack Morton Worldwide NY.

Mutz, John, and Katherine Murray (2006). *Fundraising for Dummies.* Hoboken: Wiley.

National Association of Broadcasters (1991). *A Broadcaster's Guide to Special Events and Sponsorship Risk Management.* Washington, DC: NAB.

Nichols, B. (2008). *Professional Meeting Management*, 5th ed. Birmingham, AL: Professional Convention Management Association. Available from: www.pcma.org

Norris, D. M., J. F. Loften, & Associates (1995). *Winning with Diversity: A Practical Handbook for Creating Inclusive Meetings, Events, and Organizations.* Washington, DC: Foundations of Meeting Planners International, Professional Convention Management Association, Association of Association Executives, International Association of

Convention and Visitors Bureaus, and International Association of Exposition Management.

Pizam, A. (2005). *International Encyclopedia of Hospitality Management.* London: Butterworth Heinemann.

Plenert, G. (2006). *Reinventing Lean: Introducing Lean into the Supply Chain.* London: Butterworth-Heinemann.

Post, A. (2007). *Emily Post's Wedding Parties.* William Morrow.

Post, E. (1991). *Emily Post's Complete Book of Wedding Etiquette,* rev. ed. New York: HarperCollins.

Price, C. H. (1989). *The AMA Guide for Meeting and Event Planners.* Arlington, VA: Educational Services Institute.

Prochnow, Herbert (2002). *The Toastmaster's Treasure Chest.* Castle Books.

Rago, M. (2007). *Signature Weddings: Creating a Day Uniquely Your Own.* New York: Gotham Books.

Ramsborg, G. C. (1993). *Objectives to Outcomes: Your Contract with the Learner.* Birmingham, AL: Professional Convention Management Association.

Reyburn, S. (1997). *Meeting Planner's Guide to Historic Places.* New York: John Wiley & Sons.

Reynolds, R., E. Louie, and E. Addeo (2003). *The Art of the Party.* New York: Penguin Studio.

Richards, G. (2007). *Eventful Cities: Cultural Management and Urban Revitalization.* London: Butterworth-Heinemann.

Ritchie, J. R. B., and C. R. Goeldener (2009). *Tourism Principles, Practices and Philosophies,* 11th ed. Hoboken, NJ: John Wiley & Sons.

Rogers, T. (2008). *Conferences and Conventions: A Global Industry,* 2nd ed. London: Butterworth-Heinemann.

Rooney, C. (1998). *The Knot Ultimate Wedding Planner: Worksheets, Checklists, Etiquette, Calendars, and Answers to Frequently Asked Questions.* New York: Broadway Books.

Roysner, M. (2003). *Convention Center Facilities Contracts.* Dallas: Meeting Professionals International.

Rutherford Silvers, J. (2007). *Risk Management for Meetings and Events.* London: Butterworth-Heinemann.

Rutherford Silvers, J. (2003). *Professional Event Coordination.* Hoboken, NJ: John Wiley & Sons.

Saget, A. (2005). *The Event Marketing Handbook: Beyond Logistics and Planning.* Chicago: Dearborn Trade.

Scannell, E. E., and J. W. Newstrom (1998). *The Complete Games Trainers Play, Vol II.* New York: McGraw-Hill.

Schindler-Rainman, E., and J. Cole (1988). *Taking Your Meetings Out of the Doldrums,* rev. ed. San Diego, CA: University Associates.

Schmader, S. W. (1997). *Event Operations.* Boise, ID: IFEA. Available from: www.ifea.com

Schmader, S. W., and R. Jackson (1997). *Special Events: Inside and Out: A "How-to" Approach to Event Production, Marketing, and Sponsorship.* Champaign, IL: Sagamore Publishing.

Shenson, H. L. (1990). *How to Develop and Promote Successful Seminars and Workshops: A Definite Guide to Creating and Marketing Seminars, Classes and Conferences.* New York: John Wiley & Sons.

Simerly, R. G. (1993). *Strategic Financial Management for Conferences, Workshops, and Meetings.* San Francisco: Jossey-Bass.

Skinner, Bruce (2002). *Event Sponsorship.* Hoboken, NJ: John Wiley & Sons.

Soares, E. J. (1991). *Promotional Feats: The Role of Planned Events in the Marketing Communications Mix.* Westport, CT: Greenwood Publishing Group.

Sonder, Mark (2004). *Event Entertainment and Production.* Hoboken, NJ: John Wiley & Sons.

Sowden, C.L. (1992). *An Anniversary to Remember: Years One to Seventy-Five.* St. Paul, MN: Brighton Publications.

Stallard, H. et al. (1998). *Bagehot on Sponsorship, Endorsements and Merchandising,* 2nd ed. Sweet & Maxwell.

Stern, L. (2009). *Stage Management,* 9th ed. Boston: Allyn & Bacon.

Supovitz, Frank (2004). *The Sports Event Management and Marketing Playbook.* Hoboken, NJ: John Wiley & Sons.

Surbeck, L. (1991). *Creating Special Events: The Ultimate Guide to Producing Successful Events.* Louisville, KY: Master Publications.

Swarbrooke, J. (2002). *Development and Management of Visitor Attractions.* London: Butterworth-Heinemann.

Talbot, R. (1990). *Meeting Management: Practical Advice for Both New and Experimental Managers Based on an Expert's Twenty Years in the "Wonderful Wacky World" of Meeting Planning.* McLean, VA: EPM Publications.

Tarlow, Peter (2003). *Event Risk Management & Safety.* Hoboken, NJ: John Wiley & Sons.

Tassiopoulos, D. (ed.) (2000). *Event Management: A Professional and Development Approach.* Johannesburg, South Africa: Juta Education.

Tepper, B. (1993). *Incentive Travel: The Complete Guide.* San Francisco, CA: Dendrobium Books.

The 3M Meeting and Management Team with Jeannine Drew (1994). *Mastering Meetings: Discovering the Hidden Potential of Effective Business Meetings.* New York: McGraw-Hill.

Torrence, S. R. (1991). *How to Run Scientific and Technical Meetings.* New York: Van Nostrand Reinhold.

Tutera, D., C. Maring, and J. Maring (2005). *The Party Planner.* New York: Bulfinch.

Van Der Wagen, L., and B. Carlos (2004). *Event Management.* New York: Prentice Hall.

Von Drachenfels, S. (2000). *The Art of the Table: A Complete Guide to Table Setting, Table Manners, and Tableware.* New York; Simon & Schuster.

Walford, C. (1968). *Fairs, Past and Present: A Chapter in the History of Commerce.* New York: A. M. Kelly.

Washington, G., and Applewood Books Staff (1994). *George Washington's Rules of Civility and Decent Behavior in Company and Conversation.* Mount Vernon, VA: Applewood Books.

Watt, D. C. (1998). *Event Management in Leisure and Tourism.* London, UK: Pearson Education UK.

Weirich, M. L. (1992). *Meetings and Conventions Management.* Albany, NY: Delmar Publishers.

Weissinger, S. S. (1992). *A Guide to Successful Meeting Planning.* New York: John Wiley & Sons.

Wendroff, A. (2003). *Special Events: Proven Strategies for Nonprofit Fundraising.* Hoboken, NJ: Wiley.

Whitmore, J. (2005). *Business Class: Etiquette Essentials for Success at Work.* New York: St. Martin's Press.

Wiersma, E. A. (1991). *Creative Event Development: A Guide to Strategic Success in the World of Special Events.* Indianapolis: Author.

Wigger, E. G. (1997). *Themes, Dreams, and Schemes: Banquet Menu Ideas, Concepts, and Thematic Experiences.* Hoboken, NJ: John Wiley & Sons.

Wilson, J., and L. Undall (1982). *Folk Festivals: A Handbook for Organization and Management.* Knoxville: University of Tennessee Press.

Wolfson, S. M. (1995). *The Meeting Planner's Complete Guide to Negotiating: You Can Get What You Want.* Kansas City: Institute for Meeting and Conference Management.

Wolfson, S. M. (1991). *Meeting Planner's Workbook: Write Your Own Hotel Contract.* Kansas City, Missouri: Institute for Meeting and Conference Management.

Wright, R. R. (2005). *The Meeting Spectrum: An Advanced Guide for Meeting Professionals,* 2nd ed. San Diego, CA: Rockwood Enterprises.

Yeoman, I., M. Robertson, J. Ali-Knight, S. Drummond, and U. McMahon-Beattie (eds). (2003). *Festivals and Events Management: An International Arts and Culture Perspective.* London: Butterworth-Heinemann.

General Interest Business Books for Event Leaders

Axtell, R. E. (1993). *Do's and Taboos around the World,* 3rd ed. New York: John Wiley & Sons.

Axtell, R. E. (1997). *Gestures: The Do's and Taboos of Body Language around the World.* New York: John Wiley & Sons.

Baker, D. B. (2001). *Power Quotes: 4,000 Trenchant Soundbites on Leadership & Liberty, Treason & Triumph, Sacrifice & Scandal, Risk & Rebellion, Weakness & War and Other Affairs Politiques.* Detroit, MI: Visible Ink Press.

Bartlett, J. (2002). *Familiar Quotations: A Collection of Passages, Phrases, and Proverbs Traced to Their Sources in Ancient and Modern Literature,* 14th ed. Boston: Little Brown & Co.

Boothman, N. (2008). *How to Make People Like You in 90 Seconds or Less.* New York: Workman Publishing.

Collins, J. (2001). *Good to Great.* New York: HarperCollins.

Dittrich, K. (ed.) and A. Geppert. (2000). *Component Database Systems.* San Francisco: Morgan Kaufman.

Gumley, L. (2001). *Practical IDL Programming.* San Francisco: Morgan Kaufmann.

Harris, T. L. (2006). *The Marketer's Guide to Public Relations in the 21st Century.* Hoboken, NJ: John Wiley & Sons.

Howell, M. D. (1997). *From Moonshine to Madison Avenue: A Cultural History of the NASCAR Winston Cup Series.* Bowling Green, OH: Bowling Green State University Popular Press.

Hungelmann (2009). *Insurance for Dummies*, 2nd ed. Hoboken, NJ: John Wiley & Sons.

Jay, R. (2006). *The Art of the Business Lunch: Building Relationships Between 12 and 2.* New Jersey: Career Press.

Kawasaki, G. (1991). *Selling the Dream: How to Promote Your Product, Company or Ideas—and Make a Difference—Using Everyday Evangelism.* New York: HarperCollins.

Piltzeker, T., B. Barber, M. Cross, and R. Dittner (2006). *How to Cheat at Managing Microsoft Operations Manager 2005.* Sebastopol, CA: Syngress Publishing.

Wolfram, S. (2002). *A New Kind of Science.* Champaign, IL: Wolfram Media.

Yudkin, Marcia. (2003). *6 Steps to Free Publicity.* Franklin Lakes, NJ: The Career Press.

Anthropological and Folklore Resources of Interest to Event Leaders

Anderson, N. (1993). *Ferris Wheels: An Illustrated History.* Bowling Green, OH: Bowling Green State University Popular Press.

Badger, R. (1979). *The Great American Fair: The World's Columbian Exposition and American Culture.* Chicago: Nelson-Hall.

Baron, R., and N. R. Spitzer (2008). *Public Folklore.* Mississippi: University Press of Mississippi.

Browne, R. B., and A. Neal (2001). *Ordinary Reactions to Extraordinary Events.* Bowling Green, OH: Bowling Green State University Popular Press.

Calabria, F. M. (1993). *Dance of the Sleep-Walkers: The Dance Marathon Fad.* Bowling Green, OH: Bowling Green State University Popular Press.

Cameron, D. K. (1998). *The English Fair.* Alan Sutton Publishing.

Cannadine, D., and S. Price (1993). *Rituals of Royalty: Power and Ceremonial in Traditional Societies.* New York: Cambridge University Press.

Charsley, S. R. (1992). *Wedding Cakes and Cultural History.* New York: Routledge.

Ehrenreich, Barbara (2006). *Dancing in the Streets: A History of Collective Joy.* New York: Holt Paperbacks.

Farmer, S. (2002). *Sacred Ceremony: How to Create Ceremonies for Healing, Transitions, and Celebration.* Carlsbad, CA: Hay House.

Giblin, J. C. (2001). *Fireworks, Picnics and Flags: The Story of the Fourth of July Symbols.* Boston, MA: Clarion Books/Houghton-Mifflin.

Grimes, R. (2002). *Deeply into the Bone: Re-Inventing Rites of Passage.* Berkeley: University of California Press.

Grimes, R. (1995). *Readings in Ritual Studies.* Upper Saddle River, NJ: Pearson, Allyn & Bacon.

Holbrook, M. B. (1993). *Daytime Television Game Shows and the Celebration of Merchandise: The Price Is Right.* Bowling Green, OH: Bowling Green State University Popular Press.

Klausner, S. Z. (1968). *Why Man Takes Chances: Studies in Stress-Seeking.* New York: Doubleday.

Levi-Strauss, C. (1990). *The Origin of Table Manners, Vol. 3: Mythologies.* Chicago, IL: University of Chicago Press.

Liming, W. (2005). *Chinese Festivals.* China Intercontinental Press.

Mason, A. (2002). *People Around the World.* Boston: Houghton-Mifflin.

Ray, C. (2001). *Highland Heritage: Scottish Americans in the American South.* Chapel Hill: University of North Carolina Press.

Riverol, A. R. (1992). *Live from Atlantic City: The Miss America Pageant Before, After, and In Spite of Television.* Bowling Green, OH: Bowling Green State University Popular Press.

Slocum, S. K. (1992). *Popular Arthurian Traditions.* Bowling Green, OH: Bowling Green State University Popular Press.

Turner, V. W. (1982). *Celebration Studies in Festivity & Ritual.* Washington, DC: Smithsonian Institution Press.

Visser, M. (1999). *Much Depends on Dinner: The Extraordinary History and Mythology, Allure and Obsessions, Peril and Taboos, of an Ordinary Meal.* New York: Grove Press.

Veeck, B. (1972). *Thirty Tons a Day: The Rough-Riding Education of a Neophyte Racetrack Operator.* New York: Viking Press.

Visser, M. (1992). *The Rituals of Dinner: The Origins, Evolution, Eccentricities and Meaning of Table Manners.* New York: Penguin USA.

York, S. (1992). *Developing Roots & Wings: A Trainer's Guide to Affirming Culture in Early Childhood.* St. Paul, MN: Redleaf Press.

APPENDIX 2

International Special Events Society Principles of Professional Conduct and Ethics*

Each member of ISES shall agree to adhere to the following:

- Promote and encourage the highest level of ethics within the profession of the special events industry while maintaining the highest standards of professional conduct.
- Strive for excellence in all aspects of our profession by performing consistently at or above acceptable industry standards.
- Use only legal and ethical means in all industry negotiations and activities.
- Protect the public against fraud and unfair practices, and promote all practices which bring respect and credit to the profession.
- Provide truthful and accurate information with respect to the performance of duties. Use a written contract clearly stating all charges, services, products, performance expectations and other essential information.
- Maintain industry-accepted standards of safety and sanitation.
- Maintain adequate and appropriate insurance coverage for all business activities.
- Commit to increase professional growth and knowledge, to attend educational programs and to personally contribute expertise to meetings and journals.
- Strive to cooperate with colleagues, suppliers, employees, employers and all persons supervised, in order to provide the highest quality service at every level.
- Subscribe to the ISES Principles of Professional Conduct and Ethics, and abide by the ISES Bylaws and policies.

---

*Courtesy of International Special Events Society (www.ises.com)

APPENDIX 3

The Greener Appendix

The world of Green Events is ever expanding. Compiled here is a list of references from Chapter 6 (Greener Events), suggestions for further reading, suggested Greener Events, associations, and a directory of Greener Event Suppliers around the world.

Chapter References

Baragona, John (2007). *Event Solutions 2007 Annual Forecast: Forecasting the Events Industry*. Event Publishing LLC.

Barron, James (2008). December 26. Coming Soon at Steinway, Solar Power. City Room, *TheNewYorkTimes.cityroom.blogs.nytimes.com* [online] http://cityroom.blogs.nytimes.com/2008/12/26/steinway-by-barron-for-sat/?scp=11&sq=california%20solar%20power%20fair&st=cse [Accessed February 2009].

Binge and purge: Norway and the environment. (2009) *The Economist*. [online] January 22. Available from: http://www.economist.com/displaystory.cfm?story_id=12970769 [Accessed February 2009].

Blue Green Meetings (2009). [online] Available from: http://www.BlueGreenMeetings.org [Accessed January 2009].

CESweb.org (2009). [online] Available from: http://www.cesweb.org [Accessed February 2009].

Clifford, Lorenza et al (2007). *Business on a Shoestring: Working Ethically. Creating a sustainable business ... without breaking the bank*. London: A & C Black Publishers LTD.

Esty, Daniel C. and Winston, Andrew S (2006). *Green to Gold: How Smart Companies Use Environmental Strategy to Innovate, Create, Value, and Build Competitive Advantage*. New Haven: Yale University Press.

Fairtrade Foundation (2008). [online] Available from: http://www.fairtrade.org [Accessed December 2008].

Fennell, David A (2007). *Ecotourism*. London: Routledge.

Friedman, Thomas (2008). *Hot, Flat and Crowded*. London: Allen Lane.

Gardner, Seth (2006). Going Green. *The Meeting Professional*. Dallas: Meeting Planners International. Vol. 26, Num. 3, March.

Getz, Donald (2007). *Event Studies: Theory, research and policy for planned events*. Oxford: Butterworth-Heinemann.

Golding, Maxine (2008). Sprouting Up. *PCMA Convene*. Chicago: PCMA. December.

Green Events (2009). *Special Events*. [online] Available from: http://SpecialEvents.com/green_events [Accessed: January 2009].

Green Meeting Industry Council (2009). [online] Available from: http://www.GreenMeetings.info [Accessed: January 2009].

Green Meeting / Conference Initiative. United States Environmental Protection Agency (2009). [online] Available from: http://www.epa.gov/oppt/greenmeetings [Accessed: January 2009].

Green Meetings (2009). United States Enivronmental Protection Agency. [online] Available from: http://www.epa.gov/oppt/greenmeetings/ [Accessed February 2009].

Greening Live Earth

Global Warming. National Geographic News (2009). [online] Available from: http://environment.nationalgeographic.com/environment/global-warming/gw-overview.html [Accessed: February 2009].

Haunss, Kristen (2005). Johnnie Walker Has Color-Coded Birthday Bash. *BizBash*. [online] August 3, 2005. Available from: http://www.bizbash.com/newyork/content/editorial/5089_johnnie_walker_has_color-coded_birthday_bash.php [Accessed February 2009].

It's Easy Being Green! (1996). A Guide To Planning And Conducting Environmentally Aware Meetings And Events. United States Enivronmental Protection Agency. Solid Waste and Emergency Response (5306W). September 1996. Available as a PDF from: http://www.greenbiz.com/resources/resource/its-easy-being-green-a-guide-planning-and-conducting-environmentally-aware-meetin.

Jenkins, Tiffany, et al (2002). *Ethical Tourism: Who Benefits?* Oxon: Hodder & Stoughton.

Klingler, Jill (2009). Philips Transforms Raymond James Stadium For Super Bowl XLIII. *Philips Color Kinetics*. [online] January 29. Available from: http://www.colorkinetics.com/corp/news/pr/releases/2009-01-29_superbowl.html [Accessed February 2009].

Kolbert, Elizabeth (2008). The Island in the Wind: A Danish community's victory over carbon emissions. *The New Yorker*. [online] July 7. Available from: http://www.newyorker.com/reporting/2008/07/07/080707fa_fact_kolbert [Accessed February 2009].

Live Earth (2009). [online] Available from: http://www.LiveEarth.org [Accessed January 2009].

O'Steen, Danielle (2009). Start to Finish. *BizBash*. [online] January 20, 2009. Available from: http://www.bizbash.com/newyork/content/editorial/14127_al_gores_green_ball_chooses_email_invites_seedlings_for_decor_and_a_sustainable_menu.php [Accessed February 2009].

Report of the World Commission on Environment and Development: Our Common Future. (1987) UN Documents Cooperation Circle. NGO Committee on Education. [online] March 20. Available from: http://www.un-documents.net/wced-ocf.htm [Accessed February 2009].

Revolution Rickshaws (2009). [online] Available from: http://www.revolutionrickshaws.com [Accessed February 2009].

White, Martha C (2008). Green Leaders: Setting an Example. *BizBash*. [online] September 22. Available from: http://www.bizbash.com/newyork/content/editorial/12555_green_leaders_setting_an_example.php [Accessed February 2009].

Widdicombe (2008). Born Green. *The New Yorker*. May 19, p. 31.

Vegware (2009). [online] Available from: http://www.vegware.us [Accessed February 2009].

Further Resources

Books

Batten, Rhiannon (2007). *Higher Ground: How to Travel Responsibly Without Roughing It*. London: Virgin Books.

Esty, Daniel C. and Winston, Andrew S (2006). *Green to Gold: How Smart Companies Use Environmental Strategy to Innovate, Create, Value, and Build Competitive Advantage*. New Haven: Yale University Press.

Fennell, David A (2007). *Ecotourism*. London: Routledge.

Friedman, Thomas (2008). *Hot, Flat and Crowded*. London: Allen Lane.

Websites

A Greener Festival. *www.agreenerfestival.com*. UK research-based guide to Greener Events.

BlueGreen Meetings. *www.bluegreenmeetings.org*. US EPA-sponsored guide for Greener Event Planners and Suppliers.

BS8901 Register. www.bs8901register.co.uk. Directory of UK Greener Event companies and suppliers.

Center for the New American Dream. *www.newdream.org*. Campaign for greener America.

Consumer Reports: Greener Choices. *www.greenerchoices.org*. Consumer guide to green shopping.

Energy Star, US Environmental Protection Agency and US Department of Energy. *www.energystar.gov*. US Government campaign for, and practical guide to, energy efficiency and conservation.

Environment Canada: Greening Meetings. *www.ns.ec.gc.ca/greenman*.

GreenBiz.com. *www.greenbiz.com*. Green business news.

Green Power Conferences. *www.greenpowerconferences.com*. Event organizers for the sustainability sector.

Live Earth. *www.liveearth.org*. Mega-concert and entertainment producer with green ethos and political agenda.

National Biodiesel Board. *www.biodiesel.org*. US news and guide to biodiesel.

National Geographic: Green Guide. *www.thegreenguide.com*. Green lifestyle guide.

National Recycling Coalition Green Meeting Policy. *www.nrc-recycle.org/greenmeetingsp.aspx*.

Natural Weddings. *www.naturalweddings.com.au*. Australian directory and guide to planning green weddings.

Planet Green. *www.planetgreen.com*. "Planet Green is the first and only 24-hour eco-lifestyle television network with a robust online presence and community." (from website).

Repower America. *www.repoweramerica.org*. Campaign for renewable energy in America.

Special Events Magazine: Green Events,. *SpecialEvents.com/green_events*. Articles on Greener Events from industry-leading magazine.

Sustainable Business. *www.sustainablebusiness.com. Green business news.*

Sustainable Events Group. *www.thesustainableeventsgroup.com*. BS8901-certified UK sustainable events consultants.

Treehugger. *www.treehugger.com*. Online green lifestyle magazine.

US Department of Energy: A Consumer's Guide to Energy Efficiency and Renewable Energy. *apps1.eere.energy.gov/consumer.*

US Environmental Protection Agency: Green Meetings. *www.epa.gov/oppt/greenmeetings.*

Model Greener Events

Americas Lodging Investment Summit. *www.alisconference.com*. Conference of Hotel Executives.

Big Green Gathering. *www.big-green-gathering.com*. English new age nature festival.

Bonnaroo. *www.bonnaroo.com*. Tennessee music festival.

Boom Festival. *www.boomfestival.org*. Portuguese sustainable arts festival.

Eden Project. *www.edenproject.com*. Greenfield event venue in Cornwall, England.

Exit Fest. *www.exitfest.org*. Serbian music festival.

IMEX '09. *www.imex-frankfurt.com*. Worldwide exhibition for incentive travel, meetings, and events.

Latitude. *www.latitudefestival.co.uk*. English music festival.

Opportunity Green. *www.opportunitygreen.com. Green business summit.*

Organic River Festival. *www.ecofest.co.nz*. Sustainable arts festival in New Zealand.

Peats Ridge Festival. *www.peatsridgefestival.com.au*. Australian sustainable arts and music festival.

Roskilde Festival. *www.roskilde-festival.dk*. Danish music festival.

Sustainable Living Roadshow. *www.sustainablelivingroadshow.org*. Educational and entertaining eco-carnival touring the US.

T in the Park. *www.tinthepark.com*. Scottish carbon-offsetting music festival.

Associations

Atlanta Green Meetings Council
334 Spring Hill Drive
Canton, GA 30115
USA
(404) 406-0617
www.atlantagreenmeetings.com

"The Atlanta Green Meeting Council is a collection of hospitality professionals within the meetings, special events and tourism industry dedicated to the academia, economic, environmental and social responsible meetings." (from website)

Association for Green Meetings & Events (AGME)
110 Prominence Point Parkway
Suite 114-105
Canton, GA 30114
USA
(888) 447-0555
www.agmeinc.org

"The vision of AGME is to build a professional community conductive to continued learning, overall awareness and application to sustainability and socially responsible practices for the entire global hospitality society." (from website)

Convene Green Alliance (CGA)
1110 N. Glebe Road
Suite 580
Arlington, VA 22201
USA
(703) 908-0707 ext. 104
www.convenegreen.com

"CGA is a grass-roots organization initiated by the association and meetings communities as a response to the concerns and desires of their members for the environment . . . CGA offers associations established guidelines, best practices, evaluation tools and resources via educational events, our web resource center, trade media and promotion." (from website)

"Green" Hotels Association
PO Box 420212
Houston, TX 77242-0212
(713) 789-8889
www.greenhotels.com
Guidance for environmentally friendly hotels.

Green Meeting Industry Council (GMIC)
207 Third Avenue
Hattiesburg, MS 39401
USA
(888) 450-2098
www.greenmeetings.info

GMIC is a non profit 501(c)(6) membership-based organization, and the only professional green meetings organization that is a member of the Convention Industry Council. GMIC's goal is to "encourage collaboration within the meetings industry toward the development of green standards that will improve the environmental performance of meetings and events on a global basis." (from website)

International Tourism Partnership
15-16 Cornwall Terrace
London NW1 4QP
UK
+44 (0)20 7467 3600
www.tourismpartnership.org
Global ecotourism association.

Green Suppliers

Staging and Technical Equipment

Sustainable Dance Club, +31 (0)10 276 22 13, *www.sustainabledanceclub.com*: The psychadelic Sustainable Dance Floor converts the kinetic energy of dancing into electric power, emitted from LED disco lights.

Philips Color Kinetics, (888) 385-5742 (USA), +44 (0)77 8968 0934 (Europe), *www.colorkinetics.com*: energy-saving LED lighting systems.

Waste and Recycling

ACM Waste Management (UK), +44 (0)8700 777 555, *www.acm-waste.com*. Waste minimization, recycling and ethical disposal.

Collective Good, (303) 339-4101, *www.collectivegood.com*. Mobile phone recycling service.

Renewable Energy

General Energy Providers

Green Power Markets, US Department of Energy *apps3.eere.energy.gov/greenpower/markets/pricing.shtml?page=1*. A complete list of US Green Energy Networks and Utilities, by State.

Green Mountain Energy, (800) 810-7300, *www.greenmountainenergy.com*. The largest US provider of residential renewable.

Mondial Energy, http://www.mondial-energy.com.

Sustainable Waves, (619) 358-9939, *www.sustainablewaves.com*, Sustainable energy event specialists.

Biofuels

Biowillie, (866) 765-4940 ext. 1, *www.biowillieusa.com*. Willie Nelson's biodiesel.

Hydropower

Canyon Hydro, (360) 592-5552, *www.canyonhydro.com*. Commercial and residential hydropower systems.

Utility Free, (800) 799-1122, *www.utilityfree.com*. Providers of microhydropower and other renewable energy solutions.

Solar Power

Solar Home, (866) SUN-PRODUCTS, *www.solarhome.org*. Everything from solar panels to complete solar energy systems.

Wholesale Solar, (800) 472-1142, *www.wholesalesolar.com*. Discounted solar and other renewable energy products.

Wind

Aerostar, (508) 636-5200, *www.aerostarwind.com*. 25 year-old supplier of wind turbines.

Bergey Windpower Co, (405) 364-4212, *www.bergey.com*. Supplier of small wind turbines.

Wood

Green Energy Resources, (212) 730-1496, *www.greenenergyresources.com*. Sustainable wood power provider.

Nuergy, +44 (0)1506 882 720, *www.nuergy.com*. Wood pellet and biomass wood burning ovens.

Talent

EcoSpeakers.com, (866) 658-4848, *www.ecospeakers.com*.

Catering

Lean Path, (877) 620-6512, food waste calculations, www.leanpath.com.

Carbon Offsetting

Leonardo Academy's – Cleaner and Greener ® program, http://www.cleanerandgreener.org/certification/program.htm.

Sustainable Travel International – Carbon Offset and Green Tag Projects, http://www.sustainabletravelinternational.org/documents/op_carbonoffsets_projects.html.

myclimate – The Climate Protection Partnership - Projects that lead to a direct reduction of greenhouse gases and thus makes tangible climate protection possible. http://www.myclimate.org/index.php?lang=en&m=project.

*Native*Energy – Carbon Offsetting, http://www.nativeenergy.com.

Print and Marketing

Burly House, (512) 912-1371, *burlyhouse.net*. Webhosting powered by renewable energy.

Go Green Displays, (732) 602-3281, *www.gogreendisplays.com*. Recycled signage.

Rolling Press, (718) 625-6800, *www.rollingpress.com*. Eco-friendly printing.

Spitfire Agency, (415) 381-3700, *www.spitfireagency.com*. Eco-activist marketing agency.

Decor

Seed Events, (310) 927-7493, *www.seedevents.com*. Organic flowers.

Promotional Products

Clothes Made From Scrap, (386) 447-6656, *clothesmadefromscrap.com*. Customizable clothing from recycled materials.

Weisenbach Speciality Printing, http://www.weisenbach.com/.

Signature Marketing, http://www.signaturemarketing.com/homepage.

Stan Miller & Associates, http://www.promoplace.com/millerpromotions.

Gifts and Awards made from Recycled content materials

Fire & Light – engravable, recycled glass awards and gifts, http://www.fireandlight.com.
Aurora Glass, http://www.auroraglass.org/recycledglass.html.
Rivanna Natural Designs, http://www.rivannadesigns.com.

Suppliers – Misc

Organic Bouquet – organic flowers & displays, http://www.organicbouquet.com.
Madison Avenue – Reusable signs, http://www.meetingsigns.com/.
Green Seal, http://www.greenseal.org/.

Office/Building/Home Suppliers

Green Home – products and services for a green home, http://www.greenhome.com.
Green Products – building solutions and cleaners, http://www.greenproducts.net/.
Green Depot – building supplies, http://store.greendepot.com/StoreFront.bok.
Green Office – an online retailer of recycled, environmentally friendly, and sustainable business products, school supplies, and paper, http://www.thegreenoffice.com.
Dolphin Blue, http://www.dolphinblue.com.
Leading Hotels of the World- Green Initiative, http://www.lhwgreen.com/home.aspx.
Kimpton Hotels – Earth Care, http://www.kimptonhotels.com/cares_earthcare.aspx.
Fairmont Hotels – Green Partnership, http://www.fairmont.com/EN_FA/Environment.
Marriott – Green Marriott, www.**marriott**.com/**marriott**.mi?page=environmentalInitiatives.
Onyx Environmental Solutions, (312) 421-6699, *www.onyxenvirosolutions.com*.

INDEX